Accounting for Managers

Effective Techniques for Decision Making

(3rd Revised and Updated Edition)

Prof. S. Jayapandian

Financial Consultant

Ane Books Pvt. Ltd.

New Delhi ♦ Chennai

Accounting for Managers: Effective Techniques for Decision Making

S. Jayapandian

First Edition : 2006
Second Edition : 2008
Third Edition : 2025

Published by

Ane Books Pvt. Ltd.
4821, Parwana Bhawan, 1st Floor, 24 Ansari Road, Darya Ganj, **New Delhi** - 110 002, India
Tel.: +91(011) 23276843-44, Fax: +91(011) 23276863
e-mail: kapoor@anebooks.com, Website: www.anebooks.com

Branch Office:

- Avantika Niwas, 1st Floor, 19 Doraiswamy Road, T. Nagar,
Chennai - 600 017, Tel.: +91(044) 28141554, 28141209
e-mail: anebooks_tn@airtelmail.in

ISBN : 978-93-8015-606-4

Printed at : Sagar Colorscan, New Delhi.

Preface to the Third Revised and Updated Edition

It is with a measure of pride that I observe that the book is entering into its third edition. I take the opportunity to thank the publishers and the readers for their unstinting patronage.

The third edition, besides correcting a few errors in the first edition, includes cases and caselets for the users to apply in real-life situations. It would sharpen their decision-making ability and solve problems that users face at their workplace.

Problems are the order of the day. Solutions are to be found for the problems that arise in day-to-day activities. However, there is no single solution to any problem. There are alternatives. The successful manager is the one who chooses the most beneficial alternative, having regard to costs and benefits. I had occasions to hear a few executives claim that they were able to choose the best alternative on intuition. But intuitions are probabilities and might not work on all occasions in everycase. Choosing a correct alternative would depend upon the way a situation is analysed. Situations, we know, might not usually be the same everytime a problem crops up. They might not recur. However, it is the analytical skill of the manager that helps him taking correct decisions. It is therefore necessary that a manager should be well equipped with relevant data, both internal and external and analytical tools, besides possessing analytical bent of mind. Nothing should be taken as obvious. Everything should be put to decisive test by asking questions why, when, where and how.

In dealing with case studies, therefore, importance should be given to the way in which a situation has to be approached and analysed rather than how to arrive at results. Of course, correct analysis would naturally lead to arriving at appropriate decisions. The cases are thus intended to kindle the spirit of analysis in the readers and to give a practical approach on how to face a real problem.

Prof. S. Jayapandian

Preface to the First Edition

Professionals, accountants, managers, management students and inquisitive seekers of knowledge on finance are keen to understand the nuances of using accounting information in decision making. Universities have designed courses aimed at educating students on the role of accounting information in corporate decision making. A number of textbooks have sprung up to serve the needs of these sections of society. A few books have also flown into the country from abroad for the purpose. However, most of these texts are conventional in character and have distanced themselves from the modern realities of accounting practices. For example, all the texts use the traditional method of journalizing as "*so and so account Dr. To so and so account*" and follow it by a narration. When the amount of a transaction is entered in the debit column, what is the utility of writing "*Debtor*". It is redundant. Similarly narration is like what appendix is in human beings - relics of the past without any functional usefulness. All companies, even in small-scale sector presently use computer packages like Tally for accounting. The mode of journalizing in Tally or any other package is "*By* so and so account *To* so and so account". And narration is usually omitted. So also in the format of ledger. Many books still follow the traditional "T" accounting form, which is replaced by statement type ledgers. Many colleges still teach conventional methods and students and readers continue to have the same view when they enter into management courses. This makes them more formal than rational. They are taught "how to account" and not "why so accounted". The very objective of using accounting information for decision-making is relegated to the background. Forms prevail over prudence. Much of the lament of intellectuals over inferior quality of our management education stems from this background. As a teacher in management discipline for quite some time after a long debut with industry, I observe this dichotomy and in this book I am introducing modern concepts, of course with a discussion on conventional practices as a historic relic.

The book is intended to quench the thirst of professionals, academicians, managers and students involved in unraveling the mysteries of accounting information as the basis for decision making. All managerial decisions are taken either to reduce cost or to increase benefit. Readers should be clear as to why a particular aspect is cost or benefit. Concepts are explained first from the angle why and then how to use them. As the coverage has depth and breadth, professional students could get answers to many questions that were plaguing their mind till now. No doubt, the book covers the syllabi of many southern universities: Anna University, Madras University, Annamalai University, Alagappa University, Osmania University, Andhra University, Nagarjuna University, to mention a few and is an effective text for PG and UG degree courses and management courses in any part of India.

I have also deviated from the conventional practice of annexing solutions to the problems given in "Exercises" section. It is my observation, as a teacher, that students after attempting to solve a problem, rush to the solution to verify whether what they had done tallies with the answers provided. If not, they try alternative means of arriving at the answer. Their objective seems not to discover the probable solution but to arrive at the book answer somehow. Such a tendency, I am afraid, would kill the initiative of the students to strike at right solutions. What is more, I have checked up samples of solutions to problems in the books of eminent authors and found that not a few of them are incorrect but also misleading. Relying on such doubtful solutions would deprive the inquisitive students of the real application of the concepts. In order not to be instrumental to promote such "take it easy" attitude in students, I have purposefully omitted solutions to problems.

The book is primarily aimed at analysing the accounting data and using them in decision making. Chapters 1 to 14 are designed for the purpose. In this section, readers are exposed to the process of accumulating data in the books of account and their conversion into meaningful information for use in decision making. However, having regard to such of those readers, who do not have adequate background as to how these data are generated, I have slated a chapter on financial accounting to enlighten them how financial data are recorded, classified, summarized and results interpreted. In essence, this book could conveniently be used both for management accounting and financial accounting.

I have taken personal care to ensure that readability, accuracy and clearness of concepts are maintained throughout the book. In case readers observe any lapse or have suggestions to improve the text, they are welcome to contact me in email jpandian@rediffmail.com any time and from anywhere. If they find the book useful, I am sure that they would spread the message to their friends and colleagues.

Prof. S. Jayapandian

Contents

CHAPTER–1

CONCEPTS OF ACCOUNTING

Learning Objective

This is the introductory chapter on accounting. It traces the historical evolution of accounting, the need for keeping accounts for use of resources and the types of accounting one would encounter. As accounting is an art, the chances of individuals' interpretation of the terms might vary making accounting a kaleidoscope. Doctrines and standards are introduced to assign specific meaning to accounting terms.

Your father gives you five rupees in the morning and asks you to get a newspaper from the vendor at the corner of the street. You run to the paper mart, buy the paper, pay its price of three rupees and hand over the paper and the balance two rupees to your father. In the evening, mother gives you five hundred rupees and a list of things to be purchased from the grocers. You buy the things as per the list. It costs four hundred and fifty rupees. You deliver your purchases with the bill to mother. She takes a look at the bill and asks you for the balance fifty rupees. You tell her that you are keeping it as your pocket money. Your classmate in college gives you Rs.100 and requests you to buy a book available in your neighbourhood. You buy the book for Rs.75, get a receipt and deliver the book and the balance to your friend, who thanks you for the timely help. In the above instances and many such occasions you might come across daily, you were entrusted with a **mission** and provided with the requisite **resources** (money) and **authority** to achieve the mission. You had carried out the task and **reported back** what you have done with the resources. In other words, when you use resources, you become accountable to the givers. ***Accountability is, therefore, the responsibility of users to the providers of resources as to the manner in which the resources were used and the results thereof.***

Accountability

Business is an economic activity and like all economic activities involves use of resources. Resources comprise *5 ms -money, material, machine, method, and men.* Resources are the disposable portion of savings of individuals or groups. Savings in turn are the surplus of income over expenses that are required to earn the income. People prefer to maintain a part of their savings in liquid form for certain exigencies. As Keynes had propounded, three motives guide people to prefer to be in liquidity-transaction motive, precautionary motive and speculative motive. The residue of the savings, after providing for these exigencies, is finance or the resource available for use. Finance could either be used by the savers themselves or by others, whose needs for resources outstrip their ability to save. Individuals or groups might use their own resources in economic pursuits, when it is called *capital or equity* or hire resources from other people, when it is termed *debt*. Even where individuals or groups use their own resources, they become accountable for the uses, with express proofs called *vouchers*, for periodic reporting to governmental authorities for assessment of taxes. Taxes might be income tax, wealth tax, gift tax, corporate tax, sales tax etc. Failure to submit such accounts in the approved forms and within the stipulated time might expose the owners to punishment, both civil and criminal. In case of groups, individuals become additionally accountable to the constituents of the group also. Reports have also to be submitted when users, whether individuals or groups, desire to raise additional resources in the financial market or with their bankers or financial institutions for the development of business or for meeting their day-to-day *working capital* requirements. Nowadays, even moneylenders insist on performance records, in addition to collateral securities of adequate value, before lending money. Governments too become accountable to the citizen for the use of resources placed at their disposal in their capacity as the stewards of the country.

ACCOUNTABILITY MAP

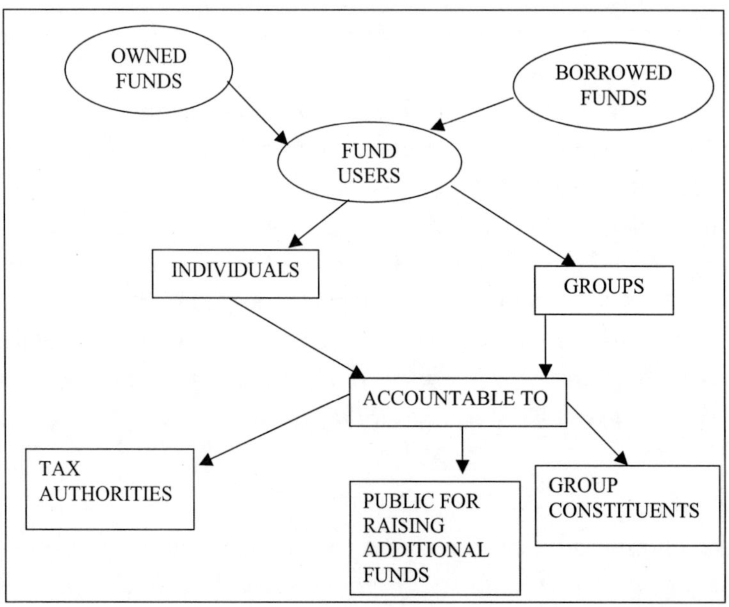

If the resources are hired by way of loans, deposits, bonds, hire purchases, leases etc., then the users become accountable to their lenders, who are concerned about the safety of their resources and the periodic realization of earnings. They are, thus, interested in the *creditworthiness* and the *financial position* of the users (for the safety of their resources) and *operating results* for the repaying capacity of the borrowers (payment of interests and repayment of principal as agreed to). For all these, the users become accountable to different sections of society, who have a stake in the business. The accountability map of the users of resources is given below:

Forms of Business Organizations: Sole Trading

That an individual or a group of individuals might promote a business is obvious. The persons who organize businesses are termed *entrepreneurs*. When an individual entrepreneur organizes a business with his owned resources and the resource he could hire from those having trust in him, we call the enterprise a *sole trading or proprietorship business*. As the sole trader is an individual, his capacity to arrange for resources and his managerial ability are limited and he has to be contended with a smaller sized business. The life of his business is linked with his personal life. His death, insanity or insolvency would put an end to his business. In other words, his business has no separate existence from him. Pan shops, bakeries, restaurants, fancy stores, shoe marts, departmental stores, dispensaries are all examples of sole trading business organizations. In law, sole trading is not recognized as an entity separate from the sole trader, who has organized it. His business and personal obligations are on par with each other. For the obligations of the business, he will be personally liable. This principle of *unlimited liability* applies to a sole trading concern. Vasuki Rani, whom we are going to learn more later, had started her business as a sole trader. She would become personally liable for her business obligations. In case her business obligations in the form of liabilities exceed her business resources represented by her assets, she has to meet the excess of obligations from out of her private resources or else will be declared insolvent.

It does not mean that sole trading, as an organization, has no merits at all. It has its own advantages. Primarily, as the sole trader is his own master, he can take prompt and timely decisions. And as timely decision is the secret of success in business, he has a better chance of becoming successful. Being the sole decision maker is not an unmixed blessing. It has got its darker side as well. As he has no one to consult, he might take wrong decisions, which might affect the business. He enjoys all the profits he earns. He takes personal interest in every detail of the business and controls costs drastically, thereby increasing profit. In businesses requiring personal contact and attention of entrepreneurs, such as those associated with arts, crafts and consumer sensitive products, sole trading has an edge over other forms of business organizations. That is why with all the economic and legal disadvantages, sole traders still thrive in specific areas.

Partnership

When a business expands requiring resources and managerial skill beyond the reach of a sole trader, he is inclined to share his business with others, who supply the needed inputs. A group is thus formed with more than one entrepreneur. Such a group might take the form of partnership, Joint Stock Company or co-operative society. Of these group-organizations, partnership is the logical extension of sole trading. Indian Partnership Act defines a partnership as a "*relation between persons, who have agreed to share the profits of the business carried on by all or any of them acting for all*". A partnership is thus a relationship borne out of an agreement between two or more persons. The agreement could be either oral or written. When oral, it is called *partnership at will.* When it is in writing and registered it is called a *registered partnership*. A partnership at will could be terminated by a oral notice, while a written notice is needed to terminate a registered partnership.

Another feature is to share the profits of the business. The proportion in which profits would be shared is an essential component of partnership deed. The partnership agreement stipulates the ratio of share in profits. When the agreement is silent, profits are to be shared equally among the partners without any regard to the capital contributed by the partners. How ever, in the event of the firm incurring losses, the sharing is in proportion to the capital outstanding at the end of the period. For example, GHO is A Partnership consisting of three partners, G H and O. G had contributed Rs. 20 lakhs as capital, H Rs.30 lakhs, while the contribution of O was Rs. 50 lakhs. In the year 2002 the business made a profit of Rs.30 lakhs. In the case where the partnership deed had not specified the ratio in which profits and losses are to be shared, each partner is entitled to Rs. 10 lakhs as share in profits. On the other hand, if the firm made a loss of Rs. 10 lakhs in 2003, the share in loss of the partners would be- G Rs.2 lakhs, H Rs. 3 lakhs and O Rs. 5 lakhs.

Partnership could be formed by a minimum of two persons and the maximum number is restricted to ten persons for banking business and twenty in the case of other businesses. Every partner in a partnership firm has the right to manage the business. It is permitted that the management be left in the hands of one or two, in which case the partners that manage the business are called ***active partners*** and the others ***sleeping partners***. In India, partnership firms by members of Hindu families are classified as ***Hindu undivided family concerns*** and are given separate treatment by the tax authorities. Partnership partakes the structural character of sole trading in many aspects, in the sense that it too has no separate legal entity apart from the persons forming it. A partnership can be formed by an oral agreement among the constituents, in which case an oral notice could dissolve it. It is an unstable form of group organization, as any one of the partners can bring about the end to the business by his resignation from the partnership without assigning any reason. The death, insolvency or insanity of any partner would also dissolve the firm. Partnership also attracts the rigors of unlimited liability just like sole trading. The principle of ***joint and several liabilities*** is another bane of this type of organization. Consequences of the acts of commission or omission of any partner are to be borne by all of them jointly and severally, whether they were party or not to such commission or omission. Promoters with special skills, whose business does not have much risk, such as chartered accountants, architects, advocates and consultants usually prefer partnership, as its Formation or dissolution are easy and does not involve legal formalities.

Limited Liability Partnership

Partnership, as we know, is an organization, where the liability of the partner is unlimited. However, in developed countries, there exists a hybrid form of partnership with limited liability except to at least one partner. The need for the introduction of limited liability in partnership has been long felt in the country. The recent report that Government is finalizing a draft act known as the Limited liability Partnership Act to permit limited liability in the operation of venture capital funds (in information technology sector) is, therefore, to be welcomed. Such an organizational set up will relieve the investors in venture capital funds of IT companies, of the rigors of unlimited liability. This concept is expected to develop the venture capital sector in the country. Once introduced, it will only be a matter of time before the applicability of the concept is enlarged to other sectors as well.

Joint Stock Company

Joint stock companies are the need-based outcome of the industrial revolution and its resultant mass scale production, which requires huge resources and managerial skills. A joint stock company "*is a voluntary association of persons formed for the purpose of some business for profit with common capital divisible into shares and possessing corporate legal entity and a common seal*". The share capital is divided into smaller denominations called *shares*, which are issued to the owners in proportion to the capital they agree to contribute. Persons who subscribe to the shares in a company are shareholders. There are two types of shares a company could issue-equity and preference. Equity shares empower the holders to participate in the management of the company. The equity shareholders are the members of the company. They meet once a year to elect directors to run the business. As the number of shareholders is large, varied and geographically spread, all of them cannot take part in the management. The management of a company is therefore entrusted to an elected body of equity shareholders called *board of directors*. The directors are elected by votes by the members at the meeting of members. Each equity shareholder is a part owner of the company and has as many votes as the number of shares he owns. The board manages the business as the representative of the shareholders and the directors hold office at the pleasure of majority shareholders. Equity shareholders are the real risk takers of the organization. They are the residual beneficiaries of the company, in the sense that in the payment of dividend and repayment of capital in the event of liquidation of the company, they stand next to preference shareholders.

The other type of shares, namely preference shares is redeemable after the lapse of a specified period and bears a predetermined rate of dividend. These shares bestow to its holders two important preferences over the equity shareholders. *Preference shareholders have preference as to the payment of dividend and the repayment of capital in the event of the winding up of the company.* In any year if the company's profits were not sufficient enough to pay dividends on both equity and preference shares, the latter would have priority. Further, in any year when the company has not made profits, the right of the preference shareholders for dividend of that year would be carried forward (unlike equity shareholders) and the accumulated dividends would first be paid when the company makes enough profits. This feature makes preference shares as *cumululative preference shares*. Thus, preference shares are redeemable and cumulative. The major set back of preference shares is that they do not give the right to their holders to manage the company. The preference shareholders cannot participate in the meeting of members and vote and do not have a say in the management of the company. There are two exceptions to this, one when the company has not declared dividend continuously for two years on these shares and two when the general body meeting decides issues affecting the rights of preference shareholders. Preference shares could be redeemed either from out of reserves or by issue of fresh shases.

The single most distinguishing feature of the joint stock company, compared to other forms of business organizations, is the concept of *separate legal entity* – it is a corporate body. A joint stock company is a legal person with its rights and responsibilities separate from the shareholders. The contractual capacity of a corporate is contained in its *memorandum of association*. The rules relating to its internal management is laid down in its *articles of association*. As joint stock company is an *artificial person* having a separate existence from its owners, the principle of unlimited liability does not apply to companies. A shareholder's responsibility to the *liabilities of the business is limited* to the extent of his committed contribution to the share capital of the company. His personal assets are not made liable to the claims on the company. By virtue of the separation of the company from its owners, this type of business organization has *perpetual succession* and death, insanity, insolvency or the relinquishment of ownership by any or all the shareholders would not threaten its existence. It is brought into existence by law and can be extinguished only by law.

Types of Companies

Companies are either public limited or private limited. *Private limited companies* have three basic restrictions - they are prohibited from inviting the public to subscribe to their share capital and debentures, the shareholders cannot transfer their shares to persons other then the members and the minimum number of members to form a private limited company is two and maximum should not exceed fifty. A *public limited company*, on the other hand, should have a minimum of seven members and there is no ceiling on the maximum. There are companies with millions of shares. Both the forms of companies are incorporated either under the Company's Act, 1956 or by any special enactment of Parliament. Companies registered under the companies act bear the word limited or its abbreviations such as Ltd or Pvt. Ltd as their suffix. In USA the corporates have the suffix of inc. meaning incorporated. Companies registered under special acts do not have this suffix, such as RBI, IDBI, LIC, UTI and nationalized banks etc. Whether a company is incorporated under the Companies Act, 1956 or under any special act, they are corporate bodies with their own memorandum of association and articles of association. *Memorandum of Association* is the charter of the company – it outlines the scope of activity of the company and any activity undertaken by the company, which is not permitted in its memorandum is ultravires and cannot be ratified even if all the members jointly desired to do so. It specifies the relationship between the company and the outsiders on important aspects such as activities that can be undertaken, borrowing powers, contracting authority etc. *Articles of Association*, on the other hand, lays down the rules for internal management of the company, such as the quorum for the board meeting, general body meeting, voting rights, meeting procedures etc. It is relevant here to dispel the misconception, if any, in the minds of some readers that public limited company is synonymous with Public Sector Company and private sector with private limited company. This need not necessarily be so. A *public sector company* is a corporate in which the government and its agencies together hold more than fifty one per cent of the paid up equity shares or voting rights. A *private sector company*, on the other hand is one in which majority of shares or voting rights is with general public or private parties that is other than government and governmental agencies. Thus, public sector companies could either be public limited or private limited. The distinction is one of major share holdings or voting rights by either governmental agencies or by the general public.

Indian Position

It might be of historic interest to learn that companies in India were recognized as separate legal entities only in 1850.The principle of limited liability was made applicable from 1857 and extended to banking and insurance companies from 1860. In 1913, private limited companies were introduced, making legal set up for corporates complete.

Cooperative Societies

The objective of joint stock companies being to make profit for its owners, the management of companies is entrusted to major money contributors or their agents. Hence this form of organization came under severe criticism of enlightened social workers in developed countries. They called companies as bourgeois or capitalistic organizations having least regard for the welfare of its minority members. These protests led to the formation of a more democratic form of business organization, the *cooperative societies.* Co-operative societies are business organizations established under the co-operative society act of the concerned States. H.Calvert, one of the pioneer cooperators, has defined a cooperative society as "*a form of organization wherein persons voluntarily associate together as human beings on the basis of equality for the economic interest of themselves*". The societies are formed for the betterment of their members. Only the members of a society can be served by the society. So any one desirous of availing the services of the society should first become its member. Cooperative societies do not issue shares to the public nor the shares are transferable. Any increase in the capital is brought about from the contributions of existing members and/ or by admitting new members. Any member desirous of quitting a society should surrender the shares to the society.

Cooperative societies are governed by their byelaws, which partake the role of the articles of association in a joint stock company. *They are owner-user based.* As Societies are formed for serving the needs of members; the profits are usually shared in proportion to the extent to which each member has used the society and not in proportion to the value of shares held by the members. Thus, societies are more democratic business organizations. The respective state governments govern cooperatives. There are different types of cooperative societies to cater to specific requirements of their members. Few examples are

- *Cooperative farming societies*
- *Cooperative producers societies*
- *Cooperative marketing societies*
- *Cooperative credit societies*
- *Cooperative banks*
- *Cooperative consumer societies*
- *Cooperative housing societies*
- *Multipurpose Cooperative societies*

Another striking difference is that co-operative societies have the principle of one man one vote irrespective of the quantum of share investment; just opposite to the principle of joint stock companies, where the number of votes of a member is related to the extent of his share holding. It is a form of democratic business organization. Co-operative societies can be organized either with limited liabilities or unlimited liabilities. Usually, co-operatives are meant for the economic upliftment of farmers, although there are urban co-operatives and industrial co-operatives, which serve other sections of society than peasants.

Accounting

Whatever might be the form of organization a businessman might chose, he is accountable to the various stakeholders in the business. The express form of accountability is to maintain accounts as per the norms of bookkeeping system. And frequently not a few new entrepreneurs are ignorant of keeping accounts. Take for example a woman entrepreneur, Vasuki Rani. Vasuki Rani, who after her engineering graduation, was not interested to get into any white collared job. She wanted to start her own business. Her father agreed to provide her with the seed capital of Rs.25, 000 and her cousins Girish and Ilkya volunteered to advance Rs.15,000 and Rs.10,000 respectively at 18% interest. With the fund of Rs.50, 000, Vasuki Rani hired a place of business in a busy locality in Chennai at a monthly rent of Rs.7, 500 and employed a helper at a salary of Rs.4, 000 per month. On 1st September 2001, she started her business activities. She was keeping a mental record of her business activities for some time. But as the business picked up briskly and the number of her business activities increased day by day, she was not that confident of remembering every thing that happens. She, therefore, began noting all her dealings chronologically in a notebook and the list of her business activities for the month of September 2001 is given in annexure 01 A at the end of this chapter. When she went through the list, she could neither make head nor tail of it. Answers were not available to many of the questions that have been plaguing her mind now days, such as

- *What happened to her money and the moneys she had borrowed from Girish and Ilkya?*
- *What is the result of her operations during the month-has she made any profit or incurred loss?*
- *Who are the parties that owe money to her and to what extent?*
- *Who are the parties to whom she owes and how much? And*
- *What are the assets she owns and what is their value?*

The dilemma in which Vasuki Rani and many new business people like her might be in is due to their overlooking an important aspect for success in business, namely maintaining proper records of the business activities. But the problem is not insurmountable. The system of recording business activities is known as *bookkeeping.* Vasuki Rani can easily learn the art of recording her business deals by going through any fundamental book on accounting. The task is made easy now days, as simple accounting packages like Tally are available. She can learn the fundamentals of accounting and with the help of the package, could herself keep proper accounts. Or else, she can employ an accounts clerk to do the job at an affordable cost.

Definition of Accounting

The word accounting usually refers to financial accounting, although it covers three groups- financial accounting, cost accounting and management accounting. First let us know what financial accounting is. Eminent writers have defined the term financial accounting but their definitions reflect the state of the accounting system prevalent in their area and at their time. As the scope of accounting function has been expanding over the time, there are perceptible variations in the definitions. The American Accounting Association has defined accounting as ***the process of identifying, measuring and communicating economic information to permit informed judgments and decisions by users of the information***. But the definition provided by the American Institute of Certified Public Accountants (AICPA) is the one that lucidly brings out the meaning and objectives of financial accounting, which could be applied in any part of the globe and at any time. In the words of AICPA, "***accounting is the art of recording, classifying and summarizing, in a significant manner and in terms of money, transactions and events, which are, in part at least, of a financial character and interpreting the results there of***".

Bookkeeping

When accountability is formalized through records, it is called ***financial accounting***. The language in which financial accounting is chronicled is ***bookkeeping.*** Prof. Carter has defined bookkeeping as "***correctly recording, in the books of accounts, all the business transactions that result in the transfer of money's worth***". Bookkeeping is the ***language*** in which business transactions are recorded. In bookkeeping language, there are only ***two words or impulses-debit(Dr.) and credit(Cr.).*** It should be borne in mind that bookkeeping is not synonymous with accounting. Although the basis of accounting is bookkeeping, bookkeeping is not accounting. Accounting is an entity where bookkeeping is a limb. Bookkeeping is a mechanical process of recording the business transaction in a set of books, as per the procedures laid down. Bookkeeping is the process of accumulating, in an understandable form, data about the business during an ***accounting period***. Accounting, on the other hand, is the technique by which the data generated by bookkeeping activity is converted into information to be used by the management in framing future policies. While bookkeeping accumulates data pertaining to the business activities, accounting processes, analyzes and interprets the data for furtherance of the interest of the business. Bookkeeping is clerical in nature while accounting is developmental in character.

Objectives of Accounting

It can be discerned from the various discussions we had so far, that the purpose of accounting is three fold, namely to

- *Ascertain the results of business operation during the accounting period,*
- *Disclose the financial strength of the business as at the end of the period and*
- *Utilize the data generated in the accounting system for making policy decisions.*

It is common knowledge and does not require any special technical training to understand that ***sales,*** also called ***turnover***, less the cost of effecting such sales, is the result of doing business. In the event of the value of sales, during the period is more than the cost, the operation has resulted in a surplus for the period and is called ***profit***. On the other hand, should the value of sales be less than the cost of sales, the operation has resulted in a deficit. Such a deficit is called ***loss***. Capital increases when the business makes profit and vice versa in case of deficit in operations. It is expedient that the businessman does not take away the entire surplus generated, but leaves something behind as a cushion against future fluctuations in the working results of the business or for further developing the business. Such left over profits are ***retained earnings***, often called as ***reserves and surplus***. The financial strength of a business is gauged by the excess of what is owned by it, called assets, over what it owes to others, called outside liabilities. The excess of assets over outside liabilities is the owner's funds, called ***net worth***. A comparison between the net worth of the owners and the borrowed funds known as ***debt-equity ratio,*** in accounting terminology, indicates the financial strength of the business. Lower the ratio of debt, compared to equity, better is the financial position of the business. Detailed discussion on these aspects is to follow in subsequent chapters.

Divisions of Accounting

Accounting has been broadly classified into three branches for functional studies

- *Financial accounting*
- *Cost accounting and*
- *Management accounting*

Although each of these branches has a specific role to play, these are not to be construed as watertight compartments. Financial Accounting is the basis for cost accounting and management accounting is the processing of the data generated in the other two branches. They are inter-related. A brief description of the three branches of accounting follows:

Financial Accounting

Financial Accounting is the technique through which one could measure the overall results of the business activities of a sole trader, partnership, corporate or society. Whatever be the nature of the business organization, the objective of financial accounting is to convert the input of the business activity of the organization into the output of useful information, ultimately to be used as basis for decision-making by the policy makers. It is an objective rendering of the historic events in the business during that particular period. It has to be within the framework of the laws of the country and the rules and practices of the profession. Financial accounting provides information about the business organization, namely its financial position and working results. This is done through recording, classifying and summarizing the business transactions and events and interpreting the results thereof. The information generated in the financial accounting section is also available to outsiders in consolidated forms of financial statement at periodic intervals.

Financial accounting encompasses the different stages of ***accounting process***, which is called by some authors as ***accounting cycle***. To be called a cycle, a process should be revolving without an end as long as the business operates. For example, operating cycle. Cash becomes inventory, then semi-finished goods, finished goods, receivables and then cash. That is cycle. In science we have nitrogen cycle, where nitrogen is absorbed by plants from atmosphere and is finally returned to atmosphere after use. Clouds become rain and water evaporates and become clouds again and this process goes on forever. These are cycles. But in accounting, the information processed from a transaction never becomes a transaction again. The reason attributed to call the accounting process as cycle is that the process of recording, classifying, summarizing and interpreting is repeated transaction after transaction and year after year. Yes, but not with the same data. We however overlook the inconsistency in the meaning of the word and follow the process. Accounting cycle, or to be precise *accounting process*, refers to the process of converting information locked up in transactions into financial reports. The various stages through which the accounting cycle revolves are

- *Identification of the aspects in transactions and events*
- *Recording the aspects in journals*
- *Posting the journals to ledgers*
- *Summarizing the ledger balances in trial balance and*
- *Preparing profit and loss account and balance sheet.*

Functions of Accountants

Readers might have, by now, had sufficient information to list the roles expected of accountants in business management. The accountant has to take all steps to translate the data in transactions and events into usable information. Basically, his role is to measure and communicate the financial and economic data hidden in transactions. For this, he has to

- *Keep records of transactions and events with supportive documents like vouchers, bills, orders etc.*
- *Interpret the message contained in transactions and events fairly without bias.*
- *Convert the information into reports.*
- *Perform mid-level managerial functions by supplying correct information to the correct person at the correct time.*
- *Comply with legal requirements, as required by the laws of the country.*

Limitations of Financial Accounting

Financial accounting system has its own limitations. As we have seen it is historical in character. It records transactions at the transacted value without any relevance to its real value.

There are chances of the interpretation of data contained in transactions tainted by the bias of the accountant. It records quantitative information, over looking important qualitative aspects. Valuable changes in technology, market conditions, customer preferences, and effectiveness of management that are sensitive to the business operation are not recorded, as they are not measurable in money or moneys worth. The information generated in financial accounting are raw and could not be used unless these are processed further. With all its limitations, financial accounting is the backbone of managerial accountability. Chapter 03 deals in detail about financial accounting.

Cost Accounting

Cost Accounting is ***the process of identifying, summarizing and interpreting information needed for planning and control, management decisions and product costing***. It is that branch of accounting, which analyzes the cost data, generated in financial accounting section and provides management with information for planning products, inventories, operations, and functions. It enables management to have effective control. In this type of accounting, the cost of producing a commodity or rendering a service is broken into smallest segments called elements and each element is analyzed critically from the point of view of usage, mix and price to arrive at optimal cost. Thus, the overall cost of production is controlled by controlling the costs of elements, thereby maximizing the profit of the business. Detailed discussion on these aspects would follow in cost accounting section of the book.

Management Accounting

Management Accounting is the process in which the data generated in the financial accounting and in the cost accounting systems are analyzed and processed with the help of statistical and other tools, modified, where necessary, to suit the specific requirements of decision making. The functions of management being planning, organizing, leading and controlling the business, management accounting provides inputs for decisions on the four areas. It is the end use of the accounting activities of the business. Detailed discussion on management accounting is to follow in the later part of the book.

Generally Accepted Accounting Principles

The definition of accounting brings out the nature and functions of financial accounting. It consists of the four clear cut activities of recording the twin aspects of transactions and events, classifying the aspects to arrive at the net value of each of the aspects, preparing a summary of the accounts and finally with the help of the summary interpret the results of the transactions. Accounting being an art is founded on the personal skills of the practitioners called ***accountants*** to interpret the impact of the transactions, guided by certain principles evolved over the years in accordance with the development of the economy and from out of a combination of traditional needs, experience and official laws. Due to the diverse situations from which the accounting practices have risen, they tend to be varied and kaleidoscopic in nature. With a view to impart an element of uniformity into the varied practices, so as to make comparative studies of the accounting data meaningful, accounting principles were later introduced. These principles stipulate the ground rules for financial accounting and are termed as ***Generally Accepted Accounting Principles (GAAP).*** According to AICPA, ***GAAP are in the category of conventions or rules developed by man from experience to fulfill the essential and useful needs and purposes in establishing reliable financial and operating information control for business activities. In this respect, they are similar to principles of commercial laws and other social disciplines***. GAAP thus, provides a general framework for financial accounting objectives, standards, concepts, assumptions, methods and rules. It is a sort of law for accountants, but could not be comparable to the natural laws, where causes lead to definite and same results. GAAP are flexible to subserve the specific needs of an accounting situation and are constantly undergoing alternations and modifications to suit the changing environment in which these are applied. Broadly, GAAP can be grouped into conventions and doctrines.

Accounting Conventions

Conventions are established usages evolved from customs among persons interacting in business, which have received the tacit approval of the society. Important among the accounting conventions are money measurement convention, historic cost convention, going concern convention and accounting period convention.

Money Measurement Convention

We have already seen in the definition of accounting that business transactions are activities and events whose value could be reduced to money or moneys worth. Transactions are to be recorded, classified, summarized and interpreted. In order to enter any activity as a transaction in financial records, the subject matter of the transaction should be capable of being exchanged for money or money's worth. For anything to have exchange value, it must be separable from the source and capable of being transferred. In order to be exchangeable and transferable, the item should be external and not an inseparable part of the source. An event like the death of a partner / director or a dispute between the finance manager and the technical manager or an industrial dispute, which would affect the business, is not a business transaction as these are not measurable in terms of moneys worth. These events ate not recorded in the books of the businessman.

Historic Cost Convention

As accounting is the recording of business transactions as and when they occur, the monetary value at which they have to be recorded assumes importance, particularly in the present day context of ever increasing prices. As transactions have to be recorded objectively, the subjective condition of different value of an asset at the time of acquisition and later is to be ignored. For instance, the purchase of a piece and land by the business at Rs.2.50 lakhs, although independent valuation places the value at Rs.3 lakhs, will be recorded in the books at Rs.2.50 lakhs only or the price actually paid for. It is, therefore, the practice in accounting to record the money value of transactions at the price at which the transaction was concluded, that is, at the historic cost.

Business Entity Convention

Legally speaking, only a joint stock company (Private limited or Public limited) has a separate legal entity apart from the persons forming it. It is a legal personality having its own rights and liabilities, which are clearly kept outside the rights and liabilities of the persons forming it. It is not so in the other forms of business organizations. In proprietorship or partnership, the legal rights and liabilities of the businesses co-exist with those of the businessmen owning the businesses. However, as far as accounting practice is concerned, the business and the businessmen constituting the business are considered separate accounting entities, whether the business is sole trading, partnership or joint stock company. That is to say, not withstanding the differential legal position, all business organizations are considered to be separate ***accounting entities*** from the persons forming them. As business operates with the objective of making profit, using the resources placed at its disposal, the business becomes the steward and is accountable to the providers of resources, whether they are owners or lenders. The accountability mat in an earlier page highlights this relationship. This stewardship character of business has given rise to the convention that the business is a separate accounting entity from the persons forming it. Unless all activities connected with the business are kept separately, without mixing them with the personal activities of the businessmen, it will be difficult, if not impossible, to ascertain, with certainty, the results of the use of those resources. Hence, the practice to treat the business as a separate accounting entity is a generally accepted principle. With the spread of specialization to business, a business might have sub-accounting entities- the production department and marketing department might become separate accounting entities, with in the overall accounting entity of the organization as a whole.

Going Concern Convention

It is the accounting principle to presume that the intention of the business is to continue for sufficiently longer period of time. However, in certain instances, where the venture is for specific purposes, such as setting up a stall in an exhibition or executing building construction for the landlord under a contract etc, the tenure of the business is short. But in all the manufacturing and service industries, business is expected to continue for a fairly long period. Hence, the terminal value of assets is not recorded every year. Cost at which each transaction is recorded is the price paid for it at the time of the transaction. Day-to-day fluctuation in the value of transactions is ignored. For example, machinery was purchased at Rs.2.35 crores on 1.4.2000. It is recorded as Rs.2.35 crores at the time of purchase and allowed to remain at that price, even though the cost of the machinery might have come down to Rs.1.75 crores the very next year. Transactions are continuous and each transaction is recorded at the historic cost. During the existence of business, new assets will be added and old assets displaced- all at the historic cost, as the business is a going concern.

Accounting Period Convention

It has been seen in the previous paragraphs that the business entity is expected to have a fairly longer life. In that event, if the businessman has to assess the results of his business endeavors, he has to wait for an unduly long period, till it is terminated. As the intention is not to close down the business, the businessman divides the life of business into relatively short accounting periods of equal lengths and evaluates its performance during periodic intervals, which might be monthly, quarterly, half-yearly or yearly. It is neither prudent nor expedient to be in a business indefinitely without knowing whether the operations have been profitable or not. In India, the customary accounting period is twelve months i.e. a year commencing from 1st April and ending with 31st March. Indian corporates have, after globalization, been increasingly adopting quarterly reporting like their western counterparts.

Doctrines

Doctrines, also called principles, on the other hand, are rules or theories conceived by accounting professionals for application in specific situations. The prominent among the accounting doctrines are Doctrine of consistency, Doctrine of conservatism, Doctrine of materiality and Doctrine of disclosure.

Doctrine of Consistency

It is essential that there is consistency or uniformity in the accounting practices followed by the business, period after period. This will ensure a meaningful study of the performance of business over the periods. Specific areas, for example, where consistency in the policies is of importance, are in the provision for depreciation and in the valuation of inventories at the end of the accounting period. There are different methods of providing depreciation on assets, such as straight-line method, written down value method, sum of the digit method, depletion method, machine hour method etc, of which a business can choose an appropriate method for adoption. For example, plant and machinery might be depreciated at written down value or straight-line method, mining lease might adopt depletion method, lathes might use machine hour method. Detailed discussion on depreciation follows in a subsequent chapter. Once a method is adopted, it should be the endeavour of the business to continue to follow the same throughout the life of the assets. Similarly, inventory valuation might be based on first in first out (FIFO), last in first out (LIFO), or weighted average (WA) methods, of which the business might follow any one consistently. It does not mean that once a particular method is adopted, the business has necessarily to stick to that method alone and that all the other methods are closed to it. Not at all. It can change the methods once in a while to cope with the changes in the situation, but not every now and then. For example, a business might adopt weighted average method for valuing its inventories when the price is fluctuating. However, it might change into LIFO subsequently when prices are affected by inflation.

Doctrine of Materiality

In recording the transactions, it should be ensured that all the relevant information regarding the activities of the business that are material to subserve the objective of the business is recorded. As to what is materiality in accounting practice, the American Accounting Association's Executive Committee has described the term as, "an Item should be regarded as material, if there is reason to believe that knowledge of it would influence the decision of an informed investor". The essence of materiality, therefore, is the relative importance of the information for use in decision-making. Value of the transaction is immaterial as long as the information is vital. For example, when the business pays a nominal penalty of Rs.100 for non-submission of periodic returns, this aspect should be highlighted by recording it specifically, although the amount is small, as it brings to the notice of all concerned about the lethargy of those running the business. On the other hand, wages paid for different shifts need not be separately recorded as such information is immaterial.

Doctrine of Conservatism

A business should follow, as far as possible, conservative methods, practiced over a period, as these have withstood the test of time. This doctrine is the outcome of the inclination on the part of the businessman to play safe. Conservatism does not mean blind following of established customs, whether relevant or not. The attitude of the business should be to adopt meaningful and beneficent changes, as and when needed, so as to reap the benefits of innovation. The conservative principle of accounting practice is evident in talking into account any revenue as income, only when it accrues. Goods sent on consignment basis are recognized as sales and recorded when the consignee sends the statement of account. On the other hand expenses are accounted even if there is a remote possibility of their occurrence, like provision for doubtful debts. Closing stock valuation at purchase price or market price, whichever is lower, is another instance of the adoption of the principle of conservatism.

Doctrine of Disclosure

The principle of adequate disclosure of the affairs of the business is a sequel to the increasing void between the business and the businessman. Gone are the days when the businessman was involved with every detail of his business. With mass scale production being the order of the day, business organizations tend to grow to a mega size, with thousands of people contributing to the owned funds and borrowed funds. The purveyors of funds are not only numerous but are also varied and located at different parts of the country and even outside the country. In the circumstances, it is neither prudent nor practical for all the fund providers to have access to details of day-to-day activities of the business. Hence, the management in large business is entrusted to an elected body of the owners known as board of directors. In a private limited company, the minimum number of directors prescribed by law is two and in a public limited company it is three. One, from among the directors, is chosen as the Chief Executive by whatever designation he is known, such as President or Managing Director or Chairman and Managing Director. The board has to disclose the relevant information to the fund providers at periodic intervals through consolidated statements of accounts. Disclosure of information is also needed by investing public to decide whether to invest in that business or not. In disclosing the required information, the management should be guided by prudence, substance over form and materiality. The onus of disclosure is on the directors of a company or the owners of any other form of business organization. A word of caution might be added here. In its earnestness to comply with the disclosure principle, the management should avoid exposing the strengths of the business to the preying eyes of the competitors. In other words, the disclosure should be to the extent of exhibiting a true and fair view of the business.

Accounting Standards

As generally Accepted Accounting Principles were optional, businessmen adopted the principles whenever they suited them and ignored when they hurt them. The flexible character of GAAP lent itself to the interpretation of the principles to the selfish end of a few entrepreneurs. The need, therefore, of imparting an element of compulsion in the implementation of GAAP was long felt. However, there was a general hesitation on the part of all concerned to make the adoption of GAAP mandatory. The impasse was broken by the rude shock inflicted on the western economy by the crash of Wall Street in 1929, when the accounting professionals felt the need to standardize GAAP and to make the vital principles compulsory for adoption by the accounting fraternity. USA took the lead in this direction, followed by UK, Australia, Canada and other Countries. The American Institute of Accountants, since renamed as the American Institute of Certified Public Accountants (AICPA) was entrusted with the task of codifying the accounting principles to be adopted as a guide by the professionals. The AICPA appointed, in 1933, the Committee on Accounting Practices, which collected and published the accounting practices in a publication entitled ***"A Statement of Accounting Practices".*** The statement evoked mixed reaction from the accounting professionals and hence could not be adopted. Finally, in 1973, Financial Accounting Standard Board (FASB) was established to set standards for the generally accepted accounting principles in the United States. USA, UK, Australia, Canada and other Countries formed the International Accounting Standards Committee (IASC) at the same time under the leadership of Sir Henry Benson, with the responsibility of formulating international standards. All the member countries agreed to adopt the standard set up by IASC. Of late, many Indian companies have adopted international standards. In case the IASC standards were not followed, it was agreed that variation from the international standard would be specifically disclosed.

International Standards

Accounting standards are, thus, the codified forms of generally accepted accounting principles. Standards consist of detailed rules to be adopted for treatment of various items in accounting, before the periodic financial reports are presented to the concerned. The main objective of setting up standards is to convey the same meaning of any accounting concept to all people in the same sense so that uniformity and comparability in financial reporting is achieved. The accounting standard will be useful when it provides for a generally understood and accepted measure of phenomenon of the business and when it aims at reducing any manipulation of the financial data. Taking the above aspects into consideration, IASC has set up quite a long list of 41 standards so far, of which the following merit mentioning:

- *Disclosure of Accounting Policies (IAS-1)*
- *Valuation and Presentation of Inventories (IAS-2)*
- *Consolidated Financial Statements (IAS-3)*
- *Depreciation Accounting (IAS-4)*
- *Information to be disclosed in Financial Statements (IAS-5)*
- *Accounting Response to Changing Prices (IAS-6)*
- *Statements of Changes in Financial Position (IAS-7)*
- *Changes in Accounting Polices (IAS-8)*
- *Accounting for Research and Development Activities (IAS-9)*
- *Contingencies and Events occurring after the Balance Sheet Date (IAS-10)*
- *Accounting for Construction Contracts (IAS-11)*
- *Accounting for Taxes and Income (IAS-12)*

- *Presentation of Current Assets and Current Liabilities (IAS-13)*
- *Reporting financial Information by segment (IAS-14)*
- *Information reflecting the effects of Changing Prices (IAS-15)*
- *Accounting for property, Plant and Equipment (IAS-16)*
- *Accounting for Leases (IAS-17).*

Standards in India

Accounting professionals in India have, by and large, been following the IASC standards, as their measurement and disclosure rules. Based on the IASC standards and taking into account the specific local conditions, the Institute of Chartered Accountants of India (ICAI) has constituted ***Accounting Standard Board (ASB),*** which is entrusted with the task of prescribing standards for practice in India. The Board so far issued standards for twenty-eight items as under:

- *Disclosure of Accounting Policies (AS-1)*
- *Valuation of Inventories (AS-2)*
- *Changes in Financial Position (AS-3)*
- *Contingencies and Events occurring after the Balance Sheet Date (AS-4)*
- *Prior Period and Extraordinary item sand Changes in Accounting Policies (AS-5)*
- *Depreciation accounting (AS-6)*
- *Accounting for Construction contracts (AS-7)*
- *Accounting for Research for Development (AS-8)*
- *Revenue Recognition (AS-9)*
- *Accounting for Fixed Assets (AS-10)*
- *Accounting for the effects of changes in foreign exchange rates (AS-11)*
- *Accounting for Government grants (AS-12)*
- *Accounting for Investments (AS-13)*
- *Accounting for Amalgamations (AS-14)*
- *Accounting for retirement benefits in the financial statements of employers (AS-15)*
- *Accounting for Segmental Reporting (AS-17)*
- *Selected part disclosures (AS-18)*
- *Leases (AS-19)*
- *Earnings per share (AS-20)*
- *Consolidated financial statements (AS-21)*

- *Accounting for taxes on income (AS-22)*
- *Investment in associates in consolidated accounts (AS-23)*
- *Discontinuing operations (AS-24)*
- *Interim financial reporting (AS-25)*
- *Intangible assets (AS-26)*
- *Financial reporting of interest in joint ventures (AS-27)*
- *Impairment of assets (AS-28)*

Of the above standards, AS-1, AS-4, AS-5, and AS-7 to AS-28 are made mandatory to corporate entities and the balance three are recommendatory. Although the three standards at AS-2, AS-3 and AS-6 are recommendatory in nature, Indian accounting professionals devote as much importance to these as they do to the other twelve and treat these on par with the mandatory standards. For non-corporate entities comprising sole proprietary concerns, partnership firms, co-operative societies, registered under co-operative societies act, trusts, Hindu undivided and families and association of persons, ICAI has made AS-1, AS-7 to AS-12 and AS-15 as mandatory. The others are, of course, recommendatory. Two more standards for IT industry on information systems and information security audits are on the anvil and are expected to be introduced.

Majority of the accounting standards are made mandatory on the accounting professionals for adherence while recording, classifying and summarizing transactions and more significantly, at the stage of interpreting the results there of i.e., preparation of financial statements. Accounting standards are, as we have already seen, prescribed with the objective of ushering in a sense of conformity in accounting practices. However, the rigidity with which the standards are being implemented uniformly to all enterprise, without having regard to the differing nature of the enterprises, which would require differential treatment, has raised many an eyebrow both in the US and in India about the efficacy of the standards. Accounting professionals feel that transparency should be built in to the standards to make their impact more realistic. It is the personal view of the author that it would be highly impracticable to have separate standards for each industry or for different sizes of enterprises to meet their specific requirements. On the other hand, in the name of transparency should any latitude be shown and the effects of standards become relaxed, the purpose of the entire exercise of bringing comparability in financial reporting will be defeated and the reliability of the accounting information will be thrown back to square one.

Internal Control System

An accountatant should follow internal control measures within the organization. Internal control, in the broadest sense, means taking all measures to

- *Protect the resources of the company against waste, misuse and fraud*
- *Ensure reliability of accounting data*
- *Comply with management's policy and*
- *Evaluate performance*

There are two types of control -accounting and administrative. Accounting control measures relate directly to the reliability of accounting information and include taking physical verification of inventory at the end of the period, reconciling ledger accounts with controlling accounts and protection of assets. Administrative controls are designed to increase operational efficiency, like quality control, budgetary control and standard costing.

Strong internal controls in accounting requires establishment of clear lines of responsibility. The organization should demarcate sections, departments or individuals responsible for specific functions, such as sales, purchases, payments, keeping records etc. The important way to achieve internal accounting control is to subdivide duties. It should be ensured that no one individual, section or department handles a transaction completely from beginning to end. For example, credit sale of goods to a person. Selling department has to procure orders, credit department to approve the credit standing of customers, stock keeper to assemble the goods, transport department to arrange for the transshipment, billing department to bill and the accounting department to record. Custody of assets should be separate from maintaining account for that asset to avoid falsification of records to conceal shortages. Other measures of achieving internal control systems are to have internal and concurring auditing, rotation of employees and serially numbering documents. Preparation of documents and its approval should be in different hands.

Summary

In this introductory chapter, readers were exposed to the background of business endeavors and the need to maintain records of the business activities. Individuals and groups use their own resources and the borrowed resources, they are accountable to the tax authorities and the purveyors of resources, who are interested in the safety of their resources and the ability of the business to service the resources as agreed upon. To meet these demands, the promoters have to accumulate financial data, through recording, classifying and summarizing transactions and by interpreting the results thereof.

The recording of the transaction is carried out in accordance with established accounting conventions and doctrines called generally accepted accounting principles. When the generally accepted accounting principles are enforced with a degree of authority for adoption, they are known as standards. There are International and Indian accounting standards to bring about comparability in accounting information locally and globally.

The function of accounting are to reveal the operating results of the business during a period, to asses the financial position as at the end of the period and to generate data for use in management decisions. It is classified into financial accounting, cost accounting and management accounting to accomplish the assigned functions. Details of the recording part of transactions, with the policies, procedures and formalities are being dealt with in chapter 2. Chapter 3 deals with the classification and summarizing of business activities. The interpretation of the results of the transactions is covered in chapters that follow.

I. QUESTIONS

1. What do you mean by accounting? What are its divisions?

2. Who is a promoter?

3. What are the types of business organizations available for business? What are their relative merits and demerits?

4. What were the questions in Vasuki Rani's mind? Are they justifiable?

5. What are the sources of resources used in economic activities?

6. How does a promoter service owned and borrowed resources?

7. What do owners expect from the business records?

8. What do lenders expect from the business records?

9. What is bookkeeping?

10. What distinguishes bookkeeping from accounting?

11. What is profit and what is loss?

12. What are the functional branches of accounting?

13. What is financial accounting? What does it strive to achieve?

14. Briefly explain what cost accounting is and its utility?

15. What do you mean by management?

16. What is the function of Management Accounting?

17. What do you understand by Generally Accepted Accounting Principles?

18. Describe briefly accounting doctrines?

19. What are the accounting conventions ?

20. Do you agree that enterprises should adopt uniform accounting practices? Why?

21. Should accounting standards be made mandatory to all?

22. Briefly trace the evolution of accounting standards?

23. What are accounting standards?

24. How many standards have so far been established internationally? Enumerate them?

25. Who are the fore runners in establishing accounting standards?

26. Who issues accounting standards in India?

27. How many standards have so far been issued in India? Enumerate.

28. What is accounting cycle?

29. What are the limitations of financial accounting system?

30. Define the term accounting standards and explain how they are used in preparing final statements?

II. QUIZ

Choose the correct alternative

1. Vasuki Rani brought money by way of (capital/loan/both)

2. Vasuki Rani's total funds at the start of business were (Rs.25, 000/Rs.50,000)

3. Business activities are also known as (accounts/transactions and events)

4. Bookkeeping and accountancy are one and the same (Yes/No)

4. Resources are (3ms/5ms)

5. Funds for business can be (owned / borrowed / both)

6. Net worth is (total funds? Owner's funds).

7. Business organization by groups is (proprietary concern/ partnership).

8. Sole trading is a business by (1,10,15, unlimited number of owners)

9. Partnership firm for banking business can have (5,10,15,20 partners)

10. Joint stock companies have unlimited liability (yes/no)

11. Private limited company means private sector company (yes / no/ might be)

12. Generally accepted accounting principles are (mandatory/optical/both)

13. Accounting standards are (flexible/rigid/both)

14. International standards issued so far are (10, 19, more)

15. Accounting standards issued in India are (10,15,17,19,21,28,30)

16. How many of Indian standards are mandatory to corporates (3,10,12,15, more)

17. Indian standards are issued by (RBI/ICAI/ICWAI/GOI, ASB)

18. International standards are set by (AICPA/FASB/IASC/GAAP).

III. EXERCISES

1. Visit any business establishment at busy time and observe what are the types of transactions that take place during an hour.
2. Keep a record of all your monetary transactions in an accounting package, such as Tally.

ANEXURE-01A

List of business activities of Vasuki Rani for the month of September 2001

	Amount Rs.
Sept.1	
Cash brought in as Capital	25,000
Opened bank account with initial deposit	10,000
Received cheques for Rs15,000 and Rs.10,000from Girish and Ilkya as loans.	
Paid rent	1,500
Bought Furniture	4,500
Bought goods for cash	5,000
Bought goods and issued cheques	20,000
Sold goods for cash	6,450
Sold goods to James	2,500
Bought goods from Ramesh	8,500
Sold goods for cash	3,750
Paid transport and coolie	75
Sept.3	
Paid insurance for the stock of goods	350
Sold goods to Haris	1,750
Bought some goods for each	2,675
Cash sales of the day	5,250
Sept.4	
Returned to Ramesh a part of goods as they were not in accordance with the description	1,150
James returned goods, as they were defective	500
Ramesh replaced returned goods	1,150

Cash sales	450
Paid in to bank	10,000
Paid Ramesh by cheque in full settlement of his account	8,250
Haris paid by cheque for Rs 1,700 and was allowed discount of Rs.50	
Sept.5	
Bought stamps	25
Bought goods from Hameedia & Co.	11,400
Cash sales	7,550
Sold goods to Stephen	1,500
Haris cheque was dishonoured.	
Sept.6	3,250
Cash sales	10,000
Deposited into bank	2,000
James paid	85
Entertainment expenses	1,450
Bought a cycle by cheque	8,400
Sold goods for cash	
Sept.7	7,500
Bought goods from Gopal	8,750
Sold goods to Hegde	4,855
Cash sales	15,000
Paid into bank	9,800
Bought a cupboard from Blue Bird & Co	
Sept.9	
Stephen paid cash	1,000
Paid Hamedia & C. by cheque in full settlement	11,000
Bought goods through cheque	24,800
Cash sales	6,650
Sold on credit to Niranjan Das	9,850
Paid cartage	60
Sept.10	
Paid for packing materials	250
Received cash for sale of goods	8,250
Sold goods to Shah & Co.	18,900
Paid Gopal by cheque	7,500

Sept.11	
Paid for advertisement	1,150
Sold for cash	11,500
Paid coolly	125
Sept.12	
Bought a typewriter from Remington Rand	18,500
Sold goods for cash	9,950
Paid the loan of Girish by cash. Interest waived	15,000
Sold to Maneklal & Co	8,850
Bought goods from Rohini Traders & Co	27,500
Paid transport on the purchase	750
Sept.13	
Paid into bank	10,000
Cash sales	14,000
Purchased through cheque	7,000
Hegde paid Rs.8,700 and was allowed discount of Rs.50	
Sold goods to Patel & Co	11,050
Sept.14	
Niranjan Das paid	9,850
Paid into bank	30,000
Sold goods for cash	8,000
Bought goods from Goswamy & Co	46,550
Sold to Bose & Co	8,800
Sept.16	
Stephen paid	500
Cash sales	14,200
Paid into bank	15,000
Issued a cheque to Remington Rand	18,500

Sept.17	
Shah & Co. paid	18,900
Deposited into the bank account	30,000
Sold for cash	12,500
Paid wages	2,500
Invested in NSC	5,000
Sold to Niranjan Das	5,500
Sept 18	
Paid Blue Bird & Co. by cheque	9,800
Maneklal & Co. paid	8,850
Repaid the loan of Ilkya by cheque; interest waived	10,000
Cash sales	14,500
Sept.19	
Paid into bank	25,000
Bought goods and paid cheque	37,000
Sold for cash	11,500
Sept.20	
Cash sales	7,000
Sold to Thanavala & Co	9,250
Bought goods from Rawal & Co	21,500
Sept.21	
Bought goods for cash	12,500
Sold goods for cash	10,450
Patel & Co. paid	5,000
Paid Goswamy & Co	20,000
Niranjan Das paid	5,500
Sept.23	
Paid into bank	28,000
Patel & Co. paid the balance Cash sales	17,000
Paid Goswamy & Co	20,000
Sold to Pilai Planits Ltd.,	8,200

Sept.24	
Thanavala & Co. paid	28,000
Paid Rawal & Co	17,000
Cash sales	20,000
Bought goods from Kapur & Co	8,200
Sept.25	
Cash sales	15, 800
Sold to Kothari & Co.	17,250
Paid Rawal & Co.	6,500
Thanavala Paid	4,250
Sept.26	
Sold goods to Niranjan Das	7,200
Cash sales of the day	9,885
Bought goods from Rawal & Co	39,870
Sept.27	
Postage expenses	155
Sold goods to Patel & Co	17,800
Cash sales	8,500
Sept.28	
Cash sales	16,550
Paid into bank	35,000
Paid Kapur & Co. by cheque in full settlement	26,250
Sold goods to Thanavala & Co	9,750
Sept.30	
Niranjan Das paid	7,200
Cash sales	16,650
Paid salaries	3,500
Rent paid	1,500
Electricity paid	900
Sold goods to Joshi & Co	11,200
Bank charges debited by bank	1,050

CHAPTER–2

ACCOUNTING FOR MANAGERS

Learning Objective

This is an introductory chapter on management accounting. The meaning and significance of management accounting are dealt with. The role a management accountant plays in providing information for decision-making is the theme of the chapter. The management accountant has to process the data available within the accounting system and supply accurate information at appropriate time to the concerned managers in the form of reports.

The aim of the book is to familiarize managers how best the accounting data could be decoded and used in managerial decision-making. It is, therefore, not my intention to load the managers with the basic procedures relating to the generation of accounting data. That would be financial accounting and for details of financial accounting, readers might refer to "Financial accounting and analysis"-2002 Himalaya Publishing House by the same author. However, I am also aware that quite a few of the managers are new to the use of accounting information and might be curious to know how the seeds of data in transactions are transformed into financial information in the statements of profit and loss account and balance sheet. To quench their thirst, I have added the fundamental aspects of financial accounting in the next chapter. Managers with basic accounting knowledge could skip chapter 3.

Accounting system has a dual task to perform in business management. It generates data relating to the business activities over a specified period. This is the ***historical function*** of accounting. The primary objective of the data collection is to ensure accountability of the resources used by the business to the providers of resources. This task we call financial accounting. The second role with which we are concerned is accounting information useful for ***management function***. The task of management is to achieve the goals of the organization through process of planning, organizing, leading and controlling. Management takes series of decisions in each of the above areas. For taking such decisions, it requires internal and external information. Internal information is sourced from the financial accounting system .The data available in financial accounting system are raw in nature and have to be processed suitably before being used as internal information for decision making. The crucial task of collecting, collating and converting the data from financial accounting system into meaningful information for use by management is carried out by ***management accountant***. Management accounting, therefore, is the intermediary stage between the generation of data and their meaningful utilization by management.

Management Accounting Defined

The era before 1950 did not use the term *management accounting*, though the function of this branch of knowledge was known and used. It was in 1950 when the Anglo-American Council of Productivity Management Accounting Team published its report on Management Accounting, that the term became a household word. The definition of management accounting, according to the team's report, was the ***"preparation of accounting information in such a way as to assist management in the creation of policy and in the day-to-day operation of an undertaking".*** The team therefore brought out the twin purpose of management accounting-

- *To provide information to management in policy making and*
- *To assist in the day-to-day operations of the business.*

After the Team's definition, a plethora of definitions of management accounting appeared. A few of these definitions are highly informative and are quoted. According to American Accounting Association, "***Management accounting is the application of appropriate techniques and concepts in processing historical and projected economic data of an entity to assist management in establishing plans for reasonable economic objectives in the making of rational decisions with a view towards these objectives***". J.Batty, a well-known author in the field has considered management accounting is "***the term used to describe the accounting methods, systems and techniques coupled with special knowledge and ability to assist management in its task of maximizing profits or minimizing loss***". He had also explained what he means by special knowledge, which is "***management economics, law, psychology etc.***". The views of Brown and Howard are that "***management accounting is concerned with the efficient management of a business through the presentation to the management of such information as will facilitate efficient and opportune planning and control***". ICMA, London has considered management accounting as ***"the application of professional knowledge and skill in the preparation of accounting information in such a way as to assist management in the formation of policies and in the planning and control of the operations of the undertaking***"

Features of Management Accounting

Management accounting is thus that part of accounting system, which ***assists*** the decision makers in framing policies and in the day-to-day operations of the business. The process of management accounting coexists with that of financial accounting. Costs are analyzed as and when they arise. The selected definitions given in the last paragraph amply highlight the salient features of management accounting. Briefly, management accounting is

- *An accounting method and system*
- *Of processing historical and projected economic data of an entity*
- *Using techniques, concepts special knowledge and skill*
- *And presenting to the management such information as would*
- *Assist Management in formulating its policies*

Role of Management Accountant

Management Accountant is the person behind the designing and developing an effective management accounting system. Mr. P.L.Tandon, an eminent economist, in his paper to the 4th All India Seminar on management accounting, held in Lucknow in 1963 had compared the role of management accountants to those of the spokes in a wheel connecting the rims to the hub. The management accountant gathers information from within the organization, blends it with the plethora of information available outside the business, sifts the requisite information from the rest, breaks the selected information into elements and reassembles them in an intelligible form and reports to the management at the right time. Perhaps in an organization, the person who knows more about the state of affairs of the business, next only to the chief executive, is the management accountant. As he is involved in the process of controlling cost, he is often designated as the ***controller or comptroller***. Irrespective of the roles, a management accountant aids management in decision-making although he is not a manager. He is an intermediary. The success of a management accountant depends upon his choosing accurately the relevant information and reporting to the appropriate person, at the opportune time and in an understandable form to enable the management to take effective decisions to achieve the goals of the organization.

The primary role of management accountant is to assist the management in taking effective decisions. Since the functions of management are to plan, organize, lead and control, management accounting provides useful information in each of the above areas of management.

Planning: Planning implies forecasting the future. Forecasting technique uses past information as the basis. Forecasting is accomplished by analyzing and exposing the past information to the changed social, political and economic environments of the economy to predict what it would be in future. Budgeting is the technique used to plan for the future. The information for budgeting is provided by the management accountant. Management accounting is thus the foundation for the process of planning by a business.

Organizing: Management accounting provides information as to the resources position of the business, its cash generating capacity, its leverage position and gives the clue for the probable mode of raising additional resources. It brings to the notice of management the current cost of capital and how best the cost could be pruned so as to achieve an optimal capital structure. It is thus an effective aid in organizing the execution of future plans.

Leading: Management accounting provides an effective means of communication for directing the execution of plans. Plans are communicated from top to bottom with the roles of each segment clearly defined. Through proper delegation of authority, the motivation to achieve the objective is enhanced. Management accountant also provides useful information to the decision makers in pricing products and services through the employment of variety of pricing bases such as marginal costing, absorption costing, incremental costing and target costing.

Controlling: Management accounting draws heavily from cost accounting to suggest proper mechanisms for controlling costs. Budgetary control and standard costing techniques ensure higher degree of control. Targets fixed in planning are compared with actual performance at periodic intervals. Variations, if any, are analyzed as to their cause, cost and location, so that corrective measures could be initiated in time to stem the slide. Management accounting facilitates internal control systems.

Information System

An important role of management accountant is to keep the management informed of the various aspects of the business from time to time. This would facilitate the management to take corrective actions whenever and wherever necessary to improve operational efficiency. In the current competitive world, information is wealth. Information is data processed or evaluated for a specific purpose. Companies with correct information at correct time would steal a march over others. A management accounting function is therefore to feed management with information through the institution and maintenance of effective system. ***Management information system*** is defined as "***an organized method of providing each manager with all the data that he needs for his decision, when he needs them and in the form which aids his understanding and stimulate his action".*** One of the contributions a good management information system could make to efficient running of a business is to provide management with time to direct more of its energies to the unsolved human and other problems prevalent in any organization. Management accountants ensure the flow of accurate information, to appropriate authorities in the form of reports. Communication within an organization could be from bottom to top and from top to bottom. When communication is from down to top, it is called a report. Communication from top to bottom levels is in the form of orders, circulars and notices. Reports are for the consideration of management, whereas orders, circulars and notices are for compliance.

The management accountant prepares periodic reports, which forms the fulcrum of management decisions. A good management information system should be

- *Accurate,*
- *Precise,*

- *Complete,*
- *Timely,*
- *In proper form or design,*
- *Consistent and*
- *Comparable.*

The success or otherwise of decisions taken by management depends upon the accuracy of the information a management accountant furnishes. Accuracy means precise and conforming to facts. It should not be based on hearsay or the personal perception of the accountant. An inaccurate information would lead to wrong decisions and impair the working of the business. Accuracy has to be ensured, if necessary, by cross checking the information with other sources. Precision relates to nature of a report. It should be exact; neither more nor less than what is relevant. Wording a report in a dubious way or with more than one interpretation would defeat the purpose of the information. It should however be borne in mind that in the name of brevity, the completeness of the report should not be lost sight of. The report should be holistic. Another characteristic of a good reporting system is to present the report in time so that management would initiate corrective action in time. A report delayed is denial of the information and would affect the business adversely. The format of the report should suit the need of management. Usually, lengthy reports are prefaced with an executive summary to save time. Another way is to reduce the report to statements and graphs for easy grasp. The report should also have consistency to aid the management to have a comparative picture. If one income statement is worked out with straight line method of depreciation and the next one with written down value method, it would lead to wrong conclusions. Flexibility is yet another quality of a good reporting system.

Forms of Reporting

Reports could be oral, written or representative depending upon the circumstances of each case. The mode of reporting has to be in accordance with the purpose. In an emergency, it would be ideal for the accountant to immediately report orally without wasting time. Yet in other situations, oral reports might not serve the purpose. It might be necessary to submit written reports. Final accounts of the business, cash flow statement and ratio analysis should usually be in written form, as their purpose is long term. In certain circumstances it might simply be represented by tables, graphs or charts. These might convey more than what a written or oral report would. The accountant should use his judgment in selecting the form of the report.

Types of Reports

Reports are classified according to purpose or functions, and periodicity. According to purpose, reports are divided into two broad categories-***external and internal***. External reports are meant for the various groups of stakeholders such as shareholders, creditors, lenders, public and governments. These reports are open to any one who needs them. As per the rules, the registrar of companies has to furnish a copy of these reports to whom so ever that need them on payment of a fee. The major reports in this category are income statements and balance sheets of companies. These reports are generic in nature and their purpose is to disseminate information on the operational results and financial position of the business. The other sets of reports are internal to the organization. These are not available to the public, including shareholders. Cost analysis, standard costing data, variance analysis, analysis of financial statements are examples of internal reports.

The objective of internal reports is to assist in managerial decisions making. Decisions are made in an organization at three levels-top management levels, middle management levels and lower management levels. Top management comprise of final decision making executives such as chief executive, Chairman and Board of directors. It is mainly concerned with strategic and policy decisions, plans and budgets to be followed by the business. Middle level consist of sectional managers like production manager, finance manager, marketing manager, personnel manager etc. Their role is to ensure the implement the decisions of top management through coordination, control and follow up. Low-level management is usually floor level and comprises of foremen, supervisors, plant in charge, godown keeper etc. They are primarily to supervise the implementation of the decisions. Internal reports are to be designed according to the needs of each level.

The reports to top management should relate to the over all operation of the business. Periodic reports on the operational results and financial position, on flow of funds, on plant capacity utilization, on behaviour of costs, sales, credit collection, stock position, levels of performance of different sections etc. Reports to middle level management relates to the variances from standards, stock levels, order positions, etc. For low levels, reports should relate to the day-to-day matters such as the requirement of materials, labour and expenses to ensure smooth activity at floor level. The management accountant should ensure that requisite reports reach the concerned levels.

According to periodicity, reports could be either routine or special. These reports are routinely made at specific intervals. For example, there could be daily reports on production, movement of goods, stock position and cash position, weekly reports on labour utilization, overtimes, plat break downs, monthly reports on performance of each section, deviations from standards, expected cash flow etc. Quarterly reporting of operational results have been made mandatory by SEBI for listed companies. Annual reports are statutory. Apart from these specific reports, certain special reports might be also necessary. For example, any recent change in governmental policy that would affect the business, any incidents or accidents within the organization that had to be attended immediately, any legal, political or social issues of the locality that has a bearing on the working of the unit, etc.

Scope of Management Accounting

The scope of management accounting is vast and covers, among other things, financial accounting, cost accounting, revaluation accounting, budgetary control, inventory control, reporting, taxation and internal auditing. We have seen in detail what financial accounting is. A detailed discussion on cost accounting will ensue. In revaluation accounting, the objective is to ensure that the real value of capital is maintained without getting diluted by change in value of money. It is accounting for change in value of money. We have slated separate chapters on these aspects. Detailed discussions on these aspects have been made in those chapters.

Techniques and Tools

Management accounting uses a number of quantitative and qualitative techniques in the process of preparing the requisite information. The commonly employed techniques are financial planning, cost accounting, standard costing, marginal costing and budgeting. The tools that are frequently used are ratios, percentage and parts of the whole. The documents analyzed include profit and loss account, balance sheet, cash flow and fund flow statements. Statistical tools like variance analysis, linear programming, regression analysis, sampling etc. are also used. We would be considering each of these techniques in detail at appropriate places. Besides, a management accountant is also expected to have accounting, costing and analytical skills to be highly effective.

Analyzing

The first step in management accounting is to analyze the data that are generated in financial accounting system. The condensed form in which the data are available are two important statements namely profit and loss account and balance sheet. The year 1950 was a landmark in the annals of management accounting system. Before 1950, financial statement analysis meant a mere comparison of the figures of the current year with that of the previous years either horizontally or vertically. In horizontal analysis, called trend analysis, the changes in the operations and financial position of the business during the year were compared to that of the previous years. Usually a period of five years was considered necessary to observe the trend. The vertical analysis, called common size analysis, entailed the reduction of the absolute figures in the profit and loss account and balance sheet to percentages. All items of costs and incomes in profit and loss account are related to sales and all assets and liabilities to total assets. The trend analysis enables the businessman to observe the improvement or otherwise of his operations and financial position to take corrective steps. In the common sized analysis, the businessman could study whether the relationship is healthy or not. We would see more of these methods in the next chapter. Although many Indian Universities still prescribe vertical and horizontal balance sheets as part of their syllabus, these techniques have outlived their utilities and are mere ornamental appendices. They are reminiscences of the past. No doubt, study of these techniques would help the analysts to appreciate the evolution of modern analytical techniques. Hence these are also added in this text.

The mode of analysis has since undergone a sea change and we now have sophisticated systems of analyzing the financial statements using ratios and percentages. With the advent of accounting packages, analysis is made less laborious and more complete and comprehensive. The improved techniques have facilitated analysis of intra-firm and inter-firm comparisons more meaningful and useful in decision-making. Analysis of the performance of a business would be incomplete if the impact of costs is not discussed. Hence, I would also be delving into that part of costing as would be necessary to process management information.

Summary

Management accounting fulfills the crucial function of providing information to management for decision making. The data available with the organization is raw and had to be processed into information before being used. This important role is assigned to the management accountant. He processes the data with the use of tools like ratio, percentage etc and converts them into useful information. The information is then fed to the concerned management through the form of reports.. Reports are vehicles of information. The success of operation of an undertaking depends to a larger extent on the quality of the information supplied by the accountant. He has to prepare the reports, having in mind its accuracy, preciseness and make available to the concerned cadre of the management at the opportune time. For this, a management accountant builds up an effective management information system within the organization.

I. QUESTIONS

1. What is management accounting?
2. What role does a management accountant play in policy decision-making?
3. What is information? What is its importance in management?
4. What are reports? How do they differ from orders?
5. What constitutes the basis of good reporting?
6. Whom should the management accountant submit reports?
7. What are the types of report a management accountant has to submit?
8. Outline the importance of an effective management information system?
9. What are the types of reports prepared by the accountant?

10. "Accounting reports are matters of necessities for a management and not matters of convenience." Comment.

II. QUIZ

Say yes or no

1. Management accounting is another name for financial accounting.
2. A management accountant prepares different types of reports
3. Reports are meant for only top management.
4. Reports have to be in writing.
5. Management accountant analyzes financial statements of a business.
6. Management accountant takes decisions based on the information.
7. Information is another name for data.
8. Policy decisions are taken on the basis of information.
9. Reports are information that passes from below to the top.
10. Orders are information from top to lower levels.

CHAPTER–3

FINANCIAL ACCOUNTING

Learning Objective

This chapter briefly explains the process and results of financial accounting. The salient features of accounting cycle are explained. How transactions and events are processed into profit and loss account and balance sheet, after going through journalizing, ledgerising and trial balancing is the theme of the chapter. It explains what costs and revenues are and how they are matched to prepare the final statements.

Financial accounting is the art of recording, classifying, summarizing and interpreting business transactions and events. Business transactions are activities involving transfer of resources for cash either from the business or into the business. If the transaction pertains to trading activities, they are called ***merchandising transactions***. If they relate to manufacturing goods or services, they are known as ***industrial transactions***. The movement of cash and resources might take place simultaneously, when it is called ***cash transactions***. Some times, there is a time gap between the movement of resources and cash. Resources move immediately and instead cash moving simultaneously, an obligation or promise to pay cash later is created. Such transactions are ***credit transactions***. When credit transactions involve obligations of any one to the business, it is called ***receivable or debtor***. On the other hand, when the business is obliged to any one, the obligation becomes ***payable or creditor*** of the business. Ultimately, when the obligations are fulfilled, cash moves. Purchase of materials, consumables, spares, tools, jigs, fixtures, plant and machineries, payments for wages, salaries, rent, interest, and taxes, transport, conveyance, carriage, advertisement and insurance, sales, borrowings, lending, raising capital etc are examples of transactions

Each business transaction involves two actions-one is a giving action and the other is a receiving action. The actions are called ***aspects***. Aspects in bookkeeping terminology are called ***accounts***. Payment of cash or promise to pay or receive cash always remains one aspect of any business transaction. The other aspect is resources. Transaction could thus be defined as ***an***

economic activity involving exchange of resources for cash or vice versa. The payment or receipt of cash might either be immediate or later. In a transaction, one of the aspects remains outside the business. But when in an economic activity, both the aspects are within the business itself, for example depreciation, such activities are called ***events.***

The first task of accounting process is to record transactions and events using the book keeping language and two words-***debtor and creditor***. One aspect of the transaction has to be debited while the other to be credited. Now the question is which of the two aspects has to be debited and which to be credited. It has been seen that of the two aspects, one aspect receives benefit and the other gives benefit. The ***aspect that receives benefit is debited and the aspect that gives benefit is credited.*** When goods are bought for cash, goods are received and as such are debited. Cash is given and therefore credited. When goods are sold for cash, goods are given and credited and cash is received and debited. When goods are bought on credit, goods are received and are debited. The business has not paid cash. Instead it has given a promise to pay later. The business is thus obliged to pay the seller later and the seller becomes the creditor of the business. As the seller has given benefit, his account is credited. Similarly, when the business sells on credit, goods are given and credited. The buyer has not paid and therefore becomes debtor to the business. As he is the receiver of benefit, his account is debited. When expenses are met, like payment of wages, salaries, insurance, transportation, electricity etc, cash is given and debited. The payment is received by persons in the name of wages, salaries etc. and hence wages, and salaries are debited.

The recording of transactions is done in a book called ***journal or the book of prime entry.*** The process of recording is ***journalizing.*** Transactions are recorded in the order in which they occur. When the same type of transactions are repeated a number of times every day, it would be advantageous to club all these transactions in separate journals pertaining to each activities. For example all transactions relating to the receipt and payment of cash could be entered in a separate journal book and named **cashbook.** All purchases other than for cash could be entered in a separate **purchases book**. All sales other than for cash could be put through a **sales book**. All sales return and purchase returned could be entered in **purchase return book** and **sales return book** respectively. In other words, journal entries could be spread over a number of specific journal books, instead of clubbing everything into one book. These additional journal books are called ***subsidiary journals.*** Any item that could not find a place in any of the subsidiary books would be booked in a residuary journal book, ***journal proper.***

From the journal, each aspect is transferred to a separate ledger account. ***Ledger*** is a head under which all aspects both debits and credits pertaining to an account are grouped. Thus, all purchase aspects would be transferred to purchases account, sales to sales account, cash to cash account, wages to wages account, rent to rent account and so forth. The ledger accounts are balanced at the end of a period called ***accounting period***. Accounting period are usually a year.

But the trend now is to have shorter accounting periods of quarter. Securities Exchange Board of India (SEBI) has made it mandatory for listed companies to issue financial statements on quarterly basis.

Accounts are classifies into personal, real and nominal according to their nature. ***Personal accounts*** relate to names of persons, whether real or artificial. Names of corporate bodies are artificial persons. All personal accounts that have received money or moneys worth from the business would be in debit and all personal accounts that had given money or moneys worth to the business would be in credit. Accounts of debtors, receivables, loans and advances etc would be in debit. Creditors, capital, lenders, subscribers to bonds and debentures are personal accounts and would be in credit. ***Real accounts*** pertain to physically existing tangible things like cash, goods, land, building, plant and machinery, equipment, fixtures, fittings, tools, spare parts, jigs, vehicles, stocks of materials, semi-finished goods and finished goods. These are real assets, which have used money or moneys worth and are debits. Sale of goods is a real account that has given money or moneys worth to the business and therefore is credit. The third category of accounts is ***nominal accounts,*** *which* are intangibles. Nominal accounts such as wages, salaries, rent, power, fuel and electricity, discounts and commissions allowed were paid for and are debits. Some nominal accounts that have given cash to the business like commission, discount, fees and royalties received, interest and dividend received on investments are credits. The three accounts therefore are governed by three golden rules. In personal account, the receiver is debited and giver credited. In real account, that which comes in is debited and that which goes out is credited. In nominal account, all costs, expenses and losses are debited and all incomes, gains and profits are credited.

It might be that some ledger accounts would have debit balances at the end of a period, while others would have credit balances. Some accounts would not have any balance at all and would be closed out. All the ledger balances are extracted at the end of the accounting period in a statement called ***trial balance.*** Trial balance would thus have all closing balances of the ledger accounts as at the end of an accounting period. It might be noted that the total of debit balances in a trial balance would tally with the total of credit balances. A specimen trial balance is furnished below.

Table 1

Trial balance of Vasuki Rani & Co., as on 31.3.2006

Particulars		Dr.	Cr.
Capital accounts			
Vasuki Rani	7,53,435		
Girish	6,54,635		
Ilkya	6,44,135		202,52,205

Current accounts			
Vasuki Rani	21,455		
Girish	12,015	33,470	
Ilkya			5.040
Opening stock		3,41,575	
Wages		36,500	
Salaries		96,550	
P F, Gratuity and bonus		20,786	
Purchases		21,71,984	
Cashbook balance		34,606	
Bank balance		3,95,060	
Bill receivable		3,14,790	
Bills payable			3,14,790
Sundry Debtors		4,13,079	
Sundry Creditors			3,43,658
Sales			30,17,489
Sales returns		2,92,770	
Purchase returns			2,98,417
Insurance		1,956	
License fees		1,050	
Stationery		2,105	
Travel & Transport		13,510	
Postage		610	
Telephone and email		9,895	
Carriage inwards		18,598	
Carriage outwards		29,896	
Discount allowed		4,075	
Discount received			3,315
Electricity		37,305	
Water charges		5,030	
Rents, rates, & taxes		37,510	
Advertisement		3,42,898	
Selling commission		30,250	
Petrol allowance for sale men		24,905	

Interest & bank charges		9,870	
Packaging Materials		7,025	
Repairs to premises		1,550	
Bad debts.		9,786	
Fixed assets-Gross	456,735		
Less:depreciation.	271,050	1,25,685	
Vehicles-Gross	522,274		
Less depreciation	143,694	3,78,580	
Franchises		2,05,450	
Goodwill		2,75,000	
Investment in NSC		1,45,000	
Advance tax		32,500	
Total		59,61,209	59,61,209

Trial balance, with appropriate modification for outstanding items of costs and benefits, supplies data for the preparation of profit and loss account and balance sheet of the business for an accounting period. Profit and loss account would reveal the operating results of business during the accounting period and balance sheet its financial position as at the end of the period. All debits in trial balance are **costs** of the business in its effort to earn income. ***Costs are resources sacrificed or foregone to achieve an objective. Since in business the objective is earning income, the cost objective is earning incomes.*** Costs are of two types-those that give one time benefit and immediately expire and those that give benefit over a period, depending upon its useful lifetime. Costs that give one time benefit are called ***expenses or revenue costs***. Examples are materials consumed, wages, salaries, rents, transport, power, fuel and electricity. These items are to be listed under costs column of profit and loss account. Costs that continue to earn income during its lifetime are ***expenditures or capital costs***, such as investment in land, building, plant and machinery, stocks of materials, semi-finished goods and finished goods. ***Expenditures are the assets*** of the business and are to be listed in balance sheet under assets column.

Some of the expenditures or assets would give benefit to the business during the next one year and then expire. These are ***current assets***. Examples are cash, bank balances, stocks, debtors, loans and advances. On the other hand, some expenditure would give benefit over a period longer than a year. These are ***fixed assets***. Useful life of fixed assets is their physical life, economic life or technological life, whichever is lower. That part of the value of fixed assets that was used up in generating income during an accounting period is ***depreciation*** and would become expense of that year. Depreciation is a cost and listed under the cost column in profit and loss account. Assets, at their ***acquired costs or original cost***, less depreciation would represent their ***book value***.

Credit balances in the trial balance could be classified in to two groups-those that are obligations and are to be returned or repaid and those that do not necessitate repayment. ***Those credit accounts that are to be repaid are liabilities and those that are not to be returned are incomes***. Share capital, bonds and debentures, borrowings, creditors are all obligations to be repaid and hence are liabilities and are listed as such in the balance sheet. Sales, discount received, commission received, interest and dividend on investments are examples of credit balances that do not necessitate repayment and are incomes. These items form the credit side of profit and loss account.

We have already seen that trial balance would have debit and credit ledger balances and that debits in trial balance are costs to the business in its attempt to earn incomes. Income could be earned only by incurring costs. Therefore profit and loss account would have ***all costs that are relevant for earning income during the accounting period***, whether paid for or not. Similarly all incomes pertaining to that period have to be taken as revenue. In other words, all costs of the accounting period are to be matched with all incomes during the period, whether received in cash or not. This is known as the ***matching principle*** in accounting. Evidence of movement of financial resources or the creation of obligations has no relevance in determining incomes or costs of the period. Certain incomes and expenses, pertaining to the accounting period might not have been received or paid in cash. Salaries due, rents due, wages due, interest due, dividend receivable, incomes on investment not yet received are all examples. They are ***outstanding incomes or expenses.*** On the other hand, all moneys received or paid might not necessarily be the incomes or expenses of that period. Advances received for supply, insurance paid in advance are a few examples. These are ***advances for supply and prepaid expenses***. To assess true profit or loss of business, these items of incomes and expenses are to be recognized for the year concerned.

Usually, such fine-tuning is done at the end of the accounting period and the process of effecting the adjustments is through passing ***closing entries.*** Functional departments furnish information regarding the items of expenses and incomes to be recognized. Stores assistant provides details of closing stock of materials, stores and spares; semi-finished goods by production manager; finished goods by costing assistant; outstanding income and expenses appropriate for the period by accountants. Appropriate adjustment for these items of costs and benefits that do not pertain to the period are made. Let us now examine some important adjustments in respect of certain costs that do not find a place in trial balance and see how the twin aspects in these events are treated by the accountant before taking up the preparation of the final accounts.

Closing Stock

Closing stock of raw materials, stores and spares, semi-finished goods and finished goods, collectively known as inventory, represent that part of the cost incurred during the accounting period, but has not contributed to the earning of revenue of that period. Technically, these are expenditures that are to be used up in the succeeding accounting period. These expenditures partake the nature of current assets. As such, the value of inventories is to be deducted from the total cost to arrive at the relevant cost attributable for the accounting period. As cost is debit, to reduce cost, it has to be credited with the value of inventories to arrive at the net cost for the period. The debit aspect of the adjustment, being expenditure, is carried to the assets' side of the balance sheet. Before passing the adjustment entries, each of the components of inventory has to be valued. The mode of valuation of the components of stock is explained in the next few paragraphs.

Materials

Raw materials are the material inputs in any production process. It is essential to assess the materials consumed by the enterprise to produce goods and services during the year. As the business continues beyond the accounting period, there is usually a stock of unused materials at the end of the period called closing stock of material. Closing stock of material is also called merchandise. Hence, wherever closing stock of material is mentioned, it should be assumed to denote inventories or merchandise. The closing stock of material of one period would be the opening stock of material of the succeeding period. Hence, every business unit, except those that have commenced their operation during the year, would have both opening and closing stock of materials. Opening stock plus materials purchased during the year, less closing balance of stock is material consumed during the period. Following formula might advantageously be used, to calculate material consumed:

$$MC = OSM + (MP - MR) - CSM,$$

Where,

MC is material consumed

OSM is opening stock of materials

MP is material purchased during the period

MR is material returned

CSM is closing stock of materials

In a business, where the opening stock of material as on 1-1-2005 was Rs.26, 85,405, purchases for the year ended 31-12-2005 was Rs.1, 15,75,560, purchases returns Rs.27, 885 and closing stock on 31.12.2005 was Rs.31, 08,750, the material consumed during the year would be Rs. 1,11, 24, 360 as under:

$$MC = Rs.26, 85,405 + (115,75,560 - 27,855) - 31,08,750$$
$$= Rs.1, 11, 24,360$$

The above illustration for working out the material consumed looks simple. But, in reality, things are quite complicated. Every prudent entrepreneur maintains a ***stock register***, where the quantity and unit price of the various materials purchased for production is separately maintained. As materials are released for production, these are entered in columns provided to arrive at closing stock. At the end of the period, the stock register would reveal the quantity of stock of materials in hand. The owner or his trusted representative would personally verify this. The quantity of opening stock and purchases, being already known, the number of units consumed could be arrived at by reducing the quantity of closing stock. In case the price of materials has remained constant through out the accounting period, it is a basic arithmetical calculation of multiplying the closing stock of units by the unit cost to arrive at stock value. However, in real life situations, cost of materials varies a number of times during the period. The price per unit of material purchased differs from purchase to purchase. In such a condition, the calculation of the closing stock of materials is not that simple. The businessman, being usually conservative, would not like to blow out his profits by valuing the closing stock at a higher cost. Further, such a decision might adversely distort his future profitability. He, therefore, adopts the policy of valuing his stock or inventory or merchandise at ***cost price or market price, whichever is lower.***

The cost price of material is historic in character and would not change with the change in market price, which is subject to fluctuations caused by demand and supply. The fluctuations might be upward or downward. In economic conditions of inflation, price would tend to show an upward swing with every purchase. In deflation, it would be on a downward trend. Combining conservative policy of cost price or market price, whichever is lower, with the prevailing price situation, there are three methods by which the price of raw materials could be valued for the purpose of closing stock – ***FIFO*** meaning ***First In First Out, LIFO*** meaning ***Last In First Out and WA*** *meaning* ***Weighted Average.***

First in First Out

FIFO implies that the materials are notionally consumed in the order in which they are procured. Thus, under this method, the opening stock is presumed to have been consumed first, followed by the first purchase, second purchase and so on. As a result, the closing stock represents the materials purchased last. This method could also be called as Last In Last Out (LILO). For example, Arabian Ltd. had opening stock of material X of 855 units at Rs.9.50 per unit as at the close of March 2002. During the accounting period, the company made four purchases- 1000 units in October @ Rs.9, 1100 units @Rs.8.50 in April, 1200 units @ Rs.8 in July, and 1050 units @ Rs.7.50 in January 2003. The issues during the years were at the rate of 250 per month for April, May and June, 275 for July, August and September, 225 for October, November and December and 260 for January, February and March. The stock register of the company would be as in Table below:

Table 2
Stock register of Arabian Ltd.

MATERIALS: X

CODE : 046

Date	Particulars	Rate / unit	Quantity purchased	Quantity issued	Balance Quantity
120028					
Apr 1	Opening stock	9.50			855
	Issues			250	605
Apr 7	Purchases	9.00	1000		1605
May 1	Issues			250	1355
June 1	Issues			250	1105
July 1	Issues			275	830
July 4	Purchases	8.50	1100		1930
Aug 1	Issues			275	1655
Sep 1	Issues			275	1380
Oct 1	Issues Purchases	8.00		225 1200	1155 2355
Nov 1	Issues			225	2130
Dec 1	Issues			225	1905
2003					
Jan 1	Issues			260	1645
Jan 6	Purchases	7.50	1050		2695
Feb 1	Issues			260	2435
Mar 1	Issues			260	2175
	Total		4350	3030	2175

The closing stock of X as on 31.3.2003 was 2175 units. By applying the formula, the quantity of materials consumed (MC = 855 + 4350 – 2175) works out to 3030 units. Under FIFO, it is thus assumed that the opening stock (855), the entire April and July purchases (1000 + 1100) and 75 units of the October purchase would have been consumed. The value of materials consumed under the method could, therefore, be worked out by multiplying the number of units consumed against their respective unit price *i.e.*, 855 @ Rs.9.50 + 1000 @ Rs.9.00+1100 @ Rs.8.50 + 75 @ Rs.8, which is Rs.27072.50. The closing stock would be Rs.16, 875 (i.e. OSM + MP – MC) = (855 × 9.5 + 1000 × 9 + 1100 × 8.5 + 1200 × 8 + 1050 × 7.5 – 27,072.50). The consumption and closing stock figures could also be worked out from the closing stock route. As the closing stock of material would represent the latest purchases, it is valued at Rs.16, 875 (1050 @ Rs.7.50 + 1125 @ Rs.8). FIFO method of valuation is resorted to when prices of materials fall with every purchase or in times of recession.

Last in First Out

LIFO method, on the other hand, is employed under conditions of increasing price levels. In this method, it is presumed that the materials purchased last are consumed first and in that reverse order. It would amount to that the opening stock is consumed last. Hence, this method is also known as *First In last Out (FILO).* The closing stock would represent the price of the earlier purchases. For example, the stock register of Diamond Traders for the year 2002 – 03 was as in Table below

Table 3
Stock Register of Diamond Traders

Material : X

Material Code : 04

Date	Particulars	Unit Rate (Rs.)	Quantity Purchased	Quantity Issued	Balance Quantity
2002					
Apr 3	Purchases	8	20,000	....	20,000
	Issues for quarter	....	....	14,000	6,000
Jul 4	Purchases	9	22,000	....	28,000
	Issued for quarter	....	....	15,500	12,500
Oct 7	Purchases	10	18,500	....	31,000
	Issued for quarter	....	....	16,000	15,000

2003. Jan.4.	Purchases	11	20,500	....	35,500
	Issued for quarter	....	....	15,000	20,500
	Total		81,000	60,500	20,500

In the above illustration, Diamond Traders had purchased 81,000 units during the year of which 60,500 have been issued for production, leaving a stock of 20,500 units. As the assumption is that the last purchases were consumed first, closing stock would be that purchased first. That is, the value of closing stock would be 20,000 units of April purchase and 500 units of July purchase, valued at Rs.1,64,500, The consumption of material for the period would have been Rs. 6,04,000, that is the total value of purchases at Rs.7,68,500 – less the closing stock of Rs.1,64,500.The consumption figure can also be worked out the other way. Total units consumed are 60,500 and the cost of material consumed Rs.6,04,000. The cost would comprise 20,500 units purchased in Jan.2003 (@ Rs. 11 each+ 18,500 units purchased in October 2002 @ Rs.10 each +21, 500 units purchased in July at Rs.9 each.

Weighted Average

Weighted Average is the other method of valuing material consumed and closing stock, when the price of the material fluctuates frequently. Even in the present day context of increasing prices, certain materials fluctuate violently. A good example is edible oils. If one has to follow the price trend of edible oils over a period, the volatility would be discernible. In these kinds of materials, neither FIFO nor LIFO would meet the doctrine of market price or cost price, whichever is less. In such cases, weighted average cost of the materials during the entire period or market price at the end of the period, whichever is lower is the benchmark for valuing the closing stock. For example, the stock register of Healthy Refineries Ltd engaged in edible oil refining is as under:

Table 4

Stock Register of Healthy Refineries Ltd

Material : Groundnut oil

Material Code : 001

Date	Particulars	Unit Rate (Rs.)	Quantity Purchased	Quantity Issued	Quantity Balance
2002					
Apr 4	Opening Balance	42,000			72
	Issued			25	47

Apr 7	Purchased	40,000	50	....	97
May 1	Issued	....	....	30	67
Jun 1	Issued			30	37
Jun 8	Purchased	41,000	50		87
Jul 1	Issued			30	57
Jul 4	Purchased	43,000	25		82
Aug 1	Issued			35	47
Aug 1	Purchased	39,000	50		97
Aug 31	Issued			40	57
	Total		175	190	57

Note: Market Price at close of August was Rs.41, 000 per tonne. Healthy Refineries Ltd had an opening balance of 72 tonnes of groundnut oil on 1st of April 2002and purchased, during the 5 months, 175 tonnes of groundnut oil at varying prices and issued 190 tonnes for refining. The closing balance was 57 tonnes. As every purchased was at different price, weighted average of the purchases, as under, would be calculated:

Table 5
Calculation of WAC

Date	Particulars	Rate per tonne (Rs.)	Quantity (tonnes)	Total (Rs.)
	Opening bal	43,000	72	30,24,000
April	Purchases	40,000	50	20,00,000
June	Purchases	41,000	50	20,50,000
July	Purchases	43,000	25	10,75,000
August	Purchases	39,000	50	19,50,000
Total			247	100,99,000
Weighted Average Price				40,887

Weighted average is worked out by dividing the total cost by the total units. As market price was Rs.41, 000, the closing stock of 57 tonnes is valued at the lower weighted average rate of Rs.40, 887 to arrive at Rs.23, 30,559. The raw material consumed, therefore, is 190 tonnes at a cost of Rs.77, 68,441 (MC = 30,24,000 + 70,75,000 – 23,30,559).

Next in First Out

As the three methods of estimating cost of the material consumed and the closing stock are based on historic costs, i.e., costs actually incurred, none of the methods consider the replacement cost of materials consumed. Should the business buy these materials at the end of the period when the finished products are sold what would these have cost the business or what would have been the cost of replacement or what would have been cost of next in? This is particularly relevant as the closing stock is going to be used in the next accounting year when the market cost of materials is different from the historic cost. This method of valuing the usage of material is known as Next In First Out (NIFO) Under this method, it is assumed that the material consumed are valued at the market price at the time of stock taking. In case NIFO is adopted, the materials consumed and the closing stocks of the illustrations contained in earlier Tables would be as under at the assumed current materials rates:

Table 6
Valuation of material consumed and closing stock under NIFO

Table No.	Qty of materials consumed units	Qty of Closing stock	Current rate per unit	Consumed cost	Value of closing stock Rs.
2	3030	2175	7.25	28178.75	15768.75
3	60500	20500	11.5	609175.00	159375.00
4	190	57	38,500.00	79,04,500.00	21,94,500.00
			OR	OR	OR
			41,00,000.00	77,90,000.00	23,09,000.00

Note: In case where the market price is lower than the historic cost price, the closing stock is valued at market price and the total cost less closing stock is taken as materials consumed. In other cases, where market price (next in) is higher than the cost of closing stock, materials consumed is considered at the market price.

Although NIFO is a relevant concept in the context of global competition, tax authorities of the country have their reservations in accepting this method, as it reduces the profit. Whatever might be the method adopted in valuing the closing stock of materials, the unused materials are expenditures and have to be deducted from the material cost incurred during the period to arrive at the cost of materials consumed to earn the income during the period. The closing stock of materials is posted to the credit side of profit and loss account to reduce cost and the other aspect, being expenditure, is shown as current asset in the balance sheet.

The above conventional method of adjusting for closing stock is giving way now a days to a more sophisticated method of showing the cost of material consumed as a deduction from the aggregate of opening stock plus purchases less closing stock. Closing stock would not appear on the credit side of P&L account but is carried to balance sheet as current asset.

Table 7
P&L A/c of Acel Inc for the year ended 31.03.2005

To Raw materials		
Opening balance	78,550	
Add : Purchases	3,43,956	
	4,22,506	
Less : Closing Stock	81,305	
Material Consumed		3,41,201

Semi-Finished Goods

The production department supplies information regarding the stock of semi-finished and finished goods. Semi finished goods or work- in process, are the stock of goods that are incomplete at the end of the period. These are in different stages of production depending upon the length of production cycle. Suppose in an industry, where the production cycle is three days, there would be three days stock of work –in- process. But the cost attributable to the semi-finished goods would vary at every stage of process. In the instant case, let us assume that the production of a batch starts on 7th August 2002. As at the end of the day, there would be one day's material and conversion cost. On 8th August, the first day's semi-finished goods would have moved to the second stage, with the addition of second day's costs and on the 9th August, the same would have absorbed third day's costs as well. As production process is continuous, there would be stock at all the three stages of semi-finished goods at any point of time-some with the cost of the first day, the next with cost of first day plus the additional costs of the second day and so on. For example, if the enterprise's raw material consumption per day is 50 Kgs @ Rs.175 per kg and the conversion cost is Rs.6,580 per day, the value of semi-finished goods in the enterprise on 9th August would be Rs. .65,730 (175 × 50 + 6580) + (175 × 50 + 6,580 + 6,580) + (175 × 6,580 + 6,580 + 6,580). Or, it would be equal to the daily material consumption × production cycle days + the mean average of the conversion cost for the production cycle × the production cycle days. It could be formulated as:

SFG = MCD × PCD + (CSD + ACFD) / 2 × PCD

Where

SPG is cost of semi-finished goods

MCD is material consumption per day

PCD is production cycle in days

CSD is conversion cost on starting day and

ACFD is Aggregate conversion cost on finishing day.

By applying the formula to the illustration, the value of SFG would be arrived at the same figure

$$SFG = (8750 \times 3) + (6580 + 19740) / 2 \times 3$$

$$= Rs.26,250 + 39,480 = Rs.65,730.$$

Instead of this cumbersome way of valuing semi-finished goods, companies convert the semi-finished goods in to equivalent of finished goods. For example, if the company has three processes, process one with 30% complete, process two with 60% complete and process three with 90% complete and the number of semi-finished goods were 290 in first state, 350 in second stage and 410 in third stage, then the number of semi-finished goods would be equivalent of 290 × .30 +350 × .60 + 410 × .90 = 666 finished goods. The cost of semi-finished goods would be equal to 666 units of finished goods.

Here again, there are two ways in which the value of closing stock of semi-finished goods could be deducted from the cost for the period. The conventional method is to show the value of semi-finished goods in the credit side of the profit and loss account, which, in effect, would amount to deduction of the stock from the prime cost. The other method, usually adopted in cost accounting, is to deduct the value of semi-finished goods directly from the prime cost. Since the profit and loss account format does not normally facilitate the deduction of semi-finished goods from the prime cost, the conventional method of showing closing stock in the credit side is still the practice followed by most. The adjustment would be to treat the value of semi-finished goods as current asset (under inventory) as it is expenditure and to credit profit and loss account to reduce the cost.

Closing stock of finished good is calculated on the basis of works cost (loosely referred to as cost of production by some analysts) or market price, whichever is lower. As closing stock of finished goods is expenditure, the cost of stock has to be deducted from the cost of production. The usual profit and loss account does not facilitate such a deduction. However, a few businessman, who have installed sophisticated costing system in their organizations, deduct the cost of finished goods from the total cost of production before closing the books, as under:

	(Rs.)
Opening stock of finished goods.	24597
Add: cost of production during the year	834610

Less : closing stock of finished goods	36291
Net cost of production	822916

In companies that follow this practice, closing stock would appear in the trial balance as a debit item, which being expenditure, is taken as current assets to the balance sheet. In other cases, closing stock of finished goods is valued at the end of the period and the adjustment entry is made. Closing stock would be posted to the credit side of trading account below sales and the other aspect, being expenditure, is shown as current asset in the balance sheet under inventory.

Prepaid Expenses

As prepaid expenses, such as unexpired insurance, partake the character of expenditure, these are to be deducted from the cost of the period. For example M/s. Multimedia insured its assets for a year on 1.7.2002 with an annual premium of Rs.1,800. When the company closed its accounts on 31st March 2003, the used up insurance premium was for nine months (Rs.1350) and the prepaid insurance was Rs.450, which has to be deducted from the cost of insurance, as it is expenditure.Prepaid expenses of Rs.450 being expenditure, is shown as current asset in balance sheet and the prepaid portion (Rs.450) is deducted from insurance of Rs.1,800, to arrive at the actual insurance expense of Rs.1350 which alone is the insurance cost for the year. This would be shown as such under the debit side of profit and loss account of M/s. Multimedia.

Outstanding Expenses

The two aspects of an outstanding expense are that it is an attributable cost of the period and that it is an obligation. The cost aspect would be added to the expenses in the profit and loss account and the obligation being repayable within the next accounting year is the current liability of the business. Sunit Ram & Co. pays its wages on the 7th of the following month. As on 31.3.2005, wages amounting to Rs.25,654 were outstanding. The wages, being relevant cost for the year ended 31.3.2005, has to be charged to the profit and loss account and the persons to whom these are due are the creditors of Sunit Ram & Co. Wages paid are already in the trial balance. The outstanding wages would be added to wages paid and posted to profit and loss account. The outstanding creditors, being obligations by the business, would be represented as current liability in the balance sheet.

Bad Debts

When a businessman wants to improve his sales, he has to sell on credit to customers with an element of risk. Some of the debtors might not pay for the goods purchased by them. The businessman tries all means to recover the debt. When it reaches a point of no return, it is treated as bad debt. Bad debts are losses to the business and hence are to be charged as such to the business. After the debts are written off, the debtors cease to exist in the books of the business and hence their accounts in the ledger are to be closed down by crediting. Sometimes, it might so happen that a debtor might become bankrupt and his estates might be able to pay a part of the debt. In such cases, when the part payment is received, cash or bank account is debited to the extent of payment and the debtor's account credited. The balance in the debtor's account would be treated as bad debt. The same would be the entry when a debtor compounds his debt.

Doubtful Debts

Bad debts are specific cases of obligations to business becoming unenforceable. Usually, bad debts arise when debtors become insolvent or absconding. There are, however, circumstances when the businessman is skeptical whether certain debtors would pay or become bad. For instance, when there is delay in payment or when the cheques given by a debtor are dishonoured, it is a case of doubtful debt. The businessman, being conservative in nature, provides for debts, which might turn out to be bad in future. As the likely loss is due for the period under consideration, the businessman provides for it by earmarking a part of the profit by way of provision for doubtful debts. The provision would thus be treated as loss of the year. The business would meet the loss as and when the debtor actually becomes bad from the provision. As this obligation is likely to be within a year, it is treated as current liability.

Discount to Debtors

The businessman with a view to encourage debtors to pay the receivable in time, evolves a credit policy, whereunder discount is allowed to debtors. Out of the debtors outstanding as at the end of the period, he estimates the likely debtors who would avail discount. The discount has not yet accrued or become due. But it might happen during the next accounting year. Since the discount, though become payable in the subsequent year, is on account of the operations for the period under consideration, a provision for discount is usually created at certain percent on the outstanding debtors. For the purpose of calculating the percentage, net debtors, after providing for bad debts and doubtful debts, are to be the basis. For example, suppose in a business the debtors as at the end of March 2002 were Rs.4,35,000 of which Rs.45,000 have become bad, 2 percent of debtors are considered doubtful and discount has to be provided at 3 percent, the debtors (Rs.4,35,000) less bad debt's (Rs.45,000) is the figure on which doubtful debt has to be calculated. That is to say, doubtful debt provision would be 2 percent on Rs.3,90,000 or Rs.7,800 and discount at 3 percent would be on the net debtors at Rs.3,82,200 or Rs.11,466. Since provision for discount is loss for the period, it has to be taken as the cost and included in the debit side of the profit and loss account. As it is a provision, it is short-term liability or current liability and shown as such in the balance sheet.

Discount by Creditors

Even though the business is entitled to discount from creditors, businessman, being conservative, usually does not take such discounts as revenues. In case it has to be created, the adjustment entry would be to debit provision for discount receivable and credit profit and loss account. Provision for discount receivable is a current asset, as it is the obligation from the creditors to the business. As and when the discount is received, the creditor is debited and the provision for discount receivable is credited.

Depreciation

Depreciation is an event. When capital assets such as building, plant and machinery, equipment, vehicles etc. are used to generate income, their economic usefulness gets diminished with every use till they become scraps. The loss in value of assets is not usually visible. The physical size and shape of the assets might look the same. But its economic utility is used up by the business over its useful life. Wear and tear, obsolescence, and fall in value, destruction or damage might cause depreciation. Such losses are costs to the business and are to be systematically provided as expenses before arriving at profits. It should, however, be noted that there is a vital difference between depreciation and other costs. While other costs causes immediate or future outward movement of financial resources, depreciation does not necessitate such cash out go. Hence, it is a notional cost.

The International Accounting Standards Committee (IASC) has defined depreciation ***as an allocation of depreciable amount of an asset over its estimated useful life***. Depreciation is allocation or an approximation. No human ingenuity could assess the exact loss in value of assets. Depreciation also does not reflect the difference between historical value and the replacement value or market value of the asset. Instances are not rare of the market value of the asset being more than the book value. Still, depreciation is provided for as it represents, in economic sense, a portion of expenditure whose benefit is used up by the business during the year and as such is a cost.

The useful life[1] of an asset is again another assumption. Usually, an asset has physical life, economic life and technological life. The useful life is assumed to be the lowest of the three.

---

1. *Readers might be puzzled how the useful life of an asset is estimated. Accountants calculate the useful life using the WDM. As we have already seen, the total depreciation of an asset on its useful life equals its original cost, whatever might be the method used. Thus, whether one uses SLM or WDM, the scrap value of the asset is taken at 5% of the cost. In other words, how many years it would take for the asset, if depreciated under WDM, to reach the level of the scrap value. If readers use their calculators and work out the example, it takes a little more than 13 years for the value of the asset to be reduced to 5% of its original cost, which we know, is the estimated scrap value of the asset. Hence the asset's useful life is assumed to be 14 years.*

Thus, if we estimate the physical life of an asset as ten years, economic life as five years and technological life as three years, the useful life of the asset is three years. On the face of it, it might seem to be a difficult task to estimate the three types of life of an asset and then decide what its useful life would be. However, the tax authorities of the country have come to the help of businessman. They do prescribe a rate of depreciation on each type of asset, based on technical analysis, which is accepted by the business world for adoption. The total depreciation that could be provided on an asset during its useful life shall not, however, exceed its historic value. There is, however, one exception. Research and Development expenditure is allowed a depreciation of 133.33 percent.

Depreciation might either be treated as factory overhead, administrative overhead or selling and distribution overhead, depending upon the positioning of the asset. Thus, depreciation on plant and machinery, factory building and equipment is factory or works overhead, depreciation on administrative building and equipment is treated as part of cost of production and depreciation on assets used by selling and distribution department is selling overhead. Depreciation caused due to the wear and tear of the assets during operation is termed *internal depreciation* while that resulting from abnormal causes unrelated to operation, such as obsolescence, fall in value, damage and destruction are called *external depreciation.*

Time Based

The methods businessman adopt to provide for depreciation vary depending upon the trade practices, the nature of the assets and their usages, or by mere passage of time. Thus the methods of depreciation are grouped into ***time based, usage passed, maintenance based and replacement based.***

Written down value method (WDV) or **the** ***residual value method or the reducing balance*** is the most familiar method of providing depreciation. Under this method a fixed percentage is provided as depreciation on the residual value of assets at the end of every year. For example, the depreciation on a fixed asset of the value of Rs.25.5 lakhs at 20% would be Rs.5 lakhs, Rs.4.08 lakhs on Rs.3.26 lakhs for the first three years as in Table below.

Table 8

Calculation of depreciation on WDV method

Year	Asset	Book value at beginning of the year	Depreciation at 20 %	Residual value at close
1	Plant and machinery	25.50	5.10	20.40
2		18.40	4.08	16.32
3		16.32	3.26	13.06

Straight-Line Method (SLM)

SLM is a system of providing for depreciation at a predetermined amount equally every year, over the useful life[1] of the asset. SLM depreciation is calculated by deducting the salvage value of the asset, at the end of its useful life, from the original cost of the asset and by dividing the resultant figure (which represents total depreciation during the useful life of the asset) by the useful life. This might be represented as:

$$SLD = \frac{OC - SV}{UL}$$

Where,

SLD is Straight Line depreciation per annum.

OC is original cost.

SV is expected salvage value

UL is useful life of asset.

Thus, in the example given above, if the useful life of the asset is 14 years, its salvage value (usually assumed at 5% of the original cost) is Rs.1.275 lakhs; the annual depreciation would be Rs.1.73 lakhs as under:

$$SLD = \frac{25.50 - 1.275}{14}$$

$$= \text{Rs.1.73 lakhs.}$$

Sum of Digits Method (SDM)

It is yet another time based method of providing for depreciation. Under the method, value of the asset during its useful life (original cost less salvage value) is divided by the sum of the digits of the life of the asset to arrive at product. In the example, the useful life of the asset being 14 years, the sum of its digits workout to 105 (1+2+3- - - - - - - -+14) and the product is 0.2307 (25.50 – 1.275/ 105). The product is multiplied by the digits of the life in reverse order. First year SDM depreciation would be 0.2307 × 14, second year 0.2307 × 13, third year 0.2307 × 12 and so on till the 14th year, when it would be 0.2307 × 1. This method is only a variant of WDM, as it also provides for higher depreciation in initial years. Table below gives a comparative picture of depreciation chargeable under each of the three time based methods explained above:

Table 9
Depreciation under time based methods.

(Rs.Lakhs)

Original Value of asset	Years	Depreciation under		
		WDV	SLM	SDM
25.50	1	5.10	1.73	3.23
	2	4.08	1.73	3.00
	3	3.26	1.73	2.77
	4	2.61	1.73	2.54
	5	2.09	1.73	2.31
	6	1.67	1.73	2.08
	7	1.34	1.73	1.85
	8	1.07	1.73	1.61
	9	0.86	1.73	1.38
	10	0.68	1.73	1.15
	11	0.55	1.73	0.92
	12	0.44	1.73	0.69
	13	0.35	1.73	0.46
	14	0.28	1.73	0.23
Total Depreciation		24.38	24.22	24.22

Usage Based

On the basis of usage, depreciation might be provided in terms of production unit method, depletion method or production hour method.

Production Unit Method

It implies the allocation of depreciation of an asset based on the number of units produced, as a percentage of its total capacity production. Suppose the asset is costing Rs.60,000 and is designed to produce 6000 articles. Depreciation per unit of production is Rs.10. The company produces 1000 articles in the first year, 2000 in the second year and 3000 in the third year. The depreciation would work out to Rs.10,000, Rs.20,000 and Rs.30,000 respectively for the three years.

Depletion Method

It is usually used for wasting assets such as mines, mineral deposits, quarrying, oil exploration etc. As these natural resources get depleted with every extraction, depreciation is charged on the basis of their exploitation. Suppose a coalmine lease is taken for Rs.45 lakhs and the mine is estimated to have coal reserves of 90,00,000 tonnes. It thus means that with the extraction of every tonne of coal, the lease value would reduce by 50 paise. If the extraction of coal in the first three years is 15,20,000 tonnes, 21,50,000 tonnes and 25,40,000 tonnes, the depreciation for the first three years would be Rs.7,60,000, Rs.10,75,000 and Rs.12,70,000.

Production Hour Method

It is similar to production unit method except that in this method, it is the number of hours the asset has been used irrespective of the quantum of units produced that determines the extent of depreciation. For example, a machine designed to work for 10,000 hours and costing Rs.25 lakhs would be depreciated at the rate of Rs.250 per operating hour. Should the machine be used for 2,000 hours in first year, 3,000 hours in second year and 4,000 hours in third year, the annual depreciation chargeable on the machine would be Rs.5,00,000, Rs.7,50,000 and Rs.10,00,000 respectively for the first three years.

Maintenance Based

Depreciation might also be provided on the basis of maintenance. Under this, the cost of repairs and maintenance of the asset during its useful life is estimated and loaded to its cost. Depreciation is charged on the loaded value. For example, the original cost of a machine is Rs.525 crores, the estimated repairs and maintenance of the machine during its useful life of 10 years is Rs.75 crores, depreciation either on straight line method or written down value method is provided on Rs.600 crores over the ten useful life of the machine. When an asset is acquired with guaranteed service through out its life, it means that the cost of maintenance is built into the price of the machine

Depreciation For Replacement

Depreciation, we have seen, is a notional cost and does not necessitate outflow of funds. It is treated as cash accrual of the business and is generally utilized to acquire assets or liquidate liabilities. Even assuming that a cautious businessman retains the entire depreciation in the form of cash or liquid assets, the aggregate depreciation funds, would fall short of the cost of replacement as the later is usually higher than the historical cost. Some shrewd businessman, therefore, could think of providing depreciation not on the historical cost, but on replacement cost. For example, the historical cost of equipment, which is expected to have a useful life of 10 years, is Rs.100 lakhs and the annual rate of inflation assumed to be 5%; the replacement cost of the equipment would be Rs.162.90 lakhs. A businessman, if he desires to follow the replacement value method of depreciation, would depreciate the asset at the cost of Rs.162.90

lakhs instead of the historical cost at Rs.100 lakhs. This would enable him to be in funds to replace the asset from out of the accumulated depreciation. But tax deduction is allowed only up to the historic cost and not on the replacement cost.

Sinking Fund Method

Whether one provides depreciation on the historical cost or the replacement cost, chances are that the accrued funds from depreciation might not be available to the businessman when needed, in the form of cash, for replacement, as he might have used the funds in the acquisition of assets or in reducing liabilities. As such, it is usually the practice for enterprises to replace their worn out assets from out of additional resources raised for that purpose. Raising additional resources at the time of replacement, either by equity or debt, depends upon the capital market conditions and the standing of the business. Either the enterprise might have no access or have access only at a high cost, which would affect the earnings of the business. To ward off these contingencies, shrewd businessmen take the depreciation fund out of the business and invest it in such a manner that the investment, together with interest thereon, is adequate enough to meet the cost of replacement as and when it is due. This process is called sinking fund methods. There are two methods of doing this namely annuity method and endowment policy method.

Annuity Method

Annuity method of providing for depreciation is to appropriate, as depreciation, an equated annual sum, which, at a predetermined rate of interest would yield funds adequate enough to replace the asset at the end of its useful life. To determine the annuity (i.e., annual sum that has to be invested) the estimated useful life of the asset has first to be estimated. Then, the prevailing rate of interest for that period has to be ascertained. Finally with the help of future value of annuity tables, which are readily available in any finance textbook, the annuity could easily be decided.

At this juncture, we might take a slight deviation to understand the significance of the annuity table and its usefulness. Annuity table indicates the future value of an equated annual amount over n years. Suppose a businessman invests Re.1 every year for 5 years at 15% interest, at the end of the fifth year, his investment would have grown into Rs.7.75 as under :

At the end of	Rs.
First year	1.15
Second year	2.47
Third year	3.20
Fourth year	5.74
Fifth year	7.75

It might be observed from the above that the annual investment of Re.1 at 15% interest would have grown into Rs.7.75 at the end of the fifth year. Of course this implies that the amount at the end of each year is reinvested at the same rate of interest. In other words, to receive an accumulated sum of Rs.7.75 at the end of the fifth year, with the rate of interest at 15%, one has to make an annual investment of Re.1. Therefore, if the funds needed at the end of 5th year were Re. 1, the amount of annuity would be 1/7.75 or Re.0.129. The annuity factor multiplied by the requisite funds for replacement would be the annuity to be invested. Suppose the replacement needs of the business are Rs.725 lakhs at the end of 5 years, one has to invest Rs.87 lakhs (725×.129) annually at 15%.

Endowment Policy Method

Endowment policy method of providing for replacement value of an asset is similar to annuity except that the equated amount is invested in an insurance policy. The value of the policy represents the replacement value and the equated installments are paid as premia towards the endowment policy.

Since depreciation provision is made at the end of an accounting year, it is given effect through a journal entry. Assuming depreciation on plant and machinery is Rs.42.50 lakhs, Buildings Rs.9.45 lakhs and vehicles Rs.2.92 lakhs. The profit and loss account is debited with the aggregate depreciation of Rs.54.87 lakhs and each of the assets credited with the extent of depreciation. Hence, in the balance sheet, the assets (which have debit balances) would stand reduced to the extent of depreciation provided as under:

Table 10
Balance sheet of Solomon Solids as on 31.3.2006

Liabilities	**Assets**		**Rs.lakhs**
	Plant & Machinery	425.00	
	Less : Depreciation	42.50	382.50
	Building	189.00	
	Less : Depreciation	9.45	179.55
	Vehicles	7.30	
	Less : Depreciation	2.92	4.38

In the above paragraphs, we have examined the costs that have to be taken into consideration while arriving at the profit or loss of a business. These are costs attributable to the accounting year. However, in the course of business, a businessman might come across instances where some of his transactions might or might not result in cost depending upon the happening of a future event. For example, the businessman might have guaranteed the payment of a client. In case the client defaults in payment, he would be liable. Such liabilities are called contingent liabilities and the businessman is expected to disclose the extent of contingent liabilities as a footnote to his balance sheet.

Intangible Accounting

Yet there are a few costs, which are on account of intangible assets and whose treatment needs special consideration. Intangible assets are expenditures that result in the acquisition of special rights, claims and privileges, which indirectly contributes to the earning of the business over its useful life. As intangible assets are abstract, they are governed, as to their character, nature, usefulness and tenure by legislations specially enacted. These regulations provide for rights and responsibilities of the users of the rights, claims and privileges. Common examples of intangible assets are patents, designs, trademarks, copyrights, technical know-how, franchises and goodwill.

Patents

Patent is a monopoly right granted to a person, who had invented a new and useful article or an improvement of an existing article or a new process of making an article for commercial exploitation, either by the inventor himself or his assignee. It is an exclusive right for a limited period to benefit the inventor for his efforts. Indian Patents Act, 1970, governs law relating to patents. The period of validity of the right has been limited to 7 years for food processes and 14 years for drugs, from the date of patenting. The right can be renewed for further periods. If not renewed, anyone can make use of the invention after the lapse of the period. Patents are to be registered with the Controller of Patents by payment of specified fees. Anyone who infringes on the patented process is liable for legal prosecution.

Designs

Designs are shapes, configurations, patterns or imitations applied to any article by an industrial process, which, in the finished article, appeals to the eye and judged solely by the eye. This right protects the owners of novel or original designs from infringement. The interested person has to get his or her design registered with the Controller General of designs, under the Indian patents & Designs Act, 1911.

Trade Marks

Trademark is a visual symbol in the form of a word, device, name, letter, brand, heading, signature or label used to indicate the connection of the goods with the registered owner of the trademark. The purpose of trade marking is to distinguish the trademarked goods from similar goods, thereby appealing to the specific demands of consumers. Trademarks were to be registered with the Register of Trademarks in terms of Trade and Merchandise Mark Act, 1958 till 2003.Under the act only 34 classes of goods were registered. Service marks were not registered. As service sector started playing a lead role in the economy after globalization, a new act "Trade Mark Act of 1999" was passed. The act came into force from 2003.In terms of the Act, trade marks of 10 classes of services are allowed to be registered. Service marks for the purpose of registration are defined as marks used in any service business, where actual tangible goods under that mark are not traded. The groups of services eligible are advertising, insurance, real estate, building construction, telecommunication, transport, education, entertainment, sporting and cultural activities, scientific and technological services, research, design, development of computer hardware, software, legal, medical and security services.

Copyrights

Copyrights are privileges allowed to producers of intellectual and artistic works for their exclusive use. It prevents the appropriation, by others, of the fruits of labour of authors in literacy, dramatic, musical or artistic work or skill, without consent. Writers and artists can get their works copyrighted with the Register of Copyrights, under the Copyrights Act, 1954. The registration gives the writers and artists and their heirs, legal representatives and assigns exclusive ownership of their work during the lifetime of the authors or artists and up to 60 years after their death.

Technical Know-How

Research and Development is an important corporate function in these days of rapid changes. Products have a life cycle comprising the stages of development, growth, saturation and decline. Hence corporates continue to improve existing product lines and introduce new product ranges to be in the reckoning. The current axiom is that creative enterprises should ***introduce new products and make their own products obsolete, otherwise competitors will do that***. It is common knowledge that technical know-how developed in the process is the exclusive right of the concerned organization. Such know-how generates income to the inventor companies during their effective life and is their intangible asset. Sometimes, the inventor shares his know-how with others, usually in different market segments, on his own terms and conditions, under a ***collaboration agreement***, for a price. The price is an adhoc one-time payment known as ***technical know-how fee*** and a recurrent annual payment called ***royalties*** for an agreed period. Royalties are charged, at certain percentage, on the sales, production or profit of the recipient corporate.

Franchises

Franchises are rights obtained by enterprises from the technical know-how developers, for exploitation of the process, product or service in specific areas for an agreed period. The nature of franchise closely resembles that of know-how arrangements, except that in case of franchises, the franchisee is always given the right to use the brand name of the innovator. This may not be so in the case of collaboration agreements, where the right to use the brand name is at the discretion of the know-how supplier and the user normally mentions that the product is made in collaboration with so and so company. Secondly, in franchise, the increasing practice is to supply the know-how with the requisite equipment to be installed at the site of the franchisee. Franchise charges would, then include the rental for the equipment in addition to royalty for the use of technology.

Intangible assets, like tangible assets, are to be written off during their effective life. The closing adjustment entry for writing off of intangible assets is given in Table

Table 11
Journal proper of Peanuts Corporation Ltd.

Date	Particulars	LF	Dr.	Cr.
	By P & L A/c		50,000	
	To Patents A/c			25,000
	To Copyright			15,000
	To Franchise A/c			10,000

In addition to the intangible assets discussed above, we also come across a few expenses incurred in a particular accounting period, which do not directly contribute to the earning of revenue. These are clubbed together as deferred revenue expenses and the commonly known items are capital issue expenses, preliminary expenses, carried forward loss balances and deferred advertisement expenses. ***Capital issue expenses*** are those that a company incurs at the time of issuing share capital or loan capital, such as bonds, debentures and deposits. Presently, issue expenses are about 10% of large mega issues and above 15% in case of medium sized issues. Where issue expenses are heavy and proceeds are expected to contribute to earning revenue over a longer period, it would be unfair to charge the entire expense in the year of occurrence. Hence, these expenses are not written off in a single year, but are deferred and written off during the period over which these are useful. For example, the issue expenses on 5-year bonds may be written off over 5 years. In case of share capital, which is used by the business as long as the company exists, a reasonable period may be assumed for writing off the expenses. Preliminary expenses, are statutorily to be written off over 10 years in equal installments. In case of mega budget advertisements, whose benefit is expected to be spread over more than the year of advertising, the expenses are treated as deferred revenue expenses and written off during the period the advertisement is presumed to be effective.

Fictitious Assets

The assets side of the balance sheet also contains the carry forward balances of losses, suffered by the business during the previous years. Loss balances carried forward are intangibles, but are not assets, as they do not contribute to the earning of revenue either directly or indirectly. These are considered as ***fictitious assets,*** although the suffix assets are a misnomer. We can simply call them as ***intangibles***. Generally, these balances are adjusted against capital and reserves of the business, to arrive at the owner's capital, also called net worth. Annually, a portion is written off from the profit and loss account, through an adjustment entry as in Table below.

Table 12
Journal proper of Beatrice Beethoven Ltd.

Date	Particulars	LF	Dr.	Cr.
	By Profit & Loss A/c		11,500	
	To Deferred revenue expenses			6,250
	Top preliminary expenses			5,250

Carried forward loss balances are primarily to be recovered from the future revenue of the business within 8 years. In case it is not absorbed within the stipulated period, the balance has to be adjusted against the equity of the owners. The justification for writing off the loss balance from future profits of the business is to allow for the fluctuating opportunities of the business. But if the business is not capable of adjusting the deferred cost within the stipulated eight years, the owners of the business have to bear the loss as a penalty for their inefficiency.

Goodwill

Goodwill is an important intangible asset of an enterprise. Although a number of business enterprises deal in the same or similar goods or services, with quality, price, after sales service etc remaining same, consumers show preference to a particular product of an enterprise over that of others. This preference leads to the reputation of the enterprise and is termed as goodwill. As a result of this special attachment of customers the concerned enterprise is able to reap abnormal profits. The additional profit accruing to the business on account of this loyalty of customers is goodwill. Goodwill is thus defined as ***"the value of reputation of a business in respect of profits expected in future, over and above normal level of profits earned by other undertakings belonging to the same class of business".*** Prof. Dicksee in his book on

"Goodwill and its treatment in accounts" describes goodwill as an aid in profit making. According to him, payment for goodwill is justified ***"when a man pays for something which places him in the position of being able to earn more money than he would be able to do by his own unaided efforts".***

From the above definitions, it transpires that goodwill is the quantified value of the reputation of the business to earn extra profit over and above what its tangible assets would have earned. The reputation, based on the preference of the customers, might have been caused by one more of the following special features, such as its location, the personal touch of the businessman, the real or imaginary product differentiation, dependability of supply and the ability of the businessman to keep his competitors at bay. Goodwill usually creates brand equity.

Creation of Intangible Assets

Intangible assets are either created or acquired from those who had created them initially. Research, development and innovation create intangible assets. The cost of intangible asset is the resources utilized by the business in its creation. In case intangibles are acquired, their value is the purchase consideration paid for such acquisition. Purchase consideration is based on the expected contribution of the intangible to the earning of revenue over its useful life. Whenever the cost of creation or acquisition is insignificant, it is treated as revenue expense of the period of incidence and charged to the profitability of the business of that period. On the other hand, should the cost be substantial, loading the entire cost to the profitability of the period of incidence would distort the operational results of the period. Therefore, the cost is capitalized and booked as an asset, to be written off during its effective life, in assumed proportion to its contribution to the earning of revenue.

Useful Life of Intangible Assets

The maximum useful lives of intangibles assets are restricted by the regulations that govern them. For example, patents have a useful life of 14 years. Hence the cost of patent should be written off within 14 years. The period of 14 years commences from the time of its registration. Thus, if a patent is acquired by another business after 4 years of its registration, the useful residual life is 10 years for the acquirer. In the event of the ability of the patent to generate income is lost during its useful life, due to development of better products or processes, it becomes obsolete and the entire amount outstanding has to be written off in that year itself.

Valuation

The valuation of goodwill is on a different footing than other intangible assets. Discernible resources are not expended in developing goodwill. Goodwill is the quantification of the entrepreneurial excellence and it is highly subjective. Goodwill remains dormant and its value is not presented in the books of the business till any change in the structure of the business is anticipated. In the case of sole trading business, it is brought into the books at the time of change in ownership of the business. When the sole trader sells his business to another or when he admits another as a partner into the business, he wants to crystallize the efforts he had taken in the past to create the name for the business. He therefore, values the goodwill and takes it as part of his capital. In this respect, goodwill reflects the valuation of the qualitative inputs of the businessman to shape the business to its present status. Goodwill thus partakes the role of ***sweat capital*** of individuals. In the case of a corporate, goodwill is created when the pattern of share holding is about to undergo change. This may be before the issue of fresh shares to the public. But usually it is at the time of takeover of the company by another. If Vasu desires to take Girish and Ilkya as partners and she desired to create goodwill of Rs.2,50,000, the journal entry required is at Table.

Table 13
Journal proper of Vasu & company

Date	Particulars	LF	Dr.	Cr.
	By Goodwill a/c		2,50,000	
	To Vasu's Capital			2,50,000

The valuation of goodwill is not an easy task. There are varieties of causes for the creation of name for the business and each business may have to adopt a different norm for the valuation of goodwill. As the value of goodwill that has to be raised should be acceptable to the buyer, the decision is really ticklish. Usually, goodwill is valued as the difference between the price paid for the enterprise as a whole less the net of assets over liabilities. Suppose a business has net assets (both of fixed and current) of Rs.27.50 lakhs and total liabilities (including share capital and reserves) of Rs.11.50 lakhs and the purchase consideration for the business is Rs.33.5 lakhs, the value of goodwill will be Rs.17.50 lakhs.

The value of goodwill, being subjective, depends upon the negotiated price. Hence it reflects the relative strength of bargaining of the parties. The valuation tends to be arbitrary in nature. Therefore, prior to arriving at an agreed price for goodwill, both the buyer and seller of the business do calculate the expected value of goodwill based on any one or more of the following methods, namely.

- *Certain multiples of the average profits / or turnover over a number of past years,*
- *The capitalization of expected future returns over a specified number of years or*
- *The present value of the super profits likely to be earned by the business.*

Multiples of Profit/ Turnover Method

This is based on the historic data of the performance of the business. Under this, the average net profit or turnover for the past five to seven years is calculated and the value of goodwill is estimated as certain multiples there of. For example, if the average net profit of Hari's business for the past five years were Rs.2,75,000 and goodwill is to be estimated as a multiple of three years, then the value of goodwill will be Rs.8,25,000. In case of certain service industries, like that of the lawyers or doctors, the multiple will be on the basis of average turnover and not average profit.

Capitalization of Expected Returns Method

Under this method, the stream of expected cash inflows, over a period (usually over the residual life of the major assets) is estimated. The cash flow is discounted with the desired rate of return of the buyer. From the summation of the discounted cash flows, the current book value of the assets is subtracted. The excess, if any, is considered the value of goodwill. For example, the current book value of the assets of Humayun was Rs.51 lakhs. The residual life of his major assets is 6 years. The expected annual cash inflows during the useful life of major assets are Rs.25 lakhs, Rs.27 lakhs, Rs.24 lakhs, Rs.22 lakhs, Rs.20 lakhs and Rs.18 lakhs respectively. The desired rate of return of the buyer is 18%. The present value of the future incomes for six years would

$$25/1.18 + 27/1.18^2 + 24/1.18^3 + 22/1.18^4 + 220/1.18^5 + 18/1.18^6 = 81.88 \text{ lakhs}$$

Present value could also be worked out by using the discount tables. Form the present value thus arrived at current book value of assets at Rs.51 lakhs is deducted, leaving a residual value of Rs.30.88 lakhs, which is the value of goodwill under the capitalization of expected return method.

PV of Super Profit Method

The next method of valuation is based on the hypothesis that the value of goodwill should roughly correspond to the present value of the abnormal profits or super profits the business is likely to earn over the next few years. As the utility of goodwill as an earning asset is subject to changes in the taste and preference of customers, technological upgradation of the competitors etc., the buyer would normally prefer to evaluate super profits for as short a period as possible, say three to four years. The summation of the discounted cash flows of the expected super profits of the business will be considered as a fair value of goodwill. For example, Ramdas' expected cash flows from super profits for the next 3 years were Rs.47 lakhs, Rs.45 lakhs, and Rs.43 lakhs respectively. The market rate of capitalization for similar industries is 25%. The sum total of discounted cash flows for the 3 years would be Rs.88.4 lakhs, which is the value of goodwill under this method.

Treatment of Goodwill

Once goodwill is created, it will be shown as an intangible asset. As a portion of assets is written off annually, notionally representing their contribution to the earning of revenue of that year, it is logical that goodwill too has to be written off. However, there is a difference between other assets (both tangible and intangible) and goodwill. Other assets have a cost, either cost of development by the business or by the seller. But, goodwill is created by the business without incurring any monetary cost. Hence, tax authorities do not allow the writing off of goodwill as an allowable cost. Goodwill has, therefore, to be adjusted against the distributable profits of the owners. Or in other words, it will reduce the wealth of the owners, who had purchased the business. However, once it has been treated as an intangible asset, it has to be amortized. As regards the methods of amortization of goodwill, the accepted accounting conventions, setup by the Accounting Principle Board of US, has prescribed the following alternatives:

- *To retain the goodwill at its full value till a reduction or amortization is desired,*
- *To retain the cost as an asset and to amortize a portion over an assumed life period. (Goodwill can be written off within forty years of its creation.)*
- *To reduce the value of goodwill from the equity of the owners.*

The third method, namely to reduce goodwill from the equity (accumulated reserves and surplus of the business) during the year of its creation itself, is an ideal choice, provided the retained earnings of the company are quite substantial to absorb the amount of goodwill. In that case, the following journal entry has to be passed:

Table 14
Journal proper of Casual-ware Ltd.

Date	Particulars	LF	Dr.	Cr.
	By Reserves & Surplus a/c		7,50,000	
	To Goodwill a/c			7,50,000

Few Modern Breeds

Global competition and the resultant consumer domination have widened the horizon of intangible assets. Businessmen all over the world are increasingly realizing that apart from the tangible assets and conventional intangibles, discussed in the foregoing paragraphs, a few non-conventional intangibles also contribute significantly to the revenue earning capacity of business. Eminent researchers have attempted to identify and quantify these intangibles. We may consider a few important modern concepts on intangibles.

Intellectual Capital

The first that gives an overall assessment of the non-conventional intangibles is the concept of intellectual capital. Stewart has described intellectual capital as "*intellectual material, comprising knowledge, information, intellectual property and experience that can be put to use to create wealth*". It is the collective brain power and not attributable to any single segment of human resource, structural advantages and customer capital. It is the synergy created by all these factors collectively. NRI Research, Evanston, Illinois, has evaluated the concept. They have developed a technique named calculated intangible value model (CIVM) to measure the ability of the intellectual capital to outperform other business in the industry, with similar tangible assets. CIVM is a simple application of the industrial return on assets (ROA), to the tangible assets of a business, to arrive at normal industry return on assets of the business. The return so arrived at is deducted from the actual profit of the business. The excess return is attributable to the *intellectual capital.* When the excess return is discounted at the cost of capital of the business, the value of intellectual capital emerges. For example Zealot Enterprises has an average operating profit of Rs.46.20 crores for the last three years. Its assets (for three years) averaged Rs.378.12 crores. The average industry return on assets is 10%. The cost of capital of Zealot is 15%. Applying CIVM to the information of Zealot, it's intellectual capital is valued at Rs.56 crores, as in Table below:

Table 15
Zealot enterprises
Assessment of intellectual capital. (Rs.Crores)

1. Average tangible assets of Zealot	378.12
2. Average ROA of the industry	10%
3. Expected profit applying industry norm (1× 2)	37.8
4. Actual profit of Zealot	46.2
5. Profit attributable to intellectual capital (4 – 3)	8.4
6. Cost of capital	15%
7. Capitalization intellectual capital of Zealot (5/6)	56.0

Human Resource As An Asset

A number of factors contribute to the creation of intellectual capital. Among these, the single largest contribution comes from human resources. The recently expired management

Guru, Peter Druker had been, for quite sometime, emphasizing on ***knowledge workers*** and their twin contribution -in their capacity as owners of companies and as employees. Measurement of human capital has been attempted by a number of economists, among whom Lew and Schwatz stand out unique. Their model, named after them, calculates the future earnings of employees till their retirement and discounts the remuneration at the cost of capital to arrive at the value of human resources. Major IT companies have already introduced this in their annual reports. For example, Infosys has valued its human resources at Rs.28,334 crores as on 31.03.2005 using 13.63% (its cost of capital) as the discount factor. The relevant figure for the previous period was Rs.21,139 crores.

Brand Names

Brand names do contribute to the earning of revenues over and above tangible assets. The earning capacity of brands had been so acclaimed that brands are equated with equity and the phrase brand equity is in common usage. Brands are treated as intangible assets and are valued by using generic brand earning multiple approach developed by Michael Bikin. Under this approach, brand strength of a company is determined on the basis of seven factors, namely, leadership, stability, market, internationality, trend, support and protection. These factors are suitably weighted according to the importance of their contribution in creating brand equity. The cumulative weighted average will be the value of the brand. As the degree of contribution by each of the factors is assumed to vary from company to company, the valuation of brands are highly subjective. Again, IT companies have taken the lead in valuing brands. Infosys in its annual report as on 31.03.2005 has valued its brand at Rs.14,153 crores (previous year Rs.8,185 crores).

Indian Experience

It is heartening to note that many Indian corporates are also veering slowly towards the recognition of these intangibles. A few blue chip companies such as Infosys, Wipro, HCL, Satyam Computers and Dr.Reddy's Lab., besides the public sector giant BHEL have made attempts to assess these intangible assets. In their latest annual reports, they had evaluated intangible assets like intellectual capital, market value addition, brand valuation, human resources capital and economic value addition. A word of caution may here be added. These valuations are not entered in the assets side of balance sheet of the companies, but are shown as annexure in annual reports. These intangible assets, no doubt, create and strengthen the goodwill of the business in the long run and increase its market capitalization.

Relevant Revenue

We would now consider what items are to be treated as income for the purpose of arriving at operating results. Economists have attempted to define revenue ever since economic thoughts began to shape. But the concept did not get any single definition that would be comprehensive. It was considered as *receipts or returns from any source*. Receipts from any source are very broad and vague and if adopted without restraints might distort the very purpose of preparing final accounts. Receipts on issue of shares, bonds or debentures or deposits or loans are not revenue. The Financial Accounting Standard Board (FASB) of the US considers as revenue ***all inflows or other enhancements of assets of an entity or settlement of its liabilities (or combination of both) during a period, from delivery or producing goods, rendering services or other activities, that constitute the entity's ongoing major or central operation***. The Institute of Charted Accountants of India (ICAI) defines revenue as ***"the gross inflow of cash, receivables or other consideration, arising out of activities of an enterprise from the sale of goods, from rendering services and from the use, by others, of the enterprise resources, yielding interest, royalties and dividends"*** If we consider the nature of income from the accounting point of view, we observe that ***all credit balances, which do not create any obligation for repayment either immediately or in future, are revenues or incomes.***

A better appreciation of the term revenue could be had from the intention of the originators of the word, revenue. The term revenue has derived from the French verb ***revenir***, meaning returning back or coming back. All business activities start with an outlay i.e. investment of resources. Investment need not necessarily mean employment of cash in fixed or floating assets. It also includes investment in processes and people. Benefits stemming out of that investment are revenues. Or in other words, the French considered capital assets as a ***stock*** and the revenues as ***flows*** from the normal investments in a business, either in the form of sales or service charges or incidental receipts without causing any obligation for repayment.

The flow of revenues, by its very nature, might confine to a particular accounting period or might sprawl over more than that period. As revenue is the flow from the outlay, it would be possible to accurately assess the extent of the revenue flow only when the outlay is fully exhausted. As business has perpetual existence and businessman goes on investing on a continuous basis, the determination of revenue for a particular period becomes difficult. It could not be measured exactly, but has necessarily to be approximated as fair as possible. Revenue recognition for a period, therefore, has its limitations. Hence, efforts are made to recognize and measure the extent of revenue as nearest to reality as possible, keeping the conservative nature of the businessman in mind. If he has to err, the businessman would like to err by underrating revenues, rather than blowing up his income for the period.

Turnover

The best known and often repeated source of revenue is turnover or sales for a trading or manufacturing organization and service charges in the form of freight, commission, brokerage, premium, franchise, royalty etc. for tertiary sector industries. The term sale is very broad and covers, within its ambit, a few transactions that resemble the nature of sale, even though these are not strictly sales from the accountants' point of view. Hence, it is necessary to clearly demarcate the boundaries of a transaction to be conclusively treated as sales or not. Legally speaking, sale has been defined by sale of Goods Act as ***a transaction where under the property in the goods is transferred from the seller to the buyer for a price.*** According to this legal definition, to consummate sale, two important conditions are to be complied with. The first criterion is transfer of property in the goods and the second is that the transfer should be for a price. Transfer of property means the transfer of ownership and not the mere possession. For concluding whether a particular exchange of goods amounts to transferring the ownership or not, the intention of the parties transferring the goods is crucial. When the owner gives the goods to another without any intention of transferring the ownership, such as for safe custody or for repairs or for raising a loan, such transactions are not sales, but are ***bailments*** or ***pledges***. On the other hand, when two parties have agreed, with the intention of one party transferring the ownership in the goods at a price and the other party intends to accept it, the transaction is sale. Hence, to constitute a sale, only **the *intention to transfer ownership of goods at a price is needed, irrespective of the physical transfer or possession of the goods or the payment of the price.*** Another test of ownership is the transfer of risk associated with the goods. With the transfer of ownership, the seller transfers the risk in the goods to the buyer, even if the goods remain in the possession of the seller.

Agreement to Sell

Having considered what constitutes sale, the next question is when sale is considered to have taken place – at the time of conclusion of the contract or later. In case of majority of sales, that is sales without any conditions, sale is assumed to have taken place as soon as the agreement is concluded. But in cases where the sales agreement is subject to the fulfillment of certain conditions, such transactions are not to be considered as sales, but *agreements to sell.* Agreements to sell are commonly referred to as *conditional sales*. They are not sales, as property in the goods would not pass on to the buyer till the stipulated conditions are fulfilled. The stipulations might be passage of time or the happening of an event. For example, an agreement to sell the standing paddy crop for an agreed price would not be sale, till the crop is harvested. Suppose in the meantime, the crop is destroyed due to natural calamities, the agreement to sell would become void, as the precondition could not be fulfilled.

Consignments

These are days of mass scale production. A few mega producers sell their products through a well-knit chain of depots and branches. However, in small and medium sized organizations, the volume of sales might not warrant countrywide branches and depots. Such units might have their depots in important strategic sales centers and in the rest of the market, operate through agents and distributors on ***consignment*** basis. Under this arrangement, the vendors send their goods to the agents and instruct them to sell the goods on terms and conditions stipulated by the vendors. The agents are custodians of the vendors' goods till they are sold. On effecting sales, the agents send periodic ***account sales***. The vendors recognize sales on receipt of account sales. Till then, the goods in the custody of the agents form part of the stock in trade of the vendors. This type of transaction is known as consignment. Consignments are, thus, bailment of goods.

Sale on Approval Basis

Similar to consignment is the sale on approval basis. Under this, the seller sends the goods directly to the consumer (instead of his agents) and allows him a time period for accepting the goods. Common examples of on-approval sales are mail order business. If the consumer accepts the goods within the stipulated time, it becomes sale. In case the consumer retains the goods beyond the stipulated period, his inaction is considered as tacit approval and sale is recognised there after. In sales on approval basis, the consumer should not make use of the goods before his acceptance. In case he makes use of the goods, it also amounts to implied approval and sale is recognized. Now a days, sale on approval basis is enlarged into use and return if not satisfied offer. Here, the use of the goods by the customer is allowed for a stipulated period and he could return the goods, if he is not satisfied with the quality or utility of the goods as promised by the vendor. In these types of transactions, the price of the goods is usually collected upfront i.e. before allowing the customer to use the product and the price is refunded, if the customer returns the goods after use with in the allowed period. Therefore, sale has to be recognized only after the expiry of the stipulated time in this type of arrangement.

Installment Credit

Sale of goods, particularly capital goods and consumer durables, such as machinery, equipment, gadgets, white goods etc on installment credit is a variation from normal sales. Here, the vendor enters into an agreement with the buyer for transfer of the goods to the latter on his making a prescribed down payment. The buyer becomes the owner of the goods, possesses it and uses it. The seller has, no doubt, the right of lien on the goods till all installments are paid. He takes back the goods on default of any installment. Sale is recognized in installment credits the moment down payment is made. A seemingly similar, but basically different arrangement is *hire purchase*. Hire purchase is an agreement to sell. The hire Purchase Act, 1972 defines hire purchase as an ***"agreement under which goods are let on hire and under which the hirer has the option to purchase them in accordance with the terms of agreement".*** Here, the vendor parts with the possession of the goods on receipt of down payment, but the property in the goods remain with him till all the installments are received. The buyer in hire purchase agrees to pay the price of the product, together with interest at agreed rate, over a specified number of periodic equated installments. Only on the payment of the last installment, the hirer would become the owner of the goods.

The question, therefore, is when should the vendor of hire-purchase goods book the transaction as sale-whether immediately after the conclusion of the agreement and accepting down payment or during the tenure of the hire purchase period or on the receipt of the last installment. There are different practices in this regard. One of the practices is to debit the cost of goods to the personal account of the hirer and to credit the hire-purchase account. The down payment is credited to the personal account of the hirer. The personal account of the hirer is debited with interest on the outstanding amount at the end of the period. The interest is treated as income of the period. When the installment is received at the end of the period, the entire installment is credited to the personal account of the hirer . At the time of preparing the profit and loss account for the year, the hire-purchase account is treated as sale of the year. When all the installments are received, the hirer's account would be amortized and he becomes the owner.

In yet other cases, particularly in hire purchase of small value goods, such as televisions, refrigerators, furniture, domestic appliances, musical instruments, computers etc, only the amount of installments is treated as revenue. For example, on 1st October, 2005, Quick Freeze Ltd sold on hire-purchase basis a refrigerator of the value of Rs.10,000 to Walter Ltd. The terms were Rs.2000 down payment and the balance to be paid in 12 monthly installments of Rs.903 each. The hire-vendor closes his books at the end of March. Interest rate could be worked out as 12% by using the annuity table. The vendor would recognize Rs 5418 as revenue for the year 2005-06 comprising part of price of refrigerator (Rs.5063) and interest for the period at 12% (Rs.355). The residual value of the refrigerator amounting to Rs. 2937 is treated as stock of finished goods. This is logical, as the hirer has the option, in law, to return the goods any time before the last installment. In the event of the client defaulting payment of installments, the vendor would terminate the contract and repossess the goods. The sale price, less the principal amount recovered, would be the value of repossessed stock, till it is resold. On sale of the repossessed goods, surplus, if any, would be treated as profit and loss would be booked as cost. It might be noted that the hirer is not liable for any loss on resale.

Quantum Meruit

Recognising the time of sale in capital goods, with process time extending more than a year and also in customer's contracts spread over longer periods is another grey area for the accountant. There is a time gap of more than one accounting year, between the time of undertaking the work and that of completing it. The work might have started in year one and completed in year four. In such cases could sales be recognized as soon as the work is taken up or to wait till it is completed? The former option would be too hasty and the latter denying the benefit to the extent of task accomplished during a year. In these cases, revenue is recognized on the principle of quantum meruit or to the extent of work completed.

Generally Accepted Accounting Practices (GAAP), detailed discussions on which were held in chapter 1, had laid down the pro-rata principle of recognizing sales in long-term contracts. As per GAAP guidelines, no revenue could be recognized till one fourth of the work is completed. When the work completed is more than one – fourth, but less than one – half, one-third of the estimated profit could be recognized as revenue. When the work completed is more than one-half, two-thirds of the estimated profits could be recognized as revenue. When the work is almost complete, the share of profit would be estimated total profit × value of work certified/contract price × cash received / work certified. The recognition is done taking into account the relationship between cash received and work certified. A simple formula for calculation of revenue recognizable is estimated profit × 1/3 or 2/3 × cash received/ work certified. For example, on 1st May 1999 General Constructions (Private) Limited had concluded an agreement with M/s Meena Agencies for constructing their industrial complex over four years. The understanding was to bill on quantum meruit basis. General Constructions had a profit margin of 20% (Rs.59 lakhs) built in to the contract price, which was finalised at Rs.3.56 crores. The profit included cushions for inflation. During 1999-2000, the work was slow and General constructions billed Meena for Rs.60 lakhs. The billing was for Rs.1.10 crores during 2000-01, Rs.1.20 crores during 2001-02 and the balance in2002-03. The architect certified all the bills. Cash received was 80% of the work certified in all situations. As the work in the first year has fallen short of one-fourth of the contracted value, General Constructions could not book any revenue for that year. However, the expenses in the year, in excess of the billed amount, are treated as loss on the contract. In 2000-01, General Constructions could book profit of Rs.15.73 lakhs (59 ×1/3 × 1.36 /1.70), being one-third of the profit multiplied by the cash received as a fraction of work certified. Work completed is up to that period (Rs.60lakhs in 1999-2000 and Rs.1.10 crores in 2000-01). In 2001-02 the company could book additionally Rs. 15.73 lakhs, being two-thirds of the profit on the billing of Rs.1.20 crores. In 2002-03, the company could book the balance of profit of Rs.27.54 lakhs as revenue, assuming that the contractors had received cash in full for the entire contract.

Service Charges

So far, we have been discussing the revenue recognition procedure in merchandise or manufacturing activities. Does the mode of recognizing revenue differs in service industries? The recognition of revenue in services industries is according to the terms of contract of service. Certain service contracts make specific performance as its essence. For example, installation fees, service guarantee fees, agency commissions, financial service fees etc. These are contracts where the fee is the revenue and it could be recognized only when the service is specifically performed to the satisfaction of the customers. Installation fees are payable for the erection of equipment. Special equipment, such as process plants, when supplied to a customer, contains an element of installation fee as part of the cost of equipment. Where the customer has no technical knowledge or competence to correctly install the equipment, he agrees to pay a fee to the suppliers towards installation. The fee is due only when the equipment is installed to the satisfaction of the customer. In fact, the fee has to be recognized as revenue only when the supplier has successfully taken trial runs as per the terms of contract. Usually, installation would have teething problems. It is the duty of the supplier to rectify the defects to the satisfaction of the customer, before recognizing the fee as revenue.

The supplier might also guarantee the effective functioning of the equipment for certain number of years. Specific fee for this purpose is included as part of the cost of the equipment. In such cases, the businessman should segregate, at the time of sale, the fee from the cost of the equipment and treat the gross value of equipment less the fee, as revenue of the year of sale. The guarantee fee component has to be recognized as revenue, usually equally, over the period for which guarantee has been extended. Costs, if any, incurred as a consequence of the guarantee obligation, had to be treated as expenses of the year concerned.

The next category of service charges comprises agency commission and financial charges. When an agent acts on behalf of the principal, he is entitled to the agreed commission only on fulfilling the conditions of the agency agreement. A selling agent of goods becomes entitled to commission on the value of goods sold by him during a period, as per the account sale submitted by him. Sometimes he is given an extra commission to take responsibilities for collection of receivables. These commissions are called ***delcredre commission.*** The commission receivable by advertising agents is recognized as revenue only after the advertisement is published. Similarly, commission receivable by insurance agent is recognized as revenue only on the issue or the renewal of the policy. Financial services, such as arranging for the loans or for issue of securities, are carried out by ***merchant bankers***. They are entitled to the agreed commission only on the specific performance of the service. That is, on the sanctioning of the loan by the financial institution or bank and on the issue of the concerned securities to the public. It might be added here that documentation and disbursement of the loan is not part of the specific performance by the merchant bankers, unless such services are also included as part of the contracts. It is not part of merchant banker's obligation to ensure that the underwriter fulfills his commitment by subscribing to the shortfall, if any, in public subscription. Once the underwriting agreement is completed and the issue is made, specific performance of the merchant bankers is complete and the commission is booked as revenue.

Technical Know-How Fees

As against the specific service contracts discussed above, there are significant numbers of continuing long-term service contracts, which generate revenue over a period. Royalty fees receivable for the know-how supply is a familiar example under this group. A businessman, who has technical know-how in his possession under a patent, might part with or share the know-how with another for commercializing in particular areas and for specific periods. Such contracts are called *technical know-how agreements*. The supplier of know-how, under this agreement, is usually entitled to a one time technical know-how fee as well as long-term periodic royalty. Technical know-how fee is for specific performance of imparting the know-how to the satisfaction of the customer. Once this is done and after successful trial runs, the businessman becomes entitled to the know-how fee, which is recognized as his revenue for the period. Royalties are, on the other hand, fees received by the supplier of the know-how over a specific period, at certain percentage on the value of sales or profit or the volume of production, as the case might be. Royalties are recognized as revenues at the end of each year, measured as per the barometers indicated above.

Franchise Fees

Franchises are akin to royalties with a difference. Royalties are paid for the use of technical know-how of a process in possession of the vendor. However, the product to be manufactured by the user of the know-how might not be marketed under brand name of the supplier. In franchise, the user is allowed to use the brand name of the franchiser. In certain cases, it is only the brand name for which franchise is paid. Further, many franchisers supply equipment, plant and machinery and production facilities along with technical know-how. Thus, the franchisee need not invest in manufacturing facilities. The best example in this category is the mineral water business. Here, the entire equipment of the franchiser is installed at the premise of the franchisee and fee is levied at certain paise per liter of water produced. Franchise fees, therefore, are levied both for the use of the equipment and the process know-how. In some franchises, such as Cocoa Cola, the product essence itself is supplied and the franchiser has simply to blend the product and sell. Franchise charges are usually recognized as revenue on yearly basis, measured according to the volume of output.

Royalties

Royalties are paid for the use of mineral deposits, such as for querying coal mining, iron ore extraction or exploring oil. The modalities are that a lease rent, based on the expected deposit of the mineral, oil etc. is agreed to and royalty is charged on the basis of the actual extraction of the deposit. For example, suppose a coal mine is estimated to have 5 million tonnes of coal of a particular quality. The owner of the mine fixes the lease say at Rs.5 crores and the period of lease is 15 years. It amounts to that the lessee has to pay Rs.10 per tonne of coal extracted as royalty. In case 5,00,000 tonnes are extracted in the first year, revenue is recognized by the lessor for 5 lakh tonnes at the rate of Rs.10 per tonnes, which is Rs.50 lakhs. In the second year, if the coal extracted were 10 lakh tonnes, the lessor's revenue would be Rs.1 crore. This would continue, till the lease period or the exhaustion of the mine, whichever is earlier.

Holding of Assets

Revenue for a business also stems from holding of assets. A business might invest its surplus funds in short-term securities and earn an income, without sacrificing liquidity of the business. In this connection, money market instruments, such as treasury bills, commercial papers etc are ideal assets to be held by the enterprise, as these have high liquidity and fair returns. Revenue, in the form of interest, is recognized at periodic intervals or on the amortization of such assets. Another method of short-term investment is to have ***speculative inventories***. A fund rich enterprise could buy or import scarce raw materials in bulk, from cheaper markets and sell the excess over its requirement at higher rates, reaping *trading profits*, which are recognized as revenue to the business in the year of occurrence.

Long term holding of assets by an organisation would also generate revenue. An organisation might invest its surplus cash in the shares/bonds of other companies and realize revenue by way of income and capital appreciation. Companies also acquire shares with a view to ultimately taking over the latter. Such takeovers result in additional revenues in future due to ***synergies*** associated with mergers. Further, an enterprise also invests in its subsidiaries or sister concerns and reaps the benefit of periodic dividends and capital appreciation. Dividends are recognized as revenues in the same accounting period, where as capital appreciation is recognized only on the sale of the investments.

Others Holding Company's Assets

Revenue might also accrue to the business by others holding the assets of the enterprise. Assets of the company, when they are in excess of its requirement, are let out for others to use. A charge is levied for such use. For example, when the company's vehicles are leased out to others, it generates a periodic income, which could be recognized at the end of the concerned period. Leasing companies earn their major income from letting out their assets.

Receipts of Cash

In some cases, revenue is recognized only on receipt of cash. Professional code of conduct restricts certain professionals from legally enforcing their claim for reward for the services rendered by them. Doctors, solicitors, accountants and similar professionals are prevented, by their respective professional codes, from legally enforcing their rights for remuneration for their services. It is, therefore, logical that revenues for their services are recognized only when received in cash. For them, cash accounting is the ideal method.

Recognising and estimating revenue pertaining to the accounting period is the prime function of the accountant. He culls out the data from the accounting records of the business organisation. Information about the sales figures are available in trial balance, but are spread over three accounting heads – sales account, (Cr.), which represents the cash sales made during the period, sales day book total (Cr.), which indicates the extent of credit sales effected by the business and sales returns or inward returns account (Dr.). Sales, for the purpose of the profitability statement, are the synthesis of these accounts, that is, cash sales plus credit sales less sales return is the net sales to be recognized.

Profit & Loss Account in Single Entry

Profit and loss account in single entry is a probability statement. In single entry profit is the excess of assets over liabilities of the current year less the capital at the beginning of the year. In that system, the total of assets less liability would reveal the owner's capital as at the end of the year. From this, the owner's capital of the previous year is deducted to ascertain the results of business during the year. If there is excess, it is profit; if deficit it is loss. Zelus Corporation, which maintains its books on single entry system, has the following assets and liabilities, as at the end of March 2004 and 2005.

Table 16

Zelus Corporation

Assessment of profitability **(Rs. in Lakhs)**

Particulars	2005	2004
1. Assets – Net fixed assets	75.42	57.24
2. Net current assets	16.89	13.15
3. Total assets (1 + 2)	92.31	70.39
4. Total outside Liabilities	29.13	23.46
5. Owners' Capital (3 – 4)	63.18	46.93
6. Profit (5 of 2005– 5 of 2004)	16.25	

Owner's fund as at the end of 2005, over that of 2004, would be the result of the operation during the year(profit or loss). In this case, it has resulted in a profit of Rs.16.25 lakhs (63.18 – 46.93). The businessman would have to deduct additional capital, if any brought in during the year and has to add back any drawings made from the capital to this figure to arrive at the profit proper.

Profit and Loss Account in Double Entry

This method of calculating profit is primitive, as it does not take into account all items of costs and incomes pertaining to the period, which are outstanding and prepaid. Besides, this form of reporting would not facilitate analysis of the results, for which details of costs and revenues are essential. The inadequacy of the system had prompted many businesses to abandon it in favour of double entry bookkeeping. In double entry system of bookkeeping, which we follow in this book, the method of preparing profit or loss is refined and scientific. Here, the statement is prepared taking into account all the items of revenues and costs attributable for the period of reporting. If the revenue is more than cost, it is profit, otherwise it is loss.

Profit and loss account is conventionally prepared in the form of a "T" account. Costs, after adjustments for outstanding and prepaid, are listed under the debit side and the revenues under credit side. In addition to costs, opening stock heads the debit side and closing stock the tail end of the credit side. The rationale is very clear – the opening stocks are used up during the current accounting year and are therefore costs to the business. The closing stocks are part of the costs that have not been used up in the process of generating revenues during the period and should, therefore, be excluded from the cost. Including the closing stocks in the credit side of profit and loss account amounts to reducing the debit (cost) side.

The title of the profit and loss account ends with the suffix ***for the year ended***. The phrase "for the year ended" signifies that the statement contains data pertaining to the whole of the accounting year. It is the aggregate of the happenings during one accounting period. Profit and loss account of current period is presented with the figures of the previous period. Each side of the profit and loss account has three columns- particulars, inner column, and outer column. Particulars column indicates the items of expenses or revenues. The inner column is meant for carrying out adjustments. The outer column presents the costs or incomes attributable for the period. Side by side with the current period's figure, appear the figures for the immediately preceding accounting period. All businesses give the previous period's figure against each expense and revenue to enable the readers of the statement to have a comparative picture of the performance of the business in the current period vis-à-vis the previous period. After all items are posted, both the debit side and the credit side are totaled up. If the credit total is higher than the debit total, the difference is profit and vice-versa.

We have seen, in the last few chapters, the tasks that precede actual preparation of profit and loss account. The businessman has to prepare a trial balance, find out the errors, if any, rectify them, prepare a revised trial balance incorporating the effects of rectification, pass adjusting entries in respect of outstanding and prepaid expenses and accrued incomes and make closing entries. Once these preliminary works are accomplished, preparation of profit and account is an intelligent grouping of expenses in the debit side and the revenue items in the credit side of the profit and loss account. Presently, a number of businessmen prepare their profit and loss account in tabular form.

Trial balance is the basis from which the preparation of profit and loss account commences. It contains, at its debit side expenses and assets. Revenues and liabilities are listed on the credit balances. It would not be difficult for an experienced accountant to segregate expenses from assets and revenues from liabilities and prepare profit and loss account and balance sheet. A beginner may show some hesitation. One can easily pick out the expenses and revenues and prepare the profit and loss account if he recollects that a) expenses are expired costs, which have already been used up by the business during the accounting period itself, b) assets are expenditures, which are to be used up in following accounting periods, c) revenues are inflows without obligation for repayment and d) liabilities are receipts with obligations for repayment.

Use of Inner Column

Expenses are lined up in the income statement according to a specific order. It begins with direct costs, followed by factory overheads, administrative overheads and selling and distribution overheads in that order. Non-operating expenses form the tail end. Such an arrangement would enable the readers to analyze the operations of the business. So also the revenue side. Sales or turnover occupies the top slot, followed by closing stock and ends up with non-co-operating incomes. At the time of entering an item from the trial balance into the profit and loss account, it should be verified whether it would need to be adjusted for outstandings, prepayments or accruals. If any adjustment is necessary, then the amount of the item is entered in inner column. Items of expenses and revenues entered in the inner column are extended to the outer column after carrying out adjustments. If no adjustment is needed, the figure is straight away entered in the outer column.

Illustration

Let us illustrate, with a few examples, how to fill up the inner and outer columns of profit and loss account. Suppose wages appear in the trial balance at Rs.6, 45,751 and an adjustment entry had been passed in the journal proper for the outstanding wages of Rs.50,175 (by debiting outstanding wages account and crediting creditors for wages account). It indicates that the actual wages for the period was not only what was paid and appeared in trial balance, but also what was due and outstanding. The above factors would appear in the profit and loss account as in the following table.

Table 17
Debit side of Profit and Loss account of Armanian Co. for the year ended 31.03.2005. 31.03.2005.

Particulars			2005
To	Wages	6,45,751	
	Add : Outstanding	50,175	
			6,95,926

Adjustment entry for prepaid expenses is to credit the concerned expense account and debit prepaid expenses. For example, out of total insurance paid at Rs.1700, insurance prepaid is Rs.1050. Adjustment entry for the prepaid insurance would be –

By Prepaid insurance Rs.1050

To Insurance expenses Rs.1050..

As the entire insurance amount of Rs.1700, shown in trial balance, is not used up during the year, the unused part is expenditure (asset). Insurance cost would be shown in the profit and loss account as in table below. The other aspect, being expenditure would find its place in the assets side of balance sheet.

Table 18
Debit side of Profit and Loss account of Armanian Co. For the year ended 31.03 2005.

Particulars		2005
By Insurance	1700	
Less Prepaid	1050	650

In case of purchases, both the figures for gross purchases and purchase returns or returns outward would be in the trial balance. Purchases would be in debit and purchase returns in credit. In the profit and loss account, the net purchases would appear in the outer column as in table below.

Table 19

Debit side of Profit and Loss account of Armanian Co. for the year ended 31.03.2005

S. No	Particulars		2005
	By Purchases	12,26,500	
	Less : Returns	1,10,250	
			11,16,250

Similarly, in the credit side of the profit and loss account, sales returns or returns inward is adjusted to the sales and the net sale is shown in the outer column. Both the figures would appear in trial balance – sales as credit and returns inwards as debit. The net sales figure would appear in the outer column as in Table below.

Table 20

Credit side of (Profit and Loss account) of Armanian Co. for the year ended 31.03.2005

Particulars		2005
By Sales	16,54, 010	
Less : Returns	1,92,055	14,61,955

Let us now proceed to prepare Profit and Loss Account of Miss Biba Ganguly as on 31.12.2004 from the following trial balanceas on 31st December 2004:

Table 21

	Debit	Credit
Capital		20,000
Plant and machinery	25,000	
Office furniture and fittings	1,300	
Stock on 1.1.2004	24,000	
Motor vehicle	6,000	
Sundry debtors	22,850	
Cash in hand	200	
Cash at bank	3,250	
Wages	75,000	

Salaries	7,000	
Purchases	1,06,750	
Sales		2,40,000
Bills receivable	3,600	
Bills payable		2,800
Sundry creditors		26,000
Returns inwards	3,000	
Provision for doubtful debts		1,250
Drawings	3,500	
Returns outwards		2,750
Rent	3,000	
Factory lighting	400	
Insurance	3,150	
General expenses	500	
Bad debts	1,250	
Discount	3,250	1,850
	2,94,650	2,94,650

The following adjustments are to be effected:

I. Stock on 31st December 2004 Rs.26,000

ii. Furniture to be depreciated by 5%

iii. Factory lighting due for 3 months Rs.150

iv. Write off further bad debts Rs.350

v. Provision for doubtful debts to be increased to Rs.1,500 and provision for discount on debts at 2% to be made

vi. During the year machinery was purchased for Rs.10,000 but it was debited to purchases account

Solution

Before attempting to prepare the final accounts, adjustment entries in respect of the additional information are to be passed in journal proper as under

Rs.

i. By Closing stock account To Trading account	26,000	26,000
ii. By Profit and loss account To Depreciation on Furniture	65	65
iii. By Profit and loss account To Outstanding creditors for Factory lighting	150	150
iv. By Bad debts To Sundry debtors	350	350
v. By Profit and loss account To Provision for doubtful debts	250	250
vi. By Profit and loss account To Provision for discount	420	420
vii. By Machinery account To Purchases account	10,000	10,000

The two aspects of the adjustment entries are to be incorporated into the final accounts.

In (i) Closing stock is a current asset and is taken to the assets' side of balance sheet. Trading account is credited to reduce the cost.

In (ii) profit and loss account is debited with depreciation and in the balance sheet, the value of the asset furniture is reduced to that extent.

In (iii) profit and loss account is debited with the outstanding cost of factory lighting and as the amount has not yet been paid, the person to whom it is due becomes a creditor in balance sheet.

In (iv) Additional bad debts being non-operating cost is debited to profit and loss account and the value of debtors is reduced to that extent.

In (v) profit and loss account is debited with additional probable loss arising out of doubtful debtors and the provision is a liability to the business.

In (vi) Expected discount on debtors is a contingent loss to the business and the provision is a liability.

In (vii) The wrong entry rectified by giving the due debit to plant and machinery and the wrong debit given to purchases is removed by giving a credit.

The trading and profit and loss account and balance sheet of MissBiba Ganguly would be as under

Table 22
Financial statements of Miss Biba Ganguly
Trading and profit and loss account for the year ended 31.12.2004

	Rs.		Rs.
To Opening stock	24,000	By Sales 2,40,000	
To Purchases 1,06,750		Less returns 4,650	2,35,3
Less returns 2,750		By Closing stock	50
Less machinery 10,000	94,000		26,000
To Wages	75,000		
To Factory Lighting 400	550		
Add. Outstanding 150			
	1,93,550		2,61,3
		By Gross profit	50
			67,800
	7,000	By Discount received	1,850
	3,000		
To Rent	3,150		
To Insurance	500		
To General expenses			
To Discount 3,250	3,670		
Add Provision 420	65		
To Depreciation			
To Bad debts 1,250	1,600		
To Prov. For D.Debts	250		
	19,235		69,650
		By Profit transferred to capital	50,415

Balance sheet of Miss Biba Ganguly as on 31.12.2004

Liabilities		Rs.	Assets		Rs.
Capital	20,000		Plant and machinery	25,000	
Less Drawings	3,500		Add Purchased	10,000	35,000
Add Net profit	50,415	66,915	Furniture	1,300	
Bills payable		2,800	Less Depreciation	65	1,235
Sundry creditors		26,000	Motor vehicle		6,000
Outstanding creditors for			Sundry debtors	22,850	
factory lighting		150	Less Bad debts	350	22,500
Provision for DD		1,500	Closing stock		26,000
Provision for discount		420	Bills receivable		3,600
			Cash in hand		200
			Cash at bank		3,250
		97,785			97,785

Let us consider a partnership account. Sumir & Co., a partnership firm with Satyaprasad, Rajesh Khanna and Sunil Sharma as partners, is engaged in the manufacturing and export of computer monitors. The partners have agreed to share profits equally. Each partner is entitled to a salary of Rs.2000 P.M. out of profits. Capital and current accounts are charged interest at 5%. Tax at 35% and reserve at 50% of profit after tax. The trial balance of the firm for the year ended 31 March 2006 was as under:

Table 23

Trial balance of Sumir & Co. as on 31.3.2006

Particulars		Dr.	Cr.
Capital accounts of			
SatyaPrasad	54,45,000		
RajeshKhanna	33,35,000		
SunilSharma	32,20,000		120,00, 000
Reserves and Surplus			21,06,043
Current accounts of			
Satya Prasad		82,500	
Rajesh Khanna			21,500
Sunil Sharma		40,955	
Opening stock			
-Raw materials		16,90,858	

-Semi finished goods		1,09,840	
-Finished goods		22,87,655	
Wages		9,72,543	
Consumables		97,865	
Power and fuel		3,45,279	
Lighting – factory		69,755	
-Office		21,560	
Doubtful debt reserve			35, 850
Packaging materials		85,065	
Transport		42,581	
Travel and conveyance		24,185	
Telephone, Fax, Email		52,,092	
Advertisement		5,27,290	
Insurance		9,270	
Purchases		57,13,459	
Returns		61,954	54,095
Sales			108,75,643
Carriage inwards		98,756	
Carriage outwards		45,765	
Bad debts		81,205	
Interest on IDBI loans		1,01,475	
Salaries		1,56,780	
Legal expenses		14,099	
Selling commission		1,37,410	
Hedging expenses		95,575	
Discount		45,1230	34,321
Profit on sale of assets			1,05,120
Interest			2,10,245
Export incentives			6,14,550
Loan from IDBI			12,50,000
Sy. Debtors/creditors		15,45,855	7,59,417
Plant & machinery	8572050		
Land	126,789		
Building	1234,972		
Vehicles	865,990		
Furniture	210,234	110,10,035	
Investment		25,00,000	

Following additional information are made available. Let us prepare a trading, profit and loss account and appropriation account for the firm:

- *Closing stock : Raw materials Rs.17,75,401 (MP Rs.16,15,950) Semi finished goods Rs.1,12,037 and Finished goods Rs.23,56,285 (MP Rs.25,65,850).*
- *Depreciate : Plant & Machinery by 10%*
- *Building by 2.8%*
- *Vehicles by 40%*
- *Furniture & fixtures by 30%.*
- *Outstanding expenses:*
- *Wages Rs.97,235*
- *Salaries Rs.38,538*
- *Insurance was paid on Oct.1, 1998 for a year.*
- *Maintain doubtful debt reserves at 3% on debtors.*
- *One of the debtors, owing Rs.16250, has become bankrupt and his estate would pay a dividend of 30 paise per rupee.*
- *Provide for discount on debtors at 2% and creditors at 1%.*
- *Capitalize advertisement cost and write off in 3 years beginning from current year in the ratio of 3 : 2 : 1.*
- *Investment was made last year at 13%.*
- *IDBI loan availed of in April 1998 at 16% interest..*
- *An old hydraulic press, with book value of Rs.2,13,185 was sold for Rs.1,98,550 during the year and was included in the sales.*
- *10 monitors sold on hire purchase basis on 1.4.98 for Rs.50,000, were included in sales, although two installments aggregating 40% of the price are due next year.*
- *A Hero Honda bought at a price of Rs.45,000 for the son - in – law of Satyaprasad has been included in the purchase account.*
- *5 monitors, priced Rs.4000 each, were taken from the stock for the use in a school run by Rajesh Khanna. No entry was passed in respect of this transaction.*
- *Cement and Steel costing Rs.68,500, purchased for the construction of the private garage of Sunil Sharma, was included in the purchase account.*
- *Wages include wages of Rs.12,450 paid for fabrication of machinery by the firm for its use.*

- *In December, a fire broke out in the factory destroying stock of materials of the value of Rs.86,550. Insurance claim for the loss has been admitted at Rs.72,000 the value of the destroyed stock has been included in the closing stock.*
- *Purchase of stationery included in purchases book Rs.5450.*

Adjustments entries needed before profitability is estimated, is given in seriatim together

Table 24

Adjustment entrieswith explanations, wherever needed:

(1) By closing Stock - Raw Material - Semifinished goods - Finished goods To Tradin/Manufacturing account Explanation: Market price of raw material was less than the cost price. As per accounting norm market price or cost price whichever is lower had to be taken as stock, the stock at market price is taken.	1615950 112037 2356285	4084272
(2) By Trading and P&L account (Depreciation) To Plant and machinery To Building To Vehicles To Furniture Explanation: Before working out depreciation, the value of assets is to be established. Wages of Rs.12,450 paid for fabrication of equipment had wrongly been included under wages, instead of under plant and machinery. This should be removed from wages and added to plant and machinery. Please see adjustment 10. Further, an old hydraulic press sold for Rs.1,98,550 had been wrongly entered in the sales book. The book value of the sold machine was Rs.2,13,185. Hence there was a loss of Rs.14,635 on sale of the machinery. The rectification would have to take three aspects, namely to remove the wrong credit given to sales	1308346	837,131 61,749 346,396 63,070

by debiting sales with Rs1,98,550, by debiting loss on sale by Rs.14,635 and by crediting plant and machinery with Rs.2,13,185(being the book value). Please see adjustment 15. Thus, the net value of plant and machinery, before depreciation would be Rs.8,37,1315(8,57,2050-2,13, 185 +12,450).Depreciation at the rate of 10% would, therefore, be 837131.		
(3) By Wages By salaries To Outstanding Creditors	97,235 38,538	1,35,773
(4) By Prepaid insurance To insurance Explanation: Only six months of insurance has been used up. Balance six months is unexpired; hence prepaid.	4,635	4,635
(5) ByProfit and loss account To Reserve for discount To Reserve for doubtful debts Explanation: Debtors on whom doubtful debt reserve had to be created have to be calculated net of bad debts. Thus, from the gross debtors of Rs.15,45,855, bad debtor for Rs.16,250 has to be deducted to arrive at debtors eligible for discount, which is Rs.15,29,605. Discount at 2% has to be created on these eligible debtors, which works out to Rs.30,592. The debtors on whom provision for doubtful debts are to be made are also Rs.15,29,605, which at 3% is Rs.45,888. As against this, the Co. had already created reserve for doubtful debts of Rs.35, 850.Additonal provision to be made this year is Rs.10,038. It may also be noted that the entire amount outstanding (Rs.16,250) in the account of the debtor, which has become bad, would not be eligible for discount, even though his estate may pay 30% of the debt.	40,630	30,592 10,038
(6) By bad debts To Debtors Explanation: the estate of an insolvent debtor would pay only 30%. Hence 70% of his outstanding at Rs.16,250 (which is Rs.11,375)would become bad. It may be noted that the adjustment for bad debts is over and above the bad debt written off during the year and shown in the trial balance.	11,375	11,375

(7) By Profit and Loss account To Advertisement Explanation: Total advertisement cost at Rs.5,27,290 has to be capitalized and written off over 3 years in the ratio of 3 : 2 : 1. For the first year, the share would be 3/6 = 2,63,645.	2,63,645	 2,63,645
(8) By debtors for interest To Interest accrued Explanation: Investment of Rs.25 lakhs at 13% should have given a yearly interest of Rs.3,25,000. Of this, Rs.2,10,245 has been received. The balance Rs.1,14,755 is accrued. Entry for accrued income is	1,14,755	 1,14,755
(9) By Interest To IDBI (Outstanding creditor) Explanation: Interest at 16% on IDBI loan of Rs.12.50 lakhs for 9 months is Rs.1,50,000. As against this, Rs.1,01,475 has been paid. The balance due is Rs.48,525.This entry is for outstanding interest.	48,525	 48,525
(10) By Sales By Loss on sale of machinery To Plant and machinery Explanation: This adjustment has two components. One, sale of hydraulic press for Rs.1,98,550 has been wrongly included in sales. So the unwanted credit given to sales is to be removed by a debit to sales of Rs.1,98,550 and plant and machinery by a credit for the same amount. Second, the book value of the machinery sold being Rs.2,13,185 (as against the sale price of Rs.1,98,550), the sale of machinery has resulted in a loss of Rs.14,635. To give effect to this the loss on sale of machinery account is debited and the machinery account is credited. In the end, the entire book value of Rs.2,13,185 of the press would be credited to plant and machinery, as the asset had been removed from the business.	1,98,550 14,635	 2,13,185

(11) By Sales To HP Party Explanation: We have already seen that the practice in hire purchase sale of smaller value articles is to treat the entire value of hire purchase deal as a liability of the hired and the installments are treated as sales. In this case, out of the sale value of Rs.50,000, ,only 2 installments for 40% of sale value is yet to be received. The balance 60% (Rs 30,000) had been receives and to be recognized as revenue. As sales was credited with the entire value of Rs.50,000 sales is debited with Rs. 20,000 to remove excess credit and the hired account is debited..	20,000	20,000
(12) By Satyaprasad's drawings account To Purchases account Explanation: The purchase of Hero Honda for the personal use of partner is a personal transaction of the partner and not the purchase for the business. Hence it is removed from purchases through a credit and debited to the drawings (personal) account of the partner.	45,000	45,000
(13) By Rajesh Khanna's drawings account To Sales account Explanation: Taking 5 monitors from stock for the personal use of the partner (Rajesh Khanna) in his school amounts to deemed sale to him. Hence, credit sales account and debit drawings account of Rajesh Khanna.	20,000	20,000
(14) By Sunil Sharma's drawing account To Purchases account Explanation: This is a private purchase of the partner and hence amounts to drawal from the business. Purchase account was wrongly debited instead of the personal account of Sunil Sharma. To rectify this error, Sunil Sharma's drawing account has to be debited and purchases account has to be credited.	68,500	68,500
(15) By Plant and machinery To Wages account Explanation: wages paid for fabrication of machinery is assets account and has to be included as cost of the machinery.	12,450	12,450

(16) By Profit and loss account	14,550	
By Insurance co. account	72,000	
To Closing stock Explanation: Destruction of stock (Rs.86,550) is a loss to the business.. The destruction has depleted the stock, hence stock would be reduced by crediting Rs.86,550. Insurance company becomes debtor to the business when it accepts liability. So, the insurance company has to be debited by Rs 72,000, the extent admitted. As the admission of loss was within the year of loss, it would go to reduce the loss to business to that extent. Hence the net loss would be Rs.14,550, which is debited to profit and loss account. In case the admission of claim materializes after the closure of account, the entire loss would be debited to the profit and loss account of the year. The claim would be treated as miscellaneous income in the year of admission.		
(17) By Stationery account	5,450	
To Purchases account Explanation: Purchase of stationery is not purchase of goods. It has been wrongly included in purchases account instead of stationery account. Wrong debit given to purchase has to be removed by crediting it and stationary account should be given its due debit.		5,450

Table 25

Sumir& Co.

Trading, Profit and Loss account for the ended 31 March, 2006

Opening Stock			Sales	10875643	
Raw Material	690858		Less:P M	198550	
SFG	109840	4088353	HP Stock	20000	
FG	2287655		Returns	61954	
			Add: Rajesh	20000	
Purchases	5713459		Closing Stock-		
Less:SP Drgs	45000		Raw material	1615950	
Stationery	5450		SFG	112037	
SS Drawings	68500		FG	2356285	
Returns	54095	5540414	Less destroyed	86,550	39,97,68

Wages 972543 Less: P&M 12450 Add: Outst 97235	1057328			
Power & Fuel	345279			
Packaging Mat	85065			
Carriage Inwards	98756			
Consumables	97865			
Lighting – Fact	69755			
Depreciation : Mach	837131			
	12219946			14699411
Lighting – Office	21560	Gross Profit		2479465
Transport	42581	Discount		34321
Travel & Conveyance	24185	Profit on sales of Assets Less: Loss on Sale of mach	105120 14635	90485
Telephone, Fax, email	52092	Int. on Invest 210245 Add. Accrued 114755		325000
Insurance 9270 Less: Prepaid 4635	4635	Export incentives		614550
Carriage outward	45765			
Bad debts 81205 Add: Debtors 11375	92580			
Int.IDBI loan 151475 Add: Outstanding 48525	200000			
Salaries 156780 Add: Outstanding 38538	195318			
Legal expenses	14099			
Selling Commission	87410			
Hedging expenses	95575			
Depreciation Building 61749 Vehicles 346396 Furniture & Fix 63070	471215			

Discount 45123 Add: Provision 30592	75715		
Reserve for DubtfulDebts	10038		
Advertisement	263645		
Loss due to fire 86550 Less: Insurance 72000	14550		
Stationery	5450		
	1716413		3543821
		Profit	1827408

P & L Appropriation account.

To Partners Salaries SatyaPrasad 24000 R.Khanna 24000B S.Sharma 24000	72000		
To Interest on Capital SatyaPrasad 272250		Interest on current Account SatyaPrasad	4125
R.Khanna 166750 S.Sharma 161000	600000	Sunil Sharma	2048
To Interest on RK's Current a/c	1075		
To Taxation	406177		
To Reserves	377166		

To Share of Profit Satyaprasad 125721 R.Khanna 125721 S.Sharma 125721	377166		
	1833581		1833581

Balance sheet as on 31.3.2006

LiabilitiesB		31.3.2006	Assets		31.3.2006
Capital a/cs of			Plant &		
S.Prasad	54,45,000		Machinery	85,72,050	
R.Khanna	33,35,000		Add wages	12,450	
S.Sharma	32,20,000	120,00,000	Less sale	2,13,185	
Reserves	21,06,043		Less Depreciat	8,37,131	
Add for year	3,77,166	24,83,209	Land		
Current a/cs			Building	12,34,972	
S.Prasad	- 82,500		Less Depreciat	61,749	
Less Purchases	- 45,000		Vehicle	8,65,990	
Less Int.drawings	- 4,125		Less Depreciat	3,46,396	
Add Salaries	24,000		Furniture	2,10,234	
Int. on Capt.	2,72,250		Less Depreciat	63,070	
Profit	1,25,721	2,90,346	Investment		
R.Khanna	21,500		Advertisement	5,27,290	
Less sales	20,000		Less P & L a/c	2,63,645	
Add Salaries	24,000		Sundry Debtors	15,45,855	
Int. Current a/c	1,075		Less bad debts	11,375	
Int. Capital	166,750		Insurance prepaid		
Profit	1,25,721	3,19,046	Insurance Co.		
S.Sharma	- 40,955		For interest		
Less sales	- 68,500		Closing Stock-		
Int.on drawings	- 2,048		Raw materials	16,15,950	
Add Salaries	24,000		SFG	1,12,037	
Interest on Cap	161,000		FG	23,56,285	
Profit	1,25,721	1,99,218	Less fire losses	86,550	

IDBI Loan		12,50,000		
Reserve for DD	35,850	7,59,417		
Add P&L	10,038	45,888		
Outstanding Creditors				
-for wages	97,235			
- for salaries	38,538	1,35,773		
Outs. Creditors (IDBI)		48,525		
Provision for Discount		30,592		
Provision for Taxation		4,06,177		
Hire purchase sale a/c		20,000		
		179,88,191		179,88,191

Summary

The enterprise, in order to know its performance during an accounting period, has to prepare final accounts. Final accounts are prepared in two parts – profit and loss accounts to ascertain the operational results of the business and balance sheet to know what others owe to the business and what the business owes to others. For the former, the revenues earned by the business and the cost attributable to the earning of that revenue are to be taken into account. This is known as the ***matching principle in accountancy.*** The balance sheet lists all expenditures as assets and all obligations as liabilities. In this chapter, we have examined the need, nature and method of adjusting transactions and events to recognize costs. At the end of an accounting period, the business would carry forward stocks in the form of raw materials, semi-finished goods and finished goods. The business would also have expenses outstanding and prepaid. As this affects cost attributable for the period, their values have to be properly adjusted to arrive at fair cost. So also certain expenditures like building, plant and machinery, equipment, furniture, vehicles etc, which have contributed to the earning of income during the period, have to be treated as costs, as these are used up during the accounting period. These adjustments are collectively known as closing entries.

Closing Stock of raw materials is valued for the purpose of adjustment on the principle that the closing stock represents purchase price or market price whichever is lower. Any one of the methods, namely, FIFO, LIFO, WA or NIFO could be used to value the stock depending upon the economic conditions. In the event of inflation, either LIFO or NIFO method is appropriate, as it equates the cost of production to the current market price. FIFO is the method suitable during times of deflation. In case of fluctuating market price, Weighted Average Method is adopted. Closing stock of semi-finished goods is valued at works cost for the period of process cycle. Finished goods are valued at cost of production or market price, whichever is lower. The adjustment entry for the closing stock is to debit the stock, which is expenditure to be treated as asset in balance sheet, while credit is given to the profit and loss account with a view to reduce cost.

Outstanding expenses are unpaid costs attributable to the accounting period and have to be added to their respective heads and taken to the cost side of the profit and loss account. Since these expenses are not paid but are due, the business owed the amount to the persons who have given the benefit. Hence, they are creditors of the business. On the other hand, prepaid expenses are expenditures, whose benefits would accrue to the business in future period or periods. As such they are assets. At the same time, prepaid expanses are to be deducted from the concerned expenses, as it is not the appropriate cost. Crediting the captioned head of account would reduce cost.

Depreciation is yet another event that has to be accounted at the end of the period, although the benefit is used up continuously by the enterprise. Depreciation is a provision for wear and tear, obsolescence, damage, loss or reduction in the value of the asset. Depreciation is a notional cost, as it does not necessitate outflow of funds. It is an item of internal cash accrual. Businessmen chose from different methods of depreciation depending upon trade practices or nature of assets. Briefly, there are two methods of depreciation- written down value method and straight-line method. Other methods or variations of either. Whatever the method of depreciation one might adopt in India, the aggregate depreciation shall not exceed the historical cost of the asset. The tax authorities in the country recognize written down value method in selected cases. The adjusting entry for depreciation is to debit the depreciation (as it is a cost) and to credit the concerned assets to bring down the value for its use during the year.

Revenue is the result of cost. Costs are resources sacrificed with a view to earn revenues. Surplus of revenue over cost attributable for earning such revenue results in profit, which increases the wealth of the enterprise. Revenue is a flow and its realistic measurement is necessary to project a fair and true picture of the operational results of the business over a period. Businessmen are conservative by not exaggerating their income during an accounting period. They prefer to defer the recognition of revenue even if there is a little doubt. On the other hand, they recognize costs even if there is a remote chance of its happening.

Intangible assets are valued at the cost at which they are created or acquired. Should the cost of creation or acquisition be insignificant, they are written off as revenue expenses in the year in which the cost was incurred. However, when the amount spent is quite large and the writing off the entire expenditure in the year of occurrence will distort the operational results of the business, these expenditures are capitalized and written off according to assumed proportion of their contribution to the earning capacity of the business. Modern concepts of intangible assets have transgressed the conventional areas. Intellectual capital, human resources capital and brand equity are considered as intangible assets capable of contributing to the earning of the business, over and above tangible assets.

Revenue recognition and measurement are vital steps in the preparation of profit and loss account. Generally speaking, revenue might be recognized at any of the following stages.

- *At the point of sale*
- *During the process of*
- *For service contracts, service charges are recognised as revenue only when the task is completed to the satisfaction of the customer.*
- *Holding assets Revenue by way of interest, dividend and capital gains are recognised on investments of the business in short term or long-term securities and assets. Revenue is also recognised when others hold the assets of the business as in the case of leasing.*
- *On receipt of payment*

I. QUESTIONS

1. What is matching principle?
2. What are closing entries? Why does a businessman pass closing entries?
3. What are the sources of information regarding costs and incomes?
4. What is inventory? What are its components?
5. Why should closing stock to be deducted from the cost?
6. How is the consumption of material arrived at?
7. What do you understand by stock register?
8. Describe LIFO, FIFO, WA and NIFO methods of valuing materials and the impact of each method on profitability of the business?
9. What is the principle of material valuation?
10. Which method of material valuation you would recommend under (a) inflation (b) deflation (c) fluctuating prices?
11. How are semi-finished goods valued?
12. What is the basis on which finished goods are valued?
13. How are prepaid expenses adjusted at the end of the year?
14. Give a hypothetical example of an outstanding expense and pass adjusting entries?
15. What are bad debts? Distinguish bad debts from doubtful debts?

16. When does a businessman offer discount on debtors? Whether discount on debtors would reduce the receivables?

17. Define depreciation? Why do entrepreneurs provide depreciation?

18. Why is depreciation called notional cost?

19. What is a useful life an asset?

20. Does depreciation find a place in the factory cost, cost of production and cost of sales?

21. What are the methods of providing depreciation? Why should there be so many methods? Do the tax authorities accept all the methods?

22. How does the straight-line method of depreciation determine?

23. What is salvage value?

24. Is there any difference between treatments of the aspects of closing entries in the final account and that of the ledger heads from the trial balance?

25. Enumerate the methods of calculating depreciation. Discuss briefly the merits and limitations of these methods.

26. What are the various methods of inventory valuation? Discuss the impact of each method on working results.

27. explain the accounting treatment of merchandising transactions?

Hint: Merchandising means inventories.

28. What do you understand by the term revenue?

29. Describe the characteristics of revenue?

30. What is accrual accounting? How does it differ from cash accounting?

31. Define the term sales?

32. What are the main attributes of a valid sale?

33. When do sales legally take place?

34. What are agreements of sale? How do they differ from sales?

35. How do sales vary from bailments?

36. How does revenue arise by holding of assets?

37. Why do you consider revenue recognition as an approximation?

38. How are revenues from service industries recognised?

39. When do the following fees recognised as revenue:

(a) Technical know-how fees;

(b) Royalties;

(c) Financial service charges;

(d) Agent's commission;

(e) Architect's commission;

40. What do you understand by quantum meruit? How does it apply in long-term construction contracts?

41. What are consignments? How are revenues recognized in consignments?

42. How are net sales computed for the income statement?

43. Write short notes on the following:

(a) Sale on approval basis;

(b) Franchises;

(c) Hire-purchase agreements;

(d) Installment credits

44. Explain the steps involved in the preparation of final accounts.

45. Which of the following inflow are revenues and why?

- *Cash received on deposits from public*
- *Commission received*
- *Interest received on investments*
- *Sale of obsolete assets*
- *Money received from debtors*
- *Goods sent on approval basis*
- *Lease rent received*

46. Do you recognize sale in the following instances? State reasons?

a. Sold goods for credit

b. Sent goods on consignment

c. Hire purchase sale of goods of low value Rs.10,500 with Rs.2000 down payment and the balance on 4 quarterly installments, when no installment has fallen due?

d. Goods sent on installment credit, where only down payment is received.

e. Doctors' fee of Rs.5200 due from a patient.

47. What are tangible assets? How do intangible assets differ from them?

48. Give a few examples of intangible assets?

49. Briefly explain patents, designs, trademarks, copyrights, technical know-how and franchises?

50. What do you mean by goodwill?

51. How do you value intangibles?

52. How are intangible assets accounted?

53. What do you know about deferred revenue expenses?

54. Explain, with examples, fictitious assets?

55. What are the different methods of valuing goodwill? Explain briefly each of them?

56. What do you understand by the term intellectual capital? Can you suggest a method of evaluating it?

57. Do human resources constitute the assets of a business?

58. What is the cost of human resources in business evaluation?

59. What factors create brand strength in a business?

60. What are capital issue expenses?

II. QUIZ

Say yes or no

- *Closing entries are passed when the business is closed down*
- *Closing entries are necessary to have a fair view off the results*
- *Cost incurred and cost attribute Table are one and the same*
- *Inventory includes raw material, semi-finished goods and finished good*
- *Closing stock of raw materials are valued on the basis of cost price or*
- *market price, whichever is higher*
- *In inflation prices tend to rise*
- *NIFO is the best method to adopt when the price of material fluctuates frequently*
- *FIFO would increase the profit in times of inflation*
- *The extent of semi-finished goods in a business would depend upon its process cycle*
- *Finished goods are always valued at cost of production*
- *Prepaid expenses are expenditures*
- *Outstanding expenses are disputed costs*

- *Bad debts are caused by wrong selection of debtors*
- *Doubtful debts are contingent liabilities*
- *Depreciation does no involve any outward movement of funds*
- *The useful life of an asset in all methods of depreciation is same*
- *Aggregate depreciation on asset represents its replacement value*
- *Adjustment entries would be posted to only one of the final accounts*
- *namely profit and loss account or balance sheet*
- *All receipts are revenues.*
- *Revenue invariably causes an immediate inward movement of funds.*
- *Hire purchase and installment credit are two terms signifying same contract.*
- *Sales conclude with transfer of goods.*
- *Goods sent on consignment are to be recognised as sales.*
- *Royalty is one-time payment for technical know-how*
- *Service contracts are usually specific performance contracts.*
- *In quantum meruit contracts, profit is booked every year on the quantum of work accomplished.*
- *Revenue might also arise from others holding the assets of the business.*
- *All intangibles are fictitious assets.*
- *Deferred revenue expenses directly contribute to the earning capacity of the business.*
- *Intangible assets are created, not acquired.*
- *Patents have 50 years validity.*
- *Trademarks are visual symbols.*
- *Creation of goodwill consumes resources.*
- *Goodwill is allowed to be written off as a deduction from income by tax authorities.*
- *Deferred revenue expenses are also called fictitious assets.*
- *Capitalization of expected returns is a method of valuing goodwill.*
- *Knowledge worker is the concept developed by Stewart.*

III. EXERCISES

1. Omego Oragon Limited had a opening stock of material of 10,93,768 kgs valued at Rs.75.47 lakhs on 30.4.2005. During the year, the company had made the following purchases and issues.

Date	Purchases		Issues
2005	Rate / kg	Qty / kgs	Kgs
May 1	7.00	12,50,000	11,75,000
June 1	7.10	11,25,000	10,95,000
July 1	7.20	12,15,000	12,10,000
Aug 1	7.30	13,00,000	12,70,000
Sept 1	7.40	12,25,000	11,95,000

The company closes its books on 30th September for its half yearly reports. Find out the value of closing stock if the company uses LIFO method of valuing stock.

2. In the example given above, what would be the value of stock if the company employs FIFO or Weighted Average Method.

3. How would you value the semi-finished goods of Peanuts India Ltd. manufacturing pistons where its process cycle is 7 days. The company uses raw materials per day of Rs.89.45 lakhs, direct wages per day being Rs.32.90 lakhs?

4. Qubeck Limited, manufacturers of electrical equipments have costed the value of finished goods 3 sq units as under on 31.3.98.

Prime cost	Rs.146.50 lakhs
Factory overheads	Rs.41.50 lakhs
Administrative overheads	Rs.27.15 lakhs
Selling overheads	Rs.32.60 lakhs

The market price of similar equipments on 31.3.98 was Rs.58,500 per unit. How would you value the closing stock of finished goods?

5. Diamond Levers Limited brought forward as opening stock, raw materials of Rs.37.50 lakhs (375 units) and had purchased during the year 1500 units at Rs.1100 each. At the end of the year, the closing stock was 4050 units. What would be the cost of material consumed during the year under i) FIFO and ii)FILO methods of stock valuation. What is the impact of FIFO on the profitability of the company?

6. Donaldson and Company's trial balance showed wages of Rs.72.10 lakhs. The company reports that one-month's wages (Rs.6.15 lakhs) due during the year 120027-98 was paid subsequent to the date of the final closing on 31.3.98. Show how the transaction is incorporated into the final accounts of the company?

7. Mrinal Enterprises had closed its books of account as on 30.6.98 and had extracted a trial balance. One of the items in the trial balance is insurance premium of Rs.60,600 paid on 30.9.120027 for a period of one year. How would you treat the unexpired part of insurance while preparing final accounts?

8. Laminated Lamps and co had, on 31.3.98, a debtors portfolio of Rs.85.10 lakhs. After the closing of the books and extraction of the balances to the trial balance but before preparation of final accounts, it came to the knowledge of the co that M/s.Sampsons, one of the debtors with an outstanding balance of Rs.48,500 had become bankrupt and his estates could pay only ten paise per rupee as dividend. The Sales Manager also reported that 25 percent of the debtors are likely to avail of the terms of sales, which is 3/115/30. The accountant felt that 4 percent of the debtors might turn out to be bad. How are the above developments treated while preparing profit and loss account?

9. Albatross Alkaline Limited had been purchasing goods on credit. As on 30.9.98, the trial balance shows bills payable of rs.25.36 lakhs. Of this, 40 percent of the purchases offer discount at 3 percent. Show the aspects would appear in the final accounts as on 30.9.98?

10. Shershah and Co's trial balance as on 31.3.98 showed, among other things, the following debit accounts :

Land	Rs.21.56 lakhs
Buildings	Rs.9.70 lakhs
Plant & Machinery	Rs.162.65 lakhs
Furniture & Fittings	Rs.13.50 lakhs
Vehicles	Rs.18.10 lakhs
Franchise	Rs.13.35 lakhs

Provide depreciation on written down basis at 5 percent on buildings, 20 percent on plant and machinery, 30 percent on furniture and fittings and 40 percent on vehicles. The period of the franchise is 5 years. Show how the aspects are dealt with in final accounts?

11. Should the company (in exercise10) choose straight-line method of depreciation, what would be the depreciation on these assets?

12. Cambridge Peanuts Ltd had acquired during 120027-98, assets of the value of Rs.92.10 lakhs on which the company had decided to charge depreciation on sum of the digits of life methods. Income tax authorities allow written down value depreciation of 20 percent on these assets. What would be the depreciation chargeable, under the method, on the investment during its useful life?

13. Eiffel Construction Company had acquired two equipment coded and Q for rs.46 lakhs and Rs.52 lakhs respectively during the accounting year. O could work for 4600 hours, while Q could produce 1020 units. As on 31.3.98, when the company's financial year ends, the company had decided to charge depreciation at production units method on Q and production hour method on O. If O had been used, during the year, for 1400 hours an Q had produced 210 units, what would be the chargeable depreciation for the equipments?

14. Prosperous Prospectors had taken granite mine on lease for Rs.148 lakhs. The estimated deposit of 592, 00,000 cubic feet of granites. During the first 4 years, the company had extracted 62,00,000 cft, 97,00,000 cft, 101,00,00 cft and 126,00,000 cft of granites. What would be the depreciation for these years?

15. Devdas Musicals wanted to purchase a modern sound system from Enlightened Entertainment. The latter quoted Rs.1,25,000 for the equipment without any repairs and maintenance during its lifespan of 4 years. Devdas Musicals are aware that the system needs scouldt maintenance for 6 months but thereafter, the maintenance would be at the compounded rate of 10% every half year. Calculate depreciation under repairs and maintenance method during the life of the instrument?

16. Hannan and Co. had recently purchased a heavy-duty lathe at Rs.48 lakhs. The effective life of the equipment is estimated to be 8 years, at the end of which the company proposes to replace it with a new machine. The industry is not expected to undergo any marked technological innovations for a longtime to come. However, the inflationary trend of the country is expected to be 4 percent per annum in the next decade. Hannan wanted to provide depreciation on annuity method so that at the end of the life of the lathe, there would be adequate funds to replace it without resorting to any other source. The rate of interest on 8-year investment is 12 percent. What would be the annuity the company has to provide for?

17. Explain the objectives of providing depreciation

X ltd, purchased a machine for Rs.60,000 on 1.1.98.Depreciation is provided@ 10% p.a. on diminishing balance method. Prepare machinery account for the year 2000in each of the following alternative cases:

- *If the machine is sold on 1.7.200 for Rs.28,600.*
- *If a new machine costing Rs.60,000 is purchased on 1.7.2000 after surrendering the old one and paying cash Rs.35,000.*

18. Pals Constructions Ltd. have undertaken the construction of a dam over Beas for the Government of Himachal Pradesh at an estimated cost of Rs.42.50 Crores. The construction began in June 1995 and were to be completed in 4 years. Payments to be made on quantum meruit basis. The yearly expenditure on the project are:

Year	Work certified (Rs in Crores)	Expenditure incurred (Rs.in Crores)
1995-96	2.75	3.15
1999-97	11.55	9.26
2000-98	22.40	20.86
1998-99	5.80	6.73
Total	42.50	34.00

The built in margin of profit was 25% on the estimated cost. The work was completed in time and within estimates. What would be the revenue Pals Constructions would recognize every year during the contract period?

19. Hire and Prosper Ltd., engaged in the hire purchase sale of high value equipment, has sold on 1.4.98 a multistage boiler to Lunar Manufacturing Company Ltd., Lucknow at Rs.27.35 Crores. Down payment 20% and balance at equated four annual installments of Rs.6.38 Crores each.

- *What is the rate of interest charged on hire purchase? (Hint : use Annuity table).*
- *What would be the revenue recognised in the year ended 31-3-1999*

- *Lunar Manufacturing Co. was paying the installment regularly upto end March 1999; became sick and closed down in June 1999. Hire and prosper repossessed the boiler and was able to find a ready bùyer for the second hand boiler at Rs.17.45 Crores. How would Hire & Prosper treat it in its books?*

20. Begwandas ledger accounts show cash sales of Rs.241,52,115 and credit sales of Rs.453,07,501 for the year ended 31.3.1999. The sale is first subjected to 3% central excise and then 5% sales tax. Returns Inward book shows a balance of Rs.11, 43,123. What would be the value of sale for the purpose of profit and loss account?

21. Chandler bought a motorbike on hire purchase basis. The cost of the bike was Rs.43,000. Chandler has to make a down payment of 10% and the balance in ten equal monthly installments of Rs. 4086, which includes interest on monthly opening balance at 12%. How would you account for the principal and interest in the books of the seller, when he receives the installments? Would it be different if Chandler has purchased the bike on installment credit?

22. Randir Constructions Ltd's tender for the construction of Hitec City in Bangalore at an estimated Rs.515.75 lakhs had been accepted. The tender value includes a profit margin of 20% on cost. The contract has to be executed over 3 years. Payment to be made on *quantum meruit* basis. Randir Construction had incurred an expenditure of Rs.110 lakhs in the first year, Rs.305 lakhs in the second year and completed the work in the third year. There was no escalation in the cost. What part of the profit would be recognized as revenue in the first, second and third year?

23. Sun Sun Shipbuilders have agreed to fabricate a 1500 tonnes freighter for Sri Lanka Govt. at an estimated cost of Rs.126 Crores and over a five-year period. Sun billed the Sri Lanka Govt. for the following, year wise :

1 year	Rs.24 Crores
2 year	Rs.32 Crores
3 year	Rs.45 Crores
4 year	Rs.20 Crores
5 year	Rs . 5 Crores
Total	Rs. 126 Crores

What would be the revenue recognised by Sun Sun on the assumption that the tender price included 25% profit margin on sales?

24. Damodar Coal Ltd. had taken mining lease for 10 years from the West Bengal Government for mining coal in Asansol area. The mine is estimated to have a deposit of 50 million tonnes of high-grade goal. The lease agreement provides for the payment of Rs.50 Crores on pro-rata basis of exploitation. Damodar Coal Ltd had extracted 25 lakh tonnes in the first year. What would be the revenue recognised to the West Bengal Govt. in each of these years?

25. Tan-Am Inc, an American Corporation, had entered into collaboration agreement with Pan-Indian Ltd. for the supply of technical know-how for the manufacture of ductile iron spun pipes, which is currently manufactured in India only by Electrosteel Castings. The collaboration agreement provides for a royalty of 5% for 3 years on the sales value. Pan India Ltd. sold 725 tonnes in 2000 @ Rs.12,500 per tonne, 965 tonnes in 2001 @ Rs.13,100 per tonnes and 1010 tonnes in 2002 @ Rs.13,250. What would be revenue recognizable by Tan-Am from Royalty on the basis of the dollar-rupee exchange rate of Rs.40 in 2000, Rs.42 in 2001 and Rs.44.50 in 2002?

26. Mona Enterprises, a proprietary engaged in trading, has the following information for the year ended 31 March 2006:

S.No.	Particulars	Amount
1	Sundry Creditors	13,86,095
2	Sundry Debtors	12,39,845
3	Stock 1-4-98	11,93,415
4	Bills payable	73,700
5	Power & fuel	13,24,560
6	Capital	27,90,000
7	Machinery	47,15,695
8	Purchases returns	3,15,610
9	Building	60,296
10	Furniture	7,40,485
11	Miscellaneous income	1,02,876
12	Cash in hand	21,342
13	Sale	133,72,441
14	Morgan's drawings	37,410
15	Sales returns	4,72,895
16	Salaries	61,189
17	Traveling expenses	51,695
18	Bad debts	26,912
19	Insurance	14,750
20	Purchases	64,94,440
21	Telephone & Email	17,616
22	Miscellaneous expenses	5,050
23	Postage	3,675
24	Printing charges	12,124

Additional Information:

- *Closing Stock 9,42,454*

- *Insurance premium is paid for one year from 1 July, 2005*
- *Depreciation on machines at 20% and furniture at 15%.*
- *Outstanding wages Rs.14,750 and Salaries Rs.9950.*

You are required to prepare a trial balance from the above and after taking into account the adjustments, prepare a profit and loss account for the year ended 31 march 2006.

27. From the following profit and loss account of Choudry of Jaipur as On 31 March2006, prepare two-tier Trading and Profit and Loss account for the period:

Profit and loss account for the ended 31 March, 2006

Particulars			Particulars	
Opening Stock		373452	Sales 3759701 Less: returns 341791	3417910
Purchases Less: returns	925437 337689	2587748	Discount received	4505
Salaries Add:Outst.	148678 13837	162515	Interest on Investment	7698
Insurance Less: Prepaid	6078 1520	4558	Closing Stock	361254
Repairs		6125		
Wages Add:Outst.	176884} 14740	191624		
Electricity		9678		
Transport		17,860		
Travel		6871		
Carriage Inwards		10517		
Carriage Outwards		18715		
Discount allowed Add: Provision	8410 1275	9685		
Bad debts Add: Provision	9104 2751	11855		
Depreciation - Fixed Assets		7650		

Depreciation-Vehicles & Furniture	23456		
	34,44,309		3793366
		Profit	349057

28. Trial Balance of M/s. Khan & Chand Co., engaged in manufacturing of pistons for motorbikes, as on 31 December 2005 was as under:

Khan & Chand Co
Trial Balance as on 31 December 2005

Particulars	Debit	Credit
Stock on 1.1.2005 -Raw Material -Semi finished goods -Finished goods	 246912 53497 641972	
Capital : Feroz Khan		 5901200 4878690
Purchases Sales returns Wages	6370342 197530 1580024	
Bills payable		1185180
Manufacturing expenses	790119	
Salaries	696121	
Discount		49382
Insurance	14814	
Telephone, mail and Fax	19876	
Advertisement	98765	
Sundry creditors		1148130
Bad debts	29629	
Land & Building	888559	
Returns Outward		345670

Plant & Machinery	5913550	
Furniture	98765	
Sales		12162671
Sundry debtors:	2508631	
Drawings accounts :FerozKhan	375900257050	
Cash in handCash at bank	493824839485	
Total	25670923	25670923

Additional Information

- *Feroz and Khan share profit and loss in the ratio of 2:1*
- *Stock on 31-3-1999 -Raw material Rs.3,95,060*
  -Semi – finished goodsRs. 45,318
  - Finished goodsRs. 7,18,518
- *Outstanding –Salaries Rs.1,48,147*
  –Wages Rs.2,07,406.
- *Provide depreciation on Land & Building 5%*
  Furniture 20%
  Plant & Machinery 25%
- *Insurance is paid for 15 months upto June 30, 1999.*
- *Provide doubtful debts at 5% and discount at 3% on debtors.*
- *Write off bad debts Rs.39,506.*
- *Partners charge interest on their capital and drawings at 5%.*
- *Feroz is the active partner and is eligible for a salary of Rs.3,000 pm which has to be provided out of profit.*
- *Tax provision to be made at 35% reserves at 25% of after tax profit.*
- *Prepare Profit and Loss account and appropriation account for the year ended 31 December 2005.*

29. From the following data of ABC & Co., prepare trading, profit and loss account and balance sheet as on 31.12.1995.

Cash in hand	2,400
Purchases	2,40,000
Stock on 1.1 95	70,000
Debtors	1,00,000
Plant and machinery	1,20,000

Furniture	30,000
Bills receivable	40,000
Rent and taxes	20,000
Wages	32,000
Salaries	37,600
Capital	2,00,000
Bills payable	44,000
Creditors	48,000
Sales	4,00,000

Adjustments

i. Closing inventory on 31.12.1995 Rs.50,000

ii. Outstanding wages Rs.5,000

iii. Goods withdrawn for personal use Rs.2,000

vi. Depreciation on plant and machinery at 10% and on furniture @ 5%.

30. The extract of the balance sheet of Peculiars India Ltd for the year-ended 31.3.2003 was as under: (Rs.Lakhs)

Fixed Assets (Average for 3 Years	3421.65
Less : Depreciation	2845.55
Net Fixed assets	576.10
Net current Assets	412.40
Capital employed	988.50
Represented by Net worth	795.30
Debt	193.20
Total	988.50

The company's profit after tax for the year was Rs.148.20 lakhs. It is envisaged that the profitability is expected to improve at the compounded rate of 8% in the next five years. Recent evaluation of the company's major assets revealed that they have useful life of 5 years. The desired rate of return for Peanuts is 16% after tax. Estimate the value of goodwill under capitalization of expected return method?

31. Jain Departmental Stores, started as a small outfit, grew into a conglomeration and presently has a chain of 21 stores in the Twin City of Hyderabad and Secunderabad. The promoters of the unit are the three Jain brothers – Arvind, Manek and Pritesh. The unit is negotiating for the take over of Multifoods, for which it proposes to induct Shantilal as a partner. Jain brothers have approached you to evaluate the goodwill of their firm on PV of super profit model. The following information about Jain Departmental Stores is made available to you:

	2005 (Actual)	2006	2007	2008 (Expected)
Profits after tax	92.45	99.86	100.93	109.00
Capital employed	513			
Industrial average	14%			
Return on capital employed	15.5%	16.75%	18 %	19%

Estimate goodwill of Jain Departmental Stores?

32. Boxfree Ltd's balance sheet for the past three year showed:

B	**2003**	**2004**	**2005**
Net fixed assets	603.10	618.19	656.51
Current assets	1487.55	1666.06	2015.93
Total tangible assets	2090.65	62284.25	2672.44
Profit for the year	75.37	131.62	169.25
Average cost of capital	13.5%	14.58%	15.91%
Average return on assets of the			
Industry	15.0%	16.35%	17.84%

You are required to assess the value of intellectual capital for the company?

CHAPTER–4

UNDERSTANDING FINANCIAL STATEMENTS

Learning Objective

This chapter would make the readers understand the various items in profit and loss account and balance sheet. Profit and loss account is expected to reveal information on the operations of the business during the accounting period. Balance sheet is meant to enlighten the readers about the financial strength. These statements are to be processed to get the requisite information with the tools of ratios, percentages and parts of. As ratios establish relationships of interrelated figures, the data are to be rationally grouped for analysis.

Companies prepare two statements at the end of the accounting period. They are profit and loss account or income statement and balance sheet. The two statements are together known as ***final accounts*** of a company. Conventionally, the final accounts were presented as T accounts, since they resemble capital " T ". The left side of T contains the costs and the right side incomes. In the balance sheet, the left hand side of T has all the liabilities of the business and the right hand side all assets. Increasingly, the practice has changed and currently most of the businesses present their final accounts in a statement form. The latter is more convenient and useful for analysis purposes. A copy of the final accounts of HDFC bank for the year ended 31.03.2004 together with notes is furnished as annexure to this chapter.

Readers might have noticed that the styling of the two statements differs. The profit and loss account is worded as profit and loss account ***for the year ended*** 31st March, 2005 whereas the balance sheet is worded as balance sheet ***as on*** 31.03.2005. Profit and loss account is the summary of all the operations of the business during the accounting year. It is the cumulative data of the period. Balance sheet on the other hand presents the position of the company at the end of the last accounting period. The position would have been different before and after that date. It is like a still photograph.

A closer look at the statements would reveal that the various items of costs and incomes are listed in the profit and loss account and the liabilities and assets in the balance sheet. The arrangements of the items follow a specific order. Consider the profit and loss account. The costs are segmented into four groups. The first part of the cost side or debit side of profit and loss account would contain the ***factory or works cost,*** followed by ***administrative or office cost, selling and distribution cost*** and finally ***non-operating costs***. Factory cost is the cost incurred in factory. It is the production cost. It consists of ***prime cost*** and factory overheads. Prime cost is the ***direct cost.*** Direct costs are costs that are traceable to the products and comprise direct materials and direct labour. ***Factory overheads*** are indirect costs incurred in factory. Indirect costs are, no doubt, essential for the operation of the business, but are not identifiable to the product. Overheads comprise indirect materials, indirect labour and all expenses. Factory materials overheads include consumables, stores and spares. Factory labour overheads are salaries and wages paid to foremen, godown keeper, maintenance team, watch and ward, gardener etc. Works expenses are power, fuel, electricity, carriage inwards, depreciation on plant and machinery, laboratory equipment and factory buildings and expenses of factory cleaning and lighting.

The next two segments cover other operating expenses incurred in administering the business and marketing the products. ***Office overheads*** again are indirect materials and labour and expenses caused in administering the business. Salaries, including salary of managing director, stationary, travel, transport, communication, and depreciation on office equipment, vehicles and buildings are some of the administrative costs. Salaries of sales person, advertisement, traveling expenses of sales personnel, depreciation on equipment, vehicles used for selling and buildings, carriage outward etc are ***selling overheads.*** Administrative and selling costs are also known as ***operating costs.*** Factory costs together with administrative costs is called cost of production. Cost of production and selling overheads are known as cost of sales. All other items of costs that are incidental to the operation are non-operating costs. Interest, taxes, discount and commission allowed, bad debts, loss on sale of assets, capital issue expenses are examples of non-operating costs. All the costs are adjusted for outstanding expenses.

The income or revenue side, that is the credit side of profit and loss account would have at its head ***sales or turn over*** of the business, followed by closing stock and non-operating incomes. Turnover includes net sale of goods and services. In cases of franchising companies, turn over also includes franchises, technical know how fees, erection and commissioning fees received. Non-operating incomes are revenues that are not directly related to the main operation of the business but are incidental. Dividend and interest received from investments, commission and discount received, profit on sale of assets and investments are some of the non-operating incomes. Receipt of money from debtors written off as bad in the past, would also be treated as non-operating income.

The liabilities in a balance sheet are classified according to the period of their repayment into three groups. ***Any liability to be repaid within one year is termed as current liabilities***. Sundry creditors, bills payable, bank borrowings for working capital, any other form of working capital borrowings such as commercial papers, bills rediscounting and provisions for taxation, for dividend, for bad and doubtful debts are current liabilities. Any obligation to be discharged over a period longer than one year is ***term liabilities or fixed liabilities***. Term loans from financial institutions, borrowings through issue of bonds, debentures and deposits and external commercial borrowings, issue of ADRs (American Depository Receipts) and GDRs (Global Depository Receipts) are term liabilities. There is yet another liability which the company has to discharge only when it closes down its business. This is the equity or owners' fund. That is, it is paid only when the business is dissolved or wound up. No doubt it is now permissible to repay a part of the networth to the shareholders in the form of ***buy back of shares,*** even when the business is on. Such repayments are restricted to the extent of accumulated reserves of the business. Fixed liabilities and current liabilities, with the exception of provisions are called ***outside liabilities*** of a business, as these are obligations to other than owners of the business. These are to be repaid even when the business is on. But the liabilities to the shareholders or the businessmen represented by networth are ***internal liabilities*** and are to be repaid only when the business ceases to exist.

The assets of the company are grouped into four categories. Such of those assets that generate income over a period longer than one year are called ***fixed or block assets.*** Land, buildings, plant and machinery, equipment, fixtures, fittings and vehicles are fixed assets. Fixed assets are presented at their original costs less depreciation up to the date of the financial statements. Any fixed asset acquired or fabricated but not yet put into operation are called ***works in progress*** and are added at the end of the fixed assets. Works in progress are non-current assets, as they have not yet been used in the generation of income. The second category of assets are also long term in nature but are not directly related to the main business of the company. These are ***investments*** made by the company outside the business. There are occasions when companies do invest in assets outside their business. Such investments might be in real assets like land, buildings, gold and other precious metals or in financial assets like shares, bonds, and debentures, in deposits or in derivatives. The reason behind such investments might be treasury operations or for acquisitions. The surplus funds of business are invested outside with a view to get a higher rate of return than what the business could generate within. That is treasury operation. The other purpose might be to acquire another entity. Takeovers by corporates are on the increase, as size is becoming the criterion for effectiveness. These investments might bring income to the business by way of interests, dividends and capital appreciation. Since these assets are not used in the normal operation of the business, they are classified as ***non-current assets***. The income generated by such investments is ***non-operating incomes***.

Next group of assets are current assets. ***Current assets are those assets which could be converted into cash within one year or which would be used up by the business within one year.*** Cash, bank balances, inventories, debtors, receivables, loans and advances and marketable securities are current assets. The last category is intangibles. Some authors call it erroneously as ***fictitious assets***. These are not assets as the main function of an asset is to generate income. When the asset generates income directly, it is called ***tangible assets.*** Examples are land building, plant and machinery and equipment. When the assets contribute to the earnings of the business indirectly, they are ***intangible assets***. Goodwill, franchises, patents, copyrights and trademarks are intangible assets. Intangibles like miscellaneous assets, past loss balances, preliminary expenses do not contribute to the earnings either directly or indirectly. These are to be written off from future profits. We simply call then as intangibles, which would reduce the owners' fund.

Liabilities and assets are also arranged in the balance sheet in an order. The way in which liabilities and assets are arranged in balance sheet is termed ***marshalling.*** There are two methods of marshalling liabilities and assets. The first and very commonly used is the ***permanency preference method***. In permanency preference method, both liabilities and assets are arranged according to their longevity. Liabilities that are to be paid last would appear in the top slot and others would follow in descending order. The most permanent liability is owners' funds or networth or equity and the liabilities side starts with equity. The next in longevity is term loans or fixed liabilities, which item is shown after equity. Current liabilities occupy the next slot and provision forms the tail end of liabilities. As far as assets are concerned, the near permanent assets are fixed assets, which are shown on top. This is followed by investments, current assets and intangibles like miscellaneous expenses, past loss balances and preliminary expenses to be written off.

The second method of marshalling is known as ***liquidity preference method***. As the name implies, assets are arranged in the order of their realisability or liquidity and liabilities in the order of their urgency for payment. Liquid assets form the top slot followed by less liquid assets and finally illiquid assets. Current assets, being most liquid, would occupy the top position followed by investments and fixed assets. Intangibles would be the last. In the liabilities' side, those obligations that are to be discharged first would be on top. Current liabilities and provisions are shown at the top, followed by term liabilities. Equity is the last in the line.

Profit and loss accounts are prepared in different ***tiers,*** depending upon the specific requirements of the business concerned. In small businesses, which do not have any manufacturing activity, it is a ***single tiered*** one. All costs are given in the debit side and all incomes in the credit side and the profit or loss is arrived at. In a ***two tiered*** profit and loss account, the first part of the profit and loss account is termed as ***trading or manufacturing account*** with only factory costs and operating incomes. The surplus of operating incomes over factory costs is the ***gross profit*** that is carried over to the next tier, which is the actual profit and loss account. In case of proprietary concerns, the income statement would at best be a two tiered one. In partnerships and joint stock companies yet another tier is added in the name of ***profit and loss appropriation account.*** The profit or loss of the business is transferred to this tier for making appropriations for taxation, dividend, reserves etc. The unappropriated profit is carried forward to the balance sheet as ***surplus,*** to be appropriated next year.

Another aspect to be observed in the presentation of the financial statements is that the figures pertaining to the previous year are given side by side with those of the current year. The objective of such a presentation is to enable the readers to have a comparative analysis of the operational results and financial position of the current year with that of the previous year. At the end of the balance sheet, contingent liabilities are given as a footnote. Contingent liabilities are probable liabilities of the business. The contingent liabilities would become real liabilities on the happening of certain events. For example, the company giving a guarantee on behalf of a client to a third party regarding the payment to be made by the client. As long as the client keeps up his payment, the liability would be contingent to the company. In case the client defaults, the company would become directly liable to the third party.

We have already seen that financial accounting accomplishes the task of pooling data in transactions into two important statements- profit and loss account and balance sheet. Profit and loss account is a storehouse of data on the operations of the business during an accounting period. Balance sheet contains plethora of information as to the financial position of the business as on the last day of the accounting period. The information contained in these two statements is essential to the entrepreneurs who start the business. They are eager to find answers to questions such as the results of their efforts during the period, whether they have made any profit or incurred loss and what is the strength of their business. Besides the businessmen, there are various segments of society that are also interested, though might not be in the same sense and degree, in the results of the business. Since businesses utilize the resources of the society, in addition to the resources of individuals and groups, cross sections of the society become ***stakeholders*** in the business, directly or indirectly. Different sections of society that are interested in the financial statements are

- ***Shareholders****: In a corporation, most of the shareholders do not have direct access to the day-to-day management of the business. Only a handful of them, elected in the shareholders meeting as directors form the* ***board of directors*** *and run the business as representatives of shareholders. The board carries on the business with the assistance of professional managers, who are usually not shareholders. Further, the current trend in corporate governance is to have a majority of independent directors. Independent directors are those who have no relationship with the promoters. Bulk of the shareholders is, therefore, eager to know whether their nominees are conducting the* *business with their interests in mind. The financial statements are the documents that could quench their thirst.*

- ***Management:*** *Managers of the company would like to make use the data in these statements, after processing, for formulating policy decisions.*
- ***Employees:*** *The employees of the business want to ensure that the business would continue and that they would prosper along with the business. They too are eager to know their bargaining power for fringe benefits like bonus. They are therefore interested in financial statements.*
- ***Fund providers:*** *They are keen to ensure the safety of their funds and the ability of the business to service the funds as agreed upon. The financial statements would provide the information needed by them.*
- ***Suppliers:*** *The suppliers of inputs such as materials and utilities are anxious that the business would continue so that their supplies would also continue. In case of suppliers for credit, they would like to ensure that payments for their supplies would be made in time. They too look to the financial statements.*
- ***Governments:*** *The governments, both at centre and in states, are keen to study the financial statements of the business to verify that the business has been paying the taxes according to their earnings and in accordance with the law of the country. They would also be interested in the growth of the business from the point of view of future revenues, employment generation and contributions to the national income.*
- ***Researchers:*** *Academicians and analysts are interested in the reports for their research, which would indirectly contribute to investors' decision as to invest in a particular company or not.*
- ***Public:*** *General public would be interested in the safety of environment and the potentiality of employment opportunities. They too are interested in the operations of the company as revealed by the statements.*

The question that has to be addressed now is whether the above segments of society, which are interested in various information about the business, would be able to obtain the requisite information from the financial statements as they are presented? The answer is both yes and no. Yes to some extent but not fully. Financial statements are presented in myriad of ways that an average individual would see only a silhouette of the information needed by him. In this context, information in financial statements might be compared to icebergs. Only the tip of iceberg is seen above the surface of water. What is underneath and hidden in water is enormous and all that would make things different. Look at the statements of Down Town Enterprises, a sole trading business, as given in Table below.

Table 1
Down Town Enterprises
Trading and Profit & Loss a/c for the year ended 31.03.2006. (Rs.in lakhs)

	2005	2006		2005	2006
To Opening stock	34.20	45.00	By Sales	305.02	420.75
To Purchases	146.25	225.00	By Closing stock	45.00	35.00
To Carriage inwards	1.95	2.50			
To Factory Rent	1.67	1.80			
To Manufacturing wages	14.89	20.00			
To Coal and gas	0.74	1.00			
	199.70	295.30		350.02	455.75
To Conveyance charges	8.93	10.00	By Gross profit	150.32	160.45
To Carriage outwards	1.23	1.50	By Discount	2.87	3.30
To Discounts allowed	0.23	0.35			
To Insurance	0.31	0.60			
To Office Rent	3.45	3.60			
To Printing and stationery	0.43	0.60			
To General admin. expenses	2.10	2.80			
To Advertisement	4.22	15.00			
To Salaries	17.20	18.00			
To Depreciation	5.98	7.875			
To Bad debts	0.21	0.30			
To Interest	1.10	1.30			
To Tax	2.35	3.00			
	47.74	64.925		153.19	163.75
			By net profit	105.45	98.825

Down Town Enterprises
Balance sheet as on 31.03. 2004

Liabilities	2005	2006	Assets	2005	2006
Capital 35.00		69.00	Plant and machinery	54.78	75.00
Add Net Profit 105.45	140.45	98.825	Less Depreciation	5.98	7.50
IDBI loan	20.00	10.00	Net Plant and machinery machinery	48.80	67.50
Sundry Creditors	3.87	5.00	Furniture	7.50	7.50

Bills payable	1.64	2.00	Less Depreciation	—	0.375
Reserve for bad debts	0.47	1.50	Net Furniture	7.50	7.125
Outstanding creditors			Investments	32.00	40.00
for expenses	0.69	0.90	Sundry Debtors	12.34	20.00
			Closing Stock	45.00	35.00
			Bills receivable	2.12	3.00
			Cash in hand	3.64	2.00
			Cash With bank	15.41	11.00
			Preliminary expenses	-	1.10
			Insurance prepaidi	0.31	0.50
	167.12	187.225		167.12	187.225

The above financial statements are that of a proprietary business. There is no legal compulsion on proprietary and partnership concerns to present financial statements to the public. It is sufficient that these business organizations present their financial statements to tax authorities and providers of funds. There is no prescribed form in which these organizations are expected to present their financial statements. As such, there are varied forms in which their financial statements are prepared. In the case of corporate bodies, however, acts under which they are incorporated compel the corporates to present balance sheet data in prescribed formats. This is done with the objective of making the information more transparent. Even then most corporates present a sketchy one-page balance sheet, stowing away all details in schedules, which an ordinary individual would find it difficult to understand. Further, the acts are not that specific as to the presentation of income statements. They have only laid down certain norms. Corporates adhere to the legal norms in letters but not in spirit. Presented below is the profit and loss account and balance sheet of a well-run textile unit (name changed) with important schedules.

Table 2

Surya Prakash Textiles Ltd.

Balance sheet as on 31.3.2003. Rs.000)

Liabilities	**2003**	**2002**	**Assets**	**2003**	**2002**
Share capital Schedule1	94054	33797	Fixed assets Schedule4		
Reserves	371257	219499	Gross block Less: Depreciation	665939 152069	613751 30165
Secured loans Sched.2	466511	500445	Net block	513870	483586
Unsecured loansSched.3	33133	55003	Add: Capital work in Progress.	87419	4280

Current liabilities	128025	66840	Investment. Schedule5	14950	5777
Provisions	8783	8449	Current assets Sched.6	467593	390390
			Miscellaneous exp.		
			Preliminary & Capital issue exp.	17931	
	1101763	884033		1101763	884033

Profit and Loss a/c for the year ended 31.3.2003

Expenses			Income		
Material consumed (Sch1)	587110	531960	Sales	1003639	901318
Yarn purchased	100524	26129	Miscellaneous income(Sch2)	124481	17966
Processing charges	3960	10754			
Stores consumed	30962	24839			
Power & fuel	86996	59856			
Excise duty	47915	38430			
Payments to employees	51370	40198			
Selling & admn. Exp.	90101	63905			
Finance charges	90529	57786			
Managerial remuneration	1672	1540			
Depreciation	24052	14890			
Less: Increase in stock (Finished goods)	(27724)	(2269)			
	1087468	868020		1128120	919284
			Profit	40652	51264

Note: Finance charges include bond interest of Rs.301.56 lakhs (Rs.167.35 lakhs previous year)

Profit and Loss appropriation a/c as on 31.03.2003

	2005	2006		2005	2006
Provision for dividend	7884	8449	Profit for the year	40652	51264
			Add: Previous year adjustments	34	(133)
			Less: Prov. for tax	5250	

Reserves	28398	44999	Profit after tax Add: Previous year surplus	35436 3622	51131
Balance (surplus)	2776	3622			
	39058	57070		39058	

Schedule 1 to Balance Sheet **(Rs.000)**

	2003	2002	
Share capital.			
Authorized.			
1,25,00,000 (previous year 75,00,000) Equity shares of Rs.10 each	125000	75000	
Issued:95,00,000 (previous year 35,00,000)			
Equity shares of Rs.10 each		95000	35000
Subscribed & paid up:			
94,10,000 (previous year 34,00,000) Equity shares of Rs.10 each fully called up	94100	34000	
Less: Calls in arrears	46	203	
Paid up	94054	33797	

Schedule 2 to Balance Sheet

Secured loans

	2003	2002
From Amco Bank cash credit. Hypothecation of stock	321961	500445
15% 2003 Debentures secured against the assets	144550	- -
Total	466511	500445

Schedule 3 to Balance Sheet

Unsecured loans

	2003	2002
Public deposits repayable in 2002	24500	46000
Loans from directors	500	9000
Others – repayable with in a year	8133	3
	33133	55003

Note : Debentures of the value of Rs.373.45 lakhs were redeemed during the year as against Rs.246.89 lakhs in 2002.

Schedule 4 to Balance Sheet

Assets	Gross block				Depreciation				Net block	
	As on 31.3.98	During the year	Deletions	As on 31.3.98	As on 31.3.98	During the year	Deletions	As on 31.3.99	As on 31.3.99	As on 31.3.98
Land & Building	57163	2858		60021	16502	4501		21003	39018	40661
Plant & Machinery	478236	66213	10234	534215	88288	19226	3582	103932	430283	389948
Furniture & Fixtures	9376	1283	345	10314	819	3821	2062	2578	7736	8557
Vehicles, Cranes forks etc.	68976	1016	8603	61389	24556	4442	4442	24556	36833	44420
	613751	71370	19182	665939	130165	31990	10086	152069	513870	483586
Capital work in progress	4280	83139		87419				87419	87419	4280
	618031	54509	19182	753358	130165	31990	10086	152069	601289	487866

Note: Scrap sale Rs.9265.

Schedule 5 to Balance Sheet

	2003	2002
Investments		
90 days treasury bills	1516	2945
Shares of subsidiaries (Not listed)	7968	2160
Other shares (Quoted M P: Rs.42, 70,000 previous year Rs.7,50,000)	5466	672
	14950	5777

Schedule 6 to Balance Sheet

Current assets		
	2003	2002
Cash	3512	2987
Receivables	55074	96734
Loans and advances	56891	3106
Inventories	352116	287563
Total	467593	390390

Schedule 1 to Profit and Loss Account

Materials Consumption	2003		2002	
	Qty. (Kgs '000)	Value (Rs.'000)	Qty. (Kgs '000)	Value (Rs.'000)
Opening stock	475	123671	327	96452
Add: Purchases	2110	607799	1882	559179
Less: Closing stock	515	144360	475	123671
Material consumption	2150	587110	2684	531960

Schedule 2 to Profit and Loss Account

Miscellaneous income		
	2003	2002
Insurance claim	——	17250
Commission received	16654	245
Discount received	28079	410
Sale of waste cotton	79748	61
	124481	17966

Could you make something out of the above financial statements? If so, I am sure you have a good accounting background. But an average non-accounting manager might not. Therefore, whether it is the financial statement of a sole trader, partnership or joint stock company, the seekers of information do not get what they look for straightaway from the statements. Further, unless readers have knowledge about the financial accounting terms that are used, they would not understand what these statements imply. For a proper understanding of the data contained in the financial statements one has to delve deeper. How one should proceed with the task of unraveling the mysteries latent in financial reports would be seen shortly. Before that, the reasons why financial reports are not transparent on the face of it need to be known.

Variations in Presentation

Accounting, being an art, is influenced by the perception of the individuals who write the books as to the interpretation of the data contained in business transactions. It is this individuality of the accountants that manifests itself in the variety of ways in which financial reports are made. Particularly, the reports of non-corporate bodies are highly susceptible for personalized versions. First, because the non-corporate bodies are under no compulsion to follow any given format to present information. Secondly, it is not even necessary for these business organizations to make public their financial data, except to tax authorities and to fund providers at their discretion. In view of the reasons stated above, differing accounting practices are prevalent in the following areas:

- *Methods of providing for depreciation*
- *Treatment of preliminary expenses*
- *Conversion of foreign subsidiary's financial reports into home currency*
- *Mode of valuation of inventories*
- *Treatment of goodwill and other intangible assets*
- *Recognition of profit on long-term contracts*
- *Valuation of fixed assets and investments*
- *Treatment of contingent liabilities*

Businesses could provide depreciation either on straight line or written down value methods. Preliminary expenses might be treated as capital expenditures just like preoperative expenses and added to cost of assets. Assets of foreign subsidiaries might be converted under any of the methods acceptable. Inventories might be valued either under first in first out, last in first out or weighted average method. Goodwill and other intangible assets might be written off or left at their original value, revenue recognition might be postponed on long-term contracts; fixed assets might have been revalued, investments might be taken at the cost or market price and contingent liabilities might be ignored. Any of these factors could distort the information in the financial statements.

Readers would agree that the presentation of data in the profit and loss account varies from company to company. As an example, consider the presentation of stocks in the income statement of corporates like Surya Prakash Textiles Ltd. Materials consumed has been shown as cost and increase or decrease in stock of semi-finished goods as a deduction or addition to the cost. This is followed by a schedule, wherein the opening stock, materials purchased during the year and closing stocks are indicated to arrive at materials consumed during the year. The closing stock is then taken to the balance sheet as current asset. Yet, in other financial reports, opening stocks and purchases are shown as costs and closing stocks adjusted by crediting in the income statement.

So also are the data presentations in balance sheets. Although Companies Act, 1956 has prescribed the format for presenting balance sheet of corporates; many corporates follow the form without the sprit. As such, it would be difficult to make any meaningful analysis of the data as presented. It is, therefore, necessary that the data of the financial reports be meaningfully grouped, before undertaking the analysis. Each analyst has his own way of grouping. However, for the purpose of analysis in this book, grouping adopted is what is usually followed by auditors and analysts world over with suitable modification for local conditions. The suggested grouping is as per the table below.

Table 3
Grouping of data from Income Statement

	Current year	Previous year
1. Turn over		
2. Less: works cost		
3. Gross profit (1-2)		
4. Less: Administration, selling and general exp.		
5. Operating profit (3-4)		
6. Less: Interest		
7. Less: Other non-operating costs		
8. Add: Non-operating profits		
9. Profit before tax (5-6-7+8)		
10. Less: Taxation		
11. Less: Preference dividend, if any		
12. Profit after tax (9-10-11)		
13. Internal accruals (12+ depreciation)		

Grouping of data from Balance Sheet

	Current year	Previous year
1. Share capital		
2. Add: Reserve & Surplus		
3. Less: Intangibles		
4. Net worth (1+ 2+ 3)		
5. Add: Fixed liabilities		
6. Less: Non-current assets		
7. Capital employed (4 + 5 - 6)		
8. Gross fixed assets		
9. Less: Depreciation		
10. Net fixed assets (8 - 9)		
11. Liquid assets		
12. Inventories		
13. Current assets (11 + 12)		
14. Less: Current liabilities		
15. Net current assets (13 - 14)		
16. Capital investments (10 + 15)		
17. Market price of stock on the date of Balance sheet		

Readers, by now, are familiar with the generality of the terminology used in the groupings. For the purpose of analysis, the terms have been assigned clear-cut meanings to avoid any misconception later. The specific meanings attributed to the terms that are not explained earlier are explained in the following paragraphs:

Gross Profit

Turnover less works cost is gross profit. Gross profit is the measure of efficiency in the area of production in a manufacturing organisation and trading efficiency in trading concerns. It gives a signal to the management whether things are normal in production or it needs closer monitoring and control.

Operating Profit

Operating profit is also known as *Earnings before Interest and Taxes* (EBIT) or *Profit Before Interest and Taxes* (PBIT). It measures the overall effiency of operation. Deducting administrative and selling overheads from gross profit gives operating profit. It is also the return the business has generated during the period and is the numerator for calculating return on investment (ROI).

Profit Before Tax

Operating profit plus non-operating income less non-operating expenses is the profit before tax. From this, when tax is deducted, profit after tax (PAT) or net income after tax (NIAT) arises. Net profit less preference dividend, if any and dividend tax is the distributable profit of the business or the earnings for equity.

Internal Cash Accruals

The profit generated by the business during an accounting period is its internal cash accruals. It comprises of profit after tax and after preference dividends and dividend tax with deprecation added back. In other worlds, it is the funds generated internally from operation.

Share Capital

The paid up capital of the company plus the paid up amount on forfeited shares before those shares are reissued, is the share capital of the company. For the purpose of paid-up capital, preference capital is also included, unless it is redeemable within 12 months. Bonus shares issued are also part of paid-up capital for the purpose of analysis, although the issue of bonus shares does not cause any inflow of funds.

Reserves and Surplus

Reserves include capital and revenue reserves. When a part of the profit after tax is retained, it is revenue reserve. When reserves are from out of capital receipts such as on revaluation of assets, premium on share issues, paid-up part of the forfeited shares (after such shares are reissued) these are all capital reserves. Surplus is that part of the distributable profit, which is not specifically appropriated as at the end of the accounting period. It is carried forward and added to the profit of the subsequent accounting year for appropriation. Surplus is, thus, a *transitional reserve.*

Intangibles

Detailed discussions on the nature, character, cause and treatment of intangibles had already been held in chapter 3. Intangibles, for the purpose of analysis, include goodwill and other fictitious assets, such as deferred expenses, balance of preliminary expenses to be written off and carried forward loss balance of the previous years. As intangibles are claims by the business on the businessman, these are to be treated as offsetting balances of the owner's net worth and are to be deducted from the owners' funds to arrive at networth.

Net Worth

It is the worth of the business to the owners. In corporate organizations owners are shareholders. Hence it is also known as *shareholders' worth or equity*. Net worth is arrived at by deducting intangibles from share capital and reserves and surplus. This is also referred to as book value of equity and is used as a criterion for measuring the growth rate of businesses. It has been the practice of analysts to include preference capital as part of equity, which is debatable. Preference is a hybrid of debt and equity. It has certain features of debt and equity. It gives the holders preference over equity shareholders as regards payment of dividend and repayment of capital when the business is wound up. It also guarantees a specified rate of dividend, even in years when the company does not earn any profit. Although a company need not pay dividend to preference shareholders in years when it does not make profit, the claim for dividend is accumulated and has to be met when it makes adequate profits. Only thing is the preference shareholders could not claim dividend as a matter of right like lenders. If the company could not pay dividend to preference shareholders for two consecutive years or for three years over a period of five years, preference shareholders would be entitled to attend general body meeting and vote. Preference shareholders could never have a claim on the reserves of the company. In view of the above and the fact that only redeemable preference shares could only be issued by the Indian companies after 1956, preference shares resemble more of debt than equity. In the circumstances, I prefer to include preference shares as part of debt and not equity.

Fixed Liabilities

Also referred to as time or term liabilities, these have a fixed period of maturity. The period should be more than a year from the date of the balance sheet to qualify as term liability. Bonds and debentures, public deposits, term loans from financial institutions, external commercial borrowings are all examples of fixed liabilities. Normally, balance sheets do not depict individual items of fixed liabilities and current liabilities separately. Instead, these are classified under secured and unsecured loans and given as schedule. Fixed liabilities and current liabilities are to be gleaned from these schedules.

Non-Current Assets

These are also known as non-operating assets. These are assets that do not aid either directly or indirectly in the designated operations of the business in the way in which plant and machinery contribute, but are incidental to the investment policy of the business. Non-current assets represent investments outside the business in bonds, shares, deposits etc. of subsidiaries, sister concerns, gilt-edged securities and other real, financial and physical assets. Capital work in progress is treated as non-current assets, as they are yet to contribute to the earning of income. For the purpose of analysis, non-current assets are grouped into marketable securities and others. Marketable securities, such as treasury bills, quoted and frequently traded stocks are segregated from investments and added to current assets. The balance of non-current assets is deducted from the networth and fixed liabilities to arrive at capital employed.

Capital Employed

It is the active or effective capital that is employed in the operation of the business. It comprises of net worth plus fixed liabilities less non-current assets. Capital employed reveals how the sources of the funds are utilized by the business in assets. It is the denominator in the calculation of return on investment.

Gross Fixed Assets

Gross fixed assets represent the original or historic cost of the assets in use in the business as at the end of the financial year. It consists of gross block assets as at the end of the previous year, plus additional assets acquired during the accounting year, less assets removed due to obsolescence, damage or destruction. The efficient use of the gross block would indicate the effective use of the funds in the business during the accounting period. Deducting accumulated depreciation, as at the end of the year, from gross block would give net fixed assets. As we have already seen, capital work-in-progress and assets acquired or fabricated but not yet put to use, called *uappropriated assets*, are to be excluded from the net block to arrive at the aggregate funds used in fixed assets.

Liquid Assets

Current asset, as we know, are assets that are to be converted into cash within twelve months from the date of the balance sheet. Though current assets are liquid, compared to fixed assets, the degree of liquidity differs from asset to asset. Those groups of current assets, which are more liquid, are classified as liquid or quick assets. Cash, receivables, loans and advances and marketable securities are all quick assets. By this measure, inventories are less liquid. It does not mean that the ready salability of inventories is less than that of receivables. In fact it might so happen that some scarce raw materials and finished goods might be more readily convertible into cash. Still, these are not considered as liquid. The reason is on account of the functional characteristics of these assets. Raw materials are meant to be converted in to finished goods, finished goods, when sold, create receivables and on realization of receivables liquidity ensues. Thus, in the chain of working capital assets, stock of raw materials and finished goods are way down in liquidity than receivables. Since business is a going concern, sale of stock of raw materials and finished goods would break the chain and the going concern convention would be thrown to the winds. That is why current assets less inventories are considered more liquid. Business liquidity, therefore, implies the quality of assets that could be converted into cash without impairing the continuity of the business.

Capital Investment

Capital investments are the assets-real, physical and financial, in which funds of the business are invested. It is operational capital employed from the uses side. Investment is equal to net fixed assets plus current assets over current liabilities. Or in other words, investment is net fixed capital and net working capital. Readers should not mistake capital investments with investment in non-current assets. Investment here refers to investment in the normal operation of the business such as plant and machinery, land and building, equipments and appliances, vehicles and other miscellaneous assets.

Market Price

It is the price at which the shares of a business are quoted in any stock exchange where they are listed. The price prevailing in the exchange as at the end of the accounting period is usually taken. This might not be price at the time of analysis.. Readers might note that the market capitalization, which is market price per share multiplied by number of equity shares outstanding, is the measure of the wealth of shareholders.

The next step in analysis is to rearrange the data of the financial reports of selected company into the grouping as discussed above. Let us take the reports of Down Town Enterprises and group the data. See table below. I have added notes how the figures are worked out.

Table 4
Down Town Enterprises.
Grouping of data from Income Statement

Rs lakhs	2004	2003
1. Turn over	420.75	305.02
2. Less: works cost[1]	260.30	154.70
3. Gross profit (1-2)	160.45	150.32
4. Less: Administration, selling and general expenses [2]	59.975	43.85
5. Operating profit (3-4)	100.475	106.47
6. Less: Interest	1.30	1.10
7. Less: Other non-operating costs[3]	0.65	0.44
8. Add: Non-operating profits	3.30	2.87
9. Profit before tax (5-6-7+8)	101.825	107.80
10. Less: Taxation	3.00	2.35
11. Less: Preference dividend, if any	-	-
12. Profit after tax (9-10-11)	98.825	105.45
13. Internal accruals (12+ depreciation) [4]	106.70	111.43

Grouping of data from Balance sheet

	Current year	Previous year
1. Capital	69.00	35.00
2. Add: Reserve & Surplus	98.825	105.45
3. Less: Intangibles	1.10	-
4. Networth (1+ 2+ 3)	166.725	140.45
5. Add: Fixed liabilities	10.00	20.00
6. Less: Non-current assets	40.00	32.00
7. Capital employed (4 + 5 - 6)	136.725	128.45
8. Gross fixed assets	82.50	62.28
9. Less: Depreciation	7.875	5.98
10. Net fixed assets (8 - 9)	74.625	56.30
11. Liquid assets[5]	36.50	33.82

12. Inventories	35.00	45.00
13. Current assets (11 + 12)	71.450	78.82
14. Less: Current liabilities	9.40	6.67
15. Net current assets (13 - 14)[6]	62.10	72.15
16. Capital investments (10 + 15)	136.725	128.45

Notes

[1] Works cost

Materials consumed:	2004	2003
Opening stock	45.00	34.20
Add: purchases	225.00	146.25
Less: closing stock	35.00	45.00
Materials consumed	235.00	135.45
Manufacturing Wages	20.00	14.89
Coal and gas	1.00	0.74
Carriage inwards	2.50	1.95
Factory Rent	1.80	1.67
Works cost	260.30	154.70

[2] Admin. & selling expenses:

Conveyance charges	10.00	8.93
Carriage outwards	1.50	1.23
Insurance	0.60	0.31
Office Rent	3.60	3.45
Printing and stationery	0.60	0.43
General admin.Expenses	2.80	2.10
Advertisement	15.00	4.22
Salaries	18.00	17.20
Depreciation	7.875	5.98
	59.975	43.85

[3] Other non-operating costs.

Discount	0.35	0.23
Bad debts	0.30	0.21
	0.65	0.44

[4] Cash accruals.

Profit after tax	98.825	105.45
Depreciation	7.875	5.98
	106.70	111.43

[5] Liquid assets.

Debtors	20.00	12.34
Bills receivables	3.00	2.12
Cash in hand	2.00	3.64
Cash with bank	11.00	15.41
Prepaid expenses	0.50	0.31
	36.50	33.82

[6] Net current asets.

Liquid assets	36.50	33.82_
Inventory	35.00	45.00
Current assets	71.50	78.82
Less Current liabilities		
Sundry creditors	5.00	3.87
Bill payables	2.00	1.64
Bad debt Res.	1.50	0.47
Outst. Creditors	0.90	0.69
Current liabilities	9.40	6.67
Net current assets	62.10	72.15

The grouping of corporate data is time consuming and laborious, as the information had to be gathered from the annexures and schedules. Let us take the financial statements of Surya Prakash Textiles ltd. The data, when grouped, would be as in table below:

Table 5
Surya Prakash Textiles Ltd.
I. Profit and loss account (Rs.000)

	2003	2002
1. Turnover	1003639	901318
2. Less: Works cost [1]	932889	747056
3. Gross profit	70750	154262
4. Less: Adm & selling expenses[2]	91773	65445
5. Add/deduct: Difference of closing stock of finished goods over opening stock	(27724)	(2269)
6. Operating profit (3 - 4 - 5)	6701	91086
7. Less: Finance charges	90529	57787
8. Less:Other Non-operating expenses	–	–
9. Add: Non-operating profits	124481	17966
10. PBT (6 - 7 - 8 + 9)	40653	51265
11. Less: Taxation	5250	–
12. Less: Prefer. dividend/Dividend tax	–	–
13. PAT (10 - 11 - 12)	35403	51265
14. Internal accruals (13 + depreciation)	59455	66154

II. Balance Sheet Regrouping

	2003	2002
1. Share capital	94054	33797
2. Reserves and surplus	371257	219499
3. Less: Intangibles	17931	
4. Networth (1 + 2 + 3)	447380	253296
5. Add: Fixed liabilities[3]	169550	55000
6. Less: Non-current assets[4]	13434	2832
7. Capital employed (4 + 5 - 6)	603496	305464
8. Gross fixed assets	753358	618031
9. Less: Depreciation	152069	130165
10. Net fixed assets (8 - 9)	601289	487866
11. Current assets[5]	116993	105772
12. Inventories	352116	287563
13. Liquid assets(11-12)	469109	393335

14. Current liabilities	466902	575737
15. Net current assets (11 - 14)	2207	182402
16. Capital Investment (10 + 15)	603496	305464
17. Market price	24	48

Notes: [2] Administrative and selling expense

	2003	**2002**
Selling and administrative expenses	90101	63905
Managerial remuneration	1672	1540
Total	91773	65445

[3] Fixed and current liabilities (gleaned from secured/ unsecured loans)

	Fixed liabilities		**Current liabilities**	
	2003	**2002**	**2003**	**2002**
From Schedule 2 Amco Bank Credit Card			3321961	500445
Debentures	144550			
From Schedule 3				
Public deposits	24500	46,000		
Loans from directors	500	9,000		
Others- repayable within a year			8133	
Current liabilities and provisions			136808	75289
Total	169550	55000	466902	575737

[4] Non-current assets

	2003	2002
Schedule 5.Investments	14950	5777
Less: Marketable securities	1516	2945
Non-current assets	13434	2832

[5] Liquid assets and Inventories

	2003		**2002**	
	Liquid assets	**Inventories**	**Liquid assets**	**Inventories**
Cash	3512		2987	
Receivable	106276		96734	

Loans & advances Inventories	5689	 352116	3106	2287563
Marketable securities	1516		2945	
Total	116993	352116	105772	287563

Grouping, which gives absolute financial figures, is the first step in analysis. Absolute figures are not helpful in arriving at meaningful conclusions. The figures are to be inter-related and compared. For example, the performance of the company, in our example, had resulted in a profit after tax of Rs.3.54 crores during 2003. Experienced analysts do not give much importance to this piece of information. For, when the performance of the unit during 2003 is compared with that of the previous year, it would give a different picture. The unit made a profit after tax of Rs.5.13 crores in the previous year. The performance would, thus, seem to be lack lustre during 2003. But, a look at the composition of revenue would reveal that the income of 2002 contained Rs.1.72 crores in respect of insurance claims of the previous years. Insurance claims are non-operational incomes. The profit, after deducting this unusual item of income, works out to Rs.3.41 crores in 2002. The profit of 2003 at Rs.3.54 is thus a shade better than that of the previous year. Yet, this comparison alone does not give a complete picture of the performance of the unit in 2003. Profit is a function of turnover. Hence, relating the profits of both the years to their respective turnovers and then making the comparison could assess the profitability of the unit fairly reasonably. The profit to turnover in Surya Prakash Textile works out to 3.53 percent in 2003, as against 5.69 percent in the previous year. Overlooking the composition of profit, one might now be tempted to conclude that the previous year was better. Just wait. During 2003, textile industry was undergoing recession and the performance of all textile units was affected, though at varying degrees. Suppose that the industrial average for the two years were 3.15 percent (2003) and 5.95 percent (2002), then the trend is different. During 2003, the company's performance looks quite satisfactory compared to 2002. As against the industrial average of 3.15 percent in 2003, Surya Prakash's performance at 3.53 percent was better than the industry. In the previous year, the industrial average was 5.95 whereas Surya Prakash's profitability ratio was lower at 5.69percent. Thus, the regrouped figures are to be related to interconnected data and compared with the performance of the previous period as well as that of the industry as a whole, before arriving at useful conclusions.

The comparison of the performance of a unit, interse, from year to year, is ***intrafirm analysis*** and the comparison with industrial average is ***interfirm analysis***. ***The tools*** that are used to analyze financial statements ***are ratios or percentages or parts of.*** Financial analysis is often referred to as ratio analysis, although percentages are more used. Detailed discussions on ratios would follow in the succeeding chapter. Finaneial statement of HDFC for the year ended 31.03.2004 is annexed for analysis of interested readers.

Balance sheet HDFC for the year ended 31.03.2004

Balance Sheet as at 31 March, 2004

	Schedule	As at 31-03-2004	Rs. (lacs) As at 31-03-2004
CAPITAL AND LIABILITES			
Capital	1	284,79	282.05
Reserves and Surplus	2	2,407,09	1,962,78
Employees' Stock Options (Grants) OUtstanding		1,45	6,91
Deposits	3	30,408,86	22,376,07
Borrowings	4	2,307,82	2,084,65
Subordinated debt	19(4)	600,00	200,00
Other Liabilities and Provisions	5	6,296,98	3,511,62
Total		42,306,99	30,424,08
ASSETS			
Cash and balances with Reserve Bank of india	6	2,541,98	2,081,96
Balances with Banks and Money at Call and Short notice	7	1,115,57	1,087,26
Investments	8, 19 (7)	19,256,79	13,388,08
Advances	9	17,744,51	11,754,86
Fixed Assets	10	616,91	528,58
Other Assets	11	1,031,23	1,583,34
Total		42,306,99	30,424,08
Contingent Liabilities	12	82,116,17	41,559,85
Bills for Collection		2,097,89	1,761,39

The attached notes form part of the financial statements.

In terms of our report of even date attached.
for **P.C HANSOTIA & company**
Chartered Accountants
N.P. SARDA
Partner
(Membership number 9544)
Mumbai, 16 April, 2004

For and on behalf of the Board
JAGDISH CAPOOR
Chairman ANIL AHUJA
ADITYA PURI
Managing Director
SANJAY DONGRE
Vice President (Legal)
& Company Secretary

KEKI
Dr. (Mrs.) A
Dr. VENKAT RAO
RENU KARNAD
ARVIND PANDE
BOBBY PARIKH
Directors

Rs. 10 Lacs = Rs. 1 Million

Profit and Loss Account
For the year ended 31 March, 2004

		Schedule	Year ended 31-03-2004	Year ended 31-03-2004
			Rs. (lacs)	
I.	**INCOME**			
	Interest earned	13	2,548,93	2,013,61
	Other income	14	480,03	465,55
	Total		3,028,96	2,479,16
II.	**EXPENDITURE**			
	Interest expended	15	1,211,05	1,191,96
	Operating expenses	16	810,00	577,05
	Provisions & Continencies [includes Income Tax provision of Rs. 209,46 lacs (Previous year : Rs. 183,25 lacs)	17	498,41	322,55
	Total		2,519,46	2,091,56
III.	**PROFIT**			
	Net Profit for the year		509,50	387,60
	Profit brought forward		356,13	190,38
	Transfer from Debenture Redemption Reserve		----	9,74
	Total		865,13	587,72
IV.	**APPROPRIATIONS**			
	Transfer to Statutory Reserve		127,38	96,90
	Proposed dividend		100,05	84,95
	Tax on dividend		12,82	10,88
	Dividend paid during the year		-----	10
	Transfer to General Reserve		50,95	38,76
	Transfer to Investment Fluctuation Reserve		169,11	---
	Balance carried over to Balance Sheet		405,32	356,13
	Total		865,63	587,72
V.	EARNINGS PER EQUITY SHARE (Face Value Rs. 10/- per share) (Rupees)	18		
	Basic		17.95	13.75
	Diluted		16.55	12.79

In terms of our report of even date attached.
For **P.C. HYANSOTIA & company**
Chartered Accountants
N. P. SARDA
Partner Managing Director
(Membership number 9544)
Vice President (Legal)
Mumbai, 16 April, 2004
Rs. 10 lacs = Rs. 1 Million

For and on behalf of the Board
JAGDISH CAPOOR
Chairman ANIL AHUJA
ADITYA PURI
RENU KARNAD
SANJAY DONGRE
BOBBY PARIKH
& Company Secretary

KEKI M. MISTRY
Dr. (Mrs.) AMLA SAMANTA
ANIL AHUJA
Dr. VENKAT RAO GADWAL

ARVIND PANDE

Directorrs

Cash Flow Statement for the year ended 31 March, 2004

		(Rs. lacs)
	31-03-2004	31-03-2003
Cash flows form operating activities		
Net profit before income tax	718,96	570,85
Adjustment for :		
Depreciation charge for the year (including lease equalisation charge)	126,32	109,70
Loss on revaluation of investments	10,91	2,13
Amortisation of premia on investments	93,22	50,44
Loan Loss provision	178,28	88,39
Provision for wealth tax	75	47
ESOS compensation lapsed	(4)	(12)
Other provisions and contingencies	16,70	--
Loss / (Profit) on sale of fixed assets	45	(1,08)
	1,145,55	820,78
Adjustments for :		
(Increase) in Investments	(5,981,59)	(1,436,63)
(Increase) in Advances	(6,051,86)	(5,029,53)
Increase in Borrowings	223,17	261,63
Increase in Deposits	8,032,79	4,722,26
Decrease / (Increase) in other assets	635,09	(403,13)
Increase in Other Liabilities and provisions	2,634,40	1,317,32
Decrease / (Increase) in Deposit Placements	418,22	(774,74)
	1,055,77	(522,04)
Direct taxes paid	(284,39)	(237,47)
Net cash flow form operating activities	771,38	(759,51)
Cash flows from investing activities		
Purchase of fixed assets	(214,39)	(253,43)
Proceeds from sale of fixed assets	2,48	1,69
Net Cash used in investing activities	211,91	(251,74)

Rs. 10 lacs = Rs. 1 million

Cash Flow Statement for the year ended 31 March, 2004-(Contd.)

(Rs. lacs)

	31-03-2004	31-03-2003
Cash flows form operating activities		
Money received on exercise of stock options by employees	42,91	17,98
Proceeds for issues of subordinated debt	400,00	—
Dividend provided last year paid during the year	(84,95)	(70,34)
Tax on Dividend	(10,88)	—
Dividend paind during the year on Stock Option exercised during the previous year	—	(10)
Net cash generated form / (used in) financing activities	347,08	(52,46)
Net increase / (decrease) in cash and cash equivalents	906,55	(1,063,71)
Cash and cash equivalents as at 31 March, 2004	3,301,03	2394,48

In terms of our report of even date attached	For and on behalf of the Board	KEKI M. MISTRY
For P. C. HANSOTIA & company	JAGDISH CAPOOR	Dr. (Mrs.) AMLA SAMANTA
Chartered Accountants	Chairman	ANIL AHUJAN. P. SARDA
ADITYA PURI	Dr. VSENKAT RAO GADWAL	
Partner	Managing Director	RENU KARNAD
(Membership number 9544)	SANJAY DONGRE	ARVIND PANDE
	Vice President (Legal)	BOBBY PARIKH
Mumbai, 16 April, 2004	& Company Secretary	Directors

Rs. 10 lacs = Rs. 1 million

Schedules to ACCOUNTS

		As at 31-03-2004	Rs. (lacs) As at 31-03-2004
SCHEDULE 1 - CAPITAL			
Authorised Capital		450,00	450,00
45,00,00,000 (31 March, 2003 : 45,00,00,000)			
Equity Shares of Rs. 10/-each			
Issued, Subscribed and paid-up Capital			
28,47,91,713 (31 March, 2003 : 28,20,45,713)			
Equity Shares of Rs. 10 /-each			
	Total	284,79	282,05
SCHEDULE 2 - RESERVES AND SURPLUS			
I. Statutory Reserve			
Opening Balance		324,99	228,09
Additions during the year		127,38	96,90
	Total	452,37	324,99
II. General Reserve			
Opening Balance		97,35	58,59
Additions during the year		50,95	38,76
	Total	184,30	97,35
III. Share Premium Account		405,32	356,13
IV. Share Premium Account			
Opening Balance		929,71	919,51
Additions during the year		47,68	10,20
	Total	977,39	929,71
V. Investment Fluctuation Reserve			
Opening Balance		240,08	240,08
Additions during the year		169,11	--
	Total	409,19	240,08
VI. Amalgamation Reserve			
Opening Balance		14,52	14,52
	Total	14,52	14,52

Rs. 10 lacs = Rs. 1 million

Schedules to the ACCOUNTS - (Contd.)

		As at 31-03-2004	Rs. (lac) As at 31-03-2004
VII. Debenture Redemption Reserve			
Opening Balance		—	9,74
Transfer to Profit and Loss Account		—	(9,74)
	Total	2,407,09	1,962,78
SCHEDULE 3 - DEPOSITS			
I. Demand Deposits			
(I) From Banks		771,12	426,77
(Ii) From Others		8,064,00	4,524,19
	Total	8,835,12	4,950,96
II. Saving Bank Deposits		7,804,30	4,663,14
III. Term Deposits			
(I) From Banks		391,19	476,47
(ii) From Others		13,378,25	12,285,50
	Total	13,769,44	12,761,97
	Total	30,408,86	22,376,07
SCHEDULE 4 -BORROWINGS			
I. Borrowings in India			
(i) Reserve Bank of India		—	13,47
(ii) Bank		1,555,54	1,406,60
(iii) Institutions and agencies		92,15	656,54
	Total	1,647,69	2,076,61
II. Borrowing outside India		660,13	8,04
	Total	2,307,82	2,084,65
SCHEDULES 5 -OTHER LIABILITIESAND PROV ISIOS			
I. Bills Payable		3,667,27	851,12
II. Interest Accrued		416,54	688,21
III. Others (including provisions)		2,100,30	1,876,456
IV. Proposed Dividend (including tax on dividend)		112,87	95,83
	Total	6,296,98	3,511,62

Rs. 10 lacs = Rs. 1 million

Schedules to the ACCOUNTS - (Contd.)

		As at 31-03-2004	As at 31-03-2004
			Rs. (lacs)
SCHEDULE 6 - CASH AND BALANCES WITH RESERVE BANK OF INDIA			
I. Cash in hand (including foreign currency notes)		254,19	166,68
II. Balances with Reserve Bank fo India in current accounts		2,287,79	1,915,28
	Tota	2,541,98	2,081,96
SCHEDULE 7-BALANCES WITH BANKS AND MONEY AT CALL AND SHORT NOTICE			
I. In India			
(I) Balances with Banks :			
(a) In Corrent accounts		237,49	83,43
(b) In other deposit accounts		139,83	82,63
	Tota	377,32	166,06
*Including deposit with NABARAD under the RIDF Deposit Scheme. This deposit in eligible for priority sector lending.			
(ii) Money at call short notice :			
(a) With banks		54,15	278,17
	Tota	431,47	444,23
II. Outside India			
(ii) In Current accounts		6,46	3,36
(ii) Money at call and short notice		677,64	639,67
	Tota	684,10	643,03
	Tota	1,115,57	1,087,26
SCHEDULE 8- INVESTMENTS			
Investments in India in			
(i) Government securities		11,530,55	6,356,25
(ii) Others apporved securities		6,50	11,84
(iii) Shares		107,00	108,39
(iv) Debentures and Bonds		4,044,63	4,165,58
(v) Joint Venture		2,43	2,43
(vi) Units, Certificate of Deposits and Others		3,565,68	2,742,59
	Tota	19,256,79	13,388,08

Rs. 10 lacs = Rs. 1 million

Schedules to the ACCOUNTS - (Contd.)

		Rs. (lacs)	
		As at 31-03-2004	As at 31-03-2004
SCHEDULE 9- ADVANCES			
A. (i) Bills purchasssed and discpunted		3,193,97	2,622,79
(ii) Cash Credits, Overdrafts and Loans reapayable on demand		3,740,65	2,607,80
(iii) Term Loans		10,809,89	6,524,27
	Total	17,744,51	11,754,86
B. (i) Secured by tangible assets*		15,277,11	9,990,73
(ii) Covered by Bank/Government Gurarantees		116,74	93,69
(iii) Unsecured		2,350,66	1,670,44
	Total	17,744,51	11,754,86
* Including advances against Book Debts			
C. Advances in India			
(i) Priority Sector		2,498,39	1,421,82
(ii) Public Sector		335,28	851,90
(iii) Banks		10,72	22,18
(iv) Others		14,9000,12	9,458,96
	Total	17,744,51	11,754,86
SCHEDULE 10- FIXED ASSETS			
A. Premises (including Land)			
Gross Block			
At Cost on 31 March of the preceding year		193,35	153,18
Additions during the year		58,32	40,17
Deductions during the year		(780	—
	Total	250,89	193,35
Depreciation			
As at 31 March of the preceding year		23,57	17,34
Change for the year		7,87	6,23
On deductions during the year		(38)	—
		31,06	23,57
Net Block		219,83	169,78

Rs. 10 lacs = Rs. 1 million

Schedules to the ACCOUNTS - (Contd.)

		Rs. (lacs)	
		As at 31-03-2004	As at 31-03-2004
B.	**Other Fixed Assest** (including furniture and fixtures)		
	Gross Block		
	At Cost on 31 March of the proceding year	616,93	403,90
	Additions during the year	159,26	227,62
	Deductions during the year	(9,58)	(14,59)
	Total	766,61	616,93
	Depreciation		
	As at 31 March of the preceding year	258,96	173,93
	Charge for the year	117,62	99,01
	On deductions during the year	(7,05)	(13,98)
	Total	369,53	258,96
	Net Block	397,08	357,97
C.	**Assest on Lease** (Plant and Machinery)		
	Gross Block		
	At Cost on 31 March of the preceding year	43,83	43,83
	Total	43,83	43,83
	Depreciation		
	As at 31 March of the preceding year	11,52	10,62
	Change for the year	23	90
	Total	11,75	11,52
	Lease Adjustment Account		
	As at 31 March fo the preceding year	31,48	27,92
	Charge for the year	60	3,56
	Total	32,08	31,48
	Unamoritsed cost of assets on lease	—	83
	Total	616,91	528,58

SCHEDULE 11- OTHER ASSETS

I.	Interest accrued	430,41	663,00
II.	Advance tax (net of provision)	129,78	88,86
III.	Stationery and stamps	1,66	94
IV.	Bond and share application money pending allotment	9,25	50
V.	Security Deposit for commerciaal and residental property	75,30	87,90
VI.	Cheques in course of collection	78,41	294,45
VII.	Other assets*	306,42	447,69
	Total	1,031,23	1,583,34

* Includes defrfered tax asset (net) of Rs. 52,99 lacs (previous year: **Rs. 19,74 lacs)**

Rs. 10 lacs = Rs. 1 million

Schedules to the ACCOUNTS - (Contd.)

		As at 31-03-2004	Rs. (lacs) As at 31-03-2004
SCHEDULE 12- CONTINGENT LIABILITIES			
I. Claims against the Bank not acknowledge as debts		99,28	51,05
II. Liability on account of outstandign forward exchange contracts		39444,08	19,772,55
III. Liability on account of outstanding derivative contracts		1,641,73	18,605,04
IV. Guarantees given on behalf of constituents-in India		1,892,10	1,424,70
V. Other items for which the Bank is contingently liable		100,00	1,171,51
		100,00	535,00
	Total	82,116,17	41,559,85
SCHEDULE 13- INTEREST EARNED			
I. Interest/discount on advances/bills		1,108,66	777,32
II. Income from investments		1,322,22	1,112,95
III. Interest on balance with RBI and other inter-bank funds		110,96	120,44
IV. Others		709	2,90
	Total	2,548,93	2,013,61
SCHEDULE 14-OTHER INCOME			
I. Commission, exchange and brokerage		320,35	236,46
II. Profit on sale of investments		37,78	132,46
III. Profit/ (Loss) on revaluation of investments		(10,91)	(2,13)
IV. Profit/ (Loss) on sale fo building and other assets		(45)	1,08
V. Profit on exchange transactions		74,00	44,53
VI. Miscellaneous income		59,26	53,22
	Total	480,03	465,55
SCHEDULE 15-INTEREST EXPENDED			
I. Interest on Deposits		1,038,29	1,063,29
II. Interest on RBI/Inter-bank borrowings		143,62	103,29
III. Other interes*		29,14	25,38
		1,211,05	1,191,96

* Represents interes on subordinated debt.

Rs. 10 lacs = Rs. 1 million

Schedules to the ACCOUNTS - (Contd.)

	As at 31-03-2004	Rs. (lacs) As at 31-03-2004
SCHEDULE 12- OPERATING EXDPENSES		
I. Payment to and provisions for employees	204,09	151,95
II. Rent, taxes and lighting	98,44	77,26
III. Printing & stationery	37,48	27,53
IV. Advertisement and publicity	37,06	17,51
V. Depreciation on bank's property	125,72	106,14
VI. Directors' fees, alowances and expenses	12	4
VII. Auditors' fees and expenses*	49	26
VIII. Law charges	1,25	42
XI. Postage, telegram, telephone etc.	77,00	51,92
X. Repairs and manintenance	66,17	45,67
XI. Insurance	17,90	12,26
XII. Other Expenditure**	144,28	86,09
Total	810,00	577,05

*Excludes Rs. 14 lacs (previous year : Rs. 12 lacs) payable for professional services to a firm of auditors in which partnersof the firm of statutory auditors are partners.

** Includes marketing expenses, professinal fees, travel & hotel charges, entertainmnet, registrar & transfer agency fee & system management fees.

SCHEDULE 17-PROVISIONS AND CONTINGENCIES		
I. Income tax	209,46	183,25
II. Wealth tax	75	47
III. Loan loss provision	178,28	88,39
IV. Amortisation of premia on investments	93,22	50,44
V. Others	16,70	—
Total	498,41	322,55

Rs. 10 lacs = Rs. 1 million

Schedules to the ACCOUNTS - (Contd.)

(Rupees)

	For the year	
	2003-2004	2002-2003
SCHEDULE 18- EARNINGS PER EQUITY SHARE		
Annualised Earnings per equity share have been calculated based on the net incoem after taxation of Rs. 509,50 lacs (previous year : Rs.387,60 lacs) and the average number of equity shares in issue during the year of 28,38,06,538 (previous year : 28,19,34,292).		
Following is the reconciliation between basic and diluted earnings per equity share :		
Nominal value per share	10.00	10.00
Basic earnings per sha	17.95	13.75
Effect of potential equity shares for stock options and subordinated debt per share	(1.40)	(0.96)
Diluted earnings per share	16.55	12.79
Basic earnings per equity share has been computed by dividing net income by the weighted average number of equity shares outsanding for the period. Diluted earnings per equity share has been computed using the weighted average number of equity shares and dilutive potential equity shares outstanding during the period. The following is the reconciliation of the earnings used in the computation of basic and diluted earnings per share:	**Rs. lacs**	**Rs. lacs**
Earnings used in basic earnings per share	509,50	387,60
Impact of dilution on profits	12,27	12,06
Earnings used in diluted earnings per share	521,77	399,66
The following is reconciliation of weighted average number of equity shares used in the computation of basic and diluted earnings per share:	28,38,06,538	28,19,34,292
Effect of potential equity shares for stock options outstanding and subordinated debt	3,13,76,824	3,04,31,174
Weighted averge number of equity shares used in computing diluted	31,51,83,362	31,23,65,466

Rs. 10 lacs = Rs. 1 million

Schedules to the ACCOUNTS - (Contd.)

	For the year	
	2003-2004	2002-2003
SCHEDULE 19- NOTES AND PRINCIPAL ACCOUNTING POLICIES APPENDED TO AND FORMING PART OF THE FINANCIAL STATEMENTS FOR THE YEAR ENDED MARCH 31, 2004.		
1. Capital Adequacy Ratio		(Rs. Lacs)
The Bank's capital adequacy ratio, calculated in accordance with RBI guidelines, is as follows:		
Tier 1 Capital	2,229,70	1,985,02
Tier 1 Capital	1,008,12	341,47
Total Capital	3,237,82	2,326,49
Total Risk weighted assets and contingents	27,773,82	20,917,71
Capital ratios		
Tier 1	8.03%	9.49%
Total capital	11.66%	11.12%

Tier 1 Capital includes paid up capital, statutory reserve, general reserve, balance in profit and loss account amalgamation reserve. From this, outstanding deferred tax asset, if any, is deducted.

Tier 2 Capital includes general loan loss reserves, investment flucttuation reserve and subordinated debt.

2. Business ratios/information

	2003-2004	2002-2003
Interest income as a percentage of working funds[1]	7.28%	7.89%
Net interest income as as percentage of working funds	3.82%	3.22%
Non-interest income as a percentage of working funds	1.37%	1.82%
Operating profit[2] as a percentage of working funds	2.56%	2.58%
Return on assets (average)	1.45%	1.52%
Business[3] per employee (Rs. lacs)	8,66	8,65
Profit per employee[4] (Rs. lacs)	9.39%	10.09%
Percentage of net Non Performing Assets[5] to customer assets[6]	0.12%	0.26%
Percentage of net Non Performing Assets to net advances[7]	0.16%	0.37%

Definitions :

1. Working funds is the daily average of total assets during the year.
2. Operating profit = (Interest incoem + other income - interest expense - operating expense - depricialtin on investment - profit / (loss) on sale of Fixed Assets)
3. "Business" is the total of ne advances and deposits.
4. Productivity ratios are based on average employee numbers.

Rs. 10 lacs = Rs. 1 million

Schedules to the ACCOUNTS - (Contd.)

5. Net NP As are non performing assets net of interest in suspense, specific provisions and ECGC claims received.
6. Customer assets include gross advances (but net of specific provisions), credit substitutes like debentures, commercial paper, loans and investments in securitised assets brought in and cost of assets ;eased pit/
7. Net advances are eqivalent to gross advances net of bills rediscounted, specific loan provisions, interest in suspense and ECGC claims received.

3. Reserves and Surplus

General Reserve

The Bank has made an appropriation from the Profit and Loss Account balance of Rs. 50,95 lacs (previous year : Rs. 38,76 lacs) out of profits for the year ended March 31, 20004 to General Reserve prusuant to Companies (Transfer of Profits to Reserves) Rules, 1975.

4. Subordinated Debt

Subrodinated debt outstanding as at March 31, 2004 is a long-term unsecured non-convertible debt aggregating Rs. 600 crores (previous year : Rs 200 crores).

In February 2004, the Bank raised Rs. 400 crores subordinated debt at an annualised coupon between 5.9% to 6%. This debt is subordinated to present and future senior indebtedness of the Bank amd qia;ofoes as Toer 2 risk-based capital under RBI's guidelines for assessing capital adequacy.

Based on the balance term to maturity as at March 31, 2004, only 73% of the book value of subrodinated debt is considered as Tier 2 capital for the prupose of capital adequacy computation.

Conversion clause

Of the outstanding amoun of debt, principal amount of Rs. 150 crores issued to certain Government owned Indian financial institutions contains a clause wherein, in the event of a defualt in payment of interest or principal, the primary lender shall have the right to convert and amount not exceeding 20% of such outstanding interest in principal, into fully paid equity shares at an exercise price equal to the par value of such shares. These provisions are commonly found in loan agreements of this nature. The Bank has never missed any payment on this debt or on any other debt. If the Bank were to defuault on all such debt and be obligated to issue the maximum number os shares on the basis of the amount outstanding and interest payable till March 31, 2004, such amount would approximately be 310 lac shares (previous year : 295 lac shares).

5. Other liabilities

Others in other liabilities include :

- General loan loss provisions of Rs. 158,93 lacs (previous year Rs. 114,70 lacs)
- Share application monies received Rs. 12,55 lacs (previous year: Rs. 14,65 lacs) prusuant to the exercise of employee stock options

6. Dividend paid on shares issued on exercise of stock optins

The Bank has allotted 10,52,100 shares after the balance sheet date, on April 5, 2004,prusuant to the exercise of options during the quarter ended March 2004. These shares will be eligible for full dividend, if approved at the ensuing Annual General Meeting.

Rs. 10 lacs = Rs. 1 million

Schedules to the ACCOUNTS - (Contd.)

This is in accordance with the Employees Stock Option Scheme as amended and approved by the shareholders. An amount of Rs. 42 lacs being dividend (including dividend tax) pertaining to the said shares has been appropriated from the profit and loss account as at March 31, 2004.

7. **Investments**

The book value of investments held under the three categories viz. 'Held to Maturity', 'Available for Sale and ' Held for Trading' are as under:

	As at March 31, 2004				As at march 31, 2003			
	Held for Trading	Available for Sale	Held to Maturity	Total	Held of Trading	Available for Sale	Held to Maturity	Total
Government Securities	424,43	8,443,76	2,662,36	11,530,55	374,68	4,074,53	1,907,04	6,356,25
Other Approved Secuirties	-----	6,50	----	6,50	----	11,84	----	11,84
Shares	-----	22,09	84,91	107,00	----	18,84	89,55	108,39
Bonds Debentures	198,18	2,966,59	879,86	4,044,63	22,89	2,315,64	1,828,05	4,166,58
Joint Ventures	----	----	2,43	2,43	----	---	2,43	2,43
Others	----	3,565,68	----	3,565,68	----	2,742,59	----	2,742,59
Total	622,61	15,004,632	3,629,56	19,256,79	397,57	9,163,44	3,827,07	13,388,08

- Investments as March 31, 2004 include securities held under LAF with RBI of Rs. 1,995,00 lacs (previsous year : Rs. Nil)
- Investment include securities aggregating Rs. 100,00 lacs which are kept as a margin with the Clearing Corporation India Limited.
- Other investments include commercial paper of Rs. 89,98 lacs (previouss year : Rs. 595,42 lacs) and investment in securitised paper of Rs. 2,885,71 lacs (previosu year : Rs. 1,918,92 lacs).
- The Bank has made investments in certain companies where it hold more than 25% of those companies. Such investments do not fall within the defrinition of a joint venture as given in paragraph 3 of AS 27, Financial Reporting of Interest in Joint Ventures, of the Institute of Chartered Accountants of India circular No.DBOB.NO. BP.BC. 3/21.04.141/2002, dated July 11, 2002, the Bank has classified these investments as joint ventures.
- Summary of investment portfolio

(Rs. lacs)

	March 31, 2004	March 31, 2003
Gross value of investment	19,276,28	13,396,66
Depreciation in the value of investment	19,49	8,58
Net book value	19,256,79	13,388,08

Rs. 10 lacs = Rs. 1 million

Schedules to the ACCOUNTS - (Contd.)

9. **Interest Income**

   Interest income under the sub-head income from investments includes dividend received during the year on units, equity and preference shares amounting to Rs. 76,94 lacs (previous year: 50,79 lacs).

10. Earnings from Assets Securitised-out

    The Bank has securitised-out commercial loans to a special purpose vehicle, Post securitisation, the Bank will contiue to maintain customer account relationships and service the loans transferred to this special prupose vehicle. The securitised paper is without recourse to the Bank. The Bank provides credit enhancements in the form of cash collaterals and/or by subordination of cash flow to senior pass through certificates (PTCs). The Bank does not retain any beneficial interest in the assets sold.

    During the eyar ended March 31, 2004, the Bank securitised loans with a carrrying value of Rs. 569,81 lacs (previous year: Rs. nil), which resulted in gains of Rs. 12,38 lacs (previous year: nil), being the net present value of future cash flows determined at the negotiated yield less the book value and provisions towards servicing and incidental costs of the contracts so securitised out. Future delinquencies have been provided for. The gains are disclosed under interest income.

11. **Commission, Exchange and Brokerage Income**

    Commission, exchange and brokerage incoem includes lease rentals net of equalisation charge and is also net of correspondent bank charges and brokerage paid on purchase and sale of investments.

12. Miscellaneous Income includes Rs. 54,86 lacs (Previous year: Rs. 50,85 lacs) pertaining to derivative transactions.

13. Other expenditure includes marketing expenses Rs. 49,40 lacs (previous year:Rs. 30,20 lacs) and outsourcing expenses Rs. 3030 lacs (previous year: 14,90 lacs) exceeding 1% of the total income

14. **Income Taxes**

	2003-2004	**(Rs. lacs)** **2002-2003**
The income tax expense comprises the following :		
Current incoem tax expense	242,71	172,26
Deferred income tax (benefit) / expense as reproted :	(33,25)	10,99
Income tax expense	209,46	183,25
The following is the reconcilliation of estimated incoem taxes at the statutory income tax rate to income tax expense as reported:		
Net income before taxes	718,96	570,85
Effective statutory income tax rat	35.88	36.75%
Expected income tax expense	257,96	209,79
Adjustments to reconcile expected income tax to actual tax expense :		
Permanent differences :		
Income exempt from taxes	**(52,94)**	(27,31)
Other (including adjustments for prior years), net	4,44	17
Effect of change in statutory tax rates, net	—	60
Income tax expense	209,46	183,25

Management believes that the realisation of the recongnised deferred tax assets in more likely than not based on expectations as to future taxable incoem.

Rs. 10 lacs = Rs. 1 million

CHAPTER–5

FINANCIAL STATEMENT ANALYSIS

Learning Objective

Information discernible on the face of a financial statement is insignificant compared to what is latent. This chapter, which is a continuation of the previous chapter, guides the readers to unravel the mysteries of hidden information treasures in a financial statement. Ratios, percentages and parts of are the tools used to bring the information to the surface. Analysis enables one to assess the operating efficiency and the financial position of an undertaking. For this purpose, the statements are analyzed from structural, turnover, profitability and liquidity angles. After going through the chapter, the readers would be in a position to analyze financial statements and to arrive at meaningful conclusions.

There are five ways in which financial statements are analyzed. The earliest and conventional forms of studying financial statements were ***vertical, horizontal and trend analysis***. The other two modern methods are ***ratio and cash flow analysis***. The introduction of ratio and cash flow has rendered the other three methods obsolete. Our major concentration would therefore be on ratio and cash flow analysis. However, for historic reasons, let us also have a look at the other methods for academic interest.

Vertical analysis is also known as ***common size statement analysis***. In this method, both the profit and loss account and the balance sheet are reduced to percentages. Let us first take profit and loss account. Sales are considered the critical aspect in profit and loss account. All the items of costs and benefits are presented as a percent of sales. For example, the profit and loss account of Kindhearts Ltd. for the year ended 31.03.2003 is as in table below.

Table 1
Kind hearts Ltd.
Profit and loss account for the year ended 31.03.2004

	2004	2003
Revenues.		
Sales	123,45,678	103,98,765
Discount received	72,329	61,543
Dividend on investments	12,36,987	10,54,087
Commission received	32,567	26,987
Total	136,87,561	115,41,382
Costs		
Materials consumed	44,92,741	35,29,139
Wages	13,72,478	11,72,582
Other factory overheads	7,84,062	5,27,789
Salaries	19,28,378	17,82,762
Administrative overheads	11,33,667	9,21,876
Selling and distribution overheads	12,23,456	11,36,879
Non-operating costs	4,22,380	3,92,876
Total	113,57,162	94,63,903
Profit before tax	23,30,399	20,77,479

A common size profit and loss account, if to be prepared for Kindhearts, would be as in Table 2.

Table 2
Kind hearts Ltd.
Common size Profit and loss account for the year ended 31.03.2004

	2004	%	2003	%
Revenues.				
Sales	123,45,678	100.00	103,98,765	100.00
Discount received	72,329	.59	61,543	.59
Dividend on investments	12,36,987	10.02	10,54,087	10.14
Commission received	32,567	.26	26,987	.26
Total	136,87,561	110.87	115,41,382	110.99
Costs				
Materials consumed	44,92,741	36.39	35,29,139	33.94
Wages	13,72,478	11.12	11,72,582	11.28
Other factory overheads	7,84,062	6.35	5,27,789	5.08

Salaries	19,28,378	15.62	17,82,762	17.14
Administrative overheads	11,33,667	9.18	9,21,876	8.87
Selling and distribution	12,23,456	9.91	11,36,879	10.93
overheads	4,22,380	3.42	3,92,876	3.78
Non-operating costs	113,57,162	91.99	94,63,903	91.01
Total	23,30,399	18.88	20,77,479	19.98
Profit before tax				

Common size analysis would help one to broadly understand the reasons for change in the operations. In the illustration, margin on sales have decreased from 19.98% in 2003 to 18.88% in 2004.The reasons are obvious. The materials cost has increased from 33.84% of sales in 2003 to 36.39 % in 2004.So also factory overheads and administrative overheads have increased. On the other hand salaries and selling costs have declined during 2004.

We may now reduce the balance sheet of Kindhearts Ltd. to a common size. In balance sheet, all the assets and liabilities are presented as a percent of total assets or liabilities. Table 3 is the balance sheet of Kindhearts for the period.

Table 3
Kind hearts Ltd.
Balance sheet as on 31.03.2004.

Liabilities	**2004**	**2003**
Share capital	125,00,000	120,00,000
Reserves and surplus	152,45,987	142,73,900
Fixed/term liabilities	138,54,000	99,54,831
Current Liabilities	16,34,951	12,45,678
Provisions	3,12,567	1,14,912
Total	435,48,492	375,89,321
Assets.		
Fixed assets –Gross	756,40,264	542,70,542
Less: Depreciation	527,83,132	361,93,529
Net fixed assets	228,57,132	180,77,013
Work-in-progress	72,41,780	103,45,678
Investments	85,00,000	53,00,000
Current assets	31,47,974	19,84,876
Intangibles	18,01,606	18,81,754
Total	435,48,492	375,89,321

A common size balance sheet of the company would be as in the following table.

Table 4
Kind hearts Ltd.
Common size Balance sheet as on 31.03.2004

Liabilities	2004	%	2003	%
Share capital	125,00,000	28.70	120,00,000	31.92
Reserves and surplus	152,45,987	35.01	142,73,900	37.97
Fixed/term liabilities	138,54,000	31.81	99,54,831	26.48
Current Liabilities	16,34,951	3.75	12,45,678	3.32
Provisions	3,12,567	.73	1,14,912	.31
Total	435,48,492	100.00	375,89,321	100.00
Assets.				
Fixed assets –Gross	756,40,264	173.69	542,70,542	144.38
Less; Depreciation	527,83,132	121.21	361,93,529	96.29
Net fixed assets	228,57,132	52.48	180,77,013	48.09
Work-in-progress	72,41,780	16.63	103,45,678	27.52
Investments	85,00,000	19.52	53,00,000	14.10
Current assets	31,47,974	7.23	19,84,876	5.28
Intangibles	18,01,606	4.14	18,81,754	5.01
Total	435,48,492	100.00	375,89,321	100.00

There was a proportionate increase in fixed liabilities, but reduction in reserves. Investments and current liabilities had increased. In assets increase in gross fixed assets and depreciation are sizeable. Investments and current assets had also shown increases.

The comparative analysis is horizontal in character as it makes a study of year to year progress. The change in absolute figures of the current year over the previous year with percentage changes would indicate the progress or otherwise of the company. Let us analyze the profit and loss account and balance sheet of Kind hearts Ltd.

Table 5
Kind hearts Ltd.
Comparative Profit and loss account for the year ended 31.03.2004

	2004	2003	Change	Change %
Revenues.				
Sales	123,45,678	103,98,765	19,46,013	18.72
Discount received	72,329	61,543	10,786	17.53
Dividend on investments	12,36,987	10,54,087	1,82,900	17.35
Commission received	32,567	26,987	5,580	20.68
Total	136,87,561	115,41,382	21,46,179	18.60

Costs				
Materials consumed	44,92,741	35,29,139	9,63,602	27.30
Wages	13,72,478	11,72,582	1,99.896	17.05
Other factory overheads	7,84,062	5,27,789	2,56,273	48.56
Salaries	19,28,378	17,82,762	1,45,616	8.17
Administrative overheads	11,33,667	9,21,876	2,11,791	22.97
Selling and distribution	12,23,456	11,36,879	86,577	7.62
overheads	4,22,380	3,92,876	29,504	7.51
Non-operating costs	113,57,162	94,63,903	18.93,259	20.01
Total	23,30,399	20,77,479	2,52,920	12.17
Profit before tax				

Comparative balance sheet of the company would be as below.

Table 6
Kind hearts Ltd.
Comparative Balance sheet as on 31.03.2004

Liabilities	**2004**	**2003**	**Change**	**Change %**
Share capital	125,00,000	120,00,000	25,00,000	20.83
Reserves and surplus	152,45,987	142,73,900	9,72,087	6.81
Fixed/term liabilities	138,54,000	99,54,831	38,99,169	39.17
Current Liabilities	16,34,951	12,45,678	3,89,273	31.25
Provisions	3,12,567	1,14,912	1,97,655	172.01
Total	435,48,492	375,89,321	59,59,171	
Assets.				
Fixed assets –Gross	756,40,264	542,70,542	213,69,722	39.38
Less; Depreciation	527,83,132	361,93,529	165,89,603	45.84
Net fixed assets	228,57,132	180,77,013	47,80,119	26.44
Work-in-progress	72,41,780	103,45,678	–31,03,898	–42.86
Investments	85,00,000	53,00,000	32,00,000	60.38
Current assets	31,47,974	19,84,876	11,63,098	58.60
Intangibles	18,01,606	18,81,754	–80,148	–4.26
Total	435,48,492	375,89,321	59,59,171	

Comparative analysis compares the changes in the items of profit and loss account and balance sheet and with the aid of percentages study the development or otherwise of the business between the two periods. When the study is extended for a longer period than two years, it is ***trend analysis***. In trend analysis, usually a period of five years is chosen and the changes in the items over the period compared to the base year are analyzed. For example, the following is the summarized financial statements of Donaldson Process Ltd. for 5 years up to 2004(Table 7).In the illustration, the base year is 2000 and the changes in items of profit and loss account and balance sheet in the subsequent years are indicated in absolute figures and percentages (Table 8).

Table 7
Donaldson Process Ltd.
Data for five years ended 2004 **Rs.lakhs**

	2000	2001	2002	2003	2004
Profit and loss account					
Sales	79.47	86.73	98.64	108.64	127.19
Less: Cost of sales	41.29	35.28	49.74	58.38	65.97
Operating profit	38.18	45.44	48.90	50.26	61.22
Less: Non-operating exp.	5.87	8.74	10.21	12.70	14.16
Add:Non-operating income	3.68	4.71	5.41	6.83	7.81
Profit before tax	35.99	41.41	44.10	44.39	54.87
Balance sheet					
Share capital	95.00	115.00	115.00	180.00	180.00
Reserves and surplus	179.52	186.49	231.67	292.84	342.04
Less intangibles	12.18	—	—	—	—
Net worth.	262.34	301.49	346.67	472.84	522.04
Term liabilities	168.23	152.73	140.50	137.07	115.80
Current liabilities.	84.31	97.42	106.49	124.69	138.53
Provisions	70.00	85.00	94.00	90.00	95.00
	584.88	636.30	687.66	824.60	871.37
Gross fixed assets	432.78	461.85	489.74	678.45	752.19
Less: Depreciation	186.94	201.48	225.72	256.90	281.34
Net fixed assets	245.84	260.37	264.02	421.55	470.85
Work in progress.	19.95	36.82	25.94	34.50	25.71
Current assets	299.09	289.11	337.70	328.55	334.81
Investments	20.00	50.00	60.00	40.00	40.00
	584.88	636.30	687.66	824.60	871.37

Table 8
Donaldson Process Ltd.
Trend analysis

		2000	2001	2002	2003	2004
Profit and loss account						
Sales. Absolute change	(AC)	79.47	7.26	19.17	29.17	47.72
% change		-	9.14%	**24.12%**	**36.71%**	**60.05%**
Less:Cost of sales-	(AC)	41.29	-6.01	8.45	17.09	24.68
% change			–14.56%	**20.47%**	**41.39%**	**59.77%**
Operatingprofit-	(AC)	38.18	7.26	10.72	12.08	23.04
% change			**19.02%**	**28.08%**	**31.64%**	**60.35%**
Less:Nonoperatingexp	(AC)	5.87	2.87	4.34	6.83	14.18
% change			**48.89%**	**73.94%**	**116.35%**	**241.64%**
Nonoperatingincome	(AC)	3.68	1.03	1.73	3.15	4.13
% change			**27.99%**	**47.01%**	**85.60%**	**112.23%**
Profit before tax-	(AC)	35.99	5.42	8.11	8.40	18.88
% change			**15.06%**	**22.53%**	**23.34%**	**52.50%**
Balance sheet						
Share capital-	(AC)	95.00	20.00	20.00	85.00	85.00
% change			**21.05%**	**21.05%**	**89.47%**	**89.47%**
Reserves and surplus-	(AC)	179.52	6.97	52.15	113.32	162.52
% change			**3.88%**	**29.05%**	**63.12%**	**90.53%**
Less intangibles -	(AC)	12.18	– 12.18	-	-	-
% change			**–100%**	-	-	-
Net worth-	(AC)	262.34	39.15	84.33	210.50	259.70
% change			**14.92%**	**32.15%**	**80.24%**	**98.99%**
Term liabilities-	(AC)	168.23	– 15.50	–27.73	31.16	–52.43
% change			**–9.21%**	**–16.48%**	**18.52%**	**–31.17%**
Current liabilities.	(AC)	84.31	13.11	22.18	40.38	54.22
% change			**15.55%**	**26.31%**	**47.89%**	**64.71%**
Provisions-	(AC)	70.00	5.00	24.00	20.00	25.00
% change			**7.14%**	**34.29%**	**28.57%**	**35.71%**
Total	(AC)	584.88	51.42	102.78	239.72	286.49
% change			**8.79%**	**17.57%**	**40.99%**	**48.98%**
Gross fixed assets-	(AC)	432.78	29.07	56.96	245.67	319.41
% change			**6.72%**	**13.16%**	**56.77%**	**73.80%**

Less: Depreciation- (AC) **% change**	186.94	14.54 **7.78%**	38.78 **20.74%**	69.96 **37.42%**	94.40 **50.50%**
Net fixed assets- (AC) **% change**	245.84	14.53 **5.91%**	18.18 **7.40%**	175.71 **71.47%**	507.00 **225.01%**
Work in progress. - (AC) **% change**	19.95	16.87 **84.56%**	5.99 **30.03%**	14.55 **72.93%**	5.76 **28.87%**
Current assets- (AC) **% change**	299.09	-9.98 **-3.34%**	38.61 **12.91%**	29.46 **9.85%**	35.72 **11.94%**
Investments (AC) **% change**	20.00	30.00 **150%**	40.00 **200%**	20.00 **100%**	20.00 **100%**
Total **%change**	584.88	51.42 **8.79%**	102.78 **17.57%**	239.72 **40.99%**	286.49 **48.98%**

Note: AC means actual change. Figures in bold letters are changes percent. They indicate the trend in the working and financials of the company.

Conventional analytical methods as we have seen in the above paragraphs, study absolute figures and absolute changes for analysis. Absolute figures lead to aberrations. To effectively study the operational results and financial position of companies, these figures are to be related to inter-related figures to make meaningful conclusions. Here comes ratio analysis.

Definition of Ratio

Ratios are quantification of relationships between figures that are inter-related. The inter- relationship may be cause or effect or functional. Therefore, before working out the relationship, the analyst has to identify what figures are inter-related. To give an example, there is inter- relationship between profit and a few figures in the financial statements. Profits are related to turnover, cost of sales, gross fixed assets, working capital, capital employed and net worth. Relationship between profit and sales is direct. Higher the turnover, higher should be the profit. Profit is the result of costs and hence the two are inter-related. Profit is also related to production as it is production that promotes sales. Production is a function of efficient utilization of fixed assets and working capital. Resources deployed in fixed assets and working capital is capital employed. Net worth, being the owned funds of the shareholders, has also a bearing on profitability. The inter-connection is usually between the data in profit and loss account with that in balance sheet, although quite a few relationships are from within either the profit and loss account or balance sheet itself.

Some analysts have split their hair in introducing hundred of meaningless relationships and ratios. As the objectives of analyzing financial statements are to assess the operational results of the business and to measure its financial strength, the vital areas of analysis are around profitability, solvency, liquidity and risk. In this book, relationships that matter are considered. Ratios are broadly classified into four groups – ***structural ratios, turnover ratios, profitability ratios and liquidity ratios.*** Each group of data is applied to interpret a specific area in the financial scenario of the business. Thus, structural ratios throw light on the financial position of the business with specific references to the owned funds (equity) and borrowed or levered funds (debts). It is an indication of the long-term solvency of the business. Profitability ratios tell us about the earning capacity of the business. Liquidity ratios assess the shot-term liquidity of the business. It is an indicator of the ability of the unit to meet the current commitments as and when they arise. Turnover ratios indicate the level of activity of the business. Broadly speaking, profitability ratios and turnover ratios would reveal the operational efficiency of the business, while structural ratios and liquidity ratios gauge the financial soundness of the firm.

What follows is a select list of ratios, which are, no doubt, comprehensive. However, these are, by no means, to be considered as exhaustive. But the ratios are selected carefully with an eye to amply serve the purpose of financial analysis by different segments of society, who are interested in the data.

1. Structural Ratios

- *Debt-equity ratio;*
- *Solvency ratio;*
- *Proprietary ratio;*
- *Debt capitalization ratio;*
- *Debt-service coverage ratio;*
- *Interest coverage ratio.*

2. Turnover Ratios

- *Fixed asset turnover ratio;*
- *Working capital turnover ratio;*
- *Inventory turnover ratio;*
- *Debtor's turnover ratio;*
- *Turnover to capital employed ratio.*

3. Profitability Ratios

- *Gross profitability ratio;*
- *Return on investment;*
- *Net profitability ratio;*
- *Earning per share;*

- *Price-earning ratio;*
- *Dividend payout ratio.*

4. Liquidity Ratios

- *Current ratio;*
- *Quick ratio;*
- *Average collection period.*

The calculation and the way in which these ratios are used to extricate the requisite information are discussed in the following paragraphs:

Structural Ratios

Structural ratios are indicators of the financial strength of the business. It brings out the relationship between debt and equity as a measure of the financial risk of the business. The ability of the business to service its financial commitments in the long run is measured by the solvency ratio. The share of the owners in the capital employed is another indicator of the strength. Financial strength is also measured in terms of debt servicing ability of the business. These relationships are examined in the following paragraphs.

Debt Equity Ratio

The ratio is arrived at by dividing debt by equity. I have expressed in the last chapter my reservations of preference shares being included as part of equity. In the analysis, however I have included preference shares as part of equity for the sake of conformity with other analysts. But I am really pained to note that analysts go to the extent of introducing a ratio of preference capital to equity and call it as ***capital gearing ratio***. Capital gearing is expected to reveal the relationship between total equity and preference capital. I do not understand the purpose behind such a ratio. If preference is treated as equity, it should be treated as such. Then there is no question of gearing, which characterizes debt. Otherwise preference has to be treated as debt, which is logically more valid a proposition.

Debt equity ratio is an indicator of the relationship between owned funds and borrowed funds that are used in business. Debt has its own advantages. Capital, particularly in developing countries like India, is scarce and costly. By its nature, even the scarce capital is shy of investment. The ever-increasing need for funds, therefore, has to be met through borrowed funds. Even when an entrepreneur can raise adequate volume of owned funds, he might decide to use borrowed funds, as debt brings an added benefit by way of ***financial leverage***. Financial leverage is the added benefit accruing to equity by mixing a judicious dose of debt to the pattern of funding. In case the return on investment of a business is higher than the cost of borrowings, financial leverage benefits accrue to the business. How ever, higher the debt component in the capital employed, greater is the risk of the undertaking. Any business with a higher risk rating would not have easy access to the market for additional funds. If it wants to raise additional resources, either by way of debt or equity it can do so only at an enhanced cost. Indian industry is prone traditionally to high risk. Having regard to the high debt sensitivity of the Indian industry, governmental agencies have fixed the maximum debt equity ratio as 2 : 1. That is, the share of debt in funding any proposal could at the most be twice the equity. But in developed countries, the ratio is reverse; equity is generally more than debt. With rapid globalization, Indian corporates are also slowly veering away to this attitude. Recent studies have revealed that the overall debt equity ratio of Indian companies have tilted in favour of equity (0.7 : 1). Now a day, Indian financial institutions also have started insisting on a debt equity ratio of less than 1: 1. An analysis of debt equity ratio has, therefore, to be carried out from the twin objectives – the extent of leverage benefits available to the business and the degree of financial risk associated with high leverage. Industry average would be the best guide for deciding a well-structured optimal debt-equity ratio.

Solvency Ratio

It indicates the overall ability of the business to meet its financial commitments in the long run. Equity, as a percent of total outside liabilities yields solvency ratio. It is an extension of the debt equity ratio, in the sense that debt equity ratio reveals the relationship between equity and long term debts, whereas solvency ratio shows the proportion of equity to total outside liabilities of the business – both long term and short term. Higher the proportion of solvency, sounder is the financial position of the company.

Proprietary Ratio

Proprietary ratio relates the proportion of owners' fund to the total funds deployed in the business. Proprietors' funds are net worth of a business and total funds are capital employed. The ratio is worked out by dividing equity (net worth) by capital employed. It measures the extent of shareholders' stake in the business. Higher the ratio, larger is the financial commitment of the owners to the business and better its financial strength.

Debt Capitalization Ratio

Debt capitalization ratio is also called *leverage ratio*. It reveals the extent of exposure of the business to financial risk. It is the percentage of debt to capital employed. It is the other side of proprietary ratio. Higher the debt capitalization ratio, greater is the degree of financial risk of the business.

Debt Service Coverage Ratio

This ratio measures the ability of the business to service its debt obligations. Debt service obligation comprises interest on fixed liabilities and repayment of installments during an accounting period. Servicing ability of the business is gauged by its cash generation before payment of interest. It is profit after tax less preference dividend and dividend tax, if any, with depreciation and interest on term loans added back. Dividing the servicing ability of the firm by its service obligations gives debt service coverage ratio.

DSCR = PAT – (Pref. Dividend. + Dividend tax) + Depreciation + Interest on term liabilities. / interest on term liabilities + installments.

A debt service coverage ratio of more than 1.5 : 1 is reasonable. It can range between 1.5 to 2. If the ratio is less than 1.5 : 1, it indicates that the unit is on a hamstrung cash budget. In the event of a shortfall in expected cash inflows, the business would be exposed to higher degree of liquidity problems and the consequent chances of failure to meet commitments. On the other hand, if the ratio is more than 2 : 1, it is an indication of excess repayment capacity. When a business is faced with excess liquidity, it has to consider premature liquidation of high cost debts. The excess liquidity might also be utilized to reduce share capital of the corporates through *buy back of shares.* Financial institutions like Banks, IDBI, IFCI, ICICI, and SIDBI make use of DSCR to determine the repayment schedule of term loans granted to industrial concerns. If the projected DSCR is less is less than 1.5, the institutions elongate the period of repayment. Should the DSCR exceed 2 :1, they reduce the period of repayment and absorb the excess liquidity.

Interest Coverage Ratio

Interest referred to in this ratio is restricted to interest on fixed liabilities. Coverage has the same meaning with a difference. Here, profit before tax, depreciation and interest is the coverage. Coverage divided by only interest yields interest coverage ratio. The ratio indicates the ability of the business to service only interest obligations. The use of this ratio is limited as it applies to business houses that use perpetuities for raising funds. Perpetuities are securities that do not have specific maturity dates. Hence, the service obligation on such securities is restricted to the payment of interest alone. Interest coverage ratio also finds application in rehabilitation programmes. Readers might be aware that industries, which have become sick but have potentiality to turn back within specific time frame if properly nursed, are assisted by financial institutions in the process of recovery. Such units would not be in a position to generate adequate cash in the initial years of rehabilitation to pay both interest and installments. But they should be in a position to meet at least interest commitments. Interest coverage ratio is therefore relevant in such circumstances also. The norm for interest coverage is similar to that of debt equity ratio.

Turnover Ratios

Turnover ratios are also known as ***activity ratios*** as they measure the level of activity in a business. Activity is related to fixed assets, current assets and capital employed. In current assets, components such as inventories and debtors have definite relationship with turnover.

Fixed Assets Turnover Ratio

Turnover ratios are activity ratios. They indicate the velocity of circulation of assets in generating income. A few activity ratios that have a bearing on the momentum of operation are dealt with in these paragraphs. The first is regarding the velocity of fixed assets. The ratio is arrived at by dividing turnover by gross fixed assets. The ratio indicates the effective utilization of fixed assets in the generation of income. Every unit aspires to have a higher turnover ratio. But, the ratio differs from industry to industry, depending upon its nature. Usually, the ratio is very high in value added industries such as in services. The turnover ratio is comparatively low in process industries. A comparison with industry average would show whether the fixed assets of a particular company had been effectively used.

Working Capital /Turnover Ratio

Turnover divided by working capital gives the ratio. It indicates the number of times working capital has turned over. Working capital here means networking capital, that is, current assets minus current liabilities. The contribution of working capital to the generation of income is direct, compared to that of fixed assets, which is indirect. It is also the fact that working capital forms between 30 to 60 percent of the capital employed in Indian industries. Therefore, lower the working capital, higher would be the reduction in financing cost and consequently better would be the performance. Higher the working capital ratio, better is the utilization of working capital. However, very high ratio, compared to the industrial average, might mean *overtrading* by the business. Overtrading is a condition where the company works with thin working capital margin. It is a state of riskiness, as any delay or shortage in expected cash inflow might adversely affect short-term liquidity.

Inventory /Turnover Ratio

Turnover divided by inventory is the inventory turnover ratio. The ratio measures the rapidity with which inventory has turned over. Higher the ratio, more efficient is inventory management. By way of caution, it might be added that inventory turn over ratio, much higher than that of the industry norm, means overtrading and is risky.

Debtors /Turnover Ratio

The ratio is analogous to the average collection period. Credit sales divided by average debtors would give the ratio. This ratio has to be analyzed having the credit policy of the company in mind. Debtors are a generic term comprising bills receivables and sundry debtors. Inventory and debtor are the major subdivisions of gross working capital. Should the debtor's turnover ratio be lower than warranted by the credit policy, it means sluggishness in collection. If the ratio is higher than needed by the credit policy, it might be a sign of efficient collection set up.

Turnover/ Capital Employed Ratio

Turnover, divided by capital employed, would give the ratio. It indicates the effective use of funds made available to the business. Preference is for a higher ratio. Although there is no standard fixed for the businesses as a whole, it is customary to consider a ratio of less than 1 : 1 as wanting. It might be pointed out that higher turnover ratio would reduce fixed cost per unit of production and would make the unit more competitive.

Let us apply these ratios to Cucumber Cornwallis Ltd. The balance sheet of Cucumber Cornwallis Ltd. for the year-ended 31.3.2004 is as in the following table. The turnover of the company for the year was Rs. 27,34,60,000.

Table 9
Cucumber Cornwallis Ltd.
Balance Sheet as on 31-3-2004

Liabilities	Rs.'000	Assets	Rs.'000
Issued Capital 2,000 equity shares		Land and Buildings	1,50,000
of Rs.100 each	2,00,000	Plant and Machinery	80,000
Reserves	90,000	Stock-in-trade	1,49,000
Current liabilities	1,30,000	Sundry debtors	71,000
Profit and loss a/c	60,000	Cash and bank balance	30,000
	4,80,000		4,80,000

Calculate :

1. Fixed asset turnover ratio;
2. Working capital turnover ratio;
3. Inventory turnover ratio;
4. Debtor's turnover ratio;
5. Turnover to capital employed ratio.

Solution

1. Fixed asset turnover ratio. = TO / FA

Turnover	= Rs.27,34,60,000
Fixed assets - Land and Buildings	= Rs.15,00,00,000
Plant and Machinery	= Rs. 8,00,00,000
	= Rs.23,00,00,000
FA/TO Ratio	= 27,34,60,000/23,00,00,000
	= 1.19:1

2. Working capital turnover ratio = TO / (CA-CL)

Current assets -A	= Stock-in-trade	Rs. 14,90,00,000
	Sundry debtors	Rs. 7,10,00,000
	Cash and bank balance	Rs. 3,00,00,000
		Rs. 25,00,00,000
Current liabilities-B	=	Rs. 13,00,00,000
Working capital C (A – B)	= 25,00,00,000 – 13,00,00,000	
	= Rs.12,00,00,000	
WC / TO Ratio	= 27,34,60,000 / 12,00,00,000	
	= 2.28 : 1.	

3. Inventory turnover ratio = TO / I
   = 27,34,60,000 / 14,90,00,000
   = 1.84 : 1.

4. Debtor's turnover ratio = TO / Debtors
   = 27,34,60,000 / 7,10,00,000
   = 3.65 : 1.

5. Turnover to capital employed ratio = TO / CE

Capital employed	= Net fixed assets + Net current assets
	= 23,00,00,000 + 12,00,00,000
	= Rs.35,00,00,000
TO / CE Ratio	= 27,34,60,000 / 35,00,00,000
	= 0.78 : 1.

Profitability Ratios

Profitability is the yardstick of success or failure of an enterprise. Profitability is directly related to turnover. Higher the turnover, greater should be the profits of the business. Infact the ratio of profit should increase higher than that of sales, as every increase in sales beyond breakeven point less variable cost is profit. The indirect factors that influence profits are increase in assets, increase in working capital and increase in capital employed. Profit is also related to the owned funds of shareholders or equity. Let us examine this inter-relationship through the use of ratios.

Gross Profitability Ratio

Gross profitability measures the surplus of sales over the cost of its production (in manufacturing) and service charges (in service industries). In case of trading business, it is sales less works cost which is gross profit. Gross profitability ratio is worked out by dividing cross profit by cost of sales. It indicates the production efficiency of a manufacturing or service organization. In a trading enterprise, the ratio would roughly indicate the margin on purchases. Some analysts consider profit before taxation as gross profit. Ratios in some newspapers and financial journals also subscribe to this view. How ever, the analysis in this book is based on the concept that sales less works cost as the gross profit.

Return on Investment (ROI)

ROI is an important measure of operating profit. It is also called yield on capital employed. It reveals the operational efficiency of the business. ROI is worked out by dividing operating profit by capital employed. The ratio justifies the continuation or otherwise of a line of activity. ROI should at least cover average cost of funds for the business. ROI, when it is more than average cost of funds, increases the wealth of the enterprise to the shareholders. Usually, return on capital employed is compared with the market rate of capitalization. Market rate of capitalization is the rate of return on investments in similar risk category of industries. When a particular business has a ROI greater than the market rate, its share price in the market tends to increase and vice versa.

Assets Profitability

Assets induce production and production increases sale, which in turn influences profitability. The contribution of investment in different categories of assets in the profits of a business is an indicator of the effectiveness of operation. This relationship is measured by relating ROI as a percent of concerned assets. We know that assets of a business are fixed assets and working capital assets. We also know that working capital is current assets less current liabilities. Hence we should assess the profitability of fixed assets and working capital. Fixed assets' profitability is ROI / Gross Fixed Assets. The profitability of working capital is ROI / CA – CL. Profitability of capital employed is yet another criterion of the contribution of net fixed assets and working capital to profitability. This ratio is worked out by dividing ROI by capital employed or ROI / C E. Return on the shareholders' fund or net worth is an indicator of equity earning and is calculated by dividing ROI by net worth or ROI / NW.

Du Pond Control Chart

Du Pond employed a variation of ROI for control purposes. Capital employed turnover ratio multiplied by the net profitability ratio would also give the return on investment (ROI). Capital employed turnover ratio is turnover divided by capital employed. The net profitability ratio reveals the relationship between net profit and sales and is calculated by dividing net profit by sales turnover. In effect it means that capital employed in Du Pond method is net profit divided by capital employed, as against the normal practice of operating profit divided by capital employed as (TO/CE) × (NP/TO) is equal to NP/TO. Suppose sales in a company are Rs.4,50,000, net profits Rs.45,000 and capital employed is Rs.2,25,000, then the capital turnover ratio would be 2 and the net profitability ratio is 10%. The ROI would thus be 2 × 10% is 20%. It might be observed that any change in any the constituents of the ratio would impact ROI. If the sales are Rs.3,00,000, then the ROI would be 19.99%. Du Pond first used this principle in a chart form for control purposes. And it has come to be referred as Du Pond Control Chart. A replica of the chart is given below:

DU POND CONTROL CHART

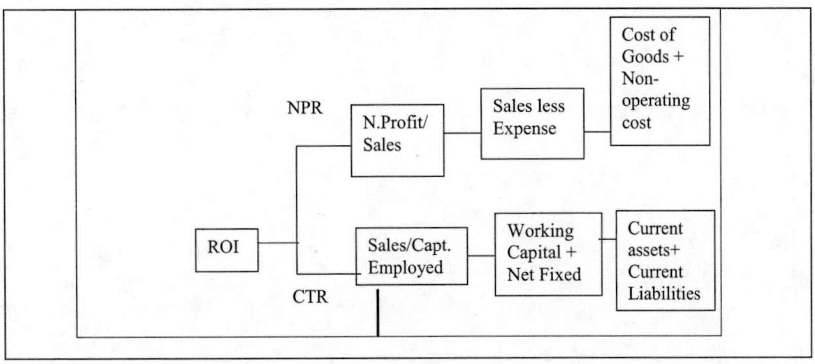

ROI = Return on investment
NPR= Net profit ratio
CTR = Capital employed turnover ratio

The above chart depicts the sequential impact of the components on the ratio, which in turn would affect the ROI. It might be relevant to point out that the chart is not very popular with the corporates now a days, as more sophisticated ratios are devised for the purpose.

Net Profitability Ratio

Net profit is the surplus after meeting all costs, both operational and non-operational and after deducting taxes. If the business has preference capital, dividend on preference capital is to be deducted. With the introduction of dividend tax, dividend tax should also be deducted to arrive at net profit. Net profit frequently referred to as PAT is thus profit after tax, after preference dividend and dividend tax. PAT is also divisible profit belonging to the owners. The value of equity or intrinsic value of the business depends on the volume of net profit. Net profit divided by turnover, would give the net profitability ratio. It indicates how profitable the working of the business is to the owners during the concerned accounting period.

The following are figures from the trading activities of Blind Traders Limited for the year ended 30th

Table 10
Blind Traders Ltd.

	Rs.
Sales	7,24,567
Purchases	3,22,432
Opening Stock	76,257
Closing Stock	98,512
Sales Returns	21,419
Purchase returns	18,350
Wages	76,492
Factory overheads:	
Depreciation on plant and machinery	1,04,752
Power and fuel	43,876
Insurance	14,238
Consumables	9,421
Selling and distribution expenses:	
Salaries	15,300
Advertising	4,700
Traveling	2,000

<u>Administrative expenses</u> :	
Salaries	27,000
Rent	2,700
Stationery, Postage etc.	2,500
Depreciation on office equipment	9,300
Other Charges	16,500
Interest	17,123
Discount received	9,000
Income from investment	3,000
Loss on Sale of Assets	4,000
Taxation	18,654
Other informations:	
Share capital 50,000 shares of Rs.10 each	5,00,000
Reserves	6,45,975
Surplus	65,432
Gross fixed assets	9,64,907
Depreciation	5,98,765
Net fixed assets	3,66,142
Current assets	2,65,987
Current liabilities	1,34,678

Let us

a. Arrange the above figures in a form suitable for analysis, and

b. Show the following ratios:

- *Gross profitability ratio;*
- *Operating ratio;*
- *Operating profit ratio;*
- *Net profit Ratio;*
- *Fixed assets' profitability ratio;*
- *Working capital profitability ratio*
- *Capital employed profitability ratio and*
- *Net worth profitability ratio.*

Solution

The above figures from the profit and loss account are to be grouped before analyzing. Detailed discussion on the methodology of grouping was done in Chapter 04.Grouping of data given in the problem in a form suitable for analysis given in the following table.

Table 11

	Rs.
1. Turn over[1]	7,03,148
2. Less: works cost[2]	5,27,537
3. Gross profit (1-2)	1,75,611
4. Less: Operating costs [3]	80,000
5. Operating profit-EBIT (3-4)	95,611
6. Less: Interest	17,123
7. Less: Other non-operating costs	4,000
8. Add: Non-operating profits[4]	12,000
9. Profit before tax (5-6-7+8)	86,488
10. Less: Taxation	18,654
11. Less: Preference dividend, if any	—
12. Net Profit (9-10-11)	67,834
13. Internal accruals (12+ depreciation)	1,81,886
14. Net worth[5]	12,11,407
15. Capital employed[6]	4,97,451

a. Notes:

	Rs.
[1] Sales - gross	7,24,567
Less : Sales returns	21,419
Net sales (Turnover)	7,03,148
[2] Works cost.	
Opening stock	76,257
Add. Purchases	3,22,432
Less. Returns	21,419
Less closing stock	98,512
Material consumed	2,78,758
Add. Wages	76,492
Add. Factory overheads:	
Depreciation	1,04,752
Power and fuel	43,876

Insurance		14,238
Consumables		9,421
Works or factory cost		5,27,537

[3]Operating costs.

Administrative costs- A

Salaries	27,000
Rent	2,700
Stationery, postage etc.	2,500
Depreciation	9,300
Other charges	16,500
	58,000

Selling and distribution costs-B

Salaries	15,300
Advertising	4,700
Traveling	2,000
	22,000
Operating costs -A+B	80,000

[4]Non-operating income

Discount received	9,000
Income from investment	3,000
	12,000

[5]Net worth

Share capital	5,00,000	
Reserves	6,45,975	
Surplus	65,432	
Net worth		12,11,407

[6] Capital employed

Net fixed assets		3,66,142
Current assets	2,65,987	
Current liabilities	1,34,678	
Net current assets		1,31,309
Capital employed		4,97,451

b. Ratios

1. Gross profit ratio or gross profit to cost of sales ratio: Gross profit ratio is the relationship between gross profit and cost of sales. The ratio indicates the production efficiency of a manufacturing organization. The ratio is worked out by dividing the gross profit by cost of sales or GP / CS.

   Gross profit =Rs. 1,75,611; cost of sales = works cost + operating cost= Rs 5,27,537 + Rs.80,000= Rs.6,07,537.

   GPR =1,75,611 / 6,07,537 × 100 = 28.91%

2. Operating ratio or operating costs to turnover ratio.. Operating ratio establishes the relationship between operating cost and sales. Operating cost comprises administrative and selling costs. The ratio is arrived at by dividing operating costs by turnover (OC / TO). The importance of the ratio is to enlighten the management as to proportion of operating costs.Cost reductions are usually attempted in this segment.

   Operating ratio = OC /TO.

   OC = Rs.80,000; Turnover = Rs. 7,03,148 .

   Operating ratio = 80,000 / 7,03,148 × 100 = 11.38%

3. Operating profit ratio or operating profit to turnover ratio. This ratio establishes the relationship between operating profit and turnover. Operating profit is profit before interest and tax or earnings before interest and taxes, commonly referred to as PBIT or EBIT. Operating profit is the real return, as interest and taxes are transfer items. Operating profit ratio is calculated by dividing operating profit by turnover(EBIT / TO).

   Operating profit ratio = EBIT / TO.

   = EBIT = Rs. 95,611; TO

   = Rs.7,03,148.

   Operating profit ratio = 95,611 / Rs. 7,03,148 × 100

   = 13.60%

4. Net profit Ratio or net profit to turnover ratio. Net profit is the profit after tax, commonly referred to as profit after tax (PAT).Profit after tax is the profit of the shareholders. It thus has a proprietary relationship with sales. PAT / TO would yield net profitability ratio.

   NPR = NP / TO

   = NP = Rs 67,834; TO = Rs 7,03,148.

   Net profitability ratio = Rs 67,834 / Rs 7,03,148 × 100 = 9.65%

5. Fixed assets' profitability ratio or profitability to fixed assets ratio. The relationship between profitability and fixed assets has already been discussed. Fixed assets by

inducing productivity influence profitability of a business. Profit for the purpose of the ratio is operating profit. It is EBIT / GFA.

Fixed assets' profitability = EBIT / GFA.

EBIT = Rs._95,611 ; GFA = Rs. 9,64,907.

Fixed assets profitability ratio = Rs.95,611 / Rs.9,64,907 × 100 = 9.91%

6. Working capital profitability ratio or profitability to working capital ratio. Working capital is the circulating asset that provides input for production. It is current assets less current liabilities. EBIT divided by working capital would give the ratio.

   Working capital profitability ratio = EBIT / WC.

   EBIT = Rs.95,611; working capital = Rs. 1,31,309.

   Working capital profitability ratio = Rs.95,611 / Rs.1,31,309 × 100 = 72.81

7. Capital employed profitability ratio or profitability to capital employed ratio. Profitability is related to capital employed, as it measures the effective use of operating funds. EBIT divided by capital employed would give the ratio.

   Capital employed profitability ratio = EBIT / CE.

   EBIT = Rs 95,611;

   Capital employed= Rs. 4,97,451

   Capital employed profitability ratio = Rs 95,611 / Rs.4,97,451 ×100 = 19.22%

8. Net worth profitability ratio or profitability to net worth ratio. As shareholders are interested in profit after tax, PAT is profit in net worth profitability ratio. The ratio establishes the rate of earning of the shareholders' funds. It also indicates the rate at which retained earnings would earn .In short it is the current growth rate of the business. The ratio is worked out by dividing PAT by net worth.

   Net worth profitability ratio = PAT / NW.

   PAT = Rs. 67,834 ; net worth = Rs. 12,11,407.

   Net worth profitability ratio =Rs.67,834 / 12,11,407 × 100 = 5.60%

Earnings Per Share

It is the earning of each share in the divisible profit pool and is the basis for strategic decisions, such as dividend payout, plough back, growth rate etc. Profit after tax divided by the number of equity shares outstanding yields earnings per share (EPS).

EPS= PAT / No. Equity Shares

EPS also exerts its weight on the market price of the shares. In income stocks, EPS divided by the desired rate of return of the investor, would determine the purchase price of the share.

Po = EPS/R

Where,

Po is the maximum price at which an investor would like to invest in a stock. In other words, it is the cut off market price for the investor. If the stock were quoted at a price equal to or below the price, the investor would invest.

R is desired rate of return of investor.

Let us apply the equation in the case of an investor, whose desired rate of return is 18%.He desires to invest in the stocks of Honolulu Ltd.The EPS of Honolulu Ltd. is Rs.5.5.The investor would consider the maximum price at which he could buy the stock by applying the formula, Po = EPS / R,which works out to Rs.30.55 per share (5.5/ .18 = 30.55).If the market price of the company's shares were quoted at Rs. 30.55 or lower, he would buy the shares.

Return on Equity

EPS should be distinguished from Return on Equity (ROE). ROE is the return on net worth or equity. Equity divided by number of equity shares is equity per share. In other words, equity is the intrinsic value of an equity share. EPS, divided by equity per share is the ROE. Where number of equity shares is not available, total earnings divided by total net worth would give ROE.

ROE = EPS / Equity Per Share.

Dividend Payout Ratio

Dividend proposed per share divided by EPS is the payout ratio. It is that portion of EPS, which is paid out to shareholders as dividend. For example, the earning per share of Glow Wears Ltd. was Rs.4 and the company declared a dividend of Rs.2.5 per share, the dividend payout ratio would be 2.5 / 4 × 100 = 62.5%. The dividend pay out depends upon two important factors. In companies where there are investment opportunities, the tendency on the part of management would be to refrain from declaring higher rate of dividend, as it needs funds for investment. The other factor which influences dividend payout is the comparison between the actual rate of capitalization and the market rate of capitalization. Actual rate of capitalization means the rate of return the company is earning on its equity. Market rate of capitalization means the prevailing rate of return for investments in similar risk category. When the actual rate of capitalization is higher than the market rate of capitalization, a lower dividend payout would increase the market value of the shares of the business. In case where the market rate of capitalization is higher than the actual rate, it is advisable to increase the payout to maintain the market price.

Market Price on Growth Securities

In growth oriented corporates, retained earnings (i.e. EPS less dividend payout) multiplied by return on equity (ROE) is the rate at which the future profits would grow.

$$G = RE \times ROE$$

Where,

G = Growth rate,

RE = Retained earnings in %

ROE = % Return on equity

For example, in a corporate with EPS of Rs.7, dividend payout of 40%, ROE of 12%, the growth rate would be 7.2% (60% of 12% = 7.2%).

Value of a Business

Market value of a business is the aggregate of the market value of debt, preferred stock and equity. It is

$$V_m = D_m + P_m + E_m$$

Where,

V_m is market value of firm

P_m is market value of preference

D_m is the market value of debt

E_m is market value of equity

It follows from the equation that $E_m = V_m - P_m - D_m$ .Market value of the firm in the short run is the market capitalization. How ever, in the long run, V_m would be the intrinsic value of the firm. Intrinsic value is the sum total of future cash flows of a business during its existence discounted at the desired rate of return.

Free Cash Flow

Value of a business, for the specific purpose of takeover and merger, is the sum of the future cash flows of the business during its useful life. Cash flow for the purpose of valuing the firm is free cash flow, which is a derivation from the normal cash flow concept we had already seen. *Free cash flow* is the profit after tax with depreciation added back less investment during the year. Life of the business is considered to be perpetual as per going concern concept, which we have seen in the first chapter. As it is not possible to estimate the life of a firm and as the discounted figures of the future cash flows in the long run would become negligible, economists have introduced *horizon* concept for the purpose of valuation of the firm. *Horizon is the point of time from where the growth of the firm would become saturated.* The useful life of a firm is split into two distinct segments –one up to the horizon period and the other after the horizon period and the discounted cash flow of the two segments would be the value of the firm. Free cash flows *up to the Horizon year* i.e. the year before horizon is expected to set in, is discounted at the desired rate of return in the normal way. Thus PV of free cashflow upto Horizon year is $C_1/(1 + R) + C_2/(1+R)^2 \ldots C_n (1 + R)^{h-1}$ and PV after Horizon value is

$1/(1 + R)^h \times FCF_h / R - G$, Where,

R is rate of return;

h is horizon year;

FCR is free cash flow;

G is growth rate of the year immediately following horizon year

An example of the calculation of the value of a firm is as follows:
Grow Quick Corporation Ltd. has projected its cash flow for the next 10 years (table 12).

Table 12

Year	Pat. +Depreciation	Investment	Free cash flow	Growth rate in profit-%
1	22.35	23.60	–1.25	—
2	25.03	28.15	–3.12	11.99
3	28.04	30.55	–2.51	12.03
4	31.40	30.05	1.16	11.98
5	35.17	28.50	6.67	12.01
6	38.25	22.80	10.45	8.76
7	42.05	18.24	23.81	9.94
8	45.44	14.59	30.85	8.06
9	48.17	11.85	36.32	6.01
10	51.11	9.30	41.81	6.10

Its desired rate of return is 18%.

In this example, 8th year is the horizon year. The value of the firm would, therefore, be the discounted cash flow upto 7th year plus the PV of horizon period. Using the formula it would be as under:

Value up to horizon $= -1.25/1.18 + -3.12/(1.18)^2 + -2.51/(1.18)^3 + 1.16/(1.18)^4 + 6.67/(1.18)^5 + 10.45/1.18^6 + 23.81/(1.16)^7$

= Rs.<u>10.03 lakhs</u>

Value after horizon $= 1/1.18^6 \times 23.81/(0.18 - .0806)$

= Rs.<u>88.65 lakhs</u>

Value of the firm = 10.03 + 88.65 = <u>Rs.98.68 lakhs</u>.

Liquidity Ratios

Liquidity is the ability of the business to meet its short-term commitments for cash without affecting operations. Short-term requirements for cash arise on account of working capital needs such as payment for materials, wages, salaries, rents, administrative and selling expenses, payment of interest, tax, and dividend and repayment of borrowings. Liquidity is basically the relationship between short-term assets (current assets) and short-term liabilities (current liabilities).

Current Ratio

Of the three important ratios that reveal the short-term liquidity of a business, current ratio is the most important. Current assets divided by current liabilities and provisions gives the ratio. The safer norm is 1.5: 1, that is, 1.5 units of current assets back up every one unit of current liability. Liquidity is the ability of the business to meet its short-term commitments as and when they arise. Short-term commitments, for the purpose of liquidity ratio are obligations payable with in a year In prescribing a ratio of 1.5, 0.5 is the safety margin to take care of unexpected delays in converting current assets into cash. Current ratio of less than 1.5: 1 indicates tight liquidity conditions, while a ratio of more than 2: 1 is a symptom of surplus liquidity. As liquid assets yield less or no return, excess liquidity would eat into profitability. On the other hand, a ratio of less than 1.5: 1 means liquidity crunch, which might lead to inability to meet the commitments as and when fall due. This is a state of insolvency. It is thus a trade off between profitability and liquidity. Business shall sacrifice profitability but not liquidity. Therefore, in the interest of continuing in business, entrepreneurs tend to keep a safer current ratio.

OPERATING CYCLE

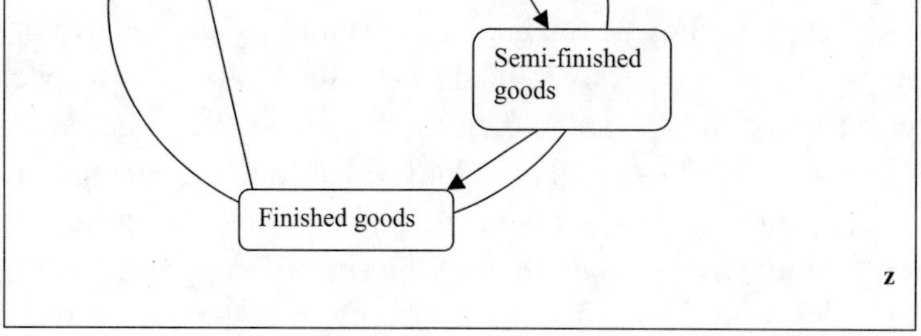

Quick Ratio

In the groups of current assets, certain assets are nearer to cash in the working capital cycle, (also called operating cycle) than others. Look at the diagram depicting the working capital cycle. All business activities commence with cash. Cash is thus the staring point of operating cycle. With cash, raw materials are acquired and wages and other input costs are met. The next phases in production are semi-finished and finished goods. When finished goods are sold, receivables result. On realization of receivables cash flows back into the kitty. A close look at the operating cycle reveals that bills receivables are at the end of the cycle and is not an integral part of the production process. Further, there are certain other items of current assets like loans and advances and marketable securities, which are not the results of operation process. These are current assets caused by non-operational policies of the business and their existence or otherwise do not impede the production process. These assets are collectively called quick assets, as these can be quickly liquidated without affecting the smooth process of operation of the business.

On the other hand, materials, semi-finished goods and finished goods, collectively termed inventory are essential for smooth operation. Thus, liquid assets are current assets less inventories. The ratio of these assets to current liabilities is called ***quick ratio or acid test ratio***. A quick ratio of 1 : 1 is considered adequate to ensure uninterrupted operation. Unfortunately, many Indian industries have a quick ratio of less than this minimum. However, with the tempo of globalization of the economy picking up, there is increasing awareness of adhering to the standard quick ratio. Currently, quick ratios of multinational Indian companies are well within the norm.

Average Collection Period

Another yardstick that indicates the liquidity of a business is the average collection period. Average collection period indicates the time taken by the business to realize receivables. Early collection of receivables within the permissible period would improve liquidity and profitability. The ratio is worked out by dividing the average receivables by credit sales of the period. Average receivable is adding receivable as on the opening date and that on closing date of the accounting period and dividing the product by two. Average collection period has to be compared with the credit policy of the business. Supposing the receivables as on the opening and closing dates of the year are Rs.27.50 lakhs and Rs.32.46 lakhs respectively and the credit sales of the period is Rs.162.45 lakhs, then the average collection period would be 67 days (Rs.27.50 lakhs + Rs.32.46 lakhs / 2) /Rs.162.45 lakhs × 365. Supposing the credit policy of the business is equal or more than the average collection period, the collection mechanism of the company is well geared. On the other hand, if the collection period at 67 days were more than the credit period allowable it would show the laxity in collection of receivables. This would affect the liquidity of the business.

The balance sheet of Zorastra Zubin Ltd. as on 31st March is in table 13.

Table 13

Liabilities	Rs.	Assets	Rs.
Share Capital	2,00,000	Land and Buildings	1,40,000
10%Preference capital	30,000	Plant and machinery	3,50,000
General Reserve	40,000	Stock	2,00,000
12% Debentures	4,20,000	Sundry Debtors	1,00,000
Sundry Creditors	1,00,000	Bills Receivables	10,000
Bills Payables	50,000	Cash at Bank	40,000
	8,40,000		8,40,000

Let us calculate the activity ratios for the company such as

(1) Current ratio

(2) Quick ratio

(3) Inventory to working Capital

(4) Debt to Equity Ratio

(5) Proprietary Ratio

(6) Capital Gearing ratio

(7) Current Assets to Fixed Assets ratio

Solution

1. Current ratio = current assets/current liabilities

Current assets A :	
Stock	2,00,000
Sundry Debtors	1,00,000
Bills Receivables	10,000
Cash at Bank	40,000
Total A	3,50,000
Current liabilities B:	
Sundry Creditors	1,00,000
Bills Payables	50,000
Total B	1,50,000
Current ratio A/B	= 2.33 : 1

2. Quich ratio = quick assets / current liabilities.

Quick assets A	= current assets less stocks and prepaid expenses	
Sundry Debtors		1,00,000
Bills Receivables		10,000
Cash at Bank		40,000
Total	A	1,50,000
Current liabilities	*B*	1,50,000
Quick ratio	A/B = 1,50,000/1,50,000 = 1 : 1	

3. Inventory to working capital = inventory/working capital

Working capital = current assets-current liabilities = 2,00,000

Inventory(stock) = 2,00,000

Inventory working capital ratio = 2,00,000/2,00,000 =1 : 1

4. Debt to Equity Ratio = Debt/equity

Debt : 12% Debentures = Rs.4,20,000

Equity :

Share Capital	= Rs. 2,00,000
Preference capital	= Rs. 30,000
General Reserve	= Rs. 40,000
	Rs. 2,70,000

Debt equity ratio = *4,20,000/2,70,000*

= 1.56: 1

5. Proprietary Ratio = Equity/capital employed.

Equity(networth) = Rs. 2,70,000

Capital employed = Net fixed assets + net current assets

Net fixed assets	= Land and Buildings :	Rs. 1,40,000
	Plant and machinery :	Rs. 3,50,000
		Rs. 4,90,000
Net current assets(working capital)		Rs. 2,00,000
Capital employed		Rs. 6,90,000

Proprietary ratio = 2,70,000/6,90,000 × %

= 39.13%.

6. Capital Gearing ratio = Preference capital/equity × %

Preference capital = Rs.30,000

Equity = Rs.2,70,000

Capital gearing ratio =30,000/2,70,000* 100

=11.11%.

7. Current assets to fixed assets ratio = GFA / GCA

As no gross fixed assets are available in the illustration, net fixed assets are taken. But the true ratio would be gross fixed assets divided by gross current assets.

= 4,90,000 / 3,50,000

= 1.4: 1.

Comprehensive Illustration

In the light of the discussions we had so far on the significance of the different groups of ratios, let us take up the analysis of the data contained in the financial statements of Surya Prakash Textile Ltd. and analyze the financial statements from all angles. Please remember that the data relates to a prominent Mumbai based textile unit. The name and date of the statement are however changed. As a pre-requisite before undertaking the analysis, the information grouped in the previous chapter is reduced to ratios with industry average, wherever required, and presented in the following Table:

Table 4.14

I. Structural ratios:

(a) Debt equity ratio: **(Rs Crores)**

	2002	**2003**
i) Fixed liabilities (debt)	1695.50	550.00
ii) Equity	4473.80	2532.96
iii) Debt equity ratio (i/ii)	0.38 : 1	0.22 : 1
iv) Industry norm	1.33 : 1	1.23 : 1

(b) Solvency ratio:

i) Equity	4473.80	2532.96
ii) Fixed liabilities	1695.50	550.00
iii) Current liabilities and provisions	4669.02	5757.37
iv) Total outside liabilities (ii + iii)	6364.52	6307.37
v) Solvency ratio (i/iv)	70.29%	40.16%

(c) Proprietary ratio:

i) Equity	4473.80	2532.96
ii) Capital employed	6034.96	3054.64
iii) Proprietary ratio (i as % of ii)	74.13%	82.92%

(d) Debt capitalization ratio:

i) Debt	1695.50	550.00
ii) Capital employed	6034.96	3054.64
iii) Debtcapitalizationratio(i %of ii)	28.1%	18%

(e) Debt service coverage ratio (DSCR):

i) Interest on bonds	301.56	167.35
ii) Bonds redeemed	373.45	246.89
iii) Service obligation	675.01	414.24
iv) Profit after tax	354.03	512.65
v) Depreciation	240.52	148.90
vi) Interest on bonds	301.56	414.89
vii)Funds for service	896.11	1076.44
viii)DSCR (vii/iii)	1.33	2.60

(f) Interest coverage ratio (ICR):

i) Interest on bonds	301.56	167.35
ii) Funds for service	896.11	1076.44
iii) ICR (ii / i)	2.97	6.43

II. Turnover ratios:

(a) Fixed assets turnover ratio (FTO):

i) Turnover	10036.39	9013.18
ii) Gross fixed assets	7533.58	6180.31
iii) FATO ratio (i/ ii)	1.33	1.46
iv) Industry average	2.45	2.36

(b) Working capital turnover ratio (WCTO):

i) Turnover	10036.39	9013.18
ii) Current assets	4691.09	3933.35
iii) Current liabilities	4669.02	5757.37
iv) Working capital (ii - iii)	22.07	1824.02

v) Working capital turnover ration (i / iv)	4.55	1.57
vi) Industry average	1.3 times	2.7 times

(c) Inventory turnover ratio (ITO):

i) Turnover	10036.39	9013.18
ii) Inventory	3521.16	2875.63
iii) ITO (i % ii)	2.86	3.13
iv) Industry norm	4.25	3.65

(d) Debtors turnover ratio (DTO):

i) Turnover	10036.39	9013.18
ii) Debtors / receivables	1062.76	967.34
iii) DTO	9.44 times	9.32 times
iv) Industrial average	11.50 times	10.00 times

(e) Turnover capital employed ratio (TCE):

i) Turnover	10036.339	9013.18
ii) Capital employed	6034.96	3054.64
iii) TCE	1.66	2.95
iv) Industrial average	3.75	3.50

III. Profitability ratios:

(a) Gross profitability ratio (GPR):

i) Turnover	10036.39	9013.18
ii) Works cost	9328.89	7470.56
iii) Gross profit (I - ii)	707.50	1542.62
iv) GPR (iii % i)	7.1%	17.12
v) Industrial average	6%	18%

(b) Return on investment (ROI):

i) Return (EBIT)	67.01	910.86
ii) Capital Investment (Capital employed)	6034.96	3054.64
iii) ROI (i as% of ii)	1.11%	2.98
iv) Industrial average	1.25%	2.5%

(c) Net profitability ratio (NPR):

i) Profit after tax	354.03	512.65
ii) Turnover	10036.39	9013.18
iii) NPR (i % ii)	3.53%	5.69%
iv) Industrial average	13.75%	12.25%

(d) Earnings per share (EPS)

i) Earnings (PAT less preference dividend/dividend tax, if any)	354.03	512.65
ii) No. of equity shares (lakhs)	94.054	33.797
iii) EPS (i / ii)	Rs.3.76	15.17
iv) Industrial average	Rs.15.60	14.57

(e) Price earning ratio (PER):

i) Market price	Rs.24	48
ii) EPS	3.76	15.17
iii) PER (i % ii) (times)	6.38	3.16
iv) Industry norm (times)	17.50	16.00

(f) Dividend payout ratio (DPOR):

i) Dividend	78.84	84.49
ii) PAT	354.03	512.65
iii) Dividend payout (i % ii)	22.27%	16.48%
iv) Retained earnings	77.73%	83.52%

(g) Economic value addition (EVA):

i) PAT	354.03	512.65
ii) Depreciation + Interest on debt	240.52	148.90
iii) Cash profit	594.55	661.55
iv) Cost of capital (10%)	603.50	305.46
v) EVA	-8.95	356.09

IV. Liquidity ratios:

(a) Current ratio (CR):

i) Current assets	4691.09	3933.35
ii) Current liabilities	4669.02	5757.37
iii) QR	1.01	0.68
iv) Industry average	1.43	1.20

(b) Quick ratio (QR):

i) Liquid assets (Note 5)	1169.93	1057.72
ii) Current liabilities	4669.02	5757.37
iii) QR	0.25	0.18
iv) Industry average	0.73	0.67

(c) Average collection period (ACP):

i) Receivable at the beginning	967.34	
ii) Receivables at the end	1062.76	967.34
iii) Average receivables	1015.05	967.34
iv) Credit sales	10036.39	9013.18
v) ACP (iii % iv) × 365	37 days	39 days
vi) Industry average	30 days	30 days

Analysis

Some analysts have stretched the analysis too far using ratios of the components of each head. They have extended the study to trivial aspects, which had led to the nickname ***thousand ratios study***. Computing and analyzing unwanted ratios would, besides adding complexity to the problem, create confusion in the minds of the users of the ratios. Hence, for our analysis, only ratios that are crucial are chosen and that too under four broad heads – structural, turnover, liquidity and profitability. The operational efficiency and financial position of the selected company are studied in the following paragraphs.

Lopsided Financial Structure

Structural ratios reveal the financial position of an enterprise. Financial position is gauged through the long-term solvency of the business. These ratios would reveal whether the business would be able to meet its commitments in the long run. The comparison is between the blend of debt and equity. The prime indicator of long-term solvency of the business is debt equity ratio. Surya Prakash Textiles Ltd. is financially sound with a low debt-equity ratio 0.38 as at the end of March 2003compared to the industrial average of 1.33. The position was a shade better in 2002 when it was only 0.22. The company is low levered. The reasons are not far to seek. The average return on capital employed works out to paltry 1.1%. No worthwhile lender would extent loans to a company with this rate. The company has necessarily to depend on its owned funds. The increase in its retained earnings is an indicator of this trend.

Low Returns

As the rate of return at 1.1%, is far below the market rate of borrowings, which ranges between 10 to 12 percent, depending upon the risk, the company could not enjoy the benefits of financial leverage. As we know, *financial leverage operates when the ROI of the business is higher than the market rate of borrowing*. Consequent to low debt component, the business has high solvency ratio at 70.20% in 2003. In the previous year, even the solvency prospect was low at 40.16%. The company had, during the year, met bulk of its requirements for funds by increasing its share capital (by over Rs.3 crores) and higher rate of retained earnings (by about 78 percent). The company is finding it difficult to service even its meager debts, its debt service coverage ratio being 1.33. The permanent solution would be to increase its earning capacity, if necessary by diversification. Otherwise, it would be an easy target for acquisition.

Higher Production Loss

As far as the earning capacity of the unit is concerned, it leaves much to be desired. The gross profitability at 8 percent compared to the industrial norm of 18 percent speaks volumes about the production inefficiency of the unit. The reasons are obvious. The miscellaneous income, during the year, includes sale of waste cotton at Rs.8.57 crores, as against a mere Rs.0.61 lakhs in the previous year. There appears to be an unprecedented higher production loss. Efficiency in production has to be looked into.

Illiquidity

The deterioration in the performance of the company had affected its liquidity. It s current ratio at 1.01 compared to industrial average of 1.43 and its quick ratio at 0.25 compared to industry norm of 0.75 are testimony to this state of affairs. The working capital position is tight and the company is working on a hamstrung cash budget.

The low turnover ratios are also indicators of the unsatisfactory operation of the unit. Fixed assets turnover ratio at 1.33 (industry 2.45) indicates inefficient use of capital assets. The phenomenal working capital turnover ratio at 454 times, rings the alarm of massive overtrading by the company. It might break down at any moment and pave the way for insolvency.

The overall performance of the company during the year is very bleak and the unit is moving towards sickness.

Fall In Market Capitalization

The low earning per share at Rs.3.76 compared to the industrial average of Rs.15.60 and the price earning ratio of 6.38 times as against industrial norm of 17.50 times are all pointers of the unsatisfactory working of the unit. As a result, the market price of shares had fallen to Rs.24 compared to market price of similar shares at Rs.273. (Market price is equal to EPS × PER. Here, the industrial EPS is Rs.15.6 and PER is 17.5 times).

Signs of Incipient Sickness

As mentioned earlier, the ROI is at the bottom; about 1.1 percent compared to the industrial average of 12.5 percent. The profitability had been eroded by high establishment costs (above Rs.9 crores) and financial charges (again above Rs.9 crores). This coupled with the economic value destroyed as at the end of the year, indicate that the company is showing symptoms of incipient sickness.

Role of Ratio Study

Ratios are effective trend indicators. They pin point the areas of strengths and weaknesses of the business. They are tools to evaluate the business and aid in the corporate financial planning. It should, however, be remembered that *ratios are not decision packages*. They are catalyst in decision-making. They feed the requisite data, in the desired form and at the appropriate time to the decision makers. Once this is done, the purpose of ratio analysis might be considered to have been fulfilled. It is then left to the decision-makers to make use the analyzed information suitably and take corrective steps.

Balance Sheets From Ratios

It has been seen from the above paragraphs how the mute data of the financial statements could be made to speak through ratios. The relationship between the ratios and the balance sheet data is very useful to the analysts in many ways. However some analysts had utilized this relationship and had embarked upon a game of constructing balance sheets from the ratios, which to me is meaningless. I am at a loss to understand the purpose behind such exercises.

What is further disgusting is that The Institute of Chartered Accountants of India and a few reputed universities have also followed up the path of these analysts and have included the construction of balance sheets from ratios as part of their syllabus. For the benefit of those students who undergo courses in these organizations, I have included an analysis of this blatantly useless exercise in the next few paragraphs. As an illustration a question from the examination papers of a well-known university in the south (updated) is below.

The following ratios are taken from the balance sheet of a company as at 31st December 2005. Draw up the balance sheet of the company.

Current ratio	2.5
Working capital	Rs.3,00,000
Liquid ratio	1.5
Stock turnover ratio	6
Gross profit ratio	20%
Debt collection period	2 months
Share holders capital	Rs.5,00,000
Reserves & Surplus	Rs.2,80,000
Fixed assets turnover ratio on cost of sales	2

Analyzed Solution

In the illustration above, a few figures are provided and others are to be calculated using the ratios. Readers would have first to arrange the available figures as a prelude to the finding of the rest. So, a proforma balance sheet has to be drawn up and given figures are to be posted to their respective sides as under:

<u>Liabilities</u>	
Share capital	5,00,000
Reserves and Surplus	2,80,000
Current liabilities	xxxxxxx
<u>Assets</u>	
Current assets	xxxxxxx
Les Current liabilities	xxxxxxx
Net Current assets	3,00,000

Next, by using the ratios, we can fill up the missing data of the balance sheet. For this, we have to proceed from known figures. Working capital, being the net of current assets over current liabilities is Rs.3,00,000. Current ratio, which is current assets divided by current liabilities, is 2.5,which indicates that for every one rupee of current liability, the current asset is Rs.2.50. The excess of current assets over current liabilities is, thus Rs.1.50. in other words, 1.5 of 2.5 is Rs.3,00,000 and therefore, 2.5 (representing current assets) is Rs.5,00,000 (3,00,000 / 1.5 × 2.5). Following the same thread, current liabilities, being current assets less working capital are Rs.2,00,000 (5,00,000-3,00,000). Liquid ratio of 1.5 means that liquid assets are 1.5 times current liabilities or Rs.3,00,000. Total current assets less liquid assets are inventories (stocks). Thus, the closing stock of the company was Rs.2,00,000 (5,00,000 – 3,00,000). The stock turnover ratio is 6 times, meaning that sales are 6 times closing stock(6×2,00,000) or Rs.12,00,000. Debt collection period is 2 months. That is. 1/6th of sales is debtors or receivables, which means sundry debtors are Rs.2,00,000. Other liquid assets, including cash, should therefore be Rs.1, 00,000(total liquid assets of Rs 3,00,000 less debtors of Rs.2,00,000). Sales less gross profit is cost of sales. In this illustration, gross profit ratio is 20% and therefore cost of sales is 80% of sale, which is Rs.9,60,000. Cost of sales is twice fixed assets, which means fixed assets are ½ of cost of sales, that is fixed assets are Rs.4,80,000. If these figures are arranged in the balance sheet, it looks as under:

Table 15

Balance sheet of—as on 31.12.2003

Liabilities	Rs.	Assets	Rs.
Share capital	5,00,000	Fixed assets	4,80,000
Reserves and Surplus	2,80,000	Stock	2,00,000
Current liabilities	2,00,00	Sundry debtors/	
		Receivables	2,00,000
		Other liquid assets	
		including cash	1,00,000
	9,80,000		9,80,000

Summary

Since the preparation of financial statements are influenced by the individual perception and understanding of the businessman, they are presented in a variety of ways. This is particularly so in case on non-corporate reporting. The multiplicity in the methods of financial reporting had rendered the reading of these statements highly complicated. With a view to usher in an element of uniformity in their presentation Generally Accepted Accounting Practices have been evolved. As the principles lacked legal sanctity, businessman adopted them when suited and discarded the principles when they hurt them. Corporates are compelled by their statutes to adhere to a uniform pattern. In non-corporate businesses, where the preparation and presentation of financial reports is not mandatory, myriad of ways are adopted. When financial reports are prepared in multiple ways, understanding the information contained therein becomes highly personalized. Any analysis would be meaningful, if the data of one period are compared with those of the previous periods and with the average industrial data. Ratios are the tools used to make the comparative study possible.

To workout ratios, data with related implication are to be grouped. Ratios of the grouped data are interpreted to assess the operations of the business during the accounting period and its financial position as at the end of the period. Ratios are analyzed under four broad categories – structural, liquidity, turnover and profitability. A number of ratios are employed under each of the groups, examining a specific aspect in the group. An over all assessment of the effective working of the company and its strength depends upon relating the inter related figures. It must also to be remembered that ratios are indicators. Ratio analysis is to provide the requisite information at the proper time to the management for taking corrective actions. Ratios are not decisions but aids in decision-making.

1. QUESTIONS

1. What information do the financial statements of a business contain ?
2. Define the term accounting ratio. Describe the various ratios used to test the solvency of a company ?
3. Why do companies and investors analyze financial statements? What do you understand by structural ratios ?
4. List out and explain the ratios used to judge the turnover ability of an organization?
5. Explain the meaning and objectives of financial statement analysis?
6. Bring out the significance of current ratio.
7. What is Ratio Analysis? Explain its usefulness in interpreting Financial Statements.
8. Briefly describe the various tools used to analyze the financial statements ?
9. List out the stakeholders interested in the financial information of a business and their purposes ?
10. What is the interest of the shareholders in analyzing financial statements?
11. Why should governments be interested in financial reports?
12. Why do the data presented in financial reports vary from company to company?
13. What documents should an analyst study, besides profit and loss account and balance

sheet, to understand the financial data?

14. Why should there be homogeneity in the presentation of financial reports?
15. What are internal accruals?
16. Explain fixed liabilities and distinguish them from current liabilities?
17. What constitute outside liabilities?
18. Explain the following terms:
    Net worth
    PBIT
    Capital employed
    Solvency
    Liquidity
    Non-current assets
    Over-trading.
19. What are quick assets?
20. How are ratios used to interpret financial information?
21. Distinguish between intra-firm and inter-firm comparisons?
22. What do you understand by return on investment? How is it calculated?
23. What is EPS? How does it differ from PER?
24. What is dividend payout? What are the reasons for high or low dividend payout?
25. What is debt-equity ratio? What does it imply?
26. Do ratio analysis amount to decision making?
27. State how debtors turnover ratio, fixed assets turnover ratio and stock turnover ratio are calculated and explain their significance?
28. From the following data, calculate gross working capital and net working capital.

Cash	20,000	Bank over draft	15,000
Bank	30,000	B/P	16,000
B / R	10,000	Creditors	8,000
Debtors	15,000	Outstanding expenses	2,000
Stock	40,000		

II. QUIZ

Say yes or no

1. Debt equity ratio is another name for debt service coverage ratio.

2. Operating profit is profit before taxation.
3. Share premium is capital reserve.
4. Data in financial reports are presented strictly according to GAAP .
5. Interest is not an operating cost but a transfer cost.
6. PAT is after taxation, preference dividend and dividend tax.
7. Fixed liabilities are fixed period obligation.
8. Paid up value of forfeited shares are transferred to capital reserves.
9. Marketable securities are included in non-current assets.
10. The following are liquid assets.
    (a) Cash
    (b) Inventories
    (c) Receivables
    (d) Loans and advances
    (e) Marketable securities
    (f) Investments
    (g) Prepaid expenses
11. Material consumed is opening stock plus purchases less returns and closing stock.
12. Intra-firm analysis is study of the data of a business with industrial average.
13. Gross profit is turnover less factory cost.
14. Capital employed is paid up share capital.
15. Dividend payout is more where the actual rate of capitalization is more than the market rate of capitalization.
16. Solvency is the capacity of the unit to meet its long term commitments.
17. Inventory is more liquid than receivables.
18. Higher debtor turnover ratio means efficient receivables management.
19. Debt equity ratio is also called leverage ratio.
20. Perpetuities are permanent sources of borrowed funds.

III. EXERCISES

1. Take the balance sheet of any company and analyze the financial statements. Using ratios, study the structure, liquidity, profitability, turnover and solvency of the firm.

2. Analyze the financial statements of the company given as Appendix 11B to Chapter 11. What do you consider about the financial position and working results of the company?
3. Comment upon the liquidity of Abel Corporation based on their following balance sheet as on 31.3.2003

Share Capital	**Rs.**		**Rs.**
Creditors	30,00,000	Fixed Assets	16,00,500
Bills Payable	8,00,000	Cash	1,00,000
Provision for Tax	2,00,000	Book Debts	6,00,000
	3,00,500	Bills Receivables	2,00,000
		Stock	17,00,500
		Prepaid Expenses	99,500
	43,00,500		43,00500

4. The following figures are extracted from the Balance sheet of Kartick Carbons Ltd. as on 31st December 2002 and 2003. Calculate Current Ratio and Acid test Ratio for the two years and commend on the liquidity position of the Company.:

	2002 Rs.	**2003 Rs.**
Stock	1,25,000	1,40,000
Debtors	1,10,000	1,16,000
Cash at bank	65,000	54,000
Creditors	98,000	1,05,000
Bills Payables	52,000	63,000
Provision for taxes	75,000	67,000
Bank Overdraft	1,05,000	1,15,000

5. Find out capital gearing ratio of Yeshwant Lal Enterprises as on 31.12.2003 from the following information from their balance sheet as on 31.12.2003.

	Rs.
Equity Share Capital	10,00,000
10% Pref. Share Capital	5,00,000
18% Debentures	8,00,000

Loan at 15% (Long period)	1,40,000
Current liabilities	3,00,000
General Reserve	8,00,000

6. Calculate liquidity ratios of Kumar Associates from the following information for the year ended 31.03.2004:

	Rs.
Stocks	3,00,000
Equity Share Capital	11,00,000
Capital Reserve	5,00,000
Sundry debtors	2,00,000
Marketable securities	5,00,000
Sundry Creditors	2,40,000
Bills Payable	1,20,000
Provision for Taxation	1,80,000
Outstanding creditors	1,60,000
Bills Receivable	1,39,000

8. From the following balance sheet of Mehta Metals Ltd. you are required to calculate: Current ratio and Solvency Ratio.

Balance Sheet as on 31st December

Share Capital	10,00,000	Fixed Assets	12,00,000
Fixed Liabilities	5,00,000	Current Assets	8,00,000
Current Liabilities	5,00,000		
	20,00,000		20,00,000

9. From the following balance sheet of Cannon Ltd., compute

1. Current Ratio
2. Liquid Ratio
3. Absolute Liquid Ratio
4. Proprietary Ratio
5. Assets-proprietorship Ratio

(i) Fixed Assets to proprietors' equity

(ii) Current Assets to proprietors' equity

6. Debt-Equity Ratio
7. Stock to Current Assets Ratio
8. Stock to Working capital Ratio
9. Current Assets to Working Capital Ratio
10. Current Assets to Liquid Assets Ratio
11. All long-term funds to Working Capital ratio
12. Tangible Assets to Working Capital Ratio
13. Capital Gearing Ratio.

Balance Sheet of Cannon Ltd As on 31st December

Liabilities	Rs.	Assets	Rs.
Equity Share Capital	2,00,000	Plan and Machinery	2,00,000
10% Preference Share Capital	1,00,000	Land and Buildings	2,00,000
20% Debentures	1,00,000	Stock	1,50,000
Reserves and Surplus	1,00,000	Debtors	50,000
Loan (long term)	50,000	Cash	1,00,000
Creditors	1,00,000		
Bank Overdraft	50,000		
	7,00,000		7,00,000

10. From the following particulars found in the trading, Profit and Loss Account of Anubama Company Ltd., work out the operation ratio of the business concern:

Trading and Profit and Loss Account of Alabama Company Ltd. for the period ending December 31

Dr. **Cr.**

Expenses	Rs.	Incomes	Rs.
To Opening Stock	1,40,000	By Net Sales	10,00,000
To Purchases	6,40,000	By Closing Stock	60,000
To Direct Expenses	30,000		
To Gross Profit	2,50,000		
	10,60,000		10,60,000

To Operating Expenses:		By Gross Profit	2,50,000
(a) Administrative Expenses	1,60,000		
(b) Selling and Distribution Expenses	30,000		
To Financial Expenses	10,000		
To Net Profit	50,000		
	2,50,000		2,50,000

11. The following is the summarized Profit and Loss Account of Taj Tarnish Products Ltd for the year ended 31st December.

Profit and loss account

	Rs.		**Rs.**
To Opening stock of Materials	1,99,500	By Sales	12,50,000
		By Stock of Materials)	1,39,000
To Purchase of Materials	3,25,250	By Stock of Finished Goods	60,000
To Direct Wages	4,20,000	By Non-operating Income	
To Manufacturing Expenses	1,14,250	Interest	3,000
To Selling & Distribution Expenses	80,000	By Profit on sale of Shares	6,000
To Administrative Expenses	1,50,000		
To Finance Charges	15,000		
To Non-operating Expenses			
Loss on sale of Assets	4,000		
To Net profit	1,50,000		
	14,58,000		14,58,000

Work out the following ratios :

(1) Gross Profit Ratio

(2) Net Profit Ratio

(3) Operating Ratio

(4) Cost Ratios (to cost of Production)

(i) Materials consumed Ratio

(ii) Labour Cost Ratio

(iii) Production Overhead Cost Ratio.

12. From the following balance sheet of Surgit Surani Ltd.and additional information, calculate :

(i) Return on Total Resources

(ii) Return on Capital Employed

(iii) Return on Shareholders' Fund

Balance sheet as on 31st December.

	Rs.		**Rs.**
Share Capital (Rs.10)	8,00,000	Fixed Assets	10,00,000
Reserves	2,00,000	Current Assets	3,60,000
8% Debentures	2,00,000		
Creditors	1,60,000		
	13,60,000		13,60,00

Net operating profit before tax is Rs.2,80,000. Assume tax rate at 35%. Dividend declared Rs.1,20,000.

13. 4 Company has capital of Rs.10,00,000; its turnover is 3 times the capital and the margin on sales is 6%. What is the return investment (ROI)?

14. Rathi Alloys International has the following information for the year ended 31st April.

Cash Sales	Rs.80,000
Credit Sales	Rs.2,00,000
Return inward	Rs.10,000
Opening Stock	Rs.25,000
Closing Stock	Rs.30,000
Gross Profit Ratio is 25%	

Find out Inventory Turnover-ratio.

15. Compute Inventory Turnover for each of the three years of Muharat Munshami Ltd. shown from the following and comment on the operating results of the company:

	2001	2002	2003
	Rs.	Rs.	Rs.
Cost of goods sold	7,60,417	8,54,413	9,55,817
Average Inventory	3,36,420	3,08,243	,10,412

16. Calculate debtor velocity from the following details.

Opening balance of debtors Rs.10,000

Credit sales during the year rs.20,000

Sales returns Rs.1,000

Discount on sales Rs.50

Cash collections during the year Rs.5,000.

Bad debts Rs.500

Bad debt provision 10%

17. Balbir Singh and Co. sells goods on cash as well as credit. The following particulars are extracted from their books of the company for the calendar year 2003.

	Rs.
Total Gross Sales	11,00,000
Cash Sales (included in above)	5,20,000
Sales Returns	97,000
Total Debtors for Sales as on 31.12.2003	1,59,000
Bills Receivable on 31.12.2003	42,000
Provision for doubtful debts on 31.12.2003	11,000
Bad debts during the year	10,000

Calculate the average collection period.

18. Calculate Debtors Velocity from the following details :

Opening Balance of Debtors Rs.10,000

Credit Sales during the year Rs.20,000

Sales returns Rs.1,000

Discount on Sales Rs.50

Cash collected from Debtors during the year Rs.5,000.

Bad Debts Rs.500

Bad Debt Provision at 10%

19. From the following figures calculate the Mona Lisa Ltd. calculate turnover ratio and the average payment period of accounts payable:

Credit purchases in 1999	Rs.10,00,000
Creditors on 1.1.1999	Rs.2,00,000
Creditors on 31.12.1999	Rs.1,00,000
Bills Payable on 1.1.1999	Rs.40,000
Bills Payable on 31.12.1999	s.60,000

20. The Capital of Eifel Eflorescence Ltd. Company is as follows :

	Rs.
10% Preference Shares of Rs.10 each	3,00,00000
Equity Shares of Rs.10 each	8,00,00,000
	11,00,00,000

The following information are made available:

Profit (after tax at 60%) Rs.2,70,00,000.

Depreciation rs.60,00,000

Equity dividend paid 20%

Market Price of equity share Rs.400.

You are required to state the following, showing the necessary workings :

(a) Dividend yield on the equity shares.

(b) Cover for the preference and equity dividends.

(c) Earnings per equity share.

(d) Price-earnings ratio

21. From the following particulars, draw up the Balance Sheet of the company :

Current Ratio	2.5
Quick Ratio	1.5
Net Working Capital	Rs.30,000
Stock Turnover Ratio (Cost of Sales/Closing Stock)	6 Times

Gross Profit Ratio	20%
Fixed Assets-Turnover Ratio (Cost of sales)	2 Times
Debtors Turnover Ratio	2 Times
Fixed Assets to Shareholders' Net Worth	0.8
Reserves & Surplus to Capital	0.5
Long-Term Loans	Rs.15,000

22. Alpha Manufacturing Co. has drawn up the following Profit and Loss Account for the year ended 31st March.

	Rs.		Rs.
To Opening Stock	26,00,000	By Sales	1,60,00,000
To Purchases	80,00,000	By Closing Stock	38,00,000
To Wages	24,00,000		
To Manufacturing Expenses	16,00,000		
To Gross Profit c/d	52,00,000		
	1,98,00,000		1,98,00,000
		By Gross profit b/d	52,00,000
To Selling & Dist. Expenses	4,00,000	By Compensation for acquisition of land	4,80,000
To Administrative Expenses	22,80,000		
To General Expenses	1,20,000		
To Value of furniture lost by fire	80,000		
To Net Profit	28,00,000		
	56,80,000		56,80,000

(a) Gross Profit Ratio

(b) Net Profit ratio

(c) Operating Ratio

(d) Operating Net Profit to Net Sales Ratio

23. Analyze vertical,ly and horizontally the under mentioned comparative condensed balance sheets,

Comparative Balance Sheet of XYZ Company.

Liabilities	2005	2006
	Rs.	Rs.
Equity Share Capital	3,00,000	4,00,000
8% Redeemable Preference		
	Share Capital	1,50,000
1,00,000		
Capital Reserve	-	20,000
General Reserve	40,000	50,000
Profit & Loss a/c	30,000	48,000
Proposed dividend	42,000	50,000
Sundry Creditors	25,000	47,000
Bills Payable	20,000	16,000
Liability for expenses	30,000	36,000
Provision for taxation	40,000	50,000
	Total	6,77,000
8,17,000		
	1996	1997
Assets	Rs.	Rs.
Good will	1,10,000	80,000
Land & Buildings	2,00,000	1,70,000
Plant	70,000	2,00,000
Investment	20,000	30,000
Sundry debtors	1,40,000	1,70,000
Stock	77,000	1,09,000
Bills receivable	20,000	30,000
Cash in hand	15,000	10,000
Cash at Bank	10,000	8,000

Preliminary expenses	15,000	10,000
Total	6,77,000	8,17,000

24. Alabama Traders sell goods for cash as well as on credit.

The following particulars are extracted from their books for the calendar year 2003. Calculate average collection period from the data

	Rs.
Total Gross Sales	20,00,000
Cash Sales (include in above)	4,00,000
Sales Returns	1,04,000
Total Debtors for sales	1,08,000
Bills Receivable	40,000
Provision for doubtful debts	20,000
Total Creditors	2,00,000

25. The following are the summarized Profit and loss account of Lama Sabaktani Ltd. for the year ending 31st December and he balance sheet as on that date:

Profit And Loss Account

		Rs.			Rs.
To Opening Stock		99,500	By Sales		8,50,000
To Purchases		5,45,250	By Closing Stock		1,49,000
To Incidental Expenses		14,250			
To Gross Profit		3,40,000			
		9,99,000			9,99,000
To Operating Expenses:			By Gross Profit		3,40,000
Selling and Distribution	30,000		By Non-operating Income :		
			Interest	3,000	
Administration	1,50,000		Profit on sale of shares	6,000	
Finance	15,000	1,95,000			
To-Non-operating Expenses:					9,000
Loss on sale of assets		4,000			
To Net Profit		1,50,000			
		3,49,000			3,49,000

Balance Sheet as on 31st December

Liabilities	Rs.	Assets	Rs.
Issued Capital		Land and Buildings	1,50,000
2,000 equity shares of Rs.100 each	2,00,000	Plant and Machinery	80,000
Reserves	90,000	Stock-n-trade	1,49,000
Current Liabilities	1,30,000	Sundry Debtors	71,000
Profit & Loss A/c	60,000	Cash and Bank	
		Balance	30,000
	4,80,000		4,80,000

From the above statements you are required to calculate the following ratios and state the purpose they serve:

(1) Gross profit ratio;

(2) Net profit ratio;

(3) Operating profit ratio;

(4) Operating ratio;

(5) Current ratio;

(6) Acid-Test Ratio.

26. From the following data of Goliath Corporate, calculate :

(a) Gross Profit Ratio

(b) Net Profit Ratio

(c) Return on Total Assets

(d) Inventory Turnover

(e) Working Capital Turnover

(f) Net Worth to Debt.

Sales	Rs.25,20,000
Cash of Sales	Rs.19,20,000
Net Profit	Rs.3,60,000
Inventory	Rs.8,00,000
Other Current Assets3	Rs.7,60,000
Fixed Assets	Rs.14,40,000
Net Worth	Rs.15,00,000
Debt	Rs.9,00,000
Current Liabilities	Rs.6,00,000

27. Extracts from accounts of Ohio Traders are as under:

	Year I		Year II	
	Assets Rs.	**Liabilities Rs.**	**Assets Rs.**	**Liabilities Rs.**
Stock	10,000		20,000	
Debtors	30,000		30,000	
Payment in Advance	2,000		—	
Cash in hand	20,000		15,000	
Sundry Creditors		25,000		30,000
Acceptances		15,000		12,000
Bank Overdraft		—		5,000
	62,000	40,000	65,000	47,000

Sales amounted to Rs.3,50,000 in the first year and Rs.4,00,000 in the second year. You are required to comment on the solvency position of the concern with the help of accounting ratios.

28. A firm has an equity base of Rs.One lakh. Following are the ratios of the firm.

Current debt to total debt 0.4

Total debt to owner's equity 0.6

Total assets turnover 2 times

Fixed asset to equity 0.6

Inventory turnover 8 times

(a) Construct the balance sheet (b) Calculate liquidity ratios.(O U MBA)

29. From the following particulars draw up the Balance Sheet of Crocodile Tears Ltd. for the year ended 31.3.2003.

Current Ratio	2.5
Quick Ratio	1.5
Net Working Capital	Rs.30,000
Stock Turnover Ratio	6 Times
(Cost of Sales/Closing Stock)	
Gross Profit Ratio	20%
Fixed Assets-Turnover Ratio	2 Times
(Fixed assets Cost of sales)	
Debtors Turnover Ratio	2 Times
Fixed Assets to Shareholders' Net Worth	0.8
Reserves & Surplus to Capital	0.5
Long-Term Loans	Rs.15,000

30. Given the following information, Prepare a Balance Sheet :

Receivable Turnover	=	4
Payables Turnover	=	6
Inventory Turnover	=	8
Capital Turnover Ratio	=	2 Times
Fixed Assets Turnover Ratio	=	8 Times
Gross Profit Ratio	=	25%

Gross profit during the year amounted to Rs.80,000. There is no long-term or overdraft. Reserves and surplus amount to Rs.28,000. Ending inventory of the year is Rs.2,000 above the beginning inventory. Notes receivable amount to Rs.5,000 and notes payable are Rs.2,000.

31. Following are the ratios relating to the trading activities of National Traders, for the year ended on 31st December.

Debtors Velocity	3 Months
Stock Velocity	8 Months
Gross Profit Ratio	2 Months
Gross Profit for the year	25%
Closing Stock is Rs.10,000, above the opening stock	
Bills Receivable	Rs.4,00,000
Bills Payable	Rs.25,000
	Rs.10,000

Find out (a) Sales

(b) Sundry Debtors

(c) Closing Sock

(d) Sundry Creditors

32. Using the following accounting variables, construct the Balance sheet of Gopinath Gulam Sahib as on 30.6.2003:

Gross Profit (20% of sales)	Rs.60,000
Shareholders Equity	50,000
Credit sales to Total Sales	80%
Total Assets Turnover	3 Times
Stock Turnover	8 Times
Average collection period	18 days
(A year = 360 days)	
Current Ratio	1.6 : 1
Long Term Debt to Equity	40%

33. Assume that Neolite Corporation has owners' equity of Rs.1,00,000. The ratios for the firm are:

Current Debt to Total Debt	O.40
Total Debt to owners' equity	0.60
Fixed Assets to owners' equity	0.60
Total Assets Turnover	2 Times
Inventory Turnover	8 Times

Complete the following balance sheet from the information given above.

Equities	**Rs.**	**Assets**	**Rs.**
Current Debt		Cash	
Long-Term Debt		Inventory	
Total Debt		Total Current Assets	
Owners Equity		Fixed Assets	
Total Equity		Total Assets	

34. In projecting the financial plan for the next year with a sale forecast of Rs.20,00,000, Xylone Xerox desires to have the following accounting ratios

Sales to Net Worth	2.5
Current Debt to Net Worth	25%
Total Debt to Net Worth	60%
Current Ratio	3.6 Times
Nert Sales to Inventory	4 Times
Average Collection period	36 days
(A year = 360 days)	
Fixed Assets to Net Worth	70%

Prepare proforma balance sheet of the firm wit a view to have the desired ratios.

35. From the following information presented by Zealoise Zen for the year ended 31st December, prepare the balance sheet. The company expects to have an annual sale of Rs.15,00,000:

Sales to Net Worth	5 Times
Current Liabilities to Net Worth	50%
Total Debts to Net Worth	60%
Fixed Assets to Net Worth	60%
Current Ratio	2
Sales to Stock	10 times
Debtors' Velocity	9 Times
Cash Sales	40% of Sales

36. You are given the following information pertaining to financial statements of Unicorn Umbrellas for the year ended 30.6.2004. Prepare Trading and profit and Loss Account and Balance Sheet as on that date:

Net Current Assets	Rs.
Paid up Capital	1,00,000
Current Ratio	3,00,000
Liquid ratio	1.8 : 1
Fixed Assets to Shareholders' Equity	1.35 : 1
Gross Profit Ratio	80%

Net Profit to Paid up Capital	25%
Stock Turnover	20%
Average Age of Outstanding Customers 36.5 days	5 Times

37. Venus Venture Capital Ltd. has given the following data showing data for the year ended 28th February:

Paid up Capital	Rs.50,000
Plant and Machinery	Rs.1,25,000
Total Sales	Rs.5,00,000
Gross profit Margin	25%
Annual Credit Sales	80% of Net Sales
Current Ratio	2
Inventory Turnover	4
Fixed Assets Turnover	2
Sales Returns	20% of Sales
Average Collection period	73 days
Bank Credit to trade credit	2
Cash to Inventory	1: 15
Total debt to Current Liabilities0	3

Construct a balance sheet for the company.

38. Toner Time Piece Ltd. was formed on 1st April 2002 for taking over the business of a partnership firm. The partners were paid the purchase consideration partly by issue of capital. The Balance sheet of 31st March 2003 shows the following position :

	Rs.		Rs.
Equity Capital	10,00,000	Goodwill	10,00,000
Debentures	2,50,000	Fixed Assets	5,00,000
Deposits from		Stock	50,00,000
Director's frieds	1,50,000	Debtors	25,00,000
Sundry Creditors	80,00,000	Cash	25,000
		Profit & Loss A/c	3,75,000
	94,00,000		94,00,000

The sales for 2002-03 were Rs.75,00,000. The company approaches you as the manager of Lend More Bank Ltd. for loan facilities. Prepare a note setting out your recommendations to your head office. Your assessment of the company's performance should be the basis of your recommendation.

39. High Sore Soft Ltd. sells computers on cash as well as credit. The following particulars are extracted from their books of accounts for the calendar year. 2003.

	Rs.
Total Gross Sales	2,00,00,000
Cash Sales (included in the above)	40,00,000
Sales Returns	14,00,000
Total Debtors for sales	14,00,000
Bills Receivable	18,00,000
Provision for doubtful debts	4,00,000
Total Creditors	2,00,000
	20,00,000

Calculate average collection period.

40. From the data of Peanuts Corporation as on 31.12.2003 compute:

(a) Working Capital

(b) Net Capital Employed

(c) Current ratio

(d) Acid Test ratio

(e) Debt-equity Ratio

(f) Fixed Asset Ratio

Peanuts Corporation

Balance sheet as on 31st December 2003

Liabilities	**Rs.Lakhs**	**Assets**	**Rs.Lakhs**
Equity Share Capital	250.00	Fixed Assets	300.00
Preference Share Capital	50.00	Current Assets:	
Reserves and Surplus	40.00	Stores	20.00
Debentures	80.00	Sundry Debtors	10.00
Bank Loan	40.00	Cash	5.00
Sundry Creditors	10.00	Bank	25.00

Proposed Dividends	10.00	Preliminary Expenses	80.00
Provision for Taxation	20.00	Brokerage on shares	20.00
		Stock	40.00
	500.00		500.00

41. You have been appointed as financial executive to the central office of AB Ltd. with special responsibility for monitoring the performance of the divisions within the company. Each division is treated as an investment center. Summaries of the divisions X and Y for the year ending 31 December2000 are given below:

Particulars	**X**	**Y**
Sales	7,00,000	9,50,000
Variable costs	3,20,000	4,10,000
Fixed overheads	2,00,000	2,90,000
Divisional assets	2,50,000	3,75,000

You are required to assess the performance of the divisions with the help of ROI.

42. From the following data, calculate

(a) Gross profit ratio

(b) Net profit ratio

(c) Return on Total assets

(d) Inventory Turnover

(e) Working Capital Turnover

(f) Net worth to Debt.

	Rs.
Sales	25,20,000
Cost of sales	19,20,000
Net profit	3,60,000
Inventory	8,00,000
Other Current Assets	7,60,000
Fixed assets	14,40,000
Net worth	15,00,000
Debt	9,00,000
Current Liabilities	6,00,000

43. From the following information, prepare a Balance sheet:

	Rs.
Working capital	75,000
Reserves and Surplus	1,00,000
Bank overdraft	60,000
Current ratio	1.75:1
Liquid ratio	1.15:1
Fixed asset to proprietor's fund	.75
Long term liabilities	Nil

CHAPTER–6

SOURCES AND USES OF FUNDS

Learning Objective

Business activities are directly related to the myriads of modes of raising funds, both short-term and long-term and their efficient utilization. Cash inflows and outflows are thus the nerve centers of a business. This chapter highlights the flow and its impact on the earning capacity of a business. Cash inflows increases the obligations of the business and outflows enhance the assets. Through cash flow analysis one could find answers to many questions that eluded him in ratio analysis.

How figures in financial statements that look so mute on the face of it, contain valid information, which could change one's perception of the enterprise has been seen. The task is accomplished by analysis of the financial statements using ratios. Ratios establish quantitative relationship between related figures and comparing this relationship with intra-firm and inter-firm data, meaningful conclusions could be arrived at. The vista of the operational performance and financial status of the business unfolds before the eyes of the analyst once the ratios are properly interpreted. However, there is a limit to which analysis could reveal information. Answers to certain questions, such as listed below, are not available from the analysis:

- *How much was the internal accrual during the year?*
- *What had happened to it?*
- *Why dividend pay out is high or low considering the profit after tax?*
- *How were assets financed during the year?*
- *What had happened to the working capital during the year?*
- *Was there any diversion of funds during the year?*

To get convincing answers to these questions, a separate document called the ***statement of sources and uses of funds or cash flow statement*** during the accounting period has to be prepared and analysed. Funds or cash for the purpose of this analysis comprise ***funds from operation***, technically called cash accruals and funds from non-operational sources. Funds from operation means profits before interests, taxes and dividends, with depreciation added back.

There is a lot of controversy among analysts as to what is cash and what is fund. Do the two words have the same meaning or do they refer to different things? Apparently, the two words seem to mean the same thing. How ever, a deeper analysis shows a slender but distinct difference between the two. According to Oxford dictionary, cash flow is "movement of money into and out of a business". It is the total flow. The dictionary does not give a definition for fund flow, but defines funds as "permanently available stock; money set apart for purpose" Considering the two definitions and having regard to the historic evolution of the words, there is a discernible difference between cash and fund. Cash is money used for meeting any requirement, whether shot-term or long- term, where as fund is for a specific requirement. Thus it is safer to assume that Cash flow refers to the overall flow of money into and out of business, while fund flow is restricted to a purpose (permanently needed) such as working capital. Should some of the readers trace the history of the evolution of the usage of financial terms, they would find that in the early financial writings, which were dominated by British authors, both the terms were interchangeably used to mean cash. After the Second World War, when USA emerged as the major financial market player, a distinct meaning was assigned to funds to mean working capital funds. The Indian writers have also switched over their allegiance to the American way of thinking in management. In this book, cash flow is given the holistic meaning, embracing all movements in cash, whereas fund flow is confined to the movement in working capital funds alone. It is gratifying to note that leading universities such as Osmania University has also subscribed to this clear-cut distinction.

Changes in Assets and Liabilities

When funds flow into the business or out of it, the movement would be reflected by changes either in the assets or the liabilities of the balance sheet. ***The inflow of funds is indicated by increase in liabilities.*** For example, the business raises funds through share issues, bond issues, deposits and any other form of borrowings or through deferment of purchases and other payments. These create obligations by the business and its liabilities increase. In other words, increase in liabilities is an indicator of inward flow of funds. It is a source of fund. On the other hand, when liabilities get reduced, on making payments, there is an outward movement of funds. ***Liquidation or reduction of liabilities is, therefore, use of fund.***

On the assets side of the balance sheet, use of funds, when assets are acquired causes increase in the value of the concerned assets. Hence, ***any increase in assets is the result of use of funds.*** When assets are acquired, not for cash but on credit, then both assets and liabilities would have increased simultaneously for the same value. Hence, the acquisition of assets on credit (i.e. without outflow of funds) would affect equally the sources and uses of funds. There would not be any net inflow or outflow of funds. It is as if funds are raised through the creation of liabilities and used for acquisition of assets. On the other hand reduction in assets implies that fund have been released into the business. For example, sale of an obsolete asset causes an inflow of funds. Similarly, balance in sundry debtors' account (which is a current asset) when gets reduced, means debtors had made payments. Hence ***reduction in asset is source of funds***. To sum up, ***any increase in asset is use of fund and any reduction, source of fund.***

On the basis of the above discussions, it might be seen that changes in the liabilities or assets of a business between two consecutive periods are indicators of changes in sources and uses of funds. Any increase in the liability of the current year over the immediately proceding year, is increase in sources of funds. So also any reduction in assets as at the end of the current balance sheet period over that of the previous year is source of funds. On the other hand, any increase in assets or reduction in liabilities at the end of the current balance sheet period compared to the previous period is use of funds. Thus, the flow of funds during the accounting period can be grouped into

Sources of Funds:

(A) Increase in liabilities and

(B) Decrease in assets

Uses of Funds:

(A) Increase in assets and

(B) Decrease in liabilities.

When all the sources and uses of funds are listed in a statement form, it is called the ***changes in sources and uses of funds***. The statements of changes in sources and uses of funds are also known as ***cash flow or fund flow statements.*** Later in this chapter, we would distinguish between a cashflow and a fund flow statements. The difference is only in details. Generally, finance managers use the term cash flow for the overall changes in the sources and uses of funds, whereas fund flow is restricted to the flow of working capital funds. The proforma of a statement of sources and uses of funds is in Table below:

Table 1

Statement of sources on uses of fund of Olea Ltd for the year ended 31.03.2005

A. Sources of funds	
Increase in share capital	
Funds from operations	
Increase in profit before tax and interest but after depreciation and provisions.	
Increase in Depreciation	
Increase in Provisions	
Increase in borrowings	
Increase in bonds	
Increase in deposits	
Increase in term loans	
Increase in bank loans for working capital	
Increase in other forms of raising funds	
Increase in current liabilities	
Reduction in assets including intangible assets	
Reduction in investments	
Reduction in current assets	
Reduction in other assets	
Reduction in intangibles such as preliminary expenses	
Total sources -A	
B..Disposition (Use or Application) of funds	
Increase in fixed assets	
Increase in current assets	
Reduction in borrowing – repayment	
Reduction in current liabilities and provisions (except cash)	
Payment of interests on fixed liabilities	
Payment of interest on working capital	
Payment of tax	
Payment of Dividend	
Any other payment	
Total uses-B	
Opening balance of cash	
Add surplus / less deficit (A – B)	
Closing balance of cash	

In preparing the above statement, increase in profit before tax with depreciation and interest added back during the year is classified as ***funds from operations***. Such profits are arrived at after including profits on sale of assets or deducting loss, if any on sale of assets. So to arrive at correct funds from operation, profits on sale of assets are to be deducted from funds from operation and loss on sale of assets are to be added back to funds from operation. Interest is not an operating cost. It is a cost arising out of management decision to finance its requirements for funds from borrowings. Hence earnings before interest is taken as funds from operation.

Preparation

Cash flow properly prepared would give an insight into the nature of the data compiled and would help in interpreting the information usefully. We would, therefore, first consider the task associated with the preparation. We have seen earlier in this chapter that changes in the sources and uses of funds have their impact on the assets and liabilities of the balance sheet. Therefore, for the preparation of the changes in source and uses of funds, figures of all liabilities and assets as at the end of two consecutive years are necessary. Given below is the balance sheet of Banberry Confectioneries Ltd. for the year-ended 31.3.2003. As is the practice, this is a real balance sheet of a large confectionery company with name and year changed:

Table 2
Banberry Confectioneries Ltd.
Balance sheet as on 31.3.2003(Rs.Lakhs)

Liabilities	2003	2002	Assets	2003	2002
Share capital	198.40	124.00	Gross F.A	1039.43	741.70
Reserves and surplus	821.52	769.07	Less: Depreciation	388.22	318.89
Secured loans	74.28	3.16			
Unsecured loans	229.42	149.99	Net fixed assets	651.21	422.81
Sundry creditors	523.86	428.86	Capital work in progress		
Provisions for tax	60.00	48.00	progress	271.66	53.92
Prov. for Dividend	32.45	27.68.	Investments	4.56	37.48
			Cash	13.84	12.37
			Other current Assets	960.09	1023.21
			Misc.expenditures	38.57	0.97
	1939.93	1550.76		1939.93	1550.76

As changes in assets and liabilities are the results of cash inflows and outflows, the first stage in preparing for cash flow statement is to work out the changes in assets and liabilities at the end of current year compared to that of the previous year. Before that a few changes are to be made in the assets side and liabilities side of balance sheet. Secured and unsecured loans are classifications done by companies according to the nature of collateral made available to the lenders. Where the company provides collateral security, it is termed secured and where the lenders depend only on the ability of the business to repay without any tangible security it is unsecured. The secured and unsecured might include term liabilities and current liabilities. For analysis purposes, fixed liabilities and current liabilities are to be gleaned from both secured and unsecured loans. These are carried out from the schedules of secured and unsecured loans attached to the balance sheet. It is observed that out of the total of secured and unsecured loans of Rs.303.70 lakhs in 2003 and Rs.153.15 lakhs in 2002,Rs.121.25 lakhs (Rs.151.58 lakhs for the previous year) were fixed liabilities and the balance were current liabilities. Further, depreciation is shown in the balance sheet as a deduction from the gross fixed assets. Gross fixed assets denote use of funds whereas depreciation is a source of funds. Hence, before working out the changes in assets and liabilities, depreciation has to be moved to the sources side, leaving the gross fixed assets alone in the assets side.

Table 3 gives rearranged figures of the balance sheet and changes that had taken place in assets and liabilities as at the end of the current year over the previous year. It might be observed that all items of liabilities, excepting fixed liabilities, have increased during the year 2003 compared to that of 2002, indicating cash inflows. The fixed liabilities have decreased, which means that funds have been used up in liquidating fixed liabilities. It is use of funds. In the assets side, excepting investments and current assets, other items have shown increases. It, therefore, reveals that funds have flown out in the acquisition of these assets. Depreciation up to date is given as liability. This rearrangement is necessitated for calculating accurately the inflow and outflow of funds. For, any increase in the gross block is use of funds and any increase in depreciation, source of funds. As the task of analyzing cashflow starts with the calculation of the flow, the increase in each of the items of assets and liabilities as at the end of 2003 over 2002 has to be ascertained. The increases and decreases in assets and liabilities of Banberry Confectioneries Ltd., is tabulated in Table 3 below:

Table 3
Banberry Confectioneries Ltd.
Balance sheet as on 31.3.2003. **(Rs.Lakhs)**

	31.3.2003	31.3.2002	Increase/ Decrease
Liabilities			
Share capital	198.40	124.00	74.40
Reserves and surplus	821.52	769.07	52.45
Depreciations	388.22	318.89	69.33
Fixed liabilities	121.25	151.58	-30.33
Current liabilities**	182.45	1.57	180.88
Sundry creditors	523.86	428.86	95.00
Provisions for tax	60.00	48.00	12.00
Prov.for dividend	32.45	27.68	4.77
Total	2328.15	1869.65	458.50

Assets			
Gross block	1039.43	741.70	297.73
Capital WIP	271.66	53.92	217.74
Investments	4.56	37.48	-32.92
Cash	13.84	12.37	1.47
Other current Assets	960.09	1023.21	-63.12
Misc. expenditure	38.57	0.97	37.60
Total	2328.15	1869.65	458.50

** Details of Calculation of term and current liabilities

Items	2003	2002
Secured	74.28	3.16
Unsecured	229.42	149.99
Total	303.70	153.15
<u>Rearranged into</u>		
Term liabilities	121.25	151.58
Current liabilities—A	182.45	1.57
Total	303.70	153.15
Current liabilities from A above	182.45	1.57
Sundry creditors from balance sheet	523.86	428.86
Total current liabilities	706.31	430.43

Cash flow statement based on the differences in the assets and liabilities of Banberry Confectioneries Ltd.is presented in Table 4. All the changes in assets and liabilities are treated either as source or use of funds except cash. All inflows are listed in the first half of the statement under the head *sources* and all outflows in the latter half under the head ***disposition or application*** or uses of funds. Cash surplus is added to the opening balance of cash to arrive at the closing balance. If there is cash deficit during the period, it is deducted from opening balance to find out the closing balance. The analyst can check the closing balance of cash from the current period to ensure that he had arithmetically constructed cash flow. Sources are grouped in to funds from operations, (which is the internal cash accruals of the business during the period) and funds from non-operational sources, including funds raised in the market, increases in current liabilities and sale proceeds of assets and investments. The components of funds from operation are increases in reserves and surpluses, depreciation, provisions and intangibles written of.

Table 4
Banberry Confectioneries Ltd.
Cash flow Statement for the year ended 31.3.2003

A.Sources of funds		
Increases in share capital		
Funds from operation:		74.40
Increases in retained earnings	52.45	
Increase in depreciation	69.33	
Increase in provision for tax	12.00	
Increase in provision for. dividend	4.77	138.55
Increases in current liabilities		180.88
Increase in sundry creditors		95.00
Decrease in Current assets		63.12
Decrease in investments		32.92
Total of A		584.87
B.Uses of funds		
Increase in Fixed assets		
Increase in work in progress		297.73
Increase in Misc. expenditures		217.74
Decreases Fixed liabilities		37.60
		30.33
Total of B		583.40
Opening balance of cash		12.37
Surplus/Deficit of cash		1.47
Closing balance		13.84

As stated earlier, the variance in the balances is also the basis from which fund flow statement is prepared. But before fund flow is attempted, a supportive statement indicating the changes in working capital is prepared as a schedule to the fund flow statement. The ***schedule of changes in working capital*** would depict the movement in the working capital assets and liabilities, such as all current assets and current liabilities, excepting provisions. As provisions are appropriations of profit, they form part of funds from operation. A proforma schedule of changes in working capital is given in Table 5.

Table 5
Proforma schedule of changes in working capital

	2003	2002	Change in working capital	
			Increases	Decreases
<u>A.Current assets</u>				
1.Stock				
2.Sundrydebtors,bills receivables				
3. Cash and bank etc				
Total of current assets. (A)				
<u>B. Current liabilities</u>				
1.Bank borrowings				
2.Sundry creditors, bills payables				
3.Outstanding expenses				
Total of current liabilities. (B)				
C.Working capital. (A-B)				
Increase/Decrease in working capital.				

The format is very clear. It would look as if only a mechanical process of choosing the items of current assets and current liabilities and completing the fund flow. But before that it is necessary to understand what type of changes would increase the working capital and what would decrease. ***Increase in current assets is increase in working capital and decrease in current assets decrease in working capital.*** This is obvious, as acquisition of current assets would have enhanced the level of working capital. Similarly, when current assets have reduced, it would have released funds, reducing pressure on working capital. Hence decreases in current assets are decline in working capital. In other words ***changes in current assets directly impact working capital.*** On the other hand, current liabilities are inflow of funds and would reduce the burden on working capital. And as such increases in current liabilities would decrease working capital needs. Decrease in current liabilities, on the other hand, would need funds for payment; hence would increase the requirement for working capital. ***Current liabilities have an inverse impact on the working capital requirements.*** It is now a matter of child's play to prepare the schedule. The schedule of changes in Baneberry's working capital is given in Table 6.

Table 6
Banberry Confectioneries Ltd.
Schedule of changes in working capital for the year ended 31.3.2003

	2003	**2002**	**Change in working capital**	
			Increases	Decreases
A.Current assets				
Cash	13.84	12.37	1.47	
Other current Assets	960.09	1023.21		63.12
Total of current assets. (A)	973.93	1035.58		
B. Current liabilities				
Current liabilities	182.45	1.57		180.88
Sundry creditors	523.86	428.86		95.00
Total of current liabilities (B)	706.31	430.43		
C. Working capital. (A-B)	267.62	605.15	1.47	339.00
Decrease in working capital.		337.53		337.53

The next step is to prepare a fund flow statement. The change in working capital is incorporated into the statement along with the left over items of Table 3. It may be remembered that the left over items represent long-term sources and uses of funds. A fund flow statement for Banberry is in Table 7.

Table 7
Banberry Confectioneries Ltd.
Fund flow statement for the year ended 31.3.2003

A. Sources of funds		
Increases in share capital		74.40
Funds from operation:		
Increases in retained earnings	52.4	
Increases in depreciation	69.33	
Increase in provision for tax	12.00	
Increase in provision for dividend	4.77	138.55
Decrease in investments		32.92
Decrease in working capital		337.53
Total of A		583.40
B.Uses of funds		

Increase in Fixed assets	297.73
Increase in work in progress	217.74
Increase in Misc. expenditures	37.60
Decreases Fixed liabilities	30.33
Total of B	583.40

The cash flow and fund flow statements in Tables 4 and 7 are based on the balance sheet position as on a particular date. However, they do not depict the total volume of the flow during the year. It merely reflects the net position as at the end of the year. In other words, the flow of funds arrived at by deducting the balances at the end of the current year from those of the previous year gives the flow as finally settled down at the end of the year. It does not show the actual quantum of flow that has taken place during the accounting period. In the process, some sources and uses of funds are not reflected in the net flow. For example, a business had outstanding borrowings of Rs.82.50 lakhs from financial institutions as on 31.3.2002.During the year 2003, it had taken an additional loan of Rs.50 lakhs and had repaid installments to the tune of Rs.21.75 lakhs. The outstanding loan as on 31-3-2003 would, then, be Rs.110.75 lakhs. The cashflow arrived at by deducting the outstanding institutional borrowings would show a net inflow of Rs.28.25 lakhs only as against the actual incremental inflow of institutional funds of Rs.50 lakhs. Besides, the net flow had not revealed the out flow, by way of repayment, of Rs.21.75 lakhs. There were two flows-an inflow of Rs.50 lakhs and an outflow of Rs.21.75 lakhs, both in the same account, which got adjusted to an extent and only the difference of Rs.28.25 lakhs was revealed by the balance sheet figures. As the objective of preparing cashflow is to assess the extent of total inflow and outflow, the net flow arrived at from the balance sheet figures has to be adjusted for flows that got squared off during the year. To do this, an analyst would need to have access to other documents like profit and loss account, profit and loss appropriation account and schedules and notes attached to the financial statements. In this analysis, net cashflow means the residual flow arrived at from the balance sheet increases and decreases and gross flow is that arrived at after adjustments during the period.

The factors that could affect the extent of the actual flow include bonus issues, sale of fixed assets, payments of interest, tax and dividend, provision for tax or dividend, payment of interest and repayment of loan installments, etc. The impact of these events on the real flow needs to be assessed and taken into account to measure the true magnitude of the cash flows. It should, however, be cautioned here that all adjustments need not necessarily affect the volume of flow. Some adjustments, as we would see in the following paragraphs, might change the composition of the flow without affecting the volume of sources or uses, while others do.

Bonus Issues

Bonus share issue is the capitalization of reserves. It is the stock dividend. When a corporation issues bonus shares to the shareholders, it converts a part of its reserve in to share capital and issues to the shareholders in certain ratio. When it is declared that the bonus issue is 2:1, it means that for every two shares held by a shareholder, one bonus share would be issued. Bonus issue is made subject to the guidelines of Securities Exchange Board of India (SEBI). The aftermath of bonus issue is that reserves would have decreased and share capital increased by the same account without any flow of funds. However, the net cash flow would show increase in share capitals as a source and the reserves as use of funds. We know that the issue of bonus has neither caused any inflow nor any outflow, but is only an adjustment between reserves and share capital. The distortion has, therefore, to be set right to show the true flow during the year. Hence, to the extent of bonus issue, increase in share capital would have to removed and added to the reserves where it belonged. Since reserves are part of funds from operation, bonus issue would have affected the funds from operation to that extent. It should therefore be added to funds from operation. Both the changes have taken place within the sources side itself. Hence, the adjustment would not affect the volume of gross flow, but would change its composition. Assuming that in the case of Banberry Confectioneries, the company had issued bonus shares for Rs.50 lakhs, then the increase in cash flow on account of share capital and reserves would be Rs.24.40 lakhs and Rs.102.45 lakhs respectively as below:

	(Rs. lakhs)
Increase in share capital as per balance sheet (Net)	74.40
Less: Bonus issue	50.00
Actual cash inflow on account of shares issued for cash	24.40
Increase in Reserves as per balance sheet	52.45
Add: Bonus issue	50.00
Actual increase in Reserves	102.45

Sale of Fixed Assets

The gross fixed assets in the balance sheet represent the value of assets that are in use as at the close of the year. During the year, a few assets might have been added and a few others deleted. Deletion usually takes place when the asset has ceased to be of use to the business. Assets cease to be of use on becoming obsolete or destroyed. Even the unusable asset has salvage value on disposal. For example, the gross fixed assets of a company at the end of 31.3.2003 was Rs.272.50 lakhs, on which depreciation upto date was Rs.186.90 lakhs. The net fixed assets was, thus, Rs.85.60 lakhs. During the year old assets with original cost of Rs.12.45

lakhs (which was depreciated to Rs.10.50 lakhs), was sold for Rs.2.85 lakhs. It is the accounting practice that once an asset is sold, its gross value and the accumulated depreciation are removed from book. The sale of the asset would have caused an inflow. Supposing that the sale price of the old asset is equal to its book value there is neither profit nor loss on sale of the asset. However, should the sales price be higher than the book value then the excess of sales price over the book value is profit to the business. If the sales price were less than the book value, it would be loss. Sale of assets would, therefore, have the following implications in the flow of funds:

- Value of gross fixed assets in the balance sheet, as at end of the period is after removing the gross value of the assets sold. Hence, the value of gross assets as shown in the balance sheet is only the incremental value and not the absolute value. To arrive at the absolute value, the gross value of the assets sold had to be added back. Therefore, the absolute value of gross fixed assets, in the example, would be Rs.284.95 lakhs (272.50 + 12.45). The additional gross flow on account of investment in fixed assets would, therefore, be Rs.12.45 lakhs more.
- The accumulated depreciation in the balance sheet at Rs.186.90 as on 31.3.2003 is also incremental in character. It is the figure after depreciation on the sold asset is removed. The removed depreciation of Rs.10.50 on the assets sold has to be added back to arrive at gross increase in depreciation. The gross depreciation should, therefore be Rs.197.40 lakhs. As a result of the adjustment, the increase in depreciation as source of funds during the year would also increase by Rs.10.50 lakhs.
- The asset sold had a book value of Rs.1.95 lakhs (original value Rs.12.45 lakhs less accumulated depreciation Rs.10.50 lakhs).
- Sales value of Rs.2. 85 lakhs was a source during the year. It should, therefore, be shown as a source of funds.
- The sale of fixed assets at Rs.2.85 lakhs, as against its book value of Rs.1.95 lakhs would have been booked in the profit and loss account of the year as non-operating profit. The funds from operation include this item of profit also. As the entire sale value of the asset (including the profit component) is taken as source of fund, the profit on sale of assets (Rs. 0.90 lakhs) has to be removed from the profit from operation to avoid duplicity.

Now let us check the adjustments for arithmetic accuracy.

Uses of funds	
Increase in gross fixed assets	**Rs.12.45 lakhs**
Sources of funds	
Increase in depreciation	Rs.10.50 lakhs
Sale of assets	Rs. 2.85 lakhs
Less reduction in funds from operation (as it is in profit on sale of asset	(–)Rs. 0.90 lakhs
	Rs.12.45 lakhs

As a result of the above adjustments, the gross source, as well as the gross use of funds would show increases of Rs.12.45 lakhs.

Payment of Taxes / Dividend / Interest

Dividend and tax payments can be accounted in two ways. It is paid and shown in the profit and loss appropriation account as deduction before arriving at the disposable profit. Alternatively, a company might create provisions for tax and dividend. In that case, tax or dividend, when actually paid, is adjusted to the respective provisions. Since interests are charges (dividend is appropriation), these are debited to the profit and loss account, before arriving at taxable profit. No provisions are made in respect of interests, as the exact amount to be paid is known in advance In case dividend or tax is paid from the profit and loss appropriation account, funds from operation would have been used up to that extent. It would have caused double impact on cash flow. That part of the profit utilized in payments is funds from operation and as such should be back to the sources under funds from operation. Secondly, the payment is use of fund and as such added to the disposition of funds. Where taxes and dividends are paid out of provisions, the figure of provisions in the balance sheet is after the payment. Hence, payments made for dividends and taxes are to be added back as sources under provisions. Since actual payments were made in respect of dividends and taxes, these are also to be treated as uses of funds. The adjustment would, therefore, necessitate increase in sources side under funds from operations and in the uses side the amounts paid would be shown as payment of taxes / dividends.

Repayment of Loan Installments

The term repayment includes payment of installments of term loans and deposits and the amortisation of debt instruments such as bonds and debentures. Repayment causes outflow of funds. But, the reduction in loans arrived at by deducting the outstanding at the end of the previous year from current year is the net outflow after adjusting for inflows by way of additional loans availed of during the year. The gross outflow would, therefore be net outflow plus additional loans during the year. The inflow through additional loan availed during the year, is to be source and shown as such.

Shares Issued at Premium or Discount

When shares are issued at premium reserves increase in the balance sheet. The swelled reserves at the end of the period are deducted from the reserves of the previous period to arrive at increase in funds from operation. This is not the correct position. The increase on account of premium is not earned profit and as such is not funds from operation. It is capital reserve. Hence this should be deducted from the accruals and shown as separate source of fund under capital reserves. Readers might recall that it is another instance of change in composition, which does not affect the sources or uses of funds. Issue of shares at discount causes capital loss and is either deducted from the reserves or charged to profit and loss appropriation .Either of the treatments would have reduced funds from operation. The amount of discount would, thus, have to be treated as source of funds under funds from operation and simultaneously shown as uses under discount on share issue.

On the basis of the following additional information made available from the records of Banberry Confectioneries Ltd., the cash flow statement of the company is reconstructed giving effect to the impact of these information on its fund flow.

Additional Information

- The company issued bonus shares of Rs.50 lakhs during the year.
- During the year, Rs.18.00 lakhs was provided for taxation.
- Assets of the original value of Rs.19.13 lakhs, on which depreciation upto date was Rs.15.32, were sold for Rs.2.86 lakhs.
- Additional shares issued for cash during the year were Rs.24.40 lakhs at 100% premium.
- The company issued additional bonds for Rs.20 lakhs during the year.
- Dividend paid during the year was Rs.2.65 lakhs.
- Interest paid during the year was Rs.4.36 lakhs.

The incremental or net cashflow of the company for the year-ended 31.3.2003 is furnished in Table 4 at page 225. The additional information would give rise to the following adjustments to it :

Bonus Issue: Rs.50 Lakhs

The net increase in capital at Rs.74.40 lakhs includes bonus issue of Rs.50 lakhs. The actual fund increase by share issue is, thus, restricted to Rs.24.40 lakhs. The amount of Rs.50 lakhs transferred from reserves for issuing bonus shares is to be added back to the sources of funds under funds from operation.

Provision For Taxation- Rs.18 Lakhs

Provision for taxation, as on 31.3.2002, was Rs.48.00 lakhs. During the year, additional provision for Rs. 18.00 lakhs was made. The balance of provision as on 31.3.2003 should have therefore risen to Rs. 66.00 lakhs. However, the balance as on 31.3.2003 was Rs.60.00 lakhs only, indicating that the difference (Rs.6.00 lakhs) had been paid as Taxes during the year.

Provision for tax as on 31.3.2002	Rs.48.00 lakhs
Additional during the year	Rs.18.00 lakhs
Balance if no tax had been paid	Rs.66.00 lakhs
Less: Actual balance as on 31.3.2003	Rs.60.00 lakhs
Tax paid during the year	Rs.6.00 lakhs

Table 4 shows net increase in provision for tax at Rs.12.00 lakhs as against the actual provision of Rs.18.lakhs. The difference has to be added as source under funds from operation, (as provisions are appropriations of profit). The payment of tax of Rs.6.00 lakhs has to be shown as use of funds.

Assets Sold: Rs.2.86 Lakhs

The book value of the assets sold (original value Rs.19.13 lakhs, less depreciation Rs.15.32 lakhs) is Rs.3.81 lakhs. Sale price being Rs.2.86 lakhs, loss on sale of the assets was Rs.0.95 lakh. When the assets were sold, their original value of Rs.19.13 lakhs would have been removed from the gross fixed assets. Similarly, accumulated depreciation on the assets sold (Rs.15.32 lakhs) would also have been removed. When sales value was received, the company would have passed the following journal entry.

By Cash	Rs. 2.86 lakhs
By Loss on sale of assets	Rs. 0.95 lakhs
By Depreciation	Rs.15.32 lakhs
To Assets	Rs.19.13 lakhs

The effects of the entry were:

- Gross fixed assets stand reduced by Rs.19.13 lakhs.
- Depreciation stands reduced by Rs.15.32 lakhs.
- Sources of funds (cash) did not include the sale proceeds of Rs.2.86 lakhs.
- Funds from operation stand reduced by loss on sale of assets of Rs.0.95 lakh.

Adjustments needed are:

Increase in gross fixed assets should be more by Rs.19.13 lakhs(use of funds).

Increase in depreciation to be more byRs. 15.32 lakhs (source of funds).

Funds from operation to be more by Rs.0.95 lakhs (source of funds).

Sources of funds on account of sale of assets should be Rs.2.86 lakhs.

These adjustments would have resulted in increase in use of funds by Rs.19.13 lakhs under fixed assets and equally in sources under funds from operation (Rs.0.95 lakh), depreciation (Rs.15.32 lakhs) and sale proceeds of assets (Rs.2.86 lakhs).

Additional Issue at 100% Premium- Rs. 24.40 Lakhs

The company's sources of funds have increased, by way of increase in capital issued for cash Rs. 24.40 lakhs and premium on shares Rs. 24.40 lakhs. Increase in share capital is accounted as source. Premium on share being capital reserve, has been included under reserves. Its inclusion under reserves would have increased funds from operation by Rs. 24.40 lakhs. As premium on issue is not operating income, the amount should be deducted from funds from operation and presented under a separated head, premium on share issue, both under the sources.

Additional Bond Issue- Rs.20 Lakhs

Fixed liabilities of the company(which includes bonds) as on 31.3.2002 were Rs.151.58 lakhs. During the year fixed liabilities should have increases by Rs. 20 lakhs when additional issue of bonds were made. Therefore, outstandings in fixed liabilities should have been Rs.171.58 lakhs if there were no amortisation. As against this, the actual balance as on 31.3.2003 was Rs.121.25 lakhs. This shows a reduction of Rs.30.33 lakhs, which is the value of term liabilities amortized during the year without taking into account the additional bonds issued. Hence, the absolute outflow would have been Rs. 20 lakhs more than the incremental outflow shown by the balance sheet differential. That is the repayment of term liabilities should have been Rs.50.33 lakhs. Therefore Rs. 20 lakhs had to be added to reduction of term liabilities. Further, the bond issue is a source of funds and has to be shown as such in the sources as a separate item.

Dividend Paid- Rs.2.65 Lakhs

Payment of dividend is use of funds. There is a provision for dividend. It was Rs. 27.68 at the end of 31.3.2002. The payment had been made from out of these provisions. Had the company made no additional provision for the year, the balance in the provisions for dividend would have been reduced to Rs.25.03.However the closing balance in the provision, as on 31.3.2003, was Rs. 32.45 lakhs. The difference (Rs.7.42 lakhs) should have been the additions made to the provisions during the year, as against which the addition in balance sheet was only Rs.4.77 lakhs. Therefore Rs.2.65 lakhs had to be added to sources under funds from operation. Simultaneously, in the uses side, Rs.2.65 lakhs has to be shown under payment of dividend.

Interest Paid- Rs.4.36 Lakhs

Interest paid would have reduced the profit from operation. Since interest is a non-operating cost, the amount of interest paid has to be added back to funds from operation and simultaneously shown as uses of fund under the head payment of interest.

Adjusted Flow

The effects of the adjustments are to be made to in Table 3, before working out adjusted cash and fund flows. The adjusted flows are thus gross flows. Table 8 shows the impact of the adjustments:

Table 8
Banberry Confectioneries Ltd.
Balance sheet ason 31.3.2003 (adjusted)

	2003	2002	Increase / Decrease	Adjustment	Final
Liabilities					
Share capital	198.40	124.00	74.40	–50.00	24.40
Reserves and surplus	821.52	769.07	52.45	+50.00+0.95	
				-24.40+4.36	83.36
Depreciations	388.22	318.89	69.33	+15.32	84.65
Premium on shares	—	—	—	+24.40	24.40
Fixed liabilities	121.25	151.58	-30.33	–20.00	–50.33
Bonds issue	—	—	—	+ 20,00	20.00
Current liabilities**	182.45	1.57	180.88	—	180.88
Sundry creditors	523.86	428.86	95.00	—	95.00
Provisions for tax	60.00	48.00	12.00	+6.00	18.00
Prov.for dividend	32.45	27.68.	4.77	+2.65	7.42
Sale of assets				+2.86	2.86
Total	2328.15	1869.65	458.50	32.14	490.64
Assets					
Gross block	1039.43	741.70	297.73	+19.13	316.86
Capital WIP	271.66	53.92	217.74		217.74
Investments	4.56	37.48	–32.92		–32.92
Cash	13.84	12.37	1.47		1.47
Other current Assets	960.09	1023.21	–63.12		–63.12
Misc. expenditure	38.57	0.97	37.60		37.60

Payment of tax				+6.00	6.00
Payment of dividend				+2.65	2.65
Payment of interest				+4.36	4.36
Total	2328.15	1869.65	458.50	32.14	490.64

It may be seen that the gross flow is higher than the net. On the basis of the adjustment revised cash flow incorporating the adjustments is in Table 9.

Table 9
Banberry Confectioneries Ltd.
Gross Cash flow for the year ended 31.3.2003 (adjusted)

		Rs.Lakh.
A.Sources of funds		
Increases in share capital		24.40
Premium on shares		24.40
Decrease in investments		32.92
Sale of assets		2.86
Funds from operation:		
Increases in retained earnings	83.36	
Increases in depreciation	84.65	
Increase in provision for tax	18.00	
Increase in provision for dividend	7.42	193.43
Increase in term liabilities (bonds)		20.00
Increases in Current liabilities		180.88
Increase in sundry creditors		95.00
Decrease in Current assets		63.12
Total of A		637.01
B.Uses of funds		
Increase in Fixed assets		316.86
Increase in work in progress		217.74
Increase in Misc. expenditures		37.60
Payment of tax		6.00
Payment of dividend		2.65
Payment of interest		4.36
Decreases Fixed liabilities		50.33
Total of B		635.54

Opening balance of cash	12.37
Surplus of cash(A-B)	1.47
Closing balance of cash	13.84

The change in working capital and the fund flow statements of the company as adjusted are given in Tables 10 and 11.

Table 10
Banberry Confectioneries Ltd.
Schedule of changes in working capital for the year ended 31.3.2003(adjusted)

	2003	**2002**	**Change in**	**WC**
A.Current assets			Increases	Decreases
Cash	13.84	12.37	1.47	
Other current Assets	960.09	1023.21		63.12
Total of current assets. (A)	973.93	1035.58		
B.Current liabilities				
Current liabilities	182.45	1.57		180.88
Sundry creditors	523.86	428.86		95.00
Total of current liabilities. (B)	706.31	430.43		
C.Working capital. (A-B)	267.62	605.15	1.47	339.00
Decrease in working capital.		337.53		
Less Increase in working capital on account of				337.53
payments for Tax			6.00	
Dividend			2.65	
Interest			4.36	
			13.01	337.53
Decrease in working capital				324.52

I am of the view that the schedule of changes in working capital is an imperfect tool and is another brain wave of Indian authors to show originality. It only indicates movement in ***working capital assets and liabilities and not working capital as a whole.*** It does not provide for the fund outflows that do not affect the current assets or liabilities. And there are quite a few of these flows. For example, payment of interest, repayment of installments, payment of dividend and taxes are all uses of working capital. These payments are not reflected in the change in current assets or liabilities statement. In the example above, I have made the adjustment for these items, by suitable modification of the schedule.

Table 11
Banberry Confectioneries Ltd.
Fund flow statement for the year ended 31.3.2003(adjusted)

A.Sources of funds		
Increases in share capital		24.40
Increase in premium on issue		24.40
Sale of assets		2.86
Decrease in investments		32.92
Increase in bonds		20.00
Funds from operation:		
Increases in retained earnings	83.36	
Increases in depreciation	84.65	
Increase in provision for tax	18.00	
Increase in provision for dividend	7.42	193.43
Decrease in working capital		324.52
Total of A		622.53
B.Uses of funds		
Increase in Fixed assets		316.86
Increase in work in progress		217.74
Increase in Misc. expenditures		37.60
Decreases Fixed liabilities		50.33
Total of B		622.53

Before we proceed further to analyze the flows, let us take a few questions from the southern universities on cash flows and fund flows. Although figures of assets and liabilities are ridiculously low and the dates are decades old, the problems are meant to ascertain the basic understanding of the concept.

From Anna University-MBA

1. Statement of financial position of Mr. A is given below: **(Rs.)**

	1.1.2000	31.12.2000
Accounts payable	29,000	25,000
Capital	7,39,000	6,15,000
	7,68,000	6,40,000

Cash	40,000	30,000
Debtors	20,000	17,000
Stock	8,000	13,000
Building	1,00,000	80,000
Other fixed assets	6,00,000	5,00,000
	7,68,000	6,40,000

Additional Information:

- There were no drawings
- There were no purchase or sale of either building or other fixed assets

Prepare statement of cash flow ?

Solution

Stage 1

Working out the balance sheet differences.

	1.1.2000	31.12.2000	Difference
	1.1.2000	31.12.2000	
Accounts payable	29,000	25,000	–4,000
Capital	7,39,000	6,15,000	–1,24,000
	7,68,000	6,40,000	–1,28,000
Cash	40,000	30,000	–10,000
Debtors	20,000	17,000	–3,000
Stock	8,000	13,000	5,000
Building	1,00,000	80,000	–20,000
Other fixed assets	6,00,000	5,00,000	–1,00,000
	7,68,000	6,40,000	–1,28,000

Stage 2

Cash flow statement of Mr. A for the year ended—

(A)Sources		Cash flow
Decrease in Debtors		3,000
Total of A		3,000
(B) Uses		
Loss in business	1,24,000	

Add Depreciation(being reduction in building and other fixed assets)	1,20,000	
Funds lost in operations		4,000
Decrease in Accounts payable		4,000
Increase in Stock		5,000
Total of B		13,000
Opening balance of cash		40,000
Less Deficit(A-B)		10,000
Closing balance of cash		30,000

When fund flow is to be worked out, the first stage would be the same as it was for cash flow. The second stage would be in two sub- stages, one a schedule of changes in working capital and the other fund flow statement proper.

Stage 3

Schedule of Changes in Working Capital of Mr. A

	1.1.2000	**31.12.2000**	**Changes in Working capital**	
			Increases	Decreases
Current Assets				
Cash	40,000	30,000		10,000
Debtors	20,000	17,000		3,000
Stock	8,000	13,000	5,000	
Total	68,000	60,000		
Current liabilities				
Accounts payable	29,000	25,000	4,000	
Total	29,000	25,000		
Working capital	-39,000	-35,000	9,000	13,000
Decrease in working capital.	4,000			4,000

Stage 4

Fund flow statement of Mr.A

Sources	
Decrease in working capital	4,000
Total	4,000

Uses		
Loss in business operation	1,24,000	
Add Depreciation(being reduction in building and other fixed assets)	1,20,000	4,000
Funds lost in operations		4,000
Total		4,000

2. From Madras University-MBA

From the following summarized balance sheets of XY Ltd as on March 31 1966 and 1967,you are required to prepare (a) Statement of changes in working capital and (b) Statement of sources and uses of funds.

Liabilities	1966	1967	Assets	1966	1967
	Rs.	Rs.		Rs.	Rs.
Equity share capital	37,500	60,000	Gross Fixed Assets	1,20,035	1,26,865
6% redeemable Pref. shares	50,000	50,000	LessDepriciation to date	45,010	49,240
Plant replacement reserve	7,500	5,000	Net Fixed Assets	75,025	77,625
Long terms loans	—	20,000	Investments	30,500	38,000
Bank loans	11,000		Inventors	49,000	52,000
Trade creditors	42,225	37,775	Debtors	44,000	42,500
Proposed dividend					
On equity shares	6,000	12,000			
P & L	50,175	51,350			
	2,04,400	2,26,125		2,04,400	2,26,125

Solution

Stage 1

Difference in balance sheet figures of XYLtd. **Rs.**

Liabilities	1966	1967	Difference
Equity share capital	37,500	60,000	22,500
6% redeemablePref. shares	50,000	40,000	–10,000
Plant replacement reserve	7,500	5,000	–2,500

Long terms loans	—	200,000	20,000
Depreciation	45,010	49,240	4230
Bank loans	11,000	—	–11,000
Trade creditors	42,225	37,775	–4450
Proposed dividend On equity	6,000	12,000	6000
P & L	50,175	51,350	1,175
Total	2,49,410	2,75,365	25,955
Assets	1966	1967	Difference
Fixed Assets	1,20,035	1,26,865	6,830
Investments	30,500	38,000	7,500
Inventories	49,000	52,000	3,000
Debtors	44,000	42,500	–1,500
Cash	5,875	16,000	10,125
Total	2,49,410	2,75,365	25,955

Stage 2

Cash flow statement of XYLtd. For the year ended31.3.1967.

A.Sources		
1.Increase in equity shares		22,500
2.Funds from operation		
Increase in P&L A/C	1,175	
Increase in Depreciation	4,230	
Increase in Proposed Dividend on equity shares	6,000	
Decrease in Plant replacement reserve	-2,500	8,905
3.Increase in term loans		20,000
4. Decrease in debtors		1,500
Total of A		52,905
B. Uses		
1.Increase in Fixed Assets		6,830
2.Decrease in Preference shares		10,000
3.Increase in investment		7,500
4.Increase in inventories		3,000

5.Decrease in bank loans	11,000
6.Decrease in trade creditors	4,450
Total of B	42,780
Opening balance of cash	5,875
Surplus (A-B)	10,125
Closing cash	16,000

Stage 3

Changes in working capital of XY Ltd. For the year ended 31.3.1967

	1966	1977	Change in Working Capital.	
			Increase	Decrease
Inventories	49,000	52,000	3,000	—
Debtors	44,000	42,500	—	1,500
Cash	5,875	16,000	10,125	—
Total of A	98,875	110,500	—	—
Current liabilities-B				
Bank loan	11,000	—	11,000	—
Trade creditors	42,225	37,775	4,450	—
Total of B	53,225	37,775		
Working capital	45,650	72,725	28,575	1,500
Increase in working capital		27,075	27,075	

Stage 4

Fund flow statement of XYLtd. For the year ended31.3.1967

A.Sources		
1.Increase in equity shares		22,500
2.Funds from operation		
Increase in P&L A/C	1,175	
Increase in Depreciation	4,230	
Increase in Proposed Dividend on equity shares	6,000	
Decrease in Plant replacement reserve	–2,500	8,905
3.Increase in term loans		20,000
Total of A		51,405

B. Uses	
1.Increase in Fixed Assets	6,830
2.Decrease in Preference shares	10,000
3.Increase in investment	7,500
4.Increase in working capital	27,075
Total of B	51,405

3. From Osmania University.

Prepare cash flow statement from the following:

Balance sheet:

	1996 Rs.	**1997 Rs.**
Liabilities:		
Capital	2,00,000	2,50,000
General Reserve	50,000	60,000
Profit & Loss A/c	30,500	30,600
Bank Loan (Long term)	70,000	—
Sundry Creditors	1,50,000	1,35,200
Provision for Taxation	30,000	35,000
	5,30,500	5,10,800
Assets	2,00,000	1,90,000
Land & Buildings	1,50,000	1,69,000
Machinery	1,00,000	74,000
Stock	80,000	64,200
Sundry Debtors	500	600
Cash	—	8,000
Bank	—	5,000
Goodwill	5,30,500	5,10,800

In 1997,dividend of Rs.23,000 was paid, machinery of book value of Rs.3,000 was sold for Rs.2,800,depreciationon on machinery Rs.12,000,income tax provided during the year Rs.33,000.

Solution

Stage 1

Difference in balance sheet figures **Rs.**

Liabilities:	**1996**	**1997**	**Difference**
Capital	2,00,000	2,50,000	50,000
General Reserve	50,000	60,000	10,000
Profit & Loss A/c	30,500	30,600	100
Bank Loan (Long term)	70,000	—	–70,000
Sundry Creditors	1,50,000	1,35,200	14,800
Provision for Taxation	30,000	35,000	5,000
	5,30,500	5,10,800	–19,700
Assets			
Land & Buildings	2,00,000	1,90,000	–10,000
Machinery	1,50,000	1,69,000	19,000
Stock	1,00,000	74,000	–26,000
Sundry Debtors	80,000	64,200	–15,800
Cash	500	600	100
Bank	—	8,000	8,000
Goodwill	—	5,000	5,000
	5,30,500	5,10,800	–19,700

Stage 2

Preparation of cash flow

Cash flow statement for the year 1997 **Rs.**

A.Sources		
1.Increase in equity shares		50,000
2.Funds from operation		
Increase in reserves	10,000	
Increase in P&L A/C	100	

Increase in provision for taxation	5,000	
Increase in depreciation on building*	10,000	25,100
3.Decrease in stock		26,000
5.Decrease in sundry debtors		15,800
Total of A		1,16,900
B. Uses		
1.Increase in machinery		19,000
2.Decrease in bank loan (long-term)		70,000
3.Increase in goodwill		5,000
3.Decrease in sundry creditors		14,800
Total of B		1,08,800
Opening balance of cash and bank		500
Surplus (A-B)		8,100
Closing stock of cash and bank		8.600

*Difference between the value of land and building between the years(Rs.2,00,000 in 1996 and Rs. 1,90,000 in 1997) had to be on account of depreciation.

Stage 3

Incorporating impacts of adjustments

There are a few adjustments in the Osmania University's question that are to be addressed.

Adjustments:

1. Dividend paid during the year Rs.30,000.

   As dividend had been paid out of profit, funds from operation should have been higher by that amount. Rs. 30,000 was paid as dividend and therefore there was a cash outflow to that extent. Uses of funds would increase by Rs.30,000.The result of this adjustment is increase in sources under funds from operation by Rs.30,000 and increase in uses of funds under dividend paid by the same amount.

2. Machinery with book value of Rs 3,000 ,on which there was depreciation of Rs.12,000 was sold for Rs.2,800.Thus the original cost of the machine sold was Rs.15,000(book value Rs.3,000 +depreciation Rs.12,000).The loss on sale of machine was Rs.200.On sale of the machine, the accountant would have removed the original cost of the concerned machinery(Rs.15,000)from the machinery account by crediting machinery Rs.15,000.He would also have removed the depreciation thereon by debiting Rs 12,000 to the

accumulated depreciation account. Further he would have debited cash by Rs.2,800 on sale of machine and also debited loss on sale of machineryRs.200 to the profit and loss account. The impact of these accounting entries on the flow of cash would be-

(a) The net increase in machinery (Rs.19,000)in the uses side of cash flow is after the removal of Rs.15,000.Hence, the actual increase in machinery during the year would be higher by Rs.15,000..This has to be added to use of funds under machinery.

(b) Depreciation of Rs.12,000 on sold machine had been removed. This should be added to depreciation in the sources side.

(c) Cash received on sale of machine Rs.2,800 is a source of funds and had to be included under the head Sale of machinery.

(d) Loss on sale of machinery Rs.200 would have been included in profit and loss account as cost. Loss on sale of machinery is non-operating cost. The cash from operation is thus reduced by Rs.200.This has to be added to the sources of funds under funds from operation.

Let us now check up our adjusted figures.

Particulars	**Sources**	**Uses**
1.Increase in depreciation	12,000	
2.increase in funds from operation	200	
3.sale of machine	2,800	
4.Increase in machinery		15,000
Total	15,000	15,000

3. Tax provision- Rs.33,000.In 1996 company had a provision Rs.30,000 for taxation. During the year it had provided a further sum of Rs.33,000.In all, the provision should have been Rs.63,000 had no tax been paid. How ever, the closing balance of tax provision was Rs.35, 000,indicating that the balance Rs.28,000 had been paid by way of taxation. The adjustment would be that the tax of Rs28,000 paid is out of provision and hence increase in provision for taxation should have been Rs.28,000.Tax being payment, is use of funds.

4. Adjusted cash flow statement

Cash flow for 1997(adjusted)

A.Sources	
1.Increase in equity shares	50,000
2.Funds from operation	

Increase in reserves	10,000	
Increase in P&L A/C	100	
Increase in provision for taxation 5,000+28,000 =	33,000	
Payment of dividend	23,000	
Loss on sale of machinery debited to P&L A/C	200	
Increase in depreciation on building	10,000	
Depreciation on machinery	12,000	88,300
3..Decrease in stock		26,000
5.Decrease in sundry debtors		15,800
6.Sale of machinery		2,800
Total of A		1,82,900
B. Uses		
1.Increase in machinery	19,000 + 15,000	34,000
2.Decrease in bank loan (long-term)		70,000
3.Increase in goodwill		5,000
3.Decrease in sundry creditors		14,800
4.Payment of dividend		23,000
5.Payment of tax		28,000
Total of B		1,74,800
Opening balance of cash and bank		500
Surplus (A-B)		8,100
Closing stock of cash and bank		8.600

Note. Although the examiners have not asked for fund flow statement, we would follow the other two stages also.

Stage 4

Changes in working capital for the year 1997

	1996	**1997**	**Change in working capital.**	
Current assets-A			Increase	Decrease
Stock	1,00,000	74,000		26,000
Sundry debtors	80,000	64,200		15,800
Cash	500	600	100	

Bank	—	8,000	8,000	
Total of A	1,80,500	1,46,800		
Current liabilities-B				
Sundry creditors	1,50,000	1,35,200	14,800	
Total of B	1,50,000	11,600	22,900	41,800
Working capital-A - B	30,500	18,900		
Decrease in WC				18,900
Increase on account of				
Payment of Dividend	23,000		23,000	
Payment of tax	28,000		28,000	
Increase in working capital	32,100		32,100	

Stage 5

Fund flow statement for the 1997

A.Sources		
1.Increase in equity shares		50,000
2.Funds from operation		
Increase in reserves	10,000	
Increase in P&L A/C	100	
Increase in provision for taxation	33,000	
Payment of dividend	30,000	
Loss on sale of machinery debited to P&L A/C	200	
Increase in depreciation on building	10,000	
Depreciation on machinery	12,000	88,300
3.Sale of machinery		2,800
Total of A		1,41,100
B. Uses		
1.Increase in Fixed Assets		34,000
2.Decrease in long term loan		70,000
3.Increase in goodwill		5,000
4.Increase in working capital		32,100
Total of B		1,41,100

Corporate Cash Flow

Our discussions on the preparation of cash flows and fund flows are based on what are normally required for the purpose of analyzing the movement of funds from and to the business. There is no statutory compulsion on any business, either corporate or non-corporate to publish flow statements along with other financial statements in their annual reports. However, corporates, whose shares are listed in any of the stock exchanges in the country, are, in terms of their listing agreements with the exchanges, required to publish cash flow statements. The Table in which the cash flow has to be reported is also prescribed in Revised Accounting Standards 3. As per the prescribed form, cashflow reporting has to be split in to three segments A, B and C, and styled as cash flow from operating activities, cash flow from investing activities and cash flow from financing activities. The divisions are to reflect the movement of funds under each of the corporate functions-operation, investing and financing. The groupings need no explanation. Cash flow from operating activities is sub-divided into two-funds from operations and adjustment for change in working capital. The latter is to reveal the changes in the flow of working capital .In effect the Table is harmonious blending of cash flow and fund flow statements in to one. The proforma in which listed companies report cashflow is as in Table below.

Table 12
Cash flow statement for the year ended

	Current year		Previous year
A. Cash flow from operation activities:			
Net profit before tax and extra ordinary items			
Adjustments for:			
Depreciation			
Foreign exchange			
Provisions			
Surplus / deficit on sale of assets			
Interest income			
Dividend income			
Operating profit before working capital changes			
Adjustment for changes in working capital:			
Adjustment for			
Trade and other receivables			
Inventories			

Trade payables and other liabilities			
Cash generated from operations			
Income taxes paid (net of refunds)			
Cash flow before extra-ordinary items			
Extra ordinary items			
Net cash from operating activities – A			
B. Cash flow from investing activities:			
Purchase of fixed assets			
Sale of fixed assets			
Purchase of investments			
Sale of investments			
Purchase of investments			
Sale of investments			
Capital subsidy received			
Net consideration received on transfer of business			
Interest received			
Dividend received			
Net cash from / used in investing activities – B			
C. Cash flow from Financing activities:			
Dividend paid			
Share capital raised			
Shares bought back / redeemed			
Market borrowings			
Repayment of borrowings			
Payment of interest			
Net cash from / used in /financing activities -C			
Net increase / decrease in cash (A + B + C)			
Cash as at beginning (opening balance)			
Cash as at the end (closing balance)			

The cash flow is given in a vertical form. *All sources are to be given in positive figures and all deployments in brackets.* It would, at the end, show the excess of deficit of cash during the year. If the opening balance of cash (which is the closing balance of cash at the end of the previous period) were adjusted to the cash surplus or deficit of the year, that would give the closing balance of cash. This can be verified with the balance sheet closing balance of cash as a check. Let us now rearrange the cashflow of Banberry Confectioneries Ltd., given in Table.9, as per the listing requirement.

Table 13
Banberry Confectioneries Ltd.
Cash flow statement for the year ended 31.3.2003
(As per listing requirements)

A. Cash flow from operating activities	
Profit before tax	82.41
Depreciation	84.65
Provision for taxation/dividend	25.42
Deficit on sale of assets written off in P&L a/c	0.95
Operating profit before working capital changes	193.43
Adjustments for	
Trade and other receivables and inventories-reduction	63.12
Trade payables and other liabilities-increase	275.88
Cash generated from operations	532.43
Income flow before extraordinary items	532.43
Extra ordinary item: writing off miscellaneous expenditures	-
Net cash from operating activities – A	532.43
B. Cash flow from investing activities:	
Purchase of fixed assets	(534.60)
Increase in miscellaneous expenses	(37.60)
Sale of fixed assets	2.86
Sale of investment	32.92
Net cash used in investing activities- B	(536.42)
C. Cash flow from financing activities:	
Dividend /Tax paid	(8.65)
Interest paid	(4.36)
Proceeds from share capital issue	24.40
Premium on share issue	24.40
Bond issued	20.00
Repayment of fixed liabilities	(50.33)
Net cash from financing activities – C	5.46

Net increases in cash (A + B + C)	1.47
Opening cash	12.37
Closing cash	13.84

Flow Analysis

Preparing cash flow becomes a mechanical process once the concept is clear. Any one with basic accounting knowledge of debit and credit can do the job effortlessly. The taste of the pudding is in its eating. The purpose of cash flow preparation is to find satisfactory answers to the questions posed in the introductory paragraph of the chapter. Let us analyse the cash flow of Banberry Confectioneries Ltd. and learn to get answers to the questions:

Internal Accruals

Internal cash accrual is the cash profit made by the business during the year. Gross cash profit comprises profit before depreciation, interest, tax and dividend. It is the funds generated in operation. Net cash accrual is after payment of interest, tax and dividend. In Banberry Confectioneries Ltd. the gross and net cash accruals for the year ended 31.3.2003 were Rs.193.43 and Rs.187.47 lakhs respectively as under:

	(Rs.lakhs)
Profit before interest, tax and dividend, but after depreciation	108.78
Add. Depreciation	84.65
Gross funds from operation	193.43
Less: Interest	4.36
Taxation	8.00
Dividend	2.65
Loss on sale of assets	0.95
Net cash accrual	187.47

The internal accruals of Rs.193.43 lakhs as percent of capital employed at Rs.1346.85 lakhs represents a return on investment of 14.36 percent.

Where is it ?

Cash accrual is used either to increase assets (including cash holdings) and / or to decrease liabilities. Banberry had used Rs.50.33 lakhs to reduce fixed liabilities and Rs.37.60 lakhs to meet miscellaneous expenses. The balance Rs.99.54 lakhs was utilized for the part financing fixed assets.

	(Rs. lakhs)
Net cash accruals	187.47
Of which	
Used for liquidating liabilities	50.33
Used for meeting miscellaneous expenses	37.60
Used for part financing fixed assets	99.54

The internal accrual available for investment was only Rs.99.54 lakhs as against the investment of Rs.534.60 lakhs which is only 18.62 % of the requirements. The company had to meet the balance of requirements from other sources, as seen in the next para.

How Assets Financed

Assets are to be financed from internal accruals and long-term resources. In the case of Banberry Confectioneries Ltd., the pattern of funding assets is as under:

		(Rs. Lakhs)
Increase in the cost of assets		534.60
Funded by		
Sale of fixed assets	2.86	
Sale of investment	33.16	
Internal accruals	99.54	
Share capital	24.40	
Share premium	24.40	
Bonds	20.00	
Long term sources		204.36
From working capital		330.24
		534.60

It is seen that out of its long-term requirements of funds for Rs.534.60 lakhs, the company could meet only Rs.204.36 lakhs from long-term sources and had to use the major part of the requirements from working capital sources.

High or Low Dividends

Dividend policy of a company is influenced by two factors, one is internal and the other is external. The former is the availability of cash. Indian laws stipulate that dividend should be paid within 42 days of its declaration. The extent of dividend declared is thus subject to the availability of cash. The fund flow projection would indicate the position. It the company's liquidity position is tight, it might restrict the pay out, even though it had made handsome profits. The second and most important aspect is the ***relationship between the market rate of capitalization and the actual rate of capitalization.*** Market rate of capitalization refers to the average rate of return companies in the same risk category earns. Actual rate of return is the **R**eturn **O**n quity of the captioned company. When the market rate of capitalization is higher than the actual rate of return of the company, it is advisable to pay higher dividends. The shareholders would not like to retain their money in the business when the market rate is higher. In such a situation if the company declares low dividends, shareholders would tend to dispose the shares and invest in other companies, where the rate is equal or higher than the market rate. The action, on the part of the investors to sell the shares of the company would depress the market price of the shares and the wealth of shareholders. This process would continue till the market rate of return equals actual rate. When the actual rate of capitalization is higher than the market rate, the company should pay less and plough back higher percentage. Shareholders would prefer retention of their money in such companies, as their wealth would grow at a faster rate. The return on capital employed in Banberry Confectioneries Ltd. at 14.36 percent is above industry average of 11.5 percent. It naturally would like to restrict its payout. Besides, it was using short-term working capital to finance its long-term needs. Its cash position is tight. So on both the counts, the company had declared a lower rate of dividend.

Working Capital

Increase in working capital, based on the genuine requirements of the business, would ensure smooth and uninterrupted functioning of business. Surplus working capital would lead to locking up funds without returns. This would increase cost of operations and reduce profitability. An effective businessman has to strike a balance between the two opposing needs of liquidity and profitability. In this illustrative case, the company had used a major part of its working capital source to finance fixed investments.

Diversion of Funds

Diversion of funds means the use of funds for purposes other than what they were meant for. Diversion could be internal or external. Internal diversion involves using short-term funds for long-term uses. External diversion is investment of funds in outside the business, usually in other concerns. The external diversion might be beneficial or detrimental to the interest of the business. In case it is invested on securities that yield higher returns, it is advantageous. On the other hand, if the funds of the business are invested in a sinking sister concern, where the directors have personal interest, it is detrimental to the interest of the company. Shrewd readers would by now have concluded that there was internal diversion of funds in the illustration during the year. About half the capital investment is met through short-term working capital sources. The company would have tight liquidity position if this trend is not reversed. It is high time that the company raises long-term resources to restore normalcy.

Cash flow analysis, as we have seen, would indicate the directional flow of funds- from where to where and to what extent. The management could keep a closer watch over the flow and take corrective measures to avoid liquidity problems, without sacrificing profitability.

Whatever we have so far seen is the ***financial cashflow*** in a business. Economists are using a concept called free ***cash flow.*** Free cash flow is that part of the funds, which is free for extraneous uses. Extraneous uses include investment in physical, financial and real assets outside the business. It is the free cash flow that is used for takeovers of other businesses. It comprises profit after tax less investments during the accounting period. The concept is also used to value firms. Present value of future free cash flows is the value of a business. For example, the following data(in lakhs of rupees) relates to an investment during its useful lifetime of 5 years.

Years	**1**	**2**	**3**	**4**	**5**
Profit after tax	125.40	137.94	151.73	166.91	183.60
Depreciation	35.09	48.12	51.10	73.10	86.35
Investment	70.45	151.02	97.22	106.94	112.29
Free cash flow	90.04	35.04	115.61	133.07	157.66

The investor's desired rate of return is 15 percent. When the free cashflow is discounted at 15%, the present value of the investment is Rs.335.31 lakhs. The conclusion is, the maximum funds to be deployed in the investment would be Rs.335.31 lakhs.

Summary

In a business organization funds flow into the business and out of it very frequently. The movement of funds is reflected in the increase and decrease of assets and liabilities. Increase in liabilities and decreases in assets are indications of inward movement of funds. On the other hand, increases in assets and decreases in liabilities cause the outward flow of funds. Hence, by measuring the changes in assets and liabilities in the balance sheet between two consecutive periods the movement of funds could be gauged. It should be remembered that movement of funds in an enterprise is continuous, whereas the flows indicated by the balance sheets represent the net flow as at the end of the accounting period. It is incremental in nature and does not reveal the total magnitude of the flow. A few flows cancel each other during the period. Therefore to ascertain the extent of gross flow, the counter flows during the period are to be recognizes. This is done through adjustments. Analysts use the term cash flow and fund flow interchangeably. But for any effective analysis, a clear-cut distinction should be made between the two. Cash flow is treated in this book as a generic term denoting all the flow during an accounting period. When the assessment of the flow is confined to the movement of working capital alone, it is called fund flow.

Cash flow study helps the analyst to follow the directional flow of funds. It helps him to find answers to the questions that are not addressed by the profitability analysis No financial analysis is, therefore, complete without analyzing movement of funds. Many Indian corporates are now presenting a cash flow statement along with other reports. It is only through cashflow analysis that meaningful answers to the queries raised above are found.

I. QUESTIONS

1. Does the analysis of financial statements enlighten the seekers of information with the needed answers to their specific questions?
2. What are the information do you think are not revealed by the ratio analysis??
3. What would be your recommendation in such situations?
4. What do you think brings about changes in assets and liabilities?
5. What happens when liabilities increase?
6. What are the changes that are caused by the efflux of funds?
7. Are the changes in the balance sheet figures adequate indication of the total flow of funds? If not, what, according to you are the adjustments to know the absolute cash flows?
8. Do cash flow and fund flow denote the same? If not how do you distinguish between the two?
9. When do companies declare higher dividends?
10. What are free cash flows? Can you think of a practical use of free cashflow?
11. What do you understand by the term growth rate? How are they calculated?
12. What constitute diversion of funds? Are there diversions beneficial to the company ?
13. When a balance sheet is available, the preparation of a funds flow statement is superfluous. Do you agree?
14. Distinguish between funds flow and cash flow.

15. Profit for the current year is Rs.14,000, opening preliminary expenses is Rs.28,000 and closing preliminary expenses is Rs.22,000. Find out the cash from operation?

II. QUIZ

Say yes or no to the following

- Ratios expose all the information one would like to know about a company.
- Liabilities cause outflow of funds.
- Whether there is increase in assets or liabilities, it prompts cash inflow.
- Cash flow is synonymous with cash profit.
- A company would do well, if it can use cheap short – term liabilities to finance its capital investment needs.
- Increased inflow of funds is the sign of growth.
- Depreciation is a use of funds.

III. EXERCISES

1. Given the following balance sheets of Dewan Bahadur Enterprises as on 31.12.2003, prepare a statement showing the changes in working capital :

Assets	**31st December**	
Cash	**2002- Rs.**	**2003-Rs.**
Accounts Receivable	3,000	4,700
Land	12,000	11,500
Stock	5,000	6,600
	8,000	9,000
	28,000	31,800
Liabilities		
Accounts Payable	7,000	4,500
Capital	20,000	25,000
Retained Earnings	1,000	2,300
	28,000	31,800

2. The following is the summarized balance sheet of Ratlam Ltd. as at 31st December 2003: Prepare a Statement showing the changes in working capital.

Balance Sheet as on 31.12.200

	2002 Rs.	2003 Rs.		2002 Rs.	2003 Rs.
Capital :			Net Fixed		
Equity Shares	1,00,000	1,00,000	Assets	95,000	1,20,000
Preference Shares		50,000	Investments	—	10,000
General Reserve	30,000	40,000	Stock	40,000	60,000
Profit and Loss	25,000	70,000	Debtors	20,000	40,000
Creditors	20,000	10,000	B/R	5,000	2,000
Bills Payables	—	2,000	Prepaid		
Bank overdraft	3,000	—	Expenses	5,000	18,000
Taxation Provision	7,000	12,000	Cash	20,000	10,000
Proposed Dividend	10,000	16,000	Advances	10,000	40,000
	1,95,000	3,00,000		1,95,000	3,00,000

3. Prepare a Statement of changes in working capital from the following balance sheets of Ramon Seth &Company as on 31st December 2003:

Balance Sheet as on 31st December

Liabilities	**2002 Rs.**	**2003 Rs.**	**Assets Rs.**	**2002 Rs.**	**2003 Rs.**
Equity Capital	5,00,000	5,00,000	Fixed Assets	6,00,000	7,00,000
Debentures	3,70,000	4,50,000	Investments	2,00,000	1,00,000
			Work-in-		
Tax Payable	77,000	43,000	progress	80,000	90,000
Creditors	96,000	1,92,000	Stocks	1,50,000	2,25,000
Interest Payable	37,000	45,000	Debtors	70,000	1,40,000
Dividend Payable	50,000	35,000	Cash	30,000	10,000
	11,30,000	12,65,000		11,30,000	12,65,000

4. From the following balance sheets of the Cosmos Symphony for the year ended 31st December 2003, prepare schedule of change in working capital and statement showing sources and application of fund:

	31-12-02 Rs.	31-12-03 Rs.		31-12-02 Rs.	31-12-03 Rs.
Share Capital	3,00,000	4,00,000	Plant and		
Sundry Creditors	1,00,000	70,000	Machinery.	50,000	60,000
Profit and Loss	15,000	30,000	Furniture and		
			Fixtures	10,000	15,000
			Stocks	85,000	1,05,000
			Debtors	1,60,000	1,50,000
			Cash	1,10,000	1,70,000
	4,15,000	5,00,000		4,15,000	5,00,000

5. From the following information relating to Anxious Andrews Ltd. as on 30.6.2002, prepare Funds Flow Statement:

(Rs.lakhs)

	2001 Rs.	2002 Rs.		2001 Rs.	2003 Rs.
Share Capital	136.50	282.00	Cash	13.65	20.23
Reserves	45.50	72.75	Accounts		
Term loans	13.65	27.30	Receivable	268.25	296.46
Retained earnings	634.72	674.69	Inventories	86.45	95.82
Accounts Payable	216.12	218.92	Fixed Assets-		
			Net	462.02	508.39
			Investments	216.12	354.76
	1046.49	1275.66		1046.49	1275.66

Additional information:

(a) The company issued bonus shares for Rs.50 lakhs

(b) Depreciation written off during the year Rs.45.45 lakhs.

6. From the following balance sheets of a company, prepare a Sources and Uses of Funds Statement for 2003:

	1 January Rs.	31st December Rs.
Assets:		
Cash	35,000	75,000

Accounts Receivable	98,000	90,000
Merchandise Inventory	87,000	1,20,000
Long-term Investments	15,000	10,000
Land	20,000	30,000
	2,55,000	3,25,000
Liabilities:		
Accounts Payable	50,000	45,000
Notes Payable (Short-term)	20,000	35,000
Notes Payable (Due Dec. 2005)	—	20,000
Capital Stock	1,25,000	1,50,000
Retained Earnings	60,000	75,000
	2,55,000	3,25,000

7. From the following balance sheets of a Competitive Consultants, prepare a schedule of Changes in Working Capital.

Balance sheet as on 31st December.

Liabilities	1999 Rs.	2000 Rs.	Assets	1999 Rs.	2000 Rs.
Share Capital	2,00,000	2,50,000	Land and		
General Reserve	50,000	60,000	Buildings	2,00,000	1,90,000
Profit and Loss	30,500	30,600	Plant and		
Bank Loan			Machinery	1,50,000	1,69,000
(Short Period)	70,000	—	Stocks	1,00,000	74,000
Creditors	1,50,000	1,35,200	Debtors	80,000	64,200
Provision for			Cash	500	600
Taxation	30,000	35,000	Bank	—	8,000
			Goodwill	—	5,000
	5,30,500	5,10,800		5,30,500	5,10,800

8. From the following balance sheets of Meghalaya Plywood Ltd., prepare a schedule of changes in working capital and statement of flow of fund for 2002:

Assets	31st Dec. 2001 Rs.	31st Dec. 2002 Rs.
Land and Buildings:	50,000	50,000
Plant	24,000	34,000
Stock	9,000	7,000
Debtors	16,500	19,500
Cash at bank	4,000	9,000
Total:	1,03,500	1,19,500
Assets		
Capital	80,000	85,000
Profit & Loss	14,500	24,500
Creditors	9,000	5,000
Mortgage	—	5,000
Total	1,03,500	1,19,500

9. Alembic Agarbatis reported current profit of Rs.70,000 after incorporating the following:

	Rs.		Rs.
Loss on sale of Equipment	10,000	Gain on sale of non-current assets	40,000
Premium on Redemption of			
Debentures	1,500	Excess provision for	
Discount on Debentures	2,000	Taxation	22,000
Depreciation on Machinery and		Dividend income on	
Buildings	20,000	Investments	4,000
Depletion of natural resources	10,000	Transfer to General	
Amortization of Goodwill	30,000	Reserve	5,000
Interim dividend	25,000	Preliminary Expenses	1,000
		Profit on Revaluation of	
		Investments	2,500

Work out funds from operations.

10. Raminco Rasin Enterprises presents the following information and requires you to calculate its funds from operation during 2003:

Profit And Loss Account for the year ended 31.12.2003

	Rs.		Rs.
To Operation Expenses	1,00,000	By Gross Profit	2,00,000
To Depreciation	40,000	By Gain on sale of	
To Loss on sale of Building	10,000	Plant	20,000
To Advertisement Suspense	5,000		
To Discount Allowed	500		
To Discount on Issue of Shares			
written off	500		
To Goodwill written off	12,000		
To Net Profit	52,000		
	2,20,000		2,20,000

11. From the following balance sheet of Prem & Company for the year ended on 31st Dec. 2002and prepare a statement showing sources and application of funds and schedule of changes in working capital.

Rs.

Liabilities	2001	2002	Assets	2001	2002
Share Capital	4,00,000	5,75,000	Plant	75,000	1,00,000
Creditors	1,06,000	70,000	Stocks	1,21,000	1,36,000
Profit & Loss	14,000	31,000	Debtors	1,81,000	1,70,000
			Cash	1,43,000	2,70,000
	5,20,000	6,76,000		5,20,000	6,76,000

12. The following is the summarized balance sheet of M/s Kumaran Sweets Ltd. as on 31st December 2002.

Liabilities	2001 Rs.	2002 Rs.	Assets	2001 Rs.	2002 Rs.
10% Preference			Machinery	2,00,000	2,30,000
Shares	1,00,000	1,10,000	Buildings	1,50,000	1,76,000
Equity Shares	2,20,000	2,50,000	Land	18,000	18,000
Share Premium	20,000	26,000	Cash	42,000	32,000
Reserves and			Debtors	38,000	38,000
surplus	1,04,000	1,34,000	Bills		

12% Debentures	70,000	64,000	Receivable	42,000	62,000
Creditors	38,000	46,000	Stock	84,000	98,000
Bills Payable	5,000	4,000			
Provision for Tax	10,000	12,000			
Dividend Payable	7,000	8,000			
	5,74,000	6,54,000		5,74,000	6,54,000

Prepare a Statement of Sources and Application of Funds.

13. Calculate Funds from Operation from the information given below by Yahu & Yahu Ltd. as on 31st March 2003:

(a) Net Profit for the year Rs.6,50,000.

(b) Gain on the sale of buildings Rs.35,500.

(c) Goodwill appeared in the beginning of the year at rs.80,000.

(d) Old machinery worth Rs.8,000 has been sold for Rs.6,500 during the year.

(e) Rs.12,500 was transferred to Reserves.

(f) Depreciation of Rs.34,500 was provided during the year on machinery and furniture

14. From the following balance sheets of a Selva Traders, a sole trader, prepare a schedule of changes in working capital and a fund flow statement for 2003:

Liabilities	**2002 Rs.**	**2003 Rs.**	**Assets**		
Capital	63,000	1,00,000	Cash	15,000	20,000
Long-Term Loans	50,000	60,000	Debtors	30,000	28,000
Trade Creditors	42,000	39,000	Stock	55,000	72,000
Bank Overdraft	35,000	25,000	Land and Buildings	80,000	1,00,000
Outstanding Expenses	5,000	6,000	Furniture	15,000	10,000
	1,95,000	2,30,000		1,95,000	2,30,000

15. From the following balance sheets of a Wayside Wears, prepare a Fund Flow statement for the month May,2003:

Liabilities	**April Rs.**	**May Rs.**	**Assets**	**April Rs.**	**May Rs.**
Share Capital	60,000	65,000	Goodwill	30,000	25,000
Profit & Loss A/c	34,000	26,000	Plant and Machinery	60,000	50,000
Current Liabilities	12,000	3,000	Current Assets	16,000	19,000
	1,06,000	94,000		1,06,000	94,000

16. The following are the summarized heads of accounts of Kiran Kumar Cycle Mart for December, 2003

Liabilities	November	December	Assets	Nov.	December
	Rs.	Rs.		Rs.	Rs.
Preference	—	10,000			
Equity Shares	40,000	40,000	Fixed Assets	41,000	40,000
General Reserve	2,000	2,000	Less:Depreciation	11,000	15,000
Profit & Loss	1,000	1,200		30,000	25,000
Debentures	6,000		Net fixed assets		
Current Liabilities:			Current Assets	20,000	24,000
			Debtors	30,000	35,000
Creditors	12,000	7,000	Stock	300	500
Provision for Tax	3,000		Prepaid expenses	1,200	3,500
Proposed Dividend	5,000	11,000	Cash		
Bank Overdraft	12,500	4,200			
		5,800			
		6,800			
	81,500	88,000		81,500	88,000

Prepare:

(a) A statement showing changes in the working capital during the month, and

(b) A statement of sources and application of funds.

17. From the following balance sheets of Honduras Households and the additional information given, calculate funds from operations for the month February 2004.

	January	February
	Rs.	Rs.
Share Capital	1,00,000	1,50,000
General reserves	30,000	30,000
Profit and Loss A/c	20,000	22,000
6% debentures	80,000	80,000
Creditors	65,000	58,000
Provision for Tax	5,000	10,000
	3,00,000	3,50,000

Land and Buildings	1,00,000	95,000
Plant and Machinery	80,000	90,000
Stocks	70,000	1,10,000
Debtors	20,000	25,000
Investments	—	10,000
Cash	10,000	10,000
Goodwill	20,000	10,000
	3,00,000	3,50,000

18. Balance sheet of National Co. for the month December, 2003 is as follows :

Liabilities & Capital	November Rs.	December Rs.	Assets	November Rs.	December Rs.
Share Capital	5,00,000	7,00,000	Land and		
Profit & Loss	1,00,000	1,60,000	Buildings	80,000	1,20,000
General Reserve	50,000	70,000	Plant and		
Sundry Creditors	1,53,000	1,90,000	Machinery	5,00,000	8,00,000
Bills Payable	40,000	50,000	Stock	1,00,000	75,000
Expenses O/S	7,000	5,000	Debtors	1,50,000	1,60,000
			Cash	20,000	20,000
	8,50,000	11,75,000		8,50,000	11,75,000

Prepare

i. Statement of change in working capital and

ii. Fund flow statement for the month and comment on the directional flow of funds.

19. From the following balance sheet of Kapil Enterprises, make out: (i) Statement of Changes in working capital (ii) Fund flow statement with comments on the directional flow.

Balance Sheet as on 30.6.2002

Liabilities	2001 Rs.	2002 Rs.	Assets	2001 Rs.	2002 Rs.
EquityShares	3,00,000	4,00,000	Goodwill	1,15,000	90,000
Preference	1,50,000	70,000	Land & Buildings	2,00,000	1,70,000
Reserves	40,000	48,000	Plant	80,000	2,00,000
Profit & Loss	30,000		Debtors	1,60,000	2,00,000
Proposed		50,000	Stock	77,000	1,09,000
Dividend	42,000	83,000	Bills Receivable	20,000	30,000
Creditors	55,000	16,000	Cash in hand	15,000	10,000
Bills Payable	20,000		Cash at Bank	10,000	8,000
Provision for		50,000			
Taxation	40,000				
	6,77,000	8,17,000		6,77,000	8,17,000

20. From the following balance sheet of Gladstone Co. Ltd. prepare a statement of changes in working capital and the funds flow statement for the year ended 31st March 2004.

Balance Sheet as on 31st March2004

Liabilities	2003 Rs.	2004 Rs.	Assets	2003 Rs.	2004 Rs.
Share Capital	3,00,000	3,50,000	Good will	1,00,000	80,000
Debentures	1,50,000	2,50,000	Machinery	4,10,000	5,40,000
Reserves	1,00,000	1,50,000	Investment	30,000	80,000
Profit & Loss	60,000	70,000	Issue		
Provision for			expenses	5,000	--
Depreciation	90,000	1,30,000	Cash at Bank	1,20,000	1,30,000
Creditors	75,000	1,10,000	Debtor	80,000	1,90,000
Bills Payable	10,000	15,000	Stock	40,000	55,000
	7,85,000	10,75,000		7,85,000	10,75,000

During the year, investment costing Rs.30,00,000 were sold for Rs.28,00,000. A new machine was purchased for Rs.45,00,000 and the payment was made in fully paid shares.

21. The following is the summarized balance sheet of Stick More Company as on 31st December 2003:

	2002	2003
Liabilities	**Rs.**	**Rs.**
Equity Share Capital	75,00,000	109,20,000
8% Debentures	18,75,000	—
Share Premium	—	4,55,000
General Reserve	11,25,000	22,75,000
Profit & Loss Account	18,00,000	30,94,000
Sundry Creditors	48,75,000	1,50,000
Proposed Dividend	52,50,000	68,25,000
Provision for Depreciation:		
Plant & Machinery	37,50,000	41,50,000
Furniture	2,25,000	1,82,000
	264,00,000	280,51,000
Assets		
Land and Buildings	39,37,500	48,25,000
Plant and Machinery (at cost)	108,75,000	125,60,000
Furniture (at cost)	3,37,500	4,55,000
Inventories	53,13,750	47,77,500
Sundry Debtors	28,12,500	38,67,500
Investments	30,00,000	13,28,000
Cash	1,23,750	2,38,000
	264,00,000	280,51,000

Additional information is as follows:

(1) Furniture which cost Rs.5,00,000, written down value Rs.1,00,000 was sold during the year 2003 for Rs.2,00,000

(2) Plant and Machinery which cost Rs.20,00,000 and in respect of Which Rs.13,00,000 had been written off as depreciation was sold during the year for Rs.3,00,000

(3) The dividend of 1999 was paid during 2003.

Prepare (a) a Statement of changes in working capital during 2003 and (b) Funds flow statement for the year.

22. The following are the summaries of the balance sheet of a Din Ilahi Ibrahim Limited as at 31st December 2003.

(Rupees)

	2002	2003
Sundry Creditors	39,50,000	41,135
Bills Payable	33,78,000	11,525
Bank Overdraft	59,51,000	—
Provision for Taxation	40,00,000	50,00050,
Reserves	50,00,000	00041,
Profit and Loss	39,69000	2202,
Share Capital	2,00,00,000	60,000
	4,62,48,000	4,53,000
Cash at Bank	2,50,000	2,700
Sundry Debtors	85,17,500	72,625
Sundry Advances	2,31,500	735
Stock	1,11,04,000	97,370
Land & Buildings	1,48,50,000	1,44,250
Plant & Machinery	1,12,95,000	1,16,200
Goodwill	—	20,000
	4,62,48,000	4,53,880

The following additional information is obtained from the general ledger:

(1) During the year, an interim dividend of Rs.26,00,000 was paid.

(2) The assets of another company were purchased for Rs.60,00,000 payable in fully paid shares of the company. These assets consisted of stock Rs.21,64,000, machinery Rs.18,36,000 and goodwill Rs.20,00,000. In addition, sundry purchases of plant were made totaling Rs.5, 65,000.

(3) Income tax paid during the year amounted to Rs.25,00,000.

(4) The net profit for the year before tax was Rs.62,53,000.

Prepare a statement showing the sources and applications of funds for the year 2003 and a schedule setting out changes in working capital.

23. The following are the summarized balance sheet of Fahien Fertilizers Ltd. as at 31st December 2003:3

	2002 Rs.	2003 Rs.		2002 Rs.	2003 Rs.
Share Capital	5,00,00,000	5,00,00,000	Land and		
Profit & Loss	1,50,00,000	2,52,00,000	Buildings (at		
Debentures	2,00,00,000	2,00,00,000	cost)	2,00,00,000	2,50,00,000
Sundry Creditors	1,20,00,000	1,05,00,000	Plant and		
Depreciation on			Machinery		
Land & Buildings	5,00,000	6,00,000	(at cost)	3,50,00,000	3,60,00,000
Plant and Machinery	30,00,000	32,00,000	Sundry		
Provisions for			Debtors	1,47,00,000	1,38,00,000
taxation	30,00,000	32,00,000	Stock	2,50,00,000	2,74,00,000
			Bank	83,00,000	1,01,00,000
			Preliminary		
			Expenses	5,00,000	4,00,000
	10,35,00,000	11,27,000		10,35,00,000	11,27,00,000

The following additional information is available:

(a) The net profit for the year ending 31st December, 2003 was Rs.2,52,00,000 and is arrived at after charging loss on sale of machinery and written off preliminary expenses and adjusting provisions for doubtful debts.

(b) During the year a part of the machinery costing Rs.7,00,000 accumulated depreciation thereon being Rs.1,00,000 was sold for Rs.5,00,000.

(c) Dividend of Rs.50,00,000 was paid during the year.

Prepare statements to show the changes in working capital for the year 2003 and the sources and applications of funds during 2003.

24. You have been given the following financial statements of Glorious Traders Ltd. as at 31st December 2003:

	2003 Rs.	2002 Rs.
Assets:		
Cash at Bank	1,45,000	1,30,000
Sundry Debtors	11,40,000	10,90,700

Stock-in-trade	11,96,000	10,42,500
Fixed assets, less Depreciation	16,00,000	13,60,000
Investments	1,10,000	1,11,250
Prepaid Expenses	1,21,000	1,14,000
	43,12,000	38,48,450
Liabilities:		
Sundry Creditors	7,98,000	6,51,450
Provision for taxation	6,72,000	5,65,000
Secured Loans from Bank	1,00,000	3,87,000
Reserve and Surplus	15,12,000	11,48,000
Share capital:		
Ordinary share of Rs.100 each	12,30,000	10,97,000
	43,12,000	38,48,450

The following further information is available from records:

1. On 31st December 2003 the accumulated depreciation on fixed assets was Rs.9,80,000 and on 31st December 2002 Rs.6,60,000. Machinery costing Rs.20,00,000 which was one-half depreciated was discarded and written off in 2003.
2. Investment costing Rs.5,00,000 were sold during the year 2003 for Rs.4,80,000 and Government Securities of the face value of Rs.4,00,000 were purchased during the year for Rs.3,75,000.Prepare:
   - *Statement of source and application of funds, and*
   - *Statement showing in details the item-wise increase or decrease in the net working capital.*

25. Following are the comparative balance sheets of Good Luck Co. as at 31st December.

Liabilities	**2002 Rs.**	**2003 Rs.**	**Assets**	**2002 Rs.**	**2003 Rs.**
Share Capital	10,00,000	11,00,000	Goodwill	50,000	40,000
Debentures	5,00,000	3,00,000	Land & Buildings	4,20,000	6,60,000
General Reserves	2,00,000	2,00,000	Plant and Machinery	6,00,000	8,00,000
Profit & Loss	1,10,000	1,90,000	Stock	2,50,000	2,10,000
Tax Provisions	40,000	1,10,000	Debtors	3,00,000	2,40,000
Creditors	50,000	40,000	Cash	3,00,000	24,000
Bills Payable	20,000	30,000	Preliminary		

Provisionfor Doubtful Debts	30,000	24,000	Expenses	30,000	20,000
	19,50,000	19,94,000		19,50,000	19,94,000

Additional Information:

(a) During the year, a part of machinery costing Rs.7,500 (Accumulated depreciation thereon being Rs.2,500) was sold for Rs.3,000.

(b) Dividend for Rs.1,00,000 was paid during the year.

(c) Income Tax Rs.50,000 was paid during the year .

(d) Depreciation for the year 2003 was provided as follows:

	Rs.
Land and Buildings	10,000
Plant and Machinery	50,000

Prepare: A schedule of change in working capital and

A statement showing the sources and application of funds.

26. The balance sheet of Hunters Hutch Ltd.as on 31st December 2003 is as follows :

Liabilities	**2002 Rs.**	**2003 Rs.**	**Assets**	**2002 Rs.**	**2003 Rs.**
Share Capital	2,00,000	2,50,000	Fixed Assets	3,50,000	4,75,000
Retained Earnings	1,60,000	3,00,000	Merchandise Inventory	1,00,000	95,000
Premium on Shares	—	5,000	Accounts Receivable	43,000	50,000
Depreciation	80,000	60,000	Prepaid Expenses	4,000	5,000
Debentures	60,000	—	Cash	15,800	10,200
Accounts Payable	37,800	40,200	Commission on share issue	25,000	20,000
	5,37,800	6,55,200		5,37,800	6,55,000

Additional Information :

(1) Net Income for the year Rs.1,40,000.

(2) An addition to the Fixed Asset was made during the year at a cost of Rs.1,65,000 and fully depreciated machinery costing Rs.40,000 was discarded, no salvage being realized.

(3) Depreciation for the year Rs.20,000.

(4) Income Tax paid was Rs.40,000.

(5) Interim Dividend paid during the year Rs.20,000. Prepare:

(a) A statement of schedule of changes in working capital.

(b) A statement of sources and application of funds.

Additional Information :

(1) Net Income for the year Rs.1,40,000.

(2) An addition to the Fixed Asset was made during the year at a cost of Rs.1,65,000 and fully depreciated machinery costing Rs.40,000 was discarded, no salvage being realized.

(3) Depreciation for the year Rs.20,000.

(4) Income Tax paid was Rs.40,000.

(5) Interim Dividend paid during the year Rs.20,000. Prepare:

(a) A statement of schedule of changes in working capital.

(b) A statement of sources and application of funds.

27. Below is the balance sheet of Kundan Mal & Co. as on 31st December 2003 and a statement of its income and reconciliation of earnings for 2003. The only item in the buildings and equipment account sold during the year was a specialized machine that originally cost Rs.15,000. The accumulated depreciation on this machine at the time of sale was Rs.8,000. The machine was sold for Rs.6,000 and full payment was received in cash. Prepare cash flow, change in working capital and fund flow statements.

Balance Sheet of Kundan Mal as on 31.12.2003.

Liabilities	2002 Rs.	2003 Rs.	Assets	2002 Rs.	2003 Rs.
Accounts Payable	58,000	94,000	Cash	74,000	37,000
Notes Payable	28,000	8,000	Accounts		
Tax Provision	86,000	12,000	Receivable	54,000	47,000
Social Security			Inventories	3,12,000	2,77,000
Provision	3,000	5,000	Prepaid		
Accrued Taxes	2,20,000	60,000	Expenses	6,000	4,000
Debentures	2,50,000	4,60,000	Land	60,000	60,000
Capital	2,31,000	2,11,000	Patents	55,000	65,000
			Buildings and		
			Equipments	4,20,000	4,80,000

			Less: Depreciation Net Buildings and Equipments	 1,05,000 3,15,000	 1,20,000 3,60,000
	8,76,000	8,50,000		8,76,000	8,50,000

Statement of income and reconciliation of earnings for 2003

	Rs.
Net sales	19,70,000
Less : Works cost	14,80,000
Gross Profit	4,90,000
Less: Operating expenses (Including depreciation of Rs.23,000 and Patent amortization of Rs.6,000)	5,00,000
Net Loss from Operation	10,000
Less: Other Revenues	7,000
Net Loss	3,000
Add: Retained earnings of 2002	2,31,000
	2,28,000
Less: Dividend paid	16,000
Less: Loss on sale of Assets	1,000
Retained earnings on 31st December 2003:	Rs.2,11,000

28. Akila Empress made a net profit of Rs.1,00,000 for the year ended 31st December 2003 after making adjustments for the under mentioned items,.

	Rs.
Loss on sale of Machinery	10,000
Depreciation on Building	4,000
Depreciation on Machinery	5,000
Preliminary Expenses written off	5,000
Provision for Taxation	10,000
Goodwill written off	5,000
Gain on sale of Buildings	8,000

What is the cash from operation for the year?

29. Statement of financial position of Ratlam Seevil Services, owned by Mason Muthiah are given below :

	1.1.2003	31.12.2003		1.1.2003	31.12.03
Accounts Payable	29,000	25,000	Cash	40,000	30,000
Capital	7,39,000	6,15,000	Debtors	20,000	
			Stock	8,000	
			Buildings	1,00,000	
			Fixed	6,00,000	
	7,68,000	6,40,000	Assets	7,68,000	6,40,000

Additional Information:

i. There were no drawings by the owner.

ii. There were no purchase or sale of either buildings or fixed assets.

Prepare Cash Flow Statement.

30. From the following balance sheets of Karaikal Canvas Ltd.as on 31st December, you are required to prepare a Cash Flow Statement : Cash Flow Statement :

	2002 Rs.	2003 Rs.		2002 Rs.	2003 Rs.
Share Capital	1,00,000	1,50,000	Fixed assets	1,75,450	2,81,700
Profit & Loss	50,000	80,000	Less. Depreciation	75,450	1,31,700
Reserves	30,000	40,000	Net Fixed assets	1,00,000	1,50,000
16% Bonds	50,000	60,000	Goodwill	50,000	40,000
Creditors	30,000	40,000	Inventories	50,000	80,000
Expenses			Debtors	50,000	80,000
outstanding	10,000	15,000	Bills Receivable	10,000	20,000
			Bank	10,000	15,000
	2,70,000	3,85,000		2,70,000	3,85,000

31. The balance sheet of Hussainy Holdings Ltd as on 31st December 2003 is below :

	2002 Rs.	2003 Rs.		2002 Rs. lakhs	2003 Rs.lakhs
	lakhs	lakhs	Fixed assets	1,520.00	2,036.73
Share Capital	1,000.00	1,600.00	Inventory	934.23	892.45

Retained Earnings	702.50	853.75	Debtors	308.63	321.79
Depreciation	626.41	846.28	Expenses		
12% Debentures	500.00	—	Prepaid	39.49	31.23
Sundry Creditors	287.94	480.68	Investment	286.33	472.19
			Cash and Bank	28.17	26.32
	3,116.85	3,780.71		3,116.85	3,780.71

Following additional information for 2003 are also given :

- Net Profit Rs.270.50 lakhs.
- Cash dividend paid during the period Rs.123.45lakhs.
- An addition to the building was made during the year at a cost of Rs.78.59lakhs and fully depreciated equipment costing Rs.36.78 lakhs was discarded and no salvage was realized.

Prepare cash Flow Statement.

32. The comparative Balance Sheets of Amalendu Gosh ltd. company are given below:

	2002 Rs.lakhs	**2003 Rs.lakhs**		**2002 Rs.lakhs**	**2003 Rs.lakhs**
	35,000.00	37,000.00	Cash	236.84	390.27
Share Capital	1,000.00	700.00	Book Debts	765.43	885.60
Debentures	180.37	220.22	Stocks	2623.70	3350.39
Creditors			Land	400.00	400.00
Provision-	349.53	461.41	Plant		
Doubtful Debts	13,000.00	14,690.00	/machinery	46,024.44	48,874.72
Depreciation	1,020.51	1,279.35	Goodwill	500.00	450.00
Profit and Loss					
	50,550.41	54,350.98		50,550.41	54,350.98

Additional information available are :

- Dividends paid amounted to Rs.175.00 lakhs.
- Goodwill amortized Rs. 50 lakhs.
- Debentures were repaid to the extent of Rs.300lakhs.

You are required to prepare a Cash Flow Statement.

33. From the following particulars Laser & Co. prepare Cash Flow and Fund Flow Statement of Kumar Associates.

	1st Jan. 2003 Rs.	**31st Dec. 2003 Rs.**
Cash	5,10,479	4,72,591

Debtors	4,72,851	4,59,742
Stock	5,34,679	6,25,369
Land	7,31,765	7,31,765
Buildings	2,54,164	2,55,137
Machinery	12,75,428	14,80,160
	37,79,366	40,24,764
Current Liabilities	6,35,951	3,42,678
Loan from Shankar repayable in 3 years	—	2,50,000
Bank term Loan	3,40,000	2,30,000
Depreciation	13,00,000	14,93,700
Capital	7,50,000	8,00,000
Reserves	7,53,415	9,08,386
	37,79,366	40,24,764
Current Liabilities	6,35,951	3,42,678
	—	2,50,000
	3,40,000	2,30,000
Loan from Shankar repayable in 3 years		
Bank term Loan	13,00,000	14,93,700
Depreciation	7,50,000	8,00,000
Capital Reserves	7,53,415	9,08,386
	37,79,366	40,24,76

34. From the following you are required to prepare a fund flow statement ,with schedule of change in working capital:

Liabilities	**1999 Rs.**	**2000 Rs.**	**Assets**	**1999 Rs.**	**2000 Rs.**
Capital	2,00,000	2,50,000	Cash	30,000	47,000
Trade Creditors	70,000	45,000	Debtors	1,20,000	1,15,000
Profit & Loss	10,000	23,000	Stocks	80,000	90,000
			Land	50,000	66,000
	2,80,000	3,18,000		2,80,000	3,18,000

35. Calculate cash from operations for Sukanya Traders :

	31st December	
	2003-Rs.	**2003-Rs.**
Debtors	50,000	47,000
Bills Receivable	10,000	12,500
Creditors	20,000	25,000
Bills Payable	8,000	6,000

Expenses Prepaid	1,000	1,200
Accrued Income	800	700
Income Received in Advance	600	750
Net Profit made	32,500	1,30,000

36. From the following balance sheets of Maxle Ltd. make out fund flows statement with statement of change in working capital.

Liabilities	**1999 Rs.**	**2000 Rs.**	**Assets**	**1999 Rs.**	**2000 Rs.**
Equity Share			Goodwill	1,15,000	90,000
Capital	3,00,000	4,00,000	Land &		
8% Redeemable			Buildings	2,00,000	1,70,000
Preference Shares	1,50,000	1,00,000	Plant	80,000	2,00,000
General Reserve	40,000	70,000	Debtors	1,60,000	2,00,000
Profit & Loss	30,000	48,000	Stock	77,000	1,09,000
Proposed	42,000	50,000	Bills Receivable	20,000	30,000
Dividend	55,000	83,000	Cash in hand	15,000	10,000
Creditors	20,000	16,000	Cash at Bank	10,000	8,000
Bills Payable					
Provision for	40,000	50,000			
Taxation	6,77,000	8,17,000		6,77,000	8,17,000

Additional Information: Depreciation of Rs.10,000 and Rs.20,000 have been charged on Plant and Land Buildings in 2000.An interim dividend of Rs.20,000 has been paid in 2000.Rs.35,000 Income tax was paid during 2000.

37. Prepare Cash Flow Statement from the following balance sheets of Pitfalls Engineering Ltd. for the year ended 31st December 2003. **Rs.**

Liabilities	**2002**	**2003**	**Asses**	**2002**	**2003**
Share Capital	17,00,000	18,35,000	Buildings	8,00,000	10,00,000
Reserves	40,000	83,700	Plant/Mach	2,50,000	
P&L a/c	1,00,000	1,30,000	Fixtures/		
Provision for			Fittings	5,000	3,70,000
Dividends	70,000	50,000	Cash	2,000	6,000
Creditors	1,00,000	95,000	Debtors	1,00,000	2,200
Bank Overdraft	8,000	18,000	Receivable	8,000	45,000
Bills Payable	14,000	13,000	Stocks	4,00,000	9,000
Mortgage Loan	10,000	70,000	Expenses		3,43,700
			Prepaid	3,000	3,100
			Investment	1,64,000	1,70,000

			Goodwill	3,00,000	3,43,000
			Preliminary Expenses	10,000	2,000
	20,42,000	22,94,700		20,42,000	22,94,700

Adjustments :

- Investments were purchased and interest received Rs.3,000 was used in writing down the book value of investments.
- The declared dividend of Rs.50,000 for 2002 was paid and interim dividend for Rs.20,000 paid out of the Profit and Loss Appropriation Account.

38. The following are the summarized balance sheets of Atlanta Traders as on 31st December 2004 :

	2003 Rs.	**2004 Rs.**
Liabilities:		
Capital	2,00,000	2,50,000
General Reserve	50,000	60,000
Profit & Loss A/c	30,500	30,600
Bank Loan (Long term)	70,000	—
Sundry Creditors	1,50,000	1,35,200
Provision for Taxation	30,000	35,000
Assets	5,30,500	5,10,800
Land & Buildings	2,00,000	1,90,000
Machinery	1,50,000	1,69,000
Stock	1,00,000	74,000
Sundry Debtors	80,000	64,200
Cash	500	600
Bank	—	8,000
Goodwill	—	5,000
	5,30,500	5,10,800

Additional Information :

During the year Ended 31st December 2003 :

(i) Dividend of Rs.23,000 was paid.

(ii) The following assets of another company were purchased for a consideration of Rs.50,000.

(a) Stock Rs.20,000 and (b) Machinery Rs.25,000.

(iii) Machinery was further purchased for Rs.8,000.

(iv) Depreciation written off : Machinery Rs.12,000.

(v) Income Tax provided during the year Rs.33,000.

(vi) Loss on sale of Machinery Rs.200 was written off to General Reserve.

39. Balance sheet of Gemini Brothers as on 1st January 2003 and 31st December 2003 were as follows : **Rs.**

	1.1.2003	31.12.2003
Assets :		
Cash	10,000	7,000
Debtors	30,000	50,000
Stock	35,000	25,000
Machinery	80,000	55,000
Land	40,000	10,000
Buildings	35,000	60,000
	2,30,000	2,47,000
Liabilities :		
Creditors	40,000	44,000
Mrs. Ram's Loan	25,000	—
Loan from Parry	40,000	50,000
Capital	1,25,000	1,53,000
	2,30,000	2,47,000

During the year a machine costing Rs.10,000 (accumulated depreciation Rs.3,000) was sold for Rs.5,000. The balance of provision for depreciation against machinery as on 1st January 2003 was Rs.25,000 and on 31st December 2003 Rs.40,000. Net Profit for the year 2003 amounted to Rs.45,000. Prepare Cash Flow Statement.

40. Quick Profit Ltd. finds on 1st January 2005 that it is short of funds with which to implement its programme of expansion. On 1st January 2004 it had a credit balance of Rs.1,80,000. From the following information, prepare a statement of cash for the Board of Directors to show how the overdraft of Rs.68,750 as at 31st December 2004 has arisen.

Figures as per Balance Sheet as at December.

	2003 Rs.	2004 Rs.
Fixed Assets	7,50,000	11,20,000
Stocks & Stores	1,90,000	3,30,000
Debtors	3,80,000	3,35,000
Bank	1,80,000(Cr.)	68,750 (O/D)
Trade Creditors	2,70,000	3,50,000
Share Capital (Rs. 10 each)	2,50,000	3,00,000
Bills Receivable	87,500	95,000

The profit for the year ended 31st December 2000 before charging depreciation and taxation amounted to Rs.2,40,000.

5,000 shares were issued on 1st January 2004 at a premium of Rs.5 per share.

Rs.1,37,500 were paid in March 2000 by way of Income Tax.

Dividend was paid as follows :

2004 (final) on the capital on 31st December 2003 at 10% less tax at 25%.

2004 (interim) 5% free of tax.

41. The financial position of M/s.Skyrock Skaters on 1st January and 31st December 2004 was as follows :

Liabilities	1 Jan. Rs.	31 Dec. Rs.	Assets	1 Jan. Rs.	31 Dec. Rs.
Current Liabilities	36,000	40,600	Cash	4,000	3,600
		20,000	Debtors	35,000	38,000
Mrs. A's Loan	30,000	25,000	Stock	25,000	22,000
		20,000	Land	20,000	30,000
Loan from Bank	1,48,000	1,54,000	Buildings	50,000	55,000
			Machinery	80,000	86,000
			DeliveryVan	—	25,000
	2,14,000	2,59,600		2,14,000	2,59,000

The delivery van was purchased in December 2000 on Hire Purchase basis : a payment of Rs.5,000 was made immediately and the balance of the amount is to be paid in 20 monthly installments of Rs.1,000 each together with interest @ 12% p.a. During the year the partners withdrew Rs.26,000 for domestic expenditure. The provision for depreciation against machinery as on 1st January 2000 was Rs.27,000 and on 31st December 2000 Rs.36,000.

You are required to prepare the Cash Flow and Fund Flow Statements.

42. Balance Sheets of a company as on 1st January and 31st December 2000 were as follows :

Liabilities	1.1.2000 Rs.	31.12.2000 Rs.	Assets	1.1.2000 Rs.	31.12.2000 Rs.
Capital	1,50,000	1,90,000	Cash	20,000	26,000
Loan	30,000	—	Debtors	54,000	76,000
Loan from Bank	60,000	80,000	Stock	48,000	42,000
Creditors	50,000	50,000	Furniture	2,000	2,000
			Machinery	90,000	65,000
			Land	36,000	45,000
			Buildings	40,000	70,000
	2,90,000	3,26,000		2,90,000	3,26,000

During the year a machine costing Rs.12,000 (accumulated depreciation Rs.4,000) was sold for Rs.5,000. The provision for depreciation against machinery as on 1st January was Rs.24,000 and on 31st December Rs.37,000. Net profit for the year 2000 amounted to Rs.60,000.

You are required to prepare:

(a) Cash Flow Statement, and

(b) Fund Flow Statement with schedule of change in working capital.

43. From the following information from profit and loss account and balance sheet of Holi Cows prepare a fund flow Statement for the year ended 31st December 2003.

Liabilities	**31.12.2002** Rs.	**31.12.2003** Rs.
Capital	70,000	70,000
Secured Loan(Repayable in 2010)	—	40,000
Creditors	14,000	39,000
Tax Payable	1,000	3,000
Profit & Loss A/c	7,000	10,000
	92,000	1,62,000
Assets		
Plant & Machinery	50,000	91,000
Inventory	15,000	40,000
Debtors	5,000	20,000
Cash	20,000	7,000
Prepaid Expenses	2,000	4,000
	92,000	1,62,000

Profit & Loss Account for the year ended 31st December 2003.

	Rs.		**Rs.**
To Opening Stock	15,000	By Sales	1,00,000
To Purchases	98,000	By Closing Inventory	40,000
To Gross Profit	27,000		
	1,40,000		1,40,000
To General Expenses	11,000	By Gross Profit	
To Depreciation	8,000		27,000
To Provision for Taxes	4,000		
To Net Profit	4,000		
	27,000		27,000

To Dividend	1,000	By Balance b/d	7,000
To Balance c/d	10,000	By Net Profit b/d	4,000
	11,000		11,000

44. Prepare a Cash Flow Statement of Angel Corporation from the following information:

Balance sheet as on 31st December 2003.

	1st January Rs.lakhs	31st December Rs.lakhs
Current Assets:		
Cash and Bank	40,000	44,400
Accounts Receivable	10,000	20,700
Inventories	15,000	15,000
Land	4,000	4,000
Business Premises	20,000	16,000
Plant and Equipment	15,000	17,000
Accumulated Depreciation	(5,000)	(2,800)
Patents and Trade Marks	1,000	900
	1,00,000	1,15,200
Current Liabilities:		
Current Liabilities	30,000	32,000
Bonds Payable	22,000	22,000
Bonds Payable Discount	(2,000)	(1,800)
Capital Stock	35,000	43,500
Retained Earnings	15,000	19,500
	1,00,000	1,15,200

Additional Information:

- Income for the period was Rs.10,000 lakhs.
- A building that costs Rs.4,000 lakhs and which had a book value of Rs.1,000 lakhs was sold for Rs.1,400 lakhs
- The depreciation charges for the period were Rs.800 lakhs.
- There was a Rs.5,000 lakh issue of Capital Stock.
- Cash dividend of Rs.2,000 lakhs and a stock dividend for Rs.3,500 lakhs were declared.

45. The condensed balance sheet of Ohio Exports India, which is a subsidiary of Ohio Orion Inc, Orion is as under.. You are required to prepare Cash Flow Statement.

Assets	**1.1.2003 $ in thosands**	**31.12.2003 $ in thosands**
Cash and Bank Balances	45,000	45,000
Sundry Debtor	33,500	21,500
Temporary Investments	55,000	37,000
Prepaid Expenses	500	1,000
Stock-in-trade	41,000	53,000
Land and Buildings	75,000	75,000
Machinery	26,000	35,000
	2,76,000	2,67,500
Liabilities:		
Sundry Creditors	51,500	48,000
Outstanding Expenses	6,500	6,000
8% debentures	45,000	35,000
Depreciation Fund	20,000	22,000
Reserve for Contingencies	30,000	30,000
Profit and Loss Account	8,000	11,500
Capital	1,15,000	1,15,000
	2,76,000	2,67,500

The following information is also available:

- 10% dividend was paid in cash.
- New machinery for $15million was purchased but old machinery costing $6 million was sold for $.2 million; accumulated depreciation was $.3million.
- $.10 million 8% debentures were redeemed by purchase from open market @$ 96 for a debenture of $100.
- $.18million investments were sold at book value.

46. Explain the difference between cash flow analysis and fund flow analysis. Statement of financial position of Mr. A is given below:

(Rs.)

	1.1.2000	**31.12.2000**
Accounts payable	29,000	25,000
Capital	7,39,000	6,15,000
	7,68,000	6,40,000
Cash	40,000	30,000
Debtors	20,000	17,000
Stock	8,000	13,000
Building	1,00,000	80,000
Other fixed assets	6,00,000	5,00,000
	7,68,000	6,40,000

Additional Information:

- There were no drawings
- There were no purchase or sale of either building or other fixed assets

Prepare statement of cash flow?

47. From the following summarized balance sheets of XY Ltd as on March 31 1966 and 1967,you are required to prepare (a) Statement of changes in working capital and (b) Statement of sources and uses of funds:

Liabilities	**1966** **Rs.**	**1967** **Rs.**	**Assets**	**1966** **Rs.**	**1967** **Rs.**
Equity share capital	37,500	60,000	Fixed Assets	1,20,000	1,26,865
6% redeemable Pref. shares	50,000	40,000	Less Depreciation	45,010	49,240
Plant replacement reserve	7,500	5,000	Net FA	75,025	77,625
Long terms loans	—	20,000	Investments	30,500	38,000
Bank loans	11,000		Inventor	49,000	52,000
Trade creditors	42,225	37,775	Debtors	44,000	42,500
Proposed dividend on equity shares	6,000	12,000	Cash	5,875	16,000
P & L	50,175	51,350			
	2,04,400	2,26,125		2,04,400	2,26,125

Additional information:

(a) Rs. 12,500 was capitalized by making equity shares fully paid up.

(b) Final dividend on preference share capital and interm dividend of Rs. 2,000 on equity shares was paid on March 31, 1967.

(c) Proposed dividend of year ending on March 31, 1966 was paid during the year 1966-67.

(d.) Difference in fixed assets replacement reserve account represents transfer to profit and loss appropriation account.

(e) Fixed assets were revalued by Rs. 1,500 in excess of the book value and the amount was credited to profit and loss account.

(f) Rs. 850 being expenditure on fixed assets which on March 31, 1966 was carried forward in Debtors A/c was transferred back to fixed assets in 1967.

(g) Fixed assets costing Rs. 3,000 (accumulated depreciation there on being Rs. 2,400 was sold for Rs. 125). The loss was charged to profit and loss account.

(h) During the year 1966-67 redeemable preference shares of Rs. 10,000 were redeemed at 10% premium for this purpose fresh issue of equity shares of Rs. 10,000 were made.

48. From the following, prepare cash flow statement:

Balance sheets

Liabilities	**31.3.1975**	**31.3.1976**
Share capital	300000	400000
8% Redeemable preference share capital	150000	100000
General Reserve	40000	70000
Profit & loss account	30000	48000
Proposed dividend	42000	50000
Creditors	55000	83000
Outstanding expenses	20000	16000
Provision for taxation	40000	50000
	677000	817000
Assets		
Goodwill	115000	90000
Land & building	200000	170000
Plant	80000	200000
Debtors	160000	200000
Bills receivable	77000	100000
Prepaid	20000	30000
Cash in hand	15000	10000
Cash with bank	10000	8000
	677000	817000

Additional information:

(a) Depreciation of Rs.10000 and Rs. 20000 were charged on plant and land& building respectively in 1996

(b) An interim dividend of Rs. 20000 has been paid in 1996. Final dividend of Rs. 20000 was paid for 1995.

(c) Income tax of Rs. 35000 has been paid in 1996.

49. From the following, determine "Funds from operation".

	Rs.
Net loss	12,000
Depreciation on Machinery	14,000
Amortisation of good will	12,000
Loss on sale of plant	4,000
Profit on sale of land	8,500
Provision for likely bad debts	2,000

50. Prepare schedule of changes and fund flow statement:

	1997-98 Rs.	**1998-99 Rs.**
Assets:		
Cash	30,000	47,000
Debtors	1,20,000	1,15,000
Stock	80,000	90,000
Land	50,000	66,000
Capital & Liabilities:		
Shares Capital	2,00,000	2,50,000
Creditors	70,000	45,000
Retained Earnings	10,000	23,000
	2,80,000	3,18,000

CHAPTER– 7

COSTS AND COST ACCOUNTING

Learning Objective

Cost causes revenue. Knowledge about costs and their behaviour are essential for their ultimate control and reduction to increase profitability. This chapter deals with the three elements of costs and their combination and how they aid managements to forecast the cost of their products and services. Understanding cost is the major step in the efforts of an enterprise to control cost. That is the objective of this chapter.

Costs are resources sacrificed to obtain a benefit (income). It is a necessary evil. Costs could be broadly divided into capital costs and revenue costs. We have christened capital costs as expenditures that contribute to generate income beyond the accounting period in which they were incurred. Land, building, plant and machinery, equipment, vehicles, etc are capital costs. Revenue costs, with which we are now concerned in this chapter, are expenses whose utility in generating income has been used up instantly. They are ***expired costs*** that are necessary to generate revenue. Even in the case of capital costs, that part of the costs that had been used up in an accounting year, represented as ***depreciation***, becomes a revenue cost of that year. No income could be earned without incurring costs. But it is the difference in the quantum of costs that have to be incurred to earn a given level of income that separates efficient organizations from inefficient ones. For example, a spinning mill produces 100 counts yarn at a cost of Rs.400 a kilogram, whereas another mill produces the same quality yarn at Rs.425 a kilogram. We call the first mill as an efficient one. The reason is that it could produce at a cheaper cost than the second mill. Lower cost makes the organization highly competitive and successful. Hence, for a business to be successful, it should be in a position to produce at a cheaper cost compared to its competitors, without sacrificing quality. Thus, a study of the cost structure of a business with a view to find ways and means of reducing costs assumes importance, particularly in the present day context of global competition.

Definition

Oxford dictionary defines cost as "***the price paid for some thing***". This is a definition from the consumer's point of view. As we are concerned with the economic use of resources in producing a thing or rendering a service, this definition falls short of our requirement. ICMA, London has given a better definition when it defined cost as "***the amount of expenditure (actual or notional) incurred on or attributable to a given thing***". The given thing is a cost object. Cost therefore means expenditure, which is a generic term covering both expenses and expenditures. The expenditures incurred might have already been paid up during the accounting period itself or are attributable for that accounting period, though not paid. In other words, expenditures for an accounting period might partly be paid up and partly outstanding. Again, the expenditures might be ***actual***, such as wages, salaries, rent, and carriage or ***notional*** such as depreciation, or reserve for doubtful debts. The expenditures are for an activity. It might be for buying a thing, producing a thing, maintaining a thing, distributing a thing or dealing with a thing. The thing is the ***cost object***. We will see later that a cost object could be a ***center or a unit***. To sum up, we might define costs as ***resources, in monetary terms, sacrificed or foregone to achieve a cost objective.***

Elements of Cost

Cost is a composite term. It denotes any or all of its *three elements-material, labour and expense.* Materials are tangible things that are used up by a business in earning an income. Raw materials, packaging materials, bought out components, consumables and spares are all examples of materials. Labour element is the monetary value of physical and mental efforts put in by human beings to earn income. Examples are wages, salaries and managerial remuneration. Expenses are intangible costs incurred in production, administration or selling and distribution. For example costs of power, fuel, electricity, depreciation, transportation, communication, stationery etc. Some of the elements of cost are traceable to the end products or services, such as materials consumed, bought out components, primary packaging materials, direct labour etc. These are *direct costs.* Costs that are not directly traceable to the products but still aid in production, administration and selling are *indirect costs.* Indirect costs are collectively called *overheads.* Depending upon the location of occurrence of overheads, they are classified into *factory overheads, administrative overheads or selling and distribution overheads.* It is thus possible that factory overheads might be *factory material overheads* (such as consumables, stores and spares), *factory labour overheads* (examples are foreman salary, watch and ward salary, godown keepers' remuneration etc.) and *factory expenses overhead* (like power, fuel, electricity, depreciation on factory buildings, plant and machinery etc.). Similarly, administrative and selling overheads would be material overheads, labour overheads and expenses in office and selling.. In the initial years of management accounting practice, expenses were also classified as direct and indirect. Certain expenses such as excise duty, power and fuel were considered direct expenses. This classification has since been discontinued and all expenses are treated as overheads, whether they are direct or indirect. Figure 1 shows the elements of cost in the form of a map.

Cost Classifications-Functional

Costs are classified according to the elements, functions, behaviour, are related to the administration of the organization, they are *administration costs*. When they are incurred for selling the products, they are *distribution or selling costs*. And when they are not related controllability and relevance to decision making. Functionally, costs are of four categories, namely production costs, administration or establishment costs, distribution and selling costs and non-operating costs. When costs are related to the process of production, they are *production costs or factory costs or works costs*. It covers direct and indirect costs that are incurred in the factory.

Figure 1
Cost Map

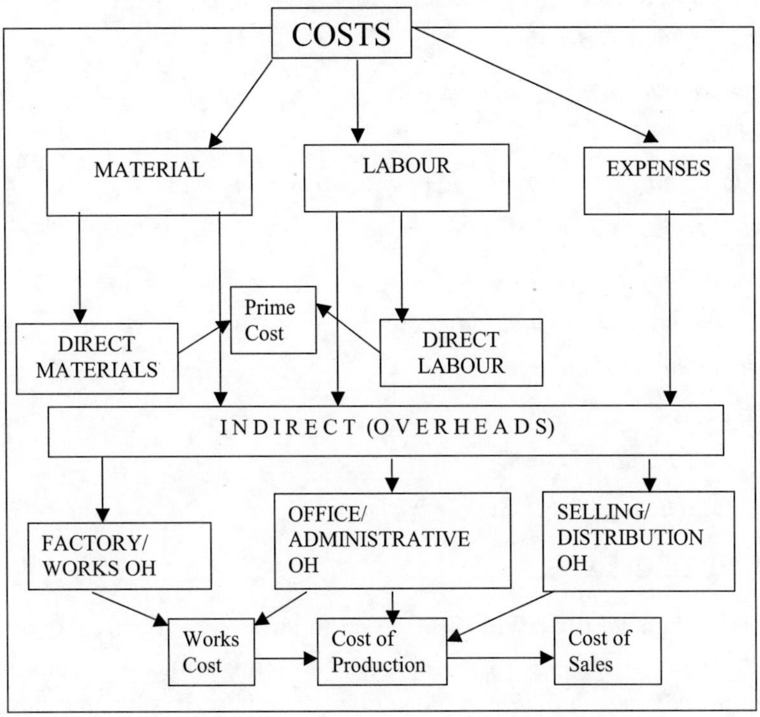

Direct materials and direct labour constitute ***prime costs***. Besides prime costs, factory overheads also form part of production costs. Prime costs plus factory overheads are ***factory costs or works costs***. Works cost less materials cost is ***conversion cost***. Works cost plus administrative overheads is ***cost of production*** and cost of production plus selling and distribution expenses are ***costs of sales.*** When costs do not relate to the core activity of the business, but are incidental or consequential to other managerial decisions or beyond the control of management, they are ***non-operating costs***. When we analyze costs, we do take only the first three cost groups into consideration, as the fourth group is not related to the core operational activities of business. Thus, interest is a cost incurred by the business as a result of the capital structure decision of the management. Similarly, discount on debtors and bad debts are due to the credit policy of the businessman. Loss on sale of assets is the consequence of replacement decisions. Loss due to fire, earthquake, cyclone or other natural calamities are incidents over which the businessman has little control. Hence these are non-operating costs. Payment of taxes and dividends are not costs to the business, but these are costs to the businessman. These are, therefore, appropriations of profits and would not find a place in the galaxy of costs.

For the purpose of taking operational and planning decisions, costs are generally grouped according to their reaction to the process of production. Some costs change with activity, while others do not. Taking into account this behavioral pattern of costs, they are classified into

- *Variable and fixed costs.*
- *Marginal and absorption costs.*
- *Product and period costs*
- *Controllable and un-controllable or relevant and irrelevant costs.*
- *Avoidable and unavoidable costs.*
- *Opportunity and incremental costs.*
- *Value added and non-value added costs.*
- *Sunk and committed costs.*
- *Imputed costs*
- *Historic and standard costs.*
- *Post manufacturing and life cycle costs.*

Variable and Fixed Costs

Different costs behave differently. Based on the way costs behave, commonly called *cost behavior*, costs are classified into variable, fixed and semivarible. A variable cost, as the name implies, *varies directly in proportion to the volume of activity*. It is like the stem of a lotus flower in a tank of water. The stem would elongate with increase in water and shrink when water recedes. Thus, at the production level of 1,000 units, if the variable cost were Rs.4,000, it would increase to Rs.40, 000 when the production increases to 10,000 units. Similarly, it would reduce to Rs.2000 if the production declines to 500 units. Of course this principle is subject to the safety valve *other things remaining constant or ceteris paribus*. Change in variable cost might not be in proportion to change in volume of activity, if there is a change in technology. But for analytical purposes it might be assumed that the *relationship between variable cost and volume of operation is direct and proportional*. As a corollary to this, *per unit variable cost would remain the same* irrespective of the change in volume of output. In the example given above, the variable cost per unit would continue to be Rs.4, whether the level of production is 1000, 10,000 or 500.

Fixed cost, also known as *period cost or time cost* behaves differently. The volume of fixed cost would remain constant up to a limit, irrespective of the level of operation. The limit is the installed capacity of the business. For example, fixed cost of a business is Rs.25, 00,000 when the production was 2500 units. The installed capacity of the business was 4000 units. The fixed cost would continue to be Rs.25, 00, 000, even if the production increases beyond 2500 unit, but up to 4000 units or declines to less than 2,500 units. It could be seen that per unit fixed cost, which was Rs.1000 at the level of production of 2500 units, would decline to Rs. 714.30 per unit when the production increased to 3500 units. However, the per unit fixed cost would increase to Rs. 5000 when production declined to 500 units. The conclusion is that *per unit fixed cost changes inversely in proportion to the level of operation*. But the volume of fixed cost would change, if the business has to produce more than 4000 units in any year. In case the business wants to produce 5000 units, it has to add fixed assets to create additional capacity. Assuming that the additional investment is Rs.100 lakhs and the weighted average cost of capital of the business is 12%, the fixed cost would go up by Rs. 12,00,000 to Rs.37, 00.000.Consequently the per unit fixed cost would also change.

Still there are some costs, which are neither fully variable nor fixed. They have an element of fixed cost combined with variable cost. These are called *semi-variable costs*. Electricity charges, for example, have a minimum charge whether the connections are used or not. Additional charges would be in proportion to the use of current in excess of the minimum. Telephone costs have rent for instrument, which is fixed irrespective of the extent of use of phone. In case of semi-variable costs, it would be the endeavor of the manager to segregate the fixed cost element and account for the variable component separately. Thus total cost of production would have the three types of costs. If we assign y for total cost, a for fixed cost, b for variable cost per unit, c for semi variable cost and x for production, then per unit cost of production would be $y / x = [a/x) + b + (c-b)/x + (c-a)/x$. If this formula is applied to business units with varying capacities, it would turn out to be that higher the volume of production, lower would be the per unit cost of production. This is the benefit of scales of operation.

Marginal and Absorption Costs

Marginal cost is the additional cost incurred to produce one more unit of the product. As fixed cost has already been absorbed, the additional cost of producing one more unit is the variable cost. Hence marginal cost is also called as variable cost. For example Memorable Manufacturing and Marketing Limited had produced 25, 700 units of FM transistor sets in May, 2003 with variable cost of 2,57,000 and fixed cost of Rs.1, 15,000. The total cost of production of the company for May 2003 was Rs. 3,72,000. Suppose the company plans to manufacture 25,701 units next month, its total cost would be Rs. 3,72,010. How? Its variable cost per unit would be Rs. 10 (2,57,000/ 25,700 = Rs.10). So the variable cost for manufacturing 25,701 units would be Rs. 2,57,010. If fixed cost of Rs.1,15,000 is added to the variable cost, the total cost would be Rs.3, 72, 010. The additional cost for manufacturing one more unit would thus be Rs. 10, which is the additional variable cost. The use of marginal cost in production decision-making would be dealt with in detail later. For the time being readers should confine their observation to the fact that marginal cost of producing anything would be its variable cost.

Product/Period Cost

According to CIMA, product cost is 'the cost of a finished product built up from its cost elements". It consists of the direct and indirect costs incurred in the factory. In other words, product costs are costs that are closely associated with production activities. It is the works cost. Period costs on the other hand are costs that are not directly related to production but aid in maintaining records about production activities and in the disposal of the products. Examples of period costs are administrative and selling and distribution costs. As these costs are caused by mere passage of time (and not connected with the volume of production activities), they are called period costs or time costs.

Controllable/ Uncontrollable Cost

Cost that could be influenced by a manager by taking prompt and appropriate action are controllable. Variable costs are generally controllable. Costs that are beyond the control of the managers are uncontrollable. For example, fluctuations in foreign exchange rates are not amenable for control as they are determined by factors beyond the reach of the manager. However, with the rapid change in technology and information system, the dividing line between a controllable and uncontrollable cost is becoming thinner. Situations once considered uncontrollable are becoming controllable. In the given examples, with the introduction of derivative trading, variety of hedging products are available to safeguard against foreign exchange fluctuations. These could be effectively used by the manager to control the once uncontrollable cost. Controllable costs are also relevant costs.

Avoidable/ Unavoidable Costs

Avoidable costs are such of the costs that could be avoided when a particular activity has been stopped. For example, if a manufacturing line is discontinued, the variable costs associated with that line are avoidable. But the fixed costs connected with the line have continuously been incurred and becomes unavoidable. There is usually a thin line of difference between avoidable cost and controllable cost. Avoidable costs might continue if not controlled effectively. For example, Binny Mills used to pay war allowances even long after the II world war ended. This is avoidable, but was not controlled.

Opportunity and Incremental Costs

In decision-making, a number of alternatives are open to the businessman. The decision maker analyzes the costs and benefits of each option and ranks them according to their net benefit. And he chooses an option that is more advantageous to his business than the others. For example, in a piece of land, one could raise either paddy or sugar cane. If paddy were raised, one would get a net income of Rs.20, 000 per annum. If he chooses to raise sugarcane in that land, he would have to forego his option of raising paddy. He would therefore expect a minimum net income of Rs.20, 000 by raising sugar cane, which is the income he had to forego by choosing to raise sugar cane. In other words, *the opportunity sacrificed in the next best alternative is the cost for the chosen alternative*. Opportunity cost therefore could be defined as the benefit a businessman has to forego in the next best alternative for choosing a particular course of action. Hence, it is logical that the cut off rate for an alternative is the opportunity cost. Incremental cost, on the other hand is the additional cost one has to bear with an increase in the activity of the business. For example, the cost of producing 10 lakh units of jotter pens is Rs. 45 lakhs and the cost of increasing the production to 15 lakh units would be Rs.65 lakhs, the incremental cost for producing 5 lakh units is Rs.20 lakhs. If increment in production were within the installed capacity, incremental cost would represent variable cost for the increased production. In the example given, assuming that the extra production was within the installed capacity of the organization, the variable cost per unit is Rs.4 (Rs.20lakhs /5 lakhs pen). Similar to incremental cost, there is a concept of decremental cost. Decremental cost is the reduction in cost due to decline in production.

Value Added and Non-Value Added Costs

Incurring certain costs, which do not enhance the functioning of the goods, but add utility to the consumers are value added costs. Doorknob of a car is a value added cost. Though it would not add to the functioning of car, it facilitates easy entry and exit to the users. The handle of a bucket is a value added cost, as it makes carrying water easy. The page tag in a book is value added cost, as it enables the reader to continue from where he had left. All these costs add value to the product without in any way improving the functioning of the goods. On the other hand if the doorknob were of silver, instead of steel, the handle is of brass or the flap is made of sandal chips, these are non-value added costs as they are ornamental and do not add value to the users.

Sunk and Committed Costs

Sunk costs are costs that have already been incurred. Constructions of building, installation of equipment are examples of sunk costs. It is the cost over which the businessman has no control. It is irrelevant for decision-making. Sometimes, it is thought that sunk cost is an unwanted cost, not beneficial to the business. This need not be. A sunk cost might be very useful and sometimes vital. It is not the nature of cost, but the time. Sunk costs are the results of past decisions, which could not be reversed without consequences. Hence, for current decision-making exercise, it becomes irrelevant. Committed costs on the other hand are costs, which have been decided but not yet incurred. Committed costs could be reversed in certain cases but not when it is legally bound. For example, rent agreement on building is a committed cost, which could be reversed by cancellation of the agreement giving due notice. Payment of tax is another committed cost, which cannot be reversed.

Imputed Costs

Imputed costs are ascribed costs. These are what a product or service actually costs, but are accounted differently by the consumers. These costs are not taken into accounting in the books of the consumers. It is the detriment suffered by providers of the product/service and a benefit to the consumers or recipients. For example, free supply of uniforms to employees. Uniforms actually costing Rs.250 a pair are supplied free to employees. Here the actual cost to the employees is zero, but the imputed cost is Rs.250. Similar is subsidized canteen facilities. The cost of food is much higher than what is charged to the workers. A course of lunch costing Rs. 25 is supplied to the workers at Rs. 5. In this example, Rs, 5 is the accounted cost by the labour, while the imputed cost for the company is Rs.25. The supply of subsidized ration by the governments is another example. Imputed costs are usually incentives aimed at motivating people to contribute to the goal of organizations.

Historic and Standard Costs

Financial accounting system records historical losts. By history we mean past. That which is over and that which could not be influenced subsequently. Historical costs are *what they were.* No doubt they are useful as basis for providing information to management for committing future costs. Standard costs on the other hand, are *what the costs should be.* Standard costs are predetermined costs for each of the elements of cost, developed on detailed assessment of their accurate requirements in quantity and value. A separate chapter dealing in detail on this subject is to follow.

Post Installation/ Life Cycle Costs

These are costs usually associated with capital goods. After an organization installs fixed assets, they require periodic maintenance, modification and upgrading till their useful lives are exhausted. These are pôst installation and life cycle costs. The estimation of these costs leads the businessman to take an important decision regarding investment in fixed assets. He could decide between owning an asset and leasing an asset, depending upon their relative life cycle costs to the business.

Costing

Having seen the attributes of costs and their classification, let us turn to the use of cost information in decision making process. Costs arise in every stage of earning income. It is continuous and omnipresent. You can see costs anywhere and at any time. Hence there is the necessity to identify costs, collect them, group them and account for them. Cost accounting performs this function. CIMA, London is against the use of the word costing. It has succinctly stated its view that ***the use of the word costing is not recommended.*** It has recommended the word cost accounting instead. Still costing is the word commonly used all over the world to the technique and process of collecting and classifying expenses according to cost elements and allocating and apportioning the expenses to the concerned cost objects, namely to cost centers or cost units or to both. So, whether it is costing or cost accounting it means the same thing to us, as we are not bogged down with the precise meaning of the word. Rather, we are keen in using the system as an aid in our attempt to control costs.

Definition

Charles T.Horngren considered cost accounting as " ***a quantitative method that accumulates, classifies, summarizes and interprets information for three major purposes: operational planning and control, special decisions and product decisions***" Chartered Institute of Management Accountants (CIMA), London has defines cost accounting as "***the process of accounting for costs from the point at which the expenditure is incurred or committed to the establishment of its ultimate relationship with cost units. In its widest sense, it embraces the preparation of statistical data, the application of cost control methods and the ascertainment of the profitability of the activities carried out or planned***'. Wilmot in his article on the cost accountant's place in management, published in Cost Accountant, October, 1936 had listed out the role of cost accounting as "***analyzing, recording, standardizing, forecasting, comparing, reporting and recommending***'. He had gone still further to identify the place of cost accountant as a " ***historian, news agent and prophet. As a historian, he must meticulously be accurate and sedulously impartial. As a newsagent, he must be up to date,***

***selective and pithy. As a prophet, he must combine knowledge and experience with foresight and courage*".**

Installation of Costing System

Organizations set up costing systems suited to their activity and size. A good costing system should aim at providing a framework for identifying costs at the points of their incurrence, ascertain the exact quantum, accumulate them to cost centers or units as the case might be and attribute them to where they should belong to. Such a system should have the cooperation and involvement of the top management, accounting and other staff, floor and line workers for successful functioning. The system should be simple and easy to follow, elastic and transparent. There are two methods of maintaining cost records in the system-integrated and non-integrated. Under integrated method, both the cost and its financial implication are recorded in one book. Under the other system, cost records are separately maintained and financial aspects are integrated later, usually at the time of compilation for analysis or presentation. For example, machine hour alone is maintained in the non-integrated method, where as the cost of machine hour in monetary value is maintained in integrated method. Although it costs to maintain a costing system, the results would more than justify the cost.

Role of Cost Accountant

The definitions have brought out the nature of cost accounting and the role expected of a cost accountant. Briefly, cost accounting is

- *A quantitative method.*
- *of accounting for costs from the point at which the expenditure is incurred or committed to the establishment of its ultimate relationship with cost units and attributing costs to cost centers or cost units, and*
- *accumulating, classifying and interpreting cost information, through*
- *analyzing, recording, standardizing, forecasting, comparing, reporting and recommending*
- *for the purpose of use in operational planning and control, in special decisions and for product decisions and*
- *application in cost control measures and in the ascertainment of the profitability of the activities carried out or planned.*

Cost Certers

The mode of operation of cost accounting is to identify centers or units of production to which the cost data could be meaningfully attributed. It therefore assumes urgency to understand what a cost center is and how it differs from a cost unit. A cost center is no doubt a cost object. According to CIMA, a cost center is " ***a location, person or item of equipment or group of these, for which cost might be ascertained and used for the purposes of cost control".*** Cost centers are thus convenient divisions of the organization for the purpose of costing. There could be three classifications of cost centers

- *Productive and unproductive cost centers;*
- *Personal and impersonal cost centers and*
- *Operation and process cost centers.*

Productive cost centers are those related to production of goods and services. Unproductive centers are those that relates to ancillary services like administration, godown, repairs and maintenance etc. ***Personal cost centers*** are either an individual or a group to which cost is attributed. Lathe operator, watchman, godown keeper, gardener are all personal cost centers. It could be a group like loading and unloading gang, shift workers, security, etc. ***Operation and process cost centers*** are the various stages of production. For example, in a textile mill, blow room, sliver section, carding section, spinning section, reeling section and winding section could all be cost centers according to this classification. It could be a branch of the organization. It could also be an activity. For example research laboratory might be treated as a cost center. Data in each cost center is maintained under different heads of expenses.

Cost Drivers

Cost driver is a factor, whose change causes a change in the cost of related cost objects. It is a causal factor. Change in cost drivers brings about change in the cost of the concerned cost object. For example, volume of output, number of set ups or number of parts in a product are cost drivers that would cause change in the manufacturing cost. More the volume higher would be the total cost of manufacture. More number of set ups or larger number of parts in a product would change manufacturing cost. Detailed discussions would follow on cost drivers in the section on activities based costing.

Cost Units

Alternatively, costs might be allocated to cost units. In small organizations, it is cost units to which cost data are usually accumulated. CIMA has defined a cost unit as "***a unit of quantity of product, service or time in relation to which costs might be ascertained and expressed***". A cost unit could thus be an end product or service. It could be a tonne of coal, a kilogram of yarn, a meter of cloth, a lorry load of tomato, a unit of electricity, a liter of petrol, a man hour or a machine hour, a passenger kilometer for a transport company, a bed for hospital, a meal for a hotel.

Profit Centers

As against cost centers, an organization might also specify certain centers as profit centers. A profit center is one to which both costs and revenues are attributed. A target profit for each profit center would be fixed in advance and the manager of the center is made responsible for achieving the target. Profit centers are more sophisticated than cost centers, as the managers are vested with adequate powers to achieve the target.

Investment Centers

Investment centers are divisions of an organization where costs and benefits of investments are accounted for. It is also a profit center. In smaller organizations, the entire unit would be an investment center. In large organizations, there could be more than one investment center. Investment centers are meant for raising funds and investing in assets. As investment decisions are crucial and irreversible, investment centers would be under the direct control the top executive of the company. A rate of return on capital employed is fixed as a target and the effectiveness of the manager responsible is measured in terms of its achievement. Business world has seen the rolling of number of heads, once the target had not been achieved.

Cost Pools

We have seen that costs are attributed to cost centers or cost units or to both on certain principles. Before attribution takes place, costs are pooled. ***A cost pool*** according to CIMA is a ***"collection of related costs, such as production overheads, that is reassigned to cost units. Overheads are often pooled along functional lines".*** The purpose behind cost pool is to group related items of costs so that attribution becomes effective. Thus, there could be repairs and maintenance cost pool for machinery, vehicles and buildings. Wages cost pool would include all production wages, factory overhead pool would include all indirect costs of the works place. It is also the practice to maintain sub-pools for variable costs, semi variable coasts and fixed costs within each pool. Cost pools are thus preparatory stages of cost attribution.

Responsibility Accounting

Responsibility accounting is the process of subdividing the organization into a number of responsibility centers each under the responsibility of a manager. This type of accounting traces the causes of variance between planned and actual performance of the responsibility centers to the individual manager and the activity concerned. R.N.Antony has characterized responsibility accounting as collection and reporting planned and actual activity information about the inputs and outputs of responsibility centers. Responsibility centers might be cost centers, profit centers or investment centers.

Cost Attribution

Cost attribution means two things. It might be cost allocation or cost apportionment. Certain costs are assigned in full to the cost centers or cost units. This is ***cost allocation***. Prime costs are allocated to production units, as they are traceable to the product. Certain other costs are incurred for more than one functional aspects. Hence they are to be shared among the concerned functions. Such sharing is ***cost apportionment***. Fixed costs are apportioned. In case of semi-variable costs, the variable portion is separated and allocated. The fixed component is apportioned in decided proportion.

It boils down to that variable costs are allocated and as such do not pose much problem. In the case of fixed costs, there are controversies as to the mode of apportionment. The question whether these costs are to be apportioned in proportion to production, time consumed, number of people working, labour cost incurred, materials used, machine hour or man hour used, space occupied, cost of investment made, return on capital employed or value added has been one of management's choice. Businessmen use any of the alternatives to allocate fixed costs, according their impact. The sectional performance in many companies is biased on account of the mode of apportionment. But general opinion on apportionment is that ***factory overheads are to be apportioned on the basis of direct wages, administrative overheads on the basis of works costs and selling and distribution costs on the basis of cost of production***. The exercises in this book are based on these rules of apportionment.

Activity Based Costing

In costing, the major area of controversy is the appropriation of overheads. In the methods of job costing and process costing, overheads are apportioned on the basis of end products or inputs. This mode of allocation would not pose any problem as long as the organization is producing a single product. In today's business environment, single products are rarities. Companies produce variety of products using different input but with the same manufacturing facilities. Cost changes with the range of items besides the volume produced. Apportionment of overheads in such cases becomes important in making crucial decisions like make or buy decisions. For example, a company produces Andin and Bindin, two components needed by automobile industry. Product Andin requires setting up of machine twice in a run and seven runs are needed to produce a given quantity. Product Bindin needs five machine sets up and six runs to produce the same quantity. If overheads are allocated on the basis of products or machine hours, there would be distortion, which might affect decision as to make the units in the factory or buy them from outside. End products or inputs are the results of a number of activities. Each activity again comprises of a number of actions. Machine set up, machine running, goods received transactions, quality control inspections, are examples of activities that are responsible for costs. Activities that drive costs are known as ***cost drivers.*** Cost drivers are activities that determine or help us to determine why a cost arose. CIMA has defined cost driver as "***an activity, which generates costs***". Activities and not the end products should thus be the basis for cost apportionment. This line of thinking is ***activity based costing***, which is assuming importance.

Activity based costing (ABC) is the collection of financial and operational performance information tracing the significant activities of the firm to product cost. ABC recognizes that it is the activities that cause costs to change. ABC involves identification of cost drivers and pools the costs of an activity in an activity cost pool before apportionment. The success of ABC therefore depends upon which cost drivers are to be chosen, how many cost pools and cost centers are to be installed. If properly installed and operated, ABC would enhance product cost accuracy, would provide most reliable and comprehensive cost data for decision making and would aid in measuring and improving departmental efficiency. ABC also contributes for strengthening of the monitoring capacity of the costing system.

Target Costing

Target costing is the process of costing a product in such a way that the sales price would give the desired rate of return. It is a Japanese technique for success in a highly competitive market economy. In a competitive market, it is the market, which determines the sales price and the company has to produce goods within the selling price after ensuring a desired rate of return. So, the company sets up a target cost for the product after deducting the required rate of return from the market determined selling price. As the company would not be in a position to influence the selling price, it has to concentrate on the reduction of the cost. Target cost is achieved through constant updating of technology and continuous improvement in the process, material and other inputs.

Costing and Value Chain

Value of a product is related to its functions and cost. Increase in the efficiency of existing functions or increase in the number of functions without any change in the cost would increase the value of the product. Decrease in cost without any change in functions would also increase the value of the product. There is thus a triangular relationship between cost, function and value. An equation that brings this relationship is

Value = Functions / cost

Cost Sheets

Cost accountants maintain cost data in the form of accounts, but presents to management in the form of cost sheet. Cost sheet is thus the format in which costs of a particular job or process are presented. The pooled data from the cost centers and cost units are given in a statement form.

The cost sheet is designed according to the needs of specific companies. Specimen of a simple cost sheet is in Table 2

Table 2
Specimen Cost Sheet.

	Units	Total Cost	Cost Per unit
Direct materials Opening stock of materials Add: Purchases of materials Less: Closing stock of materials			
Materials consumed Add: Direct labour			
Prime cost Add: Factory overheads Add: Op. stock of work in process Less: Closing stock of work in process			
Works cost or factory cost Add: Administrative expenses Add: Opening stock of finished goods Less: Closing stock of finished goods			
Cost of production Add: Selling and distribution expenses			
Cost of sales Sales Margin / profit			

Cost sheets provide information in a structured pattern for the management to act upon. Adjustments are made for stocks of semi-finished goods and finished goods. Semi- finished goods are part of factory cost and hence are adjusted at the end of factory cost before arriving at cost in the next stage. Finished goods stocks are adjusted in cost of production. Per unit cost is provided at each step to control planned figures with actuals and to enable the management to plan for future forecasts. We will see how cost sheets are prepared under the two conditions, namely when units of production are not possible due to variety and when units of production are available.

Illustration 1- When units of production not available

The following cost data of More Mileage Limited for the month of August are furnished. From the data made available, we would prepare cost sheet for the month of Ausust, 2003.

Sales.	Rs. 77,10,190
Stock of Materials	
As on 31.07.2003	Rs.32, 75,401
As on 31.08.2003	Rs.37, 98,057
Work in process	
As on 31.07.2003	Rs.15, 65,712
As on 31.08.2003	Rs.14, 96,832
Finished goods	
As on 31.07.2003	Rs.20, 74,123
As on 31.08.2003	Rs.21, 45,678
Wages	Rs.16, 57,104
Salaries	Rs. 5, 09,876
Selling expenses	Rs. 2, 34,567
Purchases	Rs.42, 67,890
Managerial remuneration	Rs. 1,74,962
Power and fuel	Rs. 4,32,109
Depreciation on	
Pland and machinery	Rs. 1, 34,678
Factory building	Rs. 54,106
Office equipmqent	Rs. 21,654
Factory lighting	Rs. 15,876
Office lighting	Rs. 4,679
Salesmen salaries	Rs. 43,210
Advertisement	Rs. 1,46,890

Solution

Before embarking upon the preparation of cost sheet, the preliminary task before us would be to group overheads into their functional heads as factory overheads, administrative overheads and selling overheads. This would facilitate the preparation of cost sheets.

Factory overheads	
Power and fuel	Rs. 4,32,109
Depreciation on	
Plant and machinery	Rs. 1,34,678
Factory building	Rs. 54, 106
Factory lighting	Rs. 15,876
Factory overheads	Rs. 6,36,769
Administrative overheads	
Salaries	Rs.5, 09,876
Managerial remuneration	Rs. 1,74,962
Depreciation:	
Office equipment	Rs. 21,654
Office lighting	Rs. 4,679
Administrative overheads	Rs. 7,11,171
Selling overheads	
Selling expenses	Rs. 2,34,567
Salesmen salaries	Rs. 43,210
Advertisement	Rs. 1,46,890
Selling overheads:	Rs. 4,24,667

Now, we are ready to prepare cost sheet. The format of a cost sheet was presented in table 2. The grouped information had to be filled into the format, as in Table 3 below:

Table 3

Cost sheet of More Mileage Limited for the month ended 31st August 2003

Particulars	Total cost (Rs.)
Opening stock of materials	32,75,401
Add: Purchases	42,67,890
Less: Closing stock	37,98,057
Materials consumed	37,45,234
Wages	.16,57,104
Prime Cost	54,02,338
Factory /works overheads	6,36,769
Opening stock- Semi- Finished goods	15,65,712
Less: Closing balance of semi finished goods	14,96,832
Works Cost/ Factory Cost	61,07,987
Add: Administrative/office overheads	7,11,171

Add: Opening stock of finished goods	20,74,123
Less: Closing stock	21,45,678
Cost of Production	67,47,603
Add: Selling & Distribution overheads	4,24,667
Cost of Sales	71,72,270
Sales	77,10,190
Margin of profit	5,37,920

Illustration 2-When units of production available

Hillary Textile Mills Ltd. has the following cost data for manufacturing 1,15, 500 Kg. of yarn for the week ended 15th June 2003. Prepase cost sheet.

Sales Price per Kg. was Rs.68.75.

Cotton :Opening stock 125,000 Kgs. at Rs.36.50 per Kg.

Purchase during the week 118,500 Kgs. price Rs.35.90 per Kg.

Closing stock 1,17,450 kgs. Value Rs. 42,16,455

The company had an opening stock of semi-finished goods of 52,487 kgs valued at Rs.24,10,203 , while the closing stock was 53,129 kgs. of the value of Rs.24,44,465 Finished goods stock as on opening date was 112,500 kgs valued at Rs.59,50,125 . The closing stock of finished goods on 15th June was 109,563 kgs.value Rs.60,32,539.

Costs for the week were

Wages	Rs. 11,78,500
Carriage inwards	Rs. 1,29,500
Carriage outwards	Rs. 1,31,250
Salaries	Rs. 1,62,450
Other Administrative expenses.	Rs. 1,34,375
Salesmen salaries	Rs. 1,48,050
Advertisement	Rs. 1,24,500
Depreciation on	
Plant and machinery	Rs. 1,71,550
Office building	Rs. 62,750
Rent for sales office	Rs. 40,000
Consumables	Rs. 76,255
Watch and ward	Rs. 7,450
Foreman's salaries	Rs. 5,750
M.D.' salary	Rs. 30,000

Solution- Preparatory work

Grouping of overheads, as a prerequisite for the preparation of the historic cost sheet, has to be done first.

Factory overheads

Carriage inwards	Rs.1, 29,500
Depreciation-P&M	Rs. 1,71,550
Factory building	Rs. 54, 106
Consumables	Rs. 76,255
Watch and ward	Rs. 7,450
Foreman salary	Rs. 5,750
	Rs. 4,53,255

Administrative overheads.

Salaries	Rs. 1, 62,450
Managerial remuneration	Rs. 30,000
Depreciation:	
Office buildings	Rs. 62,750
Other admin. expenses	Rs. 1, 34,375
	Rs. 3, 89,575

Selling overheads

Carriage outwards	Rs. 1,31,250
Rent for sales office	Rs. 40,000
Salesmen salaries	Rs. 1,48,050
Advertisement	Rs. 1,24,500
	Rs. 4,43,800

The company adopts first in first out as its policy for valuing inventories. It also values its finished goods at works cost. As the units produced are available, the cost sheet will have three columns, each for units, total cost and unit cost.

Table 4

Cost sheet of Hillary Textile Mills Ltd. for the week ended 15th June 2003

Particulars	Units (Kgs.)	Cost (Rs.)	Per unit cost
Opening stock of materials	1,25,000	45,62,500	36.50
Add: Purchases	1,18,500	42,54,150	35.90

Less: Closing stock	1,17,450	42,16,455	35.90
Materials consumed	1,26,050	46,00,195	40.87
Add: Wages	—	11,78,500	10.47
Prime Cost	**1,26,050**	**57,78,695**	**51.34**
Add: Factory overheads	—	4,53,255	4.03
Add: Opening stock of goods in process	52,487	24,10,203	45.92
Less: Closing stock of goods in process	53,129	24,44,465	46.01
Works Cost/Factory Cost	**1,25,408**	**61,97,688**	**55.06**
Add: Administrative overheads	—	3,89,575	3.46
Add: Opening stock of finished goods	1,12,500	59,50,125	52,89
Less: Closing stock of finished goods	1,09,563	60,32,539	55.06
Less: Production loss	12,845	—	—
Cost Of Production	**1,15,500**	**65,04,849**	**58..52**
Add: Selling overheads	—	4,43,800	3.94
Cost of sales	**1,15,500**	**69,48,649**	**62.46**
Sales	**1,15,500**	**79,40,625**	**68.75**
Margin		9,91,976	8.59

Hints.

- *If there was no process loss, the company should have processed 1,28,345 units. Hence the difference between what should have been processed and what actually was processed is what the company had lost in the process of manufacturing at that stage. Loss in process is normal in manufacturing industries. Even the Total quality Management (TQM) concept considers loss of 100 units out of a million products as the benchmark for best performance.*
- *Per unit cost is calculated on actual units produced. Actual units produced for the period is 1,12,563.This is worked out on the basis of factory production of 1,25,408 units less process loss of 12,845 units. It is better to work out per unit cost after arriving at the units of finished products, before adjusting for opening and closing stock of finished goods. The company had sold 1,15,500 units during the period, of which 2937 is from the opening stock of finished goods. Note that opening stock of finished goods were 1,12,500 as against the closing stock of 1,09,563, indicating 2937 from the opening stock were also sold in addition to what were produced during the period.*

Cost Emstimation

Cost sheets reveal the pattern of past cost of a business during a particular time frame. These historic costs serve as the basis for forecasting for next period. Hence, before attempting cost estimates for the future period, the historic cost sheet of the previous period needs to be prepared. It is presumed that the past pattern of cost would generally follow for the future periods as well, subject to changes observed after the previous period. Thus, variable costs in terms of units consumed would be in proportion to the level of operation envisaged, while the rate per unit might vary. Fixed costs' volume generally remains same. This could be explained through an illustration.

Illustration 3

Abhay Enterprises are manufacturers of XLP (code), an important ingredient for the assembly of personal computers. During the year ended 30 September 2003, the company had supplied 1,96,700 XLPs to IT companies all over the country. The company is preparing cost estimates for the next year. Its goal is to increase the sale of components by 10% per annum. The company had, during the year, entered into a wage settlement for three years with its employees, where under it had agreed to revise the remuneration of all categories of its employees by 15%. The cost of materials had slumped by 5%. Costs of the company for the production of 1,98,400 units during the year ended September 30, 2003 were as under:

Particulars	Units	Cost (In Rupees)
Materials cost	2,02,256	205,06,412
Wages		131,63,243
Factory overheads		120,38,864
Administrative overheads		13,93,275
Selling and distribution overheads		13,09,976
Change in goods in process	325	74,842
Opening stock of finished goods	1788	4,25,544
Sales	1,96,700	550,76,000

Note that 20% of factory overheads, 30% of administrative overheads and 40% of selling and distribution overheads are variable. The company adopts, as its strategy, to apportion factory overheads on the basis of direct labour cost, administrative overheads on the basis of works cost and selling cost on cost of production. Cost of finished goods is valued at cost of production. Keeping the selling price same, prepare estimated cost for the next year. Closing stock of semi-finished and finished goods, valued at prime cost and cost of production respectively, would increase in proportion to increase in sales. Loss in process would be proportional to production.

Solution

Before we embark upon the estimation of costs for the next year, we should have a basis from which to proceed. As we know, the basis is the historic cost sheet of the company.

Therefore, we have first to prepare the cost sheet of the company for the year ended September 30, 2003.

Table 5
Cost sheet of Abhay Enterprises for the year en

Particulars	Units	Total cost (Rs.)	Per unit cost (Rs.)
Materials	2,02,256	205,06,412	102.48
Direct labour	—	131,62,240	65.78
Prime cost	**2,02,256**	**336,68,652**	**168.26**
Factory overheads-variable	—	24,07,773	12.03
Factory overheads-fixed	—	96,31,091	48.13
Change in WIP	325	74,842	
Works cost	**2,02,581**	**457,82,358**	**228.80**
Administrative overheads- variable	—	4,17,983	2.09
Administrative overheads- fixed	—	9,75,292	4.87
Cost of production	**2,02,581**	**471,75,633**	**235.76**
Selling overhead- variable	—	5,23,990	2.62
Selling overhead –fixed	—	7,85,986	3.93
Cost of sales	**2,02,581**	**484,85,609**	**242.31**
Add; Opening stock of finished goods	1,788	4,25,544	
Less: closing stock of finished goods	3488	8,04,926	
Deemed production	2,00,881	481,06,227	242.47
Actual production	**1,98,400**	**481,06,227**	
Process loss	2481		
Cost of sales	**1,96,700**	**476,94,026**	**242.47**
Sales	**1,96,700**	**550,76,000**	**280.00**
Margin		73,81,974	37.53
Margin on cost%		15%	
Margin on sales %		13,80%	

Hints:

1. Production was 2,00,100 Kgs(deemed production less process loss). Per unit cost is based on units of production

Closing stock of finished goods (number) is arrived at by adding the excess of production over sales to opening stock. The rationale is that since all that is produced is not sold, the excess is an addition to opening stock and deficit is deduction from opening stock. Finished goods are valued at cost of production as per the problem. Hence the value of closing stock is the number of closing stock multiplied by unit cost of production.

2. Semi-variable costs have been split into variable and fixed component and presented.
3. Per unit cost is worked on actual units produced.
4. Deemed production is what should have been the production had there been no loss.
5. Process loss is the difference between the deemed production and the actual production.
6. Cost of sales is the actual units sold multiplied by their unit cost of production.
7. No scrap value is assumed for the units lost in process.
8. As no information is available about the number of processes through which the product passes, process loss is assumed at the end of the cost sheet. We will see later that in process industries, loss in process is provided at each stage.

Table 6

Estimated cost sheet of Abhay Enterprises for the year ending 30 September 2004

Particulars	**Units**	**Total cost (Rs.)**	**Cost/unit(Rs)**
Materials	2,22,482	214,29,200	98.19
Direct labour	—	166,50,233	76.29
Prime cost	**2,22,482**	**380,79,433**	**174.48**
Factory overheads-variable	—	26,48,550	12.14
Factory overheads-fixed	—	96,31,091	44.13
Change in WIP	325	63,005	0.29
Works cost	**222,840**	**504,22,079**	**231.04**
Administrative overheads-variable	—	4,59,781	2.11
Administrative overheads- fixed	—	9,75,292	4.47
Cost of production	**222,840**	**518,57,152**	**237.62**
Selling overhead- variable	—	5,76,389	2.64
Selling overhead –fixed	—	7,85,986	3.60
	222,840	532,19,527	243.86

Add; Opening stock -FG	3,488	8,04,926	3.69
Less: closing stock –FG	3,837	9,11,730	4.18
Deemed production	222,491	531,12,723	243.37
Process loss	4251	—	—
Actual production	218,240	531,12,723	243.37
Sales	216,370	605,83,600	243.37
Cost of sales (proportionate)	216,370	526,57,624	280
Margin	—	79,25,976	36.63
Margin on cost%	—	07.05%	
Margin on sales %	—	13.08%	

Notes:

1. Units of material consumed would increase by 10% on account of increased production. Price of material had decreased by 5%. Cost of material would therefore increase by 10% and then reduce by 5 %.
2. Lbour cost would increase by 10% for increase in production and by another 15% for increase in wages on account of wage settlement.
3. Variable component of overheads would increase in proportion to increase in production, but the fixed components would remain at same level. Per unit cost is based on actual production.
4. It would be practical to work out number of units' column first to arrive at the actual production of the period so that the unit cost column can be calculated. Estimated value of work in process and finished goods could be worked out from stage to stage.

Illustration 4

The following is the summarirised trading profit and loss account of Boppanna Manufactures Ltd. for the year ended 31st December 1992, in which year 800 clocks were sold by the company.

Trading Profit and Loss account of Boppanna Manufactures Ltd. for 31.12.1992.

	Rs.		**Rs.**
To Cost of materials	32,000	By Sales	1,60,000
To Direct wages	48,000		
To Manufacturing charges	20,000		
To Gross Profitc/d.	60,000		

	1,60,000		1,60,000
To Office salaries	24,000	By Gross profit b/d.	60,000
To Rent and taxes	4,000		
To Selling expenses	8,000		
To General expenses	12,000		
To Net Profit	12,000		
	60,000		60,000

The following estimates were made by the cost department of the company for the year ending 31 December 1993.

(i) The output and sales will be of 1000 clocks.

(ii) The ratio of materials will rise by 25% on the previous years level.

(iii) Wages during the year will rise by 12%.

(iv) Manufacturing cost will be 25% of the combined cost of materials and wages.

(v) Selling cost per unit will remain unchanged.

(vi) Other expenses will remain unaffected by the rise in output.

From the above information prepare a cost sheet showing the price at which the stocks would be marketed so as to show a profit of 10% on the selling price. The cost statement is to show cost per unit also.

Solution

This problem is so simple that it might not require the preparation of a historic cost sheet. Still, to be methodical, it would be advisable to prepare a historic cost sheet before taking up the estimation. The historic cost sheet is as under:

Table 7
Boppanna Manufactures Ltd. (Historic cost sheet)
Cost sheet for the year ending 31 December 1992

Particulars	Units	Cost (Rs.)	Cost per unit
Production and sale	800		
Cost of materials		32,000	40
Direct wages		48,000	60
Prime cost	800	80,000	100

Manufacturing charges			20,000	25
Works cost/Factory cost		800	100,000	125
Administrative overheads				
Office salaries	24,000			
Rent and taxes	4,000			
General expenses	12,000		40,000	50
Cost of production		800	140,000	175
Selling expenses			8000	10
Cost of sales		800	148,000	185
Sales		800	160,000	200
Profit			12,000	15

Based on the historic cost sheet, one could easily proceed to estimate the costs for the next year.

Table 8
Boppanna Manufactures Ltd
Estimated Cost sheet for the year ending 31 December, 1992

Particulars	**Units**	**Cost (Rs.)**	**Cost per unit**
Production and sale			
Cost of materials	1,000	40,000	40
Direct wages		53,760	53.76
Prime cost	**1,000**	**93,760**	**93.76**
Manufacturing charges		23,440	23.44
Works cost/Factory cost	**1,000**	**117,200**	**117.20**
Administrative overheads		40,000	40
Cost of production	**1,000**	**157,200**	**157.20**
Selling expenses		10,000	10
Cost of sales	**1,000**	**167,200**	**167.20**
Sales	**1,000**	**185,778**	**185.778**
Profit		18,577	18.577
Profit as percent of sales		10 %	

Cost sheets, as we have seen above, are generic in character and helps one to understand how to go about in the process of preparing the sheets. In actual practice, different types of cost sheets are prepared keeping in mind the specific requirements of the situation of the businessman. It might be for a specific one-time order or job, or for a batch order or for a continuous process production. Costing might be for manufacturing industry or for service industry. It might be for a single product or for multiple products. It would, therefore, be of necessity to see how costing is done under these circumstances. Detailed discussions on the different types of costing are scheduled in the chapters that follow.

Summary

Costs are resources sacrificed to achieve a cost objective. Costs comprise three elements, namely material, labour and expenses. Each of the elements might be traceable to the product, when it is called direct cost. Direct material and direct labour are the direct costs and together these are grouped as prime cost. All other costs are considered indirect and are called overheads. Depending upon the location of the overheads, these are classified into factory over heads, administrative overheads and selling and distribution over heads. Costs that are not related to operation are termed non-operative costs. Cost objectives could be centers or units. There are also profit centers and investment centers to which both costs and revenues are assigned.

Costing is the technique and process of ascertaining expenses and expenditures applicable for a specific period and attributing them to the respective cost centers or cost units or to both. Historic cost sheets act as basis for forecasting. In forecasting for the future, variable costs are allocated to the projected production and fixed costs are apportioned on an agreed basis. The basis of appropriation might be product, man-hour, machine- hour, space, investment, turnover etc. Usually factory overheads are apportioned on the basis of direct labour cost, administrative overheads on the basis of works cost and selling and distribution on the basis of cost of production. Conventionally, overheads are apportioned on the basis of outputs or inputs. But the costs of output or input are caused by activities. Therefore activity should be the basis for the allocation of overheads. This is Activity Based Costing.

In the above paragraphs we have learnt that cost is a necessary evil that every businessman had to reconcile with. A successful businessman is one who could restrain the evil to the minimum. We will see later what are the techniques one could employ to achieve the objective of cost control and cost reduction.

I. QUESTIONS

1. What do you understand by the term cost?
2. Define the term cost sheet. Draw up a model cost sheet and explain its constituents.

3. What are the basic elements of cost? Explain the cost control measure around them.
4. What is overhead? Explain how they are allocated.
5. Define a cost center? How does it differ from a cost unit?
6. What are profit centers? Are they same as investment centers?
7. Define imputed cost?
8. What constitutes prime cost?
9. What are the types of cost you might come across?
10. What is costing?
11. What is historic costing? Explain.
12. Define the term Cost and Cost accounting?
13. Discuss the functions and importance of Cost accounting?
14. "Cost accounting is an aid to management" - Explain.
15. Discuss the various methods and techniques of cost accounting methods and costing.
16. What are the essentials of a good costing system?

II. QUIZ

Say yes or no

1. Costs are not necessary to earn income.
2. Elements of cost are three in number.
3. Prime cost consists of direct material cost, direct labour cost and direct expenses cost.
4. Factory overheads include depreciation on plant and machinery.
5. Non- operating costs are part of administrative overheads.
6. Process loss is the loss in time due to labour problem.
7. All packing materials are part of selling overheads.
8. Variable cost per unit varies with volume of production.
9. Volume of fixed cost remains same upto a point.
10. Semi-variable costs are production costs.
11. Costing is the process of attributing costs to cost centers and cost units.
12. Cost centers and cost units denote the same.

13. Imputed costs are ascribed costs.

14. Relevant costs are the only costs relevant for production.

15. Marginal costs are costs for producing one more unit and are equal to variable costs.

16. Cost sheets are structured statements of cost incurred during a period.

17. Cost sheets are prepared only from the profit and loss account of the company.

18. Historic costs are costs that could not be avoided.

19. Fore casting is planning for future activities.

20. Costing is not decision making but aids in decision making.

III. EXERCISES

1. Lemuria engineers have incurred the undernoted costs for manufacturing sewing machines during October. Number of Machines manufactured for the month was1400.

Costs	RM	WIP	FG
Op. stock	1.75	0.77	1.40
Closing stock	1.90	0.62	1.65
Purchase (material)	18.40		
Direct labour	11.60		
Factory OH	1.76		
Admin. OH	0.88		
Selling OH	1.04		
Sales	39.20		

2. The following is the summarized Trading and Profit and Loss Account of Manga Rao Manufacturing Ltd. for the year ended 31 December 1992 in which year the company sold 800 clocks

Trading, Profit and loss Account

	Rs.		Rs.
To Cost of materials	32,000	By Sales	1,60,000
To Direct Wages	48,000		

To Manufacturing Charges	20, 000		
To Gross Profit	60,000		1,60,000
	1,60,000	By Gross Profit	60,000.
To Office Salaries	24,000		
To Rent and Taxes	4,000		
To Selling Expenses	8,000		
To General Expenses	12,000		
To Net Profit	12,000		
	60,000		60,000

The following estimates were made by the cost department of the company for the year ended 31December 1993.

i. Output and sales will be of 1000 clocks
ii. The ratio of materials will rise by 25% on the previous year's level.
iii. Wages during the year will rise by 12%
iv. Manufacturing cost will be 25% of the combined cost of materials and wages
v. Selling cost per unit will remain unchanged
vi. Other expenses will remain unaffected by the rise in output.

From the above information prepare a cost sheet showing the price at which the products would be marketed so as to show a profit of 10% on the selling price. The cost statement is to show cost per unit also. (Anna University- MBA).

3. Aarti Inc. has the following cost data for producing 1,20,000 kgs of products in the month of November. Prepare cost sheet for the month: of December with targeted sales of 1,50,000Kgs.

	Rs
Raw materials consumed	25,88,400
Labour	62,400
Factory overheadsZ	2,95,019
Adm. Overheads	1,21,169
Selling overheads	1,46,107
Sales	37,92,692

20% of Adm. And 40% Sales expenses are variable.

Stock positions:

	WIP Value	FG Value
Opening Stock	56,885	8,20,775
Closing Stock	49,280	8,95,583s

4. Jay Engineers are small scale job work enterprise. During 2003 the enterprise had the following information:

Raw materials	8,76,540
Direct Labour	2,04,567
Factory overhead.	1,01,675
Administrative overhead	27,498
Selling & distribution overhead	19,876
Sales	14,04,987

The unit has since received an order from Panthulu Pioneers Ltd. for a few equipment for which the material cost has been estimated as Rs. 2,10,500 and direct labour cost at Rs.1,16,345. Prepare a tender statement setting out the cost details. The unit would like to have the same return on cost. Allocate factory overheads on the basis of direct labour, administrative overheads on the basis of works cost and selling and distribution overheads on the basis of cost of production.

CHAPTER– 8

JOB COSTING

Learning Objective

This chapter deals with the basic costing method applicable to specific, non-repetitive jobs, orders, contracts and batches. As the jobs are unique and are not likely to repeat, there would be no stocks to account for. Allocation of fixed overheads is the major problem faced in this type of costing, as the unit would not be able to determine the expected volume of jobs in advance.

Costing systems adopted by businessmen are based on the nature of their operations. Certain business establishments have, as their objective, catering to specific orders for a single or group of products or services. The process of production in such units begins only after the receipt of orders. In certain other cases, the companies produce the same product or group of products repeatedly. These units estimate, well in advance, the demands for their products over a period and produce in anticipation of meeting such demands. The system of costing adopted by the former is ***job, order, contract or batch costing*** and the latter is ***process costing***.

Characteristics

CIMA has defined job costing as the "***Costing method applicable to production of goods and services where the work consists of specific jobs, contracts or batches***". Job costing is

- *The basic cost accounting method applicable to works consisting of separate contracts, jobs or batches.*
- *It is a one-of-situation, where organizations carry on the production of goods or services on a one-at-a time basis.*
- *Where production is not repetitive and consists of distinct jobs or lots.*

The difference among job, order and contract costing is one of details. Job costing is costing for a specific product or service undertaken either according to the specifications spelled out by the client or as per prototype supplied by him. It is also loosely referred to as ***terminal costing***.

Usually in jobs the client supplies materials and entrust the job of producing the goods to the business. Tailoring is a good example of such job. The client supplies clothe, gives measurement and entrust the job of stitching to the tailor. In order costing, the client places an order for the product and it is the responsibility of the unit to arrange for the requisite materials, labour etc and fulfill the order. In both job and order costing the client might pay an advance, but the main payment for the work is made only on completion of the task. In contracts, the payment is on quantum meruit basis. In all these forms of costing, the product is single and unique. In batch costing, on the other hand, a group of similar items that are closely related and which retain its identity through out one or more stages of production are undertaken. Batch production is also made for a single customer. Costing by a hosiery factory for the supply of 500 banians from a dealer is an example of batch costing. However in common parlance, job costing means costing for job, order, contract or batch. As the mode of costing is common, cost accountants treat them as a group. The basic thing to be borne in mind is that in job costing, the flow of jobs would not be uniform. Hence the entire overhead should not be loaded to a single job, as such a treatment would make the unit vulnerable in the face of competition. Partial appropriation of overheads therefore assumes importance. In the process, the enterprise might not recover its overheads in full if it does not procure sufficient jobs during the period.

The above discussions should not lead one to a conclusion that job costing is one where the process of production is of short duration or the task is small in scale. Building dams, Building ships, constructing highways, laying railway lines are all contracts coming under jobs. It could be for jobs that take years and consume huge resources to complete. The basic characteristic of a job is that it is unique and not repetitive. In job order costing system, each job is regarded as a cost unit. Hence it is one time costing.

Cost Sheets

The format of Job cost sheet is the same we had seen in the previous chapter. Certain jobs might even necessitate more than one process stage to complete. The cost attribution principle we had already seen applies to job costing as well. Thus, variable costs are allocated and fixed costs are appropriated. The production manager works out material and labour costs based on the specification of the job. The appropriation of fixed costs is usually on the basis of factory overheads on direct labour, administrative overheads on works cost and selling and distribution costs on cost of production. It is therefore necessary that the cost accountant prepare the historic cost sheet of the business for the previous period as a prerequisite before calculating the cost of the job. He then estimates the overheads on the basis of their historic relationship.

Illustration-1

Vijay Engineering Company is engaged in manufacturing components for computers. Its clientele includes such reputed companies as Satyam computers, WIPRO, Infosys HCL etc. The turn over of the company for the month of November was Rs.36,63,311. The following costs were reported for the period:

Labour wages	Rs.582,500.
Raw material used	Rs.21,43,250.
Selling expenses	Rs.162,050.
Administration costs	Rs.44,350

In the month of November, Morgan Computers International had approached the company for an assortment of components. The works manager had calculated the material cost for the order at Rs.18,67,210 and the direct labour cost at 5,07,490. The policy of the company was to allocate factory overheads on the basis of direct labour cost, administrative overheads on the basis of works cost and selling cost on cost of production. The company maintained the same margin on cost of sales.

Solution

As the first step, the cost sheet for the month of November needs to be prepared as in Table 1.

Table 1
Vijay Engineering Company
Historic cost sheet for the month of November

Description	Cost
Raw material	21,43,250
Labour	5,82,500
Factory overheads	1,53,338
Works cost	**28,79,088**
Administrative overheads	1,44,350
Cost of production	**30,23,438**
Selling overheads	1,62,050
Cost of sales	**31,85,488**
Sales	**36,63,311**
Margin	4,77,823

Since direct costs for the order have already been estimated, fixed costs need only be appropriated. The factory overhead in the previous period was 26.32 percent of direct labour cost (1,53,338/5,82,500 × 100), administrative overhead was 5.01% of works cost (1,44,350/28,79,088 100) and selling overhead was 5.36 % of cost of production (1,62,050/30,23,438 × 100).The margin on cost of sales was 15% (4,77,823/31,85,488 × 100). Having this basic information ready, preparing cost sheet for the job order becomes arithmetical. The cost sheet for the order of Morgan Computers International would be as in table 2.

Table 2
Vijay Engineering Company
Cost sheet for the order of Morgan Computers International.

Description	Cost-Rs.
Raw material	18,67,210
Labour	5,07,490
Factory overheads[1]	1,33,571
Works cost	**25,08,271**
Administrative overheads[2]	1,25,664
Cost of production	**26,33,935**
Selling overheads[3]	1,41,179
Cost of sales	**27,75,114**
Margin [4]	4,16,267
Sales	31,91,381

[1]26.32% of direct labour cost.

[2]5.01% of works cost.

[3]5.36% of cost of production.

[4] 15% on cost of sales.

The quote ex-factory for the order would be Rs. 31,91,381.It may be noted that unit cost is not given, as the order is not for a single product but for an assortment of items.

Batch Costing

Batch costing is also called operation costing. It is a variation of job order costing. In job work, each order is specific and the product/products are unique. The manufacturer does not anticipate repetition of similar orders in future and the costing system is tailored to meet this specific background. Production facilities in job order units are of general-purpose, which have the flexibility to produce a variety of products with least adjustments. The best example would be an engineering workshop. In batch, production facilities are geared to produce similar product or group of products in volume, but according to order. CIMA defines a batch production as "***Production of a group of similar articles, which maintain its identity throughout on one or more stages of production and is treated as a cost unit***" In batch process, batch runs are set for varying quantities as per the orders of individual customers. For example, a knitting unit receives orders for banians from a number of clients for varying sizes and quantities. If further orders flow in before an order is completed, the production becomes continuous. It is interrupted only for a short while when production for an order is over. In essence, it is a stage between continuous production and job order manufacturing. CIMA has described batch costing as "***a form of specific order costing; the attribution of costs to batches***". It is an extension of the principles of job costing to continuous costing. Batch costing therefore has a few characteristics such as carrying stocks and incurring process losses, which are absent in job costing.

Stocks

Job work being confined to the specific jobs or orders does not necessitate carrying stock of materials or work in process. Inputs are organized according to requirements of the specific orders and accounted for. But the same might not hold good when the company deals in batch production. In batch, products or groups of products are similar and the order is by individual clients. The frequency of orders for similar products is high. There might as well be repeat orders by the same client. Usually the process of production does not end with completion of a single batch order, but would continue for the other orders too. Hence the company could advantageously carry material stock by buying large quantities of materials with quantum discounts. Stocks would also be there in each of the processes due to continuity. Adjustments for stocks are thus to be made in batch costing. The mode of treating stocks in cost statements had already been explained. To repeat, *work-in-process are to be adjusted in works cost and finished goods stocks in cost of production*. The opening stock of goods in process is what the company had carried forward from the previous period and is presumed to be consumed first in the next period. Opening stock is thus an addition to the cost of that particular period. The closing stock on the other hand implies carrying forward a part of the cost of a period to the next period. Hence it is not a relevant cost for that period and has to be removed from the cost of that period. Closing stock is to be deducted from the cost of the period. Instead of adding the opening stock and deducting the closing stock, adjustments could also be made for the ***change in stock***. That is, if the opening stock is more than the closing stock, the difference would be added to the cost of that period. Should the closing stock be higher than the opening stock, the difference is deducted from the cost of the period.

Illustration 2

It should however be remembered that if the batches are for specific purposes or for different sizes, shapes or designs, which might not repeat immediately, there would not be any need for holding stock. For illustration, consider Kumar associates, who manufacture leather garments according to specifications of clients for exports. The company had during Sept.2003 manufactured 6000 garments with the following costs:

	Rs.
Material cost	3,96,158
Direct labour	2,94,450
Factory Overheads (25% variable)	1,83,618
Administrative Overheads (40% variable)	21,214
Selling Overheads (50% variable)	20,925
Sales	11,22,152

The company has since received an order from Hussaini Exports Ltd. for 3750 Garments of a specific sample. The production manager considers that requirements for materials and labour would be same as that for existing production. Keeping the margin on cost same, how would the company have estimated the cost for tender?

Let us examine. As a first step, we have to prepare the historic cost sheet to establish relationship between different elements.

Solution

Step 1.Preparation of historic cost sheet.

Table 3
Kumar Associates
Cost sheet for the month of September,2003

Production: 6000 units.	**Total cost (Rs.)**	**Per unit cost (Rs.)**
Material cost	396,158	66.03
Direct labour	294,450	49.07
Factory overhead-variable	48,963	8.16
Factory overhead-fixed	134,655	22.44
Works cost	**874,226**	**145.70**
Administrative overhead-variable	8,500	1.42
Administrative overhead-fixed	12,714	2.12
Cost of production	**895,440**	**149.24**
Selling overhead-variable	10,656	1.78
Selling overhead-fixed	10,269	**1.71**
Cost of sales	**916,365**	**152.73**
Sales	**11,22,152**	**187.03**
Margin	2,05,787	34.30

Based on the historic cost sheet, the relationship between the costs for the purpose of estimation has to be established. Variable overheads would be allocated in proportion to production. Fixed factory overheads at Rs. 1,34,655 as percent of direct labour cost of Rs.2,94,450 is 46%. Fixed administrative overheads at Rs. 12,714 as percent of works cost at Rs.8,74,226 is 1.45%. Fixed selling overheads at Rs. 10,269 as percent of cost of production of Rs.8,95,440 is 1.15%. The margin on cost (2,05,787/9,16,365*100) is 22.46%.

Step 2. Estimating cost for order

Table 4
Kumar Associates
Cost sheet for the order of Hussaini Exports Ltd

Batch no.1 **Lot: 3750.**

Description	Units	Cost-total	Per unit cost
Raw material[1]	3750	2,47,599	66.03
Direct labour[2]		1,84,031	49.07
Factory over head-variable[3]		30,602	8.16
Factory overhead - fixed [4]		84,654	22.95
Works cost		**5,46,886**	145.84
Administrative overhead-variable[5]		5,312	1.42
Administrative overhead - fixed[6]		7,930	2.11
Cost of production.		**5,60,128**	149.37
Selling overhead-variable[7]		6,660	1.78
Selling overhead – fixed[8]		6,441	1.71
Cost of sales		**5,73,229**	152.86
Margin[9]		1,28,747	34.33
Sales		**7,01,976**	187.19

[1] Proportionate to production-Rs.3,96,158/6000×3750 = Rs. 2,47,599.

[2] Proportionate to production-Rs.2,94,450/6000×3750 = Rs. 1,84,031.

[3] Proportionate to production- Rs. 48,963/6000×3750 = Rs. 30,602.

[4] 46% of direct labour cost of-Rs. 1,84,031 = Rs. 84,654.

[5] Proportionate to production- Rs.8,500/6000×3750 = Rs. 5,312.

[6] 1.45% of works cost -Rs.5,46,886 = Rs. 7,930.

[7] Proportionate to production-Rs.10,656/6000×3750 = Rs. 6,660.

[8] 1.15% of cost of production-Rs.5,60,128 = Rs. 6,441.

[9] 22.46% on cost of sales -Rs. 5,73,229 = Rs.1,28,747.

Quote (Ex-factory) Rs.7,01,976 for the order. This is the minimum the company could quote given the situations. It would, in practice, quote a little higher leaving room for negotiation. In yet another situation when the competition is severe, the company might quote a little lower than the minimum sacrificing a part of profit or even part of fixed cost. But the quote would never be lower than the variable component of the cost, as that would eat into the wealth of the business.

Illustration 3

In the above illustrations, we had considered cases of batch units which do not have stocks. Many batch process units, however, carry stocks at every stage of the process. There would be opening and closing stock of materials, semi-finished goods and finished goods. In processes where there is stock of finished goods, a separate statement, stock account is prepared as an annexure to the cost sheet for arriving at the margin of profit. Bacon & Co manufactures industrial tapes for orders. The company has established itself as a reliable supplier and as such its order book always gets filled up. During the month of November, the company had produced 2,18,578 tapes and sold 2,18,987 for Rs.58,32,000. The cost data for the month are:

Materials purchased 2,28,575meters of stainless steel strips, each a meter long, costing Rs.39,47,500.Direct labour cost Rs1,02,056.Factory overheads Rs.4,15,840(25% variable). Administrative overheads Rs.1,74,995(10% variable) and selling cost Rs.2,09,873(20% variable).Its Stock positions as at the end of November were:

	Raw materials		**Semi-finished**		**Finished**	
	Units	**Cost**	**Units**	**Cost**	**Unit**	**Cost**
Opening	8784	1,51,517	390	7,242	6,500	1,30,375
Closing	18,860	3,25,519	311	5,850	6,091	1,25,227

Solution

Step1. Preparing historic cost sheet.

Table 5
Cost sheet of Bacon & Co for November

Production: 2,18,578 tapes

Particulars	**Units**	**Total cost**	**Unit cost**
Materials- Opening stock	8784	1,51,517	17.25
Add: Purchases	2,28,575	39,47,500	17.27
Less: Closing stock	18,860	3,25,519	17.26
Materials Consumed	2,18,499	37,73,498	17.27

Wages		1,02,056	0.47
Factory overheads-variable		1,03,960	0.48
Factory overheads -fixed		3,11,880	1.42
Add :Opening stock-WIP.	390	7,242	18.57
Less: Closing stock-WIP	311	5,850	18.81
Works cost	**2,18,578**	**42,92,586**	**19.60**
Add. Administrative OH -V		17,499	0.08
Add. Administrative OH- F		1,57,496	0.73
Cost of Production	**2,18,578**	**44,46,458**	**20.56**
Selling overhead-variable		41,975	0.389
Selling overhead-fixed		1,67,898	0.581
Cost of sales	**2,18,578**	**46,56,331**	**21.54**

Stock account

	Units	**Total cost**	**Unit cost**
Opening stock	6,500	1,30,375	17.38
Production	2,18,578	46,56,331	**20.56**
Closing stock	6,091	1,25,227	
Cost of sales	**2,18,987**	**46,61,474**	**21.30**
Sales	**2,18,987**	**58,32,000**	**26.65**
Margin		11,70,526	

Process Loss

Loss in process is a natural phenomenon. In nature it is uncontrolled and abundant. For a single ovum to fertilize, nature wastes millions of sperms. It is a process of natural selection through trial and error method. Man, on the other hand has developed by conquering nature. He restricts the extent of loss. The more one could reduce process loss the higher is his success in business. The benchmark for Total Quality Management is to restrict the loss to less than 100 in a million. Thus, in every manufacturing activity efforts are made to minimize loss. The minimum loss recognized as inevitable is the ***normal loss***. Since normal loss is anticipated and therefore provided for, final cost is inclusive of normal loss. The cost inclusive of normal loss is ***deemed cost***. For example, if the normal loss in spinning were 10% of the material, the deemed material cost of a kilo of yarn would be 1.10 kilo of cotton. But when the quantum of loss exceeds what is normal, we call it as ***abnormal loss***. Abnormal losses are on account of inefficiencies of man, machine or material, and are to be excluded from the cost sheet and accounted straight away as business losses in profit and loss account. Some times it might so happen that the actual loss is less than the normal. This is attributed to the higher efficiencies of man, machine or material and is termed ***abnormal gains.*** Abnormal gains are ***subnormal losses***. Since abnormal gains are not due to the process, these are to be added back as costs to cost sheet to calculate the normal or deemed process cost. Abnormal gains are incomes of business and are to be included as such in the profit and loss statement. Both abnormal losses and gains are deviations from normal or deemed costs. The values of abnormal losses or gains are calculated on the basis of deemed costs. A closing stock statement or account is prepared as a part of the cost sheet for adjustment of opening and closing stocks of finished goods.

Accounting for scrap value of products lost/damaged in process is another aspect that has to be considered in batch costing. Scrap value, frequently referred to as salvage value, represents the realizable value of the products lost/damaged in process. There are two ways of accounting for it depending upon the magnitude of the value realized.. If the scrap value is insignificant, it is treated as miscellaneous income and taken straight away to the profit and loss account. Should the value is fairly sizeable, it is shown as a deduction to cost in the cost sheet.

Illustration 4

The sample case for process loss would be that of Kurnool Industries, the data for which are given below. Kurnool Industries is a small-scale unit engaged in manufacturing undergarments for men. It is located in the outskirts of Kurnool with a capacity to knit 2,00,000 pieces of banians per annum. For the year ended 31.12.2003, it had procured orders from a number of exporters, produced 1,51,985 banians and had supplied 1,50, 000 banians for Rs 46,31,479. Banians consume on an average 250 grams of yarns per piece. Other cost data are:

Stock details

	Opening stock		Closing stock	
	Units	**Value-Rs**	**Units**	**Value -Rs.**
Raw materials	19,442Kgs	9,87,654	20,054.5Kgs	10,34,560
Work in process.	11,655Pieces	2,18,654	10,115Pieces	1,78,543
Finished goods	10,680Pieces	2,58,990	12,665Pieces	3,13,491

Cost details

Purchases Rs. 83,50,740 (1,67,432 Kgs of yarn).

Direct labourRs.13,57,832. Factory OH 1,66,543, of which Rs. 87,654 is ariable. Administrative OH 1,32,654, of which Rs. 26,531is variable. Selling OH 2,65,432 of which Rs. 66,358 is variable.

Normal loss 7.5%.

Scrap value of work in process is Rs.6 per piece.

The company has now received an order for the supply of 50,000 banians from Ohio Exports Inc. Prepare a tender for the order, maintaining the same normal process loss (no abnormal loss) and margin on cost. Allocate fixed cost on principles normally adopted. Yarn price at present is Rs.51.75 per Kg.Yarn price is not expected to change in the near future.

Solution

Step 1. Historic cost sheet of Kurnool Industries for the year ended 31.12.2003.

Table 6

Production-Units: 1,51,985	Units (250 grams each)	Total	Per unit
Opening stock- materials.	77,768	9,87,654	
Add: Purchases	1,67,432	18,95,674	
Less: Closing stock (–)	80,218	10,34,560	
Material consumed	1,64,982	18,48,768	12.16
Direct labour		13,57,832	8.93
Factory overhead-variable		87,654	0.58
Factory overhead-fixed		78,889	0.52
Add: Opening Stock WIP	11,655	2,18,654	
Less: Closing Stock WIP (–)	10,115	1,78,543	
Factory Cost/ Works Cost	**1,66,522**	**34,13,254**	**22.46**
Admin. overhead-variable		26,531	0.17
Admin. overhead-fixed		1,06,123	0.70
Add: Opening stock -F.G	11,221	2,38,905	
Less: Closing stock -F.G (–)	12,939	2,76,897	
Cost of Production	**1,64,804**	**35,07,916**	**23. 08**
Selling overhead-variable		66,358	0.44
Selling overhead-fixed		1,99,074	1.31
	1,64,804	**37,73,348**	**24.83**
Normal loss (–)	12,361	—	
Deemed production	**1,52,443**	**37,73,348**	**24.75**
Abnormal loss (–)	458	11,337	
Scrap value (–)		76,914	
Production transferred to stock account	1,51,985	36,85,097	24.27

Stock account

	Units	Value
Opening stock	10,680	2,58,990
Production	1,51,985	36,85,097
Sales	1,50,000	46,31,479
Closing stock	12,665	3,13,491
Margin /Profit		10,00,883

Analysis of cost data for estimating for order..

1. Variable costs to be allotted in proportion to production.
2. Fixed factory cost as percent of direct labour = 78,889/13,57,832×100 = 5.81%
3. Fixed administrative overheads as percent of works cost = 1,06,123/34, 13,254×100 = 3.11%
4. Fixed selling overheads as percent of cost of production = 1,99,074/35,07,916×100 = 5.18%
5. Margin on cost is = 10,00,883/36,85,097×100 = 27.16%

Table 7

Production-Units :50,000	**Units (250 grams each)**	**Total**	**Per unit**
Direct material [1]	54,054	6,99,324	
Direct labour[2]		4,46,500	8.93
Factory overhead-variable[3]		29,000	0.58
Factoryoverhead-fixed[4]		25,942	0.52
Factory Cost/ Works Cost	**54,054**	**12,00,766**	12.16
Admin.overhead-variable[5]		8,500	
Admin. overhead-fixed[6]		37,280	
Cost of Production	**54,054**	**12,48,441**	**22.46**
Selling overhead-variable[7]		22,000	
Selling overhead-fixed[8]		64,466	
Normal loss (–)[9]	4,054	-	
Scrap value (–)[10]		24,324	
Production	**50,000**	**13,10,583**	
Margin[11]		3,55,954	
Sales		16,66,537	

[1] Raw material consumption(quantity) is assumed at the historic base plus for normal loss of 7.5% at Rs. 51.75 per kilo of yarn = Rs. (50,000/.925/4×51.75)=Rs.6,99,324.

[2] Direct labour=per unit×production =8.93×50,000=Rs.4,46,699.

[3] Factory variable overheads per unit×production= 0.58×50,000=Rs.29,000

[4] Fixed factory overhead= 5.81% Direct labour=5.81%×4,46,500=Rs.25,942

[5] Administrative variable overhead per unit×production=0.17×50,000=Rs.8,500

[6] Fixed administrative overhead=3.11% of works cost=3.11% ×12,00,766=Rs. 37,280

[7] Selling variable overhead per unit× production=0.44×50,000=Rs. 22,000

[8] Fixed selling overhead=5.18% of cost of production=5.18%×12,48,441=Rs. 64,466

[9] Normal loss=7.5% of deemed production=7.5%×54,054=4,054 units

[10] Scrap value=Rs.6×4,054=Rs. 24,324

[11] Margin=27.16%×cost of sales=27.16%×27.16%=Rs. 3,55,954.

Summary

There are broadly two types of costing, one is basic and confined to specific jobs or orders as and when they are received. This is job costing. The second one is process costing, where goods are produced continuously in anticipation of demand. In the case of job costing the unit arranges for the inputs and costing is done on the basis of actual consumption. There is no carrying of stock in job costing. But in batch costing the process is fairly continuous and does not confine to completion of single, specific orders. Orders are for a batch of similar products. Therefore in batch costing, there is need for holding stock at every stage of production. Further, there would be loss in process as the process is fairly continuous.

I. QUESTIONS

1. Illustrate the salient features of 'Job Order' costing. Identify its suitability for application?
2. How do you distinguish between a job order and a batch?
3. How are overheads allocated in job costing estimates?
4. Do we adjust for stocks in job costing?
5. Do job costs mean short duration tasks?
6. What types of industries normally opt for job costing?

II. QUIZ

Say yes or no

1. Job costing and batch costing are one and the same.
2. Job costing is continuous costing.
3. Adjustments for stock are necessary before arriving at job cost.
4. Job costing is one stage process.
5. Batch costing is to supply a given quantity of the same product.
6. As the process of production are done in different departments, it is called batch costing.

III. EXERCISES

1. Kumar associates, manufactures computer (PCs) for exports. It had during September manufactured 40 PCs with the following cost:

	Rs.
Material cost	3,96,158
Direct labour	2,94,450
Factory Overheads variable	48,963
Factory Overheadss fixed	1,34,655
Admin. Overheads. Variable	8,500
Admin. Overheads. Variable	12,714
Selling Overheads Variable	10,656
Selling Overheads Fixed	10,269
Sales	11,22,152

The company has received an order from Intercontinental Explorers for 25 PCs. Assuming that the cost structures remain same, prepare a tender sheet for the order with the same margin of profit on sales.

2. The following is the summarized Trading and profit and loss account of Boppanna Manufactures' Ltd. For the year ended 31 st December 1992 in which year the company sold 800 clocks.

Trading, Profit and loss Account

Sales	Rs.		Rs.
To Cost of materials	32,000	By Sales	
To Direct Wages	48,000	By Gross Profit	1,60,000
To Manufacturing Charges	20, 000		
To Gross Profit	60,000		
	1,60,000		1,60,000
To Office Salaries	24,000	By Gross Profit	60,000.
To Rent and Taxes	4,000		
To Selling Expenses	8,000		
To General Expenses	12,000		
To Net Profit	12,000		
	60,000		60,000

The following estimates were made by the cost department of the company for the year ended 31st December, 1993.

i. Out put and sales will be of 1000 clocks

ii. The ratio of materials will rise by 25% on the previous year's level.

iii. Wages during the year will rise by 12%

iv. Manufacturing cost will be 25% of the combined cost of materials and wages

v. Selling cost per unit will remain unchanged

vi. Other expenses will remain unaffected by the rise in output.

From the above information prepare a cost sheet showing the price at which the stocks would be marketed so as to show a profit of 10% on the selling price. The cost statement is to show cost per unit also

CHAPTER– 9

PROCESS COSTING

Learning Objective

Process or continuous costing is the technique adopted by manufacturing units to cost their products. In this method of costing, the additional feature from operation costing is that of transfer pricing from process to process. It could be at cost or at a margin. Since the process is continuous, stock maintaining at every stage is another feature. The components of costs in the sheet are restricted only to factory costs other operating costs such as administrative and selling overheads are accounted for in profit and loss account.

Process costing is employed in old economy industries engaged in producing goods continuously in expectation of orders. Goods are homogenous in character and are produced repeatedly. Common users of this type of costing are industries in the manufacture of chemicals, food processing, breweries, petroleum refining, paper, spinning and weaving, glass, metals etc. It is similar to batch costing except that production process does not wait for confirmed orders to commence. The production is planned based on demand forecast and sales are made as and when orders flow in. According to Charles Horngren *process costing deals with mass production of like units that usually pass in continuous fashion through a series of production steps called operations or processes*. CIMA has defined process costing as '*costing method applicable where goods or services result from a sequence of continuous or repetitive operations or processes. Costs are averaged over the units produced during the period'*. CIMA is further of the view that process costing is that form of operation costing where standardized goods are produced.

Characteristics

Major features that distinguish process costing from the rest are continuity of production, homogeneity of products, series of standardized processes and the averaged per unit cost. In process costing, each process is considered a cost center. The output of one process would become the input of the next process. It may also happen that the products of a process might become end products for certain uses and might be sold without undergoing further process. For example, in a composite textile mill, cotton is converted into yarns and yarns are used for producing clothes. But yarns might also be sold to power looms or handlooms. If the products from one process are transferred to the next, transfer might be at cost or at a margin. In a continuous process plant, each process is a cost center. But when transfers are made from one process to another with margin, such centers would become profit centers. In a process plant, the goods are usually homogenous. But it is also possible to produce a number of products from the same input. When a number of products are made from the same material stock, they are called *joint products*. For example petroleum crude is the raw material for diesel, petrol, aviation fuel, hexane etc. When more than one products are manufactured by using different inputs, it is called *co-products*. For example, automobiles. Usually, in process production, certain products, which are incidental to the main products, do emerge. These are *by-products*.

In process costing system, there would be stock at every stage of processes. The stocks in different processes would be in different stages of production and there would be no comparability in value of semi-finished goods with that of the finished goods. Under the circumstances, it would be difficult to find out per unit cost of output. To bring about a semblance of uniformity, cost accountants have introduced a concept called *equivalent units*. Equivalent units mean the equivalent of the semi-finished goods to finished goods. For example, if the stage of completion of semi-finished goods is 60% and the number of semi finished goods are 400, it is equivalent to 240 finished goods in number. As far as the value is concerned, it would be material cost in full and conversion cost in proportion to the level of completion. In the instant case, assuming raw material cost per unit as Rs.25 and the conversion cost per unit as Rs. 40, the value of semi-finished goods would be Rs.19, 600 ($25 \times 400 + 40 \times 60 \times 400$). The stock of semi-finished goods in the cost sheet thus represents equivalent to finished units.

Another important aspect of process costing is that only manufacturing costs, consisting of direct materials and conversion costs are included in the cost sheet. Direct material cost, direct labour cost and factory overheads are the components included in cost sheet under each process. As overheads are allocated and there is no universally acceptable mode of appropriation, overheads are not included in the cost sheet. The only exception is factory overheads, which could reasonably be apportioned, as in many units each process is a separate cost center and separate accounting entity. Administrative and selling overheads are thus accounted in the profitability statement, along with non-operating costs.

Transfer at Cost-Illustration

We will examine an example each of the possible alternatives under process costing. First, let us consider the case of Able Business Inc, which is engaged in the manufacture of electroplating for its holding company. It buys motherboards and carries out the process in three departments. Cost data of the company for the month of March are as under:

Table 1

Particulars	Raw materials	Dept.1	Dept.2.	Dept.3	F.G.
Opening Stock					
Units	269	240	185	155	785
Value-Rs.	11,459	3,360	8,750	8,064	64,012
Closing Stock					
Units	569	190	175	85	375
Value-Rs.	24,909	?	?	?	?
Direct labour		21,545	18,556	14,565	
Factory overhead		8,120	5,861	5,416	
Normal loss		5%	7.75%	10%	
Scrap value-Rs. per unit		5	10	20	
Transfer to next process		2300	2150	1998	

Materials purchased during the month were 2750 raw plates for Rs.1,18,800.

Sales during the month were 2408 processed plates for Rs. 2,49,165.

Solution

Table 2
Process cost sheet of Able Business Inc for the month of March on transfer at cost principle

Department 1.	Units	Cost (Total)	Per Unit
Opening Stock	240	3,360	68.00
Raw material consumed[1]	2450	105,350	52.73
Direct Labour	—	21,545	10.78
Factory overhead	—	8,120	4.06

	2690	138,375	51.44
Less Normal Loss[2]	135	—	—
Less Scrap value[4]	—	1000	5
Less Abnormal Loss[3]	65	3,520	54.16
	2,490	133,855	53.76
Closing Stock	190	10,214	53.76
Output transferred to Department 2.	2,300	123,641	53.76
Department 2			
Transferred from Department 1	2,300	123,641	53.76
Opening stock	185	8,750	47.30
Direct Labour	—	18,556	
Factory overheads	—	5,861	
	2485	156,808	63.10
Less :Normal Loss	193	—	—
Less: Scrap value[6]	—	1,600	10
Add: Abnormal gain[5]	33	2,235	67.72
Closing Stock	175	11,851	
Output transferred to Department 3	2150	145,592	67.72
Department 3			
	2150	145,592	67.72
Transferred from Department 2	155		
Opening Stock	—		
Direct Labour	—		
Factory overhead			
	2,305	173,637	75.33
	231	—	—
Less: Normal Loss	—	4,620	
Less: Scrap value[7]	76	6,193	
Closing Stock	1998	162,824	81.49
Output transferred to finished goods stock			

Finished Goods Stock A/C

	Units	Value	Per unit
Opening stock	785	64,012	64,012
Add production	1998	162,824	162,824

	2783	226,836	81.51
Less Closing stock	375	30,560	81.49
Cost of goods sold	2408	196,276	81.51
Sales	2408	249,165	103.47
Gross Profit (Margin)	—	52,889	21.96

Notes:	**Units**	**Value**
[1]Opening Stock of materials:	269	Rs. 11,459
Add: Purchases	2,750	Rs.1,18,800
Less: Closing Stock	569	Rs. 24,909
Materials Consumed	2,450	Rs.1,05,350

[2] 5% of 2,690 =135

[3] As against the expected production of 2365 units (opening stock 240 plus material fed 2450 less normal loss135 less closing stock190), the actual production was 2300, indicating abnormal loss of 65 units over and above normal expectation.

[4] Scrap value @ Rs.5 for 200units(normal loss 135 plus abnormal loss 65)

[5] Expected transfer to Department 3 should have been 2117 (transfer from Dept.1. 2300plus opening stock185 less normal loss193 less closing stock175). But the actual transfer was 2150, indicating an excess production of 33 units. The excess is abnormal gain.

[6] Scrap value @ Rs.10 for 160 (normal loss193 less abnormal gain of 33).

10% of 2220 =222

[7] As the actual loss in production was the same as the expected normal loss, scrap value @ Rs.20 for scrap of 231.

Transfer With Margin-Illustration

As stated earlier, it is the practice among quite a few large companies to load the transfer price from one process to the next with a margin. Usually, this is done with a view to assess the performance of each of the processes. The manager in charge of the process would be responsible for the targeted profit of his process. The costing procedure is similar except two additional columns to be provided for margin. Thus there would be four columns one each for units, actual cost, loaded cost and the load. Rose Mary Enterprises manufactures and markets "ALOK", which has a sustained market. Cost data of the company for the month of March is given below. Process of production is carried out in 3 divisions. Material is introduced in the first division. For the month, the company introduced 5500 units of raw materials at Rs.22 per unit; direct wages were Rs.12,505; factory overheads Rs.4400; normal loss 8%; scrap realization Rs.11 each. In Division2, wages Rs.9550; factory overheads Rs.6,200; normal loss 4.75%; scrap value Rs.14 each. Division3 had incurred the following costs: direct wages Rs.15,120; factory overheads Rs.5185; normal loss 8%; scrap Rs.17 each .

Additional information

1. The company has introduced margins from March. Margins – Division 1=5%; Division 2= 7%; Division 3= 10%.

2. Sales price Rs.50 per unit.

3. Stocks in processes are valued at actual cost .

4. Stock position at the end of March were

	Division 1		Division 2		Division3	
	Units	value	Units	value	Units	value
Opening stock	450	11,504	397	10,373	372	9,416
Closing stock	432	12,148	406	11,669	390	10,858
Units transferred	5070		4810		4400	?
Finished goods						
Opening stock						
(with loadRs.3310)					510	18,357
Closing Stock					501	?

Solution

Table 3
Rose Mary Enterprises
Cost Sheet for March
on transfer with margin principle

	Quantity-No.Uts	Cost Rs.	Loaded cost Rs.	Load Rs.
Opening stock	450	11,504	11,504	—
Material	5500	121,000	121,000	—
Direct labour		12,505	12,505	—
Factory overheads		4.400	4.400	—
	5950	149,409	149,409	—
Less: Normal loss	476	—	—	—
Less: Scrap value	—	4,928	4,928	—
Add: Abnormal gains	28	739	739	—
	5502	145,220	145,220	—
Less: Closing stock	432	11,402	11,402	—

	5070	133,818	133,818	—
Margin	—	—	6,691	6,691
Transfer to next division.	**5070**	**133,818**	**140,509**	**6,691**
Division 2.				
Transfer from division 1	5070	133,818	140,509	6,691
Opening stock	397	10,373	10,373	—
Direct labour	—	9.550	9,550	—
Factory overheads	—	6,200	6,200	—
	5467	159,941	166,632	6,691
Less: Normal loss	260	—	—	—
Less: Scrap value	—	3,72	3,724	—
Less: Abnormal loss	6	180	180	—
	5201	156,037	162,728	6,691
Less: Closing stock	406	12,180	12,195	—
	4795	144,022	150,713	6,691
Margin	—	—	10,550	10,550
Transfer to next division.	**4795**	**144,022**	**161,263**	**17,241**
Division 3				
Transfer from division 2	4795	144,022	161,263	17,241
Opening stock	372	9,416	161,263	—
Direct labour	—	15,120	9,416	—
Factory overheads	—	5,185	15,120	—
	5167	173,743	5,185	17,241
Less: Normal loss	414	—	190,984	—
Less: Scrap value	—	7,259	7,259	—
Less: Abnormal loss	13	455	455	—
	4740	166,029	183,270	17,241
Closing stock	390	13,661	13,661	—
	4350	152,368	169,609	17,241
Margin	—		16,961	16,961
Transferred to stock	4350		186,570	34,204

Stock account

	Quantity-No.Units	Cost Rs.	Loaded cost Rs.	Load Rs.
Opening stock	510	15,047	18,357	3,310
Production	4350	152,368	186,570	34,202
Closing stock	501	17,549	21,488	3,939
Cost of sales	4359	149,866	183,439	34,202
Sales	4359	217,950	217,950	—
Profit	—	68,084	34,511	33,573

Joint Product Costing

The process costing exercises we had done in the above paragraphs, relate to a single product costing. In practice, business organizations manufacture more than one product in the same process lines. Such products could either be *joint products* or *co-products*. When more than one product emerges from a single or group of raw materials, these are joint products. Production of kerosene, diesel, petrol, hexane and aviation fuel from petroleum crude is an apt example of joint products. Another common example is the manufacture of coke. Coal is the raw material and the joint products are coke, coal tar, benzol, sulphate of ammonia and gas. In the case of co-products, more than one product is manufactured in the process line, using different materials. For example, manufacture of different vehicles, like motorbikes, cars, trucks, trailers, tractors etc, in an automobile process line. According to CIMA, joint products are "two or more products separated in processing, each having a sufficiently high saleable value to merit recognition as a main product" and joint product cost is "the cost of a process which results in more than one main product". The definition distinguished a joint product from a byproduct. A by-product is a necessary evil. Its value is usually insignificant. So insignificant is the value of by products in some industries that the sale of byproducts is treated as miscellaneous income in the income statement.

In joint products, process costs for all products are common up to a stage. This stage is called *point of separation or split point*. From that stage, some products might be sold without further processing, while some others might be processed further before sale. Usually, further processing is done in separate process lines, where specific costs could be ascertained and allotted. So, in joint products, there is a joint cost for all the products up to the point of separation. Therefore, the task of sharing the common cost incurred up to the split point among the products is a significant decision. There are different methods adopted by different organizations for sharing the common cost. The principal methods are

- *Sharing the common cost in proportion to the quantity of each product or*
- *In proportion to the weight of each product or*
- *In proportion to their yield from raw materials or*
- *By assigning weightage according to importance of the emerging products or*
- *Sharing marginal cost according to volume and fixed cost according to marginal contribution or*
- *According to market value at the point of separation or*
- *According to sales volume of finished products or*
- *Net realizable value or reverse cost method*

Sharing the joint cost in proportion to *volume of production* is a simple method. The joint cost is divided by the sum of total production and multiplied by the respective quantity of each product manufactured. The joint cost for producing Ceno, Deno and Eno in Allino Industries was Rs.32,75,986 and the productions for the period were 13,000 units of Ceno, 11,500 units of Deno and 10,000 units of Eno.How would the joint cost be allotted among the products?

Solution

Cost allocation would be as per table below:

Table 4

	Production	% to total	Joint cost-Rs.	Allotment-Rs.
Ceno	13,000	37.68	32,75,986	12,34,392
Deno	11,500	33.33	32,75,986	10,91,886
Eno	10,000	28.99	32,75,986	9,49,708
Total	34,500	100.00	32,75,986	32,75,986

This method is easy but ad hoc in nature as the quantity produced might have different weight or value. Therefore some companies apportion the joint cost on the basis of the weight of each product. For example, Basilica Burlington Ltd. produces Prisom Primer, Prisom Medium and Prisom Supreme as joint products. For the month of May the company incurred joint cost of Rs.8,76,543 and produced 7,600 units of Prisom Primer, 8,200 units of Prisom Medium and 9,500 units of Prisom Supreme. The average weight of Prisom Primer was 225, grammes, Prisom Medium 200 grammes and Prisom Supreme 250 grammes. How could the joint cost be apportioned under this method?

Solution

The apportionment of joint cost would be as in the following table:

Table 5

Product	Production	Weight per unit-grams	Total Weight of products Kgs	% to total weight	Joint cost Rs.	Allocation Rs.
Prisom Primer	7,600	225	1710	29.87	8,76,543	2,61,823
Prisom Medium	8,200	200	1640	28.65	8,76,543	2,51,130
Prisom Supreme	9,500	250	2375	41.48	8,76,543	3,63,590
Total	25,300		5725	100.00	8,76,543	8,76,543

The joint cost would be allocated on the basis of the weight- 1710 Kgs., 1640 Kgs. and 2375 Kgs. respectively.The allocation would be Rs.2,61,815 to Prisom Primer, Rs.2,51,097 to Prisom Medium and Rs.3,63,631 to Prisom Supreme.

Another method of allocation is *in proportion to yield of material*. For example, 425 Kgs. of Klux and 550 kgs. of Flux are produced from a tonne of the raw material, at a joint cost of Rs.14,56,789. How would the cost be allotted?

Solution

The allocation would be as in the table below

Table 5 (a)

	Yield	Yield as %	Joint cost-Rs.	Allocation Rs.
Klux	425 Kgs.	43.59	14,56,789	6,35,014
Flux	550 Kgs.	56.41	14,56,789	8,21,775
Total	975 Kgs.	100.00	14,56,789	14,56,789

The method of allocating the joint cost by using weightage of importance method is again subjective and might be based on brand image, volume of sale, margin of profit, ready market or any other vantage a company might have. Suppose Homer Home Products Ltd. manufactured 2000 units of HH 1, 3000 units of HH 2 and 4000 units of HH 3 with joint costs of Rs.4,12,760. The company has given a weightage of 4 to HH 1, 2 to HH 2 and 1to HH3. How would the joint cost be allotted?

Solution

The joint cost allotted to the products would be as in the table below

Table 6

Products	Units ×Weight		Weighted index	Weighted index as %	Joint cost Rs.	Apportionment Rs.
HH 1	2000	×4	8000	44.45	4,12,760	1,83,449
HH 2	3000	×2	6000	33.33	4,12,760	1,37,587
HH 3	4000	×1	4000	22.22	4,12,760	91,724
Total		9000	18000	100.00	4,12,760	4,12,760

Sharing joint cost according to dual standards based on variable and fixed costs is yet another method. In this method, *variable joint costs are allocated on the basis of volume of production and fixed costs on the basis of contribution made by each product*. This seems to be more logical in the sense that variable costs vary according to volume of output and fixed costs are recovered from contribution. Consider the cost structure of Lumin Largesse Ltd., which had manufactured and sold 750 units of Illumina, 600 units of Florescenta and 500 units of Glowina in January at a variable cost of Rs.12,64,589 and fixed cost of Rs.8,65,431. The selling prices of the products are Rs. 1540, Rs.1650 and Rs.1735 respectively. How would you allot the costs under this method?

Solution

The allocation of variable or marginal cost is as follows

Table 7

	Production-units	% to total production	Variable cost	Allotment.
Illumina	750	40.54	12,64,589	5,12,671
Florescenta	600	32.43	12,64,589	4,10,137
Glowina	500	27.03	12,64,589	3,41,781
Total	1850	100	12,64,589	12,64,589

The apportionment of fixed cost is on the basis of contribution of each product. The contributions of the three products are as per the following table:

Table 8

	Illumina	Florescenta	Glowina
Sales –volume	750	600	500
Rate per unit	1540	1650	1735
Sales value	11,55,000	9,90,000	8,67,500
Variable costs	5,12,671	4,10,137	3,41,781
Contribution	6,42,329	5,79,863	5,25,719

The share of the fixed costs would be as in table

Table 9

	Contribution	% to total	Fixed cost	Allocation
Illumina	642329	36.75	8,65,431	3,18,046
Florescenta	579863	33.17	8,65,431	2,87,063
Glowina	525719	30.08	8,65,431	2,60,322
Total	1747911	100.00	8,65,431	8,60,431

The allocation of variable and fixed costs for the products would thus be as per the table below:

Table 10

Rs.	Illumina	Florescenta	Glowina	Total
Variable cost	5,12,671	4,10,137	3,41,781	12,64,589
Fixed cost	3,18,032	2,87,104	2,60,295	8,65,431
Total	3,18,032	6,97,241	6,02,076	21,30,020

Joint costs are also allocated according to market price at the point of separation .As in many cases, market price would not be available unless the product is further processed, we could only assume a notional price. Hence this method is also known as *notional sales value method.* The notional sales value is the sales value of the final product less its further processing cost. Peanuts Producers manufacture PNX and PNY.Both the products require further processing from the point of separation before marketing .The joint cost of producing 3750 PNX and 4250 PNY during the month of July was Rs.17,54,279. Further processing cost of PNX Rs.1,25,638 and PNY was Rs. 2,31,765.The sales prices of the products when fully processed were Rs.285 and Rs.305 per unit respectively. How could the joint cost be allocated between the products?

Solution

As a first step, we have to work out the notional sales of the products. The notional sales would be as in the following table:

Table 11

Products	Production	Final Sale price Rs.	Total sales Rs.	Further processing cost Rs.	Notional sales Rs.
PNX	3750	285	10,68,750	1,25,638	9,43,112
PNY	4250	305	12,96,250	2,31,765	10,64,485
Total	8000		23,65,000	3,57,403	20,07,597

The joint cost should now be allocated on the ratio of notional sales s in the table:

Table 12

Products	Notional sales Rs.	Notional sales as %	Joint cost Rs.	Allocation Rs.
PNX	9,43,112	46.98	17,54,279	8,24,160
PNY	10,64,485	53.02	17,54,279	9,30,119
Total	20,07,597	100.00	17,54,279	17,54,279

Another method of allocating joint cost is according to sales volume of finished products. In this method, joint cost up to point of separation is allocated among the products on the basis of the sales volume of each of the products. Rarebreed Chemicals had produced 7652 tonnes of Paraphyx, 6981 tonnes of Saraphyx and 8105 tonnes of Varaphyx at a joint cost of Rs.983,64,588. Paraphyx and Varaphyx were further processed, while Saraphyx was sold without further processing. The products are sold at Rs.3981 per tonne of Paraphyx, Rs.3579 per tonne of Saraphyx and Rs. 3750 per tonne of Varaphyx. Allocate the joint cost?

Solution

As a first step, sales of the products are to be calculated as in Table 13

Table 13

Products	Rate / tonne-Rs.	Production/tonnes	Sales -Rs
Paraphyx	3981	7652	304,62,612
Saraphyx	3579	6981	249,84,999
Varaphyx	3750	8105	303,93,750

After calculating sales volume of each of the products, the joint cost is divided among the products in that proportion of sales, as in the following table:

Table 14

Products	Sales volume –Rs.	% to total	Joint cost-Rs.	Allocation-Rs.
Paraphyx	304,62,612	35.49	983,64,588	349,09,592
Saraphyx	249,84,999	29.11	983,64,588	286,33,932
Varaphyx	303,93,750	35.40	983,64,588	348,21,064
Total	858,41,361	100.00	983,64,588	983,64,588

Yet another mode of sharing the joint cost among the products is *net realizable value method*. In this method, an attempt is made to assess the net realizable value of each product at the point of separation and to allocate joint cost according to that value. Net realizable value of a product would be sales less further processing cost after point of separation and net profit. The route adopted to work out the realizable value is also known as *reverse cost method*. In this method, further processing cost is available without any assumption. But the net profit has to be worked out through notional sales value method. Then, both net profit and further processing cost are deducted from the sale value of the product to arrive at the realizable value .The joint cost is apportioned according to this ratio. Improved Innovations Inc.produces Hang and Shing in its factory. The products incur common cost up to the point of separation and then are further processed before being sold. Joint cost for the production of 2340 units of Hang and 4230 units of Shang for the month of May was Rs.23,45,678. Further processing costs were Rs.54,897 for Hang and Rs.98,742 for Shang. Sale price of Hang was Rs.450 and Shang was Rs.510 per unit. Apportion joint cost under reverse cost method.

Solution

The table below indicates the working of net profit under the notional sales method.

Table 15

Products	Production	Sale price Rs.	Total sales Rs.	Further processing cost-Rs.	Notional sales Rs.
Hang	2340	450	10,53,000	54,897	9,98,103
Shang	4230	510	21,57,300	98,742	20,58,558

Using the notional sales as the basis, joint cost are allocated as per the notional sales value in the ensuing table.

Table 16

(1) Products	(2) Notional sales Rs.	(3) %of (2) to total	(4) Joint cost Rs.	(5) Allocation of Joint cost Rs.
Hang	9,98,103	32.65	23,45,678	7,65,864
Shang	20,58,558	67.35	23,45,678	15,79,814
Total	30,56,661	100	23,45,678	23,45,678

In joint product costing, the major hurdle is the mode of allocating the common cost among the joint products. Whatever method discussed above is adopted for allocation, there would be an element of subjectivity. This cannot be avoided. As the quantity of yield of different products from the common input is not under the control of the producers, the question of choosing some products and leaving some other products also does not arise. For a given input, the yield would be according to the nature and quality of the inputs. Hence, an amount of arbitrariness in allocating joint cost would not affect the overall profitability of the business and could be overlooked.

Illustration

In the above paragraphs, we were concentrating on the method of sharing joint cost among the products. As some products require further processing, the final cost of such products would comprise a share of joint cost plus the further processing cost. Chemco Corporation manufactures Amco, Beco and Ceco in three departments. Material is introduced in Department-1. After processing in Department- I, Amco is sold for Rs.57. per kg. Beco is further processed in Department- II while Ceco is processed in Department- III. Beco sells at Rs.63 per kg. and Ceco Rs.70 per kg. Information from the costing department for June reveals the following:.

Table 17

Particulars	Dept I		Dept II		Dept III	
	Kgs.	Value.	Kgs.	Value	Kgs.	Value.
Material	7450	92,195	—	—	—	—
Direct labour		61,748	—	4,521	—	34,067
Factory overheads		25,656	—	32,512	—	36,343
Transferred to Dept.II	3,545					
Transferred to Dep .III	2350					
			3,395		2,175	
Production	1,195		3,275		2,080	
Sales	1,050	5,904	615	6,109	710	9,989
Opening stock	475	—	605	—	725	—
Closing stock	485	—	4%	—	5%	—
Normal loss	2.5%					
Finished Goods			1125	35,437	845	39,073
Opening stock	540	12,690	1155	—	825	—
Closing stock	590	—				

Assuming transfer at cost and treating scrap sales accounted as miscellaneous income in the profit and loss account, allocate joint cost and work out cost sheet for each product.

Solution

Based on the allocation of joint cost on quantity transferred, joint cost is allocated and cost sheet worked out. As a first step, joint cost is calculated as in table below.

Table 18

Joint cost of Chemco Corporation for June

Particulars	Dept I	
	Kgs.	Value.inRs.
Opening stock	475	5,904
Direct Material	7,450	92,195
Direct labour	—	61,748
Factory overheads	—	25,656
	7,925	1,85,503
Less: Normal loss	199	—
Less: Abnormal loss	151	– 3626
	7,575	1,81,877
Less: Closing stock	485	11,645
	7,090	1,70,232
Transferred to Dept.II	3,545	85,116
Transferred to Dept .III	2350	56,424
Production of Amco	1,195	28,692

Further processing cost sheet of Beco and Ceco in Departments II and III respectively.

Table 19

Cost sheet of Beco and Ceco for June

Particulars	Department II-Beco		Department III-Ceco	
	Kgs.	Cost-Rs.	Kgs.	Cost- Rs.
Opening stock	615	6,109	710	9,989
Transfer from Department I	3,545	85,116	2350	56.424
Direct labour		4,521		34,067
Factory overheads		32,512		36,343
	4,160	1,28,258	3,060	1,36,823
Less: Normal loss	167	—	153	—
Less: Abnormal loss	—		7	-329
Add: Abnormal gain	7	225	—	—
	4,000	1,28,483	2,900	1,36,494
Less: Closing stock	605	19,433	725	34,124
Transferred to stock	3395	1,09,050	2175	1,02,370

Stock account of Chemco Corporation

	Amco		Beco		Ceco	
	Kgs.	**Rs.**	**Kgs.**	**Rs.**	**Kgs.**	**Rs.**
Opening stock	540	12,690	1125	35,437	845	39,073
Production	1195	28,692	3395	1,09,050	2175	1,02,370
Sales	1145	28,692	3365	2,11,995	2195	1,53,650
Closing stock Sales	590	14,166	1155	37,099	825	38,830
Profit margin		38,049		37,099		38,830

Operating Costing

Process costing technique, when used in service industry is called *operating costing*. Service industry, apart from adding greater value, also provides massive employment opportunities. The discussions we had so far on the systems of costing were confined to manufacturing activities. Manufacturing is fast loosing its grounds to services. The trend in both developed and developing countries shows that the contribution of service industries to the GDP of the country is increasing. It is nearly two thirds in developed countries. In India, its share has increased to 45% in recent years and might become dominant in the years to come. As such costing systems applicable to service industries deserve a deeper study.

Service industry could broadly be classified into three groups-public utility services, welfare services and supply services. *Public utility services* are usually performed by local administrations such as corporations, municipalities and panchayats. These are services aimed at the welfare of the society as a whole and are thus funded from the public kitty by the state and central governments and local bodies. Important utilities falling under this category are garbage removal, street cleaning, street lighting, fire fighting and policing. Costing of these services are done on socio economic considerations. *Welfare services* include establishing and maintaining schools, parks, hospitals, hotels, and canteens and laying and maintaining of roadways and railways and postal services. The governments, local bodies, non-profit organizations, social welfare associations and individuals and organizations undertake these activities. Excepting the last category of providers of these services, namely individuals and organizations, others perform this function without profit motive. The last group of services, *supply services*, is vital to the economic development of the country and includes the generation and supply of power and gas, supply of water, transportation, banking, insurance, merchant banking, broking and a host of financial, marketing and production services. This group of services is usually undertaken for monetary considerations and with profit motive.

In operating costing, the production is not any tangible goods but services. The measurement of services differs from service to service. Some of the services and the measuring units in them are

- *Garbage removal– per tonne of garbage removed*
- *Street cleaning – per square kilometer cleaned or per man hour used*
- *Street lighting – per resident*
- *Police protection – per 1000 citizen.*
- *Hospitals – per patient day or department–wise such as outpatient, ward patient, intensive care unit, operation theatre, post operation care, emergency etc. or according to the type of services such as medical service, utility service and special services.*
- *Schools – per student day.*
- *Hotels / canteens – per meal or per dish or service-wise such as boarding, lodging, beverage, canteen, laundering, shopping etc.*
- *Generation of electricity – per kwh (unit)*
- *Generation of steam– per kilogramme.*
- *Transport – passenger service is per trip or per passenger kilometer. Commercial transport per tonne, per kilometer or per trip.*

Of the various types of services, transportation occupies the core for industrial development of the country. It is the basic infrastructure for development. In this book, costing of transport services, that too road transport is considered.

Features of Transport Costing

Transports could be conveniently divided, on the basis of what they carry, into passenger transport and goods transport. The four modes of transports are road, rail, water and air. Important characteristics of transport costing are the classification of the costs into operating cost, maintenance cost and standing cost. Operating cost is the variable cost and the other two are fixed costs. Operating costs include fuel, labor, water, and consumables like grease and tyres. Standing costs include rent, establishment, insurance, license fee and road tax. Maintenance cost is the cost required to keep the vehicles in condition and includes periodic maintenance, break down maintenance etc. The cost sheet for operating costing could conveniently be devised depending upon the service and its specific requirements. For transport, the cost sheet would enable the operator to calculate the tariff to be fixed. To arrive at the tariff, it is necessary to work out running kilometer and passenger kilometer or cargo kilometer.

Running kilometer is the distance to be covered by the vehicle during a period. It is the basis on which fuel cost would be determined. It is the two-way distance between two places for the period. For example, Sunantha Transports are running four Air conditioned luxury tourists buses between Chennai and Kancheepuram.Each bus makes three trips a day for 28 days in a month. The distance between Chennai and Kancheepuram is 78 kilometers. The running kilometer would be calculated taking into account the number of vehicles, the trips, and the distance between the destinations with provisions for contingencies. Let us work out the running kilometer in the above case. One trip (to and fro) would mean 156 kilometers. Three trips per day would be 468 kilometers per day. Twenty-eight days mean 13,104 kilometers per month per bus. For four vehicles in the route, the total kilometers to cover would be 52,416. Provision should also be made for possible deviations due to accidents, roadblocks, political, religious and social processions etc. Based on past experience, deviation per month is 2%. Then the running kilometers per month for Samantha Transports would be 53,465. Running kilometer between two destinations would be same whether it is a passenger or cargo transport.

Passenger or cargo kilometer is another measurement for carriers. Passenger or cargo kilometer is the distance the passengers would have travelled per trip, per day or for the period. Passenger or cargo kilometer is calculated based on the past experience of the company or any other company operating in the route. It is the average occupancy ratio in the route and the capacity of the vehicle multiplied by the number of trips during the period. Traveling to destination and returning back constitutes one trip. In the case of Sunantha Transports each bus has seating capacity for 42 passengers. The average occupancy per trip is 85%. The passenger kilometers for 4 busses per trip would be = 22276.8 kilometers (85% of 42 passengers × distance one way 78 × trip covering two ways 2 × number of buses 4.) The total passenger kilometers for a month would be 22276.8 ×3 trips ×28 days = 18,71,251.2 kilometers.

The fuel cost of transport is worked on the basis of running kilometers and the income on the basis of passenger kilometers. If the vehicle could give 7 kilometers per liter of petrol, the requirements for petrol would be 7638 liters (53,465 running km. / kilometerage per liter7). The cost of petrol at the arte of Rs.35 per liter would be Rs.2,67,325 for a month. Another cost related to distance is engine oil. Suppose a liter of engine oil is needed for 1000 kilometers and the rate per liter is Rs.45, the cost of engine oil would be Rs.2406 per month (53,465 running km. / 1000 × rate Rs.45).Each bus needs 6 tyres.The life of a tyre is 4000 kms. Cost of a tyre is Rs.1,500. The number of tyres required by the company per month would be 321(running km. 53,465 Divided by life of tyre 4000 km. and multiplied by 6 tyres per bus into 4 buses). The tyre costs would be Rs.19,26,000 per month. Cost of consumables like grease would be Rs.400 per month. Depreciation on buses is 25% per annum and other assets 20%.

Running costs for Sunantha Transports for a month would be 4 drivers, 4 conductors and one cleaner. As the crew has to work all seven days a week, as against the norm of 6 days, an additional driver, conductor and cleaner would be needed as relievers. Thus, the total running staff would be 5 drivers, 5 conductors and two cleaners. Monthly salary for a driver Rs.5,000, conductor Rs.3,000 and cleaner Rs.2,000. Total salary of the crew per month would therefore be Rs.44,000. Besides maintenance cost of Rs.6,000 per month would have to be incurred. Administrative costs per month would be Rs.1,32,000.Cost of each bus is Rs.23 lakhs. Other capital expenditures are for Rs.21.45 lakhs. Insurance cost per year is Rs.61,560. Road tax per quarter per bus Rs.7150 and license fee per month Rs.41,000. Cost of capital to the company is 8%. Based on the above information, the cost sheet of Sunantha Transports would be

Table 20

	Cost per month Rs.
Drivers (5)	25,000
Conductors(5)	15,000
Cleaners (2)	4,000
Petrol	2,67,325
Engine oil	2406
Tyres	4,81,500
Grease etc	400
Depreciation@ 25% p.a.on bus	1,91,667
Depreciation @ 20% p.a.on other assets	35,750
Administration expenses	1,32,000
Insurance	5,130
Licence fee	41,000
Road tax	9,533
Maintenance	6,000
Cost of capital or Return on capital employed	75,633
Total cost	12,92,344
Cost per passenger kilometer	0.69
Tariff from Chennai to Kancheepuram	53.87

Summary

Process costing deals with mass production of like units that usually pass in continuous fashion through a series of production steps called operations or processes. Major features that distinguish process costing from the rest are continuity of production, homogeneity of products, series of standardized processes and the averaged per unit cost. In process costing, each process is considered a cost center. The output of one process would become the input of the next process. When a number of products are made from the same material stock, they are called joint products. When more than one products are manufactured by using different inputs, it is called co-products. For example, automobiles. Usually, in process production, certain products, which are incidental to the main products, do emerge. These are by-products. Another important aspect of process costing is that only manufacturing costs, consisting of direct materials and conversion costs are included in the cost sheet. Transfer from a division to another might be at cost or with a margin. Other features such as process loss, normal loss, abnormal loss and abnormal gain also apply to process costing. When process costing is for a joint product, there are different methods of apportioning common cost, such as in proportion to the quantity of each product or In proportion to the weight of each product or In proportion to their yield from raw materials or by assigning weightage according to importance of the emerging products or variable cost according to volume and fixed cost according to marginal contribution or according to market value at the point of separation or according to sales volume of finished products or according to net realizable value or reverse cost method.

I. QUESTIONS

1. Define process costing?
2. What are joint products? How does it differ from co-products?
3. How do you account for wastage in process?
4. What is joint cost? What are the methods used for allocating joint costs?
5. What is point of separation?
6. What are the ways in which transfers from one process to the other take place?
7. What do you understand by the term further processing cost?

II. QUIZ

Say yes or no

1. Goods produced in process costing are homogenous.
2. Abnormal gains are deducted from costs in cost sheet.
3. Joint products emanate from a single material.
4. Co-products are another name for by products.
5. Process wastage is avoidable.
6. Some joint products can be sold without further processing.
7. Process costing applies only to large organizations.

III. EXERCISES

1. Mc.Enroe & Marceilus Corporation has the following cost data of its operation in the departments of Moulding, Shaping and Finishing. Prepare process cost sheet and stock sheet, in tabular form:

Particulars	Units	Moulding	Shaping	Finishing
Raw materials	3780	107,730	—	—
Direct labour		116,887	127,645	108,155
Factory overheads		87,816	78,240	66,829
Normal loss		2.5%	3%	3%
Scrap value (per unit) Rs.		22	90	110
Semi-finished goods-				
Opening stock	Units	73	67	51
	Value	4,807	7,672	7836
Closing stock	Units	81	62	48
	Value	5600	7415	7610
Transfer (at cost)	Units	3842	3525	3404

Finished goods –Opening stock 290 units – value Rs.50,680.

Closing stock 280

Sales price Rs, 240 per unit

2. Work out the transfer cost from Dept. 1 to Dept. 11 of Mahalaya Manufacturers Ltd. for the month of December, from the following information:

   Department. 1.

   Works cost for 2854 units Rs.264,780. Opening stock for 156 units Rs. 10,145

   Closing stock for 149 units Rs. 9,872.Normal loss 5%.Transfer to Dept. 11- 2735 units. Scrap value per unit Rs.75. Transfer margin 6%.

3. Vijaya Foundries are producing Ala and Mala. The production is carried out in 3 Areas. In the 1st. Area joint cost is incurred, which is allocated to Ala and Mala in the ratio of their turnover. The company introduces 962 units of raw material each costing Rs. 213 in Area I and has incurred direct labour cost of Rs.1,53,680 and factory over head of Rs.51,227.Normal loss 2.5% in each Area. Opening stock of semi-finished goods in Area I is 26 units costing Rs.8306, in Area II are 43 units and in Area III is 31 units. Closing stock in Area I is 30 units costing Rs.10, 448, in Area II is 39 units and in Area III is 31. In all, 596 units are transferred to Area II for further processing into Ala and 344 units to Area III for processing into Mala. Ignore scrap value. Transfers are done at cost. Sales price per unit of Ala is Rs. 685 and Mala is Rs.745.Work out the allocation of joint cost between Area II and Area III from Area I.

4. Ching Chong Ltd., engaged in the manufacture of Fahien and Zahien, had allocated its joint cost from Structure section to the products for further processing. The joint cost was

Rs.987.54 lakhs, which was allocated to Fahien (5845 units) at Rs.543.15 lakhs and to Zahien at Rs.444.39 for 5962 units. Further processing costs for the products are :

Particulars	Fahien	Zahien
Direct labour	27.55 lakhs	31.20 lakhs
Fac tory overhead	12.68 lakhs	11.93lakhs
Normal loss	2%	2.5%
Opening stock-Units/cost	84 units/Rs7.14 lakhs.	62units/Rs.5.10lakhs
Closing stock-units/cost	92 units/Rs.7.65lakhs	58units/Rs.4.85lakhs

Price the products with 15% profit on cost. Ignore scrap value. No stock of finished goods.

5. Erickson Enterprises Manufactures, in three divisions, its product branded Amlok.It had introduced 5500 units of raw materials at Div.1, at a cost of Rs.22 each unit in April, 2004. Other cost data are

(Rs.)

Particulars	Div.1	Div.2	Div.3
Direct wages	12,505	9,550	15,120
Factory overheads	4,400	6,200	5,185
Normal loss	8%	4.75%	3%
Scrap realization (per unit)	11	14	17
Transfer to next division			
Quantity-Units	5070	4810	4400
Opening stock	450	397	
Quantity-Units	11,504	10,373	
Value			
Closing stock			
Units	432	406	390
Value	12,148	11,669	10,858
Finished goods			
Opening stock- units			510
Value			18,357
Closing stock—units			501

Prepare cost sheet treating transfer at cost

Selling price per unit is Rs. 50.

6. Kanaka Durga Steels Ltd. produces mild steel plates in 3stage operations. The cost data of the company for the month of December is as under. Prepare process cost sheet.

	Qty	1 STAGE	11 STAGE	111 STAGE
Direct materials.				
Quantity	2450			
Value (Rs.lakhs)		105.35		
Direct labour		21.545	18.556	14.565
Factory overheads		81.20	5.861	5.416
Opening stock-				
Quantity		240	185	155
Value (Rs.lakhs)		3.36	8.75	8.064
Closing stock-				
Quantity		190	225	85
Value (Rs.lakhs)		2.508	12.60	6.615
Normal loss %		5	7.5	10
Transfer to next stage-Qty		2300	2150	
Finished goods-				
Opening stock-quantity				750
Value (Rs.lakhs)				76.495
Closing stock- quantity				375
Scrap value-per unit -Rs.lakhs				0.022
Sales-quantity				2008
Rate-per unit (Rs.lakhs)				0.105

7. Lilliputan & Co. manufactures products Manza and Nanza. After they are processed in Department A. Manza is further processed in Department B . Nanza is further processed in Department C. The cost of 10,000 Kgs of raw materials introduced in Department A in the first week of August at Rs.7.50 per Kg. The other expenses are:

	Dept. A	Dept.B	Dept.C
Direct labour	21,548	16,440	12,119
Factory overheads	7,366	5,278	3,987
Outputs-units	9,500	4,550	4,150
Inputs- quantity	10,000kg	5,000kg	4,500 kg
Normal Loss	5%	8%	10%
Sales pr. P/U Rs.		20	21

8. Win Win Corporation markets Lim-Lim, using materials Asa and Bisa. For the month of March, the sales are expected to be 7400 units at a sales price of Rs.125 each. The company has forecast sales for the next six months as under.

April	7,500
May	8,000
June	7,750
July	8,250
Aug	8,100
Sept	7,900

Sales Price would remain at Rs.125 each. Closing stock – FG 10%, SFG 2.5% of the previous month's sales. Stock of materials 10 days production. Company operates 26 days / month. Material mix Asa2 and Bisa3. Rates Asa Rs.7 Bisa Rs.10. Lim-Lim needs 2 hrs skilled labour and 3Hrs unskilled Labour at rates of Rs.20 and Rs.10 per hour. Variable overheads Rs.5 per hour and fixed overhead Rs.50,000 per month. Ignore scrap value. No opening or closing stock of finished goods maintained. Work out process cost sheets for the six months. .

9. Kargil transports, engaged in luxury bus service between Hyderabad and Warrangal, has a fleet off 6 buses, each 40 seater. Each bus makes two trips per day. The distance (one wayO) 160 Km. The buses, on an average, operate 28 days in a month, The average occupancy of the buses is 90% Breakdown is 5%, which results in cancellation of a trip every week. The expenses of the company for December (per bus) were as under : Petrol consumption per trip 40 liters @ rs.28.50 per liter, engine oil 2 litters @ Rs.42 per liter, Grease (total for a month) / insurance (Yr.) rs.11,155, License fees (yr) Rs.18,500, Road tax (Qtr) Rs.550, 10 Kilos @ Rs.30 per Kg. Drivers wages, peta etc Rs.24,000 p.m., cleaners remuneration Rs.6000 p.m. Garage rent Rs.6,500, maintenance repairs rs.3,500, overhaul Rs.5,755, Tires Rs.18,500, Admin. OH Rs.9,500 p.m. Capital cost of buses Rs.67,50,450 each bus has four useful years life and there after could fetch salvage value of Rs.92,500 each. Rent for office Rs.2,500 per month. Collection for the month Rs.6,69,312. What is the rate of return the company earned on its capital employed? If the return has to be 15% p.a, what should be the tariff per passenger km.?

CHAPTER 10

MARGINAL COSTING

Learning Objective

This chapter highlights the importance of marginal costing, distinguishes marginal costing from absorption costing. Marginal costing is variable costing. Sales less variable cost is contribution. It is from contribution that a company recovers its fixed cost and earns profit. Contribution is an effective management tool for product and operational decision making, such as to arrive at desired sales mix, to make or buy decision, to continue or discontinue a line, shut down or continue production, to explore new market or to expand activities.

Costing of a product or service implies attribution of costs for each unit of product or service. Costs are either variable or fixed, although certain costs are mixtures of both. The semi-variable cost is split into variable component and fixed component, so that in the final analysis we have only variable and fixed costs. The question is which of these costs are relevant for product decisions, both or any one of them. There are two schools of thought on this issue. The oldest and conventional method of costing takes all costs (both variable and fixed) as components of costs of production. The other method considers only variable costs as the factor in determining cost of production. The costing systems we have so far been discussing was based on the conventional method and had taken both variable and fixed elements in arriving at the cost of a product. This is ***absorption costing, full costing or total costing.*** The cost in this method absorbs fixed costs in addition to the relevant variable cost. It is the total cost. CIMA considers absorption costing as the "***procedure which charges fixed as well as variable overheads to cost units***". Institute of Cost and Management Accountants (ICMA), UK defines absorption costing as "***the practice of charging all the costs, both variable and fixed to operations, processes or products***". Total cost as the basis for costing systems has its own limitations when it comes to decision-making. Fixed costs, being sunk costs, have no influence on product decisions. Secondly, the allocation of fixed cost in absorption costing system is arbitrary. Costs are appropriated on the basis of production, man-hour, machine hour, space occupied, sales price, margin on products, prime cost, cost of production or cost of sales. The discretionary method of allocation leads either to over recovery or under recovery of overheads. Stocks are over valued in absorption costing system, impairing fair profitability.

The alternate is ***variable or marginal costing*** method, which has been increasingly accepted *as* ***the tool of decision-making***. Marginal cost is the cost of producing one unit more or less than the existing volume of production. It is the incremental cost or differential cost over the existing cost. The Institute of Costs and Works Accountants of India (ICWAI) has defined marginal cost as "***the amount, at any given volume of input, by which aggregate costs are changed, if the volume is increased or decreased by one unit***". CIMA has defined marginal cost as "***the cost of one unit of a product or service which would be avoided if the unit were not produced***". For example Samson Ltd.'s daily production is 2500 units at a total cost of Rs.2,50,000, comprising fixed cost of Rs.2,25,000 and variable cost of Rs.25,000. If the company wants to produce 2501 units per day, then the total cost of production would increase to Rs.2,50,010. The 2501st unit is the marginal unit. The extra cost to be incurred by the company for producing the marginal unit is Rs.10. The marginal cost of production is thus Rs.10. Similarly, if it decides to confine its production to 2,499 units, the total cost of 2499 units would beRs.2,49,990 and the marginal cost is again Rs 10.. When additional unit is made within the installed capacity of the business, the marginal cost is equivalent to the ***variable cost of production***. Marginal cost is therefore synonymous with variable cost.

Marginal cost is the change in cost and marginal costing is the process of accounting for it. ICWAI has defined marginal costing as " ***the technique of determining the amount of change in the aggregate costs due to an increase or decrease of one unit over the existing level of production. As such it arises from production of additional increments to production".*** Batty, an authority on cost accounting, has defined the term as "***technique of cost accounting which pays special attention to the behaviour of costs with changes in the volume of output***". In marginal costing all variable costs are attributable to the product. Variable costs are deducted from the sales to get ***contribution***. And from the contribution all fixed costs are adjusted to arrive at profit. Thus, the marginal cost equation is S-VC=C=FC+P, where S=Sales, VC=Variable cost, C=Contribution, FC =Fixed cost and P=Profit.

Let us use the cost data of Everbright Engineers, engaged in the manufacture of black and white monitors for computers to work out cost sheet under both the methods. The company had for the month of October incurred the following costs and manufactured 1,400 monitors.

Values in Rs.Lakhs.

	Components Units/Value	**WIP Units/Value**	**FG Units/Value**
Op. stock	135 / 1.75	44/0.97-variable	66 /1.40
Closing stock	146/1.90	27/0.62-variable	77/1.65

Purchase (sets of components)	18.40
Direct labour	11.60
Factory overheads	1.76
Administrative overheads	0.88
Selling overheads	1.04
Sales	39.20

Components are accounted in sets needed for a unit of production. 40% of Factory overheads, 30% of selling overheads and 20% of Administrative overheads are variable. Finished products are valued at prime cost. The cost sheet of Everbright Engineers under absorption and marginal costing methods would be as in Table 1 and 2 respectively.

Table 1
Ever bright Engineers
Cost sheet for October 2003 (under absorption costing method).

Units Produced 1400 monitors	**Units**	**Total Cost (Rs. Lakhs)**	**Unit Cost (Rs.)**
Opening Stock - Components in sets	135	1.75	1296
Add Purchases	1405	18.40	1310
Less closing stock	146	1.90	1301
Direct materials consumed	1394	18.25	1305
Direct labour	—	11.60	828
Prime Cost	**1394**	**29.85**	**2132**
Factory overheads		1.76	126
Add. Opening stock of work in process	44	0.97	2205
Less. Closing stock of work in process	**27**	0.62	2267
Factory cost/ Works cost	**1411**	**31.96**	**2283**
Administrative overheads.		0.88	63
Add: Op. stock of finished goods	66	1.40	2120
Less: Close stock of finished goods	**77**	1.65	2132
Cost of production	**1400**	**32.59**	**2328**
Selling overheads		1.04	74
Cost of sales		**33.6 3**	**2402**
Sales		**39.20**	**2800**
Margin		5.57	398

Table 2
Ever bright Engineers
Cost sheet for October 2003 (under marginal costing method).

Units Produced 1400 monitors.	**Units**	**Total Cost (Rs. Lakhs)**	**Unit Cost (Rs.)**
Open. Stock - RM	135	1.75	1296
Add Purchases	1405	18.40	1310
Less closing stock	146	1.90	1301
Direct Materials consumed	1394	18.25	1305
Direct Labour	—	11.60	828
Prime Cost	**1394**	**29.85**	**2207**
Factory overheads variable	—	0.70	50
Add. Opening stock of WIP	44	0.97	55
Less. Closing stock of WIP	27	0.62	44
Factory cost/ Works cost	**1411**	**30.90**	**2193**
Administrative overheads- variable	—	0.18	13
Add: Op. stock- finished goods	66	1.40	2121
Less: Closing stock -finished goods	77	1.65	2143
Cost of production	**1400**	**30.83**	**2202**
Selling overheads- variable	—	0.31	22
Cost of sales	**1400**	**31.14**	**2224**
Sales	**1400**	**39.20**	**2800**
Contribution-A		8.06	576
Fixed costs.			
Factory overheads		1.06	
Administrative overheads		.70	
Selling overheads		.73	
Total fixed costs-B		2.49	178
Margin-A-B		5.57	398

Utility of Contribution

In marginal costing, the key role is assigned to contribution. Contribution is the excess of sales over variable cost. Contribution per unit is sales price per unit less variable cost per unit. It is from contribution that fixed costs are recovered and profits earned. Business entities usually face a number of production related constraints such as limitations in production facility, materials or labour availability or market for the products. The limitations might relate to any of the factors or a combination thereof. Contribution is the technique that businessmen adopt to plan his production to reap maximum profit under any of the situations.

When Production is Constraint

When production facility is the constraint, businessman would concentrate on the products that give maximum contribution per machine hour. For example, the plant capacity of Trio Tan Ltd. is geared to produce a maximum of 250 units of Ala, 400 units of Bela and 350 units of Cola per month. Market is no constraint for any of the products. The requirement of machine hour for producing Ala is 1 hour per unit, Bela 1hour30 minutes per unit and Cola 45 minutes per unit. The total machine hour available in the plant, on three-shift basis, is 690 hours per month. Operational data of the unit for April are as under. What would be the product mix for the next month that would give maximum return, having regard to the restraint on production facilities?

Table 3
Operational cost data of Trio Tan Ltd. for the month of April.

Production	**Ala 250 units**	**Bela 400 units**	**Cola 350 units**
Cost in Rupees			
Material cost per unit	36	63	42
Direct labour cost per unit	28	82	39
Factory overheads (60% variable)	48,700	53,187	49,651
Administrative overheads (25% variable)	12,365 21,745	13,369 24,731	11,870 21,360
Selling overheads (30% variable)	270	315	240
Sales price per unit			

Solution

Step.1. Working out contribution per unit for Ala, Bela and Cola.

Table 3
Worksheet on contribution per unit.

	Ala	**Bela**	**Cola**
Sales price per unit- A	270	315	240
Per unit variable cost	Rs.	Rs.	Rs.
Material Cost	36	63	42
Direct labour cost	28	82	39
Factory overheads – variable	117	80	85

Administrative overheads – variable	12	8	8
Selling overhead – variable	26	19	18
Total variable costs –B	219	252	192
Contribution –A-B	51	63	48

Working out contribution per machine hour.

Table 4
Worksheet on contribution per machine hour

	Ala Rs.	Bela Rs.	Cola Rs.
Contribution per unit	51	63	48
Machine hours needed to per unit	1	1.5	.75
Contribution per machine hour	51/1=51	63/1.5=42	48/. 75=64

Step.3.Working out production plan

Table 5
Production plan

Arranged according to contribution	Cola	Ala	Bela
Machine hour requirement per unit	.75	1	1.5
Capacity production-units	350	250	400
Machine hour allotment	350×.75 =262.5	250×1 =250	690-262.5- 250=177.5 177.5/1.5
Production plan in units for maximum return	350	250	118

Note: The priority in production would be Cola, followed by Ala and bela. Available machine hours would first be allotted to the production of Cola and then to Ala. Only left over machine hours would be used for the production of Bela, as it gives the lowest contribution per machine hour. The production plan that would give the maximum return is to produce 350 units of Cola, 250 units of Ala (their full installed capacities) and 118 units of Bela (out of the installed capacity of 400 units). Inquisitive readers might work out any other combination to verify the position.

When Material is Constraint

Sometimes it may so happen that the market for a product is large but the availability of materials is the restraining factor. This happens usually with agro based and aqua based industries. In such situations, scarce raw materials would be distributed according to their contribution per unit of material used. Mayhem Aqua Products Ltd., a Goa based marine processing unit, uses lobsters in its three products marketed in the brand names of Lobindica, Lobangrisa and Lobmangolica. Lobsters are processed in three separate divisions with different ingredients, tinned and exported to USA, UK and Japan. Production details for the month of June are given below. The availability of lobster per month is 400 kgs.

Table 6
Production details for the month of June

	Lobindica	Lobangrisa	Lobmangolica
Capacity per month-units	700	800	900
Requirement(in grams) of lobster per unit of product	350	400	250
Cost of lobster per Kg. in Rupees	800	800	800
Direct labour	17,500	16,250	14,750
Factory overheads	9,400	7,900	10,150
Administrative overheads	6,250	7,250	6750
Selling overheadsi	12,150	13,550	11,700
Sales price per tin	440	490	315

30% of factory overheads, 10% of administrative overheads and 15% of selling overheads are variable. Prioritize production plan of the company for the month of July.

Solution

Working out contribution per Kg. of Lobster and then contribution per kg. of materials to allocate the scarce materials among the products according to the contribution per kilo gramme of material.

Table 7
Worksheet on production plan

	Lobindica	Lobangrisa	Lobmangolica
Capacity per month	700	800	900
Sales price per unit-A			
Per unit variable cost	**440**	**490**	**315**
Material Cost	280	320	200
Direct labour cost	25 = (17,500/700)	20 = (16,250/800)	16 = (14,750/900)

Factory overheads – variable	4 = (2,820/700)	3 = (2,370/800)	3 = (3,045/900)
Administrative overheads – variable	1 = (625/700)	1 = (725/800)	1 = (675/900)
Selling overhead – variable	3 = (1,823/700)	3 = (2,033/800)	2 = (1,755)
Total variable costs –B	**313**	**347**	**222**
Contribution per unit–A-B	127	143	93
Materials per unit (in grams)	350	400	250
Contribution per Kg. of material	363	358	372
Order of Priority in allotment of materials (lobster)	2	3	1
Distribution of materials- in Kgs	175	—	225
Production in units for best return	500	0	900

It might be seen that since the contribution per Kg. of material in Lobmangola was the highest, it is to be produced to its full capacity of 900units.The allotment for Lobindica, which had the second highest contribution per Kg. of material was the balance 175 Kgs. and the production would be limited to 500 units. As far as Lobangrisa is concerned, it would not be processed, as there would not be any material left.

When Labour is Constraint

In certain industries, labourers are so specialized and scarce that the production plan in those industries has to be dove tailed into the availability of man-hours. Marble products in Agra and silk sarees of Kancheepuram need specialized labourers. Besides, even in other industries, labour availability on certain days might be limited. Under these circumstances, contribution per man-hour would determine the production plan of the industry. Spin Well Apparels Ltd. manufactures Wellfit, Wellsuit and Wellwear with installed capacities of 2500, 2000 and 1500 respectively. Labour is the crucial constraint in utilization of capacities. Information relating to the operation of the company for the month of January is given below. The company expects to garner 9500 man-hours for the month of February. Plan a product mix that would give maximum benefit to the company with the utilization of available man-hour.

Table 8
Operation for the month of January

Value in Rupees	Wellfit	Wellsuit	Wellwear
Man-hour requirement per unit	2.5	2	2.25
Material cost per unit	74	89	68
Labour cost per unit	83	67	79
Factory overhead per month at full capacity	24,850	26,084	22,456
Administrative overhead per month at full capacity	14,658	13,123	11,987
Selling overhead per month at full capacity	17,893	15,875	16,540
Total cost	4,49,901	3,67,082	2,71,483
Sales price per piece	225	225	225

In factory overheads 60% is variable, in administrative overheads 30% is variable and in selling overheads 20% is variable.

Solution

Step.1.Working out contribution per man-hour.

Table 9
Production plan for February

Value in Rupees	Wellfit	Wellsuit	Wellwear
Material cost per unit	74	89	68
Labour cost per unit	83	67	79
Factory OH -variable	6 = (24,850×.6/2500)	8 = (26,084×.6/2000)	9 = (22,456×.6/1500)
Admin.OH -variable	2 = (14,658×.3/2500)	2 = (13,123×.3/2000)	2 = (11,987×.3/1500)
Selling OH-variable	1 = (17,893×.2/2500)	2 = (15,875×.2/2000)	2 = (16,540×.2/1500)
Total variable cost	166	168	160
Sales price per unit	225	225	225
Contribution per unit	59	57	65
Man-hour per unit	2.5	2	2.25
Contribution per man-hour	23.6 = (59/2.5)	28.5 = (57/2)	28.90 = (65/2.25)
Order of Priority as per contribution	3	2	1
Allotment of man-hour	2125 = (9500-4000-3375)	4000 = (2000×2)	3375 = (1500 ×2.25)
Production plan- in units for best return	850	2000	1500

As contribution per man-hour at Rs.28.9 is highest in Wellwear, its capacity would be fully utilized. Secondly, Wellsuit gives the next higher contribution at Rs.28.5 per man-hour and therefore its capacity would also be fully used. The remaining man-hour of 2125 would be used for manufacturing Wellfit, where the man-hour contribution at Rs.23.6 is the lowest.

Market Constraint

These are days of global competition, where buyers constitute the market. Quality of product remaining similar between products, it is the price that determines the size of the market. High volume of sale could be possible at lower prices. In such cases it is the total contribution at different prices that would decide the production plan. For example, Letlive Company Ltd. markets its products under brand name of Comfortliv. Its marketing manager has assessed markets for Cmfortliv for the next year as follows:

At a price of Rs. 570, it can sell 25,000 units

At a price of Rs. 540, it can sell 28,000 units

At a price of Rs. 500, it can sell 31,000 units

At a price of Rs. 480, it can sell 33,000 units.

Cost information of the company for the current year (which is not likely to change in the next year), for a production of 23,500 units is as under:

Material cost	Rs.49,34,975
Direct labour cost	Rs.23,40,723
Factory overheads	Rs. 4,73,70 - of which Rs.2,23,250 is variable
Administrative overheads	Rs. 1,69,253- of which Rs. 72,169 is variable
Selling cost	Rs. 1,92,871- of which Rs. 1,15,853 is variable
Selling price per unit	Rs. 590

What should be the plan for production in the next year that would give the best returns?

Solution

Contribution at each price is as per the table below:

Table 10
Production plan for next year.

Sales price	570	540	500	480
Variable cost per unit				
Material cost	210			
Direct labour cost	100			

Factory overheads-variable	10			
Admin. overheads-variable	3			
Selling overheads-variable	5			
Total variable cost per unit	**318**	**318**	**318**	**318**
Contribution per unit	**252**	**222**	**182**	**162**
Sales volume	25,000	28,000	31,000	33,000
Total contribution at each price	63,00,000	62,16,000	56,42,000	53,46,000

The best price at which the company could maximize its returns is Rs, 570 and the volume of sale would be 25,000 units.

Besides the above product decisions, the technique of marginal costing and the concept of contribution are also used effectively to arrive at certain operational decisions such as

- *Determinations of sales mix*
- *Exploring new markets*
- *Continue or discontinue a line*
- *Make or buy*
- *Expand or retain statuesque*
- *Shut down or continue*

Determinations of Sales Mix

Single product companies have become rarity in the current scenario of global competition. The definition of marketing has radically changed from the conventional concept of *interaction of buyers and sellers* to *buyers* alone. It is the buyers that constitute a market. The market share of a company limits the total units a company could sell. But constituent of the product mix would be different. Companies produce variety of products to cater to different needs of consumers within the overall market share. Companies have often to replace their own products with new and improved versions before the market would make them obsolete. Customer retention is the main role of marketing executives today. Some products of a company cannibalize other products of the same company, but in the process give a better performance to the company as a whole. Product mix is thus the method adopted by companies to maximize profits within their market share. In the circumstances, unit contribution becomes the deciding factor. Consider the case of Kleptomania Products Ltd. which markets three products-Platitude. Latitude and Longitude. It has estimated that it could market 104960 products under any of the mix during the next financial year. Could you guide them to choose the best combination to earn the highest income.

	Platitude		Latitude		Longitude
Alternate 1.	35790	+	21670	+	47500
Alternate 2.	37930	+	17620	+	49410
Alternate 3.	36860	+	19650	+	48450

Cost data for the production during the current year are

Table 11

	Platitude	Latitude	Longitude
Material cost per unit	23	27	19
Direct labour cost per unit	17	16	14
Factory overheads-Variable per unit	9	10	7
Factory overheads-Fixed	12,34,560	9,75,923	13,25,891
Administrative overheads-variable per unit	7	6	5
Administrative overheads-Fixed	4,32,109	2,54,921	3,21,876
Selling overheads-variable per unit	8	9	6
Selling overheads-Fixed	5,67,041	3,67,890	4,54,123
Sale price per unit	140	135	125

Working out the contribution per unit.

Table 12
Worksheet on contribution per unit

	Platitude	Latitude	Longitude
Material cost per unit	23	27	19
Direct labour cost per unit	17	16	14
Factory overheads-Variable per unit	9	10	7
Administrative overheads-variable per unit	7	6	5
Selling overheads-variable per unit	7	9	6
Total variable cost	64	68	51
Sale price per unit	140	135	125
Contribution per unit	76	67	74

Based on the contribution of each of the products, the contribution in each of the alternate sales mix has to be worked out to know which of th mix gives highest return.

	Platitude		Latitude		Longitude
Contribution- Rs.					
Alternate 1.	35,790	+	21,670	+	47,500
	=27,20,040	+	14,51,890	+	35,15,000
				=76,86,930	
Alternate 2.	37,930	+	17,620	+	49,410
	=28,82,680	+	11,80,540	+	36,56,340
				=77,19,560	
Alternate 3.	36,860	+	19,650	+	48,450
	=28,01,360	+	13,16,550	+	35,91,960
				=77,09,870	

It might be seen from the above that it would be advantageous for the company to choose the second alternative for the next year.

Exploring New Markets

These are days of expanding trades. With WTO and European Common Market and the attempts of other regions to fuse into a common market, the world is shrinking in to a single global market. To be competitive in this environment, each industrial unit vies with others to expand its market horizon. Exploring new markets for the products is a strategy adopted by most of the successful corporates world over. Further with the view to have lower cost per unit, corporates have created huge capacities, which the local markets could not absorb. Thus there are two compelling reasons for companies to enter new markets- one to be competitive and the other to utilize their idle capacity. When a company enters a new market, it had to compete with existing players. Besides quality, it is the pricing of the product in the new market that assumes significance. Companies adopt piercing price strategy to establish themselves in a new market. They have to cut down their prices. But to what extent? Here comes the concept of marginal cost to aid the management. Companies could reduce prices of their products in new markets to the point of recovering marginal costs.

There would thus be two prices for the same product, one in the established market and the other in the new market.. Dual pricing has its own disadvantages. It is quite likely that the products priced lower for a new market would re-enter the established market and cut into the market share. Therefore, before embarking on dual pricing policy, a company should ensure that the low priced product does not re-enter the established market. For deciding to enter a new market at differential price, consider the case of Brindavan Products Inc.The company has an installed capacity to produce 1,00,000 umbrellas per month as against which it operates at 50% capacity due to saturation of local market. It sells umbrellas in the local markets at Rs.50 per piece. Cost data for the previous month were:

	Total		Per Unit(Rs)	
Materials consumed	Rs. 6,05,506		12.11	
Variable operating costs	Rs.6,44,496		12.89	
Fixed overheads	Rs.8,19,560	Rs.20,69,561	16.39	41.39

The company has received an export order for the supply 30,000 umbrellas per month at Rs.30 per umbrella. Exports also require special packaging, which would cost Rs.3 more per unit. The marketing manager feels that accepting the order would result in a loss of Rs.11.39 per unit, as the price offered at Rs.30 is lower than the average cost of production of Rs.41.39.As a consultant, you are asked to give your views. Should the company accept the offer?

Solution

The marketing manager has considered total cost, which also includes fixed overheads. As fixed overheads are irrelevant in decision-making, one has to see whether the price offered is higher than average variable cost. First we have to work out variable cost and see whether there is any contribution

Marginal cost of an umbrella

Material cost	Rs.12.11
Variable operating cost	Rs.12.89
Total variable costs	Rs.25.00
Additional packaging cost	Rs. 3.00
Marginal cost of export order	Rs.28.00
Export offered price	Rs.30.00
Contribution	Rs. 2.00

As the offered price is lower that the marginal cost of production, the export offer could be accepted, after ensuring that it would not cannibalize the company's local demand.

Continue or Discontinue a Line

Management might sometimes have to take decisions as to spin off or continue operation of a particular line of product whose performance is apparently not up to expectations. In such situations, the decision depends upon whether that particular line contributes or not. For example Mermaid & Co. manufactures perfumes Exalt, Confident and Beala with installed capacity of 15,000 units of Exalt, 25,000 units of confident and 35,000 units of Beala per month. The finance manager of the company has given the following data of performance for August:

Table 13
Production plan

		Exalt	Confident	Beala	
No. of units produced and sold		15,000	25,000	35,000	
Sales price per unit	Rs.	12	10	11	
Sales volume-A	Rs.	1,80,000	2,50,000	3,85,000	
Material cost	Rs.	75,000	1,00,000	1,05,000	
Labour and other					
variable costs	Rs.	60,000	75,000	70,000	
Fixed OH	Rs.	45,000	1,00,000	1,40,000	
Total costs –B	Rs.	1,80,000	2,75,000	3,15,000	
Profit/ Loss	Rs.	—	-25,000	70,000	Rs. 45,000
Aggregate profit					

An institutional director, who saw the report, recommended for the discontinuance of Confident as it has incurred a loss of Rs.25,000. The company's market is saturated. What would be your view?

The contention of the institutional director is based on the report, which is on absorption costing basis. For decision-making, the relevant is marginal costing. Should the operational data be in marginal costing pattern, it would have given an entirely different picture, as under.

Table 14
Cost sheet under marginal costing

		Exalt	Confident	Beala
No. of units produced and sold		15,000	25,000	35,000
Sales price per unit	Rs.	12	10	11
Sales volume-A	Rs.	1,80,000	2,50,000	3,85,000
Material cost	Rs.	75,000	1,00,000	1,05,000
Labour and other variablecosts.	Rs.	60,000	75,000	70,000
Total variable cost -B	Rs.	1,35,000	1,75,000	1,75,000
Contribution A-B	Rs.	45,000	75,000	2,10,000
Total contribution				3,30,000
Less: Fixed overheads				2,85,000
Profit				45,000

It may be observed that Confident had made a contribution of Rs.75,000. If it were to be discontinued, the overall performance of the company would result in a loss of R.30,000, as against the profit of Rs.45,000 with Confident. This could be seen in Table 15.

Table 15
Cost sheet if Confident is discontinued.

	Exalt	Beala	
No. of units produced and sold	15,000	35,000	
Sales price per unit	Rs. 12	11	
Sales volume-A	Rs.1,80,000	3,85,000	
Material cost	Rs. 75,000	1,05,000	
Labour and other variablecosts.	Rs. 60,000	70,000	
Total variable cost -B	Rs. 1,35,000	1,75,000	
Contribution A-B	Rs. 45,000	2,10,000	
Total contribution			2,55,000
Less: Fixed overheads			2,85,000
Loss			30,000

Conclusion is that the unit should continue producing Confident.

Make or Buy

Out sourcing materials, labour, components, products and processes has become order of the day. The main advantage is availability in time and reduction in cost. The famous Barbie doll is designed in US, materials procured from Korea and other countries, assembled in Mexico and marketed throughout the world. That is the level of outsourcing. Every company calculates cost of making a component and compares it with what is available in the market. If the cost of procuring a component is lower than the variable cost of producing it in the plant, the company does not make it, but buys it. This is a crucial decision for the company, as it has capacity to make the same component in its own plant. Sentiments do not play a role in achieving excellence. But certain aspects are scrupulously adhered to. There would not be any compromise on quality, the requisite quantity and the schedule of delivery of the bought out components. So, if a component is available at a rate less than the variable cost of making it and is available in quantity, with at least the same quality of the company's product and the supplier would not default delivery schedule, it is advisable to buy the product. Virgin Automobiles Ltd. is mainly an assembling unit for tricycles with motor. It also produces two components required for assembly, namely Zoom 2A and Zoom 3Acost of making these components for the month of May are:

Table 16
Cost sheet of Virgin Automobiles Ltd. for May

	Zoom 2A	Zoom 3A	
Material	8,66,384	2,49,085	11,15,469
Labour&othervariable costs	8,43,612	9,08,768	17,52,380
Fixed overheads-allocated	2,67,750	3,30,750	5,98,500
Total Cost	19,77,746	14,88,603	34,66,349
No.of units produced	8,500	10,500	
Per unit cost	232.68	141.77	

Bluebirds Cycles Spares Ltd. is a recently established spare part manufacturer, who had approached Virgin with proposals of supplying both Zoom 2A and Zoom 3A at Rs.210 and Rs105 respectively. The cost of buying both the components appear profitable on the face of it, as the total costs of manufacturing them in the plant are more than the price offered by Bluebirds Cycles Spares Ltd. What would be your advice to the company?

Solution

Buying both the products based on their total cost of production in the plant might lead to wrong decisions as total costs include fixed costs also. Since fixed cost is irrelevant for decision-making, our advice to the company should be based on marginal cost of the products. We have therefore to work out variable cost per unit as in table below.

Table 17
Variable cost of making the components in Virgin Automobiles Ltd.

	Zoom 2A		Zoom 3A	
	Total	Per Unit	Total	Per Unit
No. produced	8,500		10,500	
Material cost	8,66,384	101.93	2,49,085	23.72
Labour other variable costs	8,43,612	99.25	9,08,768	86.55
Total variable costs	17,09,996	201.18	11,57,853	110.27

The advice would be to ***make Zoom 2A*** in the plant, as the variable cost of making it at Rs.201.18 is cheaper than buying it at Rs.210. But Virgin should ***buy Zoom 3A*** as its price at Rs.105 is lower than the variable cost of Rs.110.27 for making it in the plant. Table 18 would justify the advantage of such buyouts.

Table 18

Cost sheet of Virgin Automobiles Ltd. When discontinuing production of Zoom 3 A and buying the component from Bluebirds Cycles Spares Ltd.

	Made – Zoom 2A(8,500)	Bought out Zoom 3A (10500)	Total cost
Material	8,66,384		
Labour& other variable costs	8,43,612		
Total variable costs	17,09,996	11,02,500	28,12,496
Fixed overheads	—	—	5,98,500
Total Cost when 3A is bought out			34,10,996
Cost when both components			
were produced in the plant	19,77,746	14,88,603	34,66,349
Savings when 3A is bought out			55,353

The total cost of the company, when it buys Zoom3A is Rs. 34,10,996 instead of making it in the factory, as against the total cost of Rs.34, 66,349 if it produces both the components in the plant. The decision to buy Zoom3A would generate a profit margin of Rs.55,353. Buying both components would also not be a correct decision, as it would increase the cost of the company by Rs. 19,651 as could be seen in Table 19.

Table 19

Cost when both the components are bought out

	Rs.
Cost of buying ZOOM 2A	17,85,000
Cost of buying ZOOM 3A	11,02,500
Total cost of buying both components	28,87,500
Fixed cost	5,98,500
Total cost to company	34,86,000
Current Cost of producing both in the plant	34,66,349
Increase in cost, if both were bought out	19,651

Note : Fixed costs of the company had to be incurred, whether it buys out or not.

As we have seen, in deciding whether to make or buy, the cost to be considered is marginal or variable cost for that particular product or component. Today information is available in plenty. But the manager has to be careful to choose the relevant information for his decision making. A recent question paper of Anna University has brought to light the need to choose the required information from among the available information. The question is as under.

The managing director of a private limited company asks for your assistance in arriving at a decision as to continue manufacture of a component X, or to buy it from an outside supplier. The component X is used in the finished products of the company. The following data are supplied.

The annual requirement of component X is 10,000 units. Lowest quotation from an outside supplier is Rs.8.00 per unit. Component X is manufactured in the machine shop. If component X is bought out, certain machinery will be sold at its book value and the residual capacity of the machine shop will remain idle.

The total expenses of the machine shop for the year ended 31.3.2004 are as follows. During the year the shop manufactured 10,000 units of X.

	Rs.
Materials	1,35,000
Direct labour	1,00,000
Indirect labour	40,000
Power and fuel	6,000
Repairs and maintenance	11,000
Rates, Taxes and Insurance	16,000
Depreciation	20,000
Other overheads	29,600

The following expenses of the machine shop apply to manufacturing component X.

	Rs.
Materials	35,000
Direct labour	56,000
Indirect labour	12,000
Power and fuel	600
Repairs and maintenance	1,000

The sale of machinery used for the manufacture of X would reduce depreciation by Rs.4,000 and insurance by Rs.2,000.

If component X is bought out the following additional expenses would be incurred.

Freight Re.1 per unit

Inspection Rs.10,000 per annum.

You are required to prepare a report to the managing director showing the comparison of expenses of machine shop when component X is made and when bought out.

I think this is the first time that Anna University has given a case study type of question in the examinations. The costs shown in the first table are for the manufacture of the finished products, whose identity is not known. The costs in the second table only relates to the manufacture of component X. In the group of costs incurred for the manufacture of 10,000 units of component X, relevant cost for decision making are following variable costs

Material cost Rs.35,000

Direct labour cost Rs. 56,000

The variable cost per unit of X is thus Rs.9.10.

If the unit decides to buy out, cost per unit of X is Rs.8.

Besides, buying out would have additional cost of Re.1 for freight and Re.1 for inspection. In all, buying out would cost the company Rs.10 per unit. However, buying out would save fixed costs of Rs.6,000 per annum(Rs.4,000 by way of reduced depreciation and Rs.2,000 in insurance) or Re.0.60 per unit of X.

Therefore, the net buy out cost per unit of X is Rs.9.40, which is higher than the variable cost of making it in the factory at Rs.9.10.It is advisable for the unit to continue to make the component X.

Expand or Not

As the horizon of markets has widened, global market is what we talk today. In global market, size is a major factor. A size, which was optimal earlier, might not be so now. Manufacturing units are therefore forced to expand their capacity. Expansion also gives the benefits of economies of scales. But the decision to expand would involve increase in fixed assets and fixed costs. Besides additional sales might necessitate reduction in sales price. Hence, before embarking up on expansion, companies assess whether the additional contribution to be generated through expansion would cover the additional fixed costs as well as the cost of capital on added assets. Malectron Video Vishion Ltd. is producer of a critical TV component with installed capacity of 5000 units per month. The company's products enjoy a good market and its capacity is fully utilized for the month of March. The demand for its components is huge. A recent market survey indicated that it could sell 10,000 units per month provided its existing price of Rs.400 per unit is reduced to Rs.375.Variable cost of production would remain at Rs.250 per unit. The company's existing fixed cost per month is Rs.2,51,550. The company is considering a proposal to increase the capacity to 10,000units per month.

Expansion would necessitate an additional investment of Rs.30 lakhs. Additional selling expenses were estimated at Rs.1 lakh per month. The cost of capital for the company is 20% before tax. Should the company go in for the expansion? Will your answer be different if the cost of capital of the company is 10%?

Solution

Expansion would involve additional investment and consequently additional fixed cost. The combined increase is called incremental cost. If the additional contribution from expansion were more than the additional cost, it would be advantageous to go in for expansion. So we have first to work out the current contribution, then the incremental contribution and cost, before deciding.

Step. 1. Existing contribution

Table 20
Malectron Video Vishion Ltd.
Contribution for March

Production-5,000 units.	Value (Rs)	Per unit (Rs)
Variable costs.	12,50,000	250
Sales	20,00,000	400
Contribution	7,50,000	150

Step 2.Estimating additional contribution.

Table 21
Incremental contribution at cost of capital of 20%

Production (proposed) :10,000	Value (Rs.)	Per unit (Rs.)
Variable costs	25,00,000	250
Sales	37,50,000	375
Gross Contribution	12,50,000	125
Existing contribution	7,50,000	
Incremental contribution-A	5,00,000	
Additional fixed cost	1,00,000	10
Additional cost of capital (20% of Rs.30 lakhs)	6,00,000	60
Incremental cost-B	7,00,000	70
Incremental contribution over incremental cost- A-B	–2,00,000	

As the incremental contribution after expansion would be negative, expansion would not be a viable proposition. However if the cost of capital of the company is 10%, then the company could go in for expansion, as the incremental contribution is more than incremental cost by Rs 1 lakh, as in the table below.

Table 22
Incremental contribution at cost of capital of 10%

Production (proposed): 10,000	**Value (Rs.)**	**Per unit (Rs.)**
Variable costs	25,00,000	250
Sales	37,50,000	375
Gross Contribution	12,50,000	125
Existing contribution	7,50,000	
Incremental contribution-A	5,00,000	
Additional fixed cost	1,00,000	10
Additional cost of capital (10% of Rs.30 lakhs)	3,00,000	30
Incremental cost-B	4,00,000	40
Incremental contribution over incremental cost-A-B	1,00,000	

Shutdown or Continue

Plants do close down temporarily, when they incur losses due to scarcity of raw materials or any other inputs, slump in market, labour problem etc. Under the situations, managements have to decide whether to shut down the plant till the situation improves or to continue operations with the limitations and continue to incur loss. Shut down involves certain unavoidable costs, besides the normal fixed costs, such as costs of maintenance, retrenchment or layoff cost and restart cost. In shut down, plants are to be maintained in proper conditions so that they could readily be restarted when conditions improve. Labour employed in production is to be paid retrenchment benefit or lay off benefit. Finally, when it is decided to restart, machine set up costs and start up costs are to be incurred. The management has, therefore, to assess the marginal cost to be incurred during shut down and compare it with the actual loss the unit might suffer had it continued its operations. As long as the plant makes a contribution, the question of shut down would not arise. In case the existing operations has resulted in cash losses[1], then the decision might be different. If the cost of shut down is less than the cash loss in operation, it should shut down. On the other hand, if the costs of shut down were higher than the expected cash loss, it should continue to operate.

Vishveshvaraiah Ginning Mills Ltd. is a case in point. Due to the failure of cotton crop during the year and the consequential increase in cotton prices, Vishveshvaraiah Ginning Mills was incurring cash losses[1]. The Mill was considering the possibility of closing down its operations till situation improves. Report for the cotton crop in the next season is good. Besides,

Government is also contemplating allowing free import of cotton within 6 months. The management of the company is, therefore, confident of the restarting the mill after 6 months. The company operated at 50% of its capacity during the immediately preceding half-year and ginned 400 bales of cotton at a sale price of Rs.2,000 each bale. The operation has resulted in a loss of Rs.1,65,725 as under.

Table 23

	Value-Rs.
Sales	8,00,000
Cost of cotton	5,04,000
Cost of labour	3,10,975
Other variable costs	35,750
Variable costs	8,50,725
Fixed cost	1,15,000
Total costs	9,65,725
Loss	1,65,725

If plant is closed, labour lay off is 10% of normal wages. During shut down, special maintenance will cost Rs.25, 000 and the restart expenses would be Rs.15,000. If it were to continue its operations, the cost pattern would be the same. Sales price of ginned cotton is also not expected to change. Should the Co. shut down or continue with the loss.The company had incurred a negative contribution (cash loss) of Rs. 50,725 in the last half-year. If continued, it would continue generate a cash loss of Rs. 50,000 for the next half-year also. But if the plant is closed and reopened after six months, what would be the extent of additional cost due to shut down it has to incur has to be worked out. If the shut down cost is less than the cash loss, the plant could be closed down. On the other hand if the shut down cost is higher than the cash operating loss, it is better to continue the plant. In the illustrative case the shut down cost would be Rs. 71,097 (Table 24 below):

Table 24

Estimation of cash loss if the unit has to shut down:

	Value-Rs.
Shut down costs	
Lay off cost	–31,097
Special maintenance cost	–25,000
Restart cost	–15,000
Total cash loss	–71,097

Since, cash loss of shut down at Rs.71,097 is more than cash loss of Rs.50,725 if the unit continues its operations, it would be advisable for the unit to continue its operations.

[1] *Cash loss means variable costs are more than sales, resulting in negative contribution*

Summary

In the previous chapters, we had considered costing a product or service with total costs that are related to its production. This is absorption costing as in this method all costs (fixed as well as variable) are absorbed to arrive at the cost of a product or service. Fixed costs are period costs and are allotted to the production costs on a basis. Since the basis is discretionary, allocation of fixed cost to cost of production would distort the real cost behind decision making. Besides fixed costs are to be incurred whether there is production or not. These are sunk costs. Hence in product decisions fixed costs are dormant players. The relevant cost for product decisions is variable costs or marginal costs.

Marginal costing is the method of costing with variable costs alone. It is the cost of producing or foregoing one additional unit to or from the existing volume. In the ultimate analysis, marginal costs represent variable costs. Sales less variable cost is contribution. And from the contribution, fixed costs are recovered and profits made. Contribution is an important concept in decision-making, particularly when there is constraint on any factors of production or marketing. It is used to take product decisions such as determinations of sales mix, exploring new markets, continue or discontinue a line, make or buy a component, expand or maintain statuesque or shut down or continue production in times of scarcity or market glut.

I. QUESTIONS

1. What is marginal cost? Explain the usefulness of marginal cost in managerial decision-making?
2. What is absorption costing? How does marginal costing differ from absorption costing?
3. How are inventories valued under absorption costing and marginal costing? How do such valuations affect profitability?
4. Name a few product decisions that are influenced by marginal costing?
5. What do you understand by the term contribution?
6. What are the practical uses of contribution?
7. What is make or buy decision?
8. When do you consider shutting down a plant?
9. What determines the decision to expand or not?
10. When raw material is a constraint, what factor would weigh with you in planning your production ?
11. What would you take into account in deciding about a sales mix to maximize your profitability and why?

II. QUIZ

Say yes or no

1. Total cost is important in determining the cost of a product
2. Marginal cost and variable cost are the same.
3. Absorption costing is the tool used in makes or buy decision.
4. Penetrating pricing is adopted to explore new markets.
5. Dual pricing is a wrong strategy as it shows differential treatment to two groups of customers.

III. EXERCISES

1. Arun Hi-Tech Ltd. is the major supplier of an important IC to WIPRO. Installed capacity of Arun is 2000 pieces per month. Currently, the capacity of Arun's factory is fully utilized. As WIPRO is getting additional orders, it had enquired Arun whether it could supply 3000 units from 6 months afterwards. The requirement would be continuous. Arun therefore proposes to increase its capacity to 3000 units by adding balancing equipment costing Rs.5,45,000. Its current selling price per unit is Rs.400. The price will continue for the enhanced order also. Arun's other cost data are: variable cost per unit Rs.275 and fixed costs were Rs 21,36,689 per annum. The cost of capital of Arun is 14%.Would you recommend for the expansion? Substantiate your answer.
2. Daredevil enterprises produces three components- Aza,Beza and Ceza and assembles Yoyo, as its product. Cost details of the components are:

(Rs)

	Aza	Belza	Ceza
D.Materials	118	142	137
Labour	81	93	66
Other variables	46	39	27
Fixed overheads	139	169	186
Total	384	443	416

The company received a quotation from Advantageous Enterprises for the supply of Aza at Rs.280, Beza at Rs.274 and Ceza at Rs.210 per piece. Which are the items you would advise the company to buy and which to make. Substatiate your answer.

3. Free From Fear Ltd. supplies the following information. Find out the amount of profit the company had earned during the year using marginal costing technique:

Fixed cost Rs.5, 00, 000,

Variable cost Rs.10 per unit

Selling price Rs.15 per unit

Output level 1,50,00 units.

4. Glow Well has the following information in respect of its products Aniza and product Biniza for June.

	Product Aniza Rs.	Product Biniza Rs.
Sales price	750	480
Direct material cost	300	300
Direct Labour hours at Re.10.50 per hour	15 hrs	2 hrs
Fixed overhead Rs.30, 000		

Present the above information to show the profitability of products during labour shortage.

5. Iniana Informatics Ltd produces two different kinds of components Casio and Dacio. The limiting factor for the company is the availability of labour. From the following information for April, find out which product is more profitable and advise future pattern of production. The company has used its labour ours to the maximum.

	Product Casino	**Product DacinoI**
	Cost per Unit-Rs.	**Cost per unit-Rs.**
Materials:	50.00	40.00
Labour 6 hrs	30.00	—
3 hrs	—	20.50
Overheads: Fixed	15.00	10.75
Variable	15.00	16.00
Total cost	110.00	87.25
Selling price	140.00	110.00
Profit	30.00	22.75
Total production for the month	500 units	600 units

The company could sell the above sales mix or

400 units of Casino and 700 units of Dacino

600 units of Casino and 500 units of Dacino

700 units of Casino and 400 units of Dacino

550 units of Casino and 550 units of Dacino

6. Fantastic Radio Manufacturing Company finds that while it costs Rs.62.5 to make each component X 2730, that same is available in the market at Rs.48.5 each, with an assurance of continued supply. The breakdown of cost of manufacturing by the company is:

	Rs.
Materials	27.50
Labour	17.50
Other Variables	5.00
Depreciation and other fixed cost	12.50
Total	62.50

Should the company make or buy?

7. Due to recession, Indo- Emirates Enterprises was running at 50% of its capacity. The following details are available.

	Cost of production per unit
Direct Materials	Rs.2000
Direct labour	Rs.1000
Variable overhear	Rs.3000
Fixed overhead	Rs.2000
Total cost	Rs.8000
Production per month	Units 20,000
Total cost of production	Rs.16,00,00, 000
Sales	Rs.14,00,00, 000
Loss	Rs.2,00,00, 000

An exporter offers to buy 5000 units per month at the rate of Rs.6500 per unit and the company hesitates to accept the offer for fear of increasing its already operating losses. What would be your advice?

8. Thermostatics Ltd. is considering a proposal to introduce a new product. There can be three models of this product, aimed at different sections of the consumer market. The company would lik to start with the most profitable model first. The relevant cost figures are as follows:

	Model I Rs.	Model II Rs.	Model III Rs.
Variable cost (per unit)			
Materials	154	122	86
Labour	106	95	58
Variable overheads	40	33	31
Total variable costs	300	250	175
Selling price (per unit)	825	775	650
Expected sales volume (mutually exclusive)	825	2,500 Units	4,500Units
Per month			
Capital Expenditure before production can commence (financed by bank at 5% p.a)	8,00,000	30,00,000	40,00,000
Fixed overheads per month attributable to new model including depreciation on capital expenditure	2,80,000	8,50,000	11,00,000

You are required to prepare a statement of return on investment for each of the models and recommend which model the company should choose .

9. Firm Fixtures proposes to install a machine to produce a component used by it. Two machines Xcalib and Xvalib are being considered for the purpose. Particulars of the machines are are as follows:

	Xcalib	Xvalib
Cost	Rs.10, 00,000	Rs.20, 00,000
Annual capacity	2, 000 Units	5, 000 Units
Effective life	10 years	10 Years
Salvage value	5%l	5%
Material per unit	300	300
Production cost per unit other than depreciation	500	450
Existing overheads per annum	Rs.1, 00,000	Rs.1, 00,000

Interest is at 9% p.a. The component is available in the market @ Rs.900 per unit .The company's requirement is 3, 000 units. Show which of the alternatives, either to make the component or to buy it in the market would be advantageous. If producing is beneficial, which of the machines the company should procure and why?

10. Carlisle Casual Ltd. has three lines of products M. N and O. The cost pattern of the Company for July was:

	M	N	O
Direct Materials	47,53,550	34,78,,915	41,78,620
Direct Labour	13,75,305	11,43,789	14,87,026
Production in units	6,310	5,412	7,450
Depreciation on			
Plant and machinery	62,57,035		
Factory Building.	2,75,350		
Office equipment	34,398		
Administrative overheads	78,465		
Selling and distribution overheads	1,16,890		

Sales price per unit M = Rs.2,500,N= Rs.1,200 and O=Rs.2,250. Overheads are to be distributed according to normal practice of factory overheads as percent of prime cost, administrative overheads as percent of works cost and selling and distribution costs as percent of cost of production . Work out cost sheets, under both absorption and marginal costing systems?

11. Explain assumptions of cost volume profit analysis.S & Co. Ltd. Had three divisions, each of which makes a different product.

(Rs.)

Divisions	**A**	**B**	**C**
Sales	1,12,000	56,000	84,000
Costs:			
Direct material	14,000	7,000	14,000
Direct labour	5,600	7,000	22,400
Variable	14,000	7,000	28,000
overhead	28,000	7,000	28,000
Fixed cost			
Total costs	61,600	35,000	92,4000

The management is considering to close down Division C. Advice whether or not division C should be closed down.

12. Outline the usefulness of process costing

50 units are introduced into a process at a cost of Rs.50.The total additional expenditure incurred by the process is Rs.30.Of the units introduced, 10% are normally spoilt in the course of manufacture. These possess a scrap value of Rs.0.25 each. Owing to an accident only 40% units are produced. You are required to prepare a process account.

13. Explain the application of marginal cost analysis for managerial decision-making.

A product –X takes 5 hours to be produced on a machine, which is used to full capacity. Its selling price is Rs.60 and marginal cost Rs.30.A component-Z used in the production of X can be made on the same machine in 2 hours. The marginal cost of producing Z is Rs.10.It can be bought at the net price of Rs.12 from the market. Should the firm make or buy the component?

14. XY Industries Ltd. is preparing its comprehensive budget for the next year. The sales manager has said that he does not wish to have a single estimate of sales but would prefer to give four forecasts along with his estimates of probabilities he attaches to them:

Sale forecasts	**Probability**
Rs.16,00,000	0.4
Rs.20,00,000	0.3
Rs.24,00,000	0.2
Rs.30,00,000	0.1

Variable costs are 40%of sales and total fixed costs are Rs.8,00,000Prepare budgeted income statement based on each of the forecasts.

15. ABC Ltd. makes a single product, which sells for Rs. 30 per unit, and there is great demand for the product. The variable cost of the product is Rs. 16 as detailed below:

	Rs.
Direct material	8
Direct labour (2hrs)	4
Variable overheads	4
	16

The labour force is currently working at full capacity and no extra time can be made available. Mr. Roy, a customer has approached the company with a request for the manufacture of a special order at Rs. 8,000. The cost of the order would be Rs. 3,000 for Direct Material and 600 labour hours will be required and variable overhead per hour shall be Rs. 2. Should the order be accepted?

CHAPTER– 11

COST, VOLUME, PROFIT ANALYSIS

Learning Objective

This chapter brings out the relationship between cost, volume and profit and its role in profit planning.. Break-even point is used as a tool. The different facets of break-even point are explored and their practical implications analyzed. The uses of profit volume ratio in determining optimal sales mix and in adjusting costs to realize maximum operating results are also dealt with.

Variable factors that contribute to profit planning decisions are cost, volume and profitability. The relationship between cost and volume, cost and profit and volume and profit is ever lasting. Cost has an inverse relationship with profit. Lower the cost higher would be the profit and vice versa. Between cost and volume, the relationship is again inverse. Higher the volume, lower would be the per unit cost. It is obvious that per unit variable cost remaining same, fixed cost when distributed over a larger volume, becomes less per unit of production. Thus the total cost per unit becomes low. Volume has a direct bearing on profit. Higher the volume, higher would be the profit. This triangular relationship leads to a number of managerial decisions relating to the operational areas of businesses. Management could achieve profit targets by varying one or more of these factors. Thus, Heiser considers this relationship as "***the most significant single factor in planning of the average business***".

We have already seen the importance of marginal cost. The cost volume profit analysis is an extension of the impact of marginal costs and contribution on operational decisions. ***Break-even point is the technique used to study the relationship between costs, volume and profit***. An enterprise should know well in advance what should be the minimum level of its operation which would cover its costs, both variable and fixed, so that its production plan would aim at a level higher than that cut off level to earn profits. The minimum level of operation that would absorb total costs is ***break-even level or break-even point***. Break-even point is thus that level of operation at which the unit would be able to recover its total costs- fixed and variable. This is the level where there is neither profit nor loss. Any incremental production over this minimum level less the incremental cost of production would amount to profit. As the incremental cost is variable cost, incremental production less marginal cost is profit.

Working knowledge about break-even point is essential to a manager, as it would put him on alert. For,

- *Even a small change in activity of the business from the break-even level would be the difference between profit and loss or between survival and extinct.*
- *It would show the leeway the business has when faced with competition and in times of economic turmoil.*

Break-Even Production

The calculation of break even point could be from thc level of units to be produced for a business to break even, the capacity or the volume of sales at which it breaks even. Break-even point could be worked out in *three methods-equation method, contribution method and graphic method.* Under equation method, break-even point is *Sales – variable cost = fixed cost.* For example, sales price per unit of Saholite produced by Sahu Salvite Ltd. is Rs.200, variable cost Rs.120 and total fixed costs Rs.48,000, the break even production would be

BEP	= S – VC	= FC
	= 200 – 120	= 48,000
	= 80	= 48,000
		= 600 units.

The second method of working out break-even production is through contribution. *Sales price per unit less variable cost per unit would yield contribution per unit of output.* Basically, it is through contribution that break-even point is assessed. Fixed cost divided by contribution would be the production in units needed to break-even. Mathematically, breakeven production is expressed in a simple formula

FC/C=BEP,

C = SP–VC

Where

BEP is break-even production.

FC is total fixed cost for the period

C is contribution per unit

SP is sales price per unit and

VC is variable cost per unit

For example, the sales price per unit of Obitu produced by Obrien Overseas Ltd. was Rs.575 and variable cost per unit was Rs.483.The contribution per unit is thus Rs.Rs.92.If the fixed cost of the company for a month was Rs.21,45,987, the breakeven production per month would be 23,326 or[21,45,987/(575–483)] =23,326.

In a trading concern, dealing with a number of products and where sales price and variable cost per unit would not be possible, contribution is total sales less total variable costs and the break even level would be in terms of sales.

The third method of calculating break-even production is through graphs. Three graphs one each for sales, variable cost and fixed cost are to be drawn and combined to arrive at the break-even production. For example, variable cost per unit is Rs.53, sales price per unit is Rs.81 and fixed cost is Rs.1,46,888, the break even production would be the point at which sales curve, variable cost curve and fixed cost curve converge. The break-even production in the example is 5246 units and the break-even sale is Rs.4, 24,926.This is indicated in a series of graphs below.

1. **Fixed cost curve**.

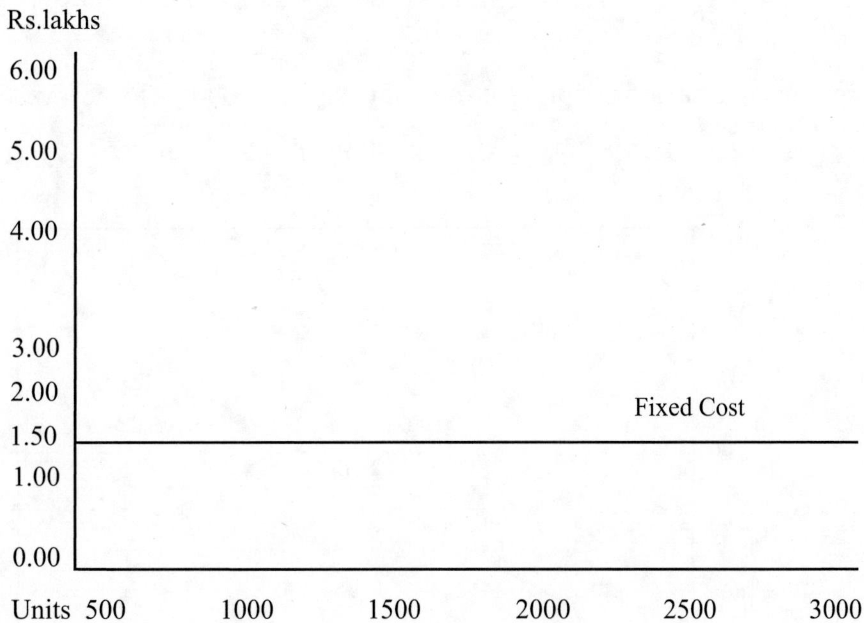

Fixed cost curve is a straight line, as fixed cost remains same irrespective of level of operation

2. Variable cost curve

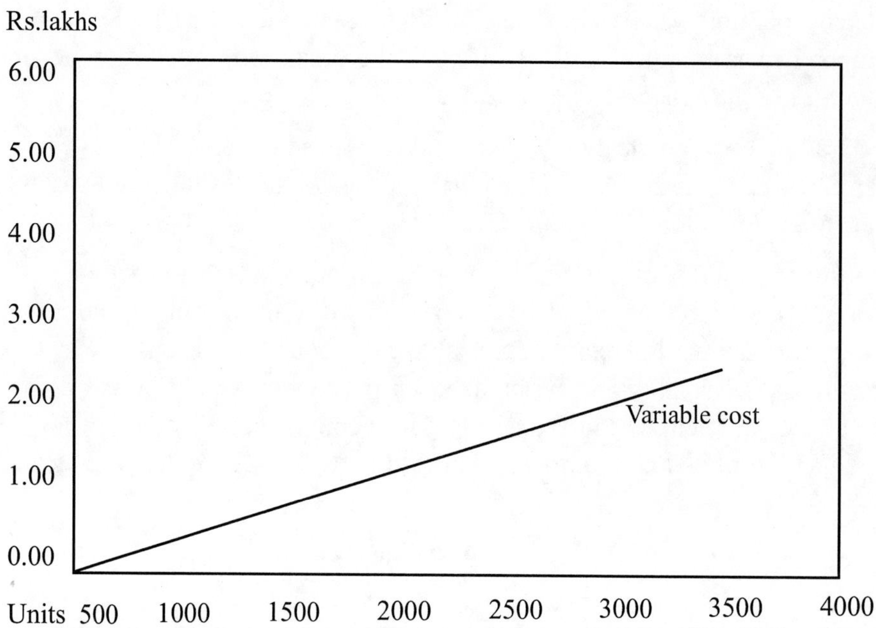

Variable cost line is linear as variable cost varies directly in proportion to the level of activity.

3. Revenue/sales curve

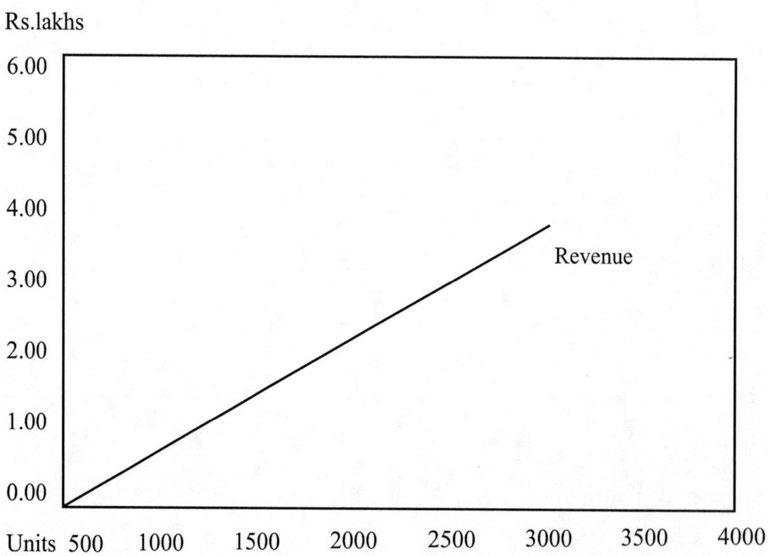

Revenue cost is also linear in character as revenues increase in proportion to volume of sale

4. **Graphic presentation of break-even point**

Note: Total cost is fixed cost plus variable cost. Variable cost curve implanted on the fixed cost

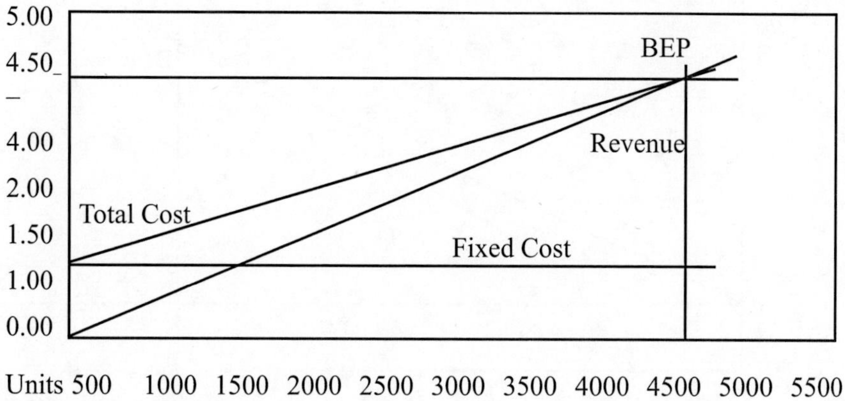

curve would be total cost curve.

Let us apply the three methods to another illustration. Concast Ltd. produces a variety of products. Its sales for the month of July was Rs.9,93,000. After covering fixed cost for the month at Rs.2,50,000, the company was able to make a profit (P) of Rs.50,000.

Note that VC is =S-FC-Profit

?VC in the illustration is = Rs.9,93,000 – 2,50,000 – 50,000

= Rs.6,93,000

1.Under equation method

BEP = S–VC = FC

= Rs.9,93,000 – 6,93,000 = 2,50,000

= Rs.3,00,000

= Rs.2,50,000 or

= 83.33%.

2.Under contribution method

BEP = FC / (S – VC).

= Rs.2,50,000 / (9,93,000 – 6,93,000)

= 83.33%.

5. Under graphical method

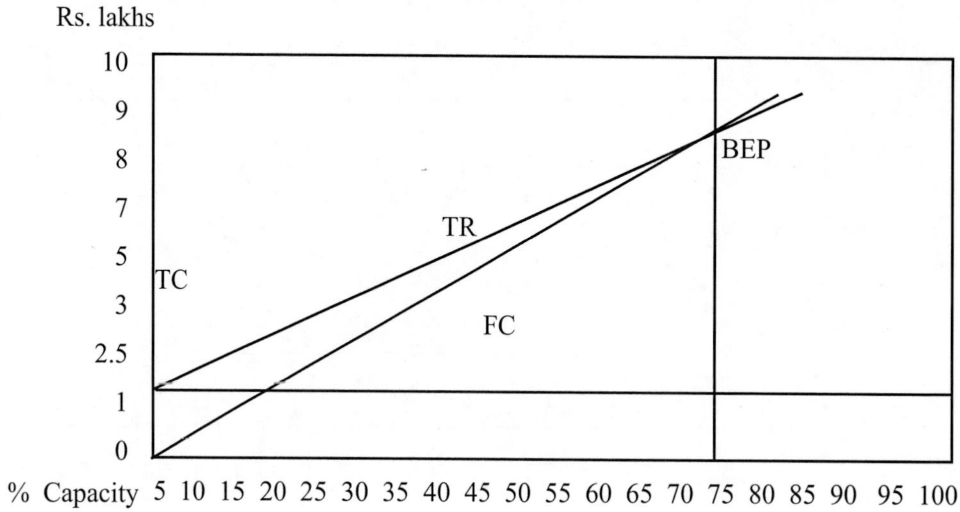

Break-even point is 83.33%

FC = Fixed cost

TC = Total cost

TR = Total revenue

BEP = Break even point

Break-Even Capacity

Break-even capacity of a unit would be the percent of break-even production to its installed capacity (IC). It would be BEP/IC×100. In the illustration given above, suppose the installed capacity of Obrien Overseas Ltd. for the production of Obitu is 3,60,000 per annum, against its monthly production of 23,326, the capacity breakeven would be 77.75% i.e. [23,326/ (3,60,000/ 12) ×100].

The above discussions bring to light an important aspect of the risk associated with the viability of a business. The extent of fixed cost in the total cost would indicate whether the business is susceptible to volatility in its operation. Higher the component of fixed cost higher would also be the break-even point. Higher break-even point would mean that the operation of the business has to be kept high to avoid losses. Consequently changes in the level of operation would affect the chances of profitability. Even a small change in the level of operation would jeopardize the results of the business and would push it to the brinks of loss. A higher break-even point would have the same impact on the profitability of the business like a higher

operating leverage. Operating leverage implies that a change in the volume of operation would bring about higher degree of change in the earnings of the firm. For a small increase in the level of operation, the earnings of the business would increase disproportionately. Similarly, a small decrease in operation would result in disproportionately larger loss. Higher proportion of fixed costs causes higher operating leverage, just like higher fixed cost increases the level of break-even. Operating leverage is synonymous with operational risk.

Profit Volume Ratio (PVR)

Break-even volume (sales) could be worked out simply by multiplying breakeven production with per unit selling price. In the illustration, break-even volume of sale per month would be Rs. 134,12,450 (23,326×575). The other way is through the route of Profit Volume Ratio, known as PVR. This ratio is also called ***contribution ratio***. This version seems to be better suited for the concept. We will use both the terms in this chapter to mean the same. PVR is calculated by dividing the contribution by sales price. In our illustration, PVR would be 92/575 = 0.16 or 16%.The formula for finding out the breakeven sales volume through the PVR route is Total Contribution/PVR. In the illustration, it would be 23,326×92 /0.16 = Rs.134,12,450.

In cases where there are comparative figures for sales and costs between two periods, PVR could be arrived at by dividing the change in profit (P_c) by change in sales (S_c). For example, Jin and Jun ltd. had sales of Rs.342.45 lakhs in the first half of 2005 and Rs.423.54 in the second half. Total costs for the periods are Rs.276.91 lakhs and Rs.341.40 lakhs respectively. PVR for the company would be 0.2047 or 20.47% as under:

Rs. lakhs.

	1 Half	II Half	Change
Sales	342.45	423.54	**81.09**
Total costs	276.91	341.40	65.54
Profits	65.54	82.14	**16.60**

PVR would thus be $=P_c/S_c=16.60/81.09=0.2047$ or 20.47%

This is no new formula, but a derivation from the earlier formula that contribution divided by sales is PVR. For, the cost of incremental sales would be marginal or variable. Hence the change in profit between two periods is the contribution for the differential sales. In this example, the differential sales are Rs.81.09 lakhs and the contribution Rs.16.60 lakhs.

PVR is a useful tool to identify various cost components in a cost pool. Given the sales and total costs for two periods, it would be only mathematical deduction to split total costs into variable and fixed. For example, Moribund Industries Ltd. had sales of Rs. 6,27,864 and

Rs.7,83,189 for the months of May and June. Total costs for the periods were Rs.4,83,159 and Rs.5,59,467 respectively. Find out variable and fixed costs and PVR for the company.

Solution

	May	**June**	**Change**
Sales	6,27,864	7,83,189	1,55,325
Costs	4,83,159	5,59,467	76,308
Profits	1,44,705	2,23,722	79,017

PVR $=P_c/S_c$=79,017/1,55,325=0.5087.

Before solving the problem, let us find out the % of variable costs to sales.

Contribution for sale of Rs.1,55,325-76,308=Rs.79,017.

Variable cost for sale of Rs1,55,325=Rs.1,55,325-Rs.79,017=Rs.76,308 or 49.12795% on sales.

1. Variable cost for sale of Rs.6,27,864×49.12795%=Rs.3,08,457.
2. Variable cost for sale of Rs.783,189=7,83,189×49.12795%=Rs.3,84,765.
3. Fixed cost =6,27,864–3,08,457– 1,44,705=Rs.1,74,702.
4. Contribution for sale of Rs.627,864=6,27,864–3,08,457= Rs.3,19,40
5. Contribution for sale of Rs.7,83,189=7,83,189–3,84,76=Rs.3,98,424

We have seen in the previous paragraphs that

- Contribution(C) divided by sales (S) is PVR($C / S = PVR$),
- Fixed cost (FC) divided by PVR is break-even sales volume ($FC / PVR = BEV$) and
- Change in profit (P_c) /change in sales (S_c) is PVR ($P_c / S_c = PVR$).

This inter-relationship between PVR, fixed cost and break-even volume results in a few permutations and combinations.

1. Since $C / S = PVR$,
2. $C = PVR \times S$
3. $S = C / PVR$
4. Since $FC/PVR = BEV$,
5. $FC = BEV \times PVR$
6. $PVR = FC / BEV$
7. Since $P_c / S_c = PVR$,

8. P_c $= PVR \times S_c$
9. S_c $= P_c / PVR$
10. $S \times PVR$ $= C$

From the above combinations, certain cross deductions could also be made, such as

11. FC/BEV = PVR
12. PVR×BEV = FC
13. P_c / PVR $= S_c$
14. $S_c \times$ **PVR** = $\mathbf{P_c}$

Thus there are more than 14uses of PVR.

The above equations could advantageously be used to find out any missing variables. For example, Quiet Performers Ltd. sold in May 24,583 units of its product "Prolific" at Rs 360 per unit. Installed capacity of the company is 26,000 units per month. Cost of sales for May was Rs.78,41,977. In April, the company sold 21,385 units for the same price and the cost of sales was Rs.69, 52,933.From the figures, which appears to be incomplete, we could easily ascertain the other figures, such as VC, FC, Contribution per unit, BEP, BEC, PVR, BEVand Margin of safety.

Solution

First let us find out variable cost.

To find out variable cost, we have to find out PVR.

Change in profit / change in sales = PVR(use no. 7).

Sales for the month of April and May were Rs.76,98,600 and Rs.88,49,880 respectively.

Change in sales is thus Rs.11,51,280 (Rs.88,49,880 – Rs.76,98,600).

Profit for the month of April was Rs.7,56,667(Sales Rs.76,98,600 less cost of sales Rs.69, 52,933).

Profit for May was Rs.10,07,903(sales of Rs.88,49,880 less cost of sales Rs.78,41,977.

Change in profit between the months is therefore Rs.2,62,236(Rs.10,07,903– Rs.7,56,667).

1. ***PVR is*** therefore 2,62,236 / 11,51,280 = ***.2278***.

Contribution is PVR × S as per use No.2 above.

2. ***Contribution*** is therefore Rs. = .2278 × Rs.88,49,880 = ***Rs. 20,16,003.***

Sales less contribution is variable cost.

3. ***Variable cost is*** Rs.88,49,880 – Rs. 20,16,003 = **<u>Rs.68,33,877.</u>**

Contribution less profit is fixed cost.

4. ***Fixed cost*** in this case is Rs. 20,16,003 - Rs.10,07,903 = ***<u>Rs.10,08,100</u>***.

5. ***BEV is*** then fixed cost plus variable cost = ***<u>Rs.78,41,977</u>***

(Rs.10,08,100 + Rs.68,,33,877)

6. ***Margin of safety*** for May would be = ***<u>Rs.10,07,903</u>***

(Rs.88,49,880 – Rs.78,41,977)

Profit volume ratio is the reflection of the level of contribution. Since contribution is the function of sales price and variable cost, PVR reflects the leeway between variable cost and sales price. Lower the variable cost higher would be the PVR. PVR could be improved by decreasing variable cost or increasing sales price. A higher PVR indicates higher profitability and vice versa. When the PVR is high, the unit could break-even at a lower volume of sales. For example, let us consider the cost structure of Deo Daniel Ltd. (DDL) and Istanbul Traders Ltd. (ITL), both engaged in export of leather goods.

Table 1

Thus there are more than 14 uses of PVR. Istanbul Traders Ltd. (ITL)

	Deo Daniel Ltd. Rs	Istanbul Traders Ltd. Rs
Sales- volume –units/month	25,000	25,000
Sale price per unit	369	383
Variable cost per unit	215	275
Fixed costs	2,15,000	2,15,000

Solution

	Deo Daniel Ltd. Rs.	Istanbul raders Ltd. Rs.
Sales price	369	383
Less Variable cost	215	275
Contribution	154	108
PVR	0.41734	0.282
Break-even volume	515,167	762,411

In the above example, higher PVR of .41734 would indicate that DDL would break-even at a sales volume of Rs.515,167, as against Rs.762,411 in the case of ITL.

Contribution ratio or PVR has its utility in ranking products according to their profitability in organizations with multi-products profile. In these days of competition, an organization is rarely confined to the production of a single commodity. When there are many products, the organization could conveniently rank them according to importance using PVR and plan its sales mix. Take for example, Noorjahan Nutrients Ltd., which has a range of five products-nutrimal, nutripal, nutrisal, nutrival and nutrigal. The cost data for the products are in Table 2.The ranking of products according to profitability is in Table 3.

Table 2
Cost data of Noorjahan Nutrients Ltd.

	Nutrimal	Nutripal	Nutrisal	Nutrival	Nutrigal
Production/month	12,000	11,000	13,000	10,000	12,500
Materials cost	20,69,520	16,47,369	120,14,062	43,45,612	29,68,250
Direct labour	12,99,240	9,20,147	9,70,089	28,50,159	16,55,875
Variable overheads	4,38,480	4,60,792	6,31,284	2,91,557	4,93,752
Sales price	425	380	1350	1040	550

Fixed costs per month were Rs.65,68,941.

Table 3
Ranking products according to profitability using PVR

Solution	Nutrimal	Nutripal	Nutrisal	Nutrival	Nutrigal
Materials cost/unit	172.46	149.76	924.16	434.56	237.46
Direct labour	108.27	83.65	74.62	285.02	132.47
Variable overheads	36.54	41.89	48.56	29.16	39.50
Total variable cost	317.27	275.30	1047.34	748.74	409.43
Sales price	425	380	1350	1040	550
Contribution	107.73	104.70	302.66	291.26	140.57
PVR	.25348	.2755	.2242	.2801	.2556
Ranking	4	2	5	1	3

As another illustration to fortify the basic concept of break-even analysis, let us consider the case of Paramount Products Ltd. engaged in the manufacture of Parafur with installed capacity of 50,000 tonnes per annum. The variable cost per tonne of Parafur was Rs.2,794 for the month ended April,. Fixed costs for the month amounted toRs.42, 71,962.The sale price per unit of Parafur was Rs.3,950.Sales for the month of was 4105tonnes. Let us work out contribution, break-even production, volume, capacity, PVR, margin of safety for paramount Products for April, 2006..

Solution

i. **Contribution**:

Contribution = sales per unit less variable cost (S-VC)
= Rs.3,950 – Rs.2,794 = **Rs.1,156**

ii. **Break-even production**:

Break-even production	= Fixed cost divided by contribution (FC / C)
	= Rs.42,71,962 / 1,156 = **3696 units**

iii. PVR:

PVR	= Contribution divided by sales price (C / SP)
	= 1156 / 3950 = **.29266**

iv. **Break-even volume**:

Break-even volume	= Fixed cost divided by PVR (FC / PVR)
	= Rs.42,71,962 / .29266 = **Rs.145,97,014**

v. **Break-even capacity** :

Break-even capacity	= Break-even production divided by installed capacity (BEP / IC)
	= 3696 / (50,000/12) × 100 = **88.72%**

vi. **Margin of safety**:

Margin of safety	= Sales less breakeven sales(S-BEV)
	= Rs.162,14,750 – Rs.145,97,014 =Rs.16,17,736
	= **9.98%**

Cash Break-Even

In the above analysis, depreciation is taken as an element of fixed costs. Costs are normally caused by an outward movement of resources, either at the time the transaction takes place or later. Depreciation is the sole exception. By providing for depreciation, the businessman is not obliged to pay any cash either immediately or in future. It is a notional cost. Practically speaking, depreciation is used as a tool in tax management. The taxable income is reduced to the extent of depreciation and tax to that extent is avoided. It is non-cash cost. It would therefore be necessary to assess break-even level of a business omitting costs that do not necessitate outflow of resources. Such break-even level is called ***cash break-even***. Cash break-even level is vital in situations of acute competition. Fixed costs devoid of depreciation divided by contribution would give cash break-even level. Manna De Manour Ltd.produces Mind Set Marvel, which is sold at Rs.2,750 per unit. The company's capacity is 17,500units per month. It had operated at a level of 15,400 units in the month of June. Its cost data for the month is materials Rs.197,89,115, direct labour Rs.11,08,845,factory variable Rs.6,46,798.Fixed costs per month was Rs.112,80,489.Depreciation for the month at Rs.4,23,678 was included in the fixed cost. What is the cash break even level of the company?

Solution.

Cash fixed cost (Fixed cost less depreciation) for the month=Rs.108,56,811.

Variable cost per unit = Rs.1,399

Sales price = Rs.2,750

Contribution per unit = Rs.1351.

PVR is = 1,351 / 2750 = .49127

1.Cash BE Production = Rs.108,56,811/Rs.1351=8036 units.

2.Cash BE Capacity = 8036/17500×100=45.92%

3.Cash BE Volume = Rs.220,99,000 (8036×2750)

or

Cash BE volume (PVR route) = Cash fixed cost / PVR)

Rs.220,99,478 (10856811% 49127).

Difference due to rounding off.

Break-Even Point For DRR

The above exercises have given us an idea as to what a break-even point is. We have considered the production or capacity of operation needed to cover costs. But covering cost is only a prerequisite for survival. The objective of organizations is to stabilize and grow. For this, organizations have to earn a desired rate of return[1] (DRR). The question now is at what level of production or capacity the organization would earn the desired rate of return. We have already stated that it is from contribution that the business has to recover its fixed costs and then earn profits. So, to earn a desired rate of return, the contribution should be adequate enough to cover both the fixed costs and desired rate of return. To state mathematically, C=FC+DRR. Let us consider the requirements of Earnest India Ltd., engaged in the manufacture of Egalite for exports. The unit has an installed capacity to manufacture 6,50,000 units per year. Its production sales details for the year ended 31st March are:

- Sales-4,19,450 units at Rs.675 per unit
- Cost-Materials Rs.1363,21,250;Direct labour Rs.398,47,750; other variable costs Rs.234,89,200; fixed overheads Rs.151,00,200; semi-varables Rs.88,08,450,of which 30% was variable.
- Cost of investment Rs.1048,62,500
- DRR: 12% on investment

Solution

The problem is solved in six steps

Step 1.

As a preparatory work we have to consolidate the costs into fixed and variable.

Fixed costs:

Fixed overheads +70% of semi-variable costs = Rs.151,00,200 + Rs.61,65,915 =Rs.212,66,115.

Variable costs:

Materials+Direct labour+other variable costs +30% of semi-variables=Rs.1363,21,250+ Rs.398,47,750+ Rs.234,89,200+ Rs.26,42,535=Rs.2023,00,735.

Variable cost per Egalite = Rs. 2023,00,735 /4,19,450=Rs.482.30

Step2.

Working out DRR

DRR = 12% on Rs.1048,62,500=Rs.125,83,500

Step 3.

Working out amount to be recovered from contribution

FC+DRR= Rs. 212,66,115+ Rs.125,83,500=Rs.1174,46,000.

Step 4.

Working out contribution

SP-VC=C=Rs.675–Rs.482.30=Rs.192.70.

Step 5.

Working out PVR

PVR=C/SP=192.70/675=.28548

Step 6.

Calculating break-even levels.

1.**BEP**=FC+DRR/C=1174,46,000/192.70 = **6,09,476 units**.

2.**BEC**=BP/IC×100=6,09,476/6,50,000×100=**93.77%.**

3.**BEV** =BP×SP=6,09,476×Rs.675 =**Rs.4113,96,300.**

OR

C/PVR=192.70×6,09,476/.28548 =**Rs.4113,98,435**.(Difference due to rounding off of PVR).

[1]*Desired rate of return is the minimum rate a company has to earn to be in business. DRR is the cut off rate. It is weighted average cost of capital or opportunity cost which ever is higher.*

Breakeven Price

Break-even point analysis finds use in pricing decisions also. When the market for a product is a constraint, the analysis would enable one to price the product effectively to face competition and optimize returns. The price break-even at a given level of operation is total cost divided by the production. Tharani Thermostat Ltd. has the following costs per month. Production 32,500 units; material cost per unit Rs.83.27; labour cost Rs.17.29; other variable costs Rs.16.28; factory overheads for the month Rs.3,19,852(25% variable); and fixed costs of Rs.21,65,974.What would be the break-even price per unit assuming that its market is confined to only 32,500 units per month? If the company wants a desired rate of return of 12%per annum on its capital employed, what would be the price? The investment of the company was Rs 672,34,879.

Solution

Break-even price without DRR.

Cost for 32,500 units

Variable cost.	Rs.
Materials cost	27,06,275
Labour cost	5,61,925
Fctory O.H.	79,963
Other Variable costs	5,29,100
Total variable cost	38,77,263
Fixed costs	
Fixed Factory cost	2,39,889
Fixed costs	21,65,974
Total cost of production	62,83,126
Per unit sales price	193.33

Break-even price with DRR

Cost of production	62,83,126
DRR 1% of Cost of capital	6,72,349

Cost of sales	69,55,475
Per unit sales price	214.00

Margin of Safety.

We have seen that break-even level is "no profit no loss" region. It is that point at which the company neither makes a profit nor incurs a loss. An upward shift from this level would take the unit to north, meaning to profitability. If the shift is downward, the unit would be southbound, that is making loss. It is therefore the gap between actual or potential level of operation of a business compared to its break-even level that determines the leeway. Economists call this leeway as ***margin of safety.*** Margin of safety would therefore mean the difference between the breakeven point and the actual or budgeted sales. Larger the margin greater would be the manoeurability of the company in the face of competition.

Limitations

Break-even point should not be considered the solution for all problems that might crop up in the profit planning exercises. It is one of the tools. It has its limitations as a technique. Two important assumptions of break-even analysis are not universally applicable. The nature of fixed cots remaining constant and that of variable cost varying in proportion to volume are true only to an extent. By improvement in process know how and purchase quantity and quality, variable cost is influenced. As far as fixed cost is concerned, the increasing popularity of activity based costing is narrowing the definition. Fixed cost no longer remains same for different volumes. A part of it becomes variable. Secondly the assumption that sales price does not vary with increased sales is not practicable. Volume of sales could be increased with reduction in sales price.

The practical application of the concept of break-even analysis is debatable. It is said that the concept is built on a number of assumptions. The theory of breakeven point is based on the economic safety valve that *other things would remain the same*. In real work situations, other things rarely remain same. It is assumed that fixed costs remain same irrespective of volume in operation and that variable costs vary according to volume of output. Any change in the behavior of these variables would affect the breakeven level. There are quite a few factors that could affect the cost behaviours, such as quality of inputs, efficiency of the factors of production and technological changes. The horizon of fixed cost is shrinking with the increasing use of activity based costing. With all these constraints, it is an important technique in profit planning decisions of businesses.

Summary

There is an enduring relationship between cost and volume, volume and profit and profit and cost. This relationship is the foundation for effective profit planning. By adjusting one or more of these variables, a business could maximize its returns. The tool through which cost, volume and profit are analyzed is breakeven point. Break-even point is that level of operation at which the sales realization would absorb both fixed and variable costs. It is a no profit or no loss region. Operation of the business above this cut off level would result in profit. The reverse is also true.

Break-even points are studied from the level of product that needs to be produced to break even, the sales volume needed to break-even, the capacity and the price at which it breaks even. The analysis is done through the use of contribution concept. Contribution is the surplus of sales over the variable costs incurred to effect those sales.

I. QUESTIONS

1. What is the relationship that exists between cost, volume and profit?
2. How is unit cost of production affected by volume?
3. What technique we use to study the above relationship?
4. What do you understand by the term break-even point?
5. What is break-even production?
6. What is break-even capacity?
7. What are the types of break-evens you know?
8. How does break-even concept help in determining price of a product?
9. What is Profit Volume Ratio?
10. What are the practical applications of profit volume ratio?
11. What is meant by contribution ratio?
12. What would the change in profit between two periods represent?
13. What is a margin of safety?
14. Do you consider the short-term view of margin of safety an adequate measure for long-term problems?

II. QUIZ

Say yes or no

1. Marginal cost is variable cost.
2. Cost is not affected by volume.
3. Profit improves with improvement in volume.
4. Sale less variable cost is contribution.
5. Fixed costs are recovered from contribution.
6. Break-even production is the number units to be produced to absorb total costs.
7. Prices are influenced by capacity.
8. Installed capacity is the capacity at which the business operates.
9. Change in profit between two periods is contribution by the incremental sales.
10. Profit volume ratio tells us that profit will increase with increase in volume.
11. Higher the fixed cost in the total cost, higher would be the profit volume ratio.
12. Break-even point is a tool in cost volume profit analysis.

III. EXERCISES

1. The selling price of Parcular produced by Futuristic Products Ltd. is Rs.100 and the marginal cost is Rs.65. During the month of April, 8000 units were produced of which 5000 were sold. There was no opening stock. Fixed costs amounted to Rs.1,80,000. Provide a statement using (a) Marginal costing and (b) Absorption costing; Show the closing stock valuation and the profit earned under each of the principles of valuation of stock.
2. The following figures are extracted from the books of Vijay Irons Ltd. for the years 1989 and 1990 whose capacity is 10,000 Tonnes p.a.

	Per Unit Rs.
Direct material	350
Direct Labour	50
Fixed overhead	200
Selling price	800

Production in 2003 was 10,00,000 units and in 2002 also it was 10,00,000 units. Sales were 8,00,000 units in 2002 and 12,00,000 units in2003.

Prepare cost statements under (a) Absorption costing and (b) Marginal Costing methods.

3. You are required to prepare income statement under (a) Absorption costing method and (b) Marginal costing method from the following data.

	Finished units
Opening Stock	5,00,000
Output	30,00,000
Less: Closing stock	2,00,000
Sales	33,00,000

	Rs.
Variable cost of production	1,78,50,000
Fixed factory overhead	35,10,000
Variable selling cost	1,70,00,000
Fixed selling cost	25,00,000
Sales	6,60,00,000

The opening stock is valued at Rs.30,95,000 as per marginal costing method and Rs36,00,000 as per absorption costing method.

4. The fixed expenses of Avenor Enterprises amount Rs.1,80,000. Its variable cost per unit of Aven is Rs.29 and selling price of Aven is Rs.44 per unit. Calculate break-even point.

5. Calculate break-even point from the following information of Brittle Traders for January.

   Sales 1,00,000 unit at Rs.105 each

   Variable cost – Rs.60 per unit

   Fixed cost –Rs.8,00,000.

   If the selling price is reduced to Rs.95, what is the new break-even point?

6. Compassionate Collaborators is considering expansion. Fixed costs per month amount to Rs.4,20,000 and are expected to increase by Rs.1,50,000 when plant expansion is completed. The present plant capacity is 80,000 units a year. Capacity will increase by 50% with the expansion. The current variable cost at Rs.435 per unit and selling price at Rs.1600 per unit are expected to remain the same under expansion also. Would you advise for the expansion? What would be the break-even point before and after expansion?

7. From the following data of Campbell Components, compute (a) composite P/V Ratio and (b) composite BEP for its products A, B and C. The total fixed cost is Rs.8,00,000

	Products		
	A	B	C
Sales Quantity (units)	2,000	3,000	5,000
Selling price per unit (Rs.)	1000	500	700
Variable cost per unit(Rs.)	600	200	350

8. Kopalan Ltd., is considering the purchase of a machine. The vendor has offered two models- A and B with following relevant information. Both the machines can produce

	A	B
	Rs.	**Rs.**
Fixed cost p.a	40,00,000	1,00,00,000
Variable cost of operating the machine per unit	800	500

Ascertain the break-even point for the machines and explain the production range in which each of the machines is better.

9. Dianand wishes to set up a sugar factory. The capacity of the plant will be 60,000 tonnes per annum. Estimated fixed costs in the first year will be Rs.120,00,000 including Rs.9,00,000 for depreciation. Selling price will be Rs.12,000 per tonne and variable cost will be Rs.9000 per tonne.

You are required to find out (i)the volume of sales at which he will neither earn profit nor incur loss.(ii) the volume of sales to ensure the payment of loan installments, if he has requested Punjab National Bank for financing his project. He has asked for a term loan of Rs.60,00,000 payable in 3 annual installments, with interest at 12% .

10. Enthrol Energia Corporation presents the following results for one year. Calculate P/V ratio, BEP and Margin of safety.

	Rs.
Sales	2,00,00,000
Variable costs	1,20,00,000
Fixed cost	50,00,000
Net profit	30,00,000.

11. From the following information supplied by Fouler Foundation, calculate

(a) Break even point

(b) Number of units that must be sold to earn a profit of Rs.6,00,000 per year.

(c) Number of units that must be sold to earn a net income of 10% on sales.

Sales	Rs.	200 per unit.
Variable cost	Rs.	140 per unit
Fixed cost	Rs.	7,92,000.

12. From the following information relating to Trinity Ltd., you are required to find out

(a) P/V ratio (b) Break even point (c) Profit (d) Margin of safety

(d) Volume of sales to earn profit of Rs.6,00,000

	Rs.
Total fixed costs	4,00,500
Total variable cost	7,00,500
Total sales	15,00,000

13. The P/V Ratio of a Filomena Fulfilment dealing in precision instruments is 0.5 and margin of safety is 40%.

You are required to work-out break even point and the net profit if the sales volume is Rs.50,00,000.If 25% of variable cost is labour cost,what will be the effect on BEP and profit when labour efficiency decreases by 5%?(Hint. Apply PVR rules)

14. Operations of Gayathri Ltd., in June disclosed a margin of safety ratio of 20% and a contribution margin ratio of 60%.

(a) Calculate the net income for the month assuming the fixed costs to be

(i) Rs.6,00,000 and (ii) Rs.2,40,000.

(b) Present the income statement to prove your answer to question (a).

15. SriVenkatesa P.Ltd.(SVP), and Thiruverkadu Amman Ltd.(TAL), sell the same type of product in the same market. Their budgeted profit and Loss Accounts for the next year are as follows:-

Sales	1,20,00,000	S.V.P.	1,00,00,000	T.A.L.
Less: Variable cost	15,00,000	Rs.	35,00,000	Rs.
Fixed cost		1,50,00,000		1,50,00,000
Budgeted net profit		1,35,00,000		1,35,00,000
		15,00,000		15,00,000

You are required to:

(a) Calculate break even point of each business

(b) Calculate the sales volume at which each business will earn Rs.5,000 profit.

(c) State which business is likely to earn greater profit in conditions of

(d) i) heavy demand for the product.

ii) low demand for the product.

Briefly give your reasons.

16. The following information is obtained from Gopu & Co., for the year ending 31st March

Sales Rs.12, 00,000.Variable cost Rs.6, 50,000.Fixed cost 4,30,000.

You are required to calculate the following

- Present P/V Ratio,Break even point and margin of safety.
- Revised P/V Ratio ,BEP and margin of safety in each of the following cases:

(1) 25% increases in selling price

(2) 10% decreases in selling price

(3) 20% increase in fixed cost

(4) 10% decrease in fixed cost

(5) 10% increase in variable cost

(6) 10% decrease in variable cost

(7) 10% increase in selling price accompanied by 10% decrease in variable cost.

(8) 10% decrease in selling price accompanied by 10% increase in variable cost.

17. Ratlam Corporation has invested Rs.10,00,000 in its plant and sets up a goal of 15% annual return on investment. Fixed costs in the factory presently amount to Rs.4,00,000 per month and variable costs amount to Rs.15 per unit produced. The company last year produced 50,000 units and sold them at Rs.25 each and earned a profit of Rs.1,00,000. How can the management achieve their targeted profit by varying (a) Fixed cost (b) variable costs (c) quantity sold and (d) increasing the price per unit?

18. The sales turnover and profit during two years were as follows:

Year	Sales	Profit
	Rs.	Rs.
2003	1,40,00,000	15,00,000
2004	1,60,00,000	20,00,000

Calculate:-

- P/V Ration

- Break even point
- Sales required to earn a profit of Rs.40,00,000
- Fixed expenses and
- Profit when sales are Rs.1,20,00,000 (Hint .PVR uses)

19. Assam Gunmetal Ltd., had furnished you with the following details relating to the year 2003.

	First half of *The year*	***Second half of The year***
	Rs.	**Rs.**
Sales	45,00,000	50,00,000
Total cost	40,00,000	43,00,000

Assuming that there is no change in prices and variable cost and that the fixed expenses are incurred equally in the both the halves, calculate:

(a) The profit volume ratio

(b) Fixed expenses

(c) Break even sales and

(d) % of margin of safety. (Hint.PVR Uses)

20. From the particulars given below by India Mercury Ltd.calculate:

(a) Break even point

(b) Profit or loss when sales are Rs.12,00,000 and Sales required to earn a profit of Rs. 5,00,000.

	Sales Rs.	**Profit/Loss (–) Rs.**
Period 1	10,00,000	–50,000
Period 2	14,00,000	1,50,000.

21. You are given the following data for the current year by Exotica Entertainers Lab..

Output	4,00,000 albums
Fixed expenses	Rs.2,00,00,000
Variable cost per album	Rs.40
Selling price per album	Rs.90

How many albums must be produced and sold in the next year, if it is anticipated that selling price would be reduced by 10%, variable cost would be Rs.42 per album and fixed cost will increase by 10%? The laboratory should make a profit equal to that of the current year.

22. Johanan Joint Venture produces a Vijay that sells for Rs.1,800 per unit. An increase of $7^1/_2$% in the cost of materials and $6^1/_4$% in the cost of labour is anticipated for the next year. Sale of units would remain same. What should be the selling price to earn the same percentage of profit as before?

The only data available are:

The material cost was 50% of cost of sales.

Wages had been 20% of cost of sales.

The overhead had been 30% of cost of sales.

The anticipated increased costs in relation to present sale price would cause a 25% decrease in the amount of the present profit.(Hint. PVR uses)

23. The following are data relating to Ramsay Ranin Ltd.

	Rs.
Present sales	1,00,00,000
Variable cost	60,00,000
Fixed cost	20,00,000

Ascertain the effect of 10% reduction in selling price on:

(a) P/V Ratio (b) Break-even point

Also calculate the sales required to maintain the present level of profit.

24. Brney Toys Ltd. earns an average net profit of Rs.30 per piece in a selling price of Rs.150 by producing and selling 60,000 pieces at 60% of the potential capacity. Composition of his cost of sales is:

Direct materials		Rs.40
Direct wages		Re.10
Works overhead	Rs.60	[50% fixed]
Sales overhead	Re.10	[25%varying]

During the current year, the company intends to produce the same number of toys but anticipates that:

- fixed charge will go up by 10%
- rates of direct labour will increase by 20%
- rates of direct material will increase by 5%
- selling price cannot be increased.

- Under these circumstances the company obtains an order for a further 20% of its capacity. What minimum price will you recommend for accepting the order to ensure the manufacturer an overall profit of Rs.18,05,000?

25. Pradesh Co. is currently working at 50% of its capacity and produces 10,000 units. At 60% of capacity, raw material cost increases by 2% and selling price falls by 2%. At 80% working, raw material cost increases by 5% and selling price falls by 5%.At 50% capacity, the product cost is Rs.180 per unit and is sold at Rs.200 per unit.

The unit cost of Rs.180 is made up as follows:

		Rs.
Material		100
Wages		30
Factory overheads	30	[40% fixed]
Administrative overheads	20	[50% fixed]

Prepare a marginal cost statement showing the estimated profit of the business when it is operated at 60% and 80% capacity.

26. From the following data, calculate break-even production, sale, capacity and PVR for the three products of Multipurpose Ltd:

	A	**B**	**C**
Budgeted(units)	10,000	15,000	20,000
Sales price per unit	40	45	30
Raw material cost	15	20	17
Direct variable cost	05	10	08
Fixed cost*	1,20,000	90,000	75,000
Mach. Hr. per unit prod	6	5	4
*FC includes			
Depreciation-Rs.	2000	1500	800

27. Zealon ltd. produces and markets JUJUBEE, with an installed capacity of 25,000 units per month. For the month of February, the unit sold 20,000 pieces at a price of Rs.28 per unit. The company has furnished the following data for the month;

Administrative expenses	Rs.34,500.
Selling expenses	Rs.58,960.
Factory overheads	Rs.74,675.

20% of administrative expenses, 40% of selling expenses and 55% of factory overheads are variable. Desired rate of return is 18% per annum on capital employed of Rs.35 lakhs. What should be the break-even level of production?

28. The Reliable Battery Co. furnishes you the following information for2003:

	First Half	**Second Half**
Sales	Rs.8, 10, 000	Rs.10, 28, 000
Profit earned	21, 800	64, 800

29. From the above you are require to compute the following assuming that the fixed cost remains the same in both the periods.

(1) P/V ration

(2) Fixed cost

(3) The amount of profit or loss where sales are Rs.6, 48, 000

(4) The amount of sales required to earn a profit of Rs. 1, 08, 000

30. Gowardan Exporters have the following data for July:

Marginal cost Rs.12, 40,000

Selling price Rs.23, 00,000

Calculate P/V ration.

The sales turnover and profits during two periods are as under:

Period I: Sales Rs.20 lakhs; Profit Rs.2 lakhs

Period II: Sales Rs.30 lakhs; Profit Rs.4 lakhs

Calculate P/V Ratio

31. The following data are obtained from the records of Shivaji Ceramics

	First Years. Rs	**Second Year - Rs**
Sales	80, 00,000	90, 00,000
Profit	10, 00,000	14, 00,000

Calculate variable cost, contribution and PVR.

32. Estimated sales of Janardhan for the April are Rs.22, 40, 000. The number of units involved coincides with the expected volume of output. Each unit sells at Rs.200.

Calculate break-even point by applying important formulae. Following details are furnished by Saravana Timber for March.Find out (a) Profit Volume Ration (b) B.E.P. (c) Margin of safety

	Rs.
Sales	1, 00, 000
Total costs	80, 000
Fixed costs	20, 000
Net Profit	20, 000

33. The following information was obtained from Vinodh & Co for February. Work out BEP, PVR and margin of safety

	Rs.
Sales	1, 60, 000
Variable costs	60, 000
Fixed costs	30, 000

34. From the following information supplied by Joyce, prepare the break-even chart.

	Rs.
Fixed Costs	2, 00,000
Variable cost	50 per unit
Sales price	100 per unit

35. P/V ratio of Jagdish Enterprises is 60% and the marginal cost of the product is Rs.50. What will be the selling price?

36. From the following data of Suhesan Software, calculate:

1. P/V ratio
2. Profit when sales are Rs.20, 00,000

Fixed expenses Rs.4, 00,000

Break-even point Rs.10, 00,000

3. New break-even point if selling price is reduced by 20%

37. Alind Alliance has a P/V ratio of 40%. By what percentage must sales be increased to offset.

(a) 10% reduction in selling price

(b) 20% reduction in selling price

38. Bala Balanur produces and sells 1000 units of Anni per month at Rs.200 per unit . Marginal cost per unit is Rs.120 and fixed cost\s are Rs.3,00,00 per month. It is proposed to reduce the selling price by 20%. Find the additional sales required to earn the same profit as before.

39. The Delhi Mixy Co manufactured and sold 1,000 mixies this year at a price of Rs.1800 each. The cost structure of a mixy is as follows:

	Rs.
Materials	600
Labour	100
Other Variable cost	150
Factory overhead fixed)	400

Due to heavy price competition, price has to be reduced to Rs.1500 for the next year. The products of the company enjoy brand equity and sale might not be problem. Assuming no change in costs, state the number of mixies that would have to be produced at the new price to ensure the same amount of total profits as that of the current year.

40. Halloween Hair oil sells variety of perfumed hair oil, bottled in 200 gramme sachets. From the data furnished by the company as at the end of July, following find out:

- Profit – volume ratio
- Break – even point
- Sales for 40% P/V ratio
- Marginal of safety from sales of Rs.3, 00, 000
- Net profit from the sales of Rs.3, 00, 000
- Required sales for the net profit of Rs.70, 000
- Required sales for the net profit of Rs.70, 000 after tax, the corporate income tax rate being 60%
- Additional sales required to cover an increase of Rs.3, 000 p.a. in the sales manager's salary.

Position of the company for the year 2003 was

	Rs.
Sales	2, 00, 000

Variable Overheads	1, 50, 000
Profit	50, 000
Fixed Overheads	15, 000
Net Profit	35, 000

41. Florescent Bloom budgets for a production of 1, 50, 000 units of its product Floboom. The variable cost per unit is Rs.140 and fixed cost is Rs.30 lakhs. The company fixes its selling price to fetch a profit of 15% on cost.

(a) What is the break-even point?

(b) What is the profit-volume ratio?

(c) If it reduces its selling price by 5%, how does the revised selling price affect the break-even and P/V ratio?

If an increase in profit of 10% over the budgeted amount is desired, what should be the sale at the reduced price?

42. The following data have been obtained from the records of a company. Calculate Break-even point.

	Year I	**Year II**
	Rs.	**Rs.**
Sales	80,000	90,000
Profit	10,000	14,000

43. Find out the break-even point from the following:

	P	**Q**	**R**
Selling Price Rs.	100	80	50
VC Rs.	50	40	20
Weightage	20%	30%	50%

Fixed cost Rs. 14,80,000(Hint. fixed cost to be shared on weightage)

44. You are given the following data for the year 2004-05:
Variable Cost Rs.6,00,000.

Fixed Cost Rs. 3,00,000.

Net Profit Rs. 1,00,000.

Sales Rs. 10,00,000

Find out:

(a) Break-even point

(b) Profit when sales amounted to Rs. 12,00,000

(c) Sales required to earn a profit of Rs. 2,00,000

45. From the following data draw a Break-even chart showing the Break-even point. Also find the new Break-even point, if selling price is reduced to Rs. 18 per unit.

Budget output	1,00,000 units
Fixed expenses	Rs. 5,00,000
Variable expenses	Rs. 10 per unit
Selling price	Rs. 20 per unit

CHAPTER– 12

STANDARD COSTING

Learning Objective

Standard costs are predetermined benchmark costs that a business would like to achieve. Normally, costs are historic in nature. Forecasts are based on past experiences. Past costs are not necessarily the ideal costs under a given situation. Changes in technology, quality of material, cost of material and efficiency of labour are constantly taking place. Costs of production should therefore be attuned to the changed environment. Standard costs are costs that ought to be in the changed situations. Fixing standards for each of the elements of cost and comparing performance with standards established is the method to ensure effectiveness in cost of production and increase in the competitiveness of the unit. This chapter highlights the need for standards, the effectiveness of standards and the control of cost.

Cost, we have seen, is the necessary evil that has to be borne to achieve an objective. But the effectiveness of an organization would depend upon how the objective could be achieved at the least cost. An enterprise, which could manufacture a product at a cost cheaper than what another unit could produce, would be highly competitive and successful. It is therefore the endeavour of every businessman to become cost effective. Cost effectiveness means controlling and reducing costs. Controlling costs involve measures to ensure that the actual cost does not exceed the budgeted. This is achieved through the technique of ***budgeting***, which we will see in a later chapter. Reducing costs, which is a better choice, is achieved through the institution of ***standard costing*** technique. In practice, companies first set up standards and then budget, realizing the benefits of both cost reduction and cost control techniques.

Cost Reduction Technique

In our discussions on costs, we had all along been assuming that the behavior of costs would continue to remain the same through out. The pattern of costs in the past would be the trend for the future as well, subject to known variations. We have been projecting future cost estimates based on the past data. In other words, we were following ***historic costing*** techniques for forecasting future costs. Happenings show that this line of thinking is obsolete. It is possible that the actual costs in the past might have been ideal in the circumstances then prevailing. Or it might be that the business had adopted the cost pattern from another unit in the industry, without analyzing whether it was the ideal. In both the cases, it might turn out to be that costs, which a business had incurred in the past were not what it should be. Alternatively, it might be that it was ideal at the time of adoption but not in the changed economic conditions. Rapid developments in the field of technology, information and research have cast their impact on the behaviour of costs. The line dividing variable cost from fixed cost is fast receding. In the circumstances, historic cost is loosing its grip in planning exercises. Instead of assuming cost to behave as it had in the past, businesses have been resetting their estimation on benchmark costs, commonly called ***standard costs***.

Definition

Standard costs are predetermined calculation of how much the costs should be under specified working conditions. Costs for each of the elements of cost are determined on the basis of scientific studies and comparative information. In terms of CIMA, standard is "***a predetermined measurable quantity set in defined conditions***". Standards are based on unquestionable natural laws and developed scientifically after detailed analysis of input requirements in quantity and value. Standard costing is a technique under which standards are fixed for each of the elements of cost based on research, empirical evidence and analysis. Standard costs are "***not what they were, but what they should be*** ". Actual cost is compared with the standards and variances are analyzed as to the location and cause and reported in time to management to take corrective action. Chartered Institute of Management Accountants, London has defined standard costing as "***the technique, which uses standards for costs and revenues for the purpose of control through variance analysis***" It elaborates the purpose of standard costing as "***the preparation and use of standard costs, their comparison with actual costs and the analysis of variance to the causes and points of incidence***". W.W.Bigg makes the purpose more lucid when he states" ***standard costing discloses the cost of deviations from standard and classifies these as to their causes, so that management is immediately informed of the sphere of operations in which remedial action is necessary***". Standard costing is not another costing system; it is a technique, which can be advantageously adopted in any of the costing systems, whether it is job costing, process costing or processing costing.

Installing Standard Costing

Standard Costing is a double-edged weapon. If it is installed properly and implemented effectively, its benefits in cost reduction would be substantial. It would boost the bottom line of the business. If it were done half heartedly, it would be a burden to the business. Care should therefore be exercised in setting up and monitoring the technique. The preparatory tasks to be undertaken by the business before implementing standards are

- *Establishing level of activity*
- *Establishing cost centers / Cost units*
- *Classifying and codifying cost heads*
- *Selecting period of standards -basis (LT) / current.*
- *Determining reasonable level of attainment*

Primarily, the company has to determine its level of activity for the chosen period. Market for the products, the chances of growth, governmental policies and plant capacity are some of the factors that have to be taken into consideration for arriving at the level of activity. Once the level of activity is reasonably established, other preparations for setting up standard could be initiated. First, the company has to decide whether it would be setting up cost centers or cost units for the purpose of ascertaining and allocating costs. We have already seen what cost centers and cost units are. In larger companies, items of costs might be many and spread over different cost centers. In those cases, it would be convenient to classify and code them, particularly in the changed situations where computer packages are used to maintain and analyze costs.

The period for which standards are to be fixed depends up on the purpose of the standard. Should the purpose be for strategic planning, longer periods, say three to five years might be chosen. Longer the period chosen for the standard, lower would be its effectiveness in controlling costs. For planning and budgeting for an accounting period, short periods are usually chosen. The successful results of standards depend to a larger extent on the realizability of the goals. It should neither be basic as could be achieved without much effort nor too ideal as could not be achieved even with the best of efforts. It should be attainable with extra efforts on the part of all concerned.

The use of the technique begins with the setting up of the ***standard output*** for the projected period. Standard output is arrived at after taking into consideration two factors, extent of market and the plant capacity. Market for the products could be assessed through market research/ survey and having relevance to the growth of the company and the industry in the past. The economic and political situation of the country should be carefully analyzed before targeting standard output. Once standard output is arrived at, standard costs for the inputs needed to achieve the output have to be assessed. Standards for each of the elements of cost have to be fixed. The process of standard costing is carried out in four stages:

- *Fixing standard for each element of cost, namely materials, labour and overheads*
- *Comparing actual performance with set standards*
- *Analyzing variances as to their location and cause and*
- *Timely reporting the findings to management for corrective action.*

Fixing Standards

The direct standard material cost consists of standard quantity of material required (usage) per unit of output and standard price per unit of material. The material usage standard is fixed based on engineering and technical specifications, after providing for probable wastage and taking into account the quality of materials. The quantity thus arrived at is verified by test runs before finalizing. Standard for price is based on forecast. For example, the manufacture of Maloney requires two materials, Malon and Oney. Research and empirical evidence have concluded that the standard quantities of materials needed per unit of Maloney are two units of Malon and one unit of Oney.Test runs have confirmed this mix. The forecast standard price per unit of Malon is Rs.5 and that of Oney Rs.7. The standard cost of direct materials for producing a unit of Maloney would be (2×5) +(1×7) = Rs.17.

The standard cost for direct labour would be based on the standard time needed for producing one unit of output and the standard rate per unit of labour. The standard time is based on the motion study on the most efficient worker. The rate per labour hour is forecast. In our illustration, supposing that the standard labour hour needed for producing a unit of Maloney is one hour and fifteen minutes and the standard rate per hour is Rs 60, the standard direct labour cost would be 1.25×60 =Rs.75.

Norms for material quantity and labour hours are usually long-term in nature and are not subjected to changes unless there are technological changes. But standards for price and rate are constantly reviewed as these are affected by market conditions. Standards for overheads are fixed separately for variable overheads and fixed overheads.

Standards for variable overheads are fixed on the basis of hours and rates. The hours are the hours worked by labour. Rates are in turn fixed on the basis of technical estimates and the normsn the industry. Fixed overheads are fixed on the basis of standard units. The important areas where standards are set in a manufacturing organization are tabulated below.

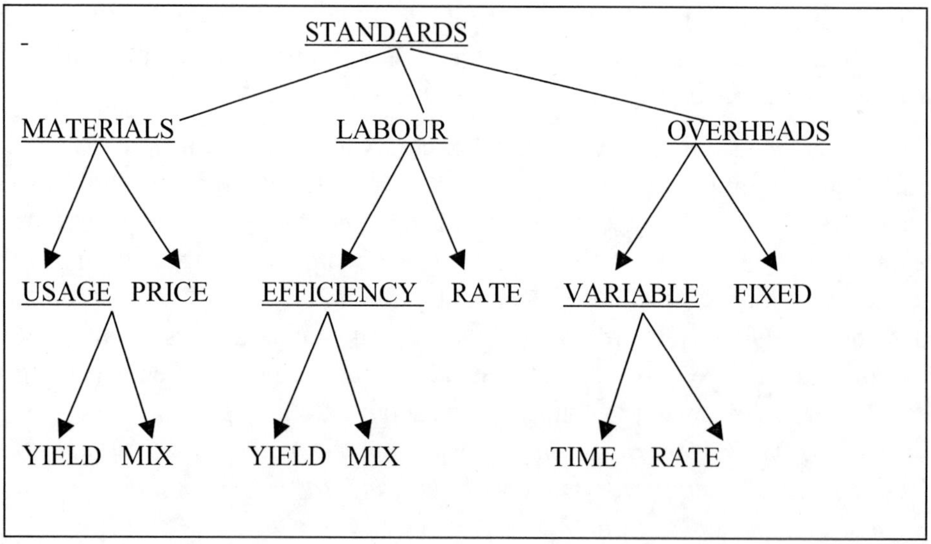

llustration-1

We may now see how standard costs for an illustrative unit is set. Future Focus Ltd. produces FFL, a testing apparatus. The company has set its standard production target for May at 1500 FFLs. Standard quantity of material needed for producing a unit was 400 grammes of mild steel. Standard price per kilogramme of mild steel was Rs.18. Standard labour hours per unit of output were 2 at the standard rate of Rs. 60 per hour. Standards for overheads were: Variable overheads rate per hour was at Rs.6 and standard for fixed overheads was Rs.13,500. Estimate standard cost for the month. Standards for sales were 1400 units at Rs 180 per unit. Statement showing standard cost for Future Focus Ltd. for the month is in Table 1

Table 1
Future Focus Ltd.
Standard cost sheet for May

Particulars	Standard quantity /unit	Total standard quantity	Standard price/ rate Rs.	Standard cost. Rs.
Standard output 1500			Per kg.	
Direct materials cost	400	600 kgs.[1]	18	10,800[2]
Direct labour cost	grammes	3000hrs.[3]	60	1,80,000[4]
Overheads-variable	2 hours	3000hrs.[5]	6	18,000[6]
Overheads-fixed			9[7]	13,500
Standard cost for standard output				2,22,300
Standard cost per unit				148.20[8]

Notes:

[1] Total quantity arrived at by multiplying the per unit requirement by standard production.= .400 × 1500 = 600 kilogrammes.

[2] Cost of material is cost per kilograms× material requirement for production = Rs.18 × 600 = Rs.10,800.

[3] Labour hour per unit × production = 2 hours× 1500 = 3000 hours.

[4] Labour cost = labour hours × labour rate = 3000 × Rs.60 = Rs.1,80,000.

[5] Labour hour is the basis for variable overheads = 3000 hours.

[6] Variable overhead hours × rate = 3000 × Rs.6 = Rs.18,000.

[7] Fixed overheads = total fixed overheads / output =Rs.13,500 / 1500 = Rs.9

[8] Standard cost per unit + total standard cost for standard output / output = Rs.2,23,300 / 1500 = Rs.148.20.

Setting up standards is no mean task. The standard set up should not be highly idealistic as would not be attainable even by best efforts of the workers. It is the carrot and donkey policy. It would breed frustration and would result in heavy labour turnover. A basic standard, on the other hand, would not bring the best in the workers and the competitiveness of the business would be lost. It would be detrimental to the business. The management should therefore be very careful in setting up standard. *The standards should be such that it should be attained with extra efforts*.

Another important input for the successful institution of standards is the active support and cooperation of all sections of employees. The employees conventionally eye any new technique with suspicion. Empirical evidence shows that workers consider standard setting as a "spying process". Unless the confidence of employees of all the sections is gained, setting up standards would at best be a ritual. The employees have to be educated on the desirability of having standards. It is heartening to note that employees of Indian companies in the post liberalization era are learning to realize the importance of competitiveness to be in job. Further, setting up standards has its financial and technical implications. The system is costly and unless its benefits are commensurate with the cost, it would be a wasteful attempt. Forecasting prices and rates are increasingly becoming risky. Lack of control over rising price levels, quality of materials and labour are some of the impediments in forecasting. Estimation of wastage in process is another grey area.

Standards are set not only for costs but also for sales. Production becomes meaningless unless what is produced is sold. After all, the taste of pudding is in its eating. Hence along with standards for costs, business organizations also set sales quantity standards and sales price standards. Standards for sales quantity and price are fixed for each product separately. ***Standard quantity by standard price is budgeted sales***. For example, if Future Focus Ltd. had set a standard price at Rs.160 for FFL, the budgeted sales of the company would be 1,400×160=Rs.2,24,000.

Comparing with Performance

Setting up of standards, we have seen, is the first step in the installation of standard costing technique. But the real usefulness of the technique starts when actual performance is compared with the standards. It is rare that the actual would equal the expected. It might be better or worse. If the performance is better, the company should identify its strengths and upgrade its standard. If the performance is less than expectation, the causes for the deviation are to be identified and corrective measures initiated to stem the rot. The proverb that a stitch in time saves nine is applicable with equal force to companies.

Let us now consider the actual performance of the company in our illustration. The company had achieved the following results for the month of May. Production 1300 units of

FFLs, materials consumed 585 kgs costing Rs.10,091. Labour hours were 2,175 and Labour cost Rs.1,72,800. Overheads for the month were: variable Rs.13,790 and fixed Rs.13,900 . Sales for the month were 1250 units at Rs.2,23,125. Statement below would give a picture of the standards prescribed and the actuals accomplished for the month:

Table 2

Future Focus Ltd.

Particulars	Quantityper unit		**Total quantity**		**Price/rate -Rs.**		**Cost-Rs**	
Std.1500 Actual 1300	Std	Actual	Std	Actual	Std	Actual	Std	Actual
Direct materials	400g.	450g.	600 kgs.	585	18/kg	17.25	10,800	10,091
Direct labour	2hrs	1.67hr	3000hrs.	2175	60/hr	79.45	1,80,000	1,72,800
O.H.-Variable			3000hrs.	2175	6/ hr	6.34	18,000	13,790
O.H.-Fixed					9/unit	10.69	13,500	13,900
Total cost							2,22,300	2,10,581
Per unit cost							148.20	161.99
Per unit cost								
Sales			1,400	1,250	180	178.50	2,52,000	2,23,125

The performance as per the above table indicates that the actual differs from standards fixed in many areas. Some of the deviations are advantageous to the business as the actual costs are less than the expected. Direct labour at 1.67 hours per unit and price of material at Rs.17.25 are advantageous to the company. All other costs are higher than expected. The actual output is 13,000 units as against the standard of 15,000 units. The actual per unit cost of production at Rs.161.99 is much higher than the standard at Rs.148.20.The overheads are also higher. The management would like to measure the extent of the differences before tracing out the area and causes of such discrepancies. From the absolute differences it would not be possible to measure the variation in terms of monetary value. Hence, the analyst has to use a few formulae and reduce the differences to monetary terms for easy comparison. This process is known as ***variance analysis***.

Principles of Variance Analysis

The basic principle of variance analysis centres around the conversion of the differences between standards and actuals into monetary value. All the variances are related to their monetary value to enable a meaningful comparison. Another principle is to analyze variances product by product. As many numbers of analyses should be carried out as the number of products a company manufactures. Such a microanalysis would guide the management to pin the spot of disharmony accurately and correct the distortion before it becomes too late. The crux of the analysis is that ***total cost variance, in whatever element it might be, is the difference between actual cost incurred and the standard cost.***

Definition

Variances are deviations of actuals from standards. CIMA has defined variance "***differences between planned, budgeted or standard cost and actual cost***". Variances might occur in the costs of materials, labour or overheads. Within the material cost, variances might be in quantity of material used or in price. Within the quantity of material itself, variances might occur in the mix of materials or the yield of materials. Similarly in labour cost, the variance might be in labour time standard or labour rate standard. Within the labour time, variances might occur in labour mix or labour efficiency. In overheads, variances might occur in variable or fixed overheads. Within variable overheads, variance might be in efficiency or in expenditure. In fixed overheads, variances might be in volume or expenditure. Within volume, it might be calendar variance, capacity variance or efficiency variance. The classifications of important variances are charted in table 3.

Variance Analysis

The variance in total direct material cost is measured by the difference between the standard material costs for actual output less actual material cost for actual output.

Standard material cost for actual output is calculated by multiplying actual output by standard material cost per unit. The assumption is what would have been the cost for actual output in case standard was adhered to.

Material Cost Variance.

In the area of direct material cost, we would analyze total material cost variance, material usage or quantity variance, material price variance, material mix variance and material yield variance. Total ***direct material cost variance*** (DMCV) would reveal the overall deviation in the cost of material consumed for the actual output over what it should have been had the cost behaved as per the standard. DMCV is the difference between standard material cost for actual output (SMCAO) and actual material cost (AMC).The formula is DMCV=SMCAO-AMC.

Figure 3
Variance chart

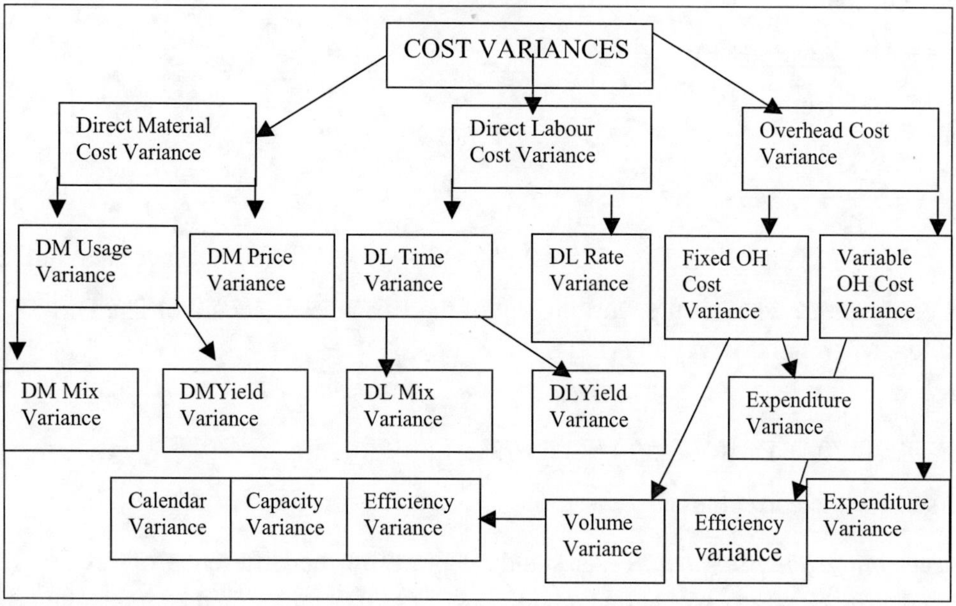

Let us apply this formula to our illustrative case of Future Focus Ltd.

<u>DMCV=SMCAO-AMC.</u>

SMCAO = 7.2×1300 = Rs.9,360

AMC = = Rs.10,091

DMCV = 9,360 – 10,091 = – Rs.731

The total material cost variance is adverse to the company.

Now let us take the composition of total material cost. Material cost is compiled by multiplying the quantity of material by the price per unit of material. Formula for ***direct material quantity (usage) variance*** (DMUV) is standard price (SP) × difference of standard quantity of material for actual output (SMAO) and actual quantity of material used (AMU).

<u>DMUV = SP × (SMAO-AMU)</u>

SP = Rs 18 per Kg.

SMUAO = 0.400×1300 = 520 Kg.

AQMU = = 585 Kg.

DMUV = 18×(520 – 585) = 18 × – 65 = – Rs. 1170.The variance is adverse.

The other component of material cost is price. ***Direct material price variance*** is actual quantity of material used (AMU) multiplied by the difference between standard price (SP) and actual price of material (AP).

DMPV = AMU × (SP – AP)

AQMU = 585 Kg.

SP = Rs.18

AP = Rs.17.249572

DMPV = 585 × (18 – 17.249572) = 585 × 0.750428 = Rs. 439. Price variance is favourable.

Readers could ***check*** whether the working out of the variances is accurate. The DMCV should be equal to DMUV +DMPV.

DMCV = – Rs.731

DMUV(– Rs.1170)+ DMPV (439) = – Rs.731.

Pat yourself for the correctness.

Direct material mix variance is standard price by the difference of revised material standard quantity (RMSQ) over actual quantity used (AQU). Dividing the total weight of actual mix (WAM) by the total weight of standard mix (TWSM) and multiplying the product by the standard weight of the component (SWC) would give ***revised material standard quantity***.

DMMV = SP (RMSQ – AQU)

Revised standard is relevant when there are more than one material used in production and when the total weight of the mix is different from the total of standard mix. In our illustration, since there is only one material used, revision in standard does not arise. Let us see the veracity of the statement.

RMSQ = TWAM / TWSM × SWC

RMSQ = 585 / 520 × 520 =585,which is the same as the standard. As only one material used and there are no components, the question of mix does not arise. There would not be any need to revise standard. As a confirmation, let us now work out the direct material mix variance for Future Focus Ltd.

DMMV = SP (RMSQ – AQU)

= Rs.18 (585 – 585) = 0

Illustration. 2

To demonstrate the principle; let us consider another illustration where more than one material is used. Popular Products Ltd. uses materials POP and ULA in its product POLAR. Standards for materials POP 3 units @ Rs.6 each and ULA 5 units @ Rs.8 each. Standard production was 2500 units for April. Actuals were production2450 POLAR, POP consumption 7425 units at total cost of Rs 43,365, ULA 12,495 units at cost of Rs 99,460.Work out direct material mix variance.

Solution

Fist let us work out revised standard quantity. For that, total standard quandity for actual output and actual quantity have to be worked out as under:

Table 4
Popular Products Ltd

Output: Std. Actual 2500 :2450	Material Std.		Standard Price- Rs.		Standard materia for actual output		Actual materials	consumed
	Per Unit of Output	Total for Std. Output	Per unit	Total std. Material cost	Total	per unit		
POP	3	7,500	6	45,000	7,350	3.07755	7,425	Rs.43,365
ULA	5	12,500	8	1,00,000	12,250	5.00	12,495	Rs.99,460
Total		20,000		1,45,000	19,600		19,920	

RMSQ =WAM/WSMAO×SWC.

POP = 19,920 / 20000 × 7500 = 7,470

ULA = 19,920 / 20000 ×12,500 =12,450

Now apply the formula, DMMV =SP (RMSQ – AMU) separately for POP and ULA.

DMMV for POP = 6 (7470–7,425) = Rs.270

DMMV for ULA = 8 (12,450–12,495) = – Rs.360

Direct material yield variance is an indicator of the extent to which the predicted yield of the material is achieved. Reduction in yield might be due to inferior quality of material and ineffective material handling or contingencies such as spoilage, chemical reactions etc.

Direct material yield variance is standard material cost per unit of output (SMCUO) into the difference between standard output for actual mix (SOAM) and actual output (AO).

DMYV = SMCUO (SOAM-AO).

Let us find out the yield variance of POP and ULA

DMYV for POP =3×6(7425/3 –2,450) = Rs. 450

DMYV for ULA = 5×8(12,495/5–2,450) = - Rs.1,960.

Direct material usage variance for the company's products would be SR(SQAO AQ)

DMUV for Pop = SR(SQAO – AQ) =Rs.6(7350–7425) = – Rs.450

DMUV for Ula = SR(SQAO – AQ) =Rs.8(12250 – 12495) = – Rs.1,960

Checking .

DMUV = DMMV + DMYV

– Rs.2410 = – 2410

Labour Cost Variances

Direct labour cost variance is worked out in similar way as material variance except that labour efficiency and rate are substituted for usage and price. This would be clear when we actually do the analysis. Direct labour cost variance is the difference of standard labour cost for actual output over actual labour cost. We know that standard labour cost is standard labour hours (efficiency) by standard labour rate per hour. Let us continue with the illustration of Popular Products Ltd. The standard and actual for labour cost for the production of Polar by the company were as below. The budgeted days for production were 10 by 14 workers working single shift. Actually it took 12 days to complete the production using 12 labours per day.

Standard output:2500 **Type of labour**	**Standard hours for 2500 units**	**Rate per hour Rs.**	**Actual** **Output :2450** **Hours**	 **Cost-Rs.**
Skilled labour	306.25	175	303.80	53,165
Semi-skilled labour	387.50	125	379.75	46,687
Unskilled labour	425.00	75	422.62	32,071
	1118.75		1106.17	1,31,923

The information given above is processed into table below for making variance analysis.

Table 5
Popular Products Ltd.

Type of labour	For a unit of output				For actual output of 2450			
	Standard		Actual		Standard		Actual	
	Hours	cost	Hours	cost	Hours	cost	Hours	cost
Skilled	0.1225	21.4375	0.124	24.15	300.13	52,523	303.80	53,165
Semi-skilled	0.1550	19.375	0.155	19.056	379.75	47,469	379.75	46,687
Unskilled	0.1700	12.75	0.1725	13.09	416.50	31,238	422.62	32,071
Total					1096.38	131,230	1106.17	1,31,923
Per unit								53,846

Now let us have a look at the variances. ***Direct labour cost variance*** (DLCV) is standard labour cost for actual output (SLCAO) less labour cost for actual output (ALC).

DLCV = SLCAO – ALC

= Rs. 1,31,230 – Rs.1,31,923 = – Rs.693(Adverse)

DLCV –Skilled = Rs.52,523 – Rs.53,165 = – Rs.642(Adverse)

DLCV –Semi-skilled = Rs.47,469 – Rs.46,687 = Rs.782(Favourable)

DLCV – Unskilled = Rs.31,238 – Rs.32,071 = – Rs.833 (Adverse)

Let us check.

DLCV = DLCV for skilled + DLCV for semi-skilled +DLCV for unskilled.

- Rs.693 = – Rs.642 + Rs.782 + – Rs.833.
- Rs.693 = – 693

Direct labour efficiency (hour) variance (DLEV) is calculated for each type of labour.It is multiplying the difference between standard labour hours for actual output (SLHAO) and actual labour hours for actual output(ALH) by standard labour rate (SLR)per hour. Formula is

DLEV = SLR(SLHAO – ALH.

In the illustration it is

DLEV- Skilled = Rs.175 (300.13 – 303.80)

= – Rs. 642.25

DLEV- Semi-skilled = Rs.125 (379.75 – 379.75)

= Rs. 0.

DLEV- Unskilled = Rs.75 (416.50 – 422.62)

= – Rs. 459.

Idle Time

In the matter of labour hours, allowance should be made for idle time caused by fatigue and factors beyond the control of workers, such as power failures and machine break downs. The actual hours worked should then be adjusted for the unavoidable idle hours. Presuming that the justifiable idle hours in the illustration are 12 hours and 30 minutes, then the adjusted actual hours worked would be 291.30(303.80 – 12.50) for skilled labour,367.25 (379.75 – 12.50) for semi-skilled labour and 410.12 (422.62 – 12.50) for unskilled labour.

DLEV- Skilled = 175 (291.30 – 300.13) = – Rs. 1,545.25

DLEV- Semi-skilled = 125 (367.25 – 416.50) = – Rs 6,156.25

DLEV- Unskilled = 75 (410.12 – 416.50) = – Rs. 478.50

This working is to show that reasonable idle hours are matters of allowances.

The other component of labour cost is ***labour rate***. The formula for working out direct labour rate variance (DLRV) is the difference between standard rate (SLR) and actual rate (ALR) multiplied by the actual hours worked by labour (ALH). Formula is

DLRV = ALH (SLR – ALR)

In the illustration, DLRV would be

DLRV for Skilled labour 303.80(175– 175) = Rs.0

Semi-skilled labour 379.75(125– 122.94) = – Rs.782.28

Unskilled labour 422.62(75 – 75.886) = – Rs.374.44

Direct labour efficiency consists of direct labour mix and direct labour yield. ***Direct labour mix variance*** (DLMV) is the standard labour rate (SLR) of the difference between revised labour standard hours(RLSH)and actual total labour hours for all groups of labours (ATLH) or SR (RSLH – ALH).Revised standard labour hours is total actual labour hours for all groups (TALH) / total standard labour hours for all groups (TSLH) × standard labour hours for that particular group of labour(SLHC).Hence, before we work out direct labour mix variance, we have to attempt revised labour standard hours.

RLSH = (TALH / TSLH) SLHC

for skilled labour = 300.13 (1106.17/ 1096.38) = 302.81

semi-skilled labour = 379.75 (1106.17/ 1096.38) = 383.141

unskilled labour = 416.50 (1106.17/ 1096.38) = 420.22

DLMV = SR (RSLH – ALH)

for skilled labour = 175 (302.81–303.80) = – Rs. 173.25

semi-skilled labour = 125 (383.14 –379.75) = Rs. 423.87

unskilled labour = 75 (420.22–422.62) = – Rs 180.00

Direct ***labour yield variance*** (DLYV) is multiplication of the difference between actual output (AO) and standard output for actual labour cost (SOALC) by the standard labour cost per unit of output (SLCUO). For the illustrative company, it would be

DLYV= SLCUO(AO - SOALC)

for skilled labour = 21.44 (2450 – 2480) = – Rs. 643.20

semi-skilled labour = 19.38 (2450 –2450) = Rs. 0

unskilled labour = 12.75 (2450 –2486) = – Rs.459

Overhead Variances

Just like materials and labour variances, overhead variances are also relationships between standard overheads for actual output and actual overheads. Instead of the words "standard overheads for actual output", the term "***recovered overheads***" is used. Thus, the formula for total overheads variance is recovered overheads (ROH) or standard overheads for actual output – Actual overheads (AOH).

TOHCV = ROH – AOH

To continue our example, presuming that for the standard production of 2500 units of Polar, cost of standard variable overheads rate per hour was Rs.11.45.Fixed overheads for the standard production were Rs. 26,390.Actual overheads costs for the production of 2450 units were: fixed overheads of Rs 32,400 and variable overheads of Rs.13,721. Processed data of the company in a suitable form for variance analysis is given in table6.

Table 6
Popular Products Ltd

Type of overheads	Standard for 2500 units			For 2450 units.			
	Hours	Rate- Rs.	Cost Rs.	Std. hours	Std.cost Rs	Actual hours	Actual cost Rs
Variable	1118.75	11.45/hr	12,810	1096.38	12,554	1106.17	13,721
Fixed		10.56/unit	26,390		25,872		32,400
Total		23.59/hr	39,200		38,426		46,121

Overhead variances could be analyzed, in addition to total, under variable and fixed components. If there are semi-variable overheads, it should first be split into variable component and fixed component and treated according to the groups they belong to. Variable overheads are measured in terms of number of labour hours, as these do not strictly vary with out put. Fixed overheads are in terms of output. Variable overheads are further analyzed under variances of efficiency and expenditure. Fixed overheads are scrutinized under volume and expenditure. Volume variances are micro analyzed into calendar variance, capacity variance and efficiency variance.

Total overhead cost variance is recovered overheads less actual overheads (ROH – AOH). Recovered overheads are standard overheads for actual output. The formula is TOHCV = ROH – AOH. The total overhead variance would be:

TOHCV = Rs.38,426 – Rs.46,121 = – Rs. 7,695.

Total overhead variance shows the macro level deviation in overheads. It is therefore necessary to the subgroups within the overhead cost. The controllable component of overheads is variable. ***Variable overhead cost variance*** would be RVOH – AVOH. The formula is:

VOHCV = RVOH – AVOH.

The variable overhead variance would then be

= Rs.12,554 – Rs.13,721 = – Rs.1,167.

Fixed overhead cost variance (FOHCV) is calculated by subtracting actual fixed overhead cost (AFOHC)from standard fixed overhead cost for actual output(SFOHCAO) As we know standard fixed overheads for actual output is also called recovered fixed overhead (RFOHC), the formula for calculation of fixed overhead variance is

FOHCV = RFOHC–AFOHC

In the illustration, it is

= Rs.25,872 – Rs.32,400 = – Rs.6,528.

Check:

TOHCV = VOHCV + FOHCV = – Rs.7,695 = – Rs. 1,167 + – Rs. 6,528.

Variable overhead efficiency (time) variance (VOHEfV)would be standard rate× standard hours for actual output less actual hours. Formula is

VOHEfV = SR(SHAO – AH)

and the variance would be :

VOHEfV = SR (SHAO – AH) = Rs.11.45 (1096.38 – 1106.17) = – Rs.112.10.

Variable overhead expenditure variance (VOHExp.V)is also called controllable variance. It is the change in the actual cost of variable overhead over the standard. It is arrived at by multiplying actual hours (AH) with the deviation of standard overhead rate per hour(SOHR) from actual overhead rate per hour (AOHR). The formula would be

VOHExp.V = AH (SOHR – AOHR)

and the expenditure variance for Popular Products would be:

VOHExp.V = AH (SOHR – AOHR) = 1106.17(Rs.11.45 – Rs.12.40) = – Rs.1,051.

Fixed overhead cost variance (FOHCV), we have already seen, is RFOH –AFOHC. FOHCV is further analyzed under two broad heads- ***volume variance and expenditure variance.*** Of the two, volume variance has three subgroups, namely ***calendar variance, capacity variance and efficiency variance.***

Fixed overhead volume variance indicates the change in the quantum of overheads between standard and actual. It is the difference between standard fixed overheads for actual output (SFOHAO) or recovered fixed overheads (RFOH) and budgeted fixed overheads (BFOH). Budgeted fixed overheads are the overheads planned for standard production.

FOHVV = RFOH – BFOH

In the illustration = Rs.25, 872 – 26,390 = – Rs.518.

Fixed overhead expenditure variance (FOHExp.V) is the difference between budgeted fixed overheads (BFOH) and actual fixed overheads (AFOH).

FOHExpV = BFOH – AFOH

In Popular Products Ltd., the budgeted overheads were Rs.26,390 as against which the actual fixed overheads were Rs.32,400. The FOHExpVwould thus be = BFOH – AFOH = Rs.26,390 – 32,400 = – Rs.6,010.

Check.

FOHCV = FOHVV + FOHExp.V

– Rs. 6,528 = – Rs.518 + – 6,010 = Rs.6,528.

Within fixed overhead volume variance, ***Fixed overhead calendar variance*** (FOHCal.V) indicates the difference between budgeted hours or days for the output and actual hours or days taken. Standard production per day was 250 units, whereas actual production per day was 204.17 units. The formula for calendar variance is the difference between Budgeted days (BH) and the actual number of hours or days worked (AH) multiplied by the standard rate per hour(SR)

FOHCal.V = SR (BH – AH)

In the example = Rs.23.59(1118.75 – 1106.17)

= Rs.296.76.

Another component of fixed overhead volume variance is ***Fixed overhead efficiency variance*** (FOHEfV). It is usually calculated for variable overheads. But it could be worked out for fixed overheads also in theory. It is arrived at by multiplying standard fixed overhead rate per hour(SFOHR) with the difference between standard hours for actual output(SHAO) and actual output (AH). It should be remembered that only variable overheads are allocated according to labour hours and not fixed overheads. Fixed overheads are allocated according to units of output. This formula presumes that fixed overheads are also influenced by labour hours. We have therefore to apply labour hours to work out the variance. The formula is

FOHEfV = SFOHR (SHAO - AH)

Applying the formula for Popular, FOHEfV would be

FOHEfV = Rs.23.59 (1096.38 – 1106.17) = – Rs.230.59.

The last subdivision of fixed overhead volume variance is *fixed overhead capacity variance.* (FOHCapV). It would indicate number of hours of fixed overheads as against the budgeted hours. The formula for FOHCapV is standard fixed overhead per hour (SFOHPH) × (actual hour worked – budgeted hours.

FOHCapV = SFOHPH (AH – BH)

In the illustration = Rs.23.59 (1106.17 – 1118.75) = – Rs. 296.76

It is rather a rule than an exception that there are quite a few changes that takes place between the time of fixing the standard and its actual implementation. Some of these changes are beyond the control of the businessman and have to be reconciled with. These changes often take place due to scarcity of materials, change in governmental policies and labour rates as a result of wage revisions. The variance caused by the revision in the standard on account of the above changes is ***revision variance*** (RV). Revision variance is thus the difference between the original standard cost for actual output (OSCAO) and the revised standard cost for actual output (RSCAO). The formula is

RV = OSCAO – RSCAO.

Supposing that in the case of Popular Products Ltd., materials are imported and the government had recently hiked the import duty on the materials by 10%. The revised rates of materials were Pop Rs.19.62 per unit as against the original standard rate of Rs.18 and Ula Rs.43.60 as against Rs. 40 per unit. The revision variance would be

for Pop = (2450 × Rs. 18) – (2450 ×Rs. 19.62)

= Rs.44,100 – Rs.48,069

= – Rs.3,969.

for Ula = Rs.98,000 – Rs.99,460

= – Rs.1,460.

There are two methods of accounting for the revision. First method is to incorporate the revised element cost and refix the standard according to revision. The other method is to continue with the original standard norms and adjust for the revision variance before arriving at the cost variance of the concerned element of cost. Of the two, the first has to preferred, as it would pinpoint the variance at the rate and price of the elements. The second would give the final variance.

Sales Variances

Standard for sales consists of volume standard for the units to be sold and the price at which each unit would be sold. Oasis Overseas Ltd. was producing two products, Oolfa and Oolta. For the month of June, the company budgeted to sell 2300 units of Oolfa at a standard of Rs.160 each. The standard price for Oolta was Rs.180 and the standard quantity to be sold was fixed at 2100 units. The actual sales were 2250 units of Oolfa for Rs.3, 55,500 and 2150 units of Oolta for Rs.3,80,550.The actual sales have differed from the standard both in terms of volumes and prices. Sales variances are analyzed under two broad groups, namely sales volume variance and sales price variance. Sales volume variances are in turn scrutinized under sales mix variances and sales quantity variances. Before we take up the variance analysis, we have to group the information in a convenient form as in Table7.

Table 7
Oasis Overseas Ltd.

Products	Standard sales			Actual sales		
	Price-Rs.	Volume	Turnover-Rs.	Price-Rs.	Volume	Turnover-Rs.
Oolfa	160	2300	3,68,000	158	2250	3, 55,500
Oolta	180	2100	3,78,000	177	2150	3,80,550
Total			7,46,000			7,36,050

From the table above, we could work out the variances. ***Total Sales variance or sales value variance*** (TSV) is the difference between total budgeted sales (TBS) and total actual sales (TAS). The formula would be

TSV = TBS – TAS

Sales value variance for Oasis Overseas Ltd = Rs.7,46,000 – Rs. 7,36,050 = – Rs.9,950.

Sales value variance for each product would be

SVOolfa = Rs.3,68,000 – Rs. 3,55,500 = – Rs. 12,500.

SVOolta = Rs. 3,78,000 – Rs.3,80,550 = Rs. 2,550.

TSV = – Rs. 9,950.

Sales volume variance (SVV) is the variation of standard realization for actual units sold(SSAU) from the budgeted sales volume(BSV).The formula for working out the variance is standard price (SP) (budgeted sales (BS) – actual sales (AS). For Oasis, it would be

Oolfa SVV = Rs.160 (2250 – 2300) = – Rs. 8,000.

Oolta SVV = Rs.180 (2150 – 2100) = Rs. 9,000

Sales price variance (SPV) is the difference of actual price at which the products were sold as against the standard price. The variance is calculated by multiplying the difference between standard sales price(SP) and actual sales price(AP) by the actual sales volume (ASV). The formula is ASV(SP – AP).For the sample case the variances would be

Oolfa = 2250 (Rs.160 – Rs.158) = – Rs.4,500.

Oolta = 2150 (Rs.180 – Rs.177) = – Rs.6,450.

Check

TSV = SVV +SPV and of Oolfa and Oolta

– Rs.9,950 = – Rs.8,000 + – Rs.4,500 + 9,000 + – Rs.6,450.

= – Rs.9,950.

Within sales volume, ***Sales mix variance*** (SMV) is the deviation in the mix of products actually sold from budgeted.SMV is the standard price (SP) × revised standard sales (RSS) – actual quantity sold (AS). Revised standard sales is total quantity of actual sales mix (TQASM) / total quantity of standard sales mix (TQSSM) × standard quantity of the component (SQC).

RSS is total actual quantity / standard quantity × standard quantity for the component (SQC).RSS in the case of

Oolfa = 4400 / 4400 × 2300 = 2300

Oolta = 4400 / 4400 × 2100 = 2100

RSS for the products are same as the standard since the total units sold is same as the standard.

The mix variance for the products Oolfa and Oollta would be

SMV – Oolfa = Rs.160 (2300 – 2250) = – Rs.8,000

SMV – Oolta = Rs.180 (2100 – 2150) = Rs.9,000

Sales quantity variance (SQV) is the deviation of revised standard sales (RSS)from budgeted sales (BS), multiplied by the standard sales price(SP). The formula is SQV = SP(BS – RSS) .

SQV Oolfa = Rs.160 (2250 – 2300) = – Rs.8,000

SQV Oolta = Rs.180 (2150 – 2100) = Rs.9,000

12.38. We have seen variances in costs and sales. Besides these, there are three important ***control ratios*** we should know. These are activity ratio, capacity ratio and efficiency ratios. Activity ratio is equivalent to capacity ratio and efficiency ratio. The formulae for these ratios are

Activity ratio = Standard hours for actual output / budgeted hours.

Capacity ratio = Actual hours worked / budgeted hours.

Efficiency ratio = Standard hours for actual output / actual hours.

We shall apply the formulae for Ramulal Brothers whose cost data are as under.

Standard hours per unit : 2

Budgeted production : 10,000 units

Actual production : 8,000

Actual hours worked : 16,400

Activity ratio is : 16,000–20,000 = – 4000

Capacity ratio is : 16,400–20,000 = – 3,600

Efficiency ratio is : 16,000–16,400 = – 400

Summary

Standard cost is a technique for reduction in the cost of the elements of cost. Standards are norms that a company should fix for the elements of cost. Standards are determined based on latest technical innovations and on empirical evidence. Standards ensure a company to reduce cost and increase its competitive strength. After the standards are stipulated, actual performance is compared with the standards and the causes and extent of deviations are analyzed he variances are reduced to monetary value to enable the management to grasp the significance of the variances and to initiate remedial measures. For this purpose, simple formulae are used. The variance formulae are summarized as under:

1. ***Direct material cost variance(DMCV)*** = Standard material cost for actual output (SMCAO) – actual materials cost (AMC).
2. ***Direct material quantity or usage variance(DMUV)*** = Standard price (SP) ×[(standard material quantity for actual output (SMQAO) – actual quantity of material used(AQMU)].
3. ***Direct material price variance(DMPV)*** = Actual quantity of material used (AQMU) × (standard price (SP)– actual price (AP).
4. ***Direct material mix variance*** *(DMMV)* = Standard price (SP) × [(Revised material standard quantity (RMSQ)– actual quantity of materials used (AQMU)].

5. ***Revised material standard quantity (RMSQ)*** = *Total weight of actual mix(TWAM) / total weight of standard mix(TWSM) × standard weight of the component(SWC)*

6. ***Direct material yield variance(DMYV)*** = Standard material cost per unit of output (SMCUO) × [standard output for actual mix (SOAM) – actual output (AO)].

7. ***Direct labour cost variance(DLCV)*** = Standard labour cost for actual output (SLCAO) – actual labour cost

8. ***Direct labour hour or efficiency variance(DLEV)*** =Standard labour rate (SLR) × [standard labour hours for actual output (SLHAO) – actual labour hours(ALH)].

9. ***Direct labour rate variance(DLRV)*** = Actual labour hours (ALH) × [standard labour rate (SLR) – actual labour rate(ALR).

10. Direc***t labour mix variance*** *(DLMV)* = Standard rate (SR) × [revised labour standard hours (RLSH) – actual labour hours (ALH)].

11. ***Revised labour standard hours(RLSH) =*** total actual labour hours (TALH)/ total standard labour hours(TSLH) × standard labour hours for the component(SLHC).

12. ***Direct labour yield variance (DLYV) =*** standard labour cost pcr unit of output (SLCUO) × [actual output (AO) – standard output for actual labour cost (SOALC).

13. ***Total overhead cost variance (TOHCV) =*** recovered overheads or standard overheads for actual output (ROH) – actual overheads (AO).

14. ***Variable overhead cost variance (VOHCV)*** = recovered variable overhead (RVOH) – actual variable overheads (AVOH).

15. ***Variable overheads efficiency variance (VOHEfV)*** = standard rate (SR) [standard hours for actual output (SHAO) – actual output (AO).

16. V***ariable overhead expenditure variance (VOHExV)*** = actual hours(AH) × [standard variable overhead rate (SVOHR) – Actual variable overhead rate (AVOHR)].

17. ***Fixed overhead cost variance (FOHCV)*** = Recovered fixed overheads (RFOH) – actual fixed overheads (AFOH).

18. ***Fixed overhead volume variance (FOHVV)*** = recovered fixed overheads (RFOH) – budgeted fixed overheads (BFOH).

19. ***Fixed overheads expenditure variance (FOHExOH)*** =Budgeted fixed overheads (BFOH) actual fixed overheads (AFOH).

20. ***Fixed overheads calendar variance (FOHCalV)*** = Standard rate × [budgeted hours (BH) –actual hours (AH).

21. ***Fixed overhead efficiency variance (FOHEfV)*** = Standard fixed overhead rate × [standard hours for actual output (SHAO) – actual hours (AH).

22. ***Fixed overhead capacity variance (FOHCapV)*** = Standard fixed overheads per hour × [actual hours(AH) – budgeted hours(BH).

23. ***Revision variance (RV)*** = Original standard cost for actual output(OSCAO) – revised standard cost for actual output(RSCAO).

24. ***Sales variance (SV)*** = Budgeted sales (BS) – actual sales (AS).

26. S***ales volume variance (SVV)*** = sales price (SP) × [budgeted sales (BS) – actual sales (AS).

27. ***Sales price variance (SPV)*** = Actual sales volume (ASV) × [standard price (SP) – actual price (AP).

28. ***Sales mix variance (SMV)*** = Standard price × [revised sales standard (RSS) – actual sales (AS).

29. ***Revised sales standard (RSS)*** = Total quantity of actual sales mix (TQASM) – total quantity of standard sales mix (TQSSM) × standard quantity of component (SQC).

28. ***Sales quantity variance (SQV)*** = standard price (SP) × [budgeted sales (BS) – revised sales standard (RSS0).

30. ***Control ratios***

i. ***Activity ratio*** = Standard hours for actual output (SHAO) –budgeted hours(BH)

ii. ***Capacity ratio*** = Actual hours (AH) – budgeted hours (BH)

iii. ***Efficiency ratio*** = Standard hours for actual output (SHAO) – actual hours(AH0

I. QUESTIONS

1. What is a standard cost?
2. How are standards fixed?
3. What is standard costing? What are the requirements for setting up a standard costing system?
4. What are Variances?
5. What is Variance Analysis? Why is it needed?
6. Describe the different types of Variances.
7. What is Material Cost Variance? Give Example?

8. Explain the following variances
   (a) Labour cost variance
   (b) Labour rate variance
   (c) Labour efficiency variance
   (d) Labour mix variance
9. What are the causes of Variances? Explain?
10. What are sales variances?
11. Expain the concepts of standard costing. What advantages are likely to be obtained from the application of standard costing as compared to historical costing?
12. What is standard costing? How does it differ from budgetary control?
13. Distinguish between
   i. Standard cost and estimated cost;
   ii. Standard cost and budgeted cost.
14. Discuss the essential components of standard costing system. What are the advantages of having a system of standard costing?
15. Write brief explanatory notes on the following
   (a) Ideal standard
   (b) Normal standard
   (c) Basic standard
   (d) Attainable standard
16. What is variance analysis? Explain and illustrate the various types of material variance
17. Distinguish between :
   (a) Material price variance and material mix variance
   (b) Labour efficient variance and Labour rate variance
18. Describe the managerial uses of variance analysis.
19. Write note on:
   (a) Setting of standards
   (b) Revision of standard
20. Discuss the cause for material price and usage variances.

II. QUIZ

Say yes or no

1. Standard costing is another type of historic costing method.
2, Standards are predetermined on the basis of technical advancement.
3. Elements are the units in fixing standards.
4. Standards can be enforced by the management on workers.
5. Deviation of actual fro, standard is variance.
6. Variance analysis helps thw management to pin point areas of failures.
7. Standards are revised when happenings necessitate.
8. Variance analysis is decision making.

III. EXERCISES

1. From the following data of Malcolm Methods, calculate the material price variance and state whether it is favourable or unfavourable:

   Standard: 10 Kg. at Rs.5 per Kg.

   Actual: 12 Kg at Rs.6 per Kg.

2. Nalco Nandid Enterprises has furnished the following data and request you to calculate material price variance, material usage variance and material mix variance for materials A and B.

Raw materials	Standard	Actual
A	40 units @ Rs.50 per unit	50 units @ Rs.50 per unit
B	60 units @ Rs.40 per unit	60 units @ Rs.45 per unit

3. Fixers Ltd. produces Fixall using 60 kgs of chemical X–L and 40 kgs. of chemical Y–L. The standard loss of production is 30%. The standard price of X–L is Rs.15 per Kg. and of Y–L is Rs.20 per Kg. The actual mixture and yield were as follows:

   X–L 80 Kgs. @ Rs.12.50 per Kg

   Y–L 70 Kgs. @ Rs.20.50 per Kg

   Actual yield 115 Kgs.

   Calculate material variances.

4. The standard estimate of Kansas Kandlin for manufacture of 1,000 units of KanKun is 400 kgs. at Rs.12.50 per Kg. When 2, 000 units of the commodity are manufactured, it is found that 820 Kgs. of materials are consumed @ Rs.12.60 per Kg. Find out material variances.

5. From the following data of Gomati Foundry, calculate material usage variance:

   Standard: 10 Kg. at Rs 12.50 per Kg

   Actual: 12 kg at Rs.12.50 per Kg.

6. For producing Peerpal, peepa is the raw material needed. Standard cost of a unit of peepa is estimated as follows:

   16 kgs. of material @ Rs.11.00 per kg.

   On completion of the unit, it was found that 20 kgs of raw material costing Rs.11.50 per kg had been consumed. Compute material variances.

7. Gemini industries manufacture GEMCO in its plants using materials Alma and Belma. Standard requirement is:

Quantity. Rate per Kg	.Kg.	Rs.
MaterialAlma	8	16.00
MaterialBelma	4	12.00

During April, 100 kgs of GEMCO were produced. The actual consumption of material is as under:

Quantity. Rate Per Kg	Kg.	Rs.			
MaterialAlma	750	17.00	Material Belma	500	18.00

Calculate:

(a) Material Cost Variance

(b) Material Price Variance

(c) Material Usage Variance

8. Given that the cost standard of Enable Endeavour Ltd. for material consumption at 40 kgs. @ Rs.10 per kg., per unit of EEL, compute the variances when actuals were:

   (a) 48 kgs. at Rs. 10 per kg.or

   (b) 40 kgs. at Rs. 12 per kg.or

   (c) 48 kgs. at Rs. 12 per kg.or

   (d) 36 kgs. for a total cost of Rs. 360.

9. From the following particulars furnished by Halo Holocene Inc. compute (a) Material cost variance (b) Material price variance, and (c) material usage variance for its detergent branded Hahes.

Quantity of materials purchased	: 3, 000 units
Value of materials purchased	: Rs.67, 654
Standard quantity of materials required per tonne of output	: 30 units
Standard rate of materials	: Rs.22.50 per unit
Opening stock of materials	: Nil
Closing stock of materials	: 500 units
Output during the period	: 80 tonnes

10. The standard cost card of Salomey Fatty Acids Ltd. shows the following details relating to the materials needed to produce one kilogram of groundnut oil.

Quantity of groundnut required per Kg. oil	: 3Kg
Price of groundnut per Kg.	: Rs. 12.50 per Kg
Actual production data:	
Production during the week	: 1000 Kgs.
Quantity used	: 2,950 Kgs..
Price of groundnut per Kg.	: Rs. 13

Calculate

(a) Material Cost Variance

(b) Material Price Variance

(c) Material Usage Variance

11. Alabama Manufacturing Company has adopted standard costing. It has furnished the following information:

Standard: for 100 Kgs. of product:	
Materials	70 Kgs.
Price of materials	Re. 11 per Kg.
Actual: Output	2, 10, 000 Kg.
Material used	2, 80, 000 Kg.
Cost of materials	Rs.30, 52, 000

Calculate:

(a) Materials usage variance

(b) Material price variance

(c) Materials cost variance

12. Following are the particulars in respect of product Zeeno,where two types of materials Ano and Bino are used:

Material input	Standard		Actual	
	Tonnes -Rates		Tonnes-Rates	
		Rs.		Rs.
An	120	10.00	140	9.50
Bino	80	7.50	60	9.00
Less: Loss	20		18	
Net production	180		182	

Your are required to calculate

(a) Material price variance

(b) Material mix variance and

(c) Material yield variance

13. The standard material cost for 100 Kg of chemical Dinopass is made up of:

Chemical Alk: 30 Kgs. @ Rs. 12.00 per kg.

Chemical Bilk: 40 Kgs. @ Rs. 15.00 per kg.

Chemical Cilk: 80 Kgs. @ Rs. 16.00 per kg.

In a batch, 500 kgs of chemical Dinopass were produced from a mix of:

Chemical Alk: 140 Kgs. At a cost of Rs.1988

Chemical Bilk: 220 kgs. At a cost of Rs. 3, 256

Chemical Cilk: 440 kgs. At a cost of Rs. 7, 260

How do yield, mix and the price factor contribute to the variance in the actual cost over standard cost?

14. The standard material cost to produce a tonne of chemical Xalto is:

300-kgs.of material Edis @ Rs. 20 per kg.

400-kgs.of material Fidis @ Rs.15 per kg.

500-kgs.of material Gidis @ Rs.16 per kg.

During a period, 100 tonnes of Xalto were produced from the usage of:

35 tonnes of material Edis at a cost of Rs.22,000 per tonnes

42 tonnes of material Fidis at a cost of Rs. 17,000 per tonnes

53 tonnes of material Gidis at a cost of Rs 15,000 per tonne

Calculate price, usage and mix variances for each material.

15. Jane Ltd. manufactures product Pitha. Standard specifications for 1,000 kg. of Pitha were as follows:

Ingredients	Qty. Kg	Price per kg Rs.	Cost Rs.
Atna	800	12.50	10,000
Bitna	200	12.00	2,800
Citna	200	16.00	3,200

Material records indicate: Consumption in January

Atna	1,57,000 kg at Rs.12.40 per kg.
Bitna	38,000 kg. At Rs.12.20 per kg.
Citna	36,000 kg. At Rs.16.10 per kg.

Actual finished production for the month of January was 2,00,000 kg.

Calculate MPV, MMV and MYV.

16. From the following data, calculate materials yield variance:

Standard Mix	Actual Mix
Material A–200 units at Rs.12	160 Units at Rs. 13
Material B–100 units at Rs.10	140 units at Rs.10
Standard loss allowed 10% of input.	Actual output is 275 units.

17. Calculate Labour Cost variances:

Standard hours: 40 @ Rs.30 per hour

Actual Hours: 35 @ Rs.34 per hour.

18. Standard hour for manufacturing two products Minoy and Ninoy are 15 hours per unit and 20 hours per unit respectively. Both products require identical kind of labour and the standard wage rate per hour is Rs.25. In the month of June, 10,000 units of Minoy and 15,000 units of Ninoy were manufactured.Total labour hours actually worked were 4,50,500 and the actual wage bill came to Rs.1, 13,10,000.

You are required to compute the labour cost variances.

19. The following are the cost data for the month of April

Actual number of working days in the month	24
Actual man-hour worked during the Month	9600
Units produced in the month	800

Actual fixed overhead incurred in the month	Rs.42,000
The company's standard cost data for the month are:	
Budgeted number of working days per month	22
Budgeted man-hour for the month	8800
Standard man-hours per unit produced	11
Standard fixed overhead rate per man-hour	0.50

Calculate fixed overhead variances

20. From the data given below, calculate labour variance for the two departments.

	Dept. A	Dept B
Actual gross wages (direct)	Rs.2,00,000	1,80,000
Standard hours	8000	6000
Standard rate per hour	Rs.30	Rs.35
Actual hours worked	8200	5800

21. The standard cost for a product is

Time : 10 hours per unit

Cost : Rs.5 per hour

The actual performance was:

Production	1000 units
Actual hours taken	10400 hours
Idle time	400 hours
Total time	10800 hours

Payment made: Rs.56160 .

Calculate.(a)Labour rate variance

(b)Labour efficiency variance

(c)Idle time variance

(d)Labour cost variance

22. From the data given above, calculate overhead variance such as:

i. Overhead cost variance
ii. Overhead efficiency variance
iii. Overhead capacity variance
iv. Overhead calendar variance

23. Following data are available from a card of a factory:

Standard Labour rate	Rs.12 per hour
Standard hours	2 per unit
Actual labour rate	Rs.12.25 per hour
Actual units produced	1000 units
Actual hours worked	1950 hours

Calculate labour variances

24. Calculate overhead variances from the following data:

	Standard	Actual
Fixed Overheads	8000	8500
Variable overheads	12000	11200
Output in units	4000	3800

25. In Hanoly Ltd. the standard units of production for the year were fixed at 1,20,000 units and estimate overhead expenditures were estimated to be

Fixed	Rs.2,41,200
Variable	Rs. 96,234
Semi-variable	Rs. 31,850

Actual production during April was 8000 units. Each month has 20 working days. During the month in question there was one statutory holiday. The actual overheads amounted to:

Fixed	Rs.21,190
Variable	Rs. .8,480
Semi-variable	Rs. 2,520

Semi-variable charges are considered to include 60 per cent expenses of fixed nature and 40 per cent of variable character

Find out:

1. Overhead Expenditure Variance
2. Overhead Volume Variance
3. Overhead Cost Variance

26. The budgeted and actual sales of Unified Producta,manufacturing and marketing a single product are furnished below

Budgeted sales 10000 units at Rs.40 per unit

Actual sales for May	5000 units at Rs.35 per unit
June	8000 units at Rs.41 per unit

Calculate month-wise:

(a) Sales price variance

(b) Sales volume variance

27. The Sales Manager of Pythagoras Pioneers engaged in the manufacturing and sales of three products, Pot, Qot and Rot gives you the following information for the month of October

Product	Budget Sales (unit)	Selling price per unit	Contribution
Pot	2000	Rs.12	Rs.6
Qot	2000	Rs.8	Rs.4
Rot	2000	Rs.5	Rs.1

Actual Sales:

Pot	1500 units for Rs.15000
Qot	2500 units for Rs.17500
Rot	3500 units for Rs.21000

You are required to calculate the following variance

i. The sales price variance

ii. The Sales volume variance

iii. The sales quantity variance

iv. The sales mix variance

28. Calculate the efficiency and activity ratios from the following figures:

Budget production	88 units
Standard hours per unit	10
Actual production	75 units
Actual working hours	600

29. The standard cost on 'Material and Labor for the making of a unit of a certain product are estimated as under:

Material 80 Kg. at Rs. 1.50 per Kg

Labour 18 hrs at Rs. 1.25 per hr

On completion of the production of a unit, it was found that 75 kg. Of material costing Rs. 1.75 per Kg. has been consumed and that the time taken was 16 hours, the wage rate being Rs. 1.50 per hour

You are required to analysis material and labour variances.

30. For unit of production A, the standard data are given below:

Material	5 Kg. @ Rs. 40 per Kg.
Labour	40 Hrs. @ Rs.11.00 per hour
Actual data	
Actual production	100 units
Material	490 Kg. @ Rs. 42 each
Labour	3960 hrs. @ Rs.11.10 per hour

Calculate material and labour variances.

31. Costa Rica enterprises has the following cost data for the month of July: The Company has adopted Standard costing system and requires you to work out the various deviations from standards on the basis of the following data: The company uses two materials for its process-A and B.

Direct material standard:

A. usage 3 kgs @ Rs. 7 per kilo.

B. usage 2 kgs @ Rs.6 per kilo.

Yield 90% in both cases.

Actual for the materials during the month were:

A: material cost Rs.169,031 and cost of materials per kilo was Rs.7.05

B: material cost Rs.98,532 and cost of material Rs. 6.95 per kg.

Direct labour standard per unit of output:

Skilled 5 hours at the rate of Rs. 80 per hour; semi-skilled 8 hours at Rs. 32 per hour. Labour fatigue time allowed 10%.

Actual labour employed are -skilled 41,580 hours at a cost of Rs.8,41,995. Semi-skilled 59,400 hours at Rs.4,90, 050.

Overhead Standard :

Total overheads Rs.92,500, 30% of which is variable. Actual overheads were -variable Rs.26, 640, fixed Rs.64,560. Standard output 7,500 units. Actual output7,200 units.

Standard price per unit of output Rs.240. Sales for the month were Rs.16,62,500. Closing stock 200 units; Opening stock – nil.

32. Aladi Ltd. manufactured 12000 units of its product LOME during the year 2003 by consuming 36,000 kgs. of raw material, which was purchased at Rs.30 per kg. The engineering section of the company had estimated 2 kg of raw material for a unit output. The standard price of the raw material was fixed for Rs. 28 per kg. Calculate material variances.

33. Compute the material variances of Gladiola Traders from the data given below

Standard mix

Material X 100 kg at Rs.30 per kg

Material Y 50 kg at Rs.40 per kg

Actual mix

Material X 120 kg at Rs.40 per kg

Material Y 30 kg at Rs.30 per kg.

34. The standard cost card of Bishwas for one kg of its product shows the following costs for material.

Material A – 3 units @ Re.10.00

Material B – 2 units @ Rs. 15.50

3600 kg of the product were manufactured during the month of April with the consumption of the following materials:

Material A – 12000 units @ Rs.11.50

Material B – 8000 units @ Rs.15.25

Calculate appropriate material variances.

35. The following standard and actual data pertaining to Subbhi Ltd.

Standards

Material X 20 Kg at Rs.30 per kg

Material Y 30 kg at Rs.30 per kg

Normal process loss is 10 per cent of input

Actual

Material X 300 Kg at Rs.30.5 per kg

Material Y 200 kg at Rs.29 per kg

Actual loss was 15 per cent on input and output 350 units.

Computer Material cost variances.

36. Two types of raw material namely, A and B are used by Shabnam Company Ltd. in the ration of 1:2 for manufacturing product "BEE". The standard price of material A and B is Rs. 13 and Rs.12 respectively the company is expecting 5 percent loss from manufacturing operations. The actual material mix was as follows:

Material A 450 kg at Rs.12.75

Material B 250 kg at Rs.12.25

Actual output was 200 kg

Calculate different material variances.

37. Following information has been taken from the records of Neelum Nelco. Calculate material variances

	Standard		Actual	
	Qty(kg)	Rate(Rs.)	Qty(kg)	Rate(Rs)
Material X	60	15.00	70	14.50
Material Y	40	13.00	30	14.00
Input	100		100	
Loss	10		9	
Output	90		91	

38. The details regarding the composition and the weekly wage rates of labour force engaged by Sandhya Sandip on a job scheduled to be completed in 20 weeks are as follow:

Category	Standard No.of Labours	Standard Weekly Wage Rate Per Labour	Actual No. of Labours	Actual Weekly Wage Rate Per Labour
Skilled	60	40	70	45
	40	25	30	27

The work is actually completed in 24 weeks.

Calculate Labour variances.

39. The standard and actual Labour force required for completing a job taking four weeks periods is given as follows:

Category	Standard No.of Workers	Standard Weekly Rate (Rs.)	Actual No. of Workers	Actual Weekly Rate (Rs.)
Men workers	50	30	45	32
Women workers	40	30	48	33

Calculate

(i) Labour cost variance

(ii) Labour rate variance

(iii) Labour efficiency variance.

40. The standard cost for a product is :

Time 10 hours per unit,

Cost Rs. 5 per hour

The actual performance was:

Production	1,000 units
Hours taken for production	10,400 hours
Idle time	400 hours
Total time	10,800 hours

Payment made Rs.56, 160 @ Rs.5.20 per hour/.

Calculate Labour variance.

41. From the following records of the Gazal Company Ltd, you are required to calculate each of the three wages variances for the two divisions:

	Division-Good	Division-Worst
Direct wages (actual)	Rs.6,000	Rs.5,000
Standard hours produced	12,000	10,000
Standard rate per hour	60 paise	40 paise
Actual hours worked	7,500	6,500

42. The following figures are extracted from the books of a company; Input 300 units of material yield a standard output of 100 units, standard price per unit of material is Rs.10, Actual quantity of material issued and used by production department 30,000 units.

Actual price per unit of material is Rs.15

Actual output = 8,500 units

No. of employees engaged = 35; standard wage rate per employee per day–Rs.13

Standard daily output per employee 6 units

Total number of days actually worked = 45 days

Actual wage rate per day per employee = Rs.12.75

Work out variances.

43. The following data are taken from the books of Everest Company Ltd.

Standard

Material X, 50 units at Rs.14 per unit

Material Y, 40 units at Rs.13 per unit

200 Men @ Rs.12 per hour for 50 hours

130 women @ Re.10 per hour for 40 hours

Normal loss, 10 units

Actual

Material X, 52 units at Rs.13.50 per unit

Material Y, 36 units at Rs.13.50 per unit

210 Men @ Rs.12 per hour for 65 hours

100 women @ Rs.10.75 per hour for 45 hours

Actual loss, 7 units

Calculate material and labour variances.

44. From the following information of Zinnamin Zalin compute the variances related to fixed expenses:

	Budget	Actual
Units of production for month	10,000	11,500
No. of days worked in the month	24	26
Efficiency of Labour (%)	100	95
Fixed overhead for the month	20,000	22,500.

45. From the following records of the Beauty Ltd., you are required to compute fixed overhead expenditure and volume.

Fixed overhead budget for July	Rs.15,000
Budgeted production of the month	70,000 units
Actual production for the month	62,000 units
Actual fixed overhead incurred	Rs.14,500

46. Calculate various overhead variance from the below given information:

	Budget	Actual
Output (in units)	9000	12000
Number of working days	16	19

Fixed overheads	Rs.45,000	Rs.57,000
Variable overheads	Rs.32,000	Rs.36,000

There was an increase of 3 per cent in capacity.

47. From the following details compute the difference overhead variances:

Budgeted variable costs	Rs.20, 000
(for 80000 direct Labour hours)	
Budget fixed costs	Rs.40,000
Normal activity (direct Labour hour)	Rs.80,000
Actual hours worked	22,000
Standard hours	20,000
Actual variable overhead costs incurred	Rs. 5,100
Actual fixed overhead costs incurred	Rs. 9,800

48. The standard output per week in a factory is 4000 units but the actual output for the week was, 4800 units. Thc total ovcrhcad cxpcnscs for thc pcriod wcrc as follows:

	Actual (Rs.)	Budget (Rs.)
Fixed	1,800	1,600
Variable	1,000	1,000
Semi-variable	2,100	1,800

The overtime work done during the week was equal to one day's work. Semi-variable expenses are one-third fixed and tow-third variable. Find out the different variances.

49. The following table shows the budgeted and actual sales for a certain period in respect of two products. Compute appropriate sales variances:

		Standard		**Actual**
	Qty	**Price**	**Qty**	**Price**
Product	**(Units)**	**(Rs.)**	**(Unit)**	**(Rs.)**
BIG	6,000	7.00	7,000	10.00
SMALL	4,000	4.00	3,200	3.50

50. From the following budgeted and actual figures, calculate variances in respect of profit.

		Standard		**Actual**
	Qty	**Price**	**Qty**	**Price**
Product	**(Units)**	**(Rs.)**	**(Unit)**	**(Rs.)**
BIG	4,000	9.00	7,000	10.00
SMALL	7,000	12.00	5,500	9.50

51 Double Beauty Manufactures Ltd. has given the following budgeted and actual figures.

Budget	Rs.
Sales-4000 units @ Rs.10 each	40000
Cost of sales @ Rs.7 each	28000
Profit	12000
Actual	
Sales - 4500 units @ Rs.9 each	40,500
Cost of sales @ Rs.6 each	27,000
Profit	13,500

Calculate the variances in respect of profit, sale and cost of sales.

52. From the data given, calculate the material price variance material usage variance and material mix variance?

material		
A	40 units @ Rs.40 per unit.	50 units @ Rs.50 per unit
B	60 units @ Rs.40 per unit	60 units @ Rs. 45 per unit

53. Gonedays Ltd., produces two commodities, Goodlook and Betterlook, in one of its departments. Each unit takes 5 hrs and 10 hrs respectively as production time. 1000 units of Goodlook and 600 units of Betterlook were produced during March. Actual man-hours spent in this production were 10000. Yearly budgeted hours are 96000.

Compute the various control ratios.

54. From the following data, calculate activity ratio of Eisen Elegant Ltd. The company manufactures two products Alan and Balan. Standard time to manufacture product A is 2 hours and product B is 10 hours. The budgeted and actual production for a day were as follows:.

	Budgeted production	Actual production
Product Alan	125 units	100 units
Product Balan	30 units	24 units

Total hours worked were 660

CHAPTER 13

BUDGETARY CONTROL

Learning Objective

Budgeting is a technique of profit planning. Planning involves forecasting future and programming action to achieve targeted goal. Companies prepare separate budgets for revenue expenses and for capital investment. After reading the chapter, readers would be in a position to appreciate the importance of different types of budgets and the modes of budgetary control. Readers would also learn how to construct the budgets for an organization. highlights the need for standards, the effectiveness of standards and the control of cost.

These are days when all activities, whether that of individuals or organizations, are planned in advance before being carried out. Precise idea as to what to do, how to do, where to do when to do and by whom are hallmarks of success in business. This process of foreseeing things in advance is planning. All organizations irrespective of their size or nature of activities plan for creating production facilities, plan for production and sale of goods and services, plan for costs and plan for profit. Even governments carry out the budgeting exercise periodically. Planning for future is budgeting. Budgeting is planning and programming action to make use of resources, project ideas of people into the future and to look back and review the actual performance as compared to the intentions. When budgeting is for creating production facilities, it is ***capital budgeting.*** When the planning process is related to the carrying out of operations of an organization, it is ***revenue budgeting.*** We are confining ourselves to the second objective in this chapter. Capital budgeting would be dealt with in another chapter.

Budget, according to the Chartered Institute of Management Accountants, London "***is a quantitative financial statement prepared and approved prior to a period of time, of the policy to be pursued during the period for the purpose of attaining the objective***". The objective, as we have seen, might be to set up production facilities or for achieving operational goals. Budget is the plan and budgeting is the process of establishing budgets relating to the responsibilities of executives to the requirements of a policy and the continuous comparison of actual results with budgeted targets either to secure, by individual action, the objective of that policy or to provide basis for its revision. In essence, budgeting is establishment of objectives, chalking out ways and means of achieving the set objective through continuous follow up, comparison of achievements at every stage with the aspirations so that the objective could be fulfilled as per design. It is the expression of management, in financial terms, of the plans to operate and finance the activities of the business during a specified period. Budget is an essential technique of management to keep the costs under control with the objective of maximizing returns.

Budgets are usually referred to as budgetary control technique. CIMA has defines budgetary control as ***"the establishment of budgets relating to the responsibilities of executives to the requirements of a policy and the continuous comparison of actual with budgeted results, either to secure by individual action the objective of that policy or to provide a basis for its revision".*** This definition of budgetary control has brought to light the essential features of an effective budgetary control system. The salient features are

- *establishment of a policy*
- *responsibilities of executives to the fulfillment of the policy*
- *continuous comparison*
- *achieving the objective or*
- *providing a basis for revision.*

The basic work on budget starts with the establishment of a policy or objective. In establishing the objective the management should take into account its strengths and weaknesses, its past performance and cause as realistic a forecast as possible. The goals to be set should be achievable. After establishing the goal, the part to be played by each executive in implementing the plan has to be assigned. The success of a budgetary control depends to a larger extent on the participation, involvement and commitment of all sections of the orgamization. Each should know what his or her part in the exercise is and should involve whole-heartedly in the preparation and execution of the budget. It is for this reason that recent management practices entrust a major role to the employees even at the stage of preparation of budgets. Many companies have budget manuals, where the responsibilities of all concerned are well defined, so that there would be complete coordination.

Success in budgeting depends to a larger extent on continuous follow up. There should be as frequent reviews of actual with targets as possible. It would make corrections easier if problems are identified at the initial stage itself. With the advancement in information technology, frequency in periods of reviews is shortened. The results of the comparison should immediately be communicated to the authorities for timely corrective measures.

Budgeting is an effective way of controlling costs. Control, as the word implies, is to see that things happen within the cost envisaged. Robert N Anthony, a well-known authority on management accounting, had defined the term control as "***the process by which managers assure that resources are obtained and used effectively and efficiently in the accomplishment of the organization's goals***". Control presupposes planning. Planning starts with forecasting .It is therefore the chain action of forecasting, planning, organizing and controlling that makes cost controls. In short, budgeting is the application of the principles of management to the area of cost control.

A good budgeting technique needs a well defined and documented ***budget manual***. The budget manual would lay down the periodicity and the process of budgeting, the format, the responsibility of the participants and the review. Period of budgets are another area of consideration. Budgets could be long-term or short-term depending upon their purpose. Strategic budgeting is long-term and provides a general future pattern to be followed by the business. Capital budgeting is also long-term. Long-term budgets are not effective as forecasting for a long period becomes more uncertain and unreliable. Short-term budgets are more likely to be achieved and hence are more important. All revenue budgets are short term in nature. Current developments in information technology have made the process of short-term budgeting less laborious. Large companies have daily budgets for cash.

For effective implementation of budgets, the ***organizational structure*** of the business should be conducive. A well-knit organization is a pre-requisite for the success of budgetary control. Flow of authority and chain of accountability of the management cadres are to be defined clearly. There should not be any ambiguity about the role of an executive. Similarly, joint authority should be avoided as it would bug pass the accountability and defeat the very objective of planned development. Usually, the full responsibility for the budget rests on the chief executive of the company. A Budget Controller or Budget Director assists him. A Budget Committee assists the Budget Controller. Budget Committee comprises the heads of all functional departments and a few experts, when needed, from outside. The Budget Controller heads the Committee.

Budgeting Process

Budgeting process begins for many organizations much before the budget period and ends only after the budget period is over. Or in other words, while a budget is still on the next budget gets ready and the process becomes continuous. The first step in budgeting is to identify the *key factor* or the limiting factor and the preparation of the key budget. CIMA says that "*anything that limits the activity of an entity. Examples are shortage of supply of a resource and restriction on sales*". Key budget would be the core for other budgets. Key factor is the single most important activity of a company, around which all other operations revolve. It is the vulnerable area of operation of the business. For many products such as consumer durables, fast moving consumer goods, textiles, iron and steel, capital equipment, etc., the key factor is market. If the extent of market for the product is fairly forecast, other operations are matters of details. So the core budget of the company would be sales budget. In certain other companies, the key factor is production. Marketing is no constraint. The company could sell any quantity it produces. In such cases, production budget is the key budget. Yet in certain other cases, availability of raw material is the key issue. Production and sales are no constraints. Cement and oil are examples. Materials budget in such cases is the starting point from other budgets emanate. Availability and mobility of skilled labour is also a key factor for certain highly technically oriented products. For example, electro optics products need skilled labour. Marble carving technicians are concentrated in Agra and silk weaving skilled labour in Kancheepuram and Mysore.These labour are less mobile. Cheap technical labour is the need for information technology based industries. Hence, in the production of these goods and services, key budget would be that of labour.

The next step in budgeting is to estimate the extent of market for the products and the availability of factors of production. Forecasting techniques are highly developed with the help of information technology. Still, future being uncertain, forecasting becomes highly risky. A forecast is the expectation of certain things to happen. According to CIMA, forecast is "***a statement of probable events***". The probable events depend upon the intention of the government and the people. What are the expected governmental expenditures that would create demands for the products of the concerned business? What plans the government has to promote economic development of the country? This question would bring out the likely demand that would be created by the governmental planning. But the most important factor is the spending intention of individuals and organizations and the extent to which they would adhere to the intention. These are assessed through surveys of intentions.

As we are living in a decentralized economy, where economic decisions are taken by individuals and entities (and not dictated to them by authorities, as in totalitarian states), a ***survey of intentions or marketing survey*** should be based on elaborate statistical sampling process. This is done through a detailed questionnaire. Care should be taken while carrying out the intention survey. The sample size and spread should be adequate to represent the target group. And the results of the survey are to be moderated to the extent of likely changes in the intention of consumers. Changes in GDP, per capita income, taste and fashion are some of the factors that could affect the intentions of customers.

The next stage in budgeting process is the preparation for budget. It is not necessary that each organization would prepare a single budget for the business entity and within the entity a number of sectional budgets. For this purpose, the organization is divided into budget centers. CIMA has defined a budget center as " a section of an entity for which control may be exercised and budget prepared".

Kinds of Budgets

Different kinds of budgets are prepared for different activities of the company. Budgets could be classified according to function and nature.

Budgets according to functions are:

- *Sales budget,*
- *Production budget,*
- *Cost (of production) budget,*
- *Materials usage budget,*
- *Materials purchase budget,*
- *Personnel budget or Labour budget,*
- *Research and development budget,*
- *Cash budget and*
- *Master budget.*
- *Capital Expenditure budget,*

Budgets according to nature are:

- *Fixed budget and*
- *Flexible budget.*

Sales Budget

With globalization looming large over the world, it is sales that is the core activity of organizations. Most of the organizations start with sales budget as their key budget. Sales budget contains the forecast sale of the business over a year, on a monthly basis. The area of sales is segmented geographically into regions-wise or state-wise. Demographically, it is divided into male and female or age wise into children, adolescent, adults and aged. Sales budget could also be segmented into domestic and exports. Sales for each segment is provided by the sales manager based on the surveys and feed back of the sales force. The budget would contain the quantity of the products proposed to be sold and the value. Separate sales budget could be prepared for each product or columnar budget for all products. A proforma sales budget for a single product is in Table 1.

Table 1
XYZ L Ltd.
Proforma Sales Budget for 6 months.

Period	Zone 1		Zone 2		Zone 3		Total		Previous (actual)	
	Qty	Value	Qty.	Value	Qty	Value	Qty	Value	Qty	Value
January										
February										
March										
April										
May										
June										
Total										
Less:										
Selling expenses										
Net Sales										

Let us prepare a sales budget for Andres Antibiotics Ltd., which produces and sells its product "Andambioles" in packs in the southern states. The company has projected sales for 6 months from July to December on the basis of data furnished by the marketing manager in table 2

Table 2
Sales forecast of Andres Antibiotics Ltd. for July to December.

Andhra pradesh-	July	August	Sept.em	Oct.	Nov.	Dec.
Quantity-packs	1100	1200	1300	1150	1250	1350
Rate-Rs	1250	1250	1250	1250	1250	1250
Sales exp.	2.5%	2.5%	2.5%	2.5%	2.5%	2.5%
Karnataka- packs						
Quantity	1050	1100	1150	1200	1075	1125
Rate-Rs	1225	1225	1225	1225	1225	1225
Sales expenses.	2.75%	2.75%	2.75%	2.75%	2.75%	2.75%
Kerala- packs						
Quantity	950	975	1025	1000	1050	1075

Rate-Rs	1275	1275	1275	1275	1275	1275
Sales exp.	2.5%	2.5%	2.5%	2.5%	2.5%	2.5%
Tamil Nadu- packs						
Quantity	1225	1275	1325	1350	1375	1350
Rate-Rs	1250	1250	1250	1250	1250	1250
Sales exp.	2.25%	2.25%	2.25%	2.25%	2.25%	2.25%

Table 3
Andres Antibiotics Ltd.
Sales Budget for Andambioles in packs **(Rs.lakhs)**

Period	Andhra pradesh		Karnataka		Kerala		Tamilnadu		Total	
	Qty	Value	Qty.	Value	Qty	Value	Qty	Value	Qty	Value
July	1100	13.75	1050	12.862	950	12.112	1225	15.132	4325	53.856
August	1200	15.00	1100	13.475	975	12.431	1275	15.937	4550	56.843
Sept.	1300	16.250	1150	13.087	1025	13.069	1325	16.562	4800	59.968
October	1150	13.375	1200	13.700	1000	12.750	1350	16.875	4700	58.700
Nov.	1250	15.625	1075	13.169	1050	13.387	1375	17.187	4750	59.368
Dec.	1350	16.875	1125	13.781	1075	13.706	1350	16.875	4900	61.237
Total	7350	91.875	6700	82.074	6075	77.455	7900	98.568	28025	349.972
Less: Sales expense		2.297		2.257		1.742		2.464		8.760
Net Sales		89.578		79.817		75.713		96.104		341.212

Responsibility for the sales budget squarely rests with the marketing manager. This leads in some cases to under estimation of sales to avoid responsibility. In corporate governance, it is the duty of every manager to undertake such tasks as would increase the wealth of the firm. It is for the CEO to counter check with sales personnel whether the forecast sales are optimal.

Production Budget

Production budget follows from sales budget. It is the quantity proposed to be sold during a period and the stock level to be maintained at the end of the period that determines the output of a company. Sales plus closing stock less opening stock is the quantity to be produced. How ever, in the case of work in process, the semi-finished units are converted to their equivalent of finished goods, as we have done in process costing. (To recall, suppose a unit has work in process of 2400 units.800 units in first process line with 40% completed, another 800 units in second process with 60% complete and the balance in third process line with 80% complete. The equivalent finished units of the work in process would be 800 × 40% +800 × 60% +800 × 80% = 1440 finished units). Usually production budgets are quantitative in nature, as financial budgets for each of the components of production, namely materials, labour and expenses are to be prepared separately. Before commencing preparation of production budget, two things are to be made clear-quantity to be sold period-wise and the level of closing stock to be maintained at each of the stages. Proforma production budget is in Table 4.

Table 4
Proforma Production Budget- (Product-wise)

		Finished goods		WIP equal to finished units.			
(1)	(2) For sales	(3) Closing stock (+)	(4) Opening stock (–)	(5) Closing stock (+)	(6) Opening stock (–)	(7) Total production	(8) Prev. year
January							
February							
March							
April							
May							
June							

To follow the example of Andres Antibiotics Ltd., suppose the closing stock of Andambioles packs for a month is 25% percent of the sales of the month, the work in process (60% complete) is 7.5% of sales of the month then the production budget for the company for the six-month would be as in Table 5. Sales for June were 4275 packs.

Table 5
Andres Antibiotics Ltd.
Production Budget for Andambioles

		Finished goods-packs.		WIP equivalent to finished units.			
(1)	(2) For sales	(3) Closg. stock (+)	(4) Opening stock (–)	(5) Closing stock (+)	(6) Open. stock (–)	(7) Total prodn.	(8) Previous year
July	4325	1081	1069	195	192	4340	4360
August	4550	1137	1081	205	195	4616	4710

Sept.	4800	137	1137	216	205	4874	4779
October	4700	1175	1200	211	216	4670	4590
Novem	4750	1187	1175	214	211	4765	4725
Decem.	4900	1225	1187	220	214	4944	4977
Total	28025					28,209	28,141

The company would have to organize for the production of 28,209 pack of Andambioles for the half year on a monthly basis. The production budget would form the basis for cost of production budgets.

Materials Budget

Once the production budget is ready, it would be the endeavour of the businessman to budget for the cost of production. Since cost of production involves materials, labour and overheads, the next step in budgeting process is to prepare separate budgets for the different costs. Materials might be direct or indirect. Whatever be the nature of materials, separate budgets are to be prepared for each material. A proforma of materials purchase budget is given below.

Table 6
Proforma Materials Purchase Budget.

	For Material .X					**Total**	**Rate**	**Total**
	For production			**Closing stock**	**Opening stock**	**Requirement**	**per unit of**	**Cost- Rs.**
Months	**Production**	**Requirement**					**material**	
(1)	**units. (2)**	**Per unit (3)**	**Total (4)**	**(5)**	**(6)**	**(4+5-6) (7)**	**(Rs) (8)**	**(7 × 8) (9)**
January								
February								
March								
April								
May								
June								
Total								

Andres Antibiotics Ltd. is using two materials for its product Andambioles-Amb and Ole. For a pack of Andambioles, the company requires 200 grammes of Amb and 300 grammes of Ole. The company maintains 3 months material requirement for production as its stock. The closing stock of materials at the end of June were 2565Kg. of Amb and 3847.5 Kg. of Ole. The cost per Kg. of Amb was Rs.34.50 and Ole Rs.29.25. The material requirement budgets for the materials would be as in the following tables.

Table 7
Andres Antibiotics Ltd.
Materials Purchase Budget for Amb.

Months	For Material .Amb. For production Production-packs	Requirement -Kg. Perpack	Requirement -Kg. Total	Closing stock (+)	Opening stock (–)	Total Requirement In Kg. (4+5-6)	Rate per unit of (Rs)	Total Cost- (7 × 8)
(1)	(2)	(3)	(4)	(5)	(6)	(7)	(8)	(9)
July	4340	0.200	868	2604	2565	907	34.50	31,291
August	4616	0.200	923.2	2769.6	2604	1088.8	34.50	37,564
September	4874	0.200	974.8	2924.4	2769.6	1129.6	34.50	38,971
October	4670	0.200	934	2802	2924.4	811.6	34.50	28,000
November	4765	0.200	953	2859	2802	1010	34.50	34,845
December	4944	0.200	988.8	2966.4	2859	1096.2	34.50	37,818
Total	28,209		5641.8			6043.2		2,08,490

Table 8
Andres Antibiotics Ltd.
Materials Purchase Budget for Ole.

Months	For Material .Amb. For production Production-packs	Requirement -Kg. Perpack	Requirement -Kg. Total	Closing stock (+)	Opening stock (–)	Total Requirement In Kg. (4+5-6)	Rate per unit of material (Rs)	Total Cost- Rs. (7 × 8)
(1)	(2)	(3)	(4)	(5)	(6)	(7)	(8)	(9)
July	4340	0.300	1302	3906	3847.5	1360.5	29.25	39,795
August	4616	0.300	1384.8	4154.4	3906	1633.2	29.25	47,771
September	4874	0.300	1462.2	4386.6	4153.4	1695.4	29.25	49,590
October	4670	0.300	1401	4203	4386.6	1217.4	29.25	28,000
November	4765	0.300	1429.5	4288.5	4203	1515	29.25	34,845
December	4944	0.300	1483.2	4449.6	4288.5	1644.3	29.25	37,818
Total	28,209		8462.7			9065.8		2,08,490

Labour Budget

After budgeting for materials, the extent and the category of labour needed to produce the budgeted quantity of goods are to be planned. Labour budget or personnel budget budgets for the number of man-hours needed for each category of labour, both direct and indirect. The company usually sets up standards for the man-hour for different types of labour needed to carry out the budgeted production and the rates thereof. A company, depending on its size, might prepare a man power requirement budget for the period and then labour cost budget for direct labour and indirect labour, as the quality and pay of the two differ. While setting up standard time for each worker, reasonable allowances for fatigue, rest, break etc have to be taken into account. A proforma of personnel budget is furnished in the table below.

Table 9
Proforma Personnel Budget(labour budget)

Production:	**Man hours for budgeted production**		**Hrs. per Worker**	**No. of personnel** ×	**Standard rate per hour-Rs.**	**Total cost Rs.**
	Standard hourperunit of output.	**Total hours**				
For production 1.Direct labor Skilled Semi-skilled Unskilled 2. Indirect Labour Skilled Semi-skilled Unskilled Total For operations 1. Administration -grade wise 2. Selling and distribution -grade wise 3.Research and Development -grade wise hours per day.						

Let us continue with the example of Andres Antibiotics Ltd. The budgeted production requires the following types of labour at rates mentioned there against. The company on an average works single shift for 20 days a month. The requirement for man-hours for production had been worked out by the works manager and the operations managers of company.

Table 10
Andres Antibiotics Ltd.

	Skilled	**Semi-skilled**	**Unskilled**
For production per 10 packs			
Andambioles			
Direct labour hours	3	4	2
Direct labour rate per hour	Rs.100	Rs.75	Rs.40
Indirect labour hours	2	1	1
Indirect labour rate per hour	Rs. 80	Rs.50	Rs.30

The requirements for administration and selling were

Administration	Skilled	Semi-skilled	Unskilled
	General Manager–1	Asst. managers–2	Messengers–2
Rate per month	Rs.25,000	Rs.8,000	Rs.3,000
Accounting	Accountant–1	Asst. accountant-1	—
Rate per month	Rs.15,000	Rs.10,000	—
Finance	—	Cashier –1	—
Rate per month		Rs.10,000	—
Selling and distribution	Salesmanager – 1	Sales reps–6	Helper –1
Rate per month	Rs.20,000	Rs.7,000	Rs.3,000
Research&development	Analyst– 1	Lab.Assistants – 2	—
Rate per month	Rs.15,000	Rs.6,000	—

Personnel budget for the company for its targeted production, based on its requirement given in table 13.10, would be as in table 11 below. Details are made for July and consolidated for the six months.

Table 11
Andres Antibiotics Ltd.
Personnel Budget(labour budget) for 6 months

	Man hours for budgeted productn.		Per day	No. oF		Stand-ard rate per hour Rs.	Total cost Rs.
	Std per 10 packs.	Total hours		Man-days	Men× Per month		
For production							
July-4340							
Direct labor							
Skilled	3	1302	8	162.7	8.14 or 9	100	1,30,200
Semi-skilled	4	1736	8	5	10.85 or11	75	1,30,200
Unskilled	2	868	8	217	5.42 or 6	40	34,720
Total				108.5			2,95,120
. Indirect Lab							
Skilled	2	868	8		5.42 or 6	80	69,440
Semi-skilled	1	434	8	108.5	2.71 or 3	50	21,700
Unskilled	1	434	8	54.25	2.71 or 3	30	13,020
Total				54.25			1,04,160
For operations							
Administration					1	25,000	25,000
General Mgr.					2	8,000	16,000
Asst.managers					1	20,000	20,000
Accountant					1	10,000	10,000
Asst accountant					1	10,000	10,000
Cashier					2	3,000	6,000
Messengers							87,000
Total							
2. Selling and							
distribution							
Manager					1	20,000	20,000
Sales					6	7,000	42,000
representatives					1	3,000	3,000
Helper							65,000
3.Research and							
Development					1	15,000	15,000
Analyst					2	6,000	12,000
Lab. Assistants							27,000
Total							5,78,280

Grand total							
For 6 months							
1.Direct labor							
Skilled	3	8462.7	8		8.82or 9	100	Rs.8,46,270
Semi-skilled	4	11283.6	8	1057.	11.75or 12	75	Rs.8,46,270
Unskilled	2	5641.8	8	8	5.88 or 6	40	Rs.19,18,212
Total				1410.			
2.Indirect				5			
Labour							
Skilled	2	5641.8	8	705.2	5.88 or 6	80	Rs. 4,51,344
Semi-skilled	1	2820.9	8	3	2.94 or 3	50	Rs. 1,41,045
Unskilled	1	2820.9	8		2.94 or 3	30	Rs. 84,627
Total							Rs. 6,77,016
For operations							
1. Admin.							
General				705.2	1	25,000	Rs. 1,50,000
Manager							
Ass. managers				3	2	8,000	Rs. 96,000
Accountant				352.6	1	20,000	Rs. 1,20,000
Asst. accountant				1	1	10,000	Rs. 60,000
Cashier				352.6	1	10,000	Rs. 60.000
Messengers				1	2	3,000	Rs. 36,000
Total							Rs. 5,22,000
2. Selling and							
distribution							
Manager					1	20,000	Rs.1,20,000
Salesrep.					6	7,000	Rs.2,52,000
Helper.					1	3,000	Rs. 18,000
Total							Rs.3,90,000
3.R &D							
Analyst					1	15,000	Rs. 90,000
Lab. Assistants					2	6,000	Rs. 72,000
Total							Rs.1,62,000
Grand total							Rs.36,69,228
× On the basis that one day rest for 6 days' work of 8hours/day.							

The above is a combined labour budget covering all operations. Although human resources management department of a company recruits personnel for both direct and indirect labour, companies, depending upon their scale of operation do prepare separate budgets for direct labour and indirect labour some times department-wise or process-wise

Overheads, as we have seen in costing, are divided into variable and fixed, depending up on their reaction to production. If they respond to the level of production, we call them as variable. If they are insensitive to the level of operation, we call them fixed. Variable costs are therefore estimated as per direct man-hour worked, while fixed costs are same for the period, as they remain constant irrespective of scale of operation. Corporates prepare manufacturing overheads budget, maintenance overheads budget, administrative overheads budget and selling and distribution overhead budget Manufacturing overhead budget is the most important among overheads budgets. A proforma of manufacturing budget is in Table 12.

Table 12
Overheads Budget for (Period).

	Man hour	**Rate per hour-Rs.**	**Total cost-Rs.**
Variable overheads.			
Indirect Material			
Indirect Labour			
Power, fuel and others inputs.			
Fixed overheads.			
Depreciation.			
Insurance.			
Salaries .			
Electricity and lighting			
Repairs and maintenance			

In Andres Antibiotics Ltd., variable overheads standard rate was Rs. 6.50 per labour hour for indirect materials and Rs. 8.25 for power and fuel. Depreciation for the year on plant and machinery was Rs.6,38,450, factory building Rs.48,430,office equipment Rs 14,750, office buildings Rs 21,375,factory insurance Rs.37,897, office insurance Rs. 14,249,salaries for administrative staff, Including managing director, Rs.1,76,370, selling and distribution staff Rs.1,38,590, electricity and lighting Rs.75,987 and repairs and maintenance Rs.1,23,450.

Table 13
Andres Antibiotics Ltd
Overheads Budget forJuly and six months July to December

	Man hour	Rate per hour-Rs.	Total cost-Rs.
Variable overheads.			
For July-Production.4340 packs			
Indirect Material	3906	6.50	25,389
Indirect Labour			
Skilled	868	80.00	69,440
Semi-skilled	434	50.00	21,700
Unskilled	434	30.00	13,020
Power, fuel and others inputs.	3906	8.25	32,225
Total - A			1,61,774
Fixed ovrheads.			
Depreciation.			
Plant and machinery			1,06,408
Factory buildings			8,072
Office equipment			2,458
Office building			3,562
Total - B			1,20,500
Insurance.			6,317
Factory			2,375
Office			8,692
Total - C			
Salaries .			87,000
Administrative			65,000
Selling and distribution			27,000
Research and development			1,79,000
Total -D			12,665
Electricity and lighting			20,575
Repairs and maintenance			33,240
Total - E			5,03,206
Grand total (A+B+C+D+E)			
For 6 months			
Indirect Material	25388.1	6.50	1,65,023
Indirect Labour			
Skilled	5641.8	80.00	4,51,344
Semi-skilled	2820.9	50.00	1,41,045
Unskilled	2820.9	30.00	84,627
Power, fuel and others inputs.	25388.1	8.25	2,09,452

Total -A			10,51,491
Fixed overheads.			
Depreciation.			
Plant and machinery			6,38,450
Factory buildings			48,430
Office equipment			14,750
Office building			21,375
Total - B			7,23,005
Insurance			
Factory			37,897
Office			14,249
Total - C			52,146
Salaries .			
Administrative			5,22,000
Selling and distribution			3,90,000
Research and development			1,62,000
Total - D			10,74,000
Electricity and lighting			75,987
Repairs and maintenance			1,23,450
Total - E			1,99,437
Grand total(A+B+C+D+E)			31,00,079

The next crucial budget for a company would be its cash budget. Cash budget is estimated cash flow. It outlines the various sources and uses of funds during a period. The period could be anything from a month to six months. With computer facilities being freely used in accounting, cash budgets could also be prepared on a day-to-day basis. Usually a six-month budget is prepared and within the over all budget, cash budgets are prepared for shorter periods. As liquidity is the hallmarks of a company's standing in the market, great care should be taken in preparing cash budgets. A proforma of a cash budget for six months is in Table 14

Table 14
Cash Budget. for 6 months)

	January	**February**	**March**	**April**	**May**	**June**
1. Receipts. Revenue receipts Capital receipts						
Total						
2.Payments. Revenue payments Capital payments						

Total						
Surplus/deficit(1–2) Add Opening balance Closing balance of cash Safety level cash						
Borrowings/investment s						

Cash budget enables a company to anticipate any shortage in cash well in advance and to arrange for the same to avoid embarrassing situations. Similarly it allows the company to plan for short-term investments in case of surpluses. Usually, every company keeps a minimum cash level to meet eventualities. Expected cash position in excess of the safety levels, are invested in marketable securities. In Andres Antibiotics Ltd. the sales budget of the company reveals the expected sales during the six month of July to December. The company sells 40% for cash and the balance for credit of one month. It is the past record of the company that 80% of its debtors pay in the next month and another 18% in the month after. 2% becomes bad. The company also enjoys credit purchases of one month. Wages and salaries are paid by 7th. of the next month. Wages for June to be paid in July were Rs.2.85 lakhs. Interest on bank borrowings at Rs.1.29 lakhs monthly. The company has to pay installments of Rs.35.00lakhs to bank during September and December. Dividend payable in July Rs.45lakhs Advance tax of Rs.12.50lakhs payable in September and December. The company has to pay unsecured loans of Rs.25.00 lakhs in October. Sales of the company for the months of May and June were Rs.50.654 lakhs and Rs. 51.678 lakhs respectively. Purchases of materials for June were Rs.37,247.The company proposes to raise additional capital of Rs.50 lakhs in November. Issue costs are expected to be 10% of issue. Investments in expansion were Rs.60 lakhs in November and Rs.38 lakhs in December. Opening balance of cash was Rs.21.35 lakhs. Minimum safety level of cash balance to be maintained is Rs.15 lakhs.

One can prepare a cash budget for the six months on the basis of the above information. Before taking up the cash budget, certain preparations become necessary. First, we have to estimate month-wise receipt on account of sales made. Please see table below.

Table 15

Calculation of month-wise sales realization **Rs.**

Months	**July**	**August**	**Sept.**	**Oct.**	**Nov.**	**Dec.**
Sales	53.856	56.843	59.968	58.700	59.368	61.237
Cash sales (40%)	21.542	22.737	23.987	23.480	23.747	24.495
Debtor's Realization of		—	—			

May sales[1]	5.471					
Debtor's Realization of					—	
June sales[2]	24.805	5.581			—	
Debtor's Realization of	—					—
July sales[3]	—	25.851	5.816			
Debtor's Realization of	—	—				
August sales[4]	—	—	27.285	6.139		
Debtor's Realization of	—	—	—			
September sales[5]		—	—	28.785	6.477	
Debtor's Realization of			—	—		
October sales[6]				—	28.176	6.340
Debtor's Realization of					—	
November sales [7]						28.497
Total sales realization	51.818	54.169	57.088	58.404	58.400	59.332

Note.

[1] Credit Sales for May was 60% of Rs. 50.654 =Rs.30.392.Of this. 80% would nave been realized in June .For July. realization would be 18% of credit sales. =Rs.5471.

[2] Credit sales for June =60% of Rs. 51.678=Rs.31.007.July realization is 80% of Rs.31.007 = Rs.24.806.August realization is 18% of Rs.31.007 = Rs.5.581.

[3] Credit sales for July is Rs.32.313. Of this realization in August is 80% = Rs.25.851 and September is 18% = Rs.5.816.

[4] Credit sales for August is Rs.34.106.Of this realizations in September and October are Rs.27.285 and Rs.6.139 respectively.

[5] Credit sales for September is Rs.35.981. Of this realization are Rs.28.785 and Rs.6.477 for October and November.

[6] Credit sales for October is Rs.35.220. Realization for November and December would be Rs.28.176 and Rs. 6.340.

[7] Credit sales for November is Rs.35.621. Realization for December would be Rs.28.497.(Note:Rs. are in lakhs)

The arranging of sources and uses of funds in the proforma would give cash budget month-wise for July to December as in Table 16.

Table 16
Andres Antibiotics Ltd
Cash Budget for July to December

	July	August	Sept.	Oct.	Nov.	Dec.
1.Receipts.						
Sales realization	51.82	54.17	57.09	58.40	58.40	59.33
Shares issue					50.00	
Total	51.82	54.17	57.09	58.40	108.40	59.33
2.Payments.						
Creditors for purchases	0.37	0.40	0.48	0.50	0.36	0.44
Wages1	2.85	2.95	3.14	3.32	3.18	3.24
FactoryOH.Variable2	1.62	1.72	1.82	1.74	1.78	1.85
Factory overheads-Fixed	0.42	0.42	0.42	0.42	0.42	0.42
Administrative overheads	0.87	0.87	0.87	0.87	0.87	0.87
Sellinganddistribution OH	0.65	0.65	0.65	0.65	0.65	0.65
Research and development	0.27	0.27	0.27	0.27	0.27	0.27
Interest	1.29	1.29	1.29	1.29	1.29	1.29
Dividend	45.00	—	—	—	—	—
Advance tax	—	—	12.50	—	—	12.50
Installments	—	—	35.00	—	—	35.00
Repayment of loans	—	—	—	25.00	—	—
Issue expenses	—	—	—	—	5.00	—
Capital investments	—	—	—	—	60.00	38.00
Total	53.34	8.57	56.44	34.06-	73.82	94.53
Surplus/deficit cash(1–2)	–1.52	45.60	0.65	24.34	34.58	–35.20
Add Opening balance	21.35	15.00	15.00	15.00	15.00	15.00
Closing balance of cash	19.83	60.60	15.65	39.34	49.58	–20.20
Safety level cash	15.00	15.00	15.00	15.00	15.00	15.00
Borrowings (+) or	—	—	—	—	—	
Investments (–).	–4.54	–45.60	–0.65	–24.34	–34.58	+35.20

Master Budget

All the functional budgets, when combined into a comprehensive one, is the ***master budget***. Master budget, in essence, is the projected operating statement of the company. It tells what the results of the future operations are planned to be. Proforma for a master budget is given in table below.

Table 17
Master Budget for the period ending 31.03.2005

	January		February		For the period	
	Budgeted	**Previous period**	**Budget**	**Previous period**	**Budget**	**Previous period**
Previous period						
Less: Purchase as per materials budget.						
Direct labour as per direct labour budget.						
Gross profit						
Less						
Factory overheads-variable						
Repairs and maintenance						
Factory overheads-fixed						
Research and development expenses						
Administrative overheads						
Selling and distribution overheads						
Operating profit						

Master budget for Andres Antibiotics Ltd. for July and for six months, July to December is furnished in Table 18.

Table 18
Andres Antibiotics Ltd.
Master budget for July and July to December

	July	**July-December**	**Previous period**
1.Sales as per sales budget	53.86	349.97	51.62
Less: Purchase as per materials budget.	0.40	2.65	2.53
Direct labour as per direct labour budget.	2.95	19.18	18.96
Factory overheads-variable			
Indirect materials	0.25	1.65	1.57
Indirect labour	1.04	6.77	6.55
Power and fuel	0.32	2.09	2.19
Factory overheads-fixed			

Repairs and maintenance	0.20	1.23	1.24
Electricity and lighting	0.13	0.76	0.73
Research and development expenses	0.27	1.62	1.84
Depreciation-Plant, machinery & building	1.14	6.87	6.66
Insurance-factory	0.06	0.38	0.38
2.Works cost	6.76	43.20	
Gross profit (1 – 2)	47.10	306.77	
Less:			
Administrative overheads-salaries	0.87	5.22	5.11
Depreciation	0.06	0.36	0.36
Insurance	0.02	0.14	0.14
Selling and distribution salaries	0.65	3.90	3.88
Selling expenses	2.30	8.76	8.98
3.Operating expenses	3.90	18.38	
4.Operating profit (2 – 3)	43.18	288.39	

The budgets we had so far discussed are fixed for a period. Companies forecast sales for the period and based on the projected sales prepare production, materials, labour, overheads and cash budgets. This method is ***fixed budgeting***. It does not allow the company manourability in case the targeted sales do not materialize. Projections change due to uncertainty of markets, change in tastes, fashion and mobility of people, availability of materials etc., which are beyond the control of the company. Companies cannot afford the luxury of revising the budgets at every stage of variation in projections to actual. As a safeguard against such eventualities, a budget, which varies with changes, is required. Hence the evolution of ***flexible budgeting***. CIMA has defined a flexible budget as "a budget designed to change in accordance with the level of activity actually attained". In essence, a flexible budget is one that provides alternatives to management in cases of actual performance deviating from projected due to causes outside management control.

There are different methods of preparing flexible budgets. But the crux of flexible budget preparation is the use of marginal costing concept in budgeting. Costs are classified into fixed and variable. Then depending up on the different levels of operation, variable costs are allocated. Fixed costs do not undergo change due to changes in the levels of activities. Flexible budgets allow managements to change their course of action without much disturbance. It is a tool to take care of exigencies, without again going through the pangs of budget preparation. Flexible budgets are prepared for the consolidated activities of an organization. Functional budgets are adjusted according to the alternative chosen. A simple format for preparing flexible budget is in the following table.

Table 19
Proforma flexible budget

	Levels of activities			
	Planned	Alternatives		
	80%	90%	70%	60%
Sales - units				
1.Sales - value				
2.Direct materials				
3.Direct labour				
4.Factory overheads-variable				
5.Factory overheads-fixed				
6Works cost(2+3+4+5)				
7.Gross profit (1 – 6)				
8.Administrativeoverheads-variable				
9.Administrative overheads-fixed				
10.Selling and distribution-variable				
11.Selling and distribution-fixed				
12..Operating cost (8+9+10+11)				
13.Operating profit (7 – 12)				

Let us apply the concept of flexible budgets to Andres Antibiotics Ltd. for its fixed budget given in table 18.The company's projected sales were for 70% of its capacity. Considering alternatives of 80%, 60% and 50%, flexible budget is prepared and presented in table 20.

Table 20
Andres Antibiotics Ltd.
Flexible budget for 6 months-July to December

	Planned	Alternatives		
Capacity	70%	80%	60%	50%
1. Sales	349.97	399.97	299.97	249.97
Direct materials	2.65	3.03	2.27	1.89
Direct labour.	19.18	21.92	16.44	13.70
Factory overheads-variable				
Indirect materials	1.65	1.89	1.41	1.18
Indirect labour	6.77	7.74	5.80	4.84
Power and fuel	2.09	2.39	1.79	1.49

Factory overheads-fixed				
Repairs and maintenance	1.23	1.23	1.23	1.23
Electricity and lighting	0.76	0.76	0.76	0.76
Research and development expenses	1.62	1.62	1.62	1.62
Depreciation-Plant and machinery				
and building	6.87	6.87	6.87	6.87
Insurance-factory	0.38	0.38	0.38	0.38
2. Works cost	43.20	47.45	38.57	33.96
3. Gross profit (1 – 2)	306.77	352.52	261.40	216.01
Administrative overheads-salaries	5.22	5.22	5.22	5.22
Depreciation	0.36	0.36	0.36	0.36
Insurance	0.14	0.14	0.14	0.14
Selling and distribution staff	3.90	3.90	3.90	3.90
salariesSelling expenses	8.76	10.00	7.50	6.25
4. Operating expenses	18.38	19.62	17.12	15.87
5. Operating profit (3 – 4)	288.39	332.90	244.28	200.14

Performance Budgeting

Yet another macro level budget is ***performance budgeting.*** It is a measure of the level of performance of the organization vis-à-vis the specific goals and overall objectives of the business. Performance reports are prepared by various functional heads and consolidated. The first step is to prepare the actual performance of the company and compare the results with budget and present the deviation to the management. The performance is compared with the master budget. As an example, Goner Ltd., budgets to sell 10,000 units of FF2 for the month of June at a selling price of Rs.90 per unit. Standard cost of material per unit of output is Rs.30, standard operating cost is Rs.3.5 lakhs and standard fixed cost Rs.2 lakhs. Due to shortage of material, only 8000 units could be sold. Material cost increased to Rs.40 per unit but sales price could not be increased due to heavy competition. Other costs remain unchanged. A performance budget for the company under these situations would appear as in Table 21.

Table 21
Performance budget for Goner Ltd. for June

	Budgeted	**Performance**
Sales– units	10,000	8,000
Sales price per unit Rs	90	90
Sales	9,00,000	7,20,000
Direct Materials	3,00,000	3,20,000

Cost of sales	3,50,000	3,50,000
Fixed cost	2,00,000	2,00,000
Cost of sales	8,50,000	8,70,000
Profit / Loss	50,000	–1,50,000

Zero Based Budgeting

Conventional methods of budgeting have their own defects. They are based on historic cost and hence there is risk of carrying forward past inefficiencies. Had the costs in the past been disproportionately higher than what it should have been, the same would continue to be the basis for future projections. Secondly, all activities are treated alike. They are not prioritized. The above two leads to inflated cost estimates, which would finally impact the profitability of the business. In the circumstances, what is needed is a fresh look at the budgeting process whereby these deficiencies could be eliminated. This exercise is carried out in ***zero-based budgeting (ZBB).***

Chartered Institute of Management Accountants, London (CIMA) has defined zero-based budget as "***a method of budgeting whereby all activities are revalued each time a budget is set. Discrete levels of each activity are valued and a combination chosen to match resources***". The combinations are called ***decision packages.*** The decision packages are arranged according to the descending order of priority and resources are allocated till they last. ZBB is an operation planning and budgeting process, which requires each manager to justify his entire budget needs in details ***from the scratch***. Past activities are not continued ipso facto without taking a fresh look at them. Each activity is revalued every time before acceptance. The query starts from why spend at all. If spending is considered necessary, then the question of which activities are to be taken up and the order in which they are to be taken up. For this, decision packages are developed. Each decision package is evaluated from the angle of cost and benefit. The decision packages are arranged in order of their importance. Allocation of resources takes place according to the importance till resources last.

Although ZBB could beneficially be applied to all economic activities; it is a highly effective technique in controlling administrative costs. Peter A Pyhrr is the person who gave a final shape to this type of budgeting technique in 1970, although it was experimented in the US Agriculture Department way back in 1961.But the efforts were dropped due to lack of support from the different sections of the Department. It was Jimmy Carter who finally implemented ZBB in his territory in 1972 when he was the Governor of Arizona. There after there was no looking back. In 1979, when Carter was the President, ZBB was introduced into the civil administration of USA. Efforts were also made in India to introduce ZBB at different periods both by central and some enterprising state governments, but have to be dropped for want of support. It is usual that any new technique would be looked upon by the existing establishment as an investigation. ZBB in India could be introduced after educating the officials as to its effectiveness in controlling costs.

There are a group of control ratios that indicates budgetary variances, which could now be seen.

Activity Ratios

Activity ratios measure the level of activity compared to the budgeted. There are three ratios relating to this namely activity, capacity and efficiency.

The formulae adopted to measure these qualities are:

For activity:

Standard hours for actual output(SHAO) / budgeted hours (BH).

For capacity:

Actual hours worked(AH) / budgeted hours (BH)

For efficiency:

Standard hours for actual output (SHAO) / actual hours (AH)

Let us apply to an illustration to be more clear.

Mathumitha Corporation produces beauty aid with a budget of 10, 000 bottles per month. Standard labour requirement per unit of output is 2 hours. For the month of June, the company produced 8,000 units with labour hours of 16,400.

Activity ratio is = SHAO / BH = 16,000 / 20,000 = 80%

Capacity ratio is = AH / BH = 16,400 / 20,000 = 82%

Efficiency ratio = SHAO / AH = 16,000 / 16,400 = 98%

Summary

Budget is a quantitative financial statement prepared and approved prior to a period of time, of the policy to be pursued during the period for the purpose of attaining the objective. Corporates prepare separate budgets for revenue costs and capital costs. Revenue budgets are functionally classified into Sales budget, Production budget, Cost (of production) budget, Materials usage budget, Materials purchase budget, Personnel budget or Labour budget, Research and development budget, Cash budget and Master budget. According to their nature, budgets might be fixed budgets and flexible budgets. Salient features of budgeting are establishment of a policy, allocation of responsibilities of executives to the fulfillment of the policy, continuous comparison of actual performance with projections for achieving the objective or providing a basis for revision, when needed. Budgets could also be conveniently based on activities. A performance budget provides information to management as to the variation between budget and performance. For controlling administrative costs, zero-based budgets are widely used.

I. QUESTIONS

1. Define "budgetary control". Explain the role of budgeting in financial control.
2. What are the objectives of budgetary control?
3. Bring out the various steps involved in budgetary control.
4. Define flexible budget.
5. What is 'cash budget'? Explain its contents giving a proforma cash budget.
6. What is zero based budgeting? Explain its features.
7. Describe the various preliminaries required for the adoption of an effective system of budgetary control
8. What are the advantages and limitations of Budgetary Control?
9. How do you classify the Budgets?
10. Briefly explain the various types of Budgets?
11. Explain the steps involved in the preparation of Sales Budget.
12. How is production Budget prepared?
13. What are the steps involved in the preparation of Materials Budget?
14. Prepare a Purchase Budget.
15. What is a Master Budget?
16. What is decision package? How is it used in Zero Base Budgeting?
17. What is Performance Budgeting? What are the steps involved in the formulation of Performance Budget?
18. How are Budgets prepared and approved? What is key factor?
19. What is activity based costing? Explain its advantages over conventional costing methods?
20. What are control ratios? What are their utilities?

II. QUIZ

Say yes or no

1. Budgets are meant for weak companies.
2. Budgets are plans for future course of action.
3. Key factor determines the starting point of budget preparation.
4. Equivalent to finished goods means the additional cost to be incurred to complete semi-finished goods.
5. Sales budgets are usually key budgets.
6. Production budget would determine what the company could sell.
7. Cash budget is another name for cash flow.
8. Zero-based budget is an effective tool for controlling administrative costs.
9. Performance budget is an assessment of the actual compared to planned.
10. Activity based costing is another name for zero based budget.
11. Zero based budget priotizes activities.
12. Budget manuals are documented forms of budgets.

III. EXERCISES

1. Draw up a flexible budget for overhead expenses on the basis of the following data and determine the overhead rate at 70%, 80% and 90% plan capacity: **(Rs)**

	Capacity levels		
	70%	80%	90%
Variable Overheads:			
Indirect labour		12,000	
Stores including spares		4,000	
Semi-variable Overheads			
Power (30% fixed, 70%			
Variable)		20,000	
Repairs and maintenance			
(60% fixed, 40% variable)		2,000	
Fixed Overheads			
Deprecation		11,000	

Insurance		3,000	
Salaries		10,000	
Total overheads		62,000	
Estimated direct labour hours		1,240 hrs	

2. Gokul & company estimates sales for next year at40.000 units of its product, GOK. Each unit of GOK needs materials A and B at the ratio of A 3 units and B 5 units. Planned opening balance for next year is 5000 units of finished goods,12000 units of material A and 20.000 units of material B.Materials on order were 7000 units of material A and 11.000 units of material B. Desired level of stock at the end of next year is finished goods 7000 units, material A 15000 units and material B 25.000 units. Expected material on order is A 8000 units and B 10000 units. Prepare materials procurement budget for Gokul & Co.

3. Xynock Ltd. expects to have a cash balance of Rs. 43,70,000 at the end of March2004. Prepare cash budget for April to June based on following information:
   - Sales for March were Rs. 346.63 lakhs and is expected to increase thereafter by 10% every month.
   - 60% of sales are for credit of 30 days and the balance for cash.
   - 95% of debtors pay after 30 days.
   - Purchase for March was Rs.125.54 lakhs.
   - Entire purchase was on one months' credit.
   - Variable production costs for the company is 30% of sales.
   - Fixed costs are Rs.35.79 lakhs per quarter. 35% of fixed costs are paid monthly and the balance at the end of 3 months.
   - Interest to be paid to banks Rs.21.25 lakhs per quarter ending March, June, September and December.
   - The company has to repay loan instalments of Rs.150 lakhs at the end of each quarter.
   - Dividend of Rs.350 lakhs to be paid in May.
   - Scrap sales of the company is Rs.12,83 lakhs every month.
   - Minimum balance to be maintained by the company from April is Rs.80 lakhs.
   - Excess cash invested in Government securities. Deficits borrowed from bank at 8% interest.

4. Explain the features of flexible budget

   XY Industries Ltd. is preparing its comprehensive budget for the next year. The sales manager has said that he does not wish to have a single estimate of sales but would prefer to give four forecasts along with his estimates of probabilities he attaches to them:

Sale forecasts	Probability
Rs.16,00,000	0.4
Rs.20,00,000	0.3
Rs.24,00,000	0.2
Rs.30,00,000	0.1

Variable costs are 40%of sales and total fixed costs are Rs.8, 00,000.Prepare budgeted income statement based on each of the forecasts (Hint: work out weighted average sales).

5. From the following information at 50% capacity prepare a flexible budget and forecast the profit or loss at 60% 70% and 90% capacity

Expenses at 50% capacity.

	Rs.
Fixed expenses	
Salaries	50,000
Rent and taxes	40,000
Depreciation	60,000
Administrative expenses	70,000
Variable expenses	
Material	2,00,000
Labour	2,50,000
Others	40,000
Semi variable	
Repairs	1,00,000
Indirect labour	1,50,000
Others	90,000

It is expected that fixed expenses will remain constant at all capacities. Semi-variable expenses will not change between 45% and 60% capacity, will rise by 10% between 60% and 75% capacity, a further increases of 5%when capacity crosses 75%.

Estimated sales are

Capacity	Sales (Rs.)
60%	11,00,000
70%	13,00,000
90%	15,00,000

6. Animation Ala Children, factory engaged in manufacturing plastic toys, is working at 40% capacity and produces 10000 toys per month. The present cost breakup for one toy is as under;

Material	Rs.10
Labour	Rs. 3
Overhead	Rs. 5 (60% fixed)

The selling price is Rs.20 per toy. If it is decided to work the factory at 50% capacity, the selling price falls by 3%. At 90% capacity the selling price falls by 5% accompanied by a similar fall in the price of material. You are required to prepare a flexible budget showing capacity utilization at 50% and 90% capacities.

7. Prepare a flexible budget for overheads of Monish Rao on the basis of data given below. Ascertain the overhead rates at 50,60 and 70 per cent capacities.

	At 50% Capacity Rs.	At 60% Capacity Rs.	At70% Capacity Rs.
Variable overheads:			
Indirect material		6,000	
Indirect labour		8,000	
Semi-variable overheads:			
Electricity (40% fixed, 60% variable)		30,000	
Repairs and maintenance (80% Fixed 20% variable)		3,000	
Fixed overheads:			
Depreciation		16,500	
Insurance		4,500	
Salaries		15,000	
Total overheads		93,000	

8. The budgeted cost of Rare Earth specializing in the production of a single product at the optimum capacity of 6,400 units per annum amounts Rs.17,04,800 as detailed below:

Fixed cost	Rs. 20,68,800
Variable costs	
Power	Rs. 1,44,000

Repairs etc	Rs. 1,70,000
Miscellaneous	Rs. 54,000
Direct material	Rs. 49,28,000
Direct labour	Rs.102,40,000
	Rs.155,36,000
Total cost	Rs.176,04,800

Having regard to possible impact on sales turnover by market trends, the company decided to have a flexible budget with a production target of 3200 and 4800units (the actual quantity proposed to be produced being left to a later date before commencement of the budget period). Prepare a flexible budget for production levels at 50% and 75% capacity. Assuming selling price per unit is maintained at Rs.4000 as at present, indicate the effect on net profit.

9. Draw up a flexible monthly budget for overhead expenses on the basis of the following data furnished by Reuben Daniel Enterprises and determine the overhead rates at 70%, 80% and 90% plant capacity levels.

	At 80% capacity
Variable overhead:	Rs.
Indirect labour	12,000
Indirect material	4,000
Semi-variable overheads	
Power (30% fixed, 70% variable)	20,000
Repairs & maintenance (60% fixed, 40% variable)	2,000
Fixed overheads:	
Depreciation	11,000
Insurance	3,000
Others	10,000
Total overheads	62,000
Estimated direct labour hours	1,24,000

10. International Books Limited is a publishing and printing company that specializes in the production of paperback books. The stock is kept in an unbound and unfinished state until it is ordered by customers. The cost of a single publication is as follows:

a. Preparation costs, and costs incurred from commissioning authors, photographs, composition, etc, for whatever quantity of publication produced, will be Rs.12000

b. Printing costs are Rs.1000 per thousand up to 50,000 and then Rs.600 per thousand for any further copies.

c. Binding and other finishing costs are Rs.600 per thousand whatever quantity is produced. The book is to be sold direct to retailers at Rs.40 per copy

Required to

Prepare table showing the production costs for 40,000, 50,000, 60,000, 70,000 and 80,000 copies of the finished publication, together with the average cost per copy for each of these quantities.

Also show the marginal cost per copy for each increment of 10000 copies, in the range 40000 and 80000 copies .

At the proposed selling price to retailers:

a. State the break even quantity

b. What would be the profit if the company produced and sold 70000 copies?

The Company has printed 70000 copies of the publication, but it has not sold as well as expected and 10,000 copies are left unsold. A Dealer has offered to buy these for Rs.11,000. Using the information given, state whether you would advise the company to accept this offer. What additional factor might also influence you recommendation?

11. Draw a material procurement budget (quantitative) from the following information:

Estimated sales of product 40,000 units. Each unit of the product requires 3 units of material A and 5 units of material B.

Estimated opening balances at the commencement of the next year

Finished product	5,000
Material A	12,000
Material B	20,000
Materials on order:	
Material A	7,000
Material B	11,000
The desirable closing balance at the end of the next year:	
Finished product	
Material A	7,000
Material B	25,000

Material on order and pipeline	
Material A	8,000
Material B	10,000

12. From the following information relating to Amar Chand & Co. for 2003 and conditions expected to prevail in 2004, prepare a budget for 2004. State the assumptions you have m

2003 Actual	Rs.
Sales	100,00,000
Raw material	53,00,000
Wages	11,00,000
Variable overheads	16,00,000
Fixed overheads	10,00,000
Prospects for 2004	
Sales	150,00,000
Raw materials Price increase	5%
Wages increase	10%
Additional fixed cost in plant	5%

13. Prepare a production budget for each month and a summarized production cost budget for the six-month period ending 31st December, from the following data of Xylophone Ltd.

The units to be sold for different months are as follows:

July	1,100
August	1,100
September	1,700
October	1,900
November	2,500
December	2,300
January, next year	2,000

There will be no work in progress at the end of any month.

Finished units equal to half the sales for the next month will be in stock at the end of each month

Budgeted production costs for the production of 2,200 units are as follows:

	Rs.
Direct material per unit	10.00
Direct wages per unit	4.00
Total factory overhead	8,800.00

14. The sales director of Bala Palani Ltd. reports that next year he expects to sell 54,000 units of product Snowball. The production manger consults his store keeper and casts his figures as follows:

Two kinds of raw materials A and B are required for manufacturing the product. Each unit of the product required 2 units of A and 3 units of B. The estimated opening balances at the commencement of the next year are:

Finished products– 11,500 units; A– 12,250 units; B- 15,100 units

The desirable closing balances at the end of next year are:

finished product –14,000 units: A–13,000 units: B–16,000 units.

Draw up a quantitative chart showing the materials budget for the next year

15. The cost of an article produced by Elavan Entertainers at a capacity level of 10,000 units is given under A. For a variation in capacity above or below this level, the individual expenses vary as indicated in B.

	A	B
Material cost	50,00	100%
Labor cost	30,000	100%
Power	3,000	80%
Repairs and maintenance	3,500	80%
Stores	2,000	100%
Inspection	800	25%
Depreciation	10,000	100%
Administrative overhead	3,600	25%
Selling overhead	4,500	50%
Total	1,07,400	
Cost per unit	10.74	

Find out the unit cost of the product under each individual expense at production levels of 8,000 units and 12,000 units.

16. Fairever Ltd. has prepared the budget for the production of one lakh units of Snowcem manufactured for a costing period as under:

Figures in Rupees.

Raw material	2.52 per unit	
Works overhead	2.50per unit	(60% fixed)
Direct Labour	0.75	

Administration overhead		
Overhead (80% fixed)	0.10	
Direct expenses	0.40per unit	
Selling overheads	0.20 per unit	(50% fixed)

Prepare a flexible budget at 60%, 70% and 80% of its capacity.

17. The following data are available in a manufacturing company for a half-yearly period.

Fixed expenses per unit at 50% of capacity. Variable expenses per unit

Wages and salaries	8.40	–	
Rent rate and taxes	5.60	Material	24.00
Depreciation	7.00	Labour	25.60
Sundry administrative Expenses	8.90	Other expenses	3.80
	23.90		53.40

Semi – variable expenses per unit at	50% of capacity
Maintenance and repair	2.50
Indirect labour	9.90
Sales department salaries, etc	2.90
Sundry administrative expenses	2.60
	17.90

Assuming that the fixed expenses remain constant for all levels of production, semi-variable remain constant between 45% and 65% of capacity,but increasing by 10% above 65% and 80% capacity and by 20% above 80% and 100% capacity. Sales at 50% capacity are Rs.85,000; 60% capacity Rs.1,00,000;75% capacity Rs.120000 90% capacity 1,50,000; and 100% Rs.1,70,000.

Prepare a flexible budget for the half-year and forecast the profits at 60%, 75%, 90% and 100% capacity.

18. The expenses budgeted for the production of 10,000 units of Rohot in Holioli Ltd. are as under:

	Per unit Rs.		
Material	70	Variable expenses(direct)	5
Labour	25	Selling expenses(10% fixed)	13

Variable overhead	20	Distribution expenses (20% fixed)	7
Fixed overheads			
(Rs.100000)	10	Administrative expenses	5
		Total	155

Prepare a budget for production of:

i. 8000 units

ii. 6000 units

Administration overheads are fixed for all levels of production.

19. Alagesan Aromatics is manufacturing two products Handsome and Lovely. A forecast about the number of units to be sold in the first seven months is given below:

Month	Handsome	Lovely
January	10,000	28,000
February	12,000	28,000
March	16,000	24,000
April	20,000	20,000
May	24,000	26,000
June	24,000	16,000
July	20,000	18,000

It is anticipated that:

- There will be no work in progress at the end of any month
- Finished units equal to half the sales for the next month will be in stock at th end of each month (including December of previous year)
- Budgeted production and production costs for the year ending 31st December are as follows

	Handsome	Lovely
Production (unit)	220000	240000
Direct materials per unit		
Direct wages per unit (Rs)	12.5	19
Total factory overheads to each type of product (Rs.)	66000	96000

Prepare for six months ending 30th June, a production budget and a summarized cost of production budget.

20. Prepare a cash budget for 6months from July to December for Casual Wear Company from the information given in the table as under: Rs. in thousands

Month	Sales Price per unit	Material	Wages	Production	Administ ration	Selling	Distribution	Develop ment
April	100	40	10.0	4.4	3000	1600	800	1000
May	120	60	11.2	4.8	2900	1700	900	1000
June	80	40	8.0	5.6	3000	1500	700	1200
July	100	60	8.0	4.6	2900	1400	900	1200
Aug.	120	70	10.0	5.6	3000	1900	1100	1400
Sept.	140	80	10.0	5.4	3000	2000	1200	1400
Oct.	160	90	10.0	5.8	3100	2250	1250	1600
Nov.	180	100	11.0	6.0	3100	2150	1250	1500
Dec.	200	110	11.6	6.4	2200	2300	1500	1600

Cash balance on July 1 was expected to be Rs.1,50,000.

Expected Capital Expenditure:

Plant and machinery to be installed in August at a cost of Rs.40,000 will be payable on September 1. Extension to Research and Development Department amounting to Rs.10,000 will be completed on August 1 payable Rs.2000 per month from completion date. Under a hire-purchase agreement Rs.4,000 is to be paid each month.

A Sales commission of 5 per cent of sales is to be paid within the month following the sales

Period of credit allowed by supplier's	3 months
Period of credit allowed to customer's	2 months
Delay in payment of overheads	1 month
Delay in payment of wages	1 month

Income tax of Rs.100000 id due to be paid on October 1. Preference share dividend of 10 per cent on Rs.200000 is to be paid on November 1.All sales and purchases are on credit.

Ten percent calls on ordinary share capital of Rs.4,00,000 is due on July 1 and September 1 respectively. Dividend from investments amounting to Rs.30,000 expected on November 1.

21. Gonedays Ltd., produces two commodities, Goodlook and Betterlook, in one of its departments. E ach unit takes 5 hrs and 10 hrs respectivelyas production time. 1000 units of

Goodlook and 600 units of Betterlook were produced during March . Actual man-hours spent in this production were 10000. Yearly budgeted hours are 96000.

Compute the various control ratios.

22. From the following data, calculate activity ratio of Eisen Elegant Ltd. The company manufactures two products Alan and Balan. Standard time to manufacture product A is 2 hours and product B is 10 hours. The budgeted and actual production for a day were as follows:

	Budgeted production	**Actual** production
Product Alan	125 units	100 units
Product Balan	30 units	24 units

Total hours worked were 660

23. Work out the control ratios with the following data:

Budgeted labour hours for the production of 24,000 units are 3 hours 15 minutes per unit. Production for the period was 21,500 units with 73,100 labour hours.

CHAPTER 14

CAPITAL BUDGETING

Learning Objective

Capital budgeting is planning for growth. This chapter deals with the need for capital budgeting, types and stages of capital budgeting. The various methods of evaluating investments and the final choice of the project are considered. Advantages of taking time value into evaluation and the role of risk in capital budgeting with tools for identifying, measuring and providing for risk are also handled. After reading the chapter, a manager would be equipped with the nuauiances of investment analysis. liabilities and the techniques available to assess the erosion.

It is the intention of every business organization to ***stabilize and grow***, in that order. Stability is the temporary position where a business is able to sustain a predetermined level of operation. Stability might be in terms of market share, sales, margin, production or any other criterion. In the initial stages of a company's promotion, it has first to stabilize and steady itself before launching its next venture. Stability is thus an intermediary step in the development of a business. It is a short-term goal. Stability is the stepping-stone for the next move, growth. To continue to be in business, the businessman should keep on running, as Alice did in Wonderland to remain where she was. The final goal of an organization would be to grow continuously, either by introducing new products or improving existing products. The market axiom is that companies should obsolete their own products by improving existing versions of products or by introducing entirely new products, otherwise competitors would do it. The objectives for stability and growth are realized through additional investments in real assets.

Planned investments in business with the view to achieve the twin objective of stability and growth are termed ***projects***. Projects are undertaken for creating facilities for the manufacture of goods or for rendering services, maintaining and improving such facilities and for better utilizing the existing facilities to generate additional revenues. The business needs ***long-term assets or capital assets*** such as land, building plant and machinery for creating and maintaining facilities. For utilizing the facilities so created and to generate income, business requires ***short-term assets or current assets*** like cash, materials and receivables. There are thus two kinds of assets in which a business has to invest- one, in fixed capital assets and the other, in working capital assets. Planned investment in projects is known as ***Capital budgeting***.

Capital investment involves finding real assets that are worth more than what they cost. The theory of value and rules relating to return are the basis for capital investment decisions. Theory of value postulates that a rupee today is worth more than a rupee tomorrow and a rupee certain is worth more than a rupee uncertain. The return rule lays down that investments are to be made when the net return is positive. According to rate of return rule, invest when the return is higher than the opportunity cost.

Capital budgeting necessitates investments in the following types of assets and expenses:

- *Land and Building*
- *Plant and machinery*
- *Equipment*
- *Miscellaneous assets*
- *Preliminary and preoperative expenses*
- *Margin money for working capital*
- *Provision for contingencies.*

Land and Building

Land and building usually refers to the factory premises with constructions, when the business owns them. Land for the purpose of capital budgeting means extend of real assets to be procured and the cost thereof Cost of land would in turn depend up on the location. In existing projects, which propose to invest in the same factory site, land would not be a cost. But in many cases, projects are to be set up at sites different from the existing factory location. In such cases, the businessman has to select sites with locational advantages. Locational advantages include proximity to market, to raw materials, to labour and other inputs, such as water, power and transports. The selected site should be above the highest flood level and should have load-bearing capacity adequate for the type of equipment to be installed. The business should acquire land adequate area of land to meet the present and future needs of the industry. Surveyor's charges, registration charges, leveling costs are included in the cost of land. An entrepreneur could select a piece of land with the above-mentioned locational advantages and construct buildings to accommodate his plant and machinery and other production facilities. He might also have his administrative and selling offices in the factory premises itself or have his office away from the factory. For logistic reasons, it is advantageous to have administrative office away from the factory premises Alternatively, an entrepreneur could avail of the ready built sheds in ***industrial estates*** set up by State and Central Governments, in selected areas, with adequate infrastructure facilities.

Plant and Machinery

Plant and Machinery is the equipment with which production activities are to be carried out. Plant refers to the complete set of equipment needed to manufacture. Machinery on the other hand refers to individual equipment. Plant is comparable to a house where machineries are doors, windows, walls etc. The plant and machinery account would contain the invoice price and all the costs incurred up to the installation of the equipment in a working condition, such as taxes, transportation, insurance, erection and commissioning charges etc.

Preliminary Expenses

Preliminary and preoperative expenses are incurred by the enterprise before it starts production. The promoter has to identify the product he is going to manufacture through a market survey. After satisfying himself as to the viability of the project, he has to prepare a project report, identify resources, arrange for funds, incorporate an organization etc. All these activities cost money. As these expenses are incurred before the project is taken up for implementation, they are called ***preliminary expenses***. Preliminary expenses are deferred revenue expenses and according to law are to be written off against the income of the business over ten equal annual installments, after it has gone into production. Tax authorities do allow preliminary expenses up to 2.50% of the cost of project.

Pre-Operative Expenses

Pre-operative expenses on the other hand, are expenses incurred after the project is taken up for implementation, but before it goes into commercial production. Interests on loans during construction period, establishment expenses during construction period, installation and commissioning fees, trial run expenses are all examples. Preoperative expenses are capitalized expenditures, in the sense that they are added to the items of capital goods for the acquisition of which they are incurred. For example, architect's fee is a preoperative expense relating to building and is, therefore, added to the cost of building. Technical know-how fee relates to the plant and machinery and is added to the cost of equipment. All items of preoperative expenses, which do not relate to any specific capital expenditure of the project, but are common to all, are added up and apportioned to the capital expenditures in proportion to their costs. For example, non-specific preoperative expenses, like interest on loan, establishment expenses etc. add up to Rs.10 lakhs and the project expenditures are: land Rs.50 lakhs, Building Rs.150 lakhs and Plant and Machinery Rs.300lakhs. The non-specific preoperative expense of Rs.10 lakhs is apportioned to land, building and plant and machinery in the proportion of 1:3:6 i.e., Rs.1 lakh to land, Rs.3 lakhs to Building and Rs.6 lakhs to Plant and Machinery. The value of the capital expenditure, called assets, would thus be: land Rs.51 lakhs, Building Rs.153 lakhs and Plant and Machinery Rs.306 lakhs. Depreciation, at the prescribed rate, is allowed on the capitalized value of the assets.

Margin Money for Working Capital

Working capital is that part of finance which is needed to maintain a given level of operation. Gross working capital consists of current assets. Current assets less current liabilities is the margin money for working capital. This part of funds has therefore to be met from the cost of project. Margin money is the real working capital needed by the business to sustain the given operating level.

Contingency Provision

It is quite possible that between the time of preparing the project report and its actual implementation, prices of the items might increase. Further, a few items might have been omitted from the project report. Provisions are made to take care of such eventualities. These are contingency provisions.

Characteristics

Capital budgeting decisions are not repetitive like working capital decisions. They are tailor made to the requirements of each situation. As such, capital budgeting has its own features. Some of the important characteristics of capital budgeting are

- *Capital budgeting involves large outlays and is requires to be prioritized.*
- *Capital budgeting decision is long-term in nature and involves problems of forecasting.*
- *Capital budgeting is highly risky and imposes heavy demand on the time and resources of management.*
- *Capital budgeting decisions are irreversible and require careful consideration.*
- *Gestation period in capital investment proposals is long and necessitates detailed planning and control.*

Outlays on capital investment are large. Lots of resources are to be committed to the project. Resources, being scarce and having alternative uses, management has to identify priorities and put the resources to their best uses. Each project is therefore evaluated from their cost and benefit angles and having regard to their technical feasibility, economic and commercial viability. The projects are then ranked in the descending order of their importance. Resources are allocated according to the rank as long as the resources last. This process is called ***capital rationing***. Projects are also prioritized according to their mutual relationship. Project that are ***mutually independent*** are considered on their relative merits. For example, a company has proposals of setting up a spinning mill and a cement factory. The setting up of the spinning mill is not a pre-requisite for putting up of the cement factory. Both are independent of each other and are decided on their merits. As regards projects that are ***dependent***, a holistic view has to be taken. For example construction of canteen in a railway station depends upon the construction of the station itself. Canteen construction would not be taken up unless construction of railway station is decided upon. Thus, setting up canteen is a dependent project.

The time gap between the decision to take up a project and its actual fruition is wide, as the gestation periods in many capital projects are long. The decision to undertake the project is based on the forecast made at the time of deciding. By the time the project is completed, the forecast might turn out to be wrong. For example, in the nineteen seventies vanaspathi was the major cooking medium in the country. The demand for vanaspathi remained largely unsatisfied. A number of units were set up in the period on the forecast that the demand for vanaspathi would continue. However, the shortage necessitated the consumers to seek substitute for cooking media and found a suitable alternate in refined oil. By the time the vanaspathi projects came into production, the demand had vaned and many units had to close down. ***Forecasting*** is therefore the major hurdle in capital budgeting.

What adds fuel to fire is that capital investment decisions once taken up are irreversible. They become sunk costs. If to be reversed, it would involve heavy loss to the investors. History is replete with instances of sound companies becoming insolvent on a single wrong capital investment decisions. We have the recent instance how Enron, the seventh globally largest company, became insolvent on a wrong investment decision in Dabholi project. Companies should therefore exercise great caution in finalizing capital investments. That is one of the reasons why capital investment decisions are entrusted to the chief executives in all corporations.

As we have seen, there is high risk in investment decisions and that the decisions are irreversible, it enjoins very high degrees of responsibilities on the management. The management at every step feels the heat of the issues concerning investment proposals. Top management usually spends quite long hours and burns midnight lamps before arriving at investment decisions and during their implementation.

The set up for planning and control in capital budgeting has to be elaborate. Every detail is to be planned in advance and resources allotted. The progress in implementation has to be compared with what is budgeted at frequent intervals. Deviations, if any, are to be corrected then and there. Business houses use PERT / CPM technique to follow up the schedule of implementation and control of costs in capital budgeting.

Kinds of Investments

Companies budget for a variety of projects. Broadly, projects could be classified into

- *New projects*
- *Expansions*
- *Diversifications*

- *Modernizations*
- *Acquisitions*
- *Research and development*
- *Replacements and*
- *Social projects*

When an entrepreneur enters in to business, he either starts a new project or takes over an existing project. If it is a new project, the entrepreneur has to make an elaborate study of the industry and prepare a feasibility report to consider whether he could take up the project or not. Feasibility studies establish the technical feasibility, commercial and economic viability and financial soundness of the project. Once all the parameters are satisfactory, the entrepreneur could decide on setting up the project and arrange for the means of financing the cost of the project. In the case of an existing business, the projects might be for expansion, diversification, and modernization or merely for replacing an unproductive machine with a new one. Expansion is vertical growth. In expansion the business plans to increase the capacity of its existing production. For example, proposal of a cement unit with an existing installed capacity of 1,00,000 tonnes per annum to increase its capacity to 1,25,000 tonnes per annum, is expansion. It could also plan for vertical integration of the production facilities. Vertical integration means adding facilities for the production of allied products. For example, a spinning mill when it plans to expand into weaving, the proposal is vertical integration and is expansion. On the other hand, if a business enters into unrelated products, we term it as diversification. WIPRO, a vegetable oil company entering into computer is diversification. Similarly, ITC, a tobacco major, entering into hotel business is diversification. Modernization is to update the process of absorbing the latest development in technology. Expansion and diversification increases the volume of output of the business, while modernization improves the quality and reduces cost. Companies too replace worned out machines with new machines. Research and development is a major area of investment, where Indian industries are way behind. Our outlay on research and development is hardly 0.2 percent of the corporate profit, whereas in developed countries, it is as much as 8 to 10%. Bulk of the research and development expenditures in India is in pharmaceutical industry. Investment in social projects such as schools, hospitals, roads, water supply are projects, which companies undertake now a days as a measure of business ethics. These are not evaluated in terms of commercial viability. They are assessed on their socio economic costs and benefits.

Steps in Capital Budgeting

The capital budgeting process involves four steps, namely

- *Identification of project ideas*
- *Calculation of cash flows of each proposal*
- *Evaluating cash flows of proposals*
- *Choosing that alternative, which gives maximum benefit or minimum cost.*

Identifying Projects

It is the corporate practice that by August, the managers of the various departments are called up on to list out their requirements for capital investments. The departmental heads discuss with the staff and lists out the requirements for the ensuing year. They estimate the cash flows for the proposals and send the project ideas to the capital budgeting committee. The chief executive officer of the company, assisted by all the functional heads, form the capital budgeting committee, which recommends proposals for implementation. The board of directors finally approves the proposals. The committee reviews all the proposals and evaluates them according to their cost and benefit and ranks them in the descending order. The projects are approved having regard to the resources that could be mobilized by the company.

Calculation of Cash Flows

Projects cause two-way movement of funds. Initially, when the project is implemented, cash flows out by way of acquisition of assets. This flow of cash from the business is negative and is indicated by – ***cash flow***, meaning that cash flew out. When investment in fixed assets and working capital is complete and the project is about to go into production, that stage is called Zero period. Investments are made during or before 0 period and income starts flowing from that point over the effective life of the investment. If the project has a longer gestation period of more than a year, then investment made in the years before 0 year is indicated as –1 year, - 2 year and so on. For example, the project of De Foe Daniel Ltd. had a gestation period of 3 years. The project was completed in 2003 and the plant went into production from 1st January, 2004.The outlay in these years were

Year 2001	Investment	Rs.125 lakhs
Year 2002	Investments	Rs.175 lakhs
Year 2003	Investments	Rs.250 lakhs

These outflows would be presented as follows for cash flow calculations:

2 year	– Rs.125 lakhs
1 year	– Rs.175 lakhs
0 year	– Rs.250 lakhs.

We have already seen that cash outflow consists of cost of land, building, plant and machinery, miscellaneous assets, preliminary and preoperative expenses, contingencies and margin money for working capital. For example, De Foe Daniel Ltd.'s investment of Rs.550 lakhs is made up of the following:

Rs. Lakhs.

Land	12.00
Buildings	65.00
Plant and machinery	297.00
Miscellaneous asset	17.00
Preliminary expenses	38.00
Preoperative expenses	31.00
Provision for contingency	55.00
Margin for working capital	35.00
Cost of project	550.00

The next step is to calculate cash inflows. Cash inflows are profit after tax of the period with depreciation added back. It is the cash generated by the project, year by year during its effective life. The effective life of a project is the lowest of its technological life, economic life or physical life. The effective life of De Foe Daniel Ltd.'s project is 7 years and the expected profitability of the company before taxes were as in Table 1. Tax rate was 40%

Table 1

Years	**2004**	**2005**	**2006**	**2007**	**2008**	**2009**	**2010**
Sales	632.50	695.75	800.11	920.13	1039.76	1164.45	1339.19
Operating costs	359.27	394.70	450.70	489.30	542.54	601.94	6880.69
Interest	45.76	39.56.	33.71.	31.17.	29.32.	26.74.	22.41.

Cash inflows for the purpose of capital budgeting means profit after tax with depreciation added back, less cash out go by way of additional investments. This is ***free cash flow***. For capital budgeting evaluation free cash flow has to be considered. The free cash inflows for De Foe Daniel Ltd.'s project during its effective life of the 7 years, presuming that the company had not made any additional investments, would be as in the following table:

Table 2

Cash flow of De Foe Daniel Ltd.'s project **Rs.lakhs**

Years	2004	**2005**	**2006**	**2007**	**2008**	**2009**	**2010**
Sales	632.50	695.75	800.11	920.13	1039.76	1164.45	1339.19
Depreciation[1]	74.65	74.65	74.65	74.65	74.65	74.65	74.65
Operatingcosts	284.62	320.05	376.05	414.65	467.89	527.29	606.04

Interest	45.76	39.56	33.71	31.17	29.32	26.74	22.41
PBT	227.47	261.49	314.70	399.66	467.90	535.77	636.09
Tax	90.99	104.60	126.28	159.86	187.16	214.31	254.44
PAT	136.48	156.89	189.42	239.80	280.74	321.46	381.65
Add.							
Depreciation	74.65	74.65	74.65	74.65	74.65	74.65	74.65
Cash inflow	211.13	231.54	264.07	314.45	355.39	396.11	456.30

[1]Cost of investment less 5% salvage value divided by life of project is annual depreciation on straight-line method. For project evaluations, straight-line method of depreciation is usually applied. Salvage value is the scrap value of investment after its useful years. Operating costs include depreciation.

Note that if the company has to make additional investment of Rs.275 lakhs in the third year to keep up its capacity, then its net cash flow during 2006 would be negative that is –10.93

We saw that the project yields returns during its effective life. It does not mean that the company would close down the project at the end of the period. It is an assumed period for working out the viability of the project. It is also presumed that on winding up, the company would release the working capital blocked in the project. Further, the investment in fixed assets would also have ***terminal value***, differently called as ***salvage value, residual value or scrap value***. Thus, the last year of the project would have two streams of inflows- one the normal operating flow and two the flow on account of salvage value. It is difficult to estimate what the salvage value of the fixed assets would be at the end of the project period. But for calculation of cash flow at the terminal year, the norms prescribed by the income-tax authorities might be considered. According to this norm, salvage value of fixed assets, excepting land, would be 5% of their historic value. Value of land to be taken at the book value, as it is not subject to depreciation. In De Foe Daniel Ltd.'s project, the salvage value of the project would be

Land	Rs. 12.00 lakhs.
Other fixed assets[1]	Rs. 23.25 lakhs
Working capital	Rs. 35.00 lakhs
Salvage value	Rs. 70.25 lakhs.

[1] Total cost of project (Rs.550 lakhs) less margin for working capital (Rs.35 lakhs), preliminary expenses (Rs.38 lakhs) and land (Rs.12 lakhs) is cost in other fixed assets (Rs.465 lakhs). 5% of the cost is salvage value = Rs.23.25.

14.18. The tabulated cash flow for De Foe Daniel Ltd.'s project would be as in the following table:

Table 3

Years	Cash flows Rs. lakhs
–2 year	– 125.00
–1 year	– 175.00
0 year	– 250.00
1 year	211.13
2 year	231.54
3 year	264.07
4 year	314.45
5 year	355.39
6 year	396.11
7 year	456.30+ 70.25 = 526.55

Cash flow calculations in replacement decisions arc a littlc different from the above method. Replacement involves removal of existing machine and installation of a new machine in its place. Hence cash flows are to be analyzed from two angles-had the existing machine been allowed to continue, what would have been the cash flows and had the new machine been installed in the place of existing machine, what would have been the flows. Then comparing the two flows, one has to work out the incremental flow. The analysis should therefore be what would be the additional cash outflow and additional inflows if a decision were taken to install the new machine. Cash flow calculation for replacement is done in seven steps:

- *Step 1: Calculating net cash outgo*
- *Step 2: Calculating depreciation on new machine*
- *Step 3: Calculating depreciation on existing machine*
- *Step 4: Calculating differential depreciation*
- *Step 5: Calculating differential cash in flows*
- *Step 6: Calculating terminal year adjustment*
- *Step 7: Tabulating incremental cash flows.*

Step 1

Net cash out go is the additional investment one has to make for replacing the equipment. It is the cost of the new machine less the present market value of the existing machine. Meena Agencies wishes to replace one of its petrol driven delivery vans by a new diesel van, which costs Rs.5 lakhs (Chassis alone). The body of the van is expected to cost Rs.2.15 lakhs. The new van will have an effective life of 4 years after which it is estimated to fetch Rs.35,000 by way of scrap. Book value of new machine after 4 years would be Rs.65,000. The existing van has a present book value of Rs.85,000 and is expected to have a physical life of 4 more years after which it will have a book value of Rs.5,000 and market value of Rs.25,000. Tax rate at 35%. The new van is expected to save by way of fuel Rs.1,60,000 per annum. Present salvage value of existing van is Rs. 30,000.

The additional cash out go in the case would Rs.6,85,000 as follows:

Step 1

Calculation of net cash outgo

Cost of chassis	Rs.5,00,000
Cost of body	Rs.2,15,000
Cost of new van	Rs.7,15,000
Less: Realization of existing van	Rs. 30,000
Incremental cash outgo	Rs.6,85,000

Step 2

Depreciation on new van:

Cost of new van	Rs.7,15,000
Less: Salvage value	Rs. 35,000
Depreciation during 4 years	Rs.6,80,000
Annual depreciation	Rs.1,70,000

Step 3

Depreciation on existing van

Current book value	Rs. 85,000
Book value after 4 years	Rs. 5,000
Depreciation for 4 years	Rs. 80,000
Annual depreciation	Rs. 20,000

Step 4

Differential depreciation:

Annual depreciation on new machine	Rs. 1,70,000
Annual depreciation on existing machine	Rs. 20,000
Differential depreciation	Rs. 1,50,000

Step 5

Differential inflows:

Annual savings in cost	Rs. 1,60,000
Less: Differential depreciation	Rs. 1,50,000
Taxable additional income	Rs. 10,000
Less: Taxation	Rs. 3,500
Additional PAT	Rs. 6,500
Add back depreciation	Rs. 1,50,000
Additional annual Cash flow	Rs. 1,56,500

Step 6

Calculating terminal year Adjustments

Salvage value of new van	Rs. 35,000
Salvage value of existing van	Rs. 5,000
Incremental salvage value	Rs. 30,000

Step 7

Tabulating incremental cash flows.

Year 0		Rs. 6,85,000
Year 1.		Rs. 1,56,500
Year 2.		Rs. 1,56,500
Year 3.		Rs. 1,56,500
Year 4.	Rs.1,56,500 +Rs.30,000	= Rs. 1,86,500

Cost of Capital

Having assessed the cash flows of each project, the management has to evaluate them to choose among them. Evaluation of projects means to ascertain whether the projects would generate a rate of return not lower than ***determined by the company***. The determined rate of return by the company would the minimum desired rate. Unless the project gives the minimum desired rate, it would not be taken up. What therefore constitutes the desired rate of return? We have seen that any investment would be financed either solely by equity or by a mixture of debt and equity. The two sources of finance have their own costs. Equity has, as its cost, the periodic payment of dividend and capital appreciation. We can call it as cost of equity or K_e. The cost of debt is the payment of periodic interest and the repayment of the principal. We can call it as cost of debt or K_d. If preference capital is used to finance, then the prescribed dividend has to be paid periodically and the amount has to be returned at the end of the stipulated period. We can call the cost of preference capital as K_p.The Company has to earn a minimum rate of return that should be adequate to service all the sources of funds used in financing the project. Minimum desired rate of return could thus be defined as ***the lowest rate of return a project should generate to service the different sources of funds used in financing the project***.

Weighted Average Cost

Thus cost of capital might consist of cost of equity, cost of debt and cost of preference. It does not happen that all the sources are used equally. Equity might be used more in certain situations and debt in yet different situations. The mix of all the sources is called ***capital structure***. When the capital structure is heavily loaded with debt we call it ***levered structure***. Usually companies endeavour to have an ***optimal capital structure***. An optimal capital structure is one where the average cost of capital is the lowest and the return on equity is the highest. There are two different schools of thoughts on optimal capital structure. One school headed by Durand is of the view that the wealth of equity shareholders could be enhanced by an optimal capital structure. The other school by Miller and Modiglioni,who opine that there is no optimal capital structure. The reduction in cost of capital by introducing fixed rate sources would be offset by the risk associated with it, which would increase the cost of equity What is gained by fixed rate sources would be neutralized by increase in equity cost, keeping the wealth of shareholders same.

The cost of capital is thus the weighted average cost of the sources of funds used for financing the project. Before taking up evaluation, one has to know what the weighted average cost of funds for a particular project is. Weighted average cost of capital is % of Equity in the capital mix × cost of equity + % of Debt in the mix × cost of debt + % of Preference in capital mix× cost of preference. Of the sources, debt has tax-shield. Interest is a charge against profit; tax burden is reduced to that extent. Hence, cost of debt would be interest payable × 1-tax rate. The formula for weighted average cost of capital is

$\% E \times K_e + \% D \times Ki\ (1-T) + \% P \times K_p$.

where

E is equity capital, D is debt, P is preference capital, K_e is cost of equity, Ki is cost of debt and K_p is cost of preference capital

Let us apply the formula to De Foe Daniel Ltd.'s project. The cost of project at Rs.550 is proposed to be financed by equity of Rs.350 lakhs at a cost of 12% and debt of Rs.200 lakhs at an interest rate of 9%. Tax rate is 35%. The weighted average cost of funds to the company would be

WACC = 63.64 % × .12 + 36.36% ×.09(1–.35) = 7.64 +2.13 =9.77 %.

Note: equity at Rs.350 out of the mix of Rs.550 is 63.64% of the mix. Debt at Rs.200 out of Rs.550 is 36.36% of the mix.

The desired rate of return of the company would be the weighted average cost of capital or the opportunity cost whichever is higher. Usually, weighted average cost of capital and opportunity cost would converge. The desired rate of return is also called the ***cut off rate or hurdle rate or discount rate.***

Evaluation Techniques

Cash flows of projects are evaluated using investment analysis techniques. There are three basic techniques of project evaluation. All other techniques are derivations of the three. These techniques have evolved over a period of time and dictated by the needs of particular situations. The techniques are

- *Accounting rate of return.*
- *Payback period method and*
- *Present value method.*

Accounting rate of return (ARR) is the earliest form of project evaluation technique. It is a simple technique of averaging returns over investments. Cash in flows during the effective life of the project are estimated and the investment is deducted from the aggregate inflow to arrive at net return over the life of the investment. The net flow divided by the number of years over which it was generated would give average annual return. Average annual return related to investment would give the accounting rate of return. The equation for ARR IS

ARR = Σ (Po+C1 + C2 + —C_n) / n /Po,

Where Po is investment,C1 to C_n are cash in flows during the life of project, and n is effective life of investment in years.Application of the formula to cash flows calculated for De Foe Daniel Ltd.'s project in Table 14.3, would give us a clear understanding of the working of ARR.

ARR = Σ (Po+C1 +C2 + —Cn) / n /Po,

= (–550 + 211.13 +231.54 +264.07+314.45+355.39+396.11+526.55) /7/550 =38.84%.

Compare the rate with the desired rate of return. It was 9.77%. As the rate of return is higher than the minimum rate required, the project is viable and could be accepted.

Average rate of return is a straightforward technique and does not require any extraordinary skill to calculate the return. Its adoption is simple. That is why even today with advanced techniques made available, ARR continues to be an evaluation technique in small enterprises. How ever it has its own defects. The technique does not take into account the time value of money. Money has the capacity to multiply by efflux of time without any effort on the part of the investor. For example, deposit Rs.100 in a bank at 6% interest per annum with instruction to invest the accumulated interest also yearly. The deposit would grow into Rs.106 at the end of first year, Rs.112.36 at the end of second year, Rs.119.10 at the end of third year and so on. Thus the time value of money is not taken into account in ARR. Another shortfall of the method is the omission of risk.

The second technique is ***pay back period***. Pay back period, as the name implies is the period over which the investment would be paid back or recovered. It is the break even point of the project, where the accumulated returns equal investment. In this technique the investor is concerned about the rapidity of the recovery of investment. Profitability does not figure in this technique. The very urgency shown in recovering the investment suggests that there is a greater risk in the continuity of the project. The risk of discontinuity might arise due to changes in governmental policies or in technology. For example, governments frequently change their policy on prohibition. Suppose a brewery has to be set up, the investor would be eager to recover the investment before the government changes its mind. In certain other industries, like computers, electronics and communication, technological changes take place faster. Each change in technology makes the products of the previous technology obsolete. The investor is thus concerned with the recovery of his investment before the next technological change. There are two methods of working out the pay back period. When the return is expected to be uniform throughout, then pay back period is the investment divided by annual return.

Pay back period $= P_o / AAR$,

Where P_o is investment

AAR is average annual return.

For example, Kavia Chemicals has invented a formula at a cost of Rs.52.50 lakhs. The formula is expected to give an annual return of Rs.17.50. The pay back period would be 52.50 / 17.50 = 3 years.

In yet other cases, for example in De Foe Daniel Ltd.'s project, the volume of cash flow varies year after year. Pay back period in those instances could be worked out by means of a Table.

Table 4
Pay back period of De Foe Daniel Ltd.'s project.

Year	Investment-opening balance	Cash inflows	Investment-closing balance
1.	550.00	211.13	338.87
2.	338.87	231.54	107.33
3.	107.33	264.07	–156.74

The pay back period for the project is less than 3 year. To be precise, it is 2 years and 4.9 months. The defects in pay back period method are that it does not give the rate of return for the project, it does not take into consideration the time value of money and it ignores risk. A few economists have attempted to answer the defect that it does not take into account time value of money by discounting the cash flows with the desired rate of return. We have calculated the DRR for De Foe Daniel Ltd.'s project at 9.77%. Let us discount the cash flow of De Foe Daniel Ltd.'s project 9.77 and rework out pay back period.

Table 5

Time value adjusted Pay back period of De Foe Daniel Ltd.'s project.

Year	Investment-opening balance	Cash inflows		Investment-closing balance
1.	550.00	211.13 / 1.0977	= 192.34	357.66
2.	357.66	231.54 / $(1.0977)^2$	= 192.16	165.50
3.	165.50	264.07 / $(1.0977)^3$	= 199.65	– 34.15

The discounted pay back period for the project would be 2 years and 9.95 months. In spite of the defects, pay back period method is a valid tool for evaluating highly uncertain projects. When uncertainty as to the governmental policy on an industry or where fast technological changes is taking place, pay back period is useful. In practice, many companies use pay back period method with present value method before taking final decision on investments.

The last but latest technique in project evaluation is ***present value method***. This approach takes into account time value of money. Let us understand, in detail, what time value of money is and how it is used in evaluating projects. We have seen in Para 14.25 that money has the ability to multiply by efflux of time, without any effort on the part of the investor. This function of money we call as ***time value***. The return a project earns is, therefore, partly for time value and only the balance is on account of the project. So, to assess the pure return on account of a project, the return due to time value of money has to be removed from the cash flow. ***Discounting*** is the technique used for the purpose.

Suppose De Foe Daniel Ltd. Had invested its funds at the opportunity cost of 10 % with instructions to reinvest the accumulated amount at the same rate, its investment would have accumulated into what is given in the table below at the end of each of the 7 years.

Table 6

Years	Accumulated investment at the end of years
1.	Rs.605.00 lakhs
2.	Rs.665.50 lakhs
3.	Rs.732.05 lakhs
4.	Rs.805.25 lakhs
5.	Rs.885.78 lakhs
6.	Rs.974.36 lakhs
7.	Rs.1071.79lakhs

Since investment is made at present and the incomes start flowing in future, it would be unfair to compare the nominal values of future returns (which are subjected to time value) with the present investment. For an effective comparison, either the present investment should be scaled up to the future or the future returns are to be brought on par with the present investment. The former is the ***cumulative cash flow method*** and the latter is ***discounted cash flow technique***. Preference is for discounted cash flow.

Table above indicated that when the market rate of return is 10 %, De Foe Daniel Ltd. is indifferent as to having Rs.605 at the end of first year or Rs.550 at present, Rs.665.50 lakhs at the end of second year or Rs.550 at present, Rs.732.05 lakhs at the end of third year or Rs.550 at present, Rs.805.25 lakhs at the end of the fourth year or Rs.550 at present, Rs.885.78 lakhs at the end of fifth year or Rs.550 at present, Rs.974.36 lakhs at the end of sixth year or Rs.550 at present, Rs.1071.79lakhs at the end of seventh year or Rs.550 at present. In other words, when the rate of return is 10%, the present value ofRs.605.00 lakhs at the end of first year, or Rs.665.50 lakhs at the end of second year or Rs.732.05 lakhs at the end of third year or Rs.805.25 lakhs at the end of fourth year orRs.885.78 lakhs at the end of fifth year orRs.974.36 lakhs at the end of sixth year or Rs.1071.79lakhs at the end of seventh year is Rs.550 lakhs. In case the company receives Re. 1 at the end of each of the years, its present value would be

550/605 = 0.9091

550/ 665.5 = 0.8264

550 / 732.05 = 0.7513

550 / 805.25 = 0.6830

550 / 885.78 = 0.6209

550 / 974.36 = 0.5645

550 / 1071.79 = 0.5132

These are ***discount factors***. Discount factors would be different for different rates of return. All books on finance would have discount tables for different rates for periods usually up to 40 years. Discount tables are given in this book as annexure at the end . Future returns multiplied by the discount factors would give the present value of future cash inflows. This process is known as ***discounting cash flow method***. Discount tables are available for absolute numbers. If the returns are in decimals, for example, 7.5%, then discount tables are of no use in assessing present value. There is yet another method of discounting cash flows by using calculators. The formula is ***C/ 1+r,*** where C is the cash flow and r is the rate of return. Applying the formula to a cash flow of Re. 1 over n years at 10% return, the factor would be $1 / 1.10 = 0.9091$, $1/(1.10)^2 =$ 8264, $(1/1.1)^3 = 0.7513$ and so on. In this method, present value of future cash flows could be arrived at by dividing the future cash flows by 1+r to the power of n years. This method could conveniently be applied even to fractional returns.

Let us apply this to the cash flows of De Foe Daniel Ltd.'s project, where the discount factor (WACC) was 9.77:

	Rs.		Rs.
Year 1	= 211.13 / 1.0977	=	192.34
Year 2	= 231.54 / $(1.0977)^2$	=	192.16
Year 3	= 264.07 / $(1.0977)^3$	=	199.65
Year 4	= 314.45 / $(1.0977)^4$	=	216.58
Year 5	= 355.39 / $(1.0977)^5$	=	222.99
Year 6	= 396.11 / $(1.0977)^6$	=	226.42
Year 7	= 526.55 / (1.0977)7	=	274.19

The sum of the discounted cash flow is the present value (PV) of the project.

Present value of project = $\sum_{t=1}^{n}$ i.e. $C / 1+r + C_2 / (1+r)^2 + C_3 / (1+r)^3 + C_n / (1+r)^n$. The present value of the cash flows of De Foe Daniel Ltd.'s project would thus be

Present value of project = $\sum_{t=1}^{n}$ i.e. 192.34+192.16+199.65 +216.58+222.99 +226.42+274.19 = Rs.1524.33 lakhs. Comparing the present value with the initial investment would make a project positive or negative. Where the present value is more than investment, the project is positive. If the present value is less than investment, the project is negative. Present value less investment is net present value (NPV). In formula, net present value is

NPV = $\sum_{t=0}^{n}$ i.e. $Po + C / 1+r + C2 / (1+r)^2 + C3 / (1+r)^3 + Cn / (1+r)^n$

When NPV is positive, project passes the test of viability. Applying the formula to the cash flows of De Foe Daniel Ltd.'s project, the NPV would be

NPV = $\sum_{t=0}^{n}$ i.e. -Rs.550 +192.34+192.16+199.65 +216.58+222.99 +226.42+274.19

= Rs 974.33lakhs.

A company before investment would evaluate cash flows and if found positive, would decide in taking up the project. Suppose the company has a basket of projects, all of which have passed the cut off test, but the resources that the company could mobilize are limited then the company would ration out the resources. If the amount to be invested in each project is same and the annual cash flows are same, it would not pose any problem in ranking the projects. But in real life situations, quantum of investments and the inflows would vary from project to project just as in the following illustration. Kavia Keltone Ltd. has a weighted average cost of capital of 15%. The company has identified three projects, of which it could afford only two. Details of the projects are:

Table 7

	Project A	Project B	Project C
Investment-Rs. Lakhs.	326.78	412.80	278.54
Return			
1 year	77.50	196.86	112.40
2 year	126.55	174.80	112.40
3year	157.00	158.25	112.40
4year.	165.25	127.69	112.40

In such a situation, the ranking of the projects under accounting rate of return, pay back period and present value methods would be

1.ARR.

Project A. = [(Σ -326.78+77.50+126.55+157.00+165.25) / 4 / 326.78 × 100] = 15.26%
Project B. = [(Σ -412.80 +196.86+174.80+158.25+127.69) / 4 / 412.80 ×100 = 14.83%

Project C. = [(Σ –278.54+112.40+112.40+112.40+112.40) / 4 / 278.54 × 100 = 15.36%

2.P B P.

Table 8

	Project A			Project B			Project C		
Yr	Opening	Returns	Closing	Opening	Return	Closing	Opening	Return	Closing
1.	326.78	77.50	249.28	412.80	196.86	215.94	278.54	112.40	166.14
2.	249.28	126.55	122.73	215.94	174.80	41.14	166.14	112.40	53.74
3.	122.73	157.00	—	41.14	158.25	—	53.74	112.40	—
4.		165.25			127.69				
PB	2years			2years			2years		
	10month			4month			6months		

3.Under discounted pay back period method

	Project A			Project B			Project C		
Yr	Opening	Returns	Closing	Opening	Return	Closing	Opening	Return	Closing
1.	326.78	77.50/ 1.15= 67.39	259.39	412.80	196.86/ 1.15= 171.18		241.62	112.40/ 1.15= 97.74	180.80
2.	259.39	126.55/ 1.152= 95.69	163.70	241.62	174.80/ 1.152= 132.17	109.45	180.80	112.40/ 1.152= 84.99	95.81
3.	163.70	157.00/ 1.153= 103.23	60.67	109.45 5.40	158.25/ 1.153– 104.05	5.40	95.81	112.40/ 1.153– 73.90	21.91
4. PB	60.67 3years8 months	165.25/ 1.154= 94.48		3 years 1month	127.69/ 1.154= 73.01		21.91 3 years 4 months	112.40/ 1.154= 64.26	

4.Under present value method

PV. of Project A.

$PV = \sum_{t=1}^{n}$ i.e. $(77.50/ 1.15) + (126.55 / 1.15^2) + (157.00 / 1.15^3 +(165.25 / 1.15^4)$

= Rs.360.79 lakhs.

PV of project Project B.

$PV = \sum_{t=1}^{n}$ i.e. $(196.86 / 1.15) +(174.80 / 1.15^2) +(158.25 / 1.15^3) +$

$(127.69 / 1.15^4)$ = Rs.480.41lakhs.

PV of Project C.

$PV = \sum_{t=1}^{n}$ i.e. $+(112.40 / 1.15) +(112.40 / 1.15^2) +(112.40 / 1.15^3) +$

$(112.40 / 1.15^4)$ = Rs.320.90lakhs

The ranking of Kavia Keltone Ltd's projects under the three techniques is in table below.

Ranking	Project A	Project B	Project C
Under ARR			
Rate of return	15.26 %	14.83 %	15.36 %

Ranking	2	3	1
Under PBP method			
Ranking	3	1	2
Under PV method			
Investment(1)	326.78	412.80	278.54
PV(2)	360.79	480.41	320.90
PI(2 / 1)	1.10	1.16	1.15
Ranking	3	1	2

The company would choose the two projects depending upon the method of evaluation it adopts. If the company adopts ARR as the method, the company would drop B as it gives a return below the cut off rate of 15%. Project C would be priority number 1 with ARR of 15.36% and A with ARR of 15.26%. Should the company adopts pay back period method, priorities change and project B with PBP of 2 years and 4 months ranks first, followed by project C with PBP of 2 years and 6 months. A is third with PBP of 2 years and 10 months. Project A would be dropped. In case the company adopts NPV method, it would be in a dilemma as all the projects are positive. There is an extended wing of NPV method, which comes to the assistance of investors in these cases. It is ***profitability index (PI)***. Profitability index is the measure of intensity of profit. It is arrived at by dividing the PV by the investment. Present Value (PV), as we know, is the sum of the discounted cash inflows of the project during its effective life. Profitability index of the three projects are:

Project A = Rs.360.79 / Rs.326.78 =1.104

Project B = Rs.480.41 / Rs.412.80 =1.164

Project C = Rs.320.90 / Rs.278.54 =1.152

The picture is now clear. Project B with PI of 1.164 ranks first, followed by Project C with PI of 1.152. A with PI of 1.104 is dropped. So in credit rationing the projects to be chosen would be determined by the method of evaluation to be adopted by the company. Today, most of the investors choose present value method, as it provides for the time value of money.

Present value method determines whether a project is positive or otherwise based on the discounting rate (which is also the DRR, the cut-off rate or hurdle rate). It tells the investors that a particular project gives more or less than the desired rate. The discounted cash flow would be either more or less than the investment. If it is more, we call it positive NPV. NPV means that the actual rate of return is more than the discount rate. If the present value is less than investment, the NPV is negative. Negative NPV indicates that the actual rate of return is less than the discount rate. It would not, however, indicate what exactly is the rate of return the project would give. This is calculated through another sub-tool of present value method, namely ***internal rate of return (IRR)***. IRR is thus that rate of return at which the discounted cash flow would equal investment. It is the point where PV – Investment = 0. Formula for IRR is

$$NPV = \sum_{t=0}^{n} = 0$$

Trial and error is the route for working out IRR. The number of try could, however, be reduced to two if we adopt interpolation technique. Discounted cash flow have to be worked out for two different rates in such a manner that one rate should give a positive PV and the other a negative PV. Roughly the IRR would be within the proximity of ARR. Therefore, ARR has to be calculated as a first step. Then two rates, one that would give a positive PV and another that would give a negative PV had to be assumed and the cash flows have to be discounted by both the rates separately. From the results, the differences are to be interpolated to arrive at the IRR. Let us apply interpolation technique to the cash flow of De Foe Daniel Ltd.'s project. The cash flow (paragraph 14.24) for seven years wereRs.211.13, Rs.231.54, Rs.264.07, Rs.314.45, Rs. Rs.355.39, Rs.396.11and Rs.526.55 on an investment of Rs. 550. The ARR was 38.84%. We should now choose one rate that might give a positive PV, say for instance 35% and another that might give a negative PV, say 45%. The following are the PVs under the rates:

At 35% = (Rs.211.13/ 1.35)+(Rs.231.54 / 1.35^2)+(Rs.264.07 / 1.35^3)+(Rs.314.45 / 1.35^4)+ (Rs.355.39 / 1.35^5)+(Rs.396.11 / 1.35^6)+(Rs.526.55 / 1.35^7) = Rs.694.57

At 50% = (Rs.211.13 / 1.45) + (Rs.231.54 / 1.45^2) + (Rs.264.07 / 1.45^3)+ (Rs.314.45 / 1.45^4)+ (Rs.355.39 /1.45^5)+(Rs.396.11 / 1.45^6)+ (Rs.526.55 / 1.45^7) = Rs.550.63.

It is by incident that we found the IRR around 45%, at which the NPV is 0.63 only (PV Rs.550.63 at 45% – investment at Rs.550) . In reality, there would be wide variation.

The variation in PV between 35% and 45% is =Rs.694.57 – Rs.550.63 = 143.94.

Or 143.94 PV would cause 10% change in discount factor.

At 35% NPV was 144.57(694.57 – 550)

For a NPV of Rs.144.47, discount factor would be = 10 / 143.94 × 144.47 = 10.04

∴ IRR would be 10.04% more than 35% = 45.04% or 45% for all practical purposes.

Let us check

Σ (Rs.211.13/1.4504)+(Rs.231.54/1.4504^2)+(Rs.264.07 / 1.4504^3)+(Rs.314.45 / 1.4504^4) + Rs.355.39 / 1.4504^5)+(Rs.396.11 / 1.4504^6)+(Rs.526.55 / 1.4504^7) = Rs. 550.17as against investment of Rs.550.The difference is due to rounding off of the discount rate and NPV.

IRR could also be used for ascertaining the feasibility of borrowings by businesses. In all investment projects, cash flow in 0 year would be negative, as ***cash flows out*** during the implementation of the project. However in cases of evaluating borrowings, cash flow in 0 year would be positive, ***as cash flows in*** when you borrow. In that case, all repayments are cash out flows. For example, Lamination Landscape Ltd. desires to borrow Rs.10,000 lakhs from Quick Loan Bank Ltd. to be repaid in three yearly installments of Rs. 4021 lakhs each. The cost of capital of the company is 11%. Let us consider whether the company could avail of the loan.

The cash flow for the proposal would work out as under:

0 year	+10,000
1 year	–4,021
2 year	–4,021
3year	–4,021

IRR of the cash flows would be 10% arrived by interpolation between 8% and 12 % as under

PV at 8% = Σ 4021 / 1.08 + 4021 / 1.082 + 4021 / 1.083

= 3725.93 + 3449.93 + 3194.38 = 10,370.24

PV at 12% = Σ 4021 / 1.12 + 4021 / 1.122 + 4021 / 1.123

= 3590.18 + 3205.52 + 2862.07 = 9,657.77

PV of 712.47(10,370.24 – 9,657.77) is caused by 4 % discount factor (12% – 4%).

∴ for a PV of 370.24 (PV at 8% 10,370.24 less investment 10,000), the discount factor should be 4 / 712.47 × 370.24 = 2 percent

∴ IRR should be 8% + 2% = 10%

Check up that the discounted cash flow would equal initial borrowings at 10% interest

At 10% , NPV = +Σ 1000 + [(– 4021 / 1.1) + (– 4021 / 1.12) + (4021 / 1.13)] = 0

Since the cost of borrowing is 10%, as against the cost of capital of the company at 11%, it is advisable for the company to borrow Rs.10,000 lakhs from Quick Loan Bank Ltd.

Defects of IRR

IRR is no doubt a good measure to know what exactly the return a particular project gives. An investor could compare the IRR with his desired rate of return and decide to invest in that project or not. But there are two known short falls of IRR. There could be more than one IRR for a particular investment proposal. This is so when the cash flows are fluctuating. That is where positive and negative cash inflows interchangeably result. For example, investment Rs.1,000 yields a net cash inflow of Rs.3,600 in the first year, net cash out flow of Rs.4,320 in the second year and net cash inflow of Rs.1,728.We have already seen that a project might have negative cash flow in any year of operation, when there is additional investment. Such a project might give either 11% or 20% as under

Table 9

Year	Cash flow	PV at 11%	PV at 20%
0	–1000	–1000	–1000
1	3600	3243	3000
2	–4320	–3506	–3000
3	1728	1263	1000
Total		1000	1000

Another defect in IRR is that in certain cash flows IRR could be negative whereas NPV would be positive. For example, investment Rs. 1000 cash flows as under:

Year 1 Rs.800
2 Rs.150
3 Rs.150
4 Rs.150
5 Rs.150
6 – Rs.150

The above proposal might give a negative IRR of 50% or a positive 15.2 %

For these inconsistencies, analysts prefer to employ net present value rather than IRR for evaluating project viability.

There is many a slip between the cup and the lip might be an old proverb but has a forceful application in current management practices. There are quite a lot of chances that many unexpected things might happen contrary to what one expects. Expectations are often based on the information available to the decision maker at the time of making the decision. Some of the information are actual while others are based on forecast. The forecasted information might turn out in either way. It might be for better or worse. Factors that are responsible for the deviation of actual from anticipated might be internal to the organization or external over which it has no control. Internal factors include managerial capabilities, organizational strengths and weaknesses and change in consumer preferences. Economical, social and political are external factors that could bring about the change over expectations. Some of these changes could be anticipated and quantified to an extent. These are ***risks***. Other deviations, which could not be envisaged, are ***uncertainties***. Economic, political and other macro level changes are uncertainties. Though we have categorized deviations into risks and uncertainties, for analysis both are interchangeably used to mean variations.

Risks are deviations of realized returns from expected returns. Some of the deviations might affect most of the industries and some are confined to a particular organization. Those variations that affect the industries as a whole are ***general or symmetrical or systemic risks***. Such of the variations that are confined to an organization are ***specific, or asymmetrical or unsystemic risks***. Specific risk are avoidable and as such do not qualify for premium. On the other hand, general risk is unavoidable and has to be borne by the investor and hence needs a premium. Higher the intensity of the risk, higher should also be the premium for shouldering such risks. The principle underlying the relationship between risk and return is ***premium for risk is commensurate with the quantum of risk***.

All the project evaluation techniques, such as accounting rate of return, pay back period and present value methods are based on the premise that the actual results of the projects would be the same as forecast. The element of risk is not taken into consideration. Suppose we expect a return of 10% on a project, the possibility of the actual return might be higher at 11%, 12% 13% or lower at 9%, 8% or 7%. For example the experience in the market is that out of 17 years, the return on investment in the industry was13% in one year, 12% in 2 years, 11% in 3 years 10% in5 years, 9% in 2 years, 8% and 7% in one year each. Therefore the probability of the project yielding a return of 10% is 31%, 11% is 19%, 12% is 13%, 13% is 6%, 9% is 19%, 8% is 6% and 7% is 6%. This gives a weighted average return of 10.14% as in table below.

Table 10

	Expected rate	Probability	Weighted average
Possibility 1	10%	0.31	3.10
Possibility 2	11%	0.19	2.09
Possibility 3	12%	0.13	1.56
Possibility 4	13%	0.06	0.78
Possibility 5	9%	0.19	1.71
Possibility 6	8%	0.06	0.48
Possibility 7	7%	0.06	0.42
Observed rate of return			10.14%

Thus, the ***observed rate of return***, which is the weighted average rate, is 10.14%. The square of the dispersion, which is the deviation of each of the expected returns from the observed returns, would give variance (σ^2). The formula would be σ^2 = S of O – E, where σ^2 is variance, S is square, O is observed return, E is expected return. The variance for the project is therefore would be as under

Table 11

Possible returns	**Observed returns**	**Variance^2**
10%	10.14%	0.0198
11%	10.14%	0.7396
12%	10.14%	3.4596
13%	10.14%	8.1796
9%	10.14%	1.2996
8%	10.14%	4.5796
7%	10.14%	9.8596
Total		28.1374

The square root of variance ($\sqrt{\sigma^2}$) is ***standard deviation (σ)***. In the illustrated case the standard deviation is 5.30 as under

$\sigma = \sqrt{28.1374} = 5.30$).

Standard deviation is usually presented in units (5.30), but could also be shown in percentages (530% in this illustration). It is thus a measure of risk. Higher is the standard deviation, higher is the risk. Suppose in the same case, the possible returns are 10% 12% and 8% and the probabilities are 0.5, 0.3 and 0.2, then the standard deviation is 2.8 as under:

Table 12

	Expected rate	**Probability**	**W.A.R**
Possibility 1	10%	0.5	5.0
Possibility 2	12%	0.3	3.6
Possibility 3	8%	0.2	1.6
Observed rate of return			10.2

Variance or dispersion of the returns is square of O – E as in statement below.

Table 13

Expected	Observed	Variance
10%	10.2%	0.04
12%	10.2%	3.24
8%	10.2%	4.84
Variance		8.12

Standard deviation is 2.85or 285%

$= \sqrt{8.12)} = 2.85$

It might be observed that the propensity of risk in the second category is lower at 2.85 as against 5.3 in the first case. Wider the degree of dispersion, higher is the risk. Standard deviation of 1 equals market risk.

We have seen that suitable premium has to be paid for bearing symmetrical risk. The quantum of premium payable for a given risk situation has to be based on a benchmark return that is free from risk. In other words, we have to relate the quantum of risk premium to a ***risk free rate of return*** **(r_f)**. There is no investment without risk. However, investments in 91 days treasury bills are presumed to be least risky. Hence the yield on 91 days treasury bills might be construed as risk free return. Treasury bills are periodically auctioned and are also available in secondary markets. The pricing of treasury bills is with upfront discount. That is, they are sold at face value less the interest component for the tenure of the bill.. For example, 91 days treasury bills of face value of Rs.100 might be auctioned at Rs.98.75. The risk free rate of return therefore would be 5.08 (1.25 / 98.75 / 91 × 365).

The market rate of return is r_m. r_m should be risk free rate of return plus premium for market risk. If we know market rate of return and the risk free rate, we could easily arrive at the premium for market risk. Should the market rate of return is 8%, and then the premium for market risk would be 2.92% (market rate of 8% less risk free rate of 5.08). Market risk premium is measured as 1. Individual projects might have the same degree of risk as the market or might have risk higher or lower than the market risk. The relationship between market risk and the risk of the individual project is called ***beta*** ( ). Beta therefore the measure of risk of individual projects compared to that of market risk. If the beta of a project is same as that of the market, then it is at unity with market and is shown as 1.If the beta of a project is higher than market, then it is more than 1.When the beta of a project is lower than that of the market, it is less than 1.Beta is the measure of premium for risk. If the beta of a project is 1, that is same as that of the market, the risk premium of the project should also be equal to the market risk premium. For example, the beta of the project of Florida Footwear is 1and the market risk premium is 2.92%, the risk premium for the project of Florida Footwear would also be 2.92% (1× 2.92). If the beta of a project is more than 1, the risk premium should be so much higher than the market risk premium. For example, if the beta of the project of Konolulu Kondara Ltd. is 1.75 and the market risk premium is 2.92%, the risk premium for the project of Konolulu Kondara Ltd. should be 1.75 times that of market risk premium or 5.11 % (1.75 × 2.92). In yet another project of Haddows Hardware Ltd., the beta is 0.75, then the risk premium for the project of Haddows Hardware Ltd. would be 2.19%(0.75 × 2.92).

Since the minimum rate of return desired on a project is risk free rate plus premium for the risk, the desired rate of return is $r = r_f + \beta (r_m - r_f)$. This equation is called ***capital assets pricing model*** (CAPM). The author of this model is William F.Sharpe, who won Nobel Prize for his formulation. CAPM is used to measure the risk premium for investment in securities particularly stocks. In portfolio management, CAPM plays a vital role in assessing the desired rate of return in a security, having regard to its riskiness. Beta in security analysis means the responsiveness of a given stock to the price movement in the market. If the price of a particular stock moves in tandem with that of the market, its beta is 1 or unity. For example, if the market price (represented by stock index) increases by 35%, or falls by 25% and the price of Reliance also increases by 35% or decreases by 25%, the beta of Reliance is 1 or unity. In case the movement in the price of a stock is greater than that of the market, its beta is more than 1. For example, if the market price increases by 30% or decreases by 20%, and the price of WIPRO's stock increases by 45% or decreases by 30%, the beta of WIPRO's stock is 1.5 or greater than 1. On the other hand, if the movement in the price of a stock is less than that of the market, its beta is less than 1. For example, the price of Hindustan Levers stock increases by 15% when the market prices have increased by 30% and decreased by 10% when the market price had decreased by 20%, then the beta of Hindustan Levers stock is 0.5 or less than 1.When the price of a security is unaffected by the market price movement, its beta is zero. A risk free investment security would thus have zero beta.

Summary

Capital budgeting is the tool for business to grow with stability. It encompasses investment in fixed assets and working capital. There are different types of projects in which a company could make investment. Basically, capital investment results either in increasing production or quality or reduction in cost of operation. As decisions in capital budgeting are not reversible, care should be exercised ininvestment. Capital budgeting involves identification of projects, calculation of likely cash flows, evaluation of cash flows and selection. Cash flows are evaluated to ensure that the investment would give a rate of return not less than the desired rate. Desired rate of return is the weighted average cost of capital or the opportunity cost. Accounting rate of return, pay back period and present value are methods of evaluating projects. Businesses employ any or all three methods of evaluating projects before choosing those that give higher return than the cost of funds or reduce costs. Investors should also look into the likely hood of their realizations matching with expectations. Risk deviates actual from expectation. Risks are primarily variances that make actual performance different from planned. Of the risks, general risks that are unavoidable need premium to shoulder. Standard deviation is used as a measurement of risk. Return for risk is worked out using CAPM.

I. QUESTIONS

1. What is capital budgeting and why it is necessary for the development of a business?
2. What are the types of investment involved in capital budgeting?
3. What are projects? What are the types of projects in which a company would invest?
4. What do you understand by the term weighted average cost of capital? How it is calculated?
5. What are interdependent and independent projects?
6. What do you mean by 'Capital Rationing'? Explain with an illustration.
7. What are the stages involved in choosing projects?
8. What are cash flows in capital budgeting? How would you calculate cash flows?
9. What are the techniques available for evaluating projects? Which of them you consider best and why?
10. Whar is Accounting rate of return? How would you calculate it?
11. What is pay back period? What are the ways of calculating pay back period? Is pay back period a useful tool in evaluating projects? When?
12. What is time value of money? Which of the techniques had adopted it/
13. What are the different discounted cash flow (DCF) techniques used in evaluating capital investment projects? Explain any one of them.
14. What is profitability index? When is it used?
15. What is IRR? What are its uses? Is it the best in present value methods?
16. What is risk?
17. Classify the factors that cause risk?
18. What are the kind of risks a project is subjected to?

19. What are systematic risks? What are their impacts?
20. When would an investor require premium for risk?
21. What is standard deviation? What are its uses?
22. What is risk free rate of return?
23. What is CAPM? In which area of investment it is generally used?
24. What t are probabilities? What are its uses in evaluating projects?

II. QUIZ

Say yes or no

1. Capital budgeting is routine in nature
2. Both long term assets and short term assets are involved in capital budgeting.
3. Companies invest in any projects that generate income.
4. Expansion means taking up an unrelated industry.
5. Modernization involves replacement of old machines with new ones.
6. Capital rationing means allocating resources on projects on priority basis.
7. Cash out flow is investment.
8. Return is profit after tax.
9. ARR means accepted rate of return.
10. Pay back period method reveals the rate of return the project is likely yield.
11. Reserves have no cost.
12. Weighted average cost of capital is the minimum rate expected from investments.
13. Money has time value.
14. Present value method discounts future returns at the desired rate,
15. Minimum desired rate is weighted average cost of capital.
16. IRR might indicate more than two rates for a project.
17. Profitability index is present value divided by investment.
18. Expected returns are usually realized returns too.
19. Probabilities of an event happening are equal.
20. CAPM is a technique to measure the reqoured risk premium.

III. EXERCISES

1. Swarna Processors Ltd. Has received a proposal from the production manager to add cloth printing to the existing activities of the company. The equipment for the additional facility is expected to cost Rs.150 lakhs, Besides, the Co. would also require, by way of addl. Working capital Rs.75 lakhs. The life of the equipment was estimated 5 years. The machine would then fetch a sale value of Rs.25 lakhs. During its life, the printing unit is expected to generate an annual sale of Rs.200 lakhs as against cost of sales of Rs.125 lakhs. The company would depreciate the equipment at the rate of Rs.20 lakh every year. Calculate the cash flow for the proposal.
2. Chiang Sun Co. has a proposal to replace one of its old machine by a new sophisticated one, which is expected to reduce costs from Rs.6.50 lakhs to Rs.5.60 lakhs annually. The purchase price of the new machine is Rs.2.20 lakhs and Rs.20,000 is required to transport and erect the new machine. The new machine has a useful life of 4 years. The old machine can also be used for the same period. The new machine would require additional tools of Rs.20,000 at the time of installation. The book value of the old machine now is Rs.80,000 and to be depreciated equally to 0. The old machine would now fetch a sales price of Rs.40,000; if sold after 4 years, Rs.10,000. The new machine, after its use would have a book value of Rs.40,000 and would have a book value of Rs.40,000 and would fetch Rs.30,000. Dep. On Straight line method; rate of tax 35% calculate cash flows.
3. Rono Ltd., desires to replace one of its machines R2 with a new sophisticated one. Cost of new machine is Rs.29 crores. The machine has effective life of 5 years after which it is expected to have a salvage value of Rs.1.8 crores. The existing machine, with a book value of Rs.9.55 crores can also work for another 5 years. Its current salvage value is Rs.8.85 crores. After 5 years, it will have scrap value of Rs1.50crores. The existing machine is depreciated at Rs.1.75 crores / annum. The new machine is expected to reduce cost of operation by Rs.7.50 crores per annum. Assuming a tax rate of 35 %, calculate cash flows for the replacement.
4. Multiproducio Ltd., proposes to replace one of its lathes at a cost of Rs.5 lakhs. The new lathe will have useful life of 4 years after which it will realize Rs.50,000 as against its book value of Rs.40,000. The old lathe can now be sold for Rs.75,000 as against its book value of Rs.80,000. The old lathe can also be operated for another 4 years at the end of which it can be sold for Rs.10,000 as against its then book value of Rs.20,000. Cost savings to the company on account of replacement would be Rs.180 lakhs per annum. Tax 40 %
5. Comprehend computers proposes to invest in a new product. The project would require investment in fixed assets of Rs.150 lakhs. Working capital needs of the project would be

Rs.75 lakhs. Project life is 4 years. Profit before tax for the investment period of four years would be Rs.100 lakhs, Rs.125 lakhs, Rs.75 lakhs, and Rs.70 lakhs. Taxation @ 35 %. Weighted average cost of capital of the company was 12 %. Would it be advisable for the company to take up the project?

6. Ferro Allies has a proposal to replace one of its old machines by a new sophisticated one, which is expected to reduce costs from Rs.16.50 lakhs to Rs.11.60 lakhs annually. The purchase price of the new machine is Rs.20.20 lakhs. The new machine has a useful life of 7 years. The old machine can also be used for the same period. The book value of the old machine now is Rs.3,80,000 and to be depreciated equally to Rs.50,000 over 7 years. The old machine would now fetch a sales price of Rs.2,40,000; if sold after 7 years, Rs.20,000. The new machine, after its use would have a book value of Rs.1,40,000 and would fetch Rs.90,000. Depreciation on straight-line method; rate of tax 35%. If desired rate of return is 12%, would you recommend the proposal?

7. From the following, rank the project under ARR,PBP and PV methods.

		A	B	C
Investments		– 10.00	– 10.00	– 10.00
Returns Years1		2.50	5.00	1.00
2.		2.50	4.00	2.00
3.		2.50	2.50	2.50
4.		2.50	2.00	3.00
5.		2.50	1.50	3.50
6.		2.50	1.00	5.00
Total		14.00	16.00	17.00

8. Calculate weighted average cost of capital for Sinnu Traders whose cost of investment is Rs.100 lakhs. The cost is to be financed by Debt Rs.35 lakhs at 14% interest, preference Rs.15 lakhs at a fixed dividend of 15%and equity Rs.50 lakhs at a cost of 18%. Rate of taxation 40%.

9. A machine purchased six years ago for Rs. 1,80,000 has been depreciated to a book value of Rs. 90,000. It originally had a projected life of 15 years and zero salvage value. A new machine will cost Rs. 2,50,000 and result in a reduced operating cost of Rs. 30,000 per year for the next nine years. The order machine could be sold for Rs. 50,000. The cost of capital is 10 per cent. The new machine will be depreciated on a straight-line basis over nine years life with Rs. 25,000 salvage value. The company's tax rate is 35%. Determine whether the old machine should be replaced.

10. If expected rate of return is 30%, do you recommend the following projects.

	Project A	Project B
Capital Cost (Rs.)	1,00,000	1,50,000
Annual Savings	30,000	50,000
Annual Savings	30,000	70,000
Annual Savings	40,000	80,000
Annual Savings	50,000	50,000

11. Using the information give below, compute the NPV.

Initial outlay Rs. 80,000

Estimate life 5 years

Profit after tax

End of the year 1. Rs. 6,000

2. Rs. 14,000

3. Rs. 24,000

4. Rs. 16,000

5. NIL

Depreciation has been calculated under straight-line method. The cost of capital may be taken at 20% per annum and the PV of Re. 1 at 20% per annum is as under

Year	1	2	3	4	5
PV factor	0.83	0.69	0.58	0.48	0.40

12. A project costs Rs.16,000 and it is expected to generate cash inflows of Rs.8,000, Rs.7,000 and Rs.6,000 at the end of each year for 3 years. Calculate NPV at 15 per cent discounting rate and also find the IRR of the project.

13. A machine will cost Rs. 1,00,000 and will provide an annual cash flow of Rs. 30,000 for six years. The cost of capital is 15 percent. Calculate the NPV and IRR and advice on the viability of investment.

14. A job, which is presently done entirely by manual labour, has a labour cost of Rs. 46,000 a year. It is proposed to install a machine to do the job. Which involves an investment of Rs. 80,000 and an additional operating cost of Rs. 10,000. Assume the machine can be written off in 5 years on straight-line depreciation basis for tax purposes. Salvage value at the end of its economic life is zero. The tax rate is 55%. Advice whether to invest in machine or continue with the labour.

CHAPTER 15

INFLATION ACCOUNTING

Learning Objective

Performances of businesses are assessed on the basis of nominal profits made by them. This, though the accepted norm, has its own pitfalls. The purchasing power of the profit gets diluted when there is increase in price levels. Shrewd businessmen do not only consider the money value of their income, but also its ability to command goods and services. Inflation accounting is the solution. The chapter discusses the impact of inflation on the various items of incomes, costs, assets and liabilities and the techniques available to assess the erosion.

Conventional accounting methods assume stability in the value of currency used for recording transactions. Value of currency is the reflection of its ***purchasing power***. Purchasing power is the ability of a given currency to command goods and services. To command a given units of goods and services, the price level of the country should remain the same. Any increase in price level would reduce the purchasing power of the currency and vice versa. When the value of a country's currency increases, consequent to the decrease in price level, the resulting economic situation is ***deflation***. When its value decreases with increase in price level, it is ***inflation.*** The increase or decrease in price level is measured by wholesale price index of selected goods and services with appropriate weightage. Our WPI is based on the price of commodities as prevailing in 1993 – 94, which was fixed as 100. WPI stood at 203.7 points in 15th July 2006. Deflation is not a usual phenomenon. Currently, Japan is reported to have a deflated economy. No country prefers deflation as it brings down the level of economic activities with its resultant unemployment, poverty and decline in standard of living.

Impact of Inflation on Profitability

The impact of inflation is beneficial to the business to an extent, particularly when its liabilities are long-term in nature and assets short-term and the rate of inflation is with in limits of say around 2 to 3 percent. But when the rate if inflation is higher and the assets of the business are of long-term duration, inflation hurts the business. It hurts both the profitability and the structure of the business. The immediate effect of inflation is the rising costs of inputs. The general assumption is that any increase in input cost would be neutralized by increase in output cost is true in monopoly conditions and in controlled economies. In free economies, towards which we are moving, it might not be possible to pass on the increase in cost of inputs to consumers particularly under the situations when

- *The demand is highly price sensitive;*
- *The market is intensely competitive;*
- *The business has long collection periods:*
- *The enterprise has huge investment in fixed assets and*
- *The method of valuation of inventory is on the basis of first in first out.*

Inflation would distort the performance of the business, whatever be its intensity. The reason is simple. The assumption that the measurement of value (i.e. money) remains stable through is proved false during inflation, when the measuring rod itself shrinks in value. Such shrinkage in value of money overstates the normal profitability and understates the value of assets held.

Increase in Input Cost

It has been seen that during inflation costs of inputs rise. The increase in cost has to be absorbed, in a free economy, by the business itself through either increase in volume of production or improvements in effiency or by both. It is, therefore, imperative for a businessman to understand where inflation is going to hurt him, so that he can take corrective measures well in time to safeguard erosion in real value of his wealth. From the input side, the impact of inflation might be on materials consumed, wages and interest paid. Increase in material cost might be either direct or indirect. When domestic prices increase, the material cost increases. This is direct increase. In case the unit consumes imported materials and there is no increase in the domestic prices of the exporter imported materials might face increased cost more on account of exchange rate fluctuations. Exchange rates are influenced by differential interest rates among countries. Interest rates are affected directly by inflation; higher the rate of inflation, higher would be the rate of interest. Thus, material costs might also be indirectly affected by inflation. No business in India works with day-to-day purchase of materials. They stock the requirements for a specific period, depending upon the lead-time and the economic order quantity. It is not unusual for Indian companies to maintain three months requirements as stock. Hence, though the material cost in the market increases during inflation, the businesses in India use stocks purchased earlier, which means at cheaper costs compared to the market rate at the time the finished products are marketed If the business utilizes the materials purchased earlier, particularly under the first in first out method, the cost of production does not truly reflect the current cost of materials consumed. This increases the profit of the business artificially. Thus profitability of businesses increases in times of inflation. Needless to add that the reverse is obvious during deflation.

Increase in Wages

Wages are the next input that are automatically pushed up by inflation, as the payment of wages is linked to any one of the cost of living indices. Cost of living indices, in turn, reflects the price levels. Therefore, excepting for a very short period, labour cost is based on the current market price. Increase in labour cost usually gets absorbed in the price of output. Interest rates tend to increase with the price level. However, due to the segmentation of the money market in the country and the predominance of fixed rate of interest in lending, the impact of inflation does not materially affect interest costs. However, with increasing opening up of the economy, the lending habit of Indian money market is fast changing into floating rate. In case the change to floating rates becomes normal, it might not be long before inflation would affect interest cost also.

Increase in Depreciation

Another cost that would affect profitability during inflation is depreciation. Depreciation is allowed as a cost only up to the extent of the historic value of assets. In times of inflation, the replacement costs of the assets would be much higher than their historic costs. If the business is temporary, then the question of replacement does not arise. But the convention of business being that of going concern, with continuity of operation, replacement costs assume significance. During inflation, the replacement costs of assets surpass their historic values. When goods are cost on the basis of historic depreciation, instead of on replacement value of assets, sales at current prices are bound to distort the true profitability.

Impact on Balance Sheet-on Liabilities

The impact of inflation on the items of balance sheet might now be examined. The real value of the shareholders investment is affected by inflation. The funds were made available to the business at the time when their purchasing power was higher than at the end of the period. Real value of shareholders funds would have, thus, lost to the extent of inflation. Similarly, outside liabilities would lose their real value in times of inflation. Although the nominal value of moneys borrowed and repaid are same, there is a disparity in their real values during inflation. Money at the time of borrowing has higher purchasing power than when repaid. Thus, the company gains in terms of real value when it uses borrowed funds during inflation. This position is just opposite to the acquisition of assets by the business. When a business acquires assets, the real value of money used in their acquisition would be higher. Due to erosion of monetary value on account of inflation, the replacement of assets would require more in terms of current prices. In the process, the real value of assets held by a business would increase during inflation. The increase in real value of the assets is of no benefit to the businessman, as he is not allowed to charge additional depreciation on the enchanced real value of assets. Instead, the higher replacement cost would increase his cost of funds.

On Assets

Assets are classified as monetary and non-monetary for the purpose of examining the impact of inflation. Monetary assets are those, which can be converted into cash, without affecting the continuous operation of business. These are cash, receivables, loans and advances and investments. In other words, monetary assets are identical to liquid assets except that they also include investments. Non-monetary assets are those that are not meant to be converted into cash, but to be used in the normal operation cycle of the business. Fixed assets and inventories are non-monetary assets. Price changes do not much affect monetary assets to any larger extent as they are rolled over and not kept for longer periods. For example, consider receivables. The debtors as at the beginning of the accounting year might have been billed at that price level, but the subsequent debtors are charged higher on the basis of the current selling prices. The impact would be confined only to the credit period In the case of loans and advances, if it is for a fixed periods, for example, electricity and telephone deposits, the book value represents the historic value of money as on the date of such advances. Thus, if a business makes an electricity advance of Rs.1.50 lakhs on the starting date i.e. 1.4.1999 when WPI was 146, as against 155.75 on 31.3.2000 or the date of financial closure, the real value of the deposit would be eroded by 6.68% (the rate of inflation during the period and would stand reduced to Rs.1.41 lakhs (or the erosion in real value is Rs.9,000).If the loans and advances are for a short period, the impact of inflation might be ignored.

On Investments

Investments are made by the businesses from out of their surplus funds. If there is temporary surplus of working capital funds, the company would invest such funds in marketable securities such as units or treasury bills or in short term deposits with banks. Banks are now accepting deposits for a minimum period of 15 days. A company also invests in shares and debentures of its subsidiaries or sister concerns. The investments, whether short-term or long-term, might be quoted or not quoted. In case of quoted securities, their market value would be readily available if these are traded. If the market value is more than the historic cost, a company in accordance with its conservative principle would not revalue the investment on market price, but would present them at their book value, which is historic cost. On the other hand, should the market value of the securities fall short of the book value, the value of the securities are shown at their market value. The principle that cost price or market price, whichever is lower, is applied in presenting investments. In the event of inflation, the real value of long-term investment would be affected. Supposing a company made investments of Rs.25 lakhs in its subsidiary on 1.4.1998, when WPI was 145, then the real value of investment as on 31.3.99 (with inflation at 3.8%) would be Rs.24.05 lakhs or an erosion of Rs.0.95 lakh.

Experiment

We have seen in the foregoing paragraphs that inflation would distort the real profitability of a business during an accounting period and its financial position as at the end of the period. A study was undertaken two decades back by Professor Ramesh Gupta of IIM, Ahmedabad on the impact of inflation on profitability of 54 companies between 1970 and 1976. The country had an average inflation of about 8% during this period. The study revealed that the gross profitability of these companies was overstated by about 33%% or about four times the rate of inflation. Conservatives as they are, entrepreneurs all over the world, therefore, would like to discount the effect of inflation to arrive at real profitability. The urge was more when the rate of inflation was high. Thus, in the 1970's, countries like USA, UK, Australia laid down standards for reporting inflation adjusted financial statements as supplements to the historic statements. Inflation accounting was made compulsory in these countries. However, with the fall in the rate of inflation to manageable levels, the compulsion had been removed. Currently, accounting standards in USA *encourage, but not insist* inflation adjusted financial statements as supplement to historic statements. When western countries were debating on the introduction of inflation accounting, the fall out was felt in India too. Indian corporates in the eighties showed interest in furnishing, as supplement to historic financial reports, inflation adjusted statements. Ashok Leyland Limited was the pioneer in the field, closely followed by another public sector giant Bharat Heavy Electricals Ltd. Sensing the importance of inflation accounting, the institute of Chartered Accountants of India had, as far back as 1982, prepared and published a guidance note on accounting for changing prices for the use of corporates. However, the enthusiasm wanted as it emerged. The report of the ICAI is perhaps gathering dust in a corner. Although the rates of inflation have become within manageable limits (as at the end of January 2005, it was around 5.2%), still, over a period, slow inflation like slow poison impairs the health of corporates. In their own interest, corporates should account for inflation atleast as a supplemental statement. Otherwise, the accumulated damage caused by slow inflation over a period would become unmanageable.

Methods

There are two well-known systems of inflation accounting, of which the entrepreneur could chose one. The earliest method known is *current purchasing power accounting* and the latest and more sophisticated is the *current cost accounting method*. Under both the methods, adjustments are to be made in both profitability statement and balance sheet. Current purchasing power (CPP) method is evolved from the recommendations of professional accounting bodies in the United Kingdom and Ireland in 1974. This method was intended to remove distortions in the financial statements due to changes in general purchasing power of money. Accounts are presented in a *stable currency* by adjusting *the various components* of the financial reports to the changed value of the currency, using a price index.

Current Purchasing Power Accounting method (CPP) divides items of balance sheet in to monetary and non-monetary items. It recommends for revaluation of *non-monetary items* of balance sheet such as capital, reserves and surplus, inventories and fixed assets based on the index on the dates of their entry or acquisition. Monetary items, such as cash, receivables, loans and advances, investments and liabilities are not restated in the balance sheet. But changes caused by current purchasing power of the currency on monetary items are treated as profit or loss in inflation adjusted income statement. Items of expenses and incomes, such as wages, materials and sales, occurring through out the period are adjusted at *average rate of inflation* during the accounting period. Items of incomes and expenses occurring on specific dates such as interest, dividend and rent paid or received are to be adjusted at the rate prevailing on the date of such transactions. Average rate of inflation is worked out by adding the rates at the beginning and at the end of the year and dividing the product by two.

The profit and loss account and balance sheet of Magnoy Ltd., Sri Lanka, was as in Table 1. The table gives an abridged version of the historic income statement and balance sheet of the company as on 31.3.2003.

Illustration

Table 1
Magnoy Ltd.
Balance sheet as on 31.3.2003

Sources of funds		(Rs.Lakhs)
Share capital		44.86
Reserves and Surplus		109.54
Fixed liabilities		27.10
		189.90
Uses of funds		
GrossFixed Assets	169.45	
Less:Depreciation	81.85	87.60
Investments		5.20
Inventories		22.35
Monetary assets		74.75
		189.90

Profit and loss account for the year ended 31-3-2003.

Revenues	(Rs. Lakhs)
Sales	711.05
Interest	4.78
	715.83
Costs	
Material consumed	74.53
Manufacturing expenses	454.57
Depreciation	16.20
Administrating and selling expenses	94.40
Interest	3.55
	643.25
Profit before tax	72.58

Additional information

- Wholesale price index – 1.4.2002 = 346, 1.6.2002 = 347, 1.8.2002 = 349, 1.10.2002 = 356, 1.12.2002 = 359, 1.1.2003 = 360, 1.2.2003 = 365, and 31.3.2003 = 368.
- The company values its inventories on first in first out method
- Investment details:

		Rs. Lakhs
Balance as on 31.3.2002		2.75
Addl. Investment on	1.6.2002	1.25
Addl. Investment on 1.10.2002	1.20	
Gross Fixes Assets as on	31.3.2002	110.23
Add: Additions on	1.8.2002	71.57
Less: Disposal on	1.1.2003	12.35
		169.45

- Rate of taxation 35%.
- Dividend payout 50%.
- Monetary assets include receivable of Rs.59.25 lakhs and cash of Rs.4.85 lakhs. The company's credit policy is one month and cash policy is minimum cash balance for 10 days.

- Interest on investment received annually on September 30. Interest borrowing is on daily balance.
- The company's fixed liabilities did not change during the year.

Solution

Before presenting inflation-adjusted statements spadework as under has to be done:

Notes:

1. The average rate of inflation would be 6.36 during the year (368 – 346 / 346 x 100).
2. Gross Fixed Assets adjustment: Rs. Lakhs.

Historic value of GFA as on 1.4.2002		110.23
CPP on 1.8.2002	110.23/346×349	= 111.19
Add: Additions on 1.8.2002		71.57
CPP as on 1.8.2002		182.76
CPP on 1.1.2003	182.76/349×360	= 188.52
Less: Disposal on 1.1.2003		12.35
CPP as on 1.1.2003		176.17
CPP on 31.3.2003	176.17 / 360×368	= 180.09

3. Depreciation on revalued FA

Historic depreciation as on 31.3.2003	81.85
Depreciation for 2003	16.20
Accumulated dep. before 31.3.2003	65.65
Historic value of GFA	169.45
Less: depreciation before 31.3.2003	65.65
Book value of FA before 31.3.2003	103.80
Rate of depreciation for 2003	16.20 / 103.80×100=15.6%
Revalued GFA	180.09
Dep. Before 31.3.2003	65.65
Revalued book value	106.44
Depreciation at 15.6%	17.85

4. Investment is a monetary asset

		(Rs.Lakhs)	
Historic value is as on 1.4.2002		2.75	
CPP value as on 1.6.2002	2.75 / 346 × 347 =	2.76	
Add: investment on 1.6.2002		1.25	4.01
CPP value on 1.10.2002	4.01 / 347×356 =	4.11	
Add: investment on 1.10.2002			1.20
			5.31
CPP value on 31.3.2003	5.31 / 356 × 368 = 5.49		

5. Inventories : As the company is adopting first in first out method, the closing stock of inventory in balance sheet would be at the CPP and hence needs no adjustment.

6. Monetary assets: Although monetary assets are not revalued under CPP method, the net difference has to be treated as gain or loss in the inflation adjusted income statements.

6. (a) Cash: The company's cash policy is to have 10 days requirement as safety levels which is Rs.4.85 lakhs. As this cash would be maintained at any point of time, its CPP value would be that as 1.4.2002. Hence the CPP of that cash as on 31.3.2003 would be 4.85 / 346 × 368 = Rs.5.16 lakhs. However, in the inflation adjusted balance sheet, the historic value only is retained. Thus, the increase of Rs.0.31 lakh in the value of cash is taken to the loss side of inflation adjusted income statement.

6 (b) Receivables: The company's credit policy being one month, the outstanding as on 04.01.2002 should have been the balance throughout the year. The CPP of the inventories would thus be, like cash, 59.25 / 346 × 368 = Rs.63.02 lakhs. The loss of Rs.3.77 would be carried to the adjusted profit and loss account, while the receivables are retained at historic value.

7. Other monetary assets: The balance monetary assets of Rs.10.65 lakhs might represent loans and advances. In case the dates on which loans and advances. In case the dates on which loans and advances were made are available, the CPP of the loans and advances would be adjusted accordingly. Since no such information is available, it might be presumed as subsisting. That is, it is always present in such situations, its CPP can be worked out in the same manner in which cash and receivables are worked out, i.e. 10.65 / 346 × 368 = Rs.11.33. The excess CPP value of Rs. 0.68 lakhs is taken as loss to the inflation adjusted profit and loss account.

Liabilities:

8. Fixed liabilities: As the volume of fixed liabilities have not changed during the year, the opening balance and closing balance are same but the CPP of the closing balance would be 27.10 / 346 ×368 = Rs.28.82 lakhs. The difference of Rs.1.72 lakhs is CPP gain and has to be taken as income in the inflation adjusted income statement.

9. Current liabilities: Just like current assets, current liabilities should have remained same throughout the year. Hence the CPP value of current liabilities would be 9.20 / 346 × 368 = Rs.9.78 lakhs. The surplus of Rs.0.58 lakhs, is gain, and to be taken to the profit and loss account.

10. Revaluation loss and gain on monetary assets:

Gain : Fixed liabilities	1.72	
Current liabilities	0.58	2.30
Loss: Cash	0.31	
Receivables	3.77	
Others	0.68	
Investments	0.29	5.05
Excess of loss	2.75	

The net loss on monetary assets is Rs.2.75 lakhs, which is adjusted to inflation-adjusted income, together with excess depreciation of Rs.1.65 lakhs.

11. Sales: Sales are made throughout the year. Hence the current purchasing power of sales would be the average rate of inflation during the year. During the year, the rate of inflation was 6.36. Average inflation during the accounting period would have been 3.18%. Historic sale or half of 711.05 is assumed to have current purchasing power of Rs.733.66 lakhs (711.05 × 1.0318).

12. Interest income on investment was received on 30 September. Thus the value of interest in terms of current purchasing power would be Rs.4.78 × the rate of inflation from 1.10.2002 which was 368–356 = 12 points or 3.37%. (12 / 356 × 100 = 3.37%). The CPP of investment would thus be Rs.4.94 lakhs (4.78 × 1.0337).

13. Material cost: As the valuation of stock by the company was FIFO, the material purchased first was assumed to have been consumed first. Or the material consumed did not represent its replacement cost. As purchases take place at periodical intervals the replacement cost would be influenced by the average rate of inflation, which has been calculated as 3.18%. Hence the current purchasing power of materials consumed would by (74.53 × 1.0337).

14. Other manufacturing costs: These are incurred continuously and hence the current purchasing power would be Rs.469.90– (Rs.454.57 × 1.03188)

15. Administrative and selling costs are also continuous costs and hence affected by the average inflation of the accounting period at 3.18%. Hence, the current purchasing power of the overheads would be Rs.97.40 lakhs (94.40 × 1.0318).

16. Interest-payment date is not available. Hence, we could assume that interest payment was in daily rests. In fact in cash credit, it is on the daily balance. Therefore, the current purchasing power of interest would be at the average rate of inflation during the accounting year. That mean the CPP of interest would be Rs.3.66 lakhs (3.55 × 1.0318). The inflation adjusted, financial statements of Magnoy Ltd. is given in Table 3 below

Table 2
Under CPP Method
Inflation adjusted financial statements of Magnoy Ltd for the year ended
Balance sheet as on 31.3.2003

Sources of funds	
Share capital	46.86
Reserves and Surplus	115.01
Revaluation reserves	1.01
Fixed liabilities (Note 8 (a)	27.10
Current liabilities (Note 8 (b)	9.20
	199.18
Uses of funds	
Gross fixed assets (Note 1)	180.09
Less: depreciation (Note 2)	83.50
	96.59
Investments (Note 3)	5.49
Inventories (Note 4)	22.35
Monetary assets (Note 5)	74.75
	199.18

Adjusted Profit and loss account for the year ended 31.3.2003

Sales (Note 11)	733.66
Interest (Note 12)	4.94
	738.60
Materials (Note 13)	76.94
Manufacturing cost (Note 14)	469.90

Administrative selling OH (Note 15)	97.40
Interest (Note 16)	3.66
Depreciation (Note 2)	17.85
Loss on monetary items (Note 10)	2.75
	668.50
Profit before tax	70.10
Impact on inflation	–2.48
OR	–3.42%

Current Cost Accounting Method

Alternative to current purchasing power method is the current cost accounting (CCA) method of inflation accounting. United Kingdom was the birthplace of CCA also. Sandiland's Committee, appointed by her majesty in 1975, had recommended the method. The Institute of Chartered accountants in England and Wales prescribed the method for adoption. The feature of this method is that non-monetary assets, such as fixed assets and inventories are to be shown at their ***value to business***. The value of these assets to the business is their *replacement value*. CCA method advocates that replacement value of non-monetary assets be calculated based on general price index and not on ascertained cost from the market. The value of fixed assets to the business is their replacement values (based on price index) or net realizable value or their economic value, which ever is higher. Inventories on the other hand are to be valued at their replacement value (again based on price index) as on the date of balance sheet or realizable value, whichever is lower. On the profitability statement, CCA stipulates

- *Adjustment for depreciation based on the replacement value of assets,*
- *To assign replacement value to the cost of goods sold,*
- *Adjustments for the cost of additional working capital needed on account of inflation,*
- *Gearing adjustments*

The historic income statement provides for depreciation at historic cost, which is less than what it should be based on replacement cost of assets. The treatment of depreciation in CCA is same as in CPP method. As regards cost of sales under CCA method, the materials and services consumed for effecting sales should be at replacement cost and not purchase cost. This stipulation is also similar to CPP method. We have already seen that excepting cost of materials consumed, all other costs are adjusted to inflation quickly and do not require any treatment in inflation accounting. The third cost is on account of additional working capital in terms of current assets to support the same level of operation. During inflation, the additional working capital required in proportion to the increase in price level or rate of inflation. CCA provides for the cost of additional working capital on account of increased prices. Gearing adjustments are the benefits accruing to the business during inflation when it uses borrowed finds. To sum up, under CCA method, adjustments are to be made for revaluation of fixed assets and inventories in balance sheet. Gearing benefit is to be taken to profit and loss account along with adjustments for materials consumed and depreciation.

Let us now use CCA method to adjust for inflation to the illustration given in Table 1. Of course a few more additional information are to be obtained such as

- *Realizable value of fixed assets and inventories and*
- *Cost of capital of the business*

Presuming that the realizable value of fixed assets is Rs.94 lakhs and inventories Rs.24 lakhs and the cost of capital to the business is 16%, the CCA method of inflation accounting is applied to the illustration and presented in Table 4 below.

Under CCA Method

Table 3

Inflation adjusted financial statements of Magnoy Ltd for the year ended31.3.2003.

Rs..Lakhs

Sources of funds		
Share capital		44.86
Reserves and Surplus		115.01
Revaluation reserves		2.72
Fixed liabilities (Note)		27.10
Current liabilities		9.20
		199.89
Uses of funds		
Gross fixed assets	180.09	
Less: depreciation	83.50	
Net Fixed Assets		96.59
Investments		5.20
Inventories		22.35
Monetary assets		74.75
		199.89

Profit and loss account for the year ended 31.3.2003

Sales	7.11.05
Interest	4.78
Gearing adjustment (Note 8a & 8b)	2.30
	718.13
Materials	76.94
Manufacturing cost	454.57
Interest	3.66
Administrative selling OH	94.40
Interest	3.55
Depreciation	17.85
Cost of additional working cash	0.51
	651.48
Profit before tax	66.65
Impact on inflation	5.93
	8.17%

Note: Additional working capital is assumed to have increased by 6.36, the rate of inflation. As the requirement of additional working capital would have increased with inflation, the additional cost would also to be averaged. Thus additional cost would be 6.36×.16% /2 = Rs.0.51 lakh.

Companies have, in the past, adopted alternative methods. The Indian pioneer, Ashok Leyland Ltd. had adopted current purchasing power method while Bharat Heavy Electricals Ltd had worked out its inflation adjustment as per the current cost accounting method. It might be seen from the foregoing paragraphs that while CPP method lays emphasis on the purchasing power of capital, CCA stresses on the productive capacity of capital. The CPP merely restates the financial statements in terms of uniform purchasing power of the currency and is a simple method. On the other hand, CCA method recognizes specific price changes but does not incorporate general inflation in price level into all the items. The reason is obvious. Inflation does not affect all items of the financial statement with the same intensity. By and large, CCA has an edge over CPP, as it takes a practical view of the impact of inflation. To conclude, the exercise on inflation accounting would bring to light the real value of the operational results and the financial position of the company. However, tax authorities do not recognize the impact of inflation on the profitability as the Companies Act, 1956 makes it obligatory on the companies to restrict depreciation to the historic value of the assets and does not extent to their replacement value.

Summary

Financial Statements are presented on the assumption that the value of the currency used in accounting continues to have same value through out the accounting period. In actual situation, the changes in the value of currency, reflecting on its purchasing power, are more often than not. As a result, the financial statements do not reflect the fair value of the assets, liabilities and profitability. Attempts have been made from seventies for adjusting the financial statements for absorbing the effects on inflation on the real profit of the business, compared to its nominal profit. Although there was an awakening in the seventies and eighties to give effect to inflation in financial reports, the enthusiasm died as it arose. The major reason for corporates not adopting inflation accounting is the relative stability in the rate of inflation over a period and not to downsize their bottom line.

There are two well-known systems of inflation accounting- Current purchasing power method and current cost accounting method. The former applies the effect of inflation on all items of the financial statement using the change in price index as basis. As the impact of inflation does not affect all items of the reports and with the same intensity, the need for the second method had risen. In CCA, efforts are made to relate the revenue to the replacement cost of consumption, so that the water in the profitability is drained of. None of the methods of inflation accounting is allowed by the tax authorities for adjusting the profits of the business. Thus, the adoption of inflation accounting is mainly to apprise the businessman of his real worth.

1. QUESTIONS

1. What do you understand by the term inflation?
2. What are the parameters of inflation?
3. Is inflation always painful to the business?
4. What is the meaning of purchasing power of money?
5. How does purchasing power affect the value of money?
6. Why should a businessman adjust his profitability to the impact of inflation?
7. What are the commonly used methods of accounting for inflation?
8. What is the Indian experience in inflation accounting?

9. What are monetary assets? How are they treated under the different methods of inflation accounting?
10. Do you consider that there is necessity for presenting inflation adjusted financial reports as a supplement to the historic reports?
11. Explain the concept of inflation accounting. What is the need and rationale for inflation accounting?

II. QUIZ

Say yes or no

1. Value of money remains same throughout
2. Value of money is the reflection of its purchasing power
3. During inflation a given unit of money would command more goods and services than before
4. Deflation is welcome, as it is a situation of lowering price level
5. Inflation affects all assets and liabilities with the same intensity
6. During inflation nominal profits of businesses increase
7. FIFO insulates the effects of inflation
8. Current purchasing power method of inflation accounting applies the effect off inflation to all items of financial reports
9. Current cost accounting method emphasis the productive capacity of capital
10. Inflation accounting is compulsory in developed countries
11. Indian Companies never adopted inflation accounting

III. EXERCISE

1. The following is the balance sheet of Roshan Lao & Company Ltd. for the year ended 31.12.2003 The whole sale price index (WPI) during the period was:

1.1.2003	348 Points
1.2.2003	356 Points
1.3.2003	360 Points
1.6.2003	365 Points

1.8.2003	377 Points
1.10.2003	385 Points
31.12.2003	396 Points

Balance sheet of Roshan Lao & Co. Ltd as on 31.12.2003

(Rs. Lakhs)

	2003		2002	
Shareholder's Funds				
Share Capital – Equity	933.39		931.90	
Share Capital – Preference	252.95		187.95	
Reserves and Surplus	11,183.00		10,862.75	
		12,369.34		11,20022.60
Subsidies		965.02		300.00
Loan Funds				
Secured Loans	5,477.64		2,736.78	
Unsecured Loans	5,207.65		5,510.55	
		10,685.29		8,247.33
Total		**24,019.65**		**20,529.93**
Application of funds				
Fixed Assets				
Gross Block	18,650.33		17,848.33	
Less: Depreciation	6,691.93		4,944.47	
Net Block	11,958.40		12,903.86	
Capital Work-in-Progress	3,437.83		2,069.43	
		15,396.23		14,973.29
Investments		4,294.59		4,282.33
Current assets, Loans and				
Advances				
Interest accrued on investments	25.61		21.07	
Inventories	1,408.61		1,343.96	
Sundry Debtors	457.10		642.72	
Cash and Bank Balances	4,897.60		2,133.51	

	6,788.92		4,141.26	
Loans and Advances	1,676.26		20031.05	
	8,465.18		**5,132.31**	
Less: Current liabilities and Provisions				
Current Liabilities	3,591.98		3,382.01	
Provisions	544.37		475.99	
	4,136.35		**3,858.00**	
Net Current Assets		4,328.83		1,274.31
Total		**24,019,65**		**20,529.93**

Work out inflation adjusted accounts under each of the methods.

CHAPTER 16

ON INTANGIBLE ASSETS

Learning Objective

After reading this chapter, readers would be in a position to appreciate the role of intangibles on the profitability of the business. One set of intangibles represent items of expenditures, such as patent rights, technical know-how, franchises and goodwill, which are assets, as they contribute indirectly to the earning of income. The other group of intangibles is deferred revenue expenses, like preliminary expenses, loss balances and other miscellaneous expenses. These do not contribute either directly or indirectly to income generation and are plain vanilla intangibles.

The word "asset" generally triggers the mind to perceive an object that can be seen, felt, possessed, used and parted with. Land, building, plant, machinery, equipment, vehicles, instruments are all assets in this sense. We usually associate assets with things that have physical existence. However, the views of an economist as to what an asset is are quite different from that of an accountant. He considers all expenditures that contribute to the earning of revenue by a business over a period longer than a year as assets. Whether the expenditure has resulted in the creation of physically recognizable objects, which directly generate income or obtaining special rights, claims or privileges, which indirectly contribute to earnings is irrelevant to him as long as they generate income. The former group of physically identifiable expenditures is termed as ***tangible assets***, while the latter group is known as ***intangible assets***.

Intangible assets are, to repeat, expenditures that result in the acquisition of special rights, claims and privileges, which indirectly contributes to the earning of the business over its useful life. As intangible assets are abstract, they are governed, as to their character, nature, usefulness and tenure by legislations specially enacted. These regulations provide for rights and responsibilities of the users of the rights, claims and privileges. Common examples of intangible assets are patents, designs, trademarks, copyrights, technical know-how, franchises and goodwill.

Patents

Patent is a monopoly right granted to a person, who had invented a new and useful article or an improvement of an existing article or a new process of making an article for commercial exploitation, either by the inventor himself or his assignee. It is an exclusive right for a limited period to benefit the inventor for his efforts. Indian Patents Act, 1970, governs law relating to patents. The period of validity of the right has been limited to 7 years for food processes and 14 years for drugs, from the date of patenting. The right can be renewed for further periods. If not renewed, anyone can make use of the invention after the lapse of the period. Patents are to be registered with the Controller of Patents by payment of specified fees. Anyone who infringes on the patented process is liable for legal prosecution.

Designs

Designs are shapes, configurations, patterns or imitations applied to any article by an industrial process, which, in the finished article, appeals to the eye and judged solely by the eye. This right protects the owners of novel or original designs from infringement. The interested person has to get his or her design registered with the Controller General of designs, under the Indian patents & Designs Act, 1911.

Trademarks

Trademark is a visual symbol in the form of a word, device, name, letter, brand, heading, signature or label used to indicate the connection of the goods with the registered owner of the trademark. The purpose of trade marking is to distinguish the trademarked goods from similar goods, thereby appealing to the specific demands of consumers. Trademarks were to be registered with the Register of Trademarks in terms of Trade and Merchandise Mark Act, 1958 till 2003. Under the Act only 34 classes of goods were registered. Service marks were not registered. As service sector started playing a lead role in the economy after globalization, a new Act "Trademark Act of 1999" was passed. The Act came into force from 2003. In terms of the Act, marks of 10 classes of services are allowed to be registered. Service marks for the purpose of registration are defined, as marks used in any service business, where actual tangible goods are under that mark are not traded. The groups of services eligible are advertising, insurance, real estate, building construction, telecommunication, transport, education, entertainment, sporting and cultural activities, scientific and technological services, research, design, development of computer hardware, software, legal, medical and security services.

Copyrights

Copyrights are privileges allowed to producers of intellectual and artistic works for their exclusive use. It prevents the appropriation, by others, of the fruits of labour of authors in literacy, dramatic, musical or artistic work or skill, without consent. Writers and artists can get their works copyrighted with the Register of Copyrights, under the Copyrights Act, 1954. The registration gives the writers and artists and their heirs, legal representatives and assigns exclusive ownership of their work during the lifetime of the authors or artists and up to 60 years after their death.

Technical Know-how

Research and Development is an important corporate function in these days of rapid changes. Products have a life cycle comprising the stages of development, growth, saturation and decline. Hence corporates continue to improve existing product lines and introduce new product ranges to be in the reckoning. The current axiom is that creative enterprises should ***introduce new products and make their own products obsolete, otherwise competitors will do that***. It is common knowledge that technical know-how developed in the process is the exclusive right of the concerned organization. Such know-how generates income to the inventor companies during their effective life and is their intangible asset. Sometimes, the inventor shares his know-how with others, usually in different market segments, on his own terms and conditions, under a ***collaboration agreement***, for a price. The price is an ad-hoc one-time payment known as ***technical know-how fee*** and a recurrent annual payment called ***royalties*** for an agreed period. Royalties are charged, at certain percentage, on the sales, production or profit of the recipient corporate.

Franchises

Franchises are rights obtained by enterprises from the technical know-how developers, for exploitation of the process, product or service in specific areas for an agreed period. The nature of franchise closely resembles that of know-how arrangements, except that in case of franchises, the franchisee is always given the right to use the brand name of the innovator. This may not be so in the case of collaboration agreements, where the right to use the brand name is at the discretion of the know-how supplier and the user normally mentions that the product is made in collaboration with so and so company. Secondly, in franchise, the increasing practice is to supply the know-how with the requisite equipment to be installed at the site of the franchise. Franchise charges would, then include the rental for the equipment in addition to royalty for the use of technology.

Intangible assets, like tangible assets, are to be written off during their effective life. The closing adjustment entry for writing off of intangible assets is given in Table 1.

Table 1
Journal Proper of Gosamy Corporation Ltd.

Particulars	LF	Dr.	Cr.
By P& L A/c		50,000	
To Patents A/c			25,000
To Copyright			15,000
To Franchise A/c			10,000

In addition to the intangible assets discussed above, we also come across a few expenses incurred in a particular accounting period, which do not directly contribute to the earning of revenue. These are clubbed together as deferred revenue expenses and the commonly known items are capital issue expenses, preliminary expenses, carried forward loss balances and deferred advertisement expenses. ***Capital issue expenses*** are those that a company incurs at the time of issuing share capital or loan capital, such as bonds, debentures and deposits. Presently, issue expenses are about 15 to 25% of large mega issues and above 25% in case of medium sized issues. Where issue expenses are heavy and are expected to contribute to earning revenue over a longer period, it would be unfair to charge the entire expense in the year of occurrence. Hence, these expenses are not written off in a single year, but are deferred and written off during the period over which these are useful. For example, the issue expenses on 5-year bonds may be written off over 5 years. In case of share capital, which is used by the business as long as the company exists, a reasonable period may be assumed for writing off the expenses. Preliminary expenses, a detailed discussion on which had been made in an earlier chart, are statutorily to be written off over 10 years in equal installments. In case of mega budget advertisements, whose benefit is expected to be spread over more than the year of advertising, the expenses are treated as deferred revenue expenses and written off during the period the advertisement is presumed to be effective.

Fictitious Assets

The assets side of the balance sheet also contains the carry forward balances of losses, suffered by the business during the previous years. Loss balances carried forward are intangibles, but are not assets, as they do not contribute to the earning of revenue either directly or indirectly. These are considered as ***fictitious assets,*** although the suffix assets are a misnomer. We can simply call them as ***intangibles***. Generally, these balances are adjusted against capital and reserves of the business, before arriving at the owner's capital, also called net worth. Annually, a portion is written off from the profit and loss account, through an adjustment entry as in Table 2.

Table 2
Journal proper of Annie Anchor Ltd.

Particulars	LF	Dr.	Cr.
By Profit & Loss A/c		11,500	
To Deferred revenue expenses			6,250
Top preliminary expenses			5,250

Carried forward loss balances are primarily to be recovered from the future revenue of the business within 8 years. In case it is not absorbed within the stipulated period, the balance has to be adjusted against the equity of the owners. The justification for writing off the loss balance from future profits of the business is to allow for the fluctuating opportunities of the business. But if the business is not capable of adjusting the deferred cost within the stipulated eight years, the owners of the business have to bear the loss as a penalty for their inefficiency.

Goodwill

Goodwill is an important intangible asset of an enterprise. Although a number of business enterprises deal in the same or similar goods or services, with quality, price, after sales service *etc.* remaining same, consumers show preference to a particular product of an enterprise over that of others. This preference leads to the reputation of the enterprise and is termed as goodwill. As a result of this special attachment of customers the concerned enterprise is able to reap abnormal profits. The additional profit accruing to the business on account of this loyalty of customers is goodwill. Goodwill is thus defined as ***"the value of reputation of a business in respect of profits expected in future, over and above normal level of profits earned by other undertakings belonging to the same class of business".*** Prof. Dicksee in his book on "Goodwill and its treatment in accounts" describes goodwill as an aid in profit making. According to him, payment for goodwill is justified ***"when a man pays for something which places him in the position of being able to earn more money than he would be able to do by his own unaided efforts".***

From the above definitions, it transpires that goodwill is the quantified value of the reputation of the business to earn extra profit over and above what its tangible assets would have earned. The reputation, based on the preference of the customers, might have been caused by one more of the following special features, such as its location, the personal touch of the businessman, the real or imaginary product differentiation, dependability of supply and the ability of the businessman to keep his competitors at bay. Goodwill usually creates brand equity.

Intangible assets are either created or acquired from those who had created them initially. Research, development and innovation create intangible assets. The cost of intangible asset is the resources utilized by the business in its creation. In case intangibles are acquired, their value is the purchase consideration paid for such acquisition. Purchase consideration is based on the expected contribution of the intangible to the earning of revenue over its useful life. Whenever the cost of creation or acquisition is insignificant, it is treated as revenue expense of the period of incidence and charged to the profitability of the business of that period. On the other hand, should the cost be substantial, loading the entire cost to the profitability of the period of incidence would distort the operational results of the period. Therefore, the cost is capitalized and booked as an asset, to be written off during its effective life, in assumed proportion to its contribution to the earning of revenue.

Useful Life of Intangible Assets

The maximum useful lives of intangibles assets are restricted by the regulations that govern them. For example, patents have a useful life of 14 years. Hence the cost of patent should be written off within 14 years. The period of 14 years commences from the time of its registration. Thus, if a patent is acquired by another business after 4 years of its registration, the useful residual life is 10 years for the acquire. In the event of the ability of the patent to generate income is lost during its useful life, due to development of better products or processes, it becomes obsolete and the entire amount outstanding has to be written off in that year itself.

Valuation

The valuation of goodwill is on a different footing than other intangible assets. Discernible resources are not expended in developing goodwill. Goodwill is the quantification of the entrepreneurial excellence and it is highly subjective. Goodwill remains dormant and its value is not presented in the books of the business till any change in the structure of the business is anticipated. In the case of sole trading business, it is brought into the books at the time of change in ownership of the business. When the sole trader sells his business to another or when he admits another as a partner into the business, he wants to crystallize the efforts he had taken in the past to create the name for the business. He therefore, values the goodwill and takes it as part of his capital. In this respect, goodwill reflects the valuation of the qualitative inputs of the businessman to shape the business to its present status. Goodwill thus par takes the role of ***sweat capital*** of individuals. In the case of a corporate, goodwill is created when the pattern of share holding is about to undergo change. This may be before the issue of fresh shares to the public. But usually it is at the time of takeover of the company by another. If Vasu desires to take Girish and Ilkya as partners and she desired to create goodwill of Rs.2,50,000, the journal entry required is at Table 3.

Table 3
Journal proper of Vasu & Co.

Particulars	LF	Dr.	Cr.
By Goodwill A/c		2,50,000	
To Vasu's Capital			2,50,000

The valuation of goodwill is not an easy task. There are varieties of causes for the creation of name for the business and each business may have to adopt a different norm for the valuation of goodwill. As the value of goodwill that has to be raised should be acceptable to the buyer, the decision is really ticklish. Usually, goodwill is valued as the difference between the price paid for the enterprise as a whole less the net of assets over liabilities. Suppose a business has net assets (both of fixed and current) of Rs.27.50 lakhs and total liabilities (including share capital and reserves of Rs.11.50 lakhs) and the purchase consideration for the business is Rs.33.5 lakhs, the value of goodwill will be Rs.17.50 lakhs.

The value of goodwill, being subjective, depends upon the negotiated price. Hence it reflects the relative strength of bargaining of the parties. The valuation tends to be arbitrary in nature.

Therefore, prior to arriving at an agreed price for goodwill, both the buyer and seller of the business do calculate the expected value of goodwill based on any one or more of the following methods, namely

- *Certain multiples of the average profits / or turnover over a number of past years,*
- *The capitalization of expected future returns over a specified number of years or*
- *The present value of the super profits likely to be earned by the business.*

Multiples of Profit/Turnover Method

This is based on the historic data of the performance of the business. Under this, the average net profit or turnover for the past five to seven years is calculated and the value of goodwill is estimated as certain multiples there of. For example, if the average net profit of Hari's business for the past five years were Rs.2,75,000 and goodwill is to be estimated as a multiple of three years, then the value of goodwill will be Rs.8,25,000. In case of certain service industries, like that of the lawyers or doctors, the multiple will be on the basis of average turnover and not average profit.

Capitalization of Expected Returns Method

Under this method, the stream of expected cash inflows, over a period (usually over the residual life of the major assets) is estimated. The cash flow is discounted with the desired rate of return of the buyer. From the summation of the discounted cash flows, the current book value of the assets is subtracted. The excess, if any, is considered the value of goodwill. For example, the current book value of the assets of Humayun was Rs.51 lakhs. The residual life of his major assets is 6 years. The expected annual cash inflows during the useful life of major assets are Rs.25 lakhs, Rs.27 lakhs, Rs.24 lakhs, Rs.22 lakhs, Rs.20 lakhs and Rs.18 lakhs respectively. The desired rate of return of the buyer is 18%. The present value of the future incomes for six years would

$$\Sigma 25/1.18 + 27/1.18^2 + 24/1.18^3 + 22/1.18^4 + 220/1.18^5 + 18/1.18^6$$

$$= 81.88 \text{ lakhs}$$

The present value could also be worked out by using the discount tables, given as annexure. Form the present value thus arrived at, current book value of assets at Rs.51 lakhs is deducted, leaving a residual value of Rs.30.88 lakhs, which is the value of goodwill under the capitalization of expected return method.

PV of Super Profit Method

The next method of valuation is based on the hypothesis that the value of goodwill should roughly correspond to the present value of the abnormal profits or super profits the business is likely to earn over the next few years. As the utility of goodwill as an earning asset is subject to changes in the taste and preference of customers, technological upgradation of the competitors *etc*., the buyer would normally prefer to evaluate super profits for as short a period as possible, say three to four years. The summation of the discounted cashflows of the expected super profits of the business will be considered as a fair value of goodwill. For example, Ramdas' expected cash flows from super profits for the next 3 years were Rs.47 lakhs, Rs.45 lakhs, and Rs.43 lakhs respectively. The market rate of capitalization for similar industries is 25%. The sum total of discounted cash flows for the 3 years would be Rs.88.4 lakhs, which is the value of goodwill under this method.

Treatment of Goodwill

Once goodwill is created, it will be shown as an intangible asset. As a portion of assets is written off annually, notionally representing their contribution to the earning of revenue of that year, it is logical that goodwill too has to be written off. However, there is a difference between other assets (both tangible and intangible) and goodwill. Other assets have a cost, either cost of development by the business or by the seller. But, goodwill is created by the business without incurring any monetary cost. Hence, tax authorities do not allow the writing off of goodwill as an allowable cost. Goodwill has, therefore, to be adjusted against the distributable profits of the owners. Or in other words, it will reduce the wealth of the owners, who had purchased the business. However, once it has been treated as an intangible asset, it has to be amortized. As regards the methods of amortization of goodwill, the accepted accounting conventions, setup by the Accounting Principle Board of US, has prescribed the following alternatives:

- *To retain the goodwill at its full value till a reduction or amortization is desired,*
- *To retain the cost as an asset and to amortize a portion over an assumed life period. (Goodwill can be written off within forty years of its creation.)*
- *To reduce the value of goodwill from the equity of the owners.*

The third method, namely to reduce goodwill from the equity (accumulated reserves and surplus of the business) during the year of its creation itself, is an ideal choice, provided the retained earnings of the company are quite substantial to absorb the amount of goodwill. In that case, the following journal entry has to be passed:

Table 4

Journal proper of X

Date	Particulars	LF	Dr.	Cr.
	By Reserves & Surplus A/c		7,50,000	
	To Goodwill A/c			7,50,000.

Few Modern Breeds

Global competition and the resultant consumer domination have widened the horizon of intangible assets. Businessmen all over the world are increasingly realizing that apart from the tangible assets and conventional intangibles, discussed in the foregoing paragraphs, a few non-conventional intangibles also contribute significantly to the revenue earning capacity of business. Eminent researchers have attempted to identify and quantify these intangibles. We may consider a few important modern concepts on intangibles.

Intellectual Capital

The first that gives an overall assessment of the non-conventional intangibles is the concept of intellectual capital. Stewart has described intellectual capital as "*intellectual material, comprising knowledge, information, intellectual property and experience that can be put to use to create wealth*". It is the collective brain power and not attributable to any single segment of human resource, structural advantages and customer capital. It is the synergy created by all these factors collectively. NRI Research, Evanston, Illinois, has evaluated the concept. They have developed a technique named calculated intangible value model (CIVM) to measure the ability of the intellectual capital to outperform other business in the industry, with similar tangible assets. CIVM is a simple application of the industrial return on assets (ROA), to the tangible assets of a business, to arrive at normal industry return on assets of the business. The return so arrived at is deducted from the actual profit of the business. This excess return is attributable to the ***intellectual capital***. When the excess return is discounted at the cost of capital of the business, the value of intellectual capital emerges. For example Zealot Enterprises has an average operating profit of Rs.46.20 crores for the last three years. Its assets (for three years) averaged Rs.378.12 crores. The average industry return on assets is 10%. The cost of capital of Zealot is 15%. Applying CIVM to the information of Zealot, it's intellectual capital is valued at Rs.56 crores, as in Table 5 below:

Table 5
Zealot enterprises
Assessment of intellectual capital. (Rs. Crores)

1. Average tangible assets of Zealot	378.12
2. Average ROA of the industry	10%
3. Expected profit applying industry norm (1*2)	37.8
4. Actual profit of Zealot	46.2
5. Profit attributable to intellectual capital (4 – 3)	8.4
6. Cost of capital	15%
7. Capitalization intellectual capital of Zealot (5/6)	56.0

Human Resource as an Asset

A number of factors contribute to the creation of intellectual capital. Among these, the single largest contribution comes from human resources. Management Guru, Peter Druker has been, for quite sometime, emphasizing on ***knowledge workers*** and their twin contribution – in their capacity as owners of companies and as employees. Measurement of human capital has been attempted by a number of economists, among whom Lew and Schwatz stand out unique. Their model, named after them, assumes the annual remuneration of employees till their termination as cost to the company and is the human capital of the business. Major IT companies in India have included the valuation in their reports. The process was, how ever, started long ago by public sector companies like Steel Authority of India and Bharat Heavy Electricals Ltd.

Broadly, there are two approaches to human capital valuation – cost-based and economic approach. The cost-based approach is further classified into three – historical cost, replacement cost and opportunity cost. The L&S model along with other methods like Likert, Flamboltz and Jaggi is part of the economic approach. Though there is little clarity on which of the various human capital valuation models is effective, the Lew and Schwatz model seems to have an edge over others in India. HR consultants say it gives an opportunity to benchmark the efficiency of their human resources as quite a few Indian companies have adopted this system. Second, the valuation is less subjective as it makes limited assumptions.

So what is the L&S Model?

Developed in 1971, it is based on the likely future earnings of an employee till his retirement. L&S advocated the estimation of future earnings during the remaining life of the employee and then arriving at the present value by discounting the estimated earnings at the employee's cost of capital.

Brand Names

Brand names do contribute to the earning of revenues over and above tangible assets. The earning capacity of brands had been so acclaimed that brands are equated with equity and the phrase brand equity is in common usage. Brands are treated as intangible assets and are valued by using earning multiple approach. Under this approach, brand strength of a company is determined on the basis of seven factors, namely, leadership, stability, market, internationality, trend, support and protection, is worked out. These factors are suitably weighted according to the importance of their contribution in creating brand equity. The cumulative weighted average will be the value of the brand. As the degree of contribution by each of the factors is assumed to vary from company to company, the valuation of brands are highly subjective. No uniform norm could therefore be adopted in valuing brand equity.

Indian Experience

It is heartening to note that Indian corporates are also veering slowly towards the recognition of these intangibles. A few blue chip companies such as Infosys, Satyam Computers and Dr. Reddy's Lab., besides the public sector giant BHEL have made attempts to assess these intangible assets. In their latest annual reports, they had evaluated intangible assets like intellectual capital, market value addition, brand valuation, human resources capital and economic value addition.

Infosys has adopted the Lew & Schwartz model to compute the value of human resources. Infosys has valued its 36,750 employees at Rs 28,334 crores ($6.4-billion). In its annual report for 2004-05, the company has reported a software delivery staff of 34,747 valued at Rs 26,550 crores and 2003 support staff value at Rs 1,784 crores. In the previous year, Infosys had valued its human capital at Rs 21,139 crores. It then had 25,634 employees, comprising of 24,110 software staff and 1,524 support personnel. Infosys revenue from software in 2005 was Rs 7129.65 crores, while its total employee cost was Rs 3539.11 crores.

Infosys had adopted the generic brand earnings-multiple model to value its corporate brand, the company said. The concept finds mention in "Valuation of Trademarks and Brand Names" by Mr Michael Birkin in "Brand Valuation", edited by Mr John Murphy.

Using the brand earnings-multiple model, Infosys based its valuation on the assumptions, among others, of the total revenues excluding other income after adjusting the cost of earnings, the annual inflation at five per cent and five per cent of the average capital employed used for purposes other than promotion of the brand and a tax rate of 33.66 per cent.

Infosys annual report said it had used various models for evaluating assets off the balance sheet to bring certain advances in financial reporting. "Such an exercise also helps the Infosys management in understanding the components that make up goodwill. The aim of such modelling is to lead a debate on the balance sheet of the next millennium," it added.

Corporate attributes including core competency, market leadership, copyrights, trademarks, brands, superior earning power, excellence in management, outstanding workforce, competition, longevity were built into this concept, the annual report said. Infosys believes the client base was its most valuable intangible asset. Marquee clients or image enhancing clients accounted for 48 per cent of Infosys' total revenues. "Marquee clients give stability to our revenues and also reduce our marketing costs," Infosys said.

A word of caution may here be added. These valuation are not entered in the books of accounts, but are presented as supplemental information to the final accounts of the corporates. These intangible assets, no doubt, create and strengthen the goodwill of the business in the long run.

Summary

This is the concluding chapter on the steps a business has to take, before actually undertaking the preparation of final accounts. Most of the intangible assets, although do not have physical existence, are created or purchased by utilizing the resources of the business. They represent expenditures, which contribute to the earning of the business during their useful life. These expenditures are treated on par with tangible assets in balance sheet. Patents, designs, trademarks, technical know-how, copyrights, franchises and goodwill are all examples of intangible assets that contribute directly or indirectly to the earning of the business. Besides, deferred revenue expenditure on account of capital issues, advertisements etc. also contribute indirectly to the earning of the business and hence are intangible assets. There are a few other intangibles, erroneously called fictitious assets, such as preliminary expenses and carried forward loss balances, which neither contribute directly nor indirectly to the revenue generating capacity of the business, but are incidental to the operations of the business. Still, they are presented on the assets side of the balance sheet and are written off periodically. Specific legislations for the intangible assets stipulate the effective life and the period over which intangibles assets are to be amortized. Whatever may be the effective life of the intangible assets, once they become obsolete, their entire outstanding value has to be written off in the year in which they had become useless. The write off is allowed as a cost in profit and loss account, except goodwill, for the creation of which resources of the business are not used up. Thus, goodwill has to be adjusted against the equity of the owners of the business.

Intangible assets are valued at the cost at which they are created or acquired. Should the cost of creation or acquisition be insignificant, they are written off as revenue expenses in the year in which the cost was incurred. However, when the amount spent is quite large and the writing off the entire expenditure in the year of occurrence will distort the operational results of the business, these expenditures are capitalized and written off according to assumed proportion of their contribution to the earning capacity of the business. Modern concepts of intangible assets have transgressed the conventional ideas. Intellectual capital, human resources capital and brand equity are considered as intangible assets capable of contributing to the earning of the business, over and above tangible assets.

I. QUESTIONS

1. What are tangible assets? How do intangible assets differ from them?
2. Give a few examples of intangible assets.
3. Briefly explain patents, designs, trademarks, copyrights, technical know-how and franchises.
4. What do you mean by goodwill?
5. How do you value intangibles?
6. How are intangible assets accounted?
7. What do you know about deferred revenue expenses?
8. Explain, with examples, fictitious assets.
9. What are the different methods of valuing goodwill? Explain briefly each of them.

10. What do you understand by the term intellectual capital? Can you suggest a method of evaluating it?

11. Do human resources constitute the assets of a business?

12. What is the cost of human resources in business evaluation?

13. What factors create brand strength in a business?

14. What are capital issue expenses?

II. QUIZ

Say Yes or No to the following

- All intangibles are fictitious assets.
- Deferred revenue expenses directly contribute to the earning capacity of the business.
- Intangible assets are created, not acquired.
- Patents have 50 years validity.
- Trademarks are visual symbols.
- Creation of goodwill consumes resources.
- Goodwill is allowed to be written off as a deduction from income by tax authorities.
- Deferred revenue expenses are also called fictitious assets.
- Capitalization of expected returns is a method of valuing goodwill.
- Knowledge worker is the concept developed by Stewart.

III. EXERCISES

1. The extract of the balance sheet of Peanuts India Ltd. for the year-ended 31.3.2003 was as under:

(Rs. Lakhs)

Fixed Assets (Average for 3 Years	3421.65
Less : Depreciation	2845.55
Net Fixed assets	576.10
Net current Assets	412.40
Capital employed	988.50
Represented by Net worth	795.30
Debt	193.20
Total	988.50

The company's profit after tax for the year was Rs.148.20 lakhs. It is envisaged that the profitability is expected to improve at the compounded rate of 8% in the next five years. Recent evaluation of the company's major assets revealed that they have useful life of 5 years. The desired rate of return for Peanuts is 16% after tax. Estimate the value of goodwill under capitalization of expected return method?

2. Jain Departmental Stores, started as a small outfit, grew into a conglomeration and presently has a chain of 21 stores in the Twin City of Hyderabad and Secunderabad. The promoters of the unit are the three Jain brothers – Arvind, Manek and Pritesh. The unit is negotiating for the take over of Multifoods, for which it proposes to induct Shantilal as a partner. Jain brothers have approached you to evaluate the goodwill of their firm on PV of super profit model. The following information about Jain Departmental Stores is made available to you:

(Rs. Crores)

	2007 (Actual)	**2008**	**2009 (Expected)**	**2010**
Profits after tax	92.45	99.86	100.93	109.00
Capital employed				513
Industrial average				14%
Return on capital employed	15.5%	16.75%	18%	19%

Estimated goodwill of Jain Departmental Stores?

3. Boxfree Ltd's balance sheet for the past three year showed:

Rs. Lakhs

	2005	**2006**	**2007**
Net fixed assets	603.10	618.19	656.51
Current assets	1487.55	1666.06	2015.93
Total tangible assets	2090.65	62284.25	2672.44
Profit for the year	75.37	131.62	169.25
Average cost of capital	13.5%	14.58%	15.9%
Average return on assets of the Industry	15.0%	16.35%	17.84%

You are required to assess the value of intellectual capital for the company?

CHAPTER 17

REVENUE RECOGNITION

Learning Objective

Readers are aware that the generation of revenue is the main objective of business. All inflows are not revenues. It should therefore clearly understood what are the inflows that could be considered revenues. This chapter deals in detail the nature and extend of inflows that are to be recognised as revenue for the accounting period.

Introduction

Profit is the surplus of revenue over the cost attributable for earning that revenue. When the volume of revenue falls short of its cost, the result is loss sustained by the business. Profit increases the value of the enterprise to the owners, while loss reduces the value. The preparation of profit and loss account depends upon the true and fair assessment of cost attributable for an accounting period and the revenue earned by the business during that period. In the earlier chapters, we have dealt, at length, with the nature and attributes of costs. In this chapter, the sources and the extent of revenue one has to take into account while preparing final accounts is considered.

Definition

Revenue has been defined differently by different authorities. Dictionary, the friend of the ignorant, defines revenue as *receipts or returns from any source* (Chambers). Receipts from any source are very broad and if adopted, without restraints, may distort the very purpose of preparing final accounts. Receipts on issue of shares, bonus or debentures or deposits or loans are not revenue. If we go back to the description of income, given in an earlier chapter, it may be recalled that receipts, which do not create any obligation for revenue. Even this definition is not all pervasive, as receipts in discharge of the obligations already created to the business, for example, payments received from debtors or receipts on sale of old assets or investments, are not revenues. In fact, if such receipts from the debtors or sale proceed from assets or investments fall short of their book value, the deficit is treated as cost. Only when the sale proceeds of assets or investments exceed their book value, the surplus is considered as revenue.

The Financial Accounting Standard Board (FASB) of the US considers all inflows or other enhancements of assets of an entity of settlement of its liabilities (or combination of both) during a period, from delivery or producing goods, rendering services or other activities, that constitute the entity's ongoing major or central operation as revenue. The Institute of Chartered Accountants of India (ICAI) defines revenue as the gross inflow of cash, receivables or other consideration, arising out of activities of an enterprise from the sale of goods, from rendering services and from the use, by others, of the enterprise resources, yielding interest, royalties and dividends.

These definitions are attempts to explain what revenue is. As better appreciation of the term revenue can be had from the intention of the originators of the word, revenue. The term revenue had arisen from the French verb revenir, meaning returning back or coming back . All business activities start with an outlay *i.e.*, investment of resources. Investment need not necessarily mean employment of cash in fixed or floating assets. It also includes investment in process and people. Any benefit coming back from that investment is revenue. Or in other words, the French considered capital asset as a stock and the revenue a flow thereof. It may therefore, be safety concluded that revenue denotes inflows from out of the normal investments in a business either in the form of sales or service charges or incidental receipts these to, without causing any obligation for repayment, either immediately or in the future.

Relevant Revenue

The flow of revenue, its very nature, may relate either to a particular accounting period or may spread over more than one period. As revenue is the flow from the outlay, it is possible to accurately assess the extent of the revenue flow only when the outlay is fully exhausted. As businessman goes on investing, on a continuous basis, the determination of revenue for a particular period becomes difficult. It cannot be measured exactly, but has necessarily to be approximated as fair as possible. Revenue recognition for a period, therefore, has it limitations. Hence, efforts are to be made to recognize and measure the extent of revenues as nearest to reality as possible, keeping the conservative nature of the businessman in mind. If he has to err, the businessman would like to err by understanding revenue, rather than blowing up his income for the period. What ever may be the professed excuses behind this attitude, the purpose of the conservatism is not to deny, but to delay, taxation.

The flow of revenue may cause either an inward movement of cash or other monetary resources or the creation of obligation to the business. Cash sales, interest received, discount received etc. are examples of the revenue causing inward moment of funds. Credit sales create obligations to be settled by movement of resources later. In either case, cash will move either immediately or in future. The question is, whether the revenue can be recognized at the point of the occurrence of the transaction, without having regard to the receipt of payments, or should it wait till payment is received. There are two accounting views prevailing on this issue. According to the first school of thought, revenue has to be recognized as and when the transaction takes place without waiting for the receipt of cash. The receipt of cash is only incidental to the credit policy, being followed by the business. This principle is known as accrual accounting. The other concept is that revenue recognition should coincide with the receipt of cash and this philosophy is called cash accounting. No doubt, most businessmen adopt the former, while very few conservative breeds among them still use the latter. We will consider later that in certain professions such as doctors, lawyers and auditors, their professional code of conduct prevents them from claiming their service fees. In such cases, cash accounting is to be followed by necessity. The discussions in the book are based on accrual accounting principles.

Turnover

The best known and often repeated source of revenue is turnover or sales for a trading or manufacturing organization and service charges in the form of freight commission, brokerage, premium etc. for tertiary sector industries. The term sale is very broad and covers, within its ambit, a few transactions that resemble the nature of sale, even though these are not actually sales from the accountants' point of view. Hence, it is necessary to clearly demarcate the boundaries of a transaction to be conclusively treated as sales or not. Legally speaking, sale has been defined by Sale of Goods Act as a transaction where – under the property in the goods is transferred from the seller to the buyer for a price. According to this legal definition, to consummate sale, two important aspects are to be fulfilled first, there should be a transfer of property and second, the transfer should be for a price. Transfer of property means the transfer of ownership and not the mere transfer of possession.

For concluding whether a particular exchanged of goods amounts to transferring the ownership or not, the intention of the parties transferring the goods is crucial. When the owner gives the goods to another, without any intentions of transferring the ownership, such as for safe custody or for repairs or for raising a loan, such transaction are not sales, but is bailments or pledges. On the other hand, when two parties have agreed, with the intention of one party transferring the ownership in the goods at a price and the other party intends to accept it, the transaction is a sale. Hence, to constitute a sale, only the intention to transfer ownership of goods at a price is needed, irrespective of the physical transfer or possession of the goods or the payment of the price. Another test of ownership is the transfer of risk associated with the goods. With the transfer of ownership, the seller transfers the risk in the goods to the buyer, even if the goods remain with the seller.

Agreement to Sell

Having considered what constitutes sale, the next question is when is sale considered to have taken place – at the time of conclusion of the contract on later. In cases of majority of sales, that is sales without any conditions, sale is assumed to have taken place as soon as the agreement is concluded. But in cases where the sales agreement is subject to the fulfillment of certain conditions, such transactions are not to be considered as sales, but agreements to sell. Agreement to sell is commonly referred to as conditional sales. They are not sales, as property in the goods will not pass on to the buyer till the stipulated conditions are fulfilled. The stipulations may be, passage of time or the happening of an event. For example, an agreement to sell the standing paddy crop for an agreed price will not be sale, till the crop is harvested. Suppose in the meantime, the crop is destroyed due to natural calamities, the agreement to sell will becomes invalid, as the precondition cannot be fulfilled.

Consignment

These are days of mass scale production. A few Mega producers sell their products through a well-knit chain of depots and branches. However, in medium sized organizations, the volume of sales may not necessitate countrywide branches and depots. Such units may have their depots in important strategic sales centers and in the rest of the market, operate through agents and distributors, on commission basis. Under this arrangement, the vendors send their goods to the agents and instruct them to sell the goods on terms and conditions stipulated by the vendors. The agents are custodians of the vendor's goods till they are sold. On effecting sales, the agents send periodic account sales. Sales are recognized by the vendors on receipt of account sales. Till then, the goods in the custody of the argents from part of the stock in trade of the vendor. This type of transaction is known as consignment. Consignments are, thus, bailments.

Sale on Approval Basis

Similar to consignment is the sale on approval basis. Under this, the seller sends the goods directly to the consumer (instead of his agents) and allows him a time period for accepting the goods. Common examples of an approval sales are mail order business. If the consumer accepts the goods within the stipulated time, it becomes sale. In case the consumer retains the goods beyond the stipulated period his inaction considered as tacit approval and sale is recognized thereafter. In sales on approval basis, the consumer can not make use of the goods before his acceptance. In case he makes use of the goods, it also amounts to implied approval and sale is recognized. Now a days, sale on approval basis is enlarged into use and return if not satisfied offer. Here, the use of the goods by the customer is allowed for a stipulated period and the can return the goods, if he is not satisfied with the quality or utility of the goods as promised by the vendor. In these types of transactions, the price of the goods is usually collected in advance *i.e.*, before allowing the customer to the use of product and the price is refunded, if the customer returns the goods after use within the allowed period. Therefore, no sale to be recognized before the expiry of the stipulated time in this type of arrangement.

Installment Credit

Sale of goods, particularly capital goods and consumer durables, such as machinery, equipment, gadget, white goods *etc.* on installment credit is a variation from normal sales.

Hence, the vendor enters into an agreement with the buyer for transfer of the goods to the latter on his making a prescribed down payment. The buyer becomes the owner of the goods, possesses it and uses it. The seller has, no doubt, the right of lien on the goods till all installments are paid. He takes back the goods on default of any installment. Sale is recognized in installment credits, the moment down payment is made. A seemingly similar, but basically different arrangement is hire purchase sale. Hire purchase is an agreement to sell. The Hire Purchase Act, 1972 defines hire purchase as an "agreement under which goods are let on hire and under which the hirer has the option to purchase them in accordance with the terms of agreement". Here, the vendor parts with the possession of the goods on receipt of down payment, but the property in the goods remain with him till all the installments are received. The buyer of hire-purchase agrees to the price of the product, together with interest, at agreed rate, over a specified number of periodic equated installments. Only on the payment of the last installment, the hirer will become the owner of the goods.

The question, therefore, is when should the vendor of hire-purchase goods book the transaction as sale-whether immediately after the conclusion of the agreement and accepting down payment or during the tenure of the hire-purchase period or on the receipt of the last installment. The down payment is credited to the personal account of the hirer. As and when the periodic installment is received, the capital recovery element of the installment is credited to the personal account of the hirer and the interest component is treated as income of the period. When all the installments are received, the hirer's account would be amortized and sale is recognized at this stage.

In yet other cases, particularly in hire-purchase of small value goods, such as televisions, refrigerators, furniture, domestic appliances, musical instruments, computers *etc.*, only the amount of installments is treated as revenue. For example, sale of a refrigerator at Rs.10,000 with Rs.2000 as down payment and the balance to be paid in 10 monthly installments of Rs.825 each was made on 1st October, 2000. The hire vendor closes his books at the end of March. The vendor will recognize as revenue for the year the down payment and six monthly installments (Rs.6950) he would have received during the accounting year as revenue. This is logical, as the hire has the option, in law, to return the goods any time before the last installment. In the event of the client defaulting in the payment of installments, the vendor will terminate the contract and repossess the goods. The sale price, less the principal amount recovered would be the value of repossessed stock, till it is resold. On sale of the repossessed goods, surplus, if any, will be treated as profit and loss will be booked as cost. It may be noted that the hirer is not liable for any loss on resale.

In case of higher value goods, such as plant and machinery, and other capital goods, the transaction is treated as sale as soon as the agreement is signed and the down payment is made. The hirer is treated as a debtor for the amount due. At agreed intervals, the hirer's account is debited with the interest on the outstanding. And when the installment is received, the hirer's account is credited with the entire amount of the installment. The procedure in respect of default is the same as that adopted in small value goods.

Quantum Meruit

Recognizing the time of sale of capital goods, with process time extending more than a year and also customer's contracts, spread over longer periods, is another grey area for the accountant. There is a time gap, more than one accounting year, between the time of undertaking the work and that of completing it. The work might have started in year one and completed in year four. Can sales be recognized as soon as the work is taken up or to wait till it is completed? The former will be too hasty and letter denying the benefit to the extent of the task accomplished. In such cases, revenue is recognized, as per the principle of accounting, to work completed or on the principle of quantum meruit or to the extent of work completed.

Generally Accepted Accounting Practices (GAAP), detailed discussions on which were held in chapter 1, had laid down the pro-rata principle of recognizing sales in long term contracts. As per GAAP guidelines, no revenue can be recognized for less than one fourth of work completed in a year. When the work completed is more than one-fourth, but less than one-half, one-third of the estimated profit can be recognized as revenue. When the work completed is more than one-half, two-thirds of the estimated profits can be recognized as revenue. For example, General Constructions (Private) Limited had concluded on 1st May 1996, an agreement with M/s Meena Agencies for constructing their industrial complex over four years, to be billed on quantum meruit basis. General Constructions had a profit margin of 20% (Rs.59 lakhs) built into the contract price, which was finalized at Rs.3.56 crores. The price included cushions for inflation. During 1996-97, the work was slow and General Constructions billed Meena for Rs.60 lakhs. The billing was for Rs.1.10 crores in 1997-98, Rs.1.20 crores in 1998-99 and the balance in 1999-2000. As the work in the first year has fallen short of one-fourth of the contracted value. General Constructions can not book any revenue for that year. However, the expenses in the year, in excess of the billed amount, are treated as loss on the contract. In 1997-98 General Constructions can book profit of Rs.9.39 lakhs, being one-third of the profit the completed work of Rs.1.70 crores (Rs.60 lakhs in 1996-97 and Rs. 1.10 crores in 1997-98). In 1998-99 the company can book Rs.22.65 lakhs, being two-thirds of the profit on the billing of Rs.2.90 crores, less the profit of Rs.9.39 lakhs already booked for 1997-98. In 1999-2000, the company can book the balance of profit of Rs.26.96 lakhs, as revenue.

Service Charges

So far, we have been discussing the revenue recognition procedure in merchandise or manufacturing activities. Does the mode of recognizing revenue differs in service industries? The recognition of revenue in services industries is according to the terms or contract of service. Certain service contract make specific performance as the essence. For example, installation fees, service guarantee fees, agency commissions, financial services fees etc. These are contracts where the fee is the revenue and it can be recognized only when the performance of the service is specifically rendered to the satisfaction of the customers. Installation fees are fees payable for the erection of equipment. Special equipment, such as process plants, when supplied to a customer, constrains an element of installation fee as part of the cost of equipment. Where the customer has no technical knowledge or competence to correctly install the equipment, he agrees to pay a fee to the suppliers towards installation. The fee is due only when the equipment is installed to the satisfaction of the customer. In fact, the fee has to be recognized as revenue only when the supplier has successfully taken trial runs and per the terms of contract. Usually, installation would have teething problems. It is the duty of the supplier to rectify the defects to the satisfaction of the customer, before recognizing the fee as revenue.

The supplier may also guarantee the effective functioning of the equipment during certain number of years. Specific fee for the purpose is included as part of the cost of the equipment. In such cases, the businessman should segregate, at the time of sale, the fee from the cost of the equipment and treat the gross value of equipment less the fee, as revenue of the year of sale. The guarantee fee component has to be recognized as revenue, usually equally, over the period for which guarantee has been extended. Costs, if any, incurred as a consequence of the guarantee obligation, has to be treated as expenses of the year concerned.

The next category of service charges comprises agency commission and financial charges. When an agent acts on behalf of the principal, he is entitled to the agreed commission only on fulfilling the conditions of the agency agreement. A selling agent of goods become entitled to commission on the value of goods sold by him during a period, as per the account sale submitted by him sometimes, he is given an extra commission to take responsibilities for collection of receivables. These commissions are called declared commission payable to advertising agents is recognized as revenue only after the advertisement is published. Similarly, commission payable to insurance agent is recognized as revenue only on the issue or the renewal of the policy. Financial services, such as arranging for the loans or for issue of securities, are carried out by merchant bankers. They are entitled to the agreed commissions only on the specific performance of the service. That is, on the sanctioning of the loan by the financial institution or bank and on the issue of concerned securities to the public. It may be added here that documentation and disbursement of the loan is not part of the specific performance by the merchant bankers, unless such services are also included as part of the contracts. It is not part of merchant banker's obligation to ensure that the underwriter fulfill his commitment by subscribing to the shortfall, if any, in public subscription. Once the underwriting agreement is completed and the issue is made specific performance of the merchant bankers is complete and the commission is booked as revenue.

Technical Know-how

As against the specific service contract discussed above, there are significant numbers of continuing long-term service contracts, which generate revenue over a period. Royalty fees receivable for the know-how supply is familiar example under a patent, may part with the know-how to another for commercializing in particular areas and for specific periods. Such contracts are called technical know-how agreements. The supplier of know-how, under this agreement, is usually entitled to a one time technical know-how fee as well as long term periodic royalty. Technical know-how fee is for specific performance of installing the know-how to the satisfaction of the customer. Once this is done and after successful trial runs, the businessman becomes entitled to the know-how fee, which is recognized as his revenue for the period. Royalties are, on the other hand, fees received by the supplier of the know-how over a specific period, at certain percentage on the value of sales or profit or the volume of production, as the case may be. Royalties are recognized as revenues at the end of each year, measured as per the barometers indicated above.

Franchises

Franchises are akin to royalties with a difference. Royalties are paid for the use of technical know-how of a process in possession of the vendor. However, the product, to the manufactured by the user of the know-how, may not bear the brand name of the franchiser. In certain cases, it is only the brand name for which franchise is paid. Further, many franchisers supply equipment, plant and machinery etc., together with technical know-how. Thus, the franchisee need not invest in manufacturing facilities. The best example in this category is the mineral water business. Here, the entire equipment of the franchiser is installed at the premise of the franchisee and fee is levied at certain paise per litter of water produced. Franchise fees, therefore, are levied both for the use of the equipment and the process know-how. In some franchises, such as Coca-Cola, the product essence itself is supplied and the franchiser is allowed only to blend and bottle the drink as per the direction of the franchiser. Franchise charges are recognized as revenue on yearly basis, measured according to the volume of output.

Royalties

Royalties are also paid for the extraction of materials, such as for querying coal, iron ore, or exploring oil *etc.* The modalities are that a lease rent, based on the expected deposit of the metal, oil etc. is agreed to and yearly royalty is charged on the basis of other actual extraction of the deposit. For example, suppose a coal mine is estimated to have 5 million tonnes of coal of a particular quality. The owner of the mine fixes the lease, based on the deposit, say at Rs scrores and the period of lease is 15 years. It amounts to that the lessee has to pay Rs 10 per tonne of coal extracted as royalty. In case 5,00,000 tonnes are extracted in the first year, revenue is recognized by the lessor for 5 lakh tonnes at the rate of Rs.10 per tonnes, which is Rs.50 lakhs. In the second year, If the coal extracted is 10 lakh tonnes, the lessor's revenue will be Rs.1 crore. This will continue, till lease period or the exhaustion on of the mine, whichever is earlier.

Holding of Assets

Revenue for a business also stems from the holding of assets. A business may invest its surplus funds in short-term securities and earn an income, without sacrificing liquidity of the business. In this connection, money market instruments, such as treasury bills, commercial papers *etc.* are ideal assets to be held by the enterprise, as these have high liquidity and fair returns. Revenue, in the form of interest, is recognized at periodic intervals or on the liquidation of such assets. Another method of short-term investment is to have speculative inventories.

A fund and sell the excess over its requirement at higher rates, reaping trading profits, which are recognized as revenue to the business in the year of occurrence.

Long term holding of assets by an organization would also generate revenue. An organization may invest its surplus cash in the shares/bonds of other companies and realize revenue by way of income and capital appreciation. Companies also acquire shares with a view to ultimately taking over the latter. Such take-over result in additional revenues in future due to synergies associated with merger. Further, an enterprise also invests in its subsidiaries or sister concerns and reaps the benefit of periodic dividends and capital appreciation. Dividends are recognized as revenue in the same accounting period, whereas capital appreciation is recognized only on the sale of the investments.

Others Holding Company's Assets

Revenue may also accrue to the business by others holding the assets of the enterprise. Assets of the company, when they are in excess of its requirement, are let out for others to use. A charge is levied for such use. For example, when the company's vehicles are leased out to others, it generates a periodic income, which can be recognized at the end of the concerned period. Leasing companies earth their major income from letting out their assets. Another instance of the assets of a business generating revenue, when they are held by others is financial instruments, such as bonds, debentures, stocks and shares, when they are pledged or mortgaged, the income generated by the instruments accrue to the business and not to the holders.

Sales Price

Sale, as we have already seen as it a price. Price is the monetary measurement of the utility in goods. What should be recognized as sales price needs closer scrutiny. When the seller extends volume discount, sale price is the marked price less the trade discount. Again, gross sale price includes central excise and state sales tax. Excise duties, at varying rates, are levied on all manufactured goods. Excise duty is meant to be paid initially by manufacturers to the Government and later to be recovered from the buyers of the goods. Further, State Governments levy commercial tax, commonly known as sales tax, which again has to be borne by the businessman initially, to be collected from the buyers of goods. Readers may be aware that taxes, where the initial incidence is shifted are called indirect taxes. Both central excise ad sales tax are indirect taxes, levied by central and state governments respectively. In determining sales for the purpose of revenue, the businessman has to recognize sales, net of excise and sales tax. This constitutes the net sales of the business for the period. From net sales, sales returns or returns inwards is deducted and the resultant is the sales to be recognized for the period.

On Receipt of Cash

In some cases, revenue can be recognized only on receipt of cash. Professional etiquette restricts certain professionals from legally enforcing their claim for reward for the services rendered by them. Doctors, solicitors, accountants and similar professionals are prevented, by their respective professionals codes, from legally enforcing their rights for remuneration for their services. It is, therefore, logical that revenue, in the case of these professionals for their services, can be recognized only when received in cash. For them, cash accounting is the ideal method.

Recognizing and estimating revenue pertaining to the accounting period is the prime function of the accountant. He culls out the data from the accounting records of the business organization. Information about the sales figure to be taken to the profit and loss account are available in trial balance, but are spread over three accounting heads – sales account, (Cr.), which represents the cash sales made during the period, sales day book total (Cr.) which indicates the extent of credit sales effected by the business and sales return or inward return account (Dr.) Sales, for the purpose of the profitability statement, is the synthesis of these accounts, that is, cash sales plus credit sales less sales return is the net sales to be recognized.

Other revenue items such as commissions, brokerage, fees, royalties, discounts received, etc., are all credit balances in the trial balance and are to be taken to the credit side of the profit and loss account after adjusting for outstanding and receipts in advance.

Summary

Revenue is the result of cost. Costs are incurred with a view to earn revenue. Revenue over the cost, attributed for earning such revenue, results in profit, which increases the wealth of the enterprise. Revenue is a flow and its realistic measurement is necessary to project a fair and true picture of the operational results of the business over a period. Businessmen are careful in not exaggerating their income during an accounting period. They prefer to defer the recognition of revenue to delay the impact to taxation.

Revenue recognition and measurement are thus vital steps in the preparation of profit and loss account. Generally speaking, revenue may be recognized at any of the following stages.

- **At the point of sale:** This is so in respect of sales without any condition. The only criterion is that the intention of the vendor should be to part with the ownership in goods to the buyer. Although sales are at a price, the receipt of pride is not an essential prerequisite to qualify for recognition as revenue.
- **During the process of production:** For manufacturer of capital goods and construction work, where the process of production spreads over more than a year, revenue is recognized on pro-rate or quantum meruit basis, even before the completion of the task.
- **On services:** For service contracts, the essence of which is that the service charges are recognized as revenue only when the task is completed to the satisfaction of the customer.
- **Holding assets:** Revenue by way of interest, dividend and capital gains are recognized on investments of the business in short term or long-term securities and assets. Revenue is also recognized when others hold the assets of the business as in the case of leasing.

- **On receipt payment:** Certain professionals, such as layers, doctors, and auditor's etc. are restrained by their professional code of conduct, to resort to legal remedies for recovering their fees for services rendered. In such cases, service charges are treated as revenues only when received in cash.

I. QUESTIONS

1. What do you understand by revenue?

2. Describe the characteristics of revenue.

3. What is accrual accounting? How does it differ from cash accounting?

4. Define the term sales.

5. What are the main attributes of a valid sale?

6. When do sales legally take place?

7. What are agreements of sale? How does it differ from sale?

8. How do sales vary from bailments?

9. How does revenue arise by holding of assets?

10. Why do you consider revenue recognition as an approximation?

11. How are revenues from service industries recognized?

12. When do the following fees recognized as revenue:

(a) Technical know-how fees;

(b) Royalties;

(c) Financial service charges;

(d) Agent's commission;

(e) Architect's fees.

13. What do you understand by quantum meruit? How does it apply in long-term construction contracts?

14. What are consignments? How are revenue recognized in consignments?

15. How are net sales computed for the income statement?

16. Write short notes on the following:

(a) Sales on approval basis;

(b) Franchises;

(c) Hire-purchase agreements;

(d) Installment credits.

17. Explain the steps involved in the preparation of final accounts.

II. QUIZ

Say yes or no to the following:

1. Estimation of revenue is an approximation as business convention is one of a going concern.
2. All receipts are revenues.
3. Revenue invariably causes an immediate inward movement of funds.
4. Hire purchase and installment credit are two terms signifying same contract
5. Sale are concluded with the transfer of goods.
6. Goods sent on consignment are to be recognized as sales.
7. Royalty is one time payment for technical know-how.
8. Service contracts are usually specific performance contracts.
9. In quantum meruit contracts, profit is booked every year on the quantum of work accomplished.
10. Revenue may also arise from others holding the assets of the business.

III. EXERCISES

1. Which of the following inflow is revenue and why?
   (a) Cash received on deposits from public
   (b) Commission received
   (c) Interest received on investments
   (d) Sale of obsolete assets
   (e) Money received from debtors
   (f) Goods sent on approval basis
   (g) Lease rent received
2. Do you recognize sale in the following instances? State reasons.
   (a) Sold goods for credit
   (b) Sent goods on consignment
   (c) Hire purchase sale of goods of low value Rs.10500 with Rs.2000 down payment and the balance on 4 quarterly installments, where no installment has fallen due?
   (d) Goods sent on installment credit, where only down payment is received.
   (e) Doctors fee of Rs.5200 due from a client.

3. Pals Construction Ltd. have undertaken the construction of a dam over Beas for the Government of Himachal Pradesh at an estimated cost of Rs.42.50 crores. The construction began in June 1995 and was to be completed in 4 years. Payments to be made on quantum meruit basis. The yearly expenditure on the project are:

Year	Work certified (Rs. in Crores)	Expenditure incurred (Rs. in Crores)
1995-96	2.75	3.15
1996-97	11.55	9.26
1997-98	22.40	20.86
1998-99	5.80	6.73
Total	42.50	34.00

The built in margin of profit was 25% on the estimated cost. The work was complement in time and within estimates. What would be the revenue Pals Construction will recognize every year during the contract period?

4. Hire and Prosper Ltd. engaged in the hire purchase sale of high value equipment, has sold on 1.4.98 a multistage boiler to Lunar Manufacturing Company Ltd. Lucknow at Rs.27.35 Crores. Down payment 20% and balance at equated four annual installments of Rs.6.38 Crores each.

   (a) What is the rate of interest charged on hire purchase? (Hint: use Annuity table)

   (b) What will be the revenue recognized in the year ended 31.3.99?

   (c) Lunar Manufacturing Co. was paying the installment regularly upto end March 1999, became sick and closed down in June 1999. Hire and Prosper repossessed the boiler and was able to find a ready buyer for the second hand boiler at Rs.17.45 Crores. How would Hire & Prosper treat it in its books?

5. Bagwandas' ledger accounts show cash sales of Rs.241, 52,115 and credit sales of Rs.453,501 for the year ended 31.3.1999. The sale is first subjected to 3% central excise and them 5% sales tax. Returns Inward book shows a balance of Rs.11. 43.123. What would be the value of sale for the purpose of profit and loss account?

6. Chandler bought a motor bike on hire purchase basis. The cost of the bike was Rs.43,000. Chandler has to make a down payment of 10% and the balance in ten equal monthly installments of Rs.4,500, which includes interest on monthly opening balanced at 12%. How will you account the installment in the books of the seller, when he receives the installments? Would it be different if Chandler has purchased the bike on installment credit?

7. Randir Constructions Ltd. tender for the construction of Hitec City in Bangalore at an estimated Rs.515.75 lakhs had been accepted. The tender value includes a profit margin of 20% on cost. The contract has to be executed over 3 years. Payment to be made on quantum meruit basis. Randir Construction had incurred an expenditure of Rs.110 lakhs in the first year. Rs.305 lakhs in the second year and completed the work in the third year. There was no escalation in the cost. What part of the profit will be recognized as revenue in the first, second and third year?

8. Sun Sun Shipbuilders have agreed to fabricate a 1500 tonnes freighter for Sri Lanka Govt. at an estimated cost of Rs.126 Crores and over a five year period. Sun Sun billed the Sri Lankan Govt for the following year wise:

   1 year Rs. 24 Crores
   2 year Rs.32 Crores
   3 year Rs.45 Crores
   4 year Rs.20 Crores
   5 year Rs. 5 Crores

   Total : Rs.126 Crores

   What would be the revenue recognizable by Sun Sun on the assumption that the tender rice included 25% profit margin on sales.

9. Damodar Coal Ltd. had taken mining lease for 10 years from the West Bengal Government for mining coal in Asansol area. The mine is estimated to have a deposit of 50 million tonnes of high-grade coal. The lease agreement provides for the payment of Rs.50 Crores on pro-rata basis annually on the basis of exploitation. Damodar Coal Ltd. had extracted 25 lakh tones in the first year, 35 lakh tonnes in the second year and 70 lakh tonnes in the third year. What would be the revenue recognizable to the West Bengal Govt. in each of these years?

10. Tan-Am Inc. an American Corporation, had entered into collaboration agreement with Pan-Indian Ltd. for the supply of technical know-how for the manufacture of ductile iron spun pipes, which is currently manufactured in India only by Electro Steel Castings. The collaboration agreement provides for a royalty of 5% for 3 years on the sales value. Pan Indian Ltd. sold 725 tonnes in 1997 @ Rs.12,500 per tonne, 965 tonnes in 1998 @ Rs.13,100 per tonne and 1010 tonnes in 1999 @ Rs.13,250. What will be revenue recognizable by Tan-Am from royalty on the basis of the dollar-rupee exchange rate of Rs.40 in 1997, Rs.41 in 1998 and Rs.42.50 in 1999?

APPENDIX

Table A.1 **Future Value Interest Factor (*FVIF*)**
$FVIF(r, n) = (1 + r)^n$

Period *n*	1%	2%	3%	4%	5%	6%	7%	8%	9%	10%	11%	12%	13%
0	1.000	1.000	1.000	1.000	1.000	1.000	1.000	1.000	1.000	1.000	1.000	1.000	1.000
1	1.010	1.020	1.030	1.040	1.050	1.060	1.070	1.080	1.090	1.100	1.110	1.120	1.130
2	1.020	1.040	1.061	1.082	1.102	1.124	1.145	1.166	1.188	1.210	1.232	1.254	1.277
3	1.030	1.061	1.093	1.125	1.158	1.191	1.225	1.260	1.295	1.331	1.368	1.405	1.443
4	1.041	1.082	1.126	1.170	1.216	1.262	1.311	1.360	1.412	1.464	1.518	1.574	1.630
5	1.051	1.104	1.159	1.217	1.276	1.338	1.403	1.469	1.539	1.611	1.685	1.762	1.842
6	1.062	1.126	1.194	1.265	1.340	1.419	1.501	1.587	1.677	1.772	1.870	1.974	2.082
7	1.072	1.149	1.230	1.316	1.407	1.504	1.606	1.714	1.828	1.949	2.076	2.211	2.353
8	1.083	1.172	1.267	1.369	1.477	1.594	1.718	1.851	1.993	2.144	2.305	2.476	2.658
9	1.094	1.195	1.305	1.423	1.551	1.689	1.838	1.999	2.172	2.358	2.558	2.773	3.004
10	1.105	1.219	1.344	1.480	1.629	1.791	1.967	2.159	2.367	2.594	2.839	3.106	3.395
11	1.116	1.243	1.384	1.539	1.710	1.898	2.105	2.332	2.580	2.853	3.152	3.479	3.836
12	1.127	1.268	1.426	1.601	1.796	2.012	2.252	2.518	2.813	3.138	3.498	3.896	4.335
13	1.138	1.294	1.469	1.665	1.886	2.133	2.410	2.720	3.066	3.452	3.883	4.363	4.898
14	1.149	1.319	1.513	1.732	1.980	2.261	2.579	2.937	3.342	3.797	4.310	4.887	5.535
15	1.161	1.346	1.558	1.801	2.079	2.397	2.759	3.172	3.642	4.177	4.785	5.474	6.254
16	1.173	1.373	1.605	1.873	2.183	2.540	2.952	3.426	3.970	4.595	5.311	6.130	7.067
17	1.184	1.400	1.653	1.948	2.292	2.693	3.159	3.700	4.328	5.054	5.895	6.866	7.986
18	1.196	1.428	1.702	2.026	2.407	2.854	3.380	3.996	4.717	5.560	6.544	7.690	9.024
19	1.208	1.457	1.754	2.107	2.527	3.026	3.617	4.316	5.142	6.116	7.263	8.613	10.197
20	1.220	1.486	1.806	2.191	2.653	3.207	3.870	4.661	5.604	6.728	8.062	9.646	11.523
25	1.282	1.641	2.094	2.666	3.386	4.292	5.427	6.848	8.623	10.835	13.585	17.000	21.231
30	1.348	1.811	2.427	3.243	4.322	5.743	7.612	10.063	13.268	17.449	22.892	29.960	39.116

(Contd)

Appendix A

Table A.1 *(Contd)*

Period *n*	14%	15%	16%	17%	18%	19%	20%	24%	28%	32%	36%	40%
0	1.000	1.000	1.000	1.000	1.000	1.000	1.000	1.000	1.000	1.000	1.000	1.000
1	1.140	1.150	1.160	1.170	1.180	1.190	1.200	1.240	1.280	1.320	1.360	1.400
2	1.300	1.322	1.346	1.369	1.392	1.416	1.440	1.538	1.638	1.742	1.850	1.960
3	1.482	1.521	1.561	1.602	1.643	1.685	1.728	1.907	2.097	2.300	2.515	2.744
4	1.689	1.749	1.811	1.874	1.939	2.005	2.074	2.364	2.684	3.036	3.421	3.842
5	1.925	2.011	2.100	2.192	2.288	2.386	2.488	2.392	3.436	4.007	4.653	5.378
6	2.195	2.313	2.436	2.565	2.700	2.840	2.986	3.635	4.398	5.290	6.328	7.530
7	2.502	2.660	2.826	3.001	3.185	3.379	3.583	4.508	5.629	6.983	8.605	10.541
8	2.853	3.059	3.278	3.511	3.759	4.021	4.300	5.590	7.206	9.217	11.703	14.758
9	3.252	3.518	3.803	4.108	4.435	4.785	5.160	6.931	9.223	12.166	15.917	20.661
10	3.707	4.046	4.411	4.807	5.234	5.695	6.192	8.549	11.806	16.060	21.647	28.925
11	4.226	4.652	5.117	5.624	6.176	6.777	7.430	10.657	15.112	21.199	29.439	40.496
12	4.818	5.350	5.936	6.580	7.288	8.064	8.916	13.215	19.343	27.983	40.037	56.694
13	5.492	6.153	6.886	7.699	8.599	9.596	10.699	16.386	24.759	36.937	54.451	79.372
14	6.261	7.076	7.988	9.007	10.147	11.420	12.839	20.319	31.961	48.757	74.053	111.120
15	7.138	8.137	9.266	10.539	11.974	13.590	15.407	25.196	40.565	64.359	100.712	155.568
16	8.137	9.358	10.748	12.330	14.129	16.172	18.488	31.243	51.923	84.954	136.969	217.795
17	9.276	10.761	12.468	14.426	16.672	19.244	22.186	38.741	66.461	112.139	186.278	304.914
18	10.575	12.375	14.463	16.879	19.673	22.901	26.623	48.039	85.071	148.023	253.388	426.879
19	12.056	14.263	16.777	19.748	23.214	27.252	31.948	59.568	108.890	195.391	344.540	597.630
20	13.743	16.367	19.461	23.106	27.393	32.429	38.338	73.864	139.380	257.916	468.574	836.683
25	26.462	32.919	40.874	50.658	62.669	77.388	95.396	216.542	478.905	1033.590	2180.081	4499.880
30	50.950	66.212	85.850	111.065	143.371	184.675	237.376	634.820	1645.504	4142.075	10143.019	24201.432

Table A.2 **Future Value Interest Factor for an Annuity *FVIFA* (*r*, *n*)** $= \dfrac{(1+r)^n - 1}{r}$

Period *n*	1%	2%	3%	4%	5%	6%	7%	8%	9%	10%	11%	12%	13%
1	1.000	1.000	1.000	1.000	1.000	1.000	1.000	1.000	1.000	1.000	1.000	1.000	1.000
2	2.010	2.020	2.030	2.040	2.050	2.060	2.070	2.080	2.090	2.100	2.110	2.120	2.130
3	3.030	3.060	3.091	3.122	3.152	3.184	3.215	3.246	3.278	3.310	3.342	3.374	3.407
4	4.060	4.122	4.184	4.246	4.310	4.375	4.440	4.506	4.573	4.641	4.710	4.779	4.850
5	5.101	5.204	5.309	5.416	5.526	5.637	5.751	5.867	5.985	6.105	6.228	6.353	6.480
6	6.152	6.308	6.468	6.633	6.802	6.975	7.153	7.336	7.523	7.716	7.913	8.115	8.323
7	7.214	7.434	7.662	7.898	8.142	8.394	8.654	8.923	9.200	9.487	9.783	10.089	10.405
8	8.286	8.583	8.892	9.214	9.549	9.897	10.260	10.637	11.028	11.436	11.859	12.300	12.757
9	9.369	9.755	10.159	10.583	11.027	11.491	11.978	12.488	13.021	13.579	14.164	14.776	15.416
10	10.462	10.950	11.464	12.006	12.578	13.181	13.816	14.487	15.193	15.937	16.722	17.549	18.420
11	11.567	12.169	12.808	13.486	14.207	14.972	15.784	16.645	17.560	18.531	19.561	20.655	21.814
12	12.683	13.412	14.192	15.026	15.917	16.870	17.888	18.977	20.141	21.384	22.713	24.133	25.650
13	13.809	14.680	15.618	16.627	17.713	18.882	20.141	21.495	22.953	24.523	26.212	28.029	29.985
14	14.947	15.974	17.086	18.292	19.599	21.015	22.550	24.215	26.019	27.975	30.095	32.393	34.883
15	16.097	17.293	18.599	20.024	21.579	23.276	25.129	27.152	29.361	31.772	34.405	37.280	40.417
16	17.258	18.639	20.157	21.825	23.657	25.673	27.888	30.324	33.003	35.950	39.190	42.753	46.672
17	18.430	20.012	21.762	23.698	25.840	28.813	30.840	33.750	36.974	40.545	44.501	48.884	53.739
18	19.615	21.412	23.414	25.645	28.132	30.906	33.999	37.450	41.301	45.599	50.396	55.750	61.725
19	20.811	22.841	25.117	27.671	30.539	33.760	37.379	41.446	46.018	51.159	56.939	63.440	70.749
20	22.019	24.297	26.870	29.778	33.066	36.786	40.995	45.762	51.160	57.275	64.203	72.052	80.947
25	28.243	32.030	36.459	41.646	47.727	54.865	63.249	73.106	84.701	98.347	114.413	133.334	155.620
30	34.785	40.568	47.575	56.805	66.439	79.058	94.461	113.283	136.308	164.494	199.021	241.333	293.199

(Contd)

Appendix A

Table A.2 *(Contd)*

Period *n*	14%	15%	16%	17%	18%	19%	20%	24%	28%	32%	36%	40%
1	1.000	1.000	1.000	1.000	1.000	1.000	1.000	1.000	1.000	1.000	1.000	1.000
2	2.140	2.150	2.160	2.170	2.180	2.190	2.200	2.240	2.280	2.320	2.360	2.400
3	3.440	3.473	3.506	3.539	3.572	3.606	3.640	3.778	3.918	4.062	4.210	4.360
4	4.921	4.993	5.066	5.141	5.215	5.291	5.368	5.684	6.016	6.362	6.725	7.104
5	6.610	6.742	6.877	7.014	7.154	7.297	7.442	8.048	8.700	9.398	10.146	10.946
6	8.536	8.754	8.977	9.207	9.442	9.683	9.930	10.980	12.136	13.406	14.799	16.324
7	10.730	11.067	11.414	11.772	12.142	12.523	12.916	14.615	16.534	18.696	21.126	23.853
8	13.233	13.727	14.240	14.773	15.327	15.902	16.499	19.123	22.163	25.678	29.732	34.395
9	16.085	16.786	17.518	18.285	19.086	19.923	20.799	24.712	29.369	34.895	41.435	49.153
10	19.337	20.304	21.321	22.393	23.521	24.709	25.959	31.643	38.592	47.062	57.352	69.814
11	23.044	24.349	25.733	27.200	28.755	30.404	32.150	40.238	50.399	63.122	78.998	98.739
12	27.271	29.002	30.850	32.824	34.931	37.180	39.580	50.985	65.510	84.320	108.437	139.235
13	32.089	34.352	36.786	39.404	42.219	45.244	48.497	64.110	84.853	112.303	148.475	195.929
14	37.518	40.505	43.672	47.103	50.818	54.841	59.196	80.496	109.612	149.240	202.926	275.300
15	43.842	47.580	51.660	56.110	60.965	66.261	72.035	100.815	141.303	197.997	276.979	386.420
16	50.980	55.717	60.925	66.649	72.939	79.850	87.442	126.011	181.868	262.356	377.692	541.988
17	59.118	65.075	71.673	78.979	87.068	96.022	105.931	157.253	233.791	347.310	514.661	759.784
18	68.394	75.836	84.141	93.406	103.740	115.266	128.117	195.994	300.252	459.449	700.939	1064.697
19	78.969	88.212	98.603	110.285	123.414	138.166	154.740	244.033	385.323	607.472	954.277	1491.576
20	91.025	102.440	115.380	130.033	146.628	165.418	186.688	303.601	494.213	802.863	1298.817	2089.206
25	181.871	212.793	249.214	292.105	342.603	402.042	471.981	898.092	1706.803	3226.844	6053.004	11247.199
30	356.787	434.745	530.321	647.439	790.948	966.712	1181.882	2640.916	5873.231	12940.859	28172.276	60501.081

Table A.3 **Present Value Interest Factor *PVIF* (*r*, *n*) = $(1 + r)^{-n}$**

Period *n*	1%	2%	3%	4%	5%	6%	7%	8%	9%	10%	11%	12%	13%
0	1.000	1.000	1.000	1.000	1.000	1.000	1.000	1.000	1.000	1.000	1.000	1.000	1.000
1	0.990	0.980	0.971	0.962	0.952	0.943	0.935	0.926	0.917	0.909	0.901	0.893	0.885
2	0.980	0.961	0.943	0.925	0.907	0.890	0.873	0.857	0.842	0.826	0.812	0.797	0.783
3	0.971	0.924	0.915	0.889	0.864	0.840	0.816	0.794	0.772	0.751	0.731	0.712	0.693
4	0.961	0.924	0.889	0.855	0.823	0.792	0.763	0.735	0.708	0.683	0.659	0.636	0.613
5	0.951	0.906	0.863	0.822	0.784	0.747	0.713	0.681	0.650	0.621	0.593	0.567	0.543
6	0.942	0.888	0.838	0.790	0.746	0.705	0.666	0.630	0.596	0.564	0.535	0.507	0.480
7	0.933	0.871	0.813	0.760	0.711	0.665	0.623	0.583	0.547	0.513	0.482	0.452	0.425
8	0.923	0.853	0.789	0.731	0.677	0.627	0.582	0.540	0.502	0.467	0.434	0.404	0.376
9	0.914	0.837	0.766	0.703	0.645	0.592	0.544	0.500	0.460	0.424	0.391	0.361	0.333
10	0.905	0.820	0.744	0.676	0.614	0.558	0.508	0.463	0.422	0.386	0.352	0.322	0.295
11	0.896	0.804	0.722	0.650	0.585	0.527	0.475	0.429	0.388	0.350	0.317	0.287	0.261
12	0.887	0.788	0.701	0.625	0.557	0.497	0.444	0.397	0.356	0.319	0.286	0.257	0.231
13	0.879	0.773	0.681	0.601	0.530	0.469	0.415	0.368	0.326	0.290	0.258	0.229	0.204
14	0.870	0.758	0.661	0.577	0.505	0.442	0.388	0.340	0.299	0.263	0.232	0.205	0.181
15	0.861	0.743	0.642	0.555	0.481	0.417	0.362	0.315	0.275	0.239	0.209	0.183	0.160
16	0.853	0.728	0.623	0.534	0.458	0.394	0.339	0.292	0.252	0.218	0.188	0.163	0.141
17	0.844	0.714	0.605	0.513	0.436	0.377	0.311	0.270	0.231	0.198	0.170	0.146	0.125
18	0.836	0.700	0.587	0.494	0.416	0.350	0.296	0.250	0.212	0.180	0.153	0.130	0.111
19	0.828	0.686	0.570	0.475	0.396	0.331	0.276	0.232	0.194	0.164	0.138	0.116	0.098
20	0.820	0.673	0.554	0.456	0.377	0.312	0.258	0.215	0.178	0.149	0.124	0.104	0.087
25	0.780	0.610	0.478	0.375	0.295	0.233	0.184	0.146	0.116	0.092	0.074	0.059	0.047
30	0.742	0.552	0.412	0.308	0.231	0.174	0.131	0.099	0.075	0.057	0.044	0.033	0.026

(*Contd*)

Appendix A

Table A.3 *(Contd)*

Period *n*	*14%*	*15%*	*16%*	*17%*	*18%*	*19%*	*20%*	*24%*	*28%*	*32%*	*36%*	*40%*
0	1.000	1.000	1.000	1.000	1.000	1.000	1.000	1.000	1.000	1.000	1.000	1.000
1	0.877	0.870	0.862	0.855	0.847	0.840	0.833	0.806	0.781	0.758	0.735	0.714
2	0.769	0.756	0.743	0.731	0.718	0.706	0.694	0.650	0.610	0.574	0.541	0.510
3	0.675	0.658	0.641	0.624	0.609	0.593	0.579	0.524	0.477	0.435	0.398	0.364
4	0.592	0.572	0.552	0.534	0.516	0.499	0.482	0.423	0.373	0.329	0.292	0.260
5	0.519	0.497	0.476	0.456	0.437	0.419	0.402	0.341	0.291	0.250	0.215	0.186
6	0.456	0.432	0.410	0.390	0.370	0.352	0.335	0.275	0.227	0.189	0.158	0.133
7	0.400	0.376	0.354	0.333	0.314	0.296	0.279	0.222	0.178	0.143	0.116	0.095
8	0.351	0.327	0.305	0.285	0.266	0.249	0.233	0.179	0.139	0.108	0.085	0.068
9	0.308	0.284	0.263	0.243	0.226	0.209	0.194	0.144	0.108	0.082	0.063	0.048
10	0.270	0.247	0.227	0.208	0.191	0.176	0.162	0.116	0.085	0.062	0.046	0.035
11	0.237	0.215	0.195	0.178	0.162	0.148	0.135	0.094	0.066	0.047	0.034	0.025
12	0.208	0.187	0.168	0.152	0.137	0.124	0.112	0.076	0.052	0.036	0.025	0.618
13	0.182	0.163	0.145	0.130	0.116	0.104	0.093	0.061	0.040	0.027	0.018	0.013
14	0.160	0.141	0.125	0.111	0.099	0.088	0.078	0.049	0.032	0.021	0.014	0.009
15	0.140	0.123	0.108	0.095	0.084	0.074	0.065	0.040	0.025	0.016	0.010	0.006
16	0.123	0.107	0.093	0.081	0.071	0.062	0.054	0.032	0.019	0.012	0.007	0.005
17	0.108	0.093	0.080	0.069	0.060	0.052	0.045	0.026	0.015	0.009	0.005	0.003
18	0.095	0.081	0.069	0.059	0.051	0.044	0.038	0.021	0.012	0.007	0.004	0.002
19	0.083	0.070	0.060	0.051	0.043	0.037	0.031	0.017	0.009	0.005	0.003	0.002
20	0.073	0.061	0.051	0.043	0.037	0.031	0.026	0.014	0.007	0.004	0.002	0.001
25	0.038	0.030	0.024	0.020	0.016	0.013	0.010	0.005	0.002	0.001	0.000	0.000
30	0.020	0.015	0.012	0.009	0.007	0.005	0.004	0.002	0.001	0.000	0.000	0.000

Table A.4 **Present Value Interest Factor for an Annuity** $PVIFA\ (r, n) = 1 - \frac{1/(1+r)^n}{r}$

Period n	1%	2%	3%	4%	5%	6%	7%	8%	9%	10%	11%	12%	13%
0	1.000	1.000	1.000	1.000	1.000	1.000	1.000	1.000	1.000	1.000	1.000	1.000	1.000
1	0.990	0.980	0.971	0.962	0.952	0.943	0.935	0.926	0.917	0.909	0.901	0.893	0.885
2	1.970	1.942	1.913	1.886	1.859	1.833	1.808	1.783	1.759	1.736	1.713	1.690	1.668
3	2.941	2.884	2.829	2.775	2.723	2.673	2.624	2.577	2.531	2.487	2.444	2.402	2.361
4	3.902	3.808	3.717	3.630	3.546	3.465	3.387	3.312	3.240	3.170	3.102	3.037	2.974
5	4.853	4.713	4.580	4.452	4.329	4.212	4.100	3.993	3.890	3.791	3.696	3.605	3.517
6	5.795	5.601	5.417	5.242	5.076	4.917	4.766	4.623	4.486	4.355	4.231	4.111	3.998
7	6.728	6.472	6.230	6.002	5.786	5.582	5.389	5.206	5.033	4.868	4.712	4.564	4.423
8	7.652	7.325	7.020	6.733	6.463	6.210	5.971	5.747	5.535	5.335	5.146	4.968	4.799
9	8.566	8.162	7.786	7.435	7.108	6.802	6.515	6.247	5.995	5.759	5.537	5.328	5.132
10	9.471	8.983	8.530	8.111	7.722	7.360	7.024	6.710	6.418	6.145	5.889	5.650	5.426
11	10.368	9.787	9.253	8.760	8.306	7.887	7.499	7.139	6.805	6.495	6.207	5.938	5.687
12	11.255	10.575	9.945	9.385	8.863	8.384	7.943	7.536	7.161	6.814	6.492	6.194	5.918
13	12.134	11.348	10.635	9.986	9.394	8.853	8.358	7.904	7.487	7.103	6.750	6.424	6.122
14	13.004	12.106	11.296	10.563	9.899	9.295	8.745	8.244	7.786	7.367	6.982	6.628	6.302
15	13.865	12.849	11.938	11.118	10.380	9.712	9.108	8.559	8.060	7.606	7.191	6.811	6.462
16	14.718	13.578	12.561	11.652	10.838	10.106	9.447	8.851	8.312	7.824	7.379	6.974	6.604
17	15.562	14.292	13.166	12.166	11.274	10.477	9.763	9.122	8.544	8.022	7.549	7.120	6.729
18	16.398	14.992	13.754	12.659	11.690	10.828	10.059	9.372	8.756	8.201	7.702	7.250	6.840
19	17.226	15.678	14.324	13.134	12.085	11.158	10.336	9.604	8.950	8.365	7.839	7.366	6.938
20	18.046	16.351	14.877	13.590	12.462	11.470	10.594	9.818	9.128	8.514	7.963	7.469	7.025
25	22.023	19.523	17.413	15.622	14.094	12.783	11.654	10.675	9.823	9.077	8.422	7.843	7.330
30	25.808	22.397	19.600	17.292	15.373	13.765	12.409	11.258	10.274	9.427	8.694	8.055	7.496

(Contd)

Appendix A

Table A.4 *(Contd)*

Period n	14%	15%	16%	17%	18%	19%	20%	24%	28%	32%	36%	40%
0	1.000	1.000	1.000	1.000	1.000	1.000	1.000	1.000	1.000	1.000	1.000	1.000
1	0.877	0.870	0.862	0.855	0.847	0.840	0.833	0.806	0.781	0.758	0.735	0.714
2	1.647	1.626	1.605	1.585	1.566	1.547	1.528	1.457	1.392	1.332	1.276	1.224
3	2.322	2.283	2.246	2.210	2.174	2.140	2.106	1.981	1.868	1.766	1.674	1.589
4	2.914	2.855	2.798	2.743	2.690	2.639	2.589	2.404	2.241	2.096	1.966	1.849
5	3.433	3.352	3.274	3.199	3.127	3.058	2.991	2.745	2.532	2.345	2.181	2.035
6	3.889	3.784	3.685	3.589	3.498	3.410	3.326	3.020	2.759	2.534	2.339	2.168
7	4.288	4.160	4.039	3.922	3.812	3.706	3.605	3.242	2.937	2.678	2.455	2.263
8	4.639	4.487	4.344	4.207	4.078	3.954	3.837	3.421	3.076	2.786	2.540	2.331
9	4.946	4.772	4.607	4.451	4.303	4.163	4.031	3.566	3.184	2.868	2.603	2.379
10	5.216	5.019	4.883	4.659	4.494	4.339	4.193	3.682	3.269	2.930	2.650	2.414
11	5.453	5.234	5.029	4.836	4.656	4.486	4.327	3.776	3.335	2.978	2.683	2.438
12	5.660	5.421	5.197	4.988	4.793	4.611	4.439	3.851	3.387	3.013	2.708	2.456
13	5.842	5.583	5.342	5.118	4.910	4.715	4.533	3.912	3.427	3.040	2.727	2.469
14	6.002	5.724	5.468	5.229	5.008	4.802	4.611	3.962	3.459	3.061	2.740	2.478
15	6.142	5.847	5.575	5.324	5.092	4.876	4.675	4.001	3.483	3.076	2.750	2.484
16	6.265	5.954	5.669	5.405	5.162	4.938	4.730	4.033	3.503	3.088	2.758	2.489
17	6.373	6.047	5.749	5.475	5.222	4.990	4.775	4.059	3.518	3.097	2.763	2.492
18	6.647	6.128	5.818	5.534	5.273	5.033	4.812	4.080	3.529	3.104	2.767	2.494
19	6.550	6.198	5.877	5.584	5.316	5.970	4.844	4.097	3.539	3.109	2.770	2.496
20	6.623	6.259	5.929	5.628	5.353	5.101	4.870	4.110	3.546	3.113	2.772	2.497
25	6.873	6.464	6.097	5.766	5.467	5.195	4.948	4.147	3.564	3.122	2.776	2.499
30	7.003	6.566	6.177	5.829	5.517	5.235	4.979	4.160	3.569	3.124	2.778	2.500

Annexures

Annexure – 1

(Please refer Chapter – 5 Page–217)

Analyse the financial statements of Tata Steels and give your view on the company's financial position and working results for 2007.

Financial Statements of Tata Steel for 2007

Profit & Loss Account (summary) for the year ended 31st March 2007

Incomes	**March, 06** (Rs. Crore)	**March, 07** (Rs. Crore)
Sales	17136.08	19772.13
Other non operating		
income	261.95	484.29
Service charges	104.91	82.47
Discount received	163.96	189.82
Expenses		
Raw materials		
consumed	3762.03	4645.06
Wages	1351.51	1454.83
Energy (Power & Fuel)	897.57	1027.84
Salaries	2060.48	2360.84
Advertising & marketing expenses	80.75	64.71
Distribution expenses	1004.32	1117.45
Others	2253.17	2418.39
Non-operating expenses	41.14	14.67
Financial charges interest	175.70	251.87
Depreciation on factory assets	733.96	804.72
PBT	5306.27	6368.33
Tax provision	1799.89	2146.18
PAT	3506.38	4222.15

Balance Sheet as on 31st March, 2007

Liabilities	March, 06	March, 07
Authorised captial	600.00	1750.00
Issued equity capital	554.07	581.07
Paid-up equity capital	553.67	580.67
Bonus equity capital	257.93	257.93
Reserves & surplus		
Free reserves		
Share premium reserves	835.26	2201.46
Other free reserves	7567.62	10378.8
Specific reserves	798.75	788.16
Borrowings Long Term		
Govt. / sales tax deferral Borrowings	1609.27	1650.26
Debentures / bonds	462.5	175
Fixed deposits	33.41	20.98
Foreign borrowings	278.07	7347.62
Borrowings from corporate bodies	12.36	8.69
Long term bank borrowings	63.47	0
Secured borrowings—long term	2191.74	3758.92
Unsecured borrowing-long term	324.41	5886.41
Current liabilities		
Short term bank borrowings	56.49	442.26
Sundry creditors	2534.03	3145.99
Interest accrued/due	24.29	47.11
Other current liabilities	277.68	624.23
Provisions		
Tax provision	250.04	448.68
Dividend provision	719.51	943.91
Other provision	1463.97	1719.48
Total liabilities	**22,505.07**	**42,527.11**

Annexure –2

(Please refer Chapter – 6 Page–289)

Prepare cash flow and fund flow statements with a statement of change in working capital of Asian Paints for the year after taking into account adjustments given at the end.

Asian Paints
Abridged Balance Sheet as on 31st March 2008

Rs. in Crores

	As on 31.03.2008	As on 31.03.2007
Funds Employed		
Shareholders Funds		
Share Capital-face value Rs. 10	195.92	95.92
Reserves and Surplus	732.58	648.16
Loan Funds		
Secured Loans—Long Term	36.70	66.90
Unsecured Loans –Long Term	58.00	58.77
Deferred Tax Liability (Net) –LT	31.52	22.15
Current liabilities	785.11	594.10
Provisions for taxation	166.49	54.15
Total	**2006.32**	**1540.15**
Application of Funds		
Fixed Assets		
Gross Block	937.89	806.20
Less: Depreciation	509.06	471.29
Net Block	428.83	334.91
Capital Work in Progress	110.39	11.62
Investments	422.88	346.53
Current Assets, Loans and Advances		

Interest accrued on investments	0.09	0.03
Inventories	538.97	434.07
Sundry debtors	251.90	235.96
Cash and Bank Balances	41.35	42.49
Other Current Assets	33.09	31.23
Loans and Advances	178.82	103.31
Total	**2006.32**	**1540.15**

Adjustments

1. The company issued bonus shares of Rs. 100 crores during the year.
2. During the year the company paid Rs. 56.28 crores as taxes.
3. Company declared and paid dividend of Rs. 47.92 crores during the year.
4. Fixed assets with book value Rs. 5.78 crores and original cost of Rs. 6.35 crores were sold for Rs. 7.12 crores during the year.

Annexure – 3

(Please refer Chapter – 7 Page–320)

1. Classify the following costs according to their nature, category, elements, functions and behaviour.

	Nature X/CX/L/I	Category P/R/N	Elements M/L/X	Functional M/A/S/NO	Traceability D/I	Behaviour V/F
1. Limestonees for a cement factory						
2. Tyres for vehicles in a transport company						
3. Paper in a printing company						
4. Grease for machines in a manufacturing company						
5. Interest paid on loans						
6. Discount received						
7. Advertising						
8. Carry forward losses						
9. Inventories						
10. Receivables						
11. Share capital						
12. Bad debts						
13. Subsidy received						
14. Batteries for cars in car manufacturing company						

15. Insurance premium on comapny car						
16. Dividend paid to shareholders						
17. Cloth in garment making						
18. Thread in garment making						
19. Lubricating oil for the sewing machine						
20. Depreciation on a chemical processing plant and machinery						
21. Power to run the machinery						
22. Electricity for lighting the shop floor						
23. Freight-in						
24. Customs duty for raw materials						
25. Royalty to author in book publishing						
26. Royalty (one shot payment) for using a foreign brand name						
27. Helpers' wages in a furniture firm						
28. Nails used in a furniture for a firm						
29. Advertising expenses						
30. Discount allowed						
31. Cash discount received (for prompt payment)						

32. Expense for government liaison						
33. Bribes paid						
34. Donations made						
35. Overtime-(factory workers)						
36. Idle time-(accounts clerks)						
37. Waste of raw material in manufacturing						
38. In Bottled perfume: the perfume						
39. In Bottled perfume: the bottle						
40. In bottled perfume: the fancy carton for each bottle						
41. Cardboard boxes to pack and deliver large orders of perfumes and other toiletries to the retail shops						
42. Civil engineer's salary in construction firm						
43. Wheat flour for bread						
44. Tailoring charges in garment making						
45. Factory rent						
46. General manager's salary						
47. Salesmen's commission						
48. Interest paid on deposits (Finance charges)						

49. Loss due to theft						
50. Cost of installing machinery						
51. Pulp in paper making						
52. Daily wages paid in road						
53. Salesmen's salary						
54. Salesmen's samples						
55. Depreciation of machinery (common for all products)						
56. Monthly rental for leased computer						
57. Fire loss						
58. Commission paid to sales agency						
59. Commission paid to raw material buying agency						
60. Rent for head office building						
61. Depreciation of delivery truck						
62. Auditor's fee						
63. Goo will						
64. Drawings by owners						

Abbreviations:

X = Expenses

CX = Expenditure

L = Liability

I = Income

P = Personal account

R = Real account

N = Nominal account

M/L/X = Materials/labour/expenses

M/A/S/NO = Manufacturing/administration/selling/non operating

D/I = Direct/indirect

V/F = Variable/fixed

2. Case of Simon Traders

Simon Traders have incurred the following costs for the production of 26,525 units of Isographs and 18,750 units of Jisographs in October, using 1225 machine hours and 3100 labour hours:

Costs	Rs.
Direct materials	?
Direct labour	34,09,350
Factory lighting	20,428
Power and fuel	4,67,891
Salaries	3,12,876
Depreciation on machine	61,845
Primary packaging materials	14,792
Administrative expenses	82,639
Selling expenses	96,238
Advertising	1,27,800
Insurance	**5,294**

Direct material costs per unit of Isograph and Isographs are Rs. 328 and Rs. 419 respectively. The production of Isograph and Jisograph requires 4 and 3 units of labour hours per unit of production.

Appropriate fixed costs on the principle of factory overhead as % of direct labour cost, administrative overheads on the basis of works cost, selling expenses on the basis of cost of production, to the two products and **work out cost of production per unit.**

3.Agri Ventures Holding Company

"It's time we reviewed the organization of our group of companies," said Mr. Mendoza, President of the Agri Ventures Trading Company (AV Trading), a wholly-owned subsidiary of the Agri Ventures Holding Company (AV Holding) at a Board meeting of AV Holding. "The prawn export business has become very competitive. Prices in Japan have dropped significantly while farm prices of prawns have been increasing. There are not 16 prawn buyers in our area compared to only four less than a year ago. Many of these buyers have their own processing facilities, some even have their own prawn farms. Because of this, they are able to pay as much as 15% more than we can for prawns and still make money. Unless we combine our trading processing and possibly our prawn growing and feed mill operations, we cannot be competitive. Prawn trading by itself is losing proposition right now," Mr. Mendoza explained.

A.V. Trading was one of the subsidiary companies owned by AV Holding, an agribusiness firm based in the Visayas, Philippiness. The other companies were.

Company	**Production**
A V Processing	Preparation, freezing and storage of prawns and dressed chicken; sale of block ice.
A V Aquaculture	Prawn production
A V Aquafeed	Production and sale of prawn feed
A V Food	Production and sale of day-old chicks, dressed chicken and poultry feed.

Except for AV Aquafeed, the subsidiaries were wholly owned by AV Holding. Ten percent of AV Aquafeed's capital stock was owned by the firm's technical consultant from Taiwan.

Each subsidiary company had its own Board of Directors and operating officers. Although the Board of each subsidiary included some members of the Board of AV Holding, the subsidiary companies were separate entities and were operated as independent companies. The companies were free to buy and sell to one another and to outside parties, even though it was expected that much of the business of each subsidiary would come from the other subsidiaries. Each subsidiary was evaluated on the basis of its profit and return on investment.

The Board of AV Holding decided on the present holding company structure and a policy of decentralization for several reasons. Firstly, it felt that the decentralized structure and policy best supported the company's diversification strategy. Each subsidiary could effectively concentrate on developing its own products and markets. Secondly, the present structure facilitated the development of younger managers in the company. Also, since each subsidiary was a separate entity, potential risk of losses to the entire company would be minimized.

A V Trading

In addition to exporting prawn to Japan, AV Trading was engaged in the marketing and distribution of construction materials as well as various agricultural products. It also supplied the other companies in the group with raw materials and supplies. Prawn exports accounted for 80% of AV Trading's total sales.

AV Trading had spent six months learning the critical aspects of the prawn export business and making the company's presence felt in the Japanese market. The orders received by AV Trading from several of Japan's major prawn buyers were evidence of its success in establishing the company's reputation as a supplier of high quality products and in creating a strong demand for the company's brands. Mr. Mendoza stressed that the demand for prawns was not a problem. He said that AV Trading could easily close contracts totaling 180 to 200 tons per month at present prices. The problem was that the prices in Japan did not cover the buying price of prawns and the costs of harvesting, processing, packing, and shipping.

The latest order of Saki Co. Ltd. was an example. Saki Co. Ltd., AV Trading's biggest buyer, wanted to confirm its order for 15,000 kilograms of AV prawns at an average price of 250 Pesos per kilogram, CIF Japan, AV Trading's estimate of the costs of the order was as follows:

	Cost per Kilogram (Pesos)
Raw Material (ex-firm)	205.00
Harvesting & Processing	20.50
Packing & Packaging materials	8.00
Freight, Insurance,	
Bank Charges & Other Costs	15.00
Total Out-of-Pocket Costs	248.50
Add: 5% Overhead Charge	12.50
Total Costs	261.00

The estimated costs were all based on current market prices and on the net weight of the final product as ordered by Saki Co. Ltd. (All prices and cost figures mentioned in the case are based on the net weight of the final product, already adjusted for prawn recovery and feed conversion factors).

Since AV Trading expected to lose Peso 11 per kilogram on the Saki order, Mr. Mendoza was inclined to reject it. Mr. Mendoza said that he wanted very much to make the shipment, if this could be done profitably, since he did not want AV Trading to become known as an unreliable supplier. The Saki order represented less than five percent of AV Trading's annual sales.

Mr. Garcia, the President of AV Holding, wondered whether he should insist that Mr. Locsin, President of AV Processing, and Mr. Gallardo, President of AV Aquaculture, lower their prices to AV Trading for the Saki order. AV Processing and AV Aquaculture had quoted market prices for their products/services and expected to make a profit on the Saki business. Messrs. Locsin and Gallardo had already indicated to Mr. Mendoza that they were not inclined to lower their prices to AV Trading. AV Trading could, of course, go to other prawn producers as well as other suppliers of harvesting and processing services. Mr. Garcia requested his technical staff to do a study of the cost situation in each of the subsidiaries involved before deciding what he should do.

AV Processing

AV processing's facilities included a large, sanitized preparation area, blast freezer, contact freezer, cold storage rooms and an ice plant. Although AV Processing's facilities were operating much below capacity during the past several months, it charged the going market rates for harvesting and processing services. These were the same rates it charged other prawn traders and producers in the area. For the Saki order, the harvesting and processing fees would amount to Pesos 20.50 per kilogram.

The out-of-pocket costs involved in harvesting would amount to Pesos 2.00 per kilogram (including fuel, labor, ice and supplies). The processing operations (i.e., preparation, packing, freezing, storage, and loading) were expected to cost Pesos 5.00 per kilogram on an out-of-pocket basis, mostly for overtime, additional labor and supplies.

A large part of AV processing's operating costs consisted of plant and administrative overhead expenses which were non-variable in nature. The major overhead expenses were electricity labor, interest equipment depreciation and supervision. At the present volume level, fixed overhead costs would amount to about Pesos 10 per kilogram of processed product.

The quality of AV Processing's services met the specifications of Japanese buyers. Its facilities were also located closer to AV Aquaculture's prawn ponds and AV Trading's present prawn buying area than other processing facilities.

AV Aquaculture operated 30 hectares of prawn ponds. The total production capacity was about 270 tons per year at an average yield of 4.5 tons per hectare, two crops per year. The present capacity utilization was already over 90 percent.

Industry capacity, in terms of number and area of prawn ventures throughout the contry, was expanding rapidly to meet the demand for prawns, mainly from Japan. An additional 40 hectares of prawn ponds were being developed by AV Aquaculture. Mr. Gallardo, president of AV Aquaculture, felt that selling the production from the additional 40 hectares would not be a problem at present supply and demand levels.

AV Aquaculture quoted the current market price of Pesos 205 per kilogram (ex-farm) for the Saki order. Direct, out-of-pocket costs would amount to Pesos 85 per kilogram as follows.

	Cost per kilogram (Pesos)
Fry	13.00
Feed	66.00
Chemicals	4.00
Electricity	2.00
Total out-of-pocket Costs	85.00

A production and administrative overhead charge of 20% was added to direct costs. Total cost for the order was therefore estimated to be Pesos 102 per kilogram.

AV Aquafeed

My Capay, President of AV Aquafeed, said that they could supply the prawn feed at P66 per kilogram, net weight of the final product on the Saki order. Related out-of-pocket costs were estimated at P52 per kilogram, mostly for raw materials, while fixed overhead costs were Pesos 18 per kilogram.

AV Aquafeed operated at less than 30% of production capacity. The mill had enough production capacity (three shifts) to meet the needs of about 1000 hectares of prawn farm.

In order to gain market share, AV Aquafeed self its prawn feed at about 5% below the price of comparable brands in the market. Since its feed was regarded as similar in quality to the better brands, sales were expected to pick up quickly over the next several months.

Mr. Garcia contemplated on the cost information and operating situation provided by his technical staff as they formulated his course of action. He planned to call a meeting of the presidents of all the subsidiary companies involved to discuss and resolve the matters raised by Mr. Mendoza in the first paragraph of this case. Had you been the consultant of this company, what would have been your advise?

Annexure – 4

(Please refer Chapter – 8 Page–335)

Case of Roofit Ltd.

The Company is engaged in manufacturing Roof leak proof with capacity of 30,000 tonnes per month. Its capacity utilization for November was only 63%. Demand is not expected to increase in future. Its cost structure for the month was

Material cost	Rs. 95,62,000
Direct labour	Rs. 27,12,540
Factory OH	Rs. 2,46,000 (30% variable)
Admin. OH	Rs. 3,72,750 (20% variable)
Selling OH	Rs. 4,76,980 (10% variable)
Sales price per tonne	Rs. 7,100

Foundation Ltd. has enquired of the company to supply 10,000 tonnes of Roof leak proof per month for exports at a price of Rs. 6,100 per tonne. The finance manager was against the order, as it fetches Rs. 1,000 less than the current sales price and would depress profit. What would be your views about accepting the Foundation's offer?

Annexure –5

(Please refer Chapter – 10 Page–392)

1. The Aasai Meal

The incident referred to in this case occurred when a controversy regarding the origin of kababs was raging in the US. An Indian firm in Lockheed -ITL (India Taste Ltd) was planning to introduce a new product. ITL was a well-thought of company with a standing of 45 years. This company was started by Mr. Prakash Kiran as an ordinary eatery, specializing in kababs and biryanis made from the recipes used in the kitchens of the royal families of Aasai. Mr. Prakash's son, Shankar modernized the business, gave it the name of ITL and introduced the facilities of ready-to-eat packed kababs. These products could be stored in ordinary (un-refrigerated) kitchen pantries for up to 9 days, heated in an oven and eaten. Some kabobs packets were also exported. A preparation called Tangri Kababs, made from chicken legs, was very popular. A packet containing two kababs and special sauce weighing 350 grams was priced at $1.5. This was ideal for couples where both the husband and the wife were employed. The technique suggested by ITL was to put the Tangri Kabob packet in the oven and while the kababs were getting heated, rotis (wheat bread) could be cooked. ITL claimed that a dinner using Tangri Kababs could be ready in 20 minutes. The system could also operate excellently if unexpected guests dropped in or if parties were planned.

However, Shankar's wife Taza had been insisting that the process of making *rotis* was cumbersome, requiring kneading of the flour to make the dough, preparing and cooking the *rotis*, etc. This was not to the liking of present generation youngsters. The last act of washing up the utensils and the crockery/cutlery was again detestable. She finally persuaded Shankar on her birthday, 24 October, to introduce pre-cooked and packed nans–a special type of wheat bread sprinkled with herbs. A microwave oven-friendly meal consisting of a packet of Tangri *Kababs* and a packet containing four *nans* and herbs in *masala* (condiments) was suggested. But these packets were to be bundled in such a way that the meal could be eaten from the packet and the containers disposed of. No mess, no washing up. This package was called an the *Aasai* Meal. The marketing department at ITL was itching to launch this product. It was universally agreed that the introduction of the Aasai meal would boost the total sales of ITL because *nans* plus herbal masala would be a much-needed supplement to *Tangri Kababs*. The additional attraction of being able to eat from the disposable packet would do wonders for families where cooking was a bother.

Unfortunately, the project sprang a leak. The cost accountants priced the *Aasai* Meal at $3 (weight 500g). Taza joined the marketing team in their protest. The cost accountants briefly explained that:

1. The price of 350 grams of microwave-friendly Tangri Kabab packet had been retained at $1.5.
2. The price of *nans* plus herbal masala capable of being heated in a microwave oven had been calculated to be $1.
3. The price of *Aasai* Meal packaging with ready-to-eat disposable containers worked out to US 50 cents, making a total of $3.

The marketing department was aghast at the *nans* plus herbal *masala* packet being priced at $1.50. They felt that the market would accept a price, between US50 to 75 cents for the *nans* and the herbal masala. Even this would be possible because the consumers had come to accept ITL products as good, healthy and tasty. Shankar called for the detailed costing. This was as shown in the table.

	Tangri Kabab	Nans plus Herbal Masals	Aasai Meal Packaging
All prices in rupees all rounded off to second decimal place.			
1. Direct materials	0.45	0.14	0.02
2. Direct labour	0.09	0.12	0.01
3. Sundry variable costs	0.03	0.03	0.01
4. Fixed production costs	0.34	0.34	0.03
5. General marketing and administrative fixed overheads	0.10	0.10	0.05
6. Total cost of manufacturing	1.01	0.73	0.12
7. Company profits @ 20% of manufacturing cost	0.21	0.15	0.01
8. Company cost and profits	1.22	0.88	0.13
9. Retailers and wholesalers margins totaling to 30% of retailers price	0.37	0.27	0.04
10. Retailers price	1.59	1.15	0.17

Total cost	$2.91
Contingency @4%	$0.09
Price	$3.00

The marketing chief argued that it was incorrect to load both *Tangri Kababs* and *nans* plus herbal *masala* packets with the same production, marketing and administrative costs. Secondly, how could *nans* plus herbal masala attract higher sundry costs compared to the *Tangri Kababs*? The cost accountant explained that total sundry expenses were divided by the number of items produced and allocated. The total production cost and the marketing and administrative expenses were distributed over the total turnover by weight. Both *Tangri Kababs* and the *nans* plus herbal masala, weighed 250 grams each and, therefore, were allocated the same amount of costs.

The marketing staff suggested an alternate costing system based on the technique of distributing the sundry variable costs and the production, marketing and administrative costs as per direct cost of the production to the company. Revised costs of *nans* plus herbal masala using this system worked out to be as follows:

Direct material and labour	0.05
Sundry variable costs	0.01
Production, marketing and administrative cost	0.12
Cost of manufacturing	0.18
Company profit	0.03
Cost plus profit	0.21
Retailers and wholesalers margins	0.07
Retailers price	0.28 or 30 cents

It was accepted that this method of overheads allocations will raise the prices of the *Tangri Kabab* packet to some extent. The cost accountants team agreed to recalculate as per the new technique, provided the management accepted this method of allocation. Shankar understood that he had a diffcult decision to make. He looked at his secretary, Yasmin, who had been taking down notes of these discussions. Efficient Yasmin understood the boss's requirement and placed the following data before him:

1. Annual sales of *Tangri Kababs* for the last three years: 30.5 tonnes, 31.7 tonnes and 29.94 tonnes, respectively.
2. Forecast of sales of *Tangri Kababs* in microwave-friendly packaging without the introduction of *Aasai* Meal: 32.5 tonnes.
3. Forecast of sale of *Aasai* Meal if priced at $3 each: 7.8 tonnes plus 30.01 tonnes of *Tangri Kababs.* The quantity of sales of *Aasai* Meal could fall after the initial reaction associated with the novelty of a new item wore off.
4. Forecast of *Aasai* Meal, if priced up to $2, is 50 tonnes.

Shankar was more confused that before. He lit his cigar and signalled Yasmin to serve some green tea with lemon. After tea was served, Yasmin suggested that Shankar may like to consider the various alternatives peacefully before arriving at a decision. Shankar did something better. He directed Yasmin to get the management consultant on the line. That consultant happens to be you. The problem is, therefore, totally yours.

What will you recommend to Shankar and why?

2. Raj singh's Decision

On receiving his M.B.A. degree in April 2010 from one of the local colleges in Bihar, Raj Singh went to work for the Electrical Components Corporation (ECC), Ludhiana, a medium-sized manufacturer of electrical controls and electronic devices. Although his bachelor degree was in mechanical engineering, summer jobs and a brief stint as an engineer in a government department before entering the M.B.A. programme had convinced Raj that he was not interested in an engineering career. Accordingly, after completing his M.B.A., he sought a finance or marketing job, though he landed up with a production job.

What, however, attracted Raj to the job offer from ECC was the fact that it presented an opportunity to assure line responsibilities after a brief training period. The position in question was that of supervisor of the parts fabrication shop at the company's manufacturing plant.

In the summer of 2010, Raj Singh assumed his new duties. At that time, the staff of the parts fabrication shop consisted of 78 machine operators and six clerks in addition to the supervisor. The shop was producing five parts which were used by other production departments in the same plant in the assembly of final products. A statement of costs incurred by the parts fabrication shop during the first quarter of 1985 is attached as Exhibit 1.

When he took over the parts fabrication shop, Raj was told by the plant manager, Mr. Sarin, that it was his responsibility to see that the five parts being produced by the shop were produced or acquired at the lowest possible cost to the company. For this reason, he had the authority to buy all or any of these parts from outside sources if he found this to be more advantageous to the company.

In order to carry out his responsibility for such make-or-buy decisions, Raj felt he needed more cost information than was supplied by the quarterly cost statement (such as Exhibit 1). He discussed his needs with the plant accountant, Mr. Chopra and together they agreed on a product line cost analysis report, which would show the actual cost of producing one unit each of the five parts during the period in question. The first such report, corresponding to the cost statement or Exhibit 1, is attached as Exhibit 2. The figures in Exhibit 2 were obtained as follows:

1. Direct Labour/Unit. Each machine operator kept a time sheet indicating the time he spent on each batch of a single part. These times were costed at the direct labour rate of Rs. 3.50/hour. The total labour cost so booked for each part was then divided by the number of units of that part.

2. Direct Materials/unit. When materials were drawn from the storeroom, an issue slip was prepared indicating the amount drawn and the part on which the materials were to be used. The amounts were totaled for each part and the totals divided by the volume of production.
3. Overhead/unit. The total of all overhead costs charged to the department was divided by the number of direct labour hours to produce a cost per hour. This figure was multiplied by the number of direct labour hours charged to each part and the product was then divided by the production quality.

After receiving the information in Exhibit 2 from Mr. Chopra, Raj Singh solicited bids on each of the five parts from several small engineering workshops in the neighbourhood. The lowest bid received on each part is given in the table alongside.

It looked more advantageous to the company to continue making each part in its own shop, and Raj Singh recommended accordingly.

In the second quarter of 1985, demand for ECC's products fell sharply because of a temporary business recession. This decline was naturally reflected in the work load in the parts fabrication shop. Because of the reduced work load, Raj Singh had laid off a few machine operators and had transferred three of them to performing maintenance of equipment which had been deferred during the period of higher production.

Part No.	Lowest Bid Rs.
101	65.00
102	90.00
103	37.50
104	60.00
105	34.50

When Raj received his product cost report for the second quarter of 1985, shown in Exhibit 3, he discovered that costs were up on all five parts, and that part 103, in particular, now cost more to make than the bid of Rs. 37.50 per unit he had received earlier. Raj called up the owner of the shop who had made that bid and asked him so he was willing to cut his earlier price. The supplier agreed to reduce the price to Rs. 37, as it would help to keep his shop busy. Raj promptly accepted the reduced offer and asked the purchasing manager of his plant to issue a purchase order to out source for 2,000 units (about a quarter's supply at the current usage rate). Raj estimated that his decision would save ECC about Rs. 7,200 just in one quarter. Assuming that the volume will not fall further, he thought he saved the company nearly Rs. 29.00 per annum.

The cost reports for the third quarter of 1985 (see exhibit 4) showed a further rise. Once again Raj checked with the sources of earlier bids, this time on parts 102 and 105, and learned that in both cases the bidders were sticking by their earlier quotes.

Questions:

1. How much the company gained or lost by Raj Singh's decision to buy Part 103 from outside?
2. What should the company do with regard to parts 102 and 105 now?
3. What was happening to the overhead costs; in total as well as per unit, over the year?
4. Subsequently, if the demand rises and if the total man hours available in Raj Singh's department is the constraint in raising internal production, in what order, he should consider buying out the various parts?
5. Are there other considerations which may influence your decision either way; make-or-buy?

Exhibit 1

Cost Statement for the first Quarter of 1985

Prime Costs:	
Labour	Rs. 1,39,756
Materials	3,11,680
Total Prime Cost	Rs. 4,51,436
Departmental Overhead:	
Departmental supervision and services	Rs. 1,00,216
Depreciation	1,20,000
Total Departmental overhead	Rs. 2,20,216
General Overhead	Rs. 1,50,000
Total Costs	**Rs. 8,21,652**

Exhibit 2

Product cost Report for the First Quarter of 1985

	Cost per Unit or Part No.				
	101	102	103	104	105
Cost element (in Rs.)					
Labour (in Rs.)	8.48	13.30	5.25	7.33	4.31
Material (in Rs.)	18.40	24.00	14.80	17.20	13.60
Total Prime Cost (in Rs.)	26.88	37.30	20.05	24.53	17.91

Overhead (in Rs.)	22.42	35.15	13.88	19.38	11.39
Total cost (in Rs.)	49.30	72.45	33.93	43.91	29.30
Production (units)	3300	4000	3200	4200	2600

Exhibit 3

Product cost Report for the Second Quarter of 1985

	Cost per Unit or Part No.				
	101	102	103	104	105
Cost element: (in Rs.)					
Labour	9.02	14.00	5.60	7.82	4.40
Material	18.43	24.01	14.78	17.20	13.52
Total Prime Cost	27.45	38.01	20.38	25.02	17.92
Overhead	30.92	48.00	19.20	26.80	14.86
Total cost	58.37	86.01	39.58	51.82	32.78
Production (Units)	2600	3200	2000	3000	2100

Exhibit 4

Product cost Report for the Third Quarter of 1985

	Cost per Unit or Part No.				
	101	102	103	104	105
Cost element (in Rs.)					
Labour	8.68	13.33		7.50	4.50
Material	18.43	24.00		17.20	13.55
Total Prime Cost	27.11	37.33		24.70	18.55
Overhead	37.60	58.00		32.14	18.00
Total cost	64.71	95.33		56.84	36.05
Production (Units)	2500	3000		2800	2000

Annexure – 6

(Please refer Chapter – 11 Page – 422)

1. Clinton Glassware breaks even at 70% of its capacity. Its variable cost forms 80% of its sales. Its fixed cost is Rs. 4,90,000. Work out:

(*a*) the breakeven volume

(*b*) variable cost

(*c*) PVR

(*d*) The sales required to have profit of Rs. 1,00,000.

2. The Big MIG House Builders

Mr. Ram Charan, an Executive Engineer with the Public Works Department of one of the Indian states resigned his job to set up a private construction firm. He intended specializing in a bidding for constructing standard houses for the "The Big House Builders". In preparation, he made the following estimates:

Estimated revenue per house	Rs. 100,000
Estimated variable costs per house	Rs. 900,000
Estimated overheads per month	Rs. 800,000

Note: 30% of overheads are variable

Required:

1. What is the *minimum* number of houses to be constructed per month to break-even?

2. If the chances of success in bidding is 50-50 what is the *minimum* number of houses for which he should bid in a year in order to *break-even*?

3. "Lala's Friendly Store" made a loss of Rs. 2,000 for the second quarter of the year.

Sales	Rs. 88,000
Costs	Rs. 90,000
Loss	Rs. 2,000

The only variable cost incurred by the store was the purchase price. Lala's mark-up on all products was 10% over the purchase price.

Required:

2.1 How much he should sell in the third quarter to *break-even*?

2.2 How much he should sell in the fourth quarter to earn a profit of Rs. 6,000 for the quarter (assuming no change in fixed costs)?

2.3 Under the current set up, if the total sales is not likely to exceed Rs. 1,10,000 in the fourth quarter, how much reduction in fixed costs is required to earn the desired profit of Rs.6,000 per quarter.

2.4 If fixed costs cannot be reduced below Rs. 9,000 per quarter, what should be his *mark-up percentage in* order to earn Rs. 6,000 per quarter? (Assume the same volume as in 2.3).

2.5 If every 5% *additional* mark-up (over and above the current 10%) is likely to result in 20% loss in volume of sales, what will be the effect (amount of profit or loss) on implementing your answer to question 2.4.

Annexure – 7

(Please refer Chapter – 13 Page–501)

1. Barney Toys Ltd. earns an average net profit of Rs. 30 per piece in a selling price of Rs. 150 by producing and selling 60,000 pieces at 60% of the potential capacity. Composition of his cost of sales is:

Direct materials	Rs. 40
Direct wages	Rs. 10
Works overhead	Rs. 60 [50% fixed]
Sales overhead	Rs. 10 [25% varying]

During the current year, the company obtains an order for a further 20% of its capacity. What minimum price will you recommend for accepting the order to ensure the manufacturer an overall profit of Rs. 18,05,000?

2. Samson enterprises has forecast a sale of $.73m, $87m, $94m, $83m and $92, $98m for the six months from July to December. Historically, 25% of the company's sales are in cash and 75% on credit. This trend is expected to continue. Past experience shows that 50% of debtors pay in the next month, 40% in the second month and 5% third, Balance becomes bad. Materials form 40% of sales, wages 10%, other expenses form 15%.

Credit for materials supplied to the company was for one month. Wages and operating expenses paid next month. The company expects to issue bonds for $ 10 in September to redeem high cost bonds of $ 12.5 m. Dividend of $ 9 m is payable in December, interest $ 6.5 m in October and tax $3m in July.

Average cash balance to be maintained is $ 1.5m. Repayment of temporary borrow. 80m to be made in August. Surplus cash to be invested in marketable securities yield 6% return per annum. Borrowing under cash credit is available from First National ..... 9% p.a. to meet any shortfall in working capital. Actual sales for April to June were $.65 m and $ 70 m respectively. Opening cash balance was $ 1.9 m. Prepare monthly cash budget for Samson Enterprises for 6 months from July.

Annexure – 8

(Please refer Chapter – 14 Page – 536)

1. The directors of Milo Ltd., are currently considering two mutually exclusive investment projects, in addition to their existing projects. Both projects are concerned with the purchase of new plant. Following data is available for each project.

Project	1	2
Cost (Immediate Outlay)	1,00,000	1,00,000
Expected Annual Net Profit/ (Loss)		
Year 1	29,000	18,000
2	(10,000)	(20,000)
	3,20,000	40,000
Estimated Residual Value	70,000	60,000

The company has an estimated cost of capital of 10% and employs the straight-line method of depreciation for all fixed assets when calculating net profit. Neither project would increase the working capital of the company. The company has sufficient funds to meet all capital expenditure requirements. The company is in 40% tax rate.

State which investment project should the company accept and why.

2. The accountant of your organisation has been abstaining for several days. In his absence, his assistant has prepared some calculations of the profitability of a project that would be discussed soon at the Board Meeting of your company. His working is reproduced below and it includes some error of principle. You can assume that there is no arithmetical error involved.

Figures in Rs. 000	20×0	20×1	20×2	20×3	20×4	20×5
Sales revenue		450	470	470	470	470
Less: Costs						
Material		126	132	132	132	132
Labour		90	94	94	94	94
Overheads		45	47	47	47	47
Depreciation		120	120	120	120	120

Working Capital	180					
Int. on W Capital		27	27	27	27	27
Devp. Costs w. off		30	30	30		
Total Costs	180	438	450	450	450	450
Profit/Loss	(180)	12	20	20	50	50
Total Profit/Loss) in Rs.	(28000					
Cost of Equipment in Rs.	6,00,000					
Return on Investment	–4.7%					

You ascertain the following additional information:

- Cost of equipment contains Rs. 1,00,000 being book value of an old machine. If it were not used for this project, it would have been scrapped with zero net realisable value. New equipment costing Rs. 5,00,000 will be purchased on the last date of financial year. All other cash flows would occur at the end of the year to which it relates.
- Development costs of Rs. 90,000 have already been spent.
- Overheads have been taken at 50% of direct labour that has been the company's normal practice. An independent assessment suggests that incremental overheads are likely to be Rs. 30,000 p.a.
- Company's cost of capital is 12%.

Ignoring taxation for computation purpose:

1. Prepare a corrected statement of the incremental cash flows from the project.
2. Calculate NPV and IRR of the project.

3. Rainbow Products is considering the purchase of a paint-mixing machine to reduce labor costs. The savings are expected to result in additional cash flows to Rainbow of $5,000 per year. The machine costs $35,000 and is expected to test for 15 years. Rainbow has determined that the cost of capital for such an investment is 12%.

[A] Compute the *payback*, net present value (NPV), and internal rate of return (IRR) for this machine. Should Rainbow purchase it? Assume that all cash flows (except the initial purchase) occur at the end of the year, and do not consider taxes.

[B] For a $500 per year additional expenditure, rainbow can get a "Good As New" service contract that essentially keeps the machine in new condition forever. Net of the cost of the service contract, the machine would then produce cash flows of $4,500 per year in perpetuity. Should rainbow products purchase the machine with the service contract?

[C] Instead of the service contract, Rainbow engineers have devised a different option to preserve and actually enhance the capability of the machine over time. By reinvesting 20% of the annual costs savings back into new machine parts, the engineers can increase the cost saving at a 4% annual rate. For example, at the end of year one, 20% of the $5,000 cost savings ($1,000) is reinvested in the machine; the net cash flow is thus $4,000. Next year, the cash flow from cost savings grows by 4% to $5,200 gross, or $4,160 net, of the 20% reinvestment. As long as the 20% reinvestment continues, the cash flows continue to grow at 4% in perpetuity.

What should Rainbow products do?

4. Suppose you own a concession stand that sells hot dogs, peanuts, popcorn, and beer at a ball park. You have three years left on the contract with the ball park, and you do not expect it to be renewed.

Long lines limits sales and profits. You have developed four different proposals to reduce the lines and increase profits.

The first proposal is to renovate by adding another window. The second is to update the equipment at the existing windows. These two renovation projects are not mutually exclusive; you could take both projects. The third and fourth proposals involve abandoning the existing stand. The third proposal is to build a new stand. The fourth proposal is to rent a larger stand in the ball park. This option would involve $1,000 in up-front investment for new signs and equipment installation; the incremental cash flows shown in later years are net of lease payments.

You have decided that a 15% discount rate is appropriate for this type of investment. the incremental cash flows associated with each of the proposals are:

Incremental Cash Flows				
Project	Investment	Year 1	Year 2	Year 3
Add a new Window				
44,000 44,000				
Update Existing Equipment		–50,000		23,000
23,000 23,000				
Build a New Stand		–125,000		70,000
70,000 70,000				
Rent a Large Stand		–1,000		12,000
13,000 14,000				

- Using the internal rate of return rule (IRR), which proposal(s) do you recommend?
- Using the net present value rule (NPV), which proposal(s) do you recommend?
- How do you explain any differences between the IRR and NPV rankings? Which rule is better?

5. MBA Tech, Inc. is negotiating with the mayor of bean city to start a manufacturing plant in an abandoned building. The cash flows for MBAT's proposed plant are:

Year 0	Year 1	Year 2	Year 3	Year 4
–1,000,000	371,739	371,739	371,739	371,739

The city has agreed to subsidize MBAT. The form and timing of the subsidy have not been determined, and depend on which investment criterion is used by MBAT. In preliminary discussions, MBAT suggested four alternatives:

[A] Subsidize the project to bring its IRR to 25%

[B] Subsidize the project to provide a two-year payback

[C] Subsidize the project to provide a NPV of $75,000 when cash flows are discounted at 20%.

[D) Subsidize the project to provide an accounting rate of return (APR) of 40%.

You have been hired by Bean City to recommend a subsidy that minimizes the costs to the city. Subsidy payments need not occur right away; they may be scheduled in later years if appropriate. Please indicate how much of subsidy you would recommend for each year under each alternative suggested by MBAT.

Which of the four subsidy plans would you recommend to the city if the appropriate discount rate is 20%.

6. You are the CEO of Value-Added Industries, Inc. (VAI). Your firm has 10,000 shares of common stock outstanding, and the current price of the stock is $100 per share. There is no debt; thus, the "market value" balance sheet of VAI looks like:

VAI Market Value Balance Sheet

Assets $1,000,000 Equity

$ 1,000,000

You then discover an opportunity to invest in a new project that produces positive cash flow with a present value of $210,000. Your total initial costs for investing and developing this project are only $110,000. You will raise the necessary capital for this investment by issuing